Resources in Reading-Language Instruction

Robert B. Ruddell
University of California, Berkeley

Evelyn J. Ahern
San Mateo City School District

Eleanore K. Hartson
San Ramon Valley Unified School District

JoEllyn Taylor
Mt. Diablo Unified School District

Prentice-Hall, Inc., *Englewood Cliffs, New Jersey*

Prentice-Hall International, Inc., LONDON
Prentice-Hall of Australia, Pty. Ltd., SYDNEY
Prentice-Hall of Canada, Ltd., TORONTO
Prentice-Hall of India Private Limited, NEW DELHI
Prentice-Hall of Japan, Inc., TOKYO

Contents

6   Decoding Instruction   *259*

7   Comprehension and Thinking Strategies   *298*

Preface

The acquisition of reading-language skills and the subsequent acquisition of knowledge are critical in determining our role in society, our influence in regional and social groups, and our upward mobility. Because of the vital importance of reading-language development to the individual child, we must search for new knowledge and field-tested ideas to improve our instructional effectiveness in the classroom. The purposes which guided the development of this collection of readings are fourfold: to illuminate issues and trends which directly affect the pre- and inservice professional development of teachers; to identify a knowledge base stemming from key disciplines and from research on reading-language instruction; to derive from this knowledge base implications for classroom practice; and to present practical field-tested ideas for classroom instruction which relate directly to the discipline and research framework.

The introduction to each chapter provides a key comprehension and discussion aid. Each introduction first sets out significant issues and offers guide questions to help the reader establish a "mental set." Critical ideas offered in the reading selections are related to the guide questions readying the reader for the detailed discussion which follows. We encourage the reader to compare ideas presented within each chapter. In Chapter 1, for example, how are Blume's ideas on humanizing teacher education compatible with Lopez's view of accountability in education? We also encourage the reader to react critically as he considers selections from different chapters; for example, what instructional programs discussed in Chapter 4 most closely approximate the needs of black and Chicano children as identified in Chapter 3? The selections must be considered in relation to the reader's experience with children in real classrooms. Of course, such experience will be limited at the preservice level and extensive for the graduate student and the inservice teacher; nevertheless, the formulation of the bridge between the ideas presented here and the real classroom must be constantly stressed.

The unique features of this collection of readings include the following:

1. An emphasis on educational change, including discussion of "programmers of the mind" versus "the new informalism," accountability, pre- and inservice professional development, school volunteers, and tutors

2. Instructional implications from linguistics, psycholinguistics, sociolinguistics, and cognitive psychology
3. Discussion of socioethnic variation and reading instruction, and the dialect and cultural variation of minority group children
4. Discussion of instructional approaches to meet learner needs, and of alternatives for reading instruction
5. Demonstration of the interrelationship of reading and language development, with specific activities for enhancing oral and written language development
6. Emphasis on approaches and techniques for developing decoding skills
7. Description of cognitive development and reading comprehension, the thinking process and reading comprehension, and listening and reading comprehension
8. Discussion of how to plan the literature program, using folklore as a mirror of culture
9. Evaluation of reading instruction, criterion-referenced measurement, individual inventories, and discussion of oral reading miscues and their meaning

The organization of the selections within a given chapter should in no way prohibit flexible use of the collection. It may be desirable, for example, to use articles from Chapter 3 concerning dialect and cultural variation in conjunction with selections from Chapter 9 dealing with evaluation and reading miscues.

The editors have drawn on a wide range of personal experience in assimilating this collection. This experience includes self-contained and departmentalized classroom instruction in the elementary school, reading specialist experience in the elementary school, teaching college and university methods courses in reading-language development, supervision of student teachers, development of innovative inservice professional development programs, and teaching graduate courses in reading-language instruction. The selection of the articles has thus been influenced by feedback from preservice student teachers, teachers in inservice development, and students working on higher degrees. To all these students the editors express their sincere appreciation.

Dr. Robert B. Ruddell is Professor of Education at the University of California, Berkeley, and spokesman for the Language and Reading Development Program at Berkeley. His professional experience includes one-room and consolidated-school teaching and reading-language supervision. He is director of the Commission on Reading of the National Council of Teachers of English, has served as chairman of the International Reading Association Studies and Research Committee, and is a member of the Commission on High Quality Teaching. He has been editorial consultant to the *Reading Research Quarterly* and *Journal of Educational Research,* and is a frequent contributor to professional journals. Dr. Ruddell has been consultant to the United States Office of Education, to state departments of education, and to local school districts. His interests range from research on basic linguistic factors influencing reading-language instruction to application of research to the development of classroom instruction.

Dr. Evelyn Jeanne Ahern is Assistant Principal for Curriculum in the San Mateo City School District, San Mateo, California. Her professional experience ranges from teaching in one-room schools to instructional leadership at elementary and secondary levels in urban schools. She has taught at California

State College at Sonoma and has conducted numerous inservice workshops for school districts in California. Dr. Ahern is currently president of the San Mateo County Reading Association and a member of the International Reading Association and the National Council of Teachers of English. Her specialty is diagnostic teaching, individualization of reading instruction, and inservice professional development of teachers. A graduate of the Colorado State College of Education, Greeley, Colorado, Dr. Ahern received her doctorate from the University of California, Berkeley.

Mrs. Eleanore K. Hartson is reading specialist for the San Ramon Valley Unified School District, Danville, California. Mrs. Hartson's professional experience includes teaching in all elementary grades. She has been a demonstration teacher at the University of California Laboratory School and a consultant to various California school districts. Her professional activities include membership in the International Reading Association and the California Teachers' Association. Her special interests include research in oral language and its relationship to written language and reading instruction, individualized reading instruction, and the diagnosis and remediation of reading difficulties. Mrs. Hartson completed her undergraduate work at Temple University and received her Master of Arts degree from the University of California, Berkeley.

Dr. JoEllyn Taylor is reading resource teacher in the Mt. Diablo Unified School District, Concord, California. Dr. Taylor is a follow-through consultant for the Far West Laboratory for Educational Research and Development in Berkeley. She has had extensive teaching experience at the elementary school level and served as key resource teacher in developing the literature and self-concept component of a United States Office of Education EPDA project during the 1970–71 school year. Her specialty is in the development of student self-esteem as related to reading competence and in the area of children's literature. Dr. Taylor completed her undergraduate work at Macalester College, St. Paul, Minnesota, and her doctorate at the University of California, Berkeley.

1

Educational Change:
New Trends and Directions

The dynamic changes in our society provide a challenge and awesome responsibility for the reading-language teacher. Although we are intensely concerned with developing communication skills for use in the present and immediate future, we must also be cognizant of the development of attitudes and learning strategies that will enable children to adapt to the inevitable changes in our society. These concerns demand that we personalize our reading and language programs—in fact the total curriculum—in such a way that the skills and knowledge developed have personal relevance for each child. But are we sufficiently equipped to develop our curricula in this manner? If not, can the answer to educational reform lie in a more humanistic approach or in a "new informalism," or do these directions merely represent a facade covering a deeper problem? Does the concept of accountability, competence-based instruction, or performance-based certification represent the solution to more effective instruction for children? What hope is present for educational change and what factors must be present to innovate and maintain positive and effective change in our schools? The articles in this chapter address these and other issues.

Robert Blume responds to the important but difficult question, *How can we humanize teacher education?* He draws heavily on Arthur Combs' interpretation of the "third force psychology" and views the teacher as "facilitator, encourager, helper, assister, colleague, and friend of his students." In brief, Blume believes that teaching is a helping relationship and not a command relationship. The article describes an innovative teacher-preparation program at the University of Florida and its technique of applying key learning principles to the classroom situation. The program is based on the belief that teachers will develop their own curriculum using their preservice professional development program as a model—in essence that "teachers teach the way they were taught."

The direction of change advocated by the "programmers of the mind" is clearly in conflict with that advocated by the "new informalists" in education. *Yet is there a middle ground between the rigid frame-by-frame programmed viewpoint and the philosophy of the unleashed child "turned loose to discover the world"?* Arthur Pearl would respond with an emphatic yes! He presents both extremes of the continuum, expressing serious concern about Skinner,

Engelmann, and Bereiter, and at the same time taking Holt, Goodman, Postman, Kohl, and Friedenberg to task. While he believes the first group represents the closed mind, he recognizes the latter group as the open mind, a "fetish with informalization." Pearl expresses the need of a strategy for changing the schools. He believes that at least in part this strategy rests with an experienced teaching staff whose major criteria of classroom interaction are represented by the acceptance of pluralism in dress, manners, behavior; accountability; negotiation; awareness of the inevitability of conflict; and rules as means rather than as goals. He sets forth a convincing argument for developing an enlightened citizenry by means of a "politically enlightened teaching force."

Pearl advocates an accountable educational system with evaluation as a basic component so that "a logical structure in the form of a plan" is present even though this "plan" may be open to negotiation with students. *But what are the values and limitations of the accountability concept, and what must be included in a successful program of accountability?*

This is a challenging question at a time when the mere mention of the word *accountability* creates heightened emotional responses both pro and con. Felix Lopez addresses the accountability issue by identifying reasons for the failure of accountability systems and by outlining basic requirements for a successful accountability program. Of central importance to his plan is the enlistment of wide participation by all levels of the educational system in establishing philosophy, trust, and shared goals. In brief, he maintains that "to be effective and accepted, both those who use it and those who will be judged by it must participate in the design, installation, administration, and review of the total accountability system." Information used in the evaluation of the system would consist of "results-oriented data," based on the effects of the teacher's performance, and "person-oriented data," consisting of ratings that describe the style of the teacher's performance. Basic to Lopez's plan is an effective accountability interview between the supervisor and the teacher.

Numerous studies on a variety of approaches to reading instruction confirm the belief that however carefully designed a reading program may be, the teacher is vital to its success. Yet not all the attributes of a good teacher can be learned in the college seminar or the extension course. Neither can the potentially excellent teacher reach his or her full excellence without quality instruction and supervision during preservice and inservice training. Opportunities to explore the world of the classroom and to communicate directly with children must be available in preservice teacher training. The opportunity to use teaching techniques based on observation of master teachers and study in the college classroom must also be present. Both the preservice and the inservice teacher must understand child growth and development, the processes involved in learning to read, and the relationship between the reading process and other language skills.

How can we provide a professional training program for both the neophyte and the experienced teacher? Robert Ruddell provides a comprehensive discussion of the elements essential for a preservice training program for the reading and language teacher. He describes in detail eight basic areas of study, which he would include in this preservice professional development program. He also emphasizes the importance of including early direct experience with children at a wide range of grade levels in classroom situations. All too often the teacher-in-training has only limited opportunity to observe and work in the classroom situation. He must, therefore, base his performance as a teacher on this narrow experience without an opportunity to explore other ways of teaching.

After the individual assumes the position of a full-time professional, there is still much to be said for continuing opportunities to upgrade teaching skills, to evaluate new materials and techniques, and to garner new ideas for dealing with specific problems. William Rutherford provides insight into the behavior of the effective classroom teacher. Although he makes no specific recommendations, his discussion provides the basis for the identification of inservice experiences essential to the successful performance of the classroom teacher. Rutherford decries the failure of teachers to follow through on the instructional objectives they have set up. He includes a guide for observing the interaction between teacher and pupils while reading instruction is taking place. He suggests that this guide may be used by a teacher who has tape-recorded his lesson.

Up to this point little attention has been given to the use of instructional personnel aside from the classroom teacher. The recent use of tutors and community participants, however, provides an important option for the teacher, which can make greater provision for individualization of instruction. *But what role can the school volunteer play in the instructional program?* Caplin reports on a sampling of programs across the nation, which are built around community volunteers. The basic aims of these programs are:

1. to relieve the teacher of nonprofessional chores,
2. to offer individual help to children not working well in a group situation (trying to develop the motivation and experiences essential for learning),
3. to enrich the school program through community resources, and
4. to stimulate an informed community to more active support of public education.

In addition to parents and high school and college students, elementary school students can become tutors of other children. Alan Gartner, Mary Kohler, and Frank Riessman describe the development and particular values of the Learning Through Teaching (LTT) program, which originated at the University of Michigan Laboratory School. One program in a Mobilization for Youth project in New York City revealed substantial gains stemming from the tutoring setting. The greater involvement of community and school resources is essential if greater individualization of instruction is to occur within the classroom setting.

The range of ideas presented in the articles focuses on improving the teacher's competence in the classroom with the effect of improving educational opportunities for the nation's youth. The value of these ideas, however, can only be determined by implementation in educational practice. Assuming these ideas are indeed successful in improving the teacher's performance, their value will be directly related to acceptance by educators. In the final article Donald Orlosky and B. Othanel Smith address the question *What are the origins and characteristics of educational change?* They discuss specific efforts toward change in instruction, curriculum, and organization and administration over the past seventy-five years; and identify each effort by source of origin with specified degrees of success, based on degree of permeation in the educational system. Their conclusions offer specific insights into educational change. These should prove valuable as the reader formulates criteria to evaluate the potential of the various ideas presented in the articles.

Obviously, we must carefully plan and coordinate many significant factors related to the child, the teacher, the institution, and the society, if successful educational change is to occur. Most important we must not lose sight of the value of the individual child and teacher in our zeal to reform the educational enterprise. In this way we can ensure reform in a positive sense and avoid regression to an earlier period where the teacher's effectiveness and the student's progress were equated with the student's performance on standardized achievement tests.

Humanizing Teacher Education

Robert Blume

University of Florida

There is no single method of teaching which can be demonstrated to be superior for all teachers. Nor will knowledge about good teaching insure superior performance. These findings from research conducted over the past 10 years have thrown teacher education into a dilemma. If not knowledge and methods, what shall we have our prospective teachers learn in college?

A study published in 1961 by the National Education Association, in which all of the research available on good and poor teaching was reviewed, failed to find any method of teaching which was clearly superior to all others.

At about the same time, Combs and Soper conducted research with good and poor teachers to determine if the good ones knew better than the poor ones the characteristics of a good helping relationship.[1] They found no significant difference between the knowledge of the two categories of teachers.

What does distinguish between good and poor teachers? Certainly we all

[1] More information concerning this study and others cited here can be found in A. W. Combs, *et al., Florida Studies in the Helping Professions,* Social Science Monograph No. 37. Gainesville, Fla.: University of Florida Press, 1969.

Reprinted by permission of Phi Delta Kappa, Inc. and the author.

think we can tell the difference, but does research bear out our beliefs?

Twenty years ago a startling finding came out of a study of various styles of psychotherapy. At that time the psychoanalysts and the Rogerians were debating whether it was more effective for the therapist to be direct and forceful in dealing with his client, or whether the client should be encouraged to think out his own solutions to problems while the therapist assumes a client-centered role.

Fiedler found that expert therapists, no matter what school of thought they belonged to, tended to advocate the same kind of relationship with their clients. In fact, these experts were more alike in their beliefs about the therapeutic relationship than were the beginners and experts in the same school. This relationship has come to be called "the helping relationship."

Combs and Soper modified the questions Fiedler used with the therapists, in order to make them appropriate for educators, and administered the instrument to a group of expert classroom teachers. They found that these teachers agreed with the expert therapists about the relationship which was most desirable and productive for helpers and helpees.

As mentioned above, when they asked poor teachers the same questions, they found that they, too, knew the answers. They concluded that a good helping relationship is something most people know about, but not all are capable of practicing.

With these questions in mind— "What does make a difference in the ability of teachers to practice the good helping relationship?" and "What shall we have future teachers learn in college?"—let us turn to some of the recent criticism of the schools.

The new critics (as opposed to the three-R's proponents of an earlier day) tell us that our schools are ineffective and dehumanizing institutions. Evidence of ineffective education surrounds us, they say. School dropouts, increasing crime, drugs and alcohol, racism—the list could go on and on— all testify to the failure of the school to educate people in a way that gives them a feeling of dignity and an understanding of their world.

Some consider this indictment too harsh. They hold that the school can't be blamed for all of society's ills. Whether or not the school is responsible for causing our problems, it is the institution responsible for producing educated people, who will in turn make the wise decisions, both large and small, that will gradually improve life. Unfortunately, we are not moving in this direction now; on the contrary, life is becoming more grim and joyless all the time, and therefore the school *is* vulnerable to the above charge.

Education must include more than the acquisition of a few more facts and a faster reading rate. It must be the instrument through which people release the tremendous creative potential that was born into all of us. Whatever methods and materials are needed to do the job—that is education.

But this isn't enough. We must also help our young to develop compassion, concern for others, faith in themselves, the ability to think critically, the ability to love, the ability to cooperate with others, the ability to maintain good health, and, above all, the ability to remain open to other people and new experiences. This is *humanistic* education.

In order to achieve this kind of school we must abandon the old patterns along with the old assumptions, and search together for a concept of education that will in Jourard's words "turn on and awaken more people to expanded perspectives of the world, new challenges, possible ways to experience the world and our own embodied being." We *can* create educational patterns that are much more exciting than anything we adults have experienced in our elementary or secondary schooling. The University of Florida has begun a program of elementary teacher education which is a radical departure from those of the past. This program has abolished courses and regularly scheduled classes, replacing them with individual study and small discussion groups. Each student becomes a member of a seminar led by the same faculty member for the two years he is enrolled in the program. Students have the opportunity to work with children every week, and almost every day, from the beginning of their teacher education to the end.

This program is based on principles which have emerged in educational literature over the past two decades, and more specifically on extensive research which Arthur Combs and his associates have conducted at the University of Florida. These principles are:

People do only what they would rather do (from Freud). That is, people behave according to choices they make from among alternatives they see available to them at the moment.

Learning has two aspects: (1) acquiring new information, and (2) discovering the *personal meaning* of that information. Information itself is useless. Only when individuals find the link between specific information and their own lives are they able to put it to use. This principle is not well understood by educators. Most of our

efforts to improve education involve new ways to deliver information to people. Very few innovations involve helping learners to discover the personal meaning of that information.

It is more appropriate for people to learn a few concepts rather than many facts.

Learning is much more efficient if the learner first feels a need to know that which is to be learned. This principle has been known for a long time, but the response of educators to it has been to artificially "motivate" students with letter grades and other rewards. None of these schemes works as well as the genuine desire to learn, and in fact they frequently get in the way of that desire by substituting artificial for real motivation.

No one specific item of information, and no specific skill, is essential for effective teaching. Any one fact or skill that could be mentioned might be missing in a very effective teacher. Furthermore, it would be presumptuous for teacher educators in the 1970s, drawing on their experience in the 40s, 50s, and 60s, to declare certain teaching skills or knowledge essential for teachers in the 80s, and 90s, and beyond. We just don't know what the job of the teacher will be in 20 years, or even 10. Hopefully it will be quite different from what it is today.

People learn more easily and rapidly if they help make the important decisions about their learning.

People learn and grow more quickly if they aren't afraid to make mistakes. They can be creative only if they can risk making errors.

Objectivity is a valuable asset for a researcher, but it is not very useful for workers in the helping professions, such as teaching. What is needed instead is the opposite of objectivity—concern and caring. As Jack Frymier has said, we want students not only to know about cold, hard facts, but to have some "hot feelings about hard facts." We must produce teachers who have developed strong values about teaching.

Teachers teach the way they have been taught—not the way they have been taught to teach. If we want elementary and secondary teachers to be warm, friendly people who relate positively and openly with their students, then we must treat them that way in our college programs. We must respect our teacher education students if we expect them to respect their pupils.

Pressure on students produces negative behaviors, such as cheating, avoidance, fearfulness, and psychosomatic illness. Students tend to become more closed in their interpersonal relationships when they are pressured.

Our teachers would be more effective if they were self-actualizers. Teachers ideally should be more healthy than "normal" people. They should be creative, self-motivated, well-liked persons.

In his book, *The Professional Education of Teachers,* Arthur Combs reviews "third force psychology," the alternative to the Freudian and stimulus-response theories which have dominated our educational thought for the past half century. Three basic principles of perceptual psychology are significant for humanistic education:

1. All behavior of an individual is the direct result of his field of perceptions at the moment of his behaving.

2. The most important perceptions an individual has are those he has about himself. The self-concept is the most important single influence affecting an individual's behavior.

3. All individuals have a basic need for personal adequacy. We all behave in ways which will, according to our view of the situation, lead to our self enhancement. Once aware of this fundamental drive toward growth and improvement, we can see that it is unnecessary to reward a child to encourage him to learn. If he already wants to learn, we need only help him, by giving him the environment which makes it easy and the materials which are appropriate for the kind of learning toward which he is motivated. We need to become aware of his motivation and plan learning experiences which will fit into it. The role of the teacher, then, is that of facilitator, encourager, helper, assister, colleague, and friend of his students.

Teaching is therefore a helping relationship rather than a command relationship. It is similar to counseling, psychotherapy, nursing, human relations work, social work, and many other helping professions.

A number of studies have been conducted at the University of Florida which have investigated the nature of the helping relationship. Combs and others have studied counselors, teachers, Episcopal priests, nurses, and college teachers to see if the more effective practitioners in these fields have different ways of perceiving than do the ineffective ones. The perceptual organizations of these professionals were examined in great detail in the following four categories:

Category 1: *The general perceptual organization.* Is he more interested in people or things? Does he look at people from the outside, or does he try to see the world as they see it? Does he look for the reasons people behave as they do in the here and now, or does he try to find historical reasons for behavior?

Category 2: *Perceptions of other*

people. Does he see people generally as able to do things or unable? As friendly or unfriendly? As worthy or unworthy? As dependable or undependable?

Category 3: *Perceptions of self.* Does he see himself as with people or apart from them? As able or unable? As dependable or undependable? As worthy or unworthy? As wanted or unwanted?

Category 4: *Perceptions of the professional task.* Does he see his job as one of freeing people or controlling them? Does he see his role as one of revealing or concealing? As being involved or uninvolved? As encouraging process or achieving goals?

The results of these studies consistently indicated that the effective helpers saw people from the inside rather than the outside. They were more sensitve to the feelings of students. They were more concerned with people than things. They saw behavior as caused by the here-and-now perceptions, rather than by historical events. They saw others and themselves as able, worthy, and dependable; they saw their task as freeing rather than controlling, and as involved, revealing, and encouraging process.

As mentioned above, one significant finding of these studies was that objectivity had a *negative* correlation with effectiveness as a helper. For example, the teacher who observes two boys fighting and tries to "get to the bottom of the problem" by asking how it started, what led up to the first blow being struck, etc., is not helping as effectively as the teacher in a similar situation who says, "Mike, I can see you are very angry with David and you want to hurt him, but I can't let you do that. How do you feel, David? Are you mad too?" The latter teacher is

not being so objective; he isn't trying to place the blame logically on one boy or the other. Instead he is trying to show the two boys that he recognizes the way they feel *at this moment,* and he wants them to know that he is a friend of each of them and will help them to express their feelings. Violence is usually an attempt to express strong feelings. The best helpers are those who help people to express these feelings without violence.

The implications of this research are important for the Florida New Elementary Program. For example, if good teachers are more sensitive to the feelings of students, we should provide more opportunities for teacher education students to enter into more personal, meaningful relationships with other students, faculty, and children. If effective teachers see others as able, well-intentioned, and dependable, they need a warm, friendly, cooperative atmosphere in which to interact with children and in-service teachers during their teacher education. If the effective teacher sees himself as able, likable, and dependable, he must be treated as a person of worth, dignity, and integrity from the very beginning of his professional program. Finally, if effective teachers see the teaching task as one of freeing and assisting, rather than controlling or coercing, we must provide teacher education which does not insist on particular methods, but which encourages students to seek their own best methods. These programs themselves should encompass a wide variety of approaches. The instructors will need to be concerned with the attitudes and perceptions of teachers, not merely with subject matter and methods.

Various members of the College of Education saw a challenge in this research and in the book Combs published in 1965. They decided to build a new program for the preparation of elementary teachers. This program consists of three parts: the seminar, the substantive panel, and field experience.

The seminar is the heart of the program. It is here most of all that the student develops a close relationship with a faculty member, one who knows him well over the entire period of his professional program. He also becomes a member of a small group of students. Thirty students are assigned to each of the three seminar leaders. They range from beginners, who have just come into the program, to seniors, who have completed all but the final phases of their work. When a student graduates, a new one is taken in to replace him. The 30 students are divided into two groups of 15 for discussion purposes, and each small group meets for two hours per week. These meetings are for the purpose of discussing everything which comes to the minds of the students and their leader relative to education. More specifically, the purpose is the discovery of the personal meaning of the information and experiences which the students are encountering in the other aspects of the program.

The seminar leader serves as advisor to each of the 30 students in his group. He is responsible for helping them schedule outside course work and for keeping the records of their work within the program. He also conducts evaluation activities for his group in the form of weekly activity sheets and the midpoint and final review conferences.

The second aspect is the substantive panel. It includes faculty members who normally teach methods, foundations, and curriculum courses. Included are math, reading, language arts, social studies, science, art, social foundations, psychological foundations, curriculum, black studies, and testing and research. In each of these areas the faculty member distributes lists of competencies for students to complete and hand in, or to discuss in faculty-student conferences. The competencies range over the entire area of didactic learnings within each of the fields mentioned. Certain competencies are required, while others are optional. In the area of curriculum, for example, there are four required competencies, and each student must do three more from a list of seven optional ones. Even the required competencies may be done in two different ways, thus carrying through the idea of giving students wide latitude for choice making. Some of the competencies involve working with a small group of children and writing a critique. The students do these while they are involved in their field experience. Others include reading in the library and writing papers summarizing the literature, or reacting to it. Students are encouraged to design their own competencies as alternatives to some of the optional ones. They write out a contract form for this purpose. The faculty member signs the contract when he has approved the design, and again when the competency has been completed. Substantive panel members conduct some small-group sessions each week to help students develop the understanding needed to complete the competencies. Students are free to sign up for these meetings or not as they choose, but if they sign up they are expected to attend. These meetings are usually offered as a series of three or four. Some competencies consist of passing a test over material which has been presented in these small-group meetings.

Obviously, the student can't work

in all substantive areas at once. He must choose which three or four he will work on each quarter, depending on his schedule of field experiences and outside classes. With this much freedom and responsibility, there is danger that students who have been spoon-fed all of their lives will goof off and get behind in their completion of the competencies. We feel this is a calculated risk worth taking, in order to gain the advantages of having students feel free to explore and probe in directions dictated by their growing interest in becoming teachers.

The field experience aspect of the program begins with level one, which consists of tutoring an individual child and observing classrooms in the Gainesville area. The student and his advisor decide when he has had enough observation experience—usually about 10 one-hour observations. The tutoring continues for an entire quarter. In level two, the student is designated "teacher assistant." He does whatever needs to be done—work with individual children or small groups, or even record keeping. Teacher assistants spend a minimum of six hours per week in the classroom. In level three, the student is designated "teacher associate." He now accepts more responsibility for planning and teaching certain groups of children within the class, or certain aspects of the curriculum for the whole class. As teacher associate he teaches two hours every day. Eventually he must do an intensive period of teaching, level four, which requires full time in the classroom for five weeks.

One of the unique aspects of this program is the flexibility of time requirements. The program is expected to take six quarters to complete, but a student who wants to push harder can complete it in as little as four quarters.

The student who needs more time to finish, or to develop confidence or maturity, might take a longer period of time. This is as it should be, we feel. If we seriously believe in individual differences in learners, we must make provision for people to go through our program at different rates.

The evaluation of each student's work within the program is handled by the seminar leader, the student himself, and the members of the substantive panel. The student completes competencies in each substantive area, and they are evaluated by the panel member. He rates them on a pass–fail basis and checks them off as the student completes his list for his area. He sends a list of the competencies completed to the seminar leader who keeps the student's records.

Approximately half-way through the program each student has a midpoint evaluation, during which he goes over his progress with the seminar leader and one member of the substantive panel. The number of competencies completed in each area, the number yet to be done, and the field experiences to date are all discussed, and a proposed timetable for completion of the program is written down in his folder. When the student has completed all of the requirements he sits for a final review in the same way, and it is determined if he is ready to teach. The seminar leader is aware of each student's progress each quarter, because he keeps all of the records, and he receives feedback from other faculty members who have observations about particular students.

One of the strongest features of the program is the participation of students in every phase of decision making. The students feel ownership in the program as a result of being on various faculty–student committees, such as a committee to write a handbook for new students, a committee to evaluate the competencies in the various substantive areas, or a committee to plan next term's schedule. Each seminar sends a representative to the bi-weekly staff meetings, not only to observe and report back, but to participate in the discussions as a full-fledged member of the group.

Within one year, two very significant, student-initiated changes were made in the program. The group petitioned the dean of the College of Education to place the entire program on a pass–fail basis rather than the letter-grading system then in use. Their logic was persuasive and the change was made.

In another case, a small group of students asked for some academic preparation for teaching in integrated schools. They were all having some teaching experience in schools that were predominantly black, and they recognized their own lack of background for teaching in those classrooms. This suggestion was followed by the creation of a faculty–student committee, which eventually planned a black-studies program and received some limited funding for its operation.

Whether students learn as much about teaching here as they would in a more standard program will have to be determined by the research which

is under way at the present time, but several perceptions are generally shared by the staff members who work most closely with these future teachers. One perception is that the students leave our campus with a solid feeling of confidence about their ability to teach.

A fact which pleases the staff is that *many* of our students ask for an intensive teaching assignment in a school which has large numbers of disadvantaged children. It isn't clear just why this is happening, but it reflects the kind of attitudes we hope to see students developing.

One coed who was having her final review conference said, "It took me almost a year in this program before I felt like these ideas were mine—and then it was easy after that." That statement summarizes what this program is trying to do: not merely to have students *learn about* principles of humanistic education, but to have them feel that they are *their* ideas.

The specific elements of the Florida New Elementary Program as still evolving, and will continue to evolve. What is more important, we believe, are the ideas on which they are based. These principles are valid for humanistic education at any level. We hope to introduce them into elementary classrooms by preparing teachers in ways that are consistent with those principles, because teachers teach the way they were taught.

What's Wrong with the New Informalism in Education?

Arthur Pearl

University of California, Santa Cruz

There are two major trends in education today, each of which is equally misleading. The first is that of the programmers of the mind, the educational engineers. Its guru is B. F. Skinner, the architect of the mindless man who has only a central nervous system to be programmed. Admiral Rickover was one of this trend's earliest proponents. Current spin-offs include Siegfried Engelmann and Carl Bereiter. The most recent disciple is Max Rafferty. The present fashion of performance contracting is a part of this vogue.

This approach is mindless, authoritarian, and anti-intellectual. For example, Engelmann recommends, in his approach to reading instruction, that his young charges jump up and down 40 times before they begin their reading lesson. There is no logic or evidence that reading is facilitated by jumping up and down.

THE BEHAVIORIST BILL OF GOODS

The behaviorist psychologists have effectively sold the bill of goods that specific skills can be learned through consistent reinforcement of desired behaviors. The reinforcement is immediate, so at superficial glance it would appear that the behaviorist is giving utility to the learning process. Not so! The reinforcement is usually extraneous to the intellectual activity; the student is forced into a *token economy*! If he learns what the instructor desires in the form and in the style and tempo that the instructor desires, he may receive from the instructor praise, a blue star, or even a piece of candy guaranteed to melt only in the mouth.

A token economy distorts the education process; the reward becomes the end in itself. Both the immediate utility of the *knowledge* and its connection to a system of thought are lacking.

TEST-TAKING SKILLS ARE NOT EDUCATION

Operant conditioning psychologists are wont to sneer, "But we get results." However, this claim doesn't hold up under much examination. The crucial factor in evaluating the effectiveness of

Reprinted from *Social Policy* (March–April 1971) by permission of Social Policy Corporation and Arthur Pearl.

a program is selection of the criteria. It is true that, in some instances, operant conditioning techniques have improved student scores on standardized achievement tests; the problem is that the test performance has little bearing on culture-carrying competence. It is also true that almost any teacher committed to students produces changes in achievement on standardized tests. Herbert Kohl (36 *Children*), whose lack of system defies all of the behaviorists' principles, reports one to two years of gain on standardized tests in six months. *The mere mastering of test-taking skills does not ensure that the test-taker is literate, articulate, knowledgeable, or analytical. Because we rarely reflect upon this truth, persons without any of these attributes succeed to advanced degrees.*

Of course, the computer, the talking typewriter, and the programmed text are important to a good education; but the roles they will play are definitely subordinate. They will only make it possible for *good teachers* to be *better.* They will also, as is the case now, make it possible for *bad teachers* to be *worse.* Technology has contributed to bureaucratic intransigence and has fortified authoritarianism. More of it will not automatically reverse these tendencies. On the contrary, there must be *well-enunciated strategies if technological advancement is to be restricted to advancing humanity.*

OVERSELLING ECSTASY

Unfortunately, it is not just the engineers who fail to see the necessity of such precaution. George Leonard, recognized as an advocate of humane education since publication of his book *Education and Ecstasy,* presents a cure for education's ills concocted of equal parts of electronic devices, biochemistries, and staged confrontations. His book is at best a journalistic tour de force in which lack of profundity is camouflaged by innumerable references. However, the references only mislead; and in every instance Leonard oversells the product.

The use of group encounters he favors so much, in which people go at each other with no holds barred and break down inhibitions through contrived physical contact, isn't where-it-is-at either. These activities may train persons to become sensitive; but it is quite clear, from years of evaluation, that most of this newfound sensitivity wears off quickly when the participants are returned to the "real world."

Leonard's fascination with psychoactive drugs is not very well balanced. He considers only the possible good things that can happen. He discounts completely the possible horror. He ignores how drugs may isolate man from his social environment and may further involute an already too involuted psychological existence. The quest for an elixir to produce inter- and intra-personal tranquility and intellectual potency is as old as man. There is nothing, Leonard's rhetoric notwithstanding, in its dismal history to lend much encouragement for the future.

CITIZENSHIP FOR HEAVEN OR HELL?

Leonard is vague about educational goals. He is particularly sloppy when he discusses democratic citizenship—for example, "To learn heightened awareness and control of emotional, sensory, and bodily states and through this, increased empathy for other people (a new kind of citizenship education). . . ."

Leonard's new kind of citizenship education picks up all of the worst elements of the old kind. One of the things wrong today is the unwillingness of the school to open up for honest examination the flaws and failures of governmental workings. Leonard closes his eyes to brutal exploitation of man by man, to the domination of political processes by the very wealthy, and to abuse of power by those elected to office. He never deals with institutionalized racism. He is oblivious to the imminent threat of totalitarianism. His goal of citizenship education could have been surrounded by a bubble emanating from the mouth of the cartoon strip character Mary Worth.

Nowhere in Leonard's book is there a recognition that dynamic leadership is required if democratic processes are to be kept alive for the limited number who now enjoy them and that even more intense effort must be made if the fruits of democracy are to be extended to the large numbers who have been denied the pleasure. Depersonalization of man through bureaucratic organization and segregation is not going to wither away—nor is the oppressiveness of school going to magically disappear. Leonard does us a disservice in arguing that they will.

Leonard's work, like so much in "education," takes on the dimensions of a fairy tale because real problems are blissfully ignored. Nowhere does he deal with the problem of political control and the possible misuse of electronics, drugs, or psychological manipulations. He assumes that as man progresses technically, he also progresses socially. History does not bear him out. He has composed a modern siren's song, one that many find as hard to resist as did the shipmates of Odysseus. He calls his approach to education "ecstacy." He has

made a common mistake; he has confused heaven with hell.

THE OPEN MIND

If the first approach can be symbolized by the closed mind, the second can be represented by the open mind, the open school, in which there are no goals and no ideology, and the student is turned loose, unleashed to discover himself and the world. This is reflected in the new fetish with informalization, as though informalizing the overregimented educational process will of itself produce significant learning and development. There is a basic Rousseauian assumption here that what is in man is basically good and intent on acquiring knowledge to promote that goodness, and that it simply needs to be let out; it does not require direction, guidance, or accountability. Education—that is, learning, personal development, and intellectual growth—is not to be painful, but rather a pleasant, open, entirely student-determined process. As the first approach has its roots in simplistic traditional education, so the new trend is rooted in Dewey and Neill and the progressive educators. Its modern advocates include such spokesmen as Paul Goodman, John Holt, Neil Postman, Herbert Kohl, and Edgar Friedenberg.

All of these new educational leaders surrender leadership to the children. John Holt ("Education for the Future," in Robert Theobold, *Social Policy for America in the '70s,* Doubleday, 1968) would not have teachers play a vital leadership role in changing and developing children; he would have each child determine his own educational goals—"School should be a place where children learn what they want to know, instead of what we think they ought to know."

Let me add here that I am in complete agreement with Holt when he accuses most schools—public schools, especially—of rigidity, irrelevance, unnecessary restrictions, lack of spontaneity, adult domination, and coerciveness. But then he throws up his hands. Just shake it all up, remove the teachers, abolish the teacher's leadership role in the classroom altogether, and thereby deny his responsibility in changing the current condition. He keeps stating: take it all off—and just that haphazardly. Regarding all learning as essentially the same, he ridicules the concept of curriculum as well as the teacher's leadership role. Because what is now taught in school is often irrelevant, Holt concludes that it is impossible to identify relevance. And so he insists:

The most we can do is try to help, by letting him know roughly what is available and where he can look for it. Choosing what he wants to learn and what he does not is something he must do for himself. . . . In short, the school should be a great smorgasbord of intellectual, artistic, creative, and athletic activities from which each child could take whatever he wanted, and as much as he wanted or as little.

I disagree. I believe that there is a body of knowledge to be taught and a position to be taken through it, and supported by it, against racism, against parochialism, against poverty and misery. It is important to remember once again that John Holt is a good man—at least by the criteria we all measure the goodness of a man. He agrees with me about most things. He is for peace and freedom, and against poverty. The problem is that his dissatisfactions have diverted his concentration so that he can only identify alternatives to what

is. As a result, this relieves the teacher of responsibility for a better society once a student makes his choice to be a racist, a jingoist, a waster of resources, or a selfish accumulator of wealth.

Holt thinks that persons can be educated to be above these frailties "by creating in the school an atmosphere of freedom, respect, and trust within which true kindness and generosity can be expected to grow. It has little or nothing to do with content, curricula, or learning, and a great deal to do with the human heart and spirit." I have less faith in the undisciplined heart and less despair over what is really possible for us to achieve through schools. John Holt exhibits an anti-intellectual distortion of equalitarianism. Because he could not eliminate fear of failure in the classroom, he assumes it cannot be done. Because what is now taught in school is irrelevant, he believes that it is impossible to identify relevance and teach it. I disagree! I believe, as I said before, that there is a body of knowledge to be taught to prevent racism and provincialism.

THE TEACHER'S LEADERSHIP ROLE

There is no place for bullies or sadists in the teaching profession! Any activity whose purpose is to inflict pain or embarrassment or to cause guilt must be eliminated from schools. But it is irresponsible to believe that the protection of the enterprise and the assurance of other students' rights will not require that some children's behavior will have to be restricted and that, in very rare instances, some children will have to be removed from the classroom. The incidence of restriction should be much less than it is now; and when it is required, the children affected must be ensured due process.

Neil Postman and Charles Weingartner oppose teacher leadership, too; they oppose what they see as its inevitable corollary—teacher domination of education. They have written a book—*Teaching as a Subversive Activity.* They see all of the structure of education as insulting to the student and good only for training students for playing the trivia game. They want a "revolution," which will become visible when "young revolutionary teachers" take the following steps:

1. Eliminate all conventional "tests" and "testing."
2. Eliminate all "courses."
3. Eliminate all "requirements."
4. Eliminate all full-time administrators and administrations.
5. Eliminate all restrictions that confine learners to sitting still in boxes made of boxes.

And specifically (in a list of 16 proposals), Postman and Weingartner recommend that teachers

Declare a moratorium on all tests and grades. That would remove from the hands of teachers their major weapons of coercion and would eliminate two of the major obstacles to their students learning anything significant.

Postman and Weingartner would scrub grades entirely. *They are all wrong!* They fail to develop accountability. They don't establish a basis for evaluating student performance that has validity. Because they have not developed educational goals that make sense in a rapidly changing world, they have no legitimate basis for evaluating students.

I believe in the evaluation of both students and faculty. I believe that both not only need evaluation—both want it. But meaningful evaluation depends upon accountability and negotiability. *A test has to be defended to students. Each question must be defended as educationally relevant.* Each question must be upheld as a necessary link in the chain that leads ultimately to the goals of occupational, political, cultural, and personal competence. The student must be encouraged to exercise his right to challenge the teacher's arguments. If his "answer" doesn't correspond with that of the teacher, he, too, should be asked to be accountable. He, too, should be asked to defend his answer in the context of the goals of education. The classroom must become the market where, as Oliver Wendell Holmes Jr. expressed it, "truth [can] be determined through open competition of thought." Assessment, which is fundamental to this competence, requires negotiation. A social contract must be established. There is no possibility of a contract if there is no commonality of goals. But even agreement on goals does not assure meaningful negotiation. There is also the elemental issue of power. Again Holmes offers legal advice that has relevance to the classroom and grading procedure: if open competition of ideas from which grades are to be given is to become a reality, then there must be the understanding that "freedom of contract begins where equality of bargaining power begins."

BINDING ARBITRATION FOR STUDENTS

The student must have access to binding arbitration and conciliation. In my classes, students can always ask for a sample of ten students to be drawn at random to determine the legitimacy of their grievances—either about tasks to be performed or evaluation of the worth of those tasks. I believe that standards should be negotiable and that the grades should be either "pass" or "haven't passed yet." *It makes little sense to me that a person who almost passes a course has to take it over, or that everyone should have to pass a course in exactly the same period of time.* Why can't a student complete this work two weeks later than the others in the class and receive full credit for his efforts? Suppose an agreed-upon standard for a class is to determine the ingredients in an unknown chemical substance. A student may not have deciphered the problem by the semester's end; but if ten days later he has finished the job, is there any earthly reason why the student shouldn't be given a "pass" for his accomplishment? Of course not.

Clearly, though more by implication than explication, Postman and Weingartner argue that one of the essentials for deflecting the world from its charted course to doom is a markedly changed school. I heartily concur with all the things they find wrong with school—dreariness, irrelevance, sterility, brutalization, etc.—but they present a solution that would in no way move the school toward widely effecting the changes we would all like to see.

SUBSTITUTING QUESTIONS FOR ANSWERS

We really do not improve education if we merely substitute questions for answers. But Postman and Weingartner identify themselves with those who recommend "inquiry training" as a reformation of current educational emphasis. They believe that they have hit upon something new and vital. They think that what they have is of the electronic age.

Inquiry training can be identified by the following characteristic teacher behaviors:

"The teacher rarely tells the students what he thinks they ought to know."

"His basic mode of discourse with students is questioning."

"He encourages student–student interaction as opposed to student–teacher interaction."

"And generally he avoids acting as a mediator or judge of the quality of ideas expressed."

"He rarely summarizes the positions taken by students on the learning that occurs."

"His lessons develop from the responses of students and not from a previously determined 'logical' structure."

"Generally, each of his lessons poses a problem for students."

"He measures his success in behavioral changes in students."

What's wrong with this behavior? Nothing, really; and everything, really! Nothing is wrong because the teacher behaviors are all desirable attributes, and everything is wrong because what is depicted is insufficient. The behaviors are not connected to educational goals. They represent processes without reference to outcomes. It is not possible even to guess what a student can *do* about saving the world from its impending disaster as a result of the described teacher behaviors. The teacher is postulated to be a part of a process designed to produce enormous change, yet he is without even a map specifying where he is and where is trying to go.

What Postman and Weingartner will not recognize is that they have generated a system that is every bit as anti-intellectual as the "fact training" they oppose. In both instances the teacher is not projected as an intellectual leader. I sympathize completely with the criticism of "right-answer"-oriented education. It *is* sterile and ritualistic. Teaching students how to pass examinations has limited utility. The information gained is not useful in the solution of real problems. Even in that rare instance in which the information can be put to use, it is almost always learned in such a way that it is minimally transferable. All of this is true, and Postman and Weingartner dispatch the advocates of performance goals neatly. They are brilliant, devastating, and witty in their denunciation of the "tough-minded," fact-dominated dolts who are gaining ascendancy in schools. But in their desperate effort to avoid Scylla, Postman and Weingartner *become* Charybdis.

There is a romantic, recurring notion that powerful and valid criticism of existing conditions automatically leads to relief from those conditions. Persons who hold such a belief stubbornly refuse to learn the lessons of history. The most reasonable and probable result of criticism without a defensible alternative is a change that is no change. I'm afraid that that is all we have to look forward to from Postman and Weingartner. The only thing subversive about their book, alas, is the title.

Asking questions can be just as sterile and ritualistic as answering questions. In fact, Postman and Weingartner warn us against this eventuality. But warning against sterility is no big thing. Everyone who favors a question-answering approach to education also opposes sterility—in fact, it can be safely said of *everyone* in education (particularly the most sterile) that he is against sterility. In practice, the warning against *stupidity* in education by educators is the *ritual* that exonerates

the practice of stupidity and allows education to exercise it with total impunity. Teachers need to define goals, goals with which students can disagree; and the students must be helped to develop processes and techniques and atmospheres for disagreeing. But the teacher must be able to say "That's a stupid question" when the discovery-method—trained child raises one.

TEACHER ACCOUNTABILITY

For good education, the student or the teacher (an arbitrary distinction) can neither a questioner nor an answerer be, all the time. What-he-is-when is determined by the goals of the enterprise. To solve man's heretofore unsolved problems, the student must have an enormous amount of facts at his command. He must continually apply those facts to the high-priority ecological puzzles. The problems must be analyzed so that manpower concerns (from the vantage points of both the individual and the greater society) are treated. The political issues (and *all* important problems will require a complex political solution) must be considered. The substantive knowledge of man must be applied to solve man's struggle for survival in such a way that the dignity of each individual is kept within the learner's consciousness. And although it is true that no important question has but one right answer, it is also true that some answers are more right than others. It is disputable whether the answer to "Who discovered America and when?" is Columbus in 1492, but that answer is quite superior to "George Wallace in 1968." The answer, regarded right (or extremely right) affects greatly how a student attacks man's major challenges to survival.

In contrast to Postman and Weingartner, I believe that a good teacher *does* start off by telling students what he thinks they ought to know—but he then has to defend to students why he believes what he believes. Not only must he be accountable to them but he must also be willing to negotiate with them. The negotiation can have meaning and be something more than a senseless tug-of-war for power only if there are agreed-upon goals that keep discussion within bounds. In the context of his functioning as an accountable authority, the teacher questions, answers, debates, disputes facts, and summarizes. He always has a logical structure in the form of a plan that can be amended or even abrogated, but only when a better plan more consistent with educational goals is forthcoming. Without continual reference to goals, without "factual" support for arguments, without new concepts introduced by the teacher, the student will wallow in his prejudices and his ignorance. It is inconceivable that an accountable educational system can, or should, avoid an evaluative system. The student has a right to know where he stands. Postman and Weingartner actually concede such a point relatively early in their book, but then vehemently deny it at the end.

Postman and Weingartner are confusing in this respect because they are obviously confused. The call for measurable indices of success isn't made with much conviction because the authors do not believe that man can really communicate very much, let alone measure anything. The main thrust of the book is a plea for recognition that men's isolation from one another is inevitable and essential. "Each man is an island," they argue. "We now know that each man creates his own unique world, that he, and

he alone, generates whatever reality he can ever know."

THE MEDIUM IS NOT THE MESSAGE

Postman and Weingartner are all entangled in the silliness of Marshall McLuhan. Because they are unable to divorce process from purpose, they assert as unassailable truth the palpable falsehood that the medium is the message. *The medium is not the message.* The medium is subordinate to the message. A message must have content. Not only must something be said in a message but that something, if it has educational value, must relate to important problems. And here is where the "inquiry" boys fall apart. They cannot make a commitment. They are unable to take sides because they cannot tell right from wrong. Weingartner and Postman, in their approach to language and perception, stress only subjectivity, imprecision, and privacy. In the end they defy all that they claim to believe. In a book that demands that teachers be limited to "three declarative sentences per class, and fifteen interrogatives," they string together hundreds of declarations and offer no interrogatives. They are shallow where they should be deep, ambiguous where they should be forthright, and cynically humorous where they should be serious.

Postman and Weingartner have written a book that opens with a bang and ends with a whimper. They start off with a powerful first chapter. That chapter, entitled "Crap Detecting," suggests that students must learn in school to separate importance from trivia and truth from misconception. It unfortunate that they did not heed the advice they offered in that first chapter. If they had, they would have written no more.

Certainly teachers should declare less and inquire more; certainly teachers should stimulate students to question more and answer less; but "inquiry," like any other tactic, remains just that. To elevate it to what it is not, to call it the essence of education, to label it the *new* education, is to do education a disservice. The ends of education should influence the means. Any educational process that fails to tie itself specifically to a long-range outcome (cultural, political, personal, and occupational) is not only inadequate but probably worthless.

Herbert Kohl's experience with his 36 *Children* is an important case in point. He managed to "make it" with his students. But it was more happenstance than design. He capitalized on his sensitivity, insight, wit, and dedication. He had no plan; he endured day by day. He had no evaluation scheme. He used informal feedback from his students and kept his antennae out for signals that indicated approaching danger or safe passage. And yet, for all that he accomplished, if he intended to keep his children in the school until they had attained the goals of education, he failed abysmally. One by one the students were overcome by the system.

Robert is not the only one of the thirty-six children who is now close to being a dropout—John, Margie, Carol, Sam—I stopped searching, don't want to know the full extent of the misery and tragedy of the children's present lives. Recently one of the kids told me: "Mr. Kohl, one good year isn't enough." (p. 205)

Herbert Kohl could not have known when the students had become educated because he had no terminal goals.

He had no theory, and he needed one. He had no strategy or tactics to win allies within the system over to his side. He needed tactics and strategy. He lacked overtures to other instructors. He was in the best tradition of the American Western folk hero. He was there all by himself when both hands of the clock were at twelve—but life isn't like the movies (although Californians obviously don't understand that); and he, not the bad guys, died in the dust.

Education must threaten ignorance and the tendency to put forth the least effort. Discipline and powerful input and stimulation from teachers are necessary. The teaching staff must challenge youngsters, interest them, lead them to confront and disagree. Only a fraction of students are self-starters. And in this sense the new trend is elitist, because it is really directed toward only this fraction.

Paul Goodman believes every mature adult can be a teacher. I disagree strongly. When my students in college played the teaching role, they came to learn very rapidly that there was more to it than simply maturity and openness; and the students whom they were teaching also wanted more than group process.

The problem with the new informalists is that they have no goals to offer, no rules to suggest. Either they produce anarchy or appeal to a tiny group of youngsters who are self-starters; or they fall back on some strong rules of their own and, like George Dennison (*The Lives of Children*), a disciple of Holt in his imposition of freedom, pick out or exclude youngsters who do not fit this pattern; or, like Edgar Friedenberg, who opposes democracy, they move toward appealing to elite, middle-class youngsters. School cannot be simply a place of questions with no answers; this is as bad as answers with no questions, the error of the educational engineers who have no appreciation of the open-ended aspect of learning.

If most "open mind" advocates are softheaded about the implicit elitism in the way they gloss over problems of preparing students for democracy, no such criticism can be leveled at Edgar Friedenberg. His explicit anti-democracy stands, in fact, as a revealing testament to the inevitable logic of democratic "open-minders" who look to him for leadership, confusing his criticism of current formal schooling with broadly based democratic goals. Edgar Friedenberg advances a most disturbing proposition. He questions the feasibility of democracy itself. He concludes that it is more accurate to reject the notion that democracy has become corrupted and perverted and recognize that "What is wrong with America may be characteristic of mass democracy itself" (*Change in Higher Education*, May–June 1969, p. 16).

Friedenberg generates a cogent argument. He points to a record of non-responsiveness to social issues:

In a society as open, invidious and competitive as ours, the kinds of people who succeed are usually incapable of responding to human demands; and the political power of the masses is used merely to express the hatreds and the envy, and to destroy anything that looks like genuine human satisfaction.

According to Friedenberg, we are presently on a collision course with disaster:

Tyranny has taken many forms in history, but the graceless vulgarity and egregious clumsy brutality of fascism are its most hideous forms; and these grow best out of the democratic process itself.

Friedenberg is dubious of reform—

The present political structure of America is precisely what is wrong, and there is no a priori reason to assume that it bears within itself the seeds of its own reform.

The hope of the future, according to Friedenberg, cannot now be accurately described, but whatever it is, it will fall outside the pale of established procedures.

But I am sure that if radical improvement in the quality of our national life can be made—and our survival depends on this—the devices by which it can be done will seem outrageous and will, indeed, cause widespread outrage.

I concur with Friedenberg on the portentous nature of our times. I differ with him on interpretation. If one perceives that education merely reflects the dominant society, then Friedenberg's assessment is correct, and we are doomed. But if one attributes some vitality to education and democracy and potential political power in a coalition of teachers and students, then there is hope.

Friedenberg's contempt for the common man's ability to perform the citizenship role concerns me. He alludes to a lack of capability. It is my view that mass democracy fails only because so little effort has been made to educate "the masses" for democracy. I believe that such education is possible. I don't believe that the masses are any less receptive to such education than the privileged who have always benefited from it, and I believe that they have the most to gain from it.

Friedenberg's pessimism may be

based on an accurate assessment of where we are going. I remain an optimist, because pessimism is a luxury I don't believe we can afford. The forces that oppose democracy are strong; and if those who support democracy are discouraged or halfhearted in their efforts, then certainly all is lost. Too often, unfortunately, these latter are just that halfhearted—and softheaded, too. They constitute the raw materials of bandwagons and the fabric of fads. They divert us from the realities of the problems of school responsibility and yet, even more important, it is in the direction they point to that our best hopes must be channeled.

In essence, education must have accountability. There must be goals that are more than those set by the youngsters, even though the youngsters must play a powerful participatory role in evaluating and contributing to the goals. No one teacher can have all the attributes or make all the inputs that are necessary. The aim is to generate all that is necessary through a wide range of teaching staff for whom the major criteria of classroom interaction are:

1. Acceptance of pluralism in dress, manners, behavior. The staff must itself be diverse enough to make advocacy of all the different groups within a school a reality.
2. Accountability. No one questions the fact that rules and regulations are essential, but the authority must explain the necessity for the restrictions, and the explanation must be based on logic and evidence.

3. Negotiation. Differences between students and staff must be reconciled on a basis of mutual concern. The staff must be willing to accept student suggestions for alternative ways of doing things.
4. Awareness of the inevitability of conflict. Teachers must not crush all who differ: they must learn to live with people who differ in values and goals.
5. Rules as means, not as goals. The educator will be in far less difficulty if he keeps rules in a proper perspective. If rules are seen only as a means to attain a legitimate goal of education, then violation of the rules can be handled rationally.

There must be a strategy for changing the schools; otherwise, teachers may simply reflect the more pernicious aspects of our society related to war, racism, and poverty. The new teachers must be able to win the youngsters, the parents, and their colleagues to a recognition that the old values are inadequate and that a new society is necessary. This must be done carefully through the whole teaching process, not by postulating advanced radical goals and posturing about them. We don't need a lot of rhetoric about change; rather, we need lots more education and politics—persuasion of people through everyday processes.

Finally, the educator has still another responsibility: he has to be an effective citizen himself. The lame-leading-the-halt approach to teaching of citizenship must be altered. If enlightened citizenship is to be obtained in the mass, it must begin with a politically enlightened teaching force.

Accountability in Education

Felix M. Lopez
Impart, Inc., Sciences Technology

Accountability refers to the process of expecting each member of an organization to answer to someone for doing specific things according to specific plans and against certain timetables to accomplish tangible performance results. It assumes that everyone who joins an organization does so presumably to help in the achievement of its purposes; it assumes that individual behavior which contributes to these purposes is functional and that which does not is dysfunctional. Accountability is intended, therefore, to insure that the behavior of every member of an organization is largely functional.

Accountability is to be distinguished from responsibility by the fact that the latter is an essential component of authority which cannot be delegated. It is the responsibility of a board of education to insure the effective education of the children in its community. Board members cannot pass this responsibility on to principals and to teachers. But they can hold teachers and principals accountable for the achievement of tangible educational effects *provided* they define clearly what effects they expect and furnish the resources needed to achieve them.

Reasons for failure

A review of accountability programs underlines its uneven, trial-and-error progress and its current inadequacies. Initiated when psychometric theory was largely underdeveloped, embedded early in unrealistic management and legislative mandates, imposed usually from above on an unwilling and uncomprehending supervisor, the program has struggled with the common conception that it is an end rather than a means and with an administrative naiveté that treats it as a student's report card. Personnel textbooks have stressed the idea that an accountability plan must be characterized by simplicity, flexibility, and economy. Ignoring the fact that these qualities are not wholly compatible, administrators have attempted to develop programs along these lines. Their inevitable failures have led to the current disillusionment and distrust and, in some quarters, to the belief that the establishment of an effective program is impossible. Nevertheless, a careful examination of efforts to establish accountability programs suggests some underlying misconceptions that explain the many failures.

Reprinted by permission of Phi Delta Kappa, Inc. and the author.

23

1. Most accountability programs have been installed in organizational settings that lack the necessary background and organizational traditions to assimilate them. Insufficient emphasis has been placed on the development of an organizational philosophy and on the determination of accountability policies before the implementation of the program.

2. The administrative procedures governing the program have not been attuned to its purposes. There has been a tendency to make the program accomplish a great deal with an oversimplified procedure. The evidence strongly suggests that despite the ardent wish for economy and simplicity, only a program designed for a specific purpose or involving a multimethod approach is likely to succeed.

3. Accountability systems have not been designed to gain acceptance by those who are covered by them nor by those who have to implement them. For the most part, they have been designed by specialists, approved at the highest levels, and imposed without explanation on those who have to implement them. This occurs because the problem is approached from an organizational rather than an individual perspective.

4. The measures of accountability so far developed have not met even minimum standards of reliability and relevancy. This failure is known as the "criterion problem" and can be summarized briefly as follows:

a. Criteria of effectiveness in a position generally lack clear specifications.

b. Objective measures, when examined closely, are usually found to be either nonobjective or irrelevant.

c. Subjective measures, when examined closely, are usually found to be biased or unreliable.

d. Seemingly adequate criteria can vary over time.

e. Position effectiveness is really multidimensional. Effectiveness in one aspect of a position does not necessarily mean effectiveness in others.

f. When effectiveness in different aspects of a position is measured, there is no sure way to combine these measures into a single index of effectiveness.

g. Different performance patterns achieve the same degree of effectiveness in the same job.

To be successful, therefore, the accountability program must meet the following requirements:

1. It must be an important communications medium in a responsive environment through which members are informed of what is to be accomplished, by whom, and how; wide participation in the obtainment of organization goals must be invited; and the attention of top management must be focused on the accomplishment of individual employees' personal goals.

2. It must reflect an organizational philosophy that inspires confidence and trust in all the members.

3. It must be based on ethical principles and sound policies that can be implemented by a set of dynamic, flexible, and realistic standards, procedures, and practices.

4. It must clearly specify its purposes so that standards, procedures, and practices can be conformed to them.

5. It must be designed primarily to improve the performance of each member in his current job duties. Other effects, such as the acquisition of information on which to base salary and promotion decisions and the personal development of the employees' capacities, may accompany the main

effect of improved job performance, but these must be considered merely by-products of the main process.

6. The manner in which the supervisor dicusses his evaluation with the subordinate constitutes the core of the process. If this is handled poorly, the program, no matter how well designed and implemented, will fail.

7. To be effective and accepted, both those who use it and those who will be judged by it must participate in the design, installation, administration, and review of the total accountability system.

These principles, then, outline the dimensions of an approach to the establishment of accountability in education. The approach encompasses three broad interventions into the current system, each aimed initially at a distinct level of the organization structure: the top, the middle, and the base, the last named being the teachers themselves. Ultimately, however, all three levels will be involved in all three phases of the accountability program.

INTERVENTION AT THE TOP

Basically, intervention at the top consists of the establishment of organizational goals by the use of a technique referred to in private industry as "Management by Objectives" (MBO) and in government as the "Planning, Programming, and Budgeting System" (PPBS). Since there are many excellent books describing these techniques in detail, we shall confine ourselves here to a brief summary of the method.[1]

[1] For example, G. S. Odiorne, *Management by Objectives*. New York: Pitman Publishing Co., 1965; and C. L. Hughes, *Goal Setting: Key to Individual and Organizational Performance*. New York: American Management Association, 1965.

Goal setting

The underlying concept of the goal-setting approach is simple: The clearer the idea you have of what you want to accomplish, the greater your chance of accomplishing it. Goal setting, therefore, represents an effort on the part of the management to inhibit the natural tendency of organizational procedures to obscure organizational purposes in the utilization of resources. The central idea is to establish a set of goals for the organization, to integrate individual performance with them, and to relate the rewards system to their accomplishment.

While there is general agreement that this method represents the surest approach to effective management, there is no primrose path to its practical implementation.

In its most commonly accepted form, MBO constitutes an orderly way of goal setting at the top, communication of these goals to lower-unit managers, the development of lower-unit goals that are phased into those set by the higher levels, and comparison of results in terms of goals. The program operates within a network of consultative interviews between supervisor and subordinate in which the subordinate receives ample opportunity to participate in the establishment of his own performance objectives. Thus, the whole concept is oriented to a value system based upon the results achieved; and the results must be concrete and measurable.

When properly administered, Management by Objectives has much to recommend it:

1. It involves the whole organization in the common purpose.

2. It forces top management to think through its purposes, to review them constantly, to relate the respon-

sibilities of individual units to pre-set goals, and to determine their relative importance.

3. It sets practical work tasks for each individual, holds him accountable for their attainment, and demonstrates clearly how his performance fits into the overall effort.

4. It provides a means of assuring that organization goals are eventually translated into specific work tasks for the individual employee.

It is, therefore, virtually impossible to conceive of an effective accountability program that does not operate within the umbrella of the goal-setting process. When properly designed and implemented, goal setting becomes an ideal basis for other forms of performance evaluation. It insures that subordinate goals and role performances are in support of the goals of the higher levels of the organization and that ultimately the institutional purposes will be achieved.

The charter of accountability

One way of implementing the goal-setting process that has been found useful in education is through the development of a charter of accountability. This approach was originally developed by the Ground Systems Group of the Hughes Aircraft Company.[2] The charter is agreed to by two individuals or groups—one in a superordinate and the other in a subordinate capacity—after consultation, discussion, and negotiation. Ultimately, the entire organization is covered by the series of charters beginning at the top with a major organization unit, say, the English department in a local high school. Each

[2] P. N. Scheid, "Charter of Accountability for Executives," *Harvard Business Review,* July–August, 1965, pp. 88–98.

teacher's goals are shaped by his unit's charter of accountability. Each unit head is held accountable for the results specified in his charter, which he draws up and which he and his superiors sign. Ultimately, all charters are combined into a system-wide charter that provides the basis of accountability for the board of education and the superintendent of schools.

A charter contains a statement of purposes, goals, and objectives. *Purpose* constitutes the organization's reason for existence and gives meaning and direction to all its activities. Purposes, therefore, are usually stated in broad inspirational terms.

Goals and *objectives* are the tangible expressions of the organization's purposes. Goals are long-range, concrete, end results specified in measurable terms. Objectives are short-range, specific targets to be reached in a period of one year, also specified in measurable terms.

Specifically, a charter of accountability contains the following features:

1. A statement of system-wide purposes or areas of concern and the purposes of the next level above the unit completing the charter of accountability.

2. A statement of the specific purposes of the unit completing the charter.

3. A description of the functional, administrative, and financial accountability necessary to accomplish the unit's purposes.

4. A set of basic assumptions about the future economic, sociopolitical, professional, and technological developments likely to affect the attainment of goals but which are beyond the control of the accountability unit.

5. A listing of the major goals of the

unit to be aimed at for the imme-
.diate five-year period.

6. A subseries of performance tasks
that provide unit supervisors with
definitive targets toward which to
orient their specialized efforts and
with which to define the resources
necessary to accomplish them.

7. Statements of the authority and
responsibility necessary to complete these tasks.

Space does not permit the full exposition of the process of establishing a
charter of accountability. Very broadly,
and quite superficially, it would follow
this pattern:

1. A central committee or council
composed of representatives of key
members of the system—school board,
local school boards, union, teachers,
parent and community groups—would
convene to define the broad purposes
of the school system. Putting it simply,
their job woudl be to answer these
questions: "What is the business of the
school system?" "What are we trying
to accomplish?" While the answers to
these questions may seem obvious, in
practice they are difficult to articulate.
Answering them serves the larger purpose of clarifying thinking about the
realistic aims of a school system. In
business, the definition of purpose has
led to dramatic changes in organization
structure, business policies, product
mix, and, ultimately, in return on investment.

The purposes delineated by this
council are then discussed widely in
the community. In particular, they
serve to determine the major areas of
concern of the school system that have
been assigned to it by the community.
Both the purposes and the areas of
concern, however, must be considered
at this point to be tentative and subject to modification by lower levels

of the system. They will provide, however, the necessary guidelines for the
goal-setting process and the development of charters of accountability by
the school districts and other lower
level units.

2. Each major subunit—school district, division, or department—meets to
define its goals and objectives and to
prepare its charter of accountability.
Since these goals and objectives can
differ substantially according to the
needs of specific localities, the criteria
of accountability will also differ. This
is the important, even crucial point
that constitutes the major advantage
of the goal-setting process. It provides
for multiplicity of measures of accountability that are tailored to the needs
and hence the goals of specific operating units. The objectives of a principal of an inner city-school will differ
from those of a principal of a suburban
school, and so must the measures of
accountability. Reading grade equiva-
lents may be an appropriate measure
of teacher effectiveness in one school
and not in the other.

3. The charters of all units are col-
lated and reviewed by the central
council or school board with the advice and assistance of the planning and
budgeting unit of the office of the
superintendent of schools. Appropriate
approvals are granted in accordance
with existing policy and legislation.
Thus, the combined charters constitute
the charter of accountability for the
board of education and the entire
school system. While there will be
some uniformity to this charter, it is
apparent that it will resemble more a
patchwork quilt than a seamless cloak
and will, therefore, adhere more closely
to the reality it attempts to reflect.

4. As each charter is approved,
subcharters are developed in the same
way for individual units in each dis-

trict. Obviously, the heads of these units will have had a voice in the formulation of the district charter so that this will not be a new task for them. But in developing the subunit charters in the schools themselves, all the members of the system will ultimately have a voice.

5. Once the charters have been adopted, they are implemented. In some cases, new inputs will eliminate or change previously stated objectives. In others, objectives will be found to be quite unrealistic. Provisions must be made, therefore, to amend the charters of accountability as experience dictates. In most cases, however, it is advisable to stick with the original charter until the year-end review and appraisal of results.

6. The evaluation of the achievement of the period's objectives is made as plans for the next charter are formulated. This is the essence of accountability: results compared to objectives. It is important to note, however, that this evaluation is made not in a punitive, policing climate to check up on people, but rather in a supportive, constructive atmosphere to find out how objectives were achieved and, if they were not, why not. Both parties to this process assume the responsibility for the results and approach the task with the idea of exploring what happened for purposes of problem solving and resetting goals and objectives.

INTERVENTION IN THE MIDDLE

The implementation of an accountability program depends, to a large extent, on the attitudes and the skills of the supervisory force. If it is skeptical, anxious, or hostile to the plan, it will fail no matter how well it is conceived. This has been the bitter experience of many firms that have attempted to install goal-setting and performance-evaluation programs without first preparing their managers and supervisors to implement them.

Thus, a second essential step in introducing accountability into a school system is the establishment of a massive supervisory development program. Such a program must be practical, intensive, and primarily participative in nature. Its purpose is not merely to disseminate information but rather to change attitudes and to impart specific skills, particularly the skill of conducting accountability interviews with subordinates.

This will not be easy. Most supervisors, principals, and teachers have had no experience with such a program to prepare them for the tasks involved. A development program must be tailor-made to meet their needs.

The development program must also begin at the top with the superintendent and the assistant superintendents. There is a practical reason for this. When presenting this subject matter to middle managers in other organizations, an almost universal response from them is, "Why can't our bosses take this course? They need it more than we do." Since the program content is likely to be quite strange, even revolutionary, to many of the lower middle-management participants, its credibility can be insured only by its being accepted at the highest levels and applied there first.

The program must enable the top-level people to examine the basic assumptions on which they operate and give them as much time as possible to get these assumptions out in the open. The specific objectives of the program would be:

1. To emphasize the influence process

in handling subordinates, managers, and supervisors, as well as teachers, and to de-emphasize the formal authority-power-coercion approach to supervision and administration.

2. To provide a deeper understanding of the communications process itself. Such a program must heighten the awareness of the supervisor as to how he comes across best to others and develop his flexibility in dealing with the broad spectrum of personalities encountered in the fulfillment of his responsibilities. Each supervisor should be given an opportunity to prepare a plan for his self-growth and development.

3. To consider ways of dealing with the more routine aspects of teaching by considering job enrichment techniques.

4. To emphasize the sociopsychological realities that education faces today. The program should make supervisors aware that they simply cannot rely on authoritarianism alone to get results with people.

The format of the program should be primarily participative in nature—that is, it should consist of learning experiences and exercises which require the supervisors to participate actively in the training sessions. Frequent use should be made of audio-visual displays, role playing, conference discussions, and case study techniques. Theoretical ideas and concepts that help develop new ways of thinking and approaching problems can be introduced and amplified through specifically designed case studies. The solutions which result from the systematic examination of these case studies should be applied directly to specific school system problems. And, finally, attention must be given to problem areas that may be unique to an individual supervisor.

INTERVENTION AT THE BASE

The third phase of the accountability system, and the most pertinent, is the development of specific instruments and techniques to evaluate how individual members of the school system are performing their assigned roles. Since this phase touches the teachers directly, it is the most difficult and also the most delicate. If it is handled properly, it can accelerate the educational development of the community's children. If it is handled poorly, or indifferently, or as just another routine task (as it so often has been in other public agencies), problems of academic retardation will persist.

Description and discussion of the design, development, and installation of individual performance standards and measures for teachers is beyond the scope of this paper.[3] There are a number of approaches to this effort utilizing both objective and subjective measures. But regardless of the measures and procedures employed, there are some general principles that warrant mention here.

Requirements of a teacher accountability program

First, an individual teacher accountability program can function effectively only within the context of a goal-setting program, such as the charter of accountability previously described, and a program of continuous supervisory

[3] Felix M. Lopez, *Evaluating Employee Performance*. Chicago: Public Personnel Association, 1968.

development in coaching and evaluation interviewing.

Second, it must be quite clear from the outset that the purpose of the accountability program is improvement of present role performance. If the measurements and standards developed are used for other purposes—such as discipline, promotion, and salary increases—the program will fail, positively and absolutely. Of course there must be a relationship between the measures of accountability and these other personnel actions, but the relationship must be indirect and antecedent rather than direct and causal.

Third, the immediate intentions of the instruments developed as part of the accountability program should be to provide the teacher (or other professional worker) with feedback on his efforts and to provide him and his supervisor with material for discussions of ways to strengthen his professional performance.

Instruments of accountability

The instruments or standards of measurement of performance must be designed to fulfill two purposes:

1. They must be meaningful and acceptable to the person who is evaluated by them.
2. They must permit quantitative consolidation in the form of means, standard scores, and percentiles to serve as criteria with which to evaluate the department, school, and district achievement of objectives.

Such instruments can be of two basic types:

1. *Results-oriented data.* These are hard data geared to the effects of the teacher's performance—attendance, standardized achievement test scores, grade point averages, etc.
2. *Person-oriented data.* These consist of ratings completed by peers, superiors, and subordinates describing the *style* of the teacher's performance—that is, his initiative, technical competence, interpersonal competence, etc. It is possible to design the instrument so that the person completing it cannot consciously control the outcome.

None of the information obtained at this level should go beyond the school principal except in a consolidated and hence anonymous form.

To insure the acceptance of these instruments, it is necessary that the teachers themselves and their supervisors actively participate in this research, design, and implementation. This is done in two ways. First, in the initial development of the program, teachers and supervisors should actively assist the professional researchers at every stage.[4] Second, and even more important, in the accountability interview, the teacher takes an active role in what is essentially a problem-solving process.

The accountability interview

The entire program described in this paper pivots around the accountability interview between supervisor and teacher. If it is conducted well throughout the school system, then the educational process in that community will thrive. If it is done poorly, the whole accountability program will fail and the school system will be in

[4] For an expansion of this principle, see Lopez, *op. cit.,* pp. 68–69.

trouble. Therefore, this encounter is crucial.

To make the interview effective, a number of conditions must exist before, during, and afterward. First, the supervisor must have discussed his own performance with his superior—the principal or the superintendent. He must also have participated in the development of his charter of accountability and that of his school or district. Both the teacher and the supervisor must be familiar with these documents.

They must also be aware of the department's and the school's goals and objectives. The supervisor must have adequate preparation in coaching and interviewing skills. Both the supervisor and the teacher must have met earlier to agree on the dimensions of the teacher's role and on acceptable standards of performance. The teacher must be given adequate time for self-evaluation, and both must have reviewed the data resulting from the accountability instruments referred to above.

During the interview, both discuss the material collected on the teacher's performance. They analyze the teacher's strengths and explore ways of capitalizing on them. They identify areas for improvement, develop an improvement plan, and choose the resources to implement it. The teacher also discusses his professional problems with his supervisor and ways in which the latter can be of greater assistance to him. They establish follow-up schedules with milestones to determine progress. And they put all of this—the plan, the schedule, and the milestones—in writing for subsequent review and follow-up.

This accountability program, sincerely pursued at all these levels, is guaranteed to achieve positive results. There will remain, however, one major obstacle—time. It is obvious that the program will make major demands on a supervisor's time. Consequently, most supervisors will assert that they do not have the time for such a meticulous and detailed approach. In part they will be wrong, and in part they will be right.

They will be wrong, first, because they are not really using the time they now have to maximum advantage. If they are like most managers, they waste a good deal of time in superfluous activities. Secondly, they will be wrong because they are mistaken in their notions of the proper functions of their job. They tend to overemphasize the professional and functional aspects of their responsibilities and to underemphasize the managerial and supervisory concerns that are of paramount importance in the organizational system.

But they will be right because their present school system, like nearly every other organizational system in the United States, requires them to perform many functions that interfere with their basic duties of manager and supervisor.[5]

The answer to this problem, which is one of the chief stumbling blocks to the implementation of an accountability program, seems to lie in a searching examination of the functions performed at each level of supervision. Many of these, upon closer examination, will be found to be delegatable, thus enriching the jobs of their subordinates and freeing them for their real responsibilities of managing one of the most vital enterprises in society—the school system.

[5] See, for example, F. M. Lopez, *The Making of a Manager: Guidelines to His Selection and Promotion.* New York: American Management Association, 1970, Chapter 4 ("What Does a Manager Do?").

Innovations in the Professional Development of Teachers

Robert B. Ruddell

University of California, Berkeley

INTRODUCTION

The critical agent of change in reading instruction is the classroom teacher. Although innovative reading programs possessing unique instructional characteristics designed to meet the needs of various pupil populations represent valuable instructional tools, this aspect of reading instruction is secondary in importance. If we are to accept this perspective, then we must shift our emphasis from finding the "magic" text to preparing the "master" teacher (34B).

Preservice educational experiences in reading and language development require careful planning and development if instructional effectiveness is to be realized in the classroom. We must move from the professional development experience offered in the fourth or fifth year of the college or university program to include experiences which provide for contact with youngsters from the freshman or sophomore year through the culminating fourth or fifth year preservice experiences. Such early experiences may include observations of innovative classroom practices, ranging from concrete to abstract concept development, aiding teachers in preparation of instructional materials, tutorial experience with children from various ethnic and achievement levels, playground leadership opportunities, and story reading and storytelling experiences with small groups of children. College and university educators must re-examine educational development programs and make provision for directed field contact with children in cooperation with public school personnel. Such experience will not only provide for a better understanding of the individual child and the nature of instruction but will also provide potential educators with one facet of information necessary in making educational career decisions.

Early preservice program counselling at the freshman or sophomore year is essential if opportunity is to be provided for developing background knowledge in such basic areas as child language and cognitive development, linguistics, sociolinguistics, and children's literature—to mention several

Robert B. Ruddell, "Innovations in the Professional Development of Teachers," in *Handbook for Developing an NDEA Institute in Reading*, ed. Jack W. Humphrey (1966). Reprinted with permission of the International Reading Association.

critical informational areas. A close relationship must be established between staff in professional schools of education and college and university staff having special competencies in areas such as those identified above. Establishing such a relationship demands that the professional educator schedule informal discussions with the college and university personnel to jointly identify special requisites important to the classroom teacher. These discussions must lead to active involvement of professors outside of the professional school in the undergraduate professional development program. The need for this involvement is illustrated by comparatively recent surveys which conclude that although 40 percent of elementary school instructional time is devoted to reading and language instruction (9) over 94 percent of teacher education programs throughout the country fail to require undergraduate course preparation in the study of the English language (10).

CONTENT AND EXPERIENCE IN THE PRESERVICE PROGRAM

It becomes clear at this point that a significant body of knowledge and experience with children is essential to the development of the effective classroom teacher. The professional school should carefully consider five general areas of content essential in the preparation of innovative reading and language teachers. These areas include the following:

1. language learning and related psychological factors,
2. linguistic implications for reading instruction,
3. methodology and reading instruction,

4. literature and the reading program,
5. innovations in reading instruction.

The development of these areas requires that the total resources of the college or university be marshaled. In addition, close relationships must be established with master teachers in local school districts so that the professional development program represents a true cooperative planning effort between the institution of higher education and public school personnel.

LANGUAGE LEARNING AND RELATED PSYCHOLOGICAL FACTORS

The preservice education experience should provide opportunity to help students examine important experiential variables related to children's language learning. Although only partial success has been attained in identifying specific variables directly related to language development, a number of significant implications for reading instruction can be obtained from an overview of language research.

The average child entering the classroom for the first time is functioning on a complex level of vocabulary and grammatical control. His vocabulary development has increased dramatically from a minute group of words used during the first and second year to many hundreds of words used by the sixth year (37, 38). The grammatical development of his language has likewise increased from one word utterances at the end of the first year to lexical class substitution in the second year (47) and the mastery of most basic grammatical fundamentals by the fourth year (14). Thus upon entering the first grade he has achieved a high degree of sophistication in his language development (42).

It is basic, however, to keep in mind in such a discussion that a wide range of variation will inevitably be present in concept and grammatical development when we consider thirty-five youngsters in any designated classroom. For example, a problem is presented when the concept-deprived child classifies the large floating object carrying men and food supplies as a *boat* when the vocabulary in the reader refers to this object as a *ship*. We must help students anticipate and be acutely aware of such difficulties and expand the child's concept of *boat* and *ship* to include size differentiation. Similar awareness and consideration must be made in understanding the provisional role structure words such as *if* and *however* play in conveying meaning.

The content of the preservice course work should include an examination of stages of concept development such as those proposed by Inhelder and Piaget (21). Bruner's discussion of concept formation, concept attainment, and learning transfer as related to the structure of subject matter would also hold significant value in such a discussion (6, 7).

Students should thus be encouraged to search for factors which produce varied degrees of language proficiency in the child. Related investigations suggest that children's language and reading achievement is a function of provision for an appropriate language model (4, 12, 28), the opportunity for parent–child interaction (4, 28), sex differences (25), intelligence differences (25, 42), auditory and visual discrimination ability (18, 48), and socioeconomic level (4, 25, 42, 44). Further, a number of studies point to the close interrelationships which exist among the language skills of speaking,

listening, reading, and writing (25, 34A, 42).

From investigations such as those indicated above we can help the student develop an added awareness of operational factors essential for language and reading development in the classroom. These include:

1. specific attention to the importance of oral language development as a base for the teaching of reading,
2. concept development encompassing the vocabulary and syntactical depth and scope utilized in the reading materials,
3. reading readiness levels precipitated by experiential and instructional variation which must be anticipated and accounted for over an extremely wide range at all grade levels, and
4. methodological approaches requiring adjustment in relation to the various types of learners encountered in the classroom.

Consideration should be given to factors encompassing a psychological framework essential to language learning experiences. From an operational point of view the following factors exemplify such a framework directly influencing the child's success in reading. (Introspectively the student may ask, "How can I implement each of the following elements in my reading program?").

Readiness. The student must be concerned with the background that the learner brings to the reading situation regardless of his reading level. The significant point is to identify the child's functioning level in word perception and comprehension skill development.

Motivation. This essential element in language learning should be considered both from an extrinsic and intrinsic point of view. The child's interest and persistence may remain at a high level in anticipation of verbal praise from his teacher. On the other hand the interest and persistence may result from functional pleasure due to the enjoyment received in participating in the vicarious experience afforded in the story. Careful consideration should be given to the importance of motivation in reading and to the examination of methods by which this factor can be strengthened in the classroom reading program.

Cues. Consideration should be given to the organization of the reading materials used in the instructional program. The rationale for the organization, sequencing, presentation, and provision for transfer of word attack and comprehension skills should be examined. This information should then be considered in light of cue adjustment relative to children possessing unique backgrounds and characteristics.

Response. Learner activity is extremely important in reading instruction. The student must observingly inquire about the nature of the response as it reflects meaningfulness and transferability for the individual child.

Reinforcement. The consequences of the reader's activity is of vital significance to the child and the teacher. The child must be provided with some feedback as to the nature of his response. The student must consider ways in which this can be accomplished most effectively for the individual youngster.

Transfer. The provision in the reading program for utilization of reading skill development in a new learning situation is of vital importance. Reading materials should be examined for this provision. The teacher will also need to carefully consider how transfer

of word recognition and comprehension skills can be effected in various content areas of the curriculum.

The significance of emphasizing discussion of these principles within a psychological framework centers about the need to help the student examine his teaching–learning environment for optimum learning conditions. Although many outstanding teachers utilize these factors on an intuitive basis, a greater conceptual awareness of learning elements should enable the student to more effectively adjust the reading program to meet the needs of individual youngsters.

LINGUISTIC IMPLICATIONS FOR READING INSTRUCTION

A significant need is present in developing basic concepts and understandings about the operation of the English language. This can be of important value to the student from the standpoint of implementing the word-study skills program and in comprehension skill development. This background should also be of consequence in extending his ability to evaluate current reading programs and in better understanding linguistically oriented articles published in such professional periodicals as *The Reading Teacher* and *Elementary English.*

Specific areas of discussion relevant to the teaching of reading and deserving consideration include the following:

1. A study of the relationship between the oral and written language systems of English should include an examination of phonemics and graphemics as related to current reading programs. The "consistencies" and "inconsistencies" of grapheme–phoneme (symbol–sound) correspondences should

be studied (20). The discussion, however, should also extend to the examination of correspondences in letter pattern context which provides for much greater regularity to English spelling (17).

e.g. hat/hæt/, hate/heyt/, heat/hiyt/

A study of the relationship of intonation (pitch or frequency, stress or loudness, and juncture or pause) to meaning as partially reflected in written punctuation can be of value to the primary grade teacher's oral reading and comprehension skills program.

e.g. Tab is in the *airplane*.
(Answer to "Where is Tab?")
Tab is in the airplane.
(Answer to "Who is in the airplane?")
Tab is in the airplane!
(Implication that Tab should not be in the airplane.)
Tab is in the airplane?
(Expression of surprise as to Tab's location.)

The effect of varied stress patterns on changes in meaning and vowel values can be utilized in clarifying certain class cleavage difficulties.

e.g. Bring the fruit *can*. /kæn/
I *can* run fast. /kən/
What is your *address*? / ædres/
Will you *address* the envelope? /ədres/

The latter examples also reassert the importance of using sentence context and avoiding isolated word introduction in developing meaningful relationships.

2. An examination of syntactical elements which produce distinct meaning changes in a sentence. The use of common structure words in sentences will require special emphasis and development for some children. Consider,

for example, the meaning contrast resulting from substitution of the following words in a given sentence: the, this; if, because; into, below; and why, what (23). Emphasizing the importance of subordination to sentence comprehension and to paragraph comprehension through word substitution and pattern expansion can be of value in developing the teacher's comprehension skills program.

e.g. He had a birthday.
Bill, my brother, had a birthday yesterday.

3. Consideration of dialect differences which may be of significant value in understanding learning problems of specific groups of children. The study of linguistic geography offers a great deal of insight relative to dialect differences in pronunciation (e.g., Midland area /r/ is retained after vowels; Southern area /r/ is lost except before vowels), lexicon (e.g., Northern area, *pail*; Midland area, *bucket*), and grammar (e.g., Northern area, *dove* as the past tense of *dive*; Southern area, *on account of* for *because*) (26). Such a study should be of definite help to the teacher confronted with teaching the child from a transient community, in a culturally different community, or if he is teaching in an area of the country where the dialect used is different from that of his own dialect area.

A greater understanding of language levels and deviations from standard English can also be an important contribution from this type of study. The use of oral-pattern practice encompassing the original development of materials or the utilization of prepared materials (e.g., tape recordings) (19) may have significant merit in meeting the responsibility of developing usage levels appropriate for different language environments. The inclusion of content following the study of phonemics and syntax should aid the student in better understanding and coping with auditory discrimination and meaning difficulties experienced by children using a language characterized by a varied dialect, vocabulary, and syntax.

4. An investigation of basic language concepts holding implications for understanding spelling change and vocabulary growth and development. From an historical standpoint major changes in the language can highlight basic language concepts. For example, the exploration of the belated effect of the Norman invasion in 1066 on a highly inflected language can lead to a more explicit understanding of the importance of word order as the carrier of meaning in the English language. The change in word pronunciation through the years coupled with foreign loan words and the slower change in recorded language can be used to explain a number of "inconsistencies" in English spelling (e.g., knight).

The influx of new words in the English language resulting from world trade and expansion can help the teacher understand the important contribution of other people and countries to the expansion of the English vocabulary (e.g., Indians: opossum, skunk; Africans: banjo, voodoo; Spanish: mustang, plaza). Language growth can also be emphasized by tracing the origin of specific words, noting how the words were used at different periods of our history, and by observing the new meanings which have been attached to words in the present space age (e.g., artificial, antenna, capsule). A depth of understanding related to vocabulary can be developed by noting how recent words have been coined using old roots (e.g., spaceship, rapid

transit, astrojet). By noting changes in the English language which have taken place throughout the years the student can more readily understand why a dictionary reflects a specific level of language usage and development during a given period of time and why it cannot be the ultimate authority on pronunciation and meaning. The examination of language content can add greatly to the student's knowledge of word study and make provision for generating a great deal of enthusiasm for vocabulary and language study with youngsters (41).

Thus classroom implications from the study of English linguistics include expanding understanding of the relationship between oral and written language leading to more effective development of phonics, syllabification, and dictionary skills; extending comprehension skills through the study of meaning resulting from changes in vocabulary and syntactical elements; and creating a broader awareness for comprehending a range of dialect and usage levels in his classroom.

METHODOLOGY AND READING INSTRUCTION

Development of reading methodology should attempt to develop a brief overview of research findings encompassing a rationale for practice and identify discussions of specific methods and techniques used in the improvement of reading instruction. The student of reading must possess a high degree of familiarity with a variety of procedures and techniques for the development of word perception and comprehension skills. To carry out effective provision for individual needs in the classroom it is essential that he possess an operational understanding of group assessment and individual reading inventories. In this manner diagnostic clues to strengths and weaknesses of the individual reader can be provided. Coordinated with reading assessment specific concern must be given to remediation techniques including the utilization of self-developed and published reading materials appropriate for a wide range of reader deficiencies. The professional school staff should consider the relative importance of the following areas in terms of the projected accomplishments for the teacher preparation program.

Word Perception Skills. Development of word perception skills should include a brief overview of research ranging from methodological investigations such as those encompassing a study of the potential merit of a phonic supplemented reading program (39) to a more basic type of experimental research considering the transferability of consistent and variable grapheme–phoneme correspondences to new words (24). Research such as that conducted throughout the country in the 27 U.S. Offices of Education sponsored first-grade reading research centers also deserves consideration (45). Even though much of methodological research lacks the rigor of carefully controlled laboratory research, partially because of the many classroom and teacher variables involved, attention should be given to the nature of the reading program studied; the type of achievement assessment made; the type of instruments utilized; and at what point in the instructional program the criterion measures were administered. In this way a great deal of clarity can be added to the interpretation of the outcomes.

The rationale used in the selection of various word attack skills and in the sequencing of the component elements of a specific skill (e.g., grapheme–phoneme correspondences) in reading programs should be examined in light of the psychological and linguistic background developed in the undergraduate program. Such an examination will help the student better understand how unique features of reading programs with a code emphasis can be utilized in strengthening the decoding skills of specific youngsters.

The practical aspects of teaching word attack skills should encompass the use of word form clues, context clues, phonic analysis, structural analysis, tactile kinesthetic exercises, and the development of dictionary skills. Following an intensive discussion of these skills application of the discussion should be carried out by working with children in classrooms established for this purpose. If actual contact with children is not possible, then observations of the development of specific skills in classrooms at several levels should be arranged.

Comprehension Skill Development. The development of comprehension skills in the reading program should receive high priority. Emphasis should be placed on the importance of children's concept development as related to the meaningful understanding of vocabulary and the utilization of comprehension skills. A brief overview of research offering implications for practice should be considered. Such an overview could well range from Thorndike's early study of mistakes in paragraph reading (46) and Judd and Buswell's study of different types of silent reading (22) to the Feifel and Lorge (15B) and the Russell and Saadeh (36) studies on meaning as related to developmental stages of thinking. This type of discussion coupled with the earlier consideration of factors related to children's language development should enable the student to build a rationale encompassing significant factors basic to comprehension skill development.

Methods and techniques utilized in the classroom can then be discussed and evaluated in light of such a rationale. The importance of operational assessment of the range of concept development in a given classroom and possible ways in which concepts can be strengthened and developed deserve strong emphasis. Establishing a reading purpose relative to levels of comprehension including factual, inference, and application levels should be considered from the applied standpoint at various grade levels and especially in the content areas. Once again classrooms should be available for the student in order that implementation or direct observation of comprehension skill development can be effected.

Meeting Individual Needs. It is essential to provide for individual learning differences in the developmental reading program. Detailed consideration should be given to the use of group and individual assessment techniques. This will require student familiarity with the administration and evaluation of group and individual reading inventories respectively isolating general class difficulties and specific individual deficiencies. A practicum should be provided in the development of diagnostic inventories related to classroom reading programs. Opportunity for the administration of such inventories as well as commercially prepared diagnostic tests is of basic importance. Techniques for remediation should encompass use of the language experience approach and the preparation of materials relative to the clues provided in the diagnostic test. The careful examination of appropriate published reading programs, reading kits, and children's books possessing high interest and limited vocabularies for remediation constitutes a valuable phase of meeting individual needs.

Discussion of classroom grouping procedures will be of significant value in helping students provide for a range of reading levels. Because of the encompassing nature of reading in the curriculum, grouping procedures should be considered not only in the developmental reading program but also in relation to the content areas of the classroom.

By briefly surveying pertinent research, developing a rationale for the word attack and comprehension skills program, and making provision for children at various levels of skills development, the preservice experience can provide the student with a basis for the evaluation, development, and improvement of his classroom program of reading instruction.

LITERATURE AND THE READING PROGRAM

The student's knowledge of children's literature is of great import to the classroom reading program. If he is familiar with literature, his awareness of children's motivations and interests can be capitalized upon in introducing quality reading experiences of immediate interest and of appropriate ability level to the individual child. The theme, plot, characterization, and writing style deserve careful consideration in the selection and adjustment of the right book to the right child in the classroom. A wide scope of literature should be considered ranging from fables and myths, to fiction and biography (1, 30).

A vast reservoir exists in children's literature for providing the child opportunity for self-reflection and understanding (e.g., deAngeli's *The Door in the Wall*), for broadening and extending meaningful concepts in subject matter areas (e.g., Averill's *Cartier Sails the St. Lawrence*), for developing greater empathy with difficulties encountered by others (e.g., Gates' *Blue Willow*), for vicarious adventures to other cultures leading to a better understanding of the world's people (e.g., DeJong's *The Wheel on the School*), and for enjoyment of realistic literary experiences (e.g., McCloskey's *Make Way for Ducklings*). Although many basal reading programs contain excellent selections chosen from quality literature, the content of the basal reader serves only as a point of departure for the literature program. Individual reading programs must be established by considering specific reading selections appropriately based on the child's interest level, his maturity and conceptual development, and his functioning reading achievement level. It is thus essential that the student know and understand both children and books on a friendly and personal basis if the right combination is to be satisfactorily achieved.

Literary appreciation can also be developed through oral language experiences. Many of the values emphasized above can be obtained through storytelling and story reading. By relating the content of a tale directly to the children, facial expression and voice intonation set the mood and carry important clues to the nature of the content (e.g., *The Three Billy-Goats Gruff*). Stories read to children can have a similar effect and may be necessary when the author's style demands an exacting recreation (e.g., Grahame's *Wind in the Willows*). Such experiences can also be of great value to the development of language comprehension skills especially for children from a concept-different environment.

The preservice program should thus emphasize and make provision for the study of children's literature and its value and application as related to a wide range of individual differences in the classroom. The utilization of literature as a basis for the study of the English language and for developing composition skills also deserves merit. The curriculum library can be of unlimited value in having available a wide selection of children's literature and in obtaining for participant availability such experimental materials as exemplified by those developed in the Nebraska Curriculum Development Center (*11*).

INNOVATIONS IN READING INSTRUCTION

Opportunity for examining recently published reading programs encompassing new approaches and techniques should be provided. The linguistic, psychological, and methodological background developed in the program can be of important value to the student in such study. Recent materials developed by publishers and curriculum centers for classroom use may be roughly grouped into the following categories (*32B*):

1. emphasis on carefully controlled grapheme–phoneme correspondences or larger linguistic units with emphasis on a consistent presentation of the orthography (*8, 13, 16, 31A, 43*);

2. emphasis on language structure which is more nearly like that used by the child in his oral language with emphasis on decoding, meaning, and comprehension (*3 9A, 13B, 15A, 31B, 33, 34C, 40*);

3. emphasis on programming reading materials in such a fashion to provide for the adjustment of individual rate and progress (8, 35);

4. emphasis on story characters presented in an interracial setting for the purpose of increasing interest through greater identification by the reader with the story setting (3, 5, 49);

5. emphasis on building communication skills and basic concepts related to the English language through the study of literature (11);

6. emphasis on building communication skills using experiences of the child with multimedia;

7. emphasis on developing communication skills using a combination of media experiences.

As the examination of these new trends proceeds, it is of the utmost importance that the student focus and utilize his classroom experience combined with his academic knowledge in order that the validity of new programs may be assessed in relation to linguistic, psychological, and methodological evidence. It is necessary to consider the proposed innovations against a background of children possessing a wide range of characteristics in order to determine program effectiveness for a given group of children.

CONCLUSIONS AND RECOMMENDATIONS

It is obvious that the experiences described above cannot fit within most preservice education programs as presently organized. The informational content and application of this content through direct experience with children must be carefully planned over a three or four year period—starting with the freshman or sophomore year at the college or university. Thus course experiences in academic majors and minors should make provision for foundation and background areas related to reading and language development; experiences with pupils from early childhood through high school should be provided through special directed study utilizing college and university personnel with such efforts being coordinated by the professional school of education; and the culminating year of the preservice experience in the professional school should be devoted to seminar settings held in the on-site location of the supervised teaching experience and formulated with the joint cooperation of the preservice student, the master teacher, and the college or university professional school personnel.

In summary the preservice professional development program should include the following:

1. study of basic language concepts, including implications for understanding children's reading and language growth and development,

2. study of the relationship between the oral language system and the written language system of English,

3. examination of syntactical elements which produce distinct meaning changes within and across sentences,

4. study of concept development, thinking strategies, and the relationship between language and thought,

5. study of socio-ethnic variables and school–community relationships,

6. study and understanding of dialect differences which will be of significant value in reading and language instruction for teachers and children (particularly low income Black, White, and Chicano young-

sters) speaking standard and non-standard English respectively,

7. study of children's literature as related to ethnic differences and development of self-concept for individual children,

8. indepth study of reading and language methodology and instruction including concepts such as the following: wider range of reading and language development will be found in most urban primary classrooms; children's reading and language development is greatly influenced by the models presented in their environmental settings; in decoding instruction sound-blending should be placed in a natural sound unit; various decoding units including context clues can be used in reading instruction and the teacher should attempt to develop a corresponding fit between a youngster's learning style and the appropriate unit or units; the child's concept development can be enhanced most effectively at the early levels through direct experience; oral language development should provide a basis for reading and written language development in an integrated language skills curriculum; a close interrelationship exists between listening comprehension and reading comprehension.

If the preservice professional experience is to result in significant improvement in preparing the master teacher, cooperative planning by the professional school personnel must account for the use of the wide range of resources available in higher education, and in the elementary, junior high, and secondary levels of public education. A basic knowledge background in reading and language related disciplines is essential to the development of highly effective classroom instruction. Early direct experience with pupils at a wide range of levels in real classrooms is also critical to the development of a successful preservice experience. And finally, the preservice experience must be viewed as the first level in developing the master teacher. Ongoing teacher renewal centers must be established and staffed with highly skilled professionals who plan for intensive inservice work in reading and language instruction. The neophyte teacher should be provided opportunity to continue the preservice education experience into the early years of public school teaching where the carefully planned professional education program will enable the individual teacher to pursue the development of competence in reading and language instruction leading to the level of master teacher.

BIBLIOGRAPHY

1. Arbuthnot, May Hill, *Children and Books.* Chicago: Scott, Foresman and Company, 1964.

2. Auston, Mary C., *The Torch Lighters.* Cambridge, Mass: Harvard University Press, 1961.

3. Baugh, Dolores, and Marjorie P. Pulsifer, *Let's See the Animals.* San Francisco: Chandler Publishing Company, 1965.

4. Bernstein, Basil, "Language and Social Class," *British Journal of Sociology,* 11:271–76, 1960.

5. Black, Irma S., *Around the City.* New York: The Macmillan Co., 1965.

6. Bruner, Jerome S., *The Process of Education.* Cambridge, Mass.: Harvard University Press, 1960.

7. Bruner, Jerome S., Jacqueline Goodnow, and George A. Austin, *A Study of Thinking.* New York: John Wiley, 1956.

8. BUCHANAN, CYNTHIA DEE, *Programmed Reading*. New York: McGraw-Hill Book Company, Inc., 1963.

9A. CLYMER, THEODORE, et al., *Reading 360*. Boston: Ginn and Co., 1970.

9B. COMMITTEE ON NATIONAL INTEREST, *The Natonal Interest and the Continuing Education of Teachers of English*. Champaign, Ill.: National Council of Teachers of English, 1964.

10. COMMITTEE ON NATIONAL INTEREST, *The National Interest and the Teaching of English*. Champaign, Ill.: National Council of Teachers of English, 1961.

11. *Curriculum for English*. Nebraska Curriculum Development Center, The University of Nebraska, 1963.

12. DAVIS, EDITH A., *The Development of Linguistic Skill in Twins, Singletons with Siblings, and Only Children from Ages Five to Ten Years*. University of Minnesota Press, Minneapolis, 1937.

13A. DOWNING, JOHN A., *The Downing Readers*. London: Initial Teaching Publishing Company, Ltd., 1963.

13B. DURR, WILLIAM, et al., *The Houghton Mifflin Readers*. Boston: Houghton Mifflin Company, 1971.

14. ERVIN, SUSAN M., and WICK R. MILLER, *Language Development*, The 62nd Yearbook of the National Society for the Study of Education, V. 62, Part I: 108–43. Chicago: University of Chicago Press, 1963.

15A. FAY, LEO, et al., *The Young America Basic Reading Program*. Chicago: Lyons and Carnahan, 1972.

15B. FEIFEL, HERMAN, and I. D. LORGE, "Qualitative Differences in the Vocabulary Responses of Children," *Journal of Educational Psychology*, 41: 1–18, 1950.

16. FRIES, CHARLES C., *A Basic Reading Series Developed Upon Linguistic Principles* (Preliminary and Experimental). Ann Arbor, Mich.: Fries Publications, 1964.

17. ———, *Linguistics and the Teaching of Reading*. New York: Holt, Rinehart and Winston, 1964.

18. GOINS, JEAN T., *Visual Perceptual Abilities and Early Reading Progress*. Supplementary Education Monographs, No. 87. Chicago: University of Chicago Press, 1958.

19. GOLDEN, RUTH I., "Changing Dialects by Using Tapes," in *Social Dialects and Language Learning* (ROGER W. SHUY, ed.). Champaign, Ill.: National Council of Teachers of English, 1964, pp. 63–66.

20. HALL, ROBERT A., JR., *Sound and Spelling In English*. Philadelphia: Chilton Co., 1961.

21. INHELDER, B., and JEAN PIAGET, *The Growth of Logical Thinking from Childhood to Adolescence*. New York: Basic Books, 1958.

22. JUDD, CHARLES H., and GUY T. BUSWELL, *Silent Reading: A Study of Its Various Types*. Supplementary Education Monographs. Chicago: University of Chicago Press, 1922.

23. LEFEVRE, CARL A., *Linguistics and the Teaching of Reading*. New York: McGraw-Hill, 1964.

24. LEVIN, HARRY, and JOHN WATSON, "The Learning of Variable Grapheme-to-Phoneme Correspondences: Variations in the Initial Consonant Position," *A Basic Research Program on Reading*. Ithaca, N.Y.: Cornell University, 1963, Cooperative Research Project No. 639.

25. LOBAN, WALTER D., *The Language*

of Elementary School Children. Champaign, Ill., National Council of Teachers of English, 1963.

26. MALMSTROM, JEAN, and ANNABELLE ASHLEY, *Dialects U.S.A.* Champaign, Ill.: National Council of Teachers of English, 1963.

27. *Manual for the Preparation of Proposals, NDEA Institutes for Advanced Study.* Title XI, Summer 1966, Academic Year 1966–67. Washington, D.C.: U.S. Department of Health, Education and Welfare, Office of Education, 1965.

28. MILNER, ESTHER, "A Study of the Relationship Between Reading Readiness in Grade One School Children and Patterns of Parent–Child Interaction," *Child Development,* 22:95–112, 1951.

29. NATIONAL EDUCATION ASSOCIATION, *Schools for the 60's.* New York: McGraw-Hill Book Company, 1963.

30. REID, VIRGINIA M. (ed.), *Children's Literature—Old and New.* Champaign, Ill.: The National Council of Teachers, 1964.

31A. RICHARDSON, JACK E., JR., HENRY LEE SMITH, JR., and BERNARD J. WEISS, *The Linguistic Readers.* New York: Harper & Row, Publishers, 1965.

31B. ROBINSON, HELEN M., et al., *Scott Foresman Reading Systems.* Glenview, Ill.: Scott, Foresman and Company, 1971.

32. RUDDELL, ROBERT B., "In a Time of Transition We Seek New and Better Ways to Teach Reading," *California Teachers Association Journal,* 61:15–16, 56–64, October 1965.

33. ———, *The Effect of Four Programs of Reading Instruction with Varying Emphasis on the Regularity of Grapheme-Phoneme Correspondences and the Relation of Language Structure to Meaning on Achievement in First-Grade Reading.* Berkeley: University of California, 1964. Cooperative Research Project No. 2699.

34A. ———, "The Effect of the Similarity of Oral and Written Patterns of Language Structure on Reading Comprehension," *Elementary English,* 42:403–10, 1965.

34B. RUDDELL, ROBERT B., and ARTHUR C. WILLIAMS, *A Research Investigation of a Literacy Teaching Model: Project DELTA.* U.S. Department of Health, Education and Welfare, Office of Education, EPDA Project No. 005262, 1972.

34C. RUDDELL, ROBERT B., BARBARA W. GRAVES, and FLOYD DAVIS, *Program BUILD.* Boston: Ginn and Co., 1972.

35. RUSSELL, DAVID H., et al., *By Myself.* Boston: Ginn and Company, 1962.

36. RUSSELL, DAVID H., and I. Q. SAADEH, "Qualitative Levels in Children's Vocabulary," *Journal of Educational Psychology,* 53:170–74, August 1962.

37. SMITH, MARY K., "Measurement of the Size of General English Vocabulary Through the Elementary Grades and High School," *Genetic Psychology Monographs,* 24:311–45, 1941.

38. SMITH, MEDORAH E., "An Investigation of the Development of the Sentence and the Extent of Vocabulary in Young Children," *Studies in Child Welfare,* Vol. 5, No. 5. Iowa City: State University of Iowa, 1926, pp. 28–71.

39. SPARKS, PAUL E., and LEO C. FAY, "An Evaluation of Two Methods of Teaching Reading," *Elementary School Journal,* 57:386–90, April 1957.

40. STOPLEN, BUELA, PRISCILLA TYLER, and ELEANOR POUNDS, *Linguistic Block Series*. Chicago: Scott, Foresman and Company, 1963.

41. STRICKLAND, RUTH G., *The Contribution of Structural Linguistics to the Teaching of Reading, Writing, and Grammar in the Elementary School*. Bulletin of the School of Education, Indiana University, Bloomington, Vol. 40, No. 1, January 1964.

42. ————, *The Language of Elementary School Children: Its Relationship to the Language of Reading Textbooks and the Quality of Reading of Selected Children*. Bulletin of the School of Education, Indiana University, Bloomington, Vol. 38, No. 4, July 1962.

43. TANYZER, HAROLD, and ALBERT J. MAZURKIEWIC, *Early-to-Read i/t/a Program*. New York: Initial Teaching Alphabet Publications, Inc., 1964.

44. TEMPLIN, MILDRED C., *Certain Language Skills in Children: Their Development and Interrelationships*. Minneapolis: University of Minnesota Press, 1957.

45. *The Reading Teacher*, May 1966. (This issue is devoted to research reports from the cooperative investigations carried out from September 1964 to May 1965 in twenty-seven U.S. Office of Education–sponsored First-Grade Reading Research Centers.)

46. THORNDIKE, E. L., "Reading and Reasoning: A Study of Mistakes in Paragraph Reading," *Journal of Educational Psychology*, 8:323–32, 1917.

47. WEIR, RUTH, *Language in the Crib*. The Hague: Mouton and Company, 1962.

48. WEPMAN, J. M., "Auditory Discrimination, Speech and Reading," *Elementary School Journal*, 60:325–33, 1960.

49. Writer's Committee of the Great Cities School Improvement Program of the Detroit Public Schools, *The Detroit Series*. Chicago: Follett Publishing Co., 1963.

An Analysis of Teacher Effectiveness in Classroom Instruction in Reading

William L. Rutherford
University of Texas at Austin

Any discussion of the essential components of an effective reading program will include one or more of the following elements: (*1*) the students; (2) the teacher; (3) teaching method; (4) instructional materials; and (5) ancillary personnel and resources, e.g., the librarian and the library. Research findings (*1, 2, 5*) have made it abundantly clear that the single most important element is the teacher. All of the other factors are important, of course, but pupil success or failure is directly related to teacher effectiveness.

But what are the characteristics of an effective reading teacher? How does one become a successful teacher of reading? It goes without saying that indisputable answers to these questions have not yet been discovered, but there is available much knowledge to guide those who would heed it. This report will present some of this information along with suggestions for incorporating it into teaching behavior.

In this discussion, teaching effectiveness will be divided into two categories, what the teacher is—how he acts and interacts with children on the personal level; and what the teacher does —how he performs his instructional duties. These categories are roughly parallel to the affective and cognitive domains of behavior.

PERSONAL CHARACTERISTICS OF TEACHERS

Research with teachers in general furnishes some insights into affective behaviors that might reasonably be generalized and applied to teachers of reading. A succinct review of this research is provided by Hamacheck (4).

Investigations of the personal characteristics of teachers revealed that effective teachers have a sense of humor, they are fair, empathetic, more democratic than autocratic, and they have good rapport with students on an individual or group basis. Effective teachers also view themselves as being related to people rather than withdrawn. They feel adequate, trustworthy, wanted, and worthy rather than the opposite of these feelings. In addition to feeling good about themselves, teachers who

William L. Rutherford, "An Analysis of Teacher Effectiveness in Classroom Instruction in Reading," in *Reading Methods and Teacher Improvement*, ed. Nila Banton Smith (1971). Reprinted with permission of William L. Rutherford and the International Reading Association.

are effective have a more positive view of students and adults and a more accepting attitude toward the ideas and values of others.

The classroom behaviors of effective teachers seem to reflect more of the following characteristics (4):

1. Willingness to be flexible, to be direct or indirect as the situation demands.
2. Ability to perceive the world from the student's point of view.
3. Ability to personalize their teaching.
4. Willingness to experiment, to try out new things.
5. Skill in asking questions (as opposed to seeing self as a kind of answering service).
6. Knowledge of subject matter and related areas.
7. Provision of well-established examination procedures.
8. Provision of definite study helps.
9. Reflection of an appreciative attitude (evidenced by nods, comments, smiles).
10. Use of conversational manner in teaching—informal, easy style.

Harris (6) reports on several studies that relate specifically to reading instruction. In a study comparing a language experience approach with a skills-centered approach, he and his collaborators found that teachers in the former method received good results with praise and poor results with criticism. Teachers in the skills-centered approach seemed to get better results when they avoided excessive praise or criticism and concentrated on skills instruction.

From other studies Harris drew these conclusions:

1. Mild criticism does not seem to effect achievement, but strong criticism negatively affects achievement.
2. No relation between the frequency of use of praise and achievement in general has been found.
3. Praise seems to be more effective when issued in relation to a specific student contribution.

INSTRUCTIONAL ACTIVITIES OF TEACHERS

Very few are the studies that have investigated the specific instructional activities of reading teachers, and even fewer have checked the relationship between these activities and student achievement.

Harris reported that good achievement tends to be associated with a high level of verbal interchange between teacher and students. Such an interchange supposedly indicates an active discussion between teacher and pupils, probably with an exchange of questions and answers.

Whereas Harris did not report on the nature of the questions asked in the verbal interchange, Guszak (3) did analyze the questioning strategies of reading teachers. He did not, however, correlate these strategies with student achievement.

The initial task in Guszak's study was to categorize the types of questions teachers ask in reading lessons. He found that most teacher questions were of the following six types:

1. Recognition—locating information from reading context.
2. Recall—recalling a fact previously read.
3. Translation—changing words, ideas, and pictures into different symbolic form.

4. Conjecture—anticipating what will or might happen without providing a rationale.
5. Explanation—providing a rationale for a response based on the context or even going beyond the context.
6. Evaluation—making judgments based on values rather than fact or inferences.

From his observations in a number of second, fourth, and sixth grade classrooms, Guszak found that 56.9 percent of all questions asked were of the recall type. Recognition questions were asked 13.9 percent of the time, and 15.3 percent were evaluation type questions, but most of the evaluation questions could be answered by a simple "yes" or "no" and required little depth of thought. Conjecture and explanation questions, which require a higher level of thinking, constituted only 6.5 and 7.2 percent, respectively, of the total questions asked.

In concluding, Guszak pointed out that most of the recall questions focused on trivial facts from the story. These questions tended to lead children away from the literal understanding of the broad text which should be the goal of comprehension instruction. He also warned that teachers who encourage the unsupported value judgments that are called for in evaluation type questions may be conditioning students for irresponsible citizenship. To combat these deficiencies in questioning strategies, Guszak recommends that teachers tape their lessons and listen to them carefully afterwards.

A constellation of teaching procedures and teacher skills were found to be associated with high reading achievement in studies by Pescosolido (7) and Wade (8).

Pescosolido observed twenty-eight fourth grade teachers twice each in an attempt to assess their teaching performance when teaching reading. He then measured the reading achievement of the students in these classes with the California Reading Test. The correlation between gains in reading and the teacher rating was .74. Seven teaching procedures were found to have a high relationship to growth in reading; (1) systematic and meaningful vocabulary development, (2) availability and use of a variety of instructional materials, (3) making appraisals of pupil attitudes toward teaching, (4) provision for a constructive independent reading program, (5) development of purposes for reading, (6) reading silently prior to oral reading, and (7) adequate preparation by the teacher for the reading lesson.

Wade constructed an instrument to test a group of teacher skills used in reading instruction in grades two through five. These skills included choosing and evaluating teaching materials, diagnosing and correcting deficiencies in certain skill areas, judging pupils' reading ability, evaluating pupil progress, and grouping homogeneously for instruction. The test was administered to a group of employed teachers, to student teachers with sixteen weeks' teaching experience, and to a group of undergraduates in education. On the test the employed teachers outscored the student teachers who outscored the undergraduates. In addition, it was found that children taught by teachers who scored in the highest quartile made significantly greater gains in reading achievement than did students taught by teachers in the lowest quartile.

From these research investigations, at least two conclusions can be drawn: (1) teachers are the success ingredient in reading instruction; and (2) teachers do differ in their teaching effectiveness, and these differences are detectable in pupil achievement.

Just exactly what it is that makes the difference in teaching effectiveness has not yet been definitely established through research. But do we need research to tell us what makes reading teachers effective? The real need now is to put into practice those things that are already known about good reading instruction. A review of some of these "knowns" in the cognitive domain of teacher behavior might be helpful at this point.

"KNOWNS" ABOUT GOOD READING INSTRUCTION

1. To read, children must be able to recognize words and get meaning from these words.
2. To do these two things effectively, children must master a wide variety of intricate skills.
3. It is the responsibility of the teacher to know these skills and to teach each child so that he masters them.
4. To fulfill this obligation, teachers must know the needs of each child and provide instruction appropriate to these needs.
5. Children's needs, not books or curriculum guides or grade level designations, must determine the instruction children receive.

It will be noted that these teacher behaviors are very similar to those Wade found to be significantly related to high reading achievement.

A teacher who respects these imperatives of good instruction will structure his reading program in the following manner:

1. Begin the instructional program

with a diagnosis of the specific reading needs of each child.
2. Design all lessons or learning experiences to meet the needs identified through diagnosis.
3. Define in precise terms what it is that children are to learn in each lesson.
4. Teach to accomplish these objectives, avoiding tasks that frustrate pupils and tasks that do not contribute to the accomplishment of the objectives, e.g., meaningless recall questions.
5. Following the lesson, evaluate to determine what *each* child knows, not just what the "answering" students know.
6. Plan the next lesson on the basis of this evaluation.

Compare this approach with the typical reading program:

1. Teachers have scores from a readiness test or achievement test or the report of a previous teacher which indicates the book the child was "in" last year. This information is used as the basis for grouping even though it furnishes very little insight into the specific reading needs of individual children.
2. The next story in the book, not the needs of children, dictates the objectives of the reading lesson.
3. Objectives are stated, if at all, in general terms that defy evaluation, e.g., "to introduce vowel sounds."
4. The questions in the teacher's guide are asked even though they may not contribute to pupil learning. Guszak found in his study that on the very first attempt, children gave acceptable responses to 90 percent of the literal comprehension questions. This suggests it may not be necessary or useful to spend time on this type of instructional activity for many children have already mastered this skill.

5. Evaluation of the lesson is accomplished through oral questioning. Because all children cannot respond to all questions and because the better students do most of the answering, it is virtually impossible for the teacher to discover what each child knows.

6. The next lesson is planned in accordance with the next story in the book, regardless of the findings of the previous evaluation.

A GUIDE FOR OBSERVING READING INSTRUCTION

A guide for observing reading instruction has been developed and used by this writer and his students to investigate the nature of reading group instruction. The instrument is designed for use by a team of two observers, but it can be used by a single observer or by a teacher who has tape recorded his lesson.

Specifically, the Guide will reveal the following things:

1. The portion of time spent in teacher talk

2. The portion of time spent in student talk

3. The number of interchanges between teacher and student

4. How much time is spent by each student talking or reading aloud

5. What types of teaching activities are included in the lesson

6. Approximate percentage of time devoted to each activity.

Here is how the Guide is used by an observer team. At five second intervals, Observer One indicates whether the teacher or a student is talking or reading or if there is silence. The observer mentally assigns a number to each student and records his number

each time he verbalizes so the number of times a child responds or performs can be ascertained.

Using the following categories, Observer Two records at five second intervals the types of instructional activities that occur.

C = Comprehension development, which includes any activities intended to teach or test understanding of material read. This encompasses everything from recall of a name or simple fact to critical analysis of a selection.

R = Word recognition includes any activities intended to improve a student's skill in "unlocking" or recognizing words.

O = Oral reading by teacher or student. This symbol should be used only when there is an actual attempt to improve oral reading skill. Such instruction usually emphasizes reading for meaning, attention to punctuation, appropriate speed, enunciation, etc. When oral reading is used primarily for *evaluating* or *improving* word recognition, it should be marked "R" (word recognition). Such would probably be the case in the following types of situations: (1) when a child is asked to read to find a word that begins or ends with the same letter or sound as some other word, or (2) when the child is asked to read so the teacher can assess his ability to use word attack skills to recognize unknown words. If the primary purpose of the oral reading is to evaluate or improve comprehension, the symbol C (comprehension) should be used. When a teacher says, "Billy, read the first sentence on page 46 and tell us how Dick's goat got out of his pen," she is using oral reading to improve or check comprehension.

S = Silent reading by teacher or student. This symbol will typically be used when an entire group is engaged in silent reading. If a single child is asked to read for some word recognition or comprehension purpose, the symbol R or C should be used.

E = Enrichment activities—discussions carried on to establish background for the story to be read would be included here. Also, relating personal experiences by teacher or students. Additional information presented by teacher or pupils to supplement the story or lesson would be categorized as an enrichment activity.

L = Listening skills—any direct attempt to improve the listening skills of students would be included in this category. Caution: teacher admonitions such as "pay attention" and "listen carefully" do not qualify as direct instruction in listening skills.

Some interesting and useful insights into reading group instruction can be gleaned through the use of this instrument. A look at a representative lesson in the primary grades will serve to illustrate this claim.

One teacher taught a lesson which, according to her objectives, was to present several word recognition skills. The observational analysis showed that less than forty percent of the lesson was devoted to these skills, while an approximately equal portion of time was spent on comprehension skills. Enrichment and silent reading activities received a combined total of twenty percent of the instructional time. No attempt was made to teach listening skills.

This lesson was discouraging for several reasons. First, it reflects the tendency of many primary teachers to spend as much or more time on com-prehension activities than is spent on word recognition. Certainly comprehension is a vital part of reading, but most children who have reading difficulties are deficient in word recognition skills, not comprehension. This suggests that more, not less, time should be spent teaching recognition skills. Among those who do have comprehension problems, there are only a relative few who need the recall and/or recognition type skills that constituted a major portion of the comprehension activities in this lesson.

For another reason this lesson gives cause for concern. The teacher apparently did not seriously intend that the lesson should accomplish the stated objectives, otherwise word recognition skills would have received a greater share of instructional time. Had the pupils mastered the recognition skills early in the lesson, it would have been appropriate to either stop the lesson or go on to another skill. But this was not the case, for the recognition activities followed the comprehension activities.

The time spent on enrichment and silent reading is also perplexing. In the first place, both activities were closely related to the comprehension instruction which really increased the total percentage of time spent teaching comprehension. In addition is the consideration of how the silent reading was accomplished. First, the story was read paragraph by paragraph or page by page with questions being asked after each reading. Only after the story had been dissected in this manner did the children have the opportunity to read the story as a whole. What possible enjoyment or connected meaning can children derive from a story read in this manner?

Judging from this lesson, and from many others observed, listening is rarely taught as a part of reading instruction. In most instances there is very little direct listening instruction during the reading period. Hopefully, this skill is being taught at some other time during the day.

A check of student–teacher interactions revealed a fairly even division between teacher talk and student talk. There was a relatively high level of verbal interchanges, a factor associated with good achievement according to Harris. However, many of the student verbalisms were one-word responses to a teacher question, meaning that these discussions were really very lively.

Further analysis of the interactions made it even more evident that the discussion wasn't animated and stimulating on the part of the class as a whole. Of the eight students in the group, one child spoke or read twenty-six times while another child performed only once and two others performed just three times. Four children accounted for seventy percent of the student responses.

These findings on student participation are interesting from another standpoint. There was no written assignment following the reading lesson, so if the teacher evaluated the lesson, it had to be through the oral responses of the children. How could the teacher possibly know anything about those children who were unresponsive? And what about the child who recited twenty-six times? Did she learn anything or was she just displaying knowledge and skill possessed before the lesson even began?

What often appears to be happening in reading instruction is that teachers are placing too much reliance on a basal reader or other structured instructional material. They base their lessons on the objectives and techniques offered in the teacher's guide. When the established program seems inadequate, they use supplemental materials, often another basal series, but taught in much the same way as the original program. This is not an incrimination of basal readers or other structured materials, they are useful tools. But they are only tools. There is no way in which a book or series taught just as it is printed, can meet the daily needs of even a single child, much less the needs of a reading group. It is imperative that teachers *adapt* materials to meet student needs.

It well may be that the principal difference between effective and ineffective teachers is that effective teachers teach *children* to read while ineffective teachers teach *materials* to children.

REFERENCES

1. BOND, GUY L., and ROBERT DYKSTRA, "The Cooperative Research Program in First-Grade Reading Instruction," *Reading Research Quarterly,* 2 (Summer 1967), 26–142.

2. FRY, EDWARD, "Comparison of Beginning Reading With i.t.a., DMS, and t.o. After Three Years," *Reading Teacher,* 22 (January 1969), 357–62.

3. GUSZAK, FRANK J., "Teacher Questioning and Reading," *Reading Teacher,* 21 (December 1967), 227–334.

4. HAMACHEK, DON, "Characteristics of Good Teachers and Implications for Teacher Education," *Phi Delta Kappan,* 50 (February 1959), 341–46.

5. HARRIS, ALBERT J., BLANCHE L. SERWER, and LAWRENCE GOLD, "Comparing Reading Approaches in First-Grade Teaching With Disad-

vantaged Children—Extended into Sceond Grade," *Reading Teacher*, 20 (May 1967), 698–703.

6. HARRIS, ALBERT J., "The Effective Teacher of Reading," *Reading Teacher*, 23 (December 1969), 195–204.

7. PESCOSOLIDO, JOHN RICHARD. "The Identification and Appraisal of Certain Major Factors in the Teaching of Reading," unpublished doctoral dissertation, University of Connecticut.

Dissertation Abstracts, 23, 1629. Ann Arbor, Michigan: University Microfilms, 1962.

8. WADE, EUGENE WELLINGTON, "The Construction and Validation of a Test of Ten Teacher Skills Used in Reading Instruction, Grades 2–5," unpublished doctoral dissertation, Indiana University. *Dissertation Abstracts*, 22, 167–68. Ann Arbor, Michigan: University Microfilms, 1960.

An Invaluable Resource:
The School Volunteer

Morris D. Caplin

Education has long been the business of the professional educator. However, during the past ten years, the educator has been receiving more and more assistance from people in the local community. At first it was mostly housewives and students. Today it includes businessmen, retired citizens, and anyone else who has free time and is willing to assist them in subjects with which they are having difficulty, to enrich them culturally, or to improve their self-image.

The School Volunteer movement received great impetus in New York City through a grant to the Public Education Association by the Ford Foundation in 1956. A further grant in 1964 established the National School Volunteer Program. Before this, volunteer service to the schools appeared to be sporadic, diffuse, and minimal, although community groups have always offered some service to schools. Under the auspices of the NSVP, activity was generated in small and large urban and suburban areas. Participation was voluntary and the service offered was advisory. Most programs were organized around guidelines set up in *School Volunteers (1)*.

This program has shown a steady growth pattern. By the end of 1964 seven programs had started. By the

Reprinted from *The Clearing House* (September 1970) by permission of Fairleigh Dickinson University.

end of 1967 there were 17, with 3 to 6 times as many volunteers as in 1964 (2). For example, Pittsburgh, during the 1967–68 school year, had 254 volunteers in 31 public schools and 100 volunteers in 8 parochial schools. This was an increase of over 200 per cent over the previous year. The volunteer dropout rate was only 3 per cent (3).

The basic aims of the School Volunteer Program are:

1. to relieve the teacher of nonprofessional chores,
2. to offer individual help to children not working well in a group situation (trying to provide the motivation and experiences essential for learning),
3. to enrich the school program through community resources, and
4. to stimulate an informed community to more active support of public education.

The kinds of services offered by volunteers fall into various categories: general classroom or school service, individual help service, and enrichment activities. Many interesting special programs have also been developed to meet specific needs.

The financing of the School Volunteer Program varies in different cities, but the budget is usually underwritten by either local citizen efforts, foundation grants, the Board of Education, federal agencies, or by any combination of these. Very often, as the value of the program is demonstrated, it is included in the Board of Education budget.

There are no set criteria for school volunteers, but, generally, they must be in good health, promise to fulfill a regularly scheduled commitment, and must enjoy working with children. Some special programs may require specific skills, and others, a college degree. All applicants are usually interviewed for placement in services that will be most enjoyed by them, and to which they can offer the best of their talents. Satisfactory job placement may well be the most important factor in retaining good volunteers.

Many methods of recruitment, such as newspapers, radio, television, posters, flyers, and letters, are used. From information gathered in many cities, the most successful method seems to be the referral by a volunteer who has been so enthusiastic that she had influenced a friend or group of friends to try it. Volunteering has been mostly a middle class activity, but volunteers are increasingly being recruited from all levels of society. The NSVP Project Report states, "There is wide recognition that neighborhood volunteers, even with limited schooling, have a great deal of wisdom and life experience to bring to the schools, especially in relation to their knowledge of the community and their understanding of the children"(4).

San Francisco is one of the cities which is very interested in involving neighborhood parents as volunteers. In their report to the Board of Education, the San Francisco Education Auxiliary states, "The unmotivated child often reflects his frustrated and apathetic parents. By calling on these people who have much experience of life, albeit little formal education, we hope to join the advantaged and disadvantaged in working together to create a better climate of learning for all our children" (5).

School volunteer service may also become a stepping-stone to paid employment and escape from poverty. For example, since October, 1966, when volunteers were first recruited from poverty areas in New York City, 63 have left to accept employment in the schools (6).

Most cities have fairly extensive programs of orientation, training, and supervision. These give volunteers basic approaches and skills that they need, as well as an understanding of the relationship of the volunteer program to the school and of the volunteer to the teacher.

Much of the evaluation of the program is done on an informal basis, but the need for evaluation has been intensified within the last year or two because of the demands for expansion of the program and the increasing use of federal and other public funds. From oral and written comments of volunteers, the professional staff, and children and their parents, it would seem that the program is a great success and that children have a more rewarding school experience because of it. It appears that the number of volunteers increases every year of its operation, and the kinds of programs in which they are participating are growing (7).

Several cities have had volunteers from major business companies. In Philadelphia, at the beginning of 1968, nine companies released workers to tutor, act as school aides, and to offer job opportunity counseling. Philadelphia Gas Works has a list of 98 tutor volunteers, and the manager of Customer Service Operations reports that "tutors often derive as much, if not more, personal satisfaction from their participation than the children do themselves" (8). Many of the volunteers have been active for over a year and a half, tutoring in arithmetic, speech, social science, and science.

Mark Leven, a principal in one of the participating schools, commented, "There is no doubt in my mind that this volunteer service is one of the most significant contributions being offered to our students by the community" (9).

In Boston, there are 650 volunteers in 75 schools, a number of whom are business men and women released for part of every day by their employers to serve in the public schools. Robert Hoddeson, an executive of Prudential Life Insurance Company, wrote of his experiences teaching creative writing. He helped the students put out their high school's first literary magazine with 64 pages of poems, stories, essays, sketches, and a one-act play. This year he is teaching conversational English to foreign-born children (10).

A program unique to Boston is one which utilizes a television assistant volunteer group who help in the schools by implementing and following up a classroom series, *Meet the Arts* and *Let's Investigate,* which is broadcast by Boston's educational channel. The volunteers, after watching the programs with the children in the classrooms, do follow-up projects in art and science with the students to help make the programs relevant to their everyday lives. This program has now been extended to provide television volunteers for *The City Child,* a new enrichment series (11).

Winnetka, Illinois makes use of the services of their older citizens. A Volunteer Pool for Community Service came into being as a by-product of the Senior Center in 1960. The Senior Center is a meeting place for retired men and women who have been successful in business and professions and have the will and desire to share their skills and knowledge with others. The Winnetka schools invite informed retirees to talk to classes in the local schools. A retired newspaperman helped some students start a school newspaper. A retired banker helped children working in their school banks. A former executive of a transportation company discussed pioneer travel with third graders. A naval officer told about his experiences at sea. Many types of students benefited from this kind of personalized learning—the underachiever, the unmotivated child, the gifted child, and the slow learner.

Some remarkable contributions to library service were made in schools in Cleveland and Boston. From a beginning of a few dozen volunteers in 4 libraries in 1959, the program had grown so much that by 1967 every one of the 136 schools in Cleveland had libraries for which volunteers had raised the money, supplied the books, and provided the staff (12). In Boston, in 1966, no elementary school had a central library. Today, under the supervision of a librarian and volunteers, every school will soon have one. Volunteers have painted, put up shelves, hung curtains, pictures, and travel posters, and processed, catalogued, and shelved thousands of books (13).

At the University of Washington in Seattle, volunteers take fifth and sixth graders on trips to places such as the state capitol, the mountains, and the theatre. Last year, 25 groups included 51 university students and 230 children from 4 schools (14).

San Francisco has an important enrichment program. Through voluntary contributions, free symphony orchestra and circus tickets have been given to hundreds of pupils. Youngsters have been bussed to Young Audience concerts, museums, and zoos. New paintings appear on school walls every month (15).

An early venture, not connected with the National School Volunteer Program, took place in 1959 in Elmont, New York, where a specialized program within the regular education system devoted itself to providing seriously disturbed children with individualized education and training (16). Childhood schizophrenics and brain damaged children were identified and selected to participate. Their age range was from five to nine, and their pattern included withdrawal with autistic overtones, as well as aggressive, hostile, and disruptive behavior.

A program was set up for these children, enlisting the aid of the community. Since there was no space in the schools at the time for this kind of individualized instruction, the Elmont Jewish Center volunteered six classrooms and other facilities during school mornings. The Board of Education provided transportation. The local Kiwanis Club paid the insurance premiums needed for the children when off school premises, bought special equipment, and provided snacks. Free services of the school psychologist, school doctor, and the Psychiatric Director of the West Nassau Mental Health Center were secured.

For the teaching staff, mothers from the community were engaged who had been successful in their own child rearing, and who were warm, emotionally stable, and dedicated women. Their age-range varied from the early 30s to the late 50s. They were interviewed by the educational administrator and two psychologists. Two mothers were teamed and assigned to a particular child twice a week. Eighteen mothers worked with six children. This allowed for substitutes. The mothers were given several orientation sessions, and a variety of educational materials. The services of a teacher was always available to them if they had questions.

In addition to individual help, group activity was also provided. The children came together for morning exercises, a "show and tell" period, music, arts and crafts, story time, physical education, and some playground activities.

After a year and a half in this program, three of the original six children were back in regular school on a half-day basis, and it was hoped the others would soon follow. As for the "teacher-moms," only 3 of the original 18 had to be replaced after the first year. They had all derived much personal satisfaction, and achieved a certain status in the community and with the professionals with whom they worked. They all reported that they had developed greater understanding and insights which helped them in their own personal lives.

This program is still in operation today. Last year it had 19 children including three Head Start 5-year-olds, and three 6-year-olds who were on a half-day program. Thirteen children between 7 and 11 years work with a certified teacher and "teacher-moms" in various flexible programs arranged for their individual needs. The program is now housed in one of the elementary schools in the district (17).

Similar programs have now been started in New Rochelle, New York, Superior, Wisconsin, Grasslands Hospital, Valhalla, New York, P.S. 89 in the Bronx, Stamford, Connecticut, Mamaroneck and Mineola, New York, and in Toronto, Canada. Evaluation by means of oral and written comments by volunteers, teachers, principals, parents, and children has been most favorable. City after city, in their literature, have praised the contributions of volunteers.

In an article appearing in *The Reporter*, a magazine edited for school volunteers in Los Angeles, the principal of a junior high school states that the volunteers, through their encouragement and interest, may well be the difference between a child finishing school or becoming a dropout (18).

It seems evident that school volunteers can and do provide invaluable assistance to the schools. If it were possible to recruit large numbers of parents from every neighborhood in every city and suburb, we might soon do away with apathy, anger, and protest, and substitute instead sympathy, patience, and understanding. Parents would benefit from the knowledge that they are helping their children and bringing new meaning to their own lives, for ". . . few people can engage in a social cause and not themselves be transformed" (19). Professional educators would no longer have to deal with a negative community climate, but would enjoy a partnership with people who will come to be their allies. When we see the extraordinary feats accomplished by the dedicated citizens of the volunteer movement, it seems incredible that any school should allow itself to be without them.

REFERENCES

1. JAMER, MARGARET T., *School Volunteers*. New York: Public Education Association, 1961.

2. NATIONAL SCHOOL VOLUNTEER PROGRAM. *Project Report, April 1964 to October 1967*. Sponsored by the Public Education Association of New York City, Inc., with a grant from the Ford Foundation.

3. SCHOOL VOLUNTEER ASSOCIATION OF PITTSBURGH. *Guidelines for the School Volunteer*, p. 1 (6-page mimeographed report.)

4. *Project Report, April 1964 to October 1967*, p. 13.

5. SAN FRANCISCO EDUCATION AUXILIARY TO THE BOARD OF EDUCATION, *Code of Ethics for School Volunteers,* and *Report to the Board of Education, June 1967,* p. 2 (8-page printed report).

6. BOARD OF EDUCATION OF THE CITY OF NEW YORK SCHOOL VOLUNTEER PROGRAM. *Annual Report, 1967–68.* 20 West 40th St., New York, N.Y., p. 11.

7. *Project Report, April 1964 to October 1967,* p. 17.

8. PHILADELPHIA GAS WORKS. *PGW News,* August 1968, p. 5.

9. *PGW News,* p. 6.

10. *Boston Sunday Globe.* "Teacher Volunteer," November 30, 1968.

11. SCHOOL VOLUNTEER PROJECT. *School Volunteer Project Information Kit.* Boston, Mass., 1968, p. 9 (13-page mimeographed pamphlet).

12. *School Volunteer Project Information Kit,* pp. 4–6.

13. *School Volunteer Project Information Kit,* p. 9.

14. HELLUM, FRANK R., *The Effectiveness of Volunteer Tutoring.* A study of the Seattle Tutoring Agency for Youth, March 1968 (17-page Xeroxed report).

15. *Report of the San Francisco Education Auxiliary to the Board of Education,* p. 3.

16. DONAHUE, GEORGE T., and SOL NICHTERN, *Teaching the Troubled Child.* New York: The Free Press, 1965.

17. PETERSON, MARTIN, *Meeting the Special Needs of Individual Children.* Elmont, N.Y., 1968 (4-page mimeographed report).

18. LOS ANGELES PUBLIC SCHOOLS. *The Reporter.* Los Angeles, California, October 1968, p. 1.

19. FANTANI, MARIO D., "Alternatives for Urban School Reform," *Harvard Educational Review,* Vol. 38, No. 1, Winter 1968, p. 15.

Every Child a Teacher

Alan Gartner, Mary Conway Kohler, and
Frank Riessman

From ancient Rome to present-day California, from the Soviet Union to Great Britain to Cuba, there is mounting evidence that a very simple principle may provide a leap in the learning of children. That children learn from their peers has long been obvious, but a more significant observation is that *children learn more from teaching other children.* Hence our premise: every child should be given the opportunity to play the teaching role.

Children have been teaching other children throughout history, in an enormous variety of settings. The method has long been occurring in one-room schoolhouses. It was central in the monitorial systems of Joseph Lancaster and Andrew Bell and has been an important ingredient in some schools employing the Montessori approach. Crossculturally, various learning through teaching derivatives can be found: in the Soviet Union, for example, where one class of pupils adopts another class; in Britain, where increasing numbers of infant schools and junior schools are using multi-age "family grouping"; in Cuba, where the

Each One Teach One approach is being applied.

In most of these programs, and in the early tutoring programs in the United States, general emphasis has gone to improving the learning of the recipient—the tutor. Generally, findings indicated that though the recipient improved in his learning, no major leaps or breakthroughs were evident on the cognitive indices utilized.

RECENT HISTORY—LEARNING THROUGH TEACHING IN THE 60s

But in the early 1960s attention was more strongly directed to the potentially significant benefits that may accrue to the tutor. Peggy and Ronald Lippitt (and associates) made studies of the effects of using older elementary and junior high school students with younger elementary grade children. The Lippitts focused upon the process of socialization among the older children and assistance to the younger children. The initial projects were at

From pp. 1–8, 47, 58–59 in *Children Teach Children* by Alan Gartner, Mary Conway Kohler, and Frank Riessman. Copyright © 1971 by Alan Gartner, Mary Conway Kohler, and Frank Riessman. By permission of Harper & Row, Publishers, Inc.

the University of Michigan Laboratory School, a neighborhood public school, and a summer day camp.

The first project involved twenty-seven sixth-graders assisting in a kindergarten. A pair of older children helped out, three days a week, for forty-five minutes. Twice weekly the older children met to discuss the experience of working with the younger ones and to improve the work done with them. The next year, 1962, the initial effort having been successful within its limited scope, the program was expanded to two Detroit public schools, with sixth-graders helping in the first through fourth grades. The Lippitts found that, in situations where fourth-grade pupils with reading problems were assigned to the tutelage of sixth-grade pupils who were also experiencing reading difficulties, not only did the fourth-graders make significant progress but the sixth-graders also learned from the experience to an extent that the child teachers were themselves the chief beneficiaries.

Later a more elaborate program was established in a Detroit public school complex—a high school, a junior high school, and an elementary school. Sixty-eight children participated. The older pupils met with the younger ones for a half hour a day three or four times a week, helping in activities that ranged from drills on spelling words, mathematics tables and vocabulary to making bookcases, sewing, and publishing a class paper. Again it appeared from evaluation of the experience that positive changes resulted for both tutors and tutees.

Working at Mobilization for Youth (MFY, a New York City antipoverty program which employed an extensive tutoring system whereby high school youngsters were prepared to tutor disadvantaged elementary school chil-

dren), Frank Riessman observed that, while the tutees enjoyed the tutoring sessions, no great improvement occurred in their learning. On the other hand, the tutors really appeared to be "turned on" by what they were doing. They were not only becoming excited about it and deriving new, heightened self-esteem from their efforts, but they also seemed much more interested in the whole learning process. They were evidently acquiring new "sets," skills and attitudes that were being transferred to many other learning experiences in which they were involved. Thus a tutor teaching arithmetic to an elementary school youngster showed self-improvement not only in mathematics but also in other subjects. Moreover, in many cases the tutors appeared to acquire a new self-conscious, analytic orientation in dealing with all kinds of problems, not just academic work.

These impressionistic observations led MFY's research staff, in particular Robert Cloward and his associates, to develop carefully controlled studies to assess what was occurring. They found striking gains in the achievement scores of the tutors, gains that far exceeded those of the tutees. For example, over a five-month period in which older children tutored younger children having reading difficulties, those tutored gained 6.0 months while the tutors gained an extraordinary 3.4 years. Unfortunately, most of the cognitive measures employed, not only at MFY but elsewhere, have thus far been largely restricted to achievement tests. A great need exists to develop new, expanded indices related to learning how to learn, creativity, analytic thinking, curiosity and the like.

Since these beginnings in the early sixties, there has been an enormously rapid spread of various types of tutorial programs. In 1968 Herbert Thelen listed some two dozen programs, each conducted by a school as part of its regular day. The National Commission on Resources for Youth, under the guidance of Mary Conway Kohler, has developed "Youth Tutoring Youth" programs that began with demonstration projects in Newark and Philadelphia in 1967 and are now in operation in over 200 school systems. A number of these programs are after-school (and/or summer) and are run in collaboration with the Neighborhood Youth Corps. And the Office of Education's new Career Opportunities Program, operating in some 130 communities in all fifty states, incorporates a National Commission-designed Youth Tutoring Youth component.

In Pocoima, California, an entire school has become involved in the development of a tutorial community project, which grew out of a research effort by the Systems Development Corporation to devise effective instructional procedures for the teaching of reading-readiness concepts to first-grade Mexican-American students. Presently, grades 4–6 tutor students in grades K–3. Inservice discussions about the learning and teaching process are conducted by the teacher who sends the tutors, using the Lippitts' Cross-Age Helping Program materials. The "receiving teacher" leads discussions, role playings and simulations on specific subject matters. After tutoring sessions, both tutors and tutees evaluate their experiences, sometimes apart, sometimes with each other.

A less elaborate but related effort is the Each One Teach One program taking place at P.S. 25, an elementary school in Yonkers, New York. And in Portland, Oregon, most of the children in the high schools are engaged in an assisting program. Elsewhere tutoring programs focus upon children with special handicaps, sometimes using "problem children" and "disabled" children as tutors; in some cities programs with classes composed of children of several ages (inter-age classes) use tutoring as a part of the regular class activity.

EDUCATIONAL TRENDS AND LTT

It is not surprising that great interest in Learning Through Teaching should arise at the present time. The LTT concept is related to a number of highly significant current trends: decentralizing of teaching, differentiated staffing, the individualization of instruction, the self-help and human potential movements, the need for more teaching resources, the growing criticism of competitiveness in schools and the demand for more cooperative learning situations, the use of the consumer of the service as a service giver, the recognition of the schools' waste and inefficiency and the demand for accountability in the schools, and the great new emphasis on participatory processes. Added to these is the anti-poverty focus, with its recognition that large numbers of disadvantaged youngsters have not been reached by the usual curriculum and forms of teaching (it is interesting to observe that Learning Through Teaching and most of the tutorial programs have begun in poverty areas) and its recognition that the teacher is not the sole repository of knowledge.

With the increasing recognition today that learning need not be a win-lose game in which some pupils presumably learn a good deal in a competitive grading system and others do not, there is a need for what William Glasser calls Schools Without Failure.

As Herbert Thelen observes,

The idea of students learning through helping each other is a very promising alternative to the traditional system of learning through competing with each other. It also makes the acquisition of knowledge and skills valuable, not in the service of competition for grades but as the means for personally significant interaction with others.[1]

It is possible, then, to move from the present nonindividualized and competitive system to an individualized and cooperative one.

Donald Durrell has commented that a great deal of time in the classroom is wasted when the teacher asks a student a question and the whole class sits passively by while the pupil responds in this one-to-one dialogue. Durrell proposes many ways whereby large numbers of youngsters can be active simultaneously. Learning through teaching allows for much more simultaneous involvement of all the youngsters; more, it constrains toward much more pervasive active participation. If the active learner learns how to learn, all the better; and if he acquires significant learning attitudes, still better.

The Lippitts and Herbert Thelen have been very much concerned about the emotional or affective benefits that surround and contextualize LTT. The Lippitts observed that it is rare for older youngsters to have the opportunity to play a constructive, socializing, positive role with younger children, but that the cross-age model allows for and encourages this greatly. Thelen notes that LTT may play an important role in combating prejudice. He states that ". . . student tutoring built into the regular classroom learning process

capitalizes on heterogeneity and therefore is a method through which racial class and integration can be achieved. It is specially intriguing to think of possibilities of Negroes helping whites, of younger children helping older ones, of ethnic minority members helping the majority." [2]

INDIVIDUALIZATION

One of the major observations in the current period is that the key to learning is individualization—the patterning of learning to suit the individual, his idiom, his style, his way of learning. In essence, an ultimate objective might be for every child to have his own teacher; perhaps one way of achieving this is to have each pupil play the teacher role. As a tutor, he learns through teaching, and he also learns as a recipient, as a tutee when he is being taught. Another way of achieving this individualization is through various computer-aided forms of programed instruction; to some extent these two approaches can be combined when the tutor uses and monitors programed materials for the tutee. But in fairness it must be said that learning through teaching essentially is an emphasis on *learning from people*. It is a people-oriented approach to learning in contrast to the more machine-oriented approaches. Another contrast is also important here: most programed learning is, by necessity, highly sequenced, ordered, and preplanned. The learning through teaching model can be much more informal, idiosyncratic, and open ended, following the needs and interests of the learner at the moment, although it *is* possible for the LTT design to be highly formalized and

---

[1] Herbert A. Thelen, "The Humane Person Defined" (paper presented at the Secondary Education Leadership Conference, St. Louis, Missouri, November 1967).

[2] *Ibid.*

sequenced. The crucial point, however, is that it is individualized; it can be attuned to the style and way of learning of the individual child as well as to the individual child acting as a teacher. A teacher for every child is by no means impossible. The new motto may very well be that everybody is teaching and everybody is learning.

A SELECTED BIBLIOGRAPHY ON LEARNING BY TEACHING

CLOWARD, ROBERT, "Studies in Tutoring." *The Journal of Experimental Education* 36, No. 1 (Fall 1967): 14–25.

Do Teachers Make a Difference? A Report on Recent Research in Pupil Achievement. Washington, D.C.: U.S. Office of Education, 1970.

LIPPITT, PEGGY, JEFFREY EISEMAN, and RONALD LIPPITT, *Cross-Age Helping Program: Orientation, Training, and Related Materials.* Ann Arbor: University of Michigan, Center for Research on Utilization of Scientific Knowledge, Institute for Social Research, 1969.

NATIONAL COMMISSION ON RESOURCES FOR YOUTH, "Final Report on Demonstration Project Proposal To Develop a Monitoring-Assessment System for Youth Tutoring Youth E & D Model In-School NYC Program." U.S. Department of Labor, Grant No. 42–9–12–134, June 30, 1969, to June 29, 1970.

NEWMARK, GERALD, and RALPH J. MELARAGNO, "Tutorial Community Project: Report on the First Year, May 1968–June 1969." Santa Monica, California: System Development Corporation, n.d.

THELEN, HERBERT A., "Learning by Teaching." Report of a Conference on the Helping Relationship in the Classroom, Stone-Brandel Center, University of Chicago, 1968.

WEINSTEIN, GERALD, and MARIO D. FANTINI, *Toward Humanistic Education—A Curriculum of Affect.* New York: Praeger Publications, 1970; published for the Ford Foundation.

See also:

ACEI, *Aides to Teachers and Children.* Washington, D.C.: The Association, 1968. Pp. 64. $1.50.

ALLEN, AUDRIANNA, "Children as Teachers." Childhood Education 43, 6 (February 1967): 345–50.

LIPPITT, PEGGY, and RONALD LIPPITT, "The Peer Culture as a Learning Environment." Childhood Education 47, 3 (December 1970): 135–38.

Educational Change:
Its Origins and Characteristics

B. Othanel Smith and Donald E. Orlosky

University of South Florida

The purpose of this essay is to report a study of educational changes attempted during the past 75 years, examine the efforts to put these ideas into practice, rate the efforts to install them as successful or unsuccessful, attribute that success or failure to particular factors, and make recommendations to those who promote educational change. The changes selected are broad, macrochanges rather than narrow and specific changes. Also, many changes have been attempted during this period for which there is no record, but on the whole it may be assumed that the changes which are included in this account are of general significance.

Four categories were used to classify changes according to their degree of success or failure.[1] The symbols used and the descriptions for degrees of success were:

4—A change that has successfully been installed and has permeated the educational system.

3—A change that has successfully been installed and is sufficiently present that instances of the change are obvious.

2—A change that has not been accepted as a frequent characteristic of schools but has left a residue that influences educational practice.

1—A change that has not been implemented in the schools and would be difficult to locate in any school system.

Changes that were rated 3 and 4 were regarded as successes and changes rated 1 and 2 were regarded as failures. The changes were also classified according to the aspect of the educational system that was the focus of change. The symbols employed in this classification were: A—instruction, B—curriculum, and C—organization and administration.

Each idea for change was classified according to its origin. Some changes originated outside of the school setting and others arose within the field of education. The changes were classified as internal or external, using these symbols: I—internal origin, within the

[1] The authors independently classified the changes, then compared the results of their work. Agreement on the inside–outside dichotomy was 88%, for the post-pre 98%, for the success–failure categories 68% (no differences exceeded one scale point), and for the focus of the change, 72%. Differences were resolved on the basis of evidence that supported the rating.

education field; and EX—external origin, outside the education field.

The fourth distinction made was between changes proposed recently and those proposed some time ago. Changes initiated after 1950 were regarded as recent; all others were listed in the pre-1950 era.

Table 1 provides an alphabetical listing by categories of the changes included in this report.

Table 1. Changes Listed According to Date of Origin, Source, Rating of Success, and Focus of Change

Change	Post-1950	Source	Rating	Focus
Ability Grouping		I	3	A
Activity Curriculum		I	2	B
Adult Education		EX	4	C
British Infant School	X	I	3	B
Carnegie Unit		I	4	C
Community School		I	2	B
Compensatory Education	X	EX	3	B
Compulsory Attendance		EX	4	C
Conservation Education		EX	3	B
Consolidation of Schools		I	4	C
Core Curriculum		I	1	B
Creative Education	X	I	1	B
Dalton Plan		I	1	A
Desegregation	X	EX	3	C
Driver Education		EX	4	B
Elective System		I	4	B
Environmental Education	X	EX	3	B
Equalization Procedures		I	4	C
Extra-class Activities		I	4	B
Flexible Scheduling	X	I	2	C
Guidance		I	4	A
Head Start	X	EX	3	C
Home Economics		EX	3	B
Individually Prescribed Instruction	X	I	3	A
International Education		I	3	B
Junior College		I	4	C
Junior High School		I	4	C
Kindergarten		I	4	C
Linguistics	X	I	3	A
Look-and-Say Method		I	3	A
Media and Technology		I	4	A
Microteaching	X	I	3	A
Middle School	X	I	3	C
Mid-year Promotion		I	1	C
New Leadership Roles		I	4	C
Nongraded Schools	X	I	3	C
Nursery Schools		EX	3	C
Open Classroom	X	I	3	A
Phonics Method		I	3	A
Physical Education		EX	4	B
Platoon System		I	1	C
Programmed Instruction		I	3	A
Project Method		I	2	A
Safety Education		I	4	B
School Psychologist	X	I	3	C
Self-contained Classroom		I	3	C
Sensitivity Training	X	I	2	A
Sex Education	X	EX	2	B
Silent Reading		I	4	A
Social Promotion		I	4	C
Special Education	X	I	4	B
Store Front Schools	X	EX	3	C
Student Teaching		I	4	A
Team Teaching	X	I	2	C
Testing Movement		I	4	C
Tests and Measurements		I	4	A
Thirty-School Experiment		I	1	B
Unit Method		I	2	B
Unit Plan		I	2	A
Updating Curriculum Content		I	3	B
Visiting Teacher		I	2	A
Vocational and Technical Education		EX	4	B
Winnetka Plan		I	1	A

It is important to observe in Table 1 that a large number of changes (*49*) originated within the school system, compared with a small number (*14*) originating from external sources. The schools initiated changes at a ratio of 3½ to 1, compared with individuals or agencies outside the schools. External changes were invariably in the areas of curriculum (eight instances) or organization and administration (six instances). The external ideas had a higher success percentage (*93%*) than the internal ideas (*64%*). These data suggest that when an idea has both outside group and school support, success probability is high.

It should not be inferred from the lower success rate of ideas originating within the field of education that ideas are likely to fail because of their origin. For instance, all efforts to alter instructional behavior originated within the education field, but it is notoriously difficult to change teaching habits. Also, the lower percentage of success is quite likely due to the fact that the professional literature reports a larger number of internal change attempts. Failures that originate outside of education are less likely to remain long enough to be recorded as an effort to change at the macro-level studied.

Changes were successfully implanted in instruction, curriculum, and organization and administration. None of these three categories was immune. Likewise, failures in all three areas suggest that each area had resisted changes or was unable to accommodate some of them. All of the successful changes in instruction came from within the education field, two-thirds of the changes in organization and administration originated within education, and half of the curricular changes came from within the field. Thus it appears that the public school is more responsive to change than is generally conceded.

Government influence was evident in such programs as Head Start, which required heavy financial support, and in compulsory attendance, where the legislative branch produced change through law.

The successful pre-1950 ideas usually involved school organization and administration. It appears to be easy to try and discard changes in curriculum and instruction, but when the machinery of organization and administration is modified the change is relatively permanent.

It should be noted that there are factors and agencies not categorized in this analysis that bear on change and are influential in the determination of educational practice. They cannot be regarded as the basis for any particular change but affect the entire spectrum of educational practice. Four such factors within education are (*1*) educational research, (2) school personnel (teachers, administrators, state departments, and university personnel), (3) educational commissions and committees, and (4) professional and extralegal organizations. The elements outside of the field of education that should be taken into account include (*1*) state and federal constitutional requirements, (2) court decisions that rule on educational practice, and (3) pressure groups in society.

Planned change should be based on a combination of past experiences, current theories, and analysis of all aspects of the field of education. The conclusions that follow encourage such an approach and can serve as guides to those who promote educational change.

1. Changes in methods of instruction are apparently more difficult to

make successfully than changes in curriculum or administration.

2. Changes in instruction are most likely to originate within the education profession. In no case in the past did a successful change in instruction come from outside of education. Changes in ways of teaching and organizing instruction are neither the result of legislation nor of social pressure, but rather are the outcome of professional wisdom and research. This is attributable partly to the fact that the teacher's behavior in the classroom is shaped by factors considerably removed from social concerns, partly to the stability of teaching patterns, and partly to the intellectual character of teaching about which the public has little information.

3. A change that requires the teacher to abandon an existing practice and to displace it with a new practice risks defeat. If teachers must be retrained in order for a change to be made, as in team teaching, the chances for success are reduced unless strong incentives to be retrained are provided.

4. Specific curricular changes such as the establishment of the elective system are often initiated from within the field of education. Successful changes in curriculum can originate either within the profession or from the outside. Neither point of origin monopolizes ideas for curricular change.

5. Curricular changes involving the addition of subjects or the updating of content are more permanent than changes in the organization and structure of the curriculum. Efforts to change the curriculum by integrating or correlating the content, or by creating new category systems into which to organize the content, are made at great risk. Complete or considerable displacement of an existing curriculum pattern is not likely to be permanent even if the

faculty initially supports the change. This can be attributed partly to cognitive strain on the faculty, partly to upsetting the expectations of pupils and consequent parental distrust, and partly to faculty mores which tend to become stronger when threatened by change.

6. Changes in the curriculum that represent additions such as new subjects or changes in the substance of subjects can be made most securely with support from legislation or organized interest groups. The failure of curricular changes to be permanent may be attributed either to lack of social support or to resistance to displacement of the existing curriculum pattern. If school authorities are successful in finding social backing for the addition of a subject to a curriculum, the change can be made with little risk of failure. On the other hand, if social opposition is pronounced, the probability of the change not being made is very high, or if it is made it is likely not to persist.

7. Efforts to alter the total administrative structure, or any considerable part of it, are likely to be unsuccessful.

8. Changes that represent additions or extensions of the educational ladder, such as junior college, are more likely to be lasting than changes that entail general modifications of the administrative organization, such as flexible scheduling.

9. The lack of a diffusion system will lead to abortive change. A change initiated in a particular school, in the absence of a plan for diffusion, no matter how loudly it may be acclaimed, is not likely to become widespread or to be permanently entrenched.

10. Changes that have the support of more than one critical element are more likely to succeed. Compulsory

education, with legal, social, and educational support, did not have to overcome as much resistance as it would have if only educators had supported it.

11. Changes will be resisted if they require educational personnel to relinquish power or if they cast doubt on educator roles. Accompanying legislative, legal, and financial impetus increases the probability of success in such changes.

12. The weight of the cognitive burden is one of the significant factors that determine the permanence of a change. If the cognitive load is light, i.e., if not many people are required to learn many new facts and procedures, a change is more likely to persist than if the burden is heavy. The weight of the burden is proportional to the number of factors entailed in the change. For example, if the total administrative structure is the object of change, the chances for successful innovation will be low. The same observation can be made about changes in methods of instruction or curricular changes.

13. The initiation of change may come from a number of sources—professionals, social groups, government, and so on—and changes may arise from research, as in the case of ability grouping, or from ideologies, as in the case of the core curriculum, or from professional wisdom, as in the platoon system. The source of the change appears to have far less to do with its staying power than the support the change receives and the strain it places upon the school personnel. The core curriculum and creative education are constant drains on the time and energy of a faculty and they consequently tend to disappear even though each may enjoy faculty support. On the other hand, international understanding tends to be more persistent as a curricular change. If requires far less time and energy of the teacher and has enjoyed no greater support from the faculty than either the core curriculum or creative education.

14. The federal government, as a change agent, will have optimum success if it takes certain facts into account. In the first place, the government acts in two ways. It passes enabling legislation empowering various federal agencies to do specified things to attain certain goals. In the second place, it acts through the courts to interpret laws, to establish norms, and to order certain actions by school officials. Programs of the U.S. Office of Education are based largely upon enabling legislation. In the development of its programs the USOE is subject to the same conditions of success as any other change agent. For example, its efforts to induce changes in methods of teaching are likely to be less successful than efforts to change curriculum content or to extend or modify the educational ladder; its efforts are likely to be more successful if it has the support of commission recommendations, organized groups, and professional personnel.

The data set forth in this report are too broad to provide insight into the sort of situational analysis that successful change entails. More refined data can be secured by intensive case studies. A few well-chosen case studies can be made to explore the underlying variables whose manipulation and control can give a change agent greater assurance of success.

The educational system in a dynamic society cannot remain stagnant. We should expect changes to be proposed that will alter the school system, since the United States is undergoing rapid change. The idiosyncrasies of a particular situation may not always con conform to the patterns revealed in this study, but it is likely that an understanding of the characteristics of the changes proposed over the last three-quarters of a century will be helpful in the development of successful procedures in the installation of educational changes.

2

Instructional Implications from the Disciplines

Reading-language instruction relies on several different bodies of knowledge to formulate a sound program for all learners. Many educators feel that reading programs of the past often failed to rely on or even consider some of the most critical information available. The various communication skills were frequently separated into discrete programs which fragmented spoken and written language learning into daily doses of reading, spelling, handwriting, phonics, grammar, and creative writing.

Careful study of linguistics and psycholinguistics has provided a valuable resource to help change this situation. With an understanding of the structure of the language, and a knowledge of theories regarding language acquisition, the educator can bring reading into focus as an extension of the language development process. The artificial barriers between the language skills disappear so the reading act can be taught on the strength of what it has in common with the other skills (semantic system, syntactic system), not just where it differs (graphic representation). Isolating sound-symbol relationships toward decoding for its own sake would no longer constitute a viable reading "lesson."

The following articles provide a general overview of specialized areas which the reader should pursue in greater depth. The selections are representative of major areas of knowledge with a high degree of relevance to reading-language programs.

It is hoped that the reader will seek other authors and viewpoints in linguistics, psycholinguistics, sociolinguistics, and psychology. The reader should also pursue original sources of views he is comfortable with and wishes to understand in greater depth. These articles are educators' translations of knowledge from the disciplines, and this knowledge is vital to the job of teaching communication between human beings. They have made their interpretations of what they believe to be the implications relevant to the child learning these skills.

The chapter is divided into two major parts. The first part is concerned with "what to teach"—the content—and concentrates on linguistics. The second part is concerned with "how to teach"—the process—and concentrates on the application of learning theory. Since process cannot be separated completely from content, the first section will, of course, have considerable information that can be applied to process. The second section, however, emphasizes process as it is used consciously by teachers.

The first section on content of teaching begins with the body of knowledge basic to all the communication skills—the knowledge of language, or linguistics. Pose Lamb describes language historically and relates the discussion to language processing.

What major changes have been made in American reading programs as a result of applying linguistic principles? Lamb highlights several distinct changes or new emphases. She stresses instruction which isolates sound–symbol associations and considers alphabet patterns in a new perpective which affects instruction in decoding and encoding.

What are the implications for the other communication skills prior to and during the process of beginning to read? Lamb discusses recommendations regarding the range of acceptability of oral language, the amount of child language in the classroom situation, and critical listening as a skill. Although they are discussed as separate entities, Lamb does not imply that these areas should be treated separately in the classroom. The teacher must integrate the reading-language program by using her knowledge of language as the base.

Language educators have taken the linguists' information on language, coupled it with the psychology of the reading process, and offered suggestions on the appropriate components and parameters of a reading program. Kenneth Goodman discusses how three major cue systems can be used by the beginning reader. The nonreader poses one of the most difficult problems in the schools today, with numerous ramifications for his functioning in the daily school program and in his future activities. As the nonreader struggles orally with the printed page, the teacher may hear word calling that varies only slightly or greatly with the meaning of the passage. Goodman makes assumptions about the instruction that child probably received during the initial stages of reading. Perhaps there was more emphasis on the graphic and phonic aspects of the reading act than on the message conveyed by the print. In another instance a child may decode the first word or two and assign the remainder of the sentence his own meaning, regardless of the meaning indicated by the symbols on the page. This child may not be able to use sound–symbol cues and lacks the language and background experience to make the bridge to the author's expression and meaning. To be satisfactory, reading materials must:

> have meaning for the reader.
> sound like language to the reader.
> contain some familiar sound–symbol relationships.

What content should be chosen for the beginning reader? The primary level teacher should compare Goodman's criteria to the program she is using. Does the content deal with experiences familiar to the children? Is it expressed in language similar to the way the children and their families speak? If such a program is not readily available for financial reasons, or if representative materials do not exist, the teacher can develop a program on the basis of the children's experiences as expressed through their language. (See the discussion on language experience in chapter 4.)

While Goodman expresses the psycholinguists' reasons for using only meaningful content with beginning readers, the sociolinguists have their own reasons for this same criteria. Donald Smith discusses the relevancy issue with regard for all persons. *How do educators grant the right to read?* Smith's article might lead the reader to ponder how the state adoption of texts, approved reading lists, and the single standard for an acceptable life style contribute to withholding a young person's right to read. Relying solely on the values of the dominant culture as a standard, educators can exclude much relevant material for minority groups. A broad perspective and awareness is needed to meet this range of needs.

Smith does not perceive the right to read as a privilege existing in isolation. He believes that the classroom teacher must face underlying social and political issues prior to realizing the right to read. She then must reveal her stand on these issues when she chooses materials for instruction. Smith is advising her to use this power wisely. (The implications of these statements are pursued in greater depth in chapter 3.)

The second section on process in teaching focuses on the relationship between understanding of the learning process and knowledge of developmental reading. Ronald J. Raven and Richard T. Salzer describe the stages of intellectual development purported by the Swiss psychologist Jean Piaget. Raven and Salzer relate each stage of cognitive development to the reading task and identify expectations for various age levels. Examination of most materials shows a demand for cognitive tasks which Piaget believes are not normally within the capability of the six-year-old (the age of the American child faced with these programs). Piaget would certainly provide reading experiences for the child of any age capable of the tasks involved, but the child of "reading age," incapable of the tasks, needs attention here. Certain solutions always emerge from the problem:

Change the materials,
Change the method,
Change the child,
Change the requirements.

Raven and Salzer would eliminate one of these solutions quite readily: To change the child in this developmental point of view would be unacceptable; the child has certain stages he must work out and work through. Certainly some changes in methods and materials would be required. Just as Goodman and Smith point out the necessity for meaning and relevancy, Piaget adds the necessity for demanding of a child only what he is cognitively capable of doing. Since the reading task requires the abilities acquired in the concrete-operational stage, including decentration, to break the task into manageable tasks would violate the respect for language as the base of the reading process. The only remaining solution is to change the requirements. Just as respect for all humans demands a wide range of acceptance of language, dress and life style, the standards for time and degree of mastery of reading skills may need to be broadened also.

In recent years a number of persons have emphasized that consideration of the learning process as cognitive is only half the picture. The affective domain is of equal importance for consideration in the child's learning process. William

Purkey's book *Self-Concept and School Achievement* documents the relationship between these two conditions. Although measurement of self-esteem (a positive self-concept) is still questionable, the most acceptable measures available (which Purkey cites in detail) do reveal the logical relationship between how the child regards himself as a learner and his subsequent achievement in a given area. Purkey refers to many studies in this area as well as the works of a considerable number of notable authors (educators, psychologists, philosophers) which reflect a high regard for the role of affective feelings in learning.

The school, as well as the family and the peer group, can contribute to the positive or negative aspect of the self-concept. Since studies (for example, the First Grade Studies funded by the Office of Education in the '60s, as reporated in the *First Grade Studies: Findings of Individual Investigations,* edited by Russell G. Stauffer, International Reading Association, 1967) have shown that the teacher contributes significantly to achievement differences, what does the teacher do deliberately to make these differences? Although there are no all-encompassing answers, research has revealed some distinct behaviors employed by effective teachers. Purkey discusses the process behaviors he deems important to effective classroom relationships and learning.

It is neither necessary nor desirable to continue to think in compartments: What would the linguist impose on a reading program? the psychologist? and so on. Instead it is possible to discover common elements among the disciplines; and although these common elements are held for different reasons, they reinforce one another. Purkey's article then helps to bring these commonalities together:

1. He speaks of accepting and respecting the child as he is. Sociolinguists advocate that dialects be regarded as acceptable means of communication. Psycholinguists believe that the child's language should serve as the base of his reading program. These views support each other, promoting a certain kind of teacher attitude, which affects her behavior and selection of materials.

2. He speaks of an environment geared to success, not failure, for individual students. The psychologists offer guidelines regarding realistic expectations for a given age and experience level. The psycho- and sociolinguists' statements regarding meaningful and relevant materials pertain here also, since the major avenue to success involves use of the known to bridge the gap to the unknown.

3. He speaks of the importance of the teacher's attitude about himself; the individual with a positive attitude is in much better position to help build positive and realistic self-concepts in her students. What helps to build this self-confidence? The linguist would help by preparing the teacher with a sound knowledge of language, on which she can build a reading-language program. The psychologist would help by acquainting the teacher with child behavior and the way learning takes place. The teacher who knows what she "is about" is more likely to convey her self-confidence which aids her effectiveness with her students and their parents.

To incorporate up-to-date knowledge from the various disciplines related to reading-language instruction is no simple task. It requires continued work by all concerned, especially classroom teachers working with researchers. This section is intended to highlight important concerns in a sound educational program for the development of communication skills. Now it is up to the teacher.

Linguistics and Language Arts

Pose Lamb

Elementary teachers in recent years have received persistent and repeated advice, even pleas, to base their teaching of the language arts [1] on a solid "linguistic" basis. Textbooks, films, programmed materials, media of every type are being produced to aid the teachers of children from kindergarten through sixth grade in making the difficult transition from "traditional, old-fashioned" techniques to more modern methods of language teaching.

IMPORTANCE OF LINGUISTIC KNOWLEDGE FOR ELEMENTARY TEACHERS

Although he may be confused and bewildered by the profusion of articles, books, and revised teaching materials purported to have a "linguistic" basis, the elementary teacher is usually eager to utilize the results of research in the language arts and to make appropriate adjustments in his teaching. However, when he attempts to investigate the field of linguistic knowledge

[1] The language arts are here defined as listening, speaking, reading, and writing.

as it applies to teaching in the elementary schools, too often he finds disagreement, confusion, and contradictory advice instead of enlightenment and help. Linguistics is a relatively new field, a modern "humanistic science" (if such a term may be permitted —it seems particularly appropriate here!). Efforts to relate linguistic knowledge to educational programs are newer still. Knowledge concerning the structure of our language is expanding quite rapidly, and some books and articles published as recently as five years ago are held in disrepute.

Why should the teacher enter this "jungle" then? Why not wait until guidelines are clearer, until the teacher is more certain of what he knows and doesn't know? Because, in the first place, materials are being produced, in the field of beginning reading especially, at an increasingly rapid rate, and elementary teachers must decide which materials to use, how much linguistic emphasis to incorporate into their spelling programs and their reading programs—and *whose* linguistic approach seems most appropriate. There is at least one other important reason for making the effort to understand

Reprinted from Pose Lamb, *Linguistics in Proper Perspective*, with permission of Charles E. Merrill.

linguistics and the implications of linguistics for elementary teaching. A few widely used teaching techniques (emphasis on isolated sounds in phonics instruction, for example, or "parsing" sentences as part of instruction in the structure of our language) are *clearly* outdated. One need not be a linguist on the "growing edge" of his field of competence to adapt and make full use of some basic linguistic principles. The proliferation of terminology ("allophones," "phonemes," "graphemes") and disagreements about the most useful approach to grammar (transformational or structural?) are of major concern to graduate students majoring in linguistics and to advanced scholars in the field, of course, but at the level of elementary school classroom practice, the areas of agreement outnumber and outweigh in importance the areas of greatest controversy among linguists.

In this book, an effort has been made to discuss, in general terms, the work of linguists as they attempt to learn more about our language, its origins, its structure, and its sounds. More specifically, an effort has been made to indicate possible and useful application of linguistics, as a field of knowledge, a discipline, pursued by respected scholar-scientists, to the language arts programs in elementary school classrooms. Oversimplification is a pitfall in any effort of this type. Unfortunately, only a few linguists have tried to explain their work so the typical classroom teacher could understand it and make changes and adaptations in terms of the new knowledge. It is the well-known problem of the "thinkers" being separated from the "doers," the theorists vs. the practitioners. In trying to relate basic elements of linguistic theory to classroom practice, undoubtedly some important understandings will be overlooked or developed in a less thorough manner than might be desirable. If, at times, the vocabulary in this book seems too non-technical, too simple to express adequately significant and complex concepts, the reader should keep in mind that the anticipated reader of this book is not the linguist, working with tape recorder and computer, comfortably conversant with Pike, Chomsky, and other scholars, but the elementary school teacher whose problems relate to *how* and *how much* to teach as well as *what* to teach in the field of language arts.

. . .

LINGUISTIC STUDY: FROM BLOOMFIELD TO CHOMSKY

Boas and Sapir were anthropologists who developed a strong interest in studying language. They also contributed a great deal to the field of descriptive analysis of language. Nevertheless, the most significant fact about their work was that it served as a solid foundation for Bloomfield's work, and today Bloomfield's work is more widely known by linguists *and* the public than that of either of the men whose work he studied so carefully. Bloomfield's major contribution was his book, *Language*, which has become a classic. The year in which *Language* was published, 1933, is a modern landmark in the field of scientific language study. Bloomfield advocated the study of language through structural analysis, *independent of a study of semantics or meaning.* He wrote:

The statement of meaning is therefore a weak point in language study, and will remain so until human knowledge is very far beyond its present state. In practice, we define the meaning of a linguistic form, wherever we can, in terms of some other science.[2]

For example, the definition of a verb as "an action word" is of little use, Bloomfield would contend, because it tells us nothing of a verb's grammatical function.

The field of linguistics is a very active one; otherwise there would be no purpose for a book of this type. Kenneth Pike, Zellig Harris, George Trager, Noam Chomsky, and Bernard Bloch are just a few linguists who have made recent contributions to linguistic knowledge.

Pike has developed a very useful guide for writing unfamiliar and previously unwritten languages—a phonetic alphabet, similar to the International Phonetic Alphabet, but with a few striking differences. Pike's alphabet, and another phonetic alphabet developed by George Trager and Henry Lee Smith, include nine different representations for vowel sounds in English; the IPA lists thirteen. (The IPA, of course, was developed to represent the sounds of many languages, not English alone). Harris has studied not only phonemes, or words, or sentences, but portions of discourse larger than a sentence. He writes:

The successive sentences of a connected discourse . . . offer fertile soil for the methods of descriptive linguistics, since these methods study the relative distribution of elements within a connected stretch of speech.[3]

Stated in terms which probably represent an over-simplification, Harris has

[2] Leonard Bloomfield, *Language* (New York: Holt, Rinehart and Winston, Inc., 1933), p. 139.
[3] Zellig Harris, "Discourse Analysis," *Language*, 28:19, 1952.

expanded the notion that sentences make words; he would add that groups of sentences make words, or words achieve their primary significance when studied in the context of a sentence or a paragraph. Harris has worked in the field of transformational grammar, which differs rather strikingly from the decomposition-by-sentence-parsing approach with which the reader is probably too familiar. Transformational grammar appears to rest on the basic assumption that all the sentences of a language are either kernel sentences or transformations of kernel sentences. The number of kernels possible or acceptable in a given language is finite or limited. It is through transformation of these kernels that we gain the infinite variety of sentences we have in English. Harris writes:

Our picture of a language then, includes a finite number of actual kernel sentences, all cast in a small number of sentence structures built out of a few morpheme classes by means of a few constructional rules; a set of combining and introducing elements; and a set of elementary transformations such that one or more transformations may be applied to any kernel sentence or group of kernel sentences, and such that any properly transformed sentences may be added sequentially by means of combiners.[4]

Transformational grammar will be dealt with in greater detail in Chapter Four, "Linguistics and the Teaching of Grammar and Usage."

Another post-Bloomfield contribution was the concept of the juncture. The significance of juncture, or pause, is illustrated by the difference in meaning conveyed by placing juncture in these utterances in different positions:

[4] Zellig Harris, "Co-occurrence and Transformation in Linguistic Structure," *Language*, 33:399, 1957.

1. a name
2. an aim

Obviously, differences in pitch also play a part in making combinations of the same "words" quite different kinds of utterances. The meaning in the following utterance is altered significantly by changes in pitch:

1. What are we having for breakfast, Mother? (Rising pitch on "Mother.")
2. What are we having for breakfast, Mother? (Falling pitch on "Mother.")

Modern linguists have identified four levels of pitch and four levels of stress.

The reader might try reading aloud the following utterance, placing the stress on the italicized words, to gain some idea of the role of stress in conveying meaning:

Are *you* going to wear that dress?
Are you going to *wear* that dress?
Are you going to wear *that* dress?
Are you going to wear that *dress*?

Variations in levels of stress become apparent as each utterance is read. "Wear" in each of the sentences probably received more stress than "are," regardless of the word receiving the most stress. Stress variation is an aid in conveying meaning in a given utterance and helps to differentiate meaning variations in similar utterances.

Change in patterns of pitch can elicit different responses from the decoder of a linguistic message—the listener. Using the suggested pitch patterns following each utterance (highest pitch is indicated by the numeral three, the lowest by the numeral one), read the utterances aloud and note the difference in meaning:

She's a good mother. (2–3–2–1)
She's a good mother. (2–2–3–2)

Most women would suspect that the second utterance was something less than a compliment, suggesting that motherhood was the woman's *only* skill or area of competence! Pitch, stress, and pause or juncture may be labeled "supra-segmental" phonemes, and linguists have helped all those who are interested in language, and how it is learned and used, to become aware of the impact of these "supra-segmental" phonemes on meaning.

Everyone is aware of the role of the lifted eyebrow, the nod, the frown, in supporting or refuting the meaning of the speaker's words. Linguists have recently determined that these are not instinctive, but are learned, and arbitrary, much as the vocabulary and syntax of a language are. Japanese people respond to an embarrassing or frustrating situation with something which sounds like our giggle; it is actually quite *unlike* our use of this form of laughter, and this difference is important in communicating between representatives of the two cultures. The patterned bodily movements which accompany speech (excluding formal gestures, for the most part) is often termed kinesis.

Finally, it might be noted that, in recounting the contributions of modern liguists, the contribution of Noam Chomsky deserves some discussion. It will be recalled that transformational grammar (in which each sentence of a language is restructured into "kernel" or elementary sentences for purpose of transform) was contrasted with traditional school grammar (in which parts of the sentence are labeled, without much discussion in depth of the function of each element). Chomsky calls his grammar "generative grammar"; he writes:

A generative grammar is a system of explicit rules that assign to each sequence of phones (sounds [5]), whether of the observed corpus (text-sentence, paragraph, etc.) or not, a structural description that contains all information about how this sequence of phones is a properly formed or grammatical sentence, and if not, in what respects it deviates from well-formedness. In particular, then, this grammar distinguishes a class of perfectly well formed (fully grammatical) sentences.[6]

It should be some comfort to the elementary teacher struggling with these sophisticated theories to know that linguists disagree among themselves. The existence of two such widely different grammatical theories as structural and transformational-generative is adequate testimony to this disagreement. Many questions remain to be answered before one of these theories gains universal acceptance, and before that happens still other theories may be proposed. The basic question regarding transformational grammar relates to the criteria to be used in judging the acceptability of any particular transformation; of Chomsky's "generative" groups, one might ask for a statement regarding the criteria for judging these "well formed" and fully grammatical sentences.[7]

[5] Words in parentheses not in original text.

[6] Noam Chomsky, "Some Methodological Remarks on Generative Grammar," *Word,* 17:221, August, 1961.

[7] A note from Paul Roberts' preface to *English Sentences* serves to confuse matters still further. Fries notes some real differences between transformational grammar and generative grammar. The preceding quotation from Chomsky also seems to suggest some basic differences. Yet Roberts writes: "Chomsky's tranformational, or generative grammar is one of the major developments in linguistics in recent years. It is a development particularly interesting for students

It should not be disturbing to find so many competing linguistic theories. This is the hallmark of a living, vigorous, and growing science. Within the next few years, additional knowledge will enable linguists, and those who teach children something of the nature of their language, to determine which approach has the most merit, and which is the most fruitful for instructional as well as research purposes. Materials have been developed to help teachers of high school pupils, and surely the linguists will soon help the elementary teacher make some needed changes in his approach to grammar and "usage."

Following is a summary of the major developments in the field of linguistics during the period since 1925:

1. This was the period during which the phoneme was conceptualized, although linguists are still arguing about the precise nature of the phoneme and disagree when asked to state a given numeral as representing the number of significant speech sounds in American English.

2. Thanks particularly to the work of Bloomfield, "meaning" assumed a different role in language study. It was Bloomfield who insisted that language should be studied through analysis of its structure, rather than through a study of semantics or meaning.

3. Some linguists have focused on

and teachers of English, since it goes a long way toward reconciling highly divergent views about English teaching—the linguistic and the traditional. Without losing sight of the valuable advances in linguistic science, Chomsky has been able to rehabilitate, and provide a theory for many features of earlier language teaching." (Quoted from Paul Roberts, *English Sentences* [New York: Harcourt Brace & World, Inc., 1962], Preface.)

analysis of large units of language, "discourse analysis," feeling that even the sentence was somewhat too small a unit to give a useful description of linguistic structures.

4. Levels of pitch and stress (four of each have been identified), and the concept of juncture have aided the linguist in his search for a more complete description of a language. Juncture refers to the pauses or near-pauses which connect various parts of a sentence. Stress refers to changes in a speaker's volume, pitch to the highness or lowness of a sound—the frequency of the vibrations of sound waves reaching the listener's ear. Pitch, stress, and juncture have a profound impact upon the rhythm of a given language and its phonology, and illustrations were included in this chapter suggesting the impact of stress, pitch, and juncture on the meaning of an utterance. Pitch, stress, and juncture have been labeled collectively supra-segmental phonemes.

5. Kinesis, supporting or refuting the meaning conveyed by a group of sounds through facial expression, smiles, etc., has been studied by linguists during the period being summarized here. One significant discovery is that these non-language aspects of language are arbitrary and are learned, just as vocabulary and syntax are learned.

6. Linguists have made full use of appropriate technological advances —the tape recorder and the computer, for example—and as a result languages can now be described with much more precision than ever before.

7. Finally, a few linguists, although not enough, have become interested in sharing their findings with classroom teachers. Particularly in the fields of reading and spelling, elementary school teachers have benefited. In work done relative to

grammar, most of the materials have been developed for high school students, but it is obviously desirable to have a fully articulated K–12 language arts program, and more "linguistically oriented" elementary school materials will almost certainly develop.[8]

IMPLICATIONS OF LINGUISTICS FOR ELEMENTARY TEACHING

Linguists have uncovered a mass of data regarding the operation and structure of language. They have devoted years to studying the changes which have occurred, to analyzing languages and developing superior methods and techniques for making such analyses. It is probably clear that no modern elementary teacher of the language arts would intentionally disregard such a significant body of knowledge. Yet, what *difference* does all this make? How will the elementary teacher change his methods of teaching, speaking, reading, and spelling, as a result of the linguistic advances reported in this chapter? The elementary teacher may feel the information in the preceding section contributes to his background information, that his general education has profited by reading something of the history of our language, and by familiarizing himself with the contributions of important linguistic scientists. One's coffee-room conversation may "sparkle" a bit more, and one's fellow teachers may be favorably impressed if the reader mentions the continual borrowing from Latin in coining new words to label our scientific and technological advances. But really, isn't

[8] A list of materials developed for use in elementary schools at the time this book was published is included with other references at the end of appropriate chapters.

this about as far as it goes? If linguists disagree about the construct of a phoneme, if not everyone agrees that transformational grammar differs from generative grammar, what can the elementary teacher (who has taken, perhaps, fifteen semester hours of course work in speech, composition, and literature and one course in teaching language arts) find to apply to his own teaching?

In a sense, this entire book represents a search for the answer to that question. The major purpose of this book is to seek out and record some findings from the field of linguistics and to point out their relevance and/or application to the teaching of reading, writing, spelling, speaking, and listening in the elementary school. In the chapters which follow, the implications of linguistic research for teaching these areas of the language arts will be discussed in some detail. In general, and as an introductory statement which can serve as an overview of this book, the implications might be summarized as follows:

1. Because we know that language is arbitrary and changing, a teacher's attitude toward sub-standard or non-standard usage is one of acceptance. Acceptance of a child from a culturally deprived or culturally disadvantaged background necessitates accepting the child's language. Otherwise communication between the child and teacher is seriously hampered—in some cases it ceases to exist. However, it should be quickly added that the teacher uses many techniques for raising the child's language level to one which will *not* hurt his opportunities to advance socially, will *not* keep him from getting a scholarship to a college he very much wants to attend, or being hired to do a job he is well equipped to do. Acceptance of a pupil's language is a neces-

sary beginning, a prerequisite to all classroom work done in language. Language is such an intensely personal characteristic—only pause to think how one feels when a small grammatical error is corrected by a peer or a superior—and although we should know better, criticism of our language ("Gee you say that funny—say it again!") is generally accepted as criticism on a more general and personal level.

One level of language is not "better" than another; this is why the term "non-standard" is preferable to "substandard" in describing such usage as "He don't do it," "Was you there?" One who uses terms such as these will be penalized in terms of social and educational advancement in our society, however, and it is for this reason the teacher helps children work toward and eventually achieve standard usage.

Standards change and what is correct today may be "prissy" or pedantic within a few years. For example, "whom" is in a state of rapid decline— linguists tell us it will probably leave our language before the time of our great-grandchildren. Many linguists believe "It's me" is as acceptable as "It's I," and grammar books used by children in 2067 may and probably will list it as correct.

2. The study of language, with the knowledge that it is an exciting, growing, changing organism, will be more interesting to children when grammarians no longer act as though they were members of a mythical American equivalent of the French Academie, setting precise standards for our language and telling us that statement A is more "correct" than statement B. Even a quick perusal of language textbooks will reveal advice that will impede rather than aid communication, and recommended patterns which are so unnatural as to elicit the comment

from Winston Churchill that something had occurred "up with which I will not put."

3. With reference to oral language, the classroom teacher will devote much more time to causing children to engage in conversations, discussions, oral reading, dramatic plays, and choral speaking. Something in excess of eighty percent of most adults' language experiences are in the speaking–listening area, and teachers can be much more effective than they presently are in helping children learn to use these important skills more effectively. Vocabulary growth is important here, and so is intonation; children can learn a great deal about pitch, stress, and juncture as clues to meaning, and they can then apply what they know to making their own speech more colorful and interesting. The skills involved are acquired, not inborn, and teachers have a responsibility to aid and abet the continuous acquisition of oral language skills.

4. In the area of listening, children can analyze the way a speaker has *used* pitch, stress, juncture, and kinesis to convey meaning, exaggerate facts, or conceal points of weakness. Critical listening—"auding," if you will—depends upon the ability to spot or identify the speaker's use of the devices just mentioned to sway his audience (whether one or one hundred) to his way of thinking. John F. Kennedy is credited with noting that Winston Churchill "marshalled the English language and sent it to war." Adolph Hitler's use of invective, his repetition of half-truths and falsehoods so often they were accepted as facts, his ability to convince audiences that he alone could lead Germany to greatness, had a great deal to do with his success as *der Fuehrer*. In a democracy especially, the ability to use judgment in responding to a speaker is very important. Linguists have helped us do this by classifying the elements in oral discourse which speakers use in combining words to convey meaning. Teachers have frequently used the technique of comparing the way different newspapers reported the same news events; similar techniques have value in discussing speeches, newscasts, etc., which have been tape recorded or which children can watch or hear "live" on radio or television.

5. In reading, the linguists have perhaps recommended more drastic changes than in any other area except grammar. Bloomfield, Fries, and Smith have wide differences of opinion on details, and some differences on basic principle, but in general they recommend:

a. more emphasis, at an early level, on learning the alphabetic principle, if not the alphabet itself;

b. a beginning vocabulary of words which follow consistent patterns— usually consonant–short vowel– consonant patterns (pan, rug, etc.);

c. an absence of work on isolated speech sounds. It is almost impossible to repeat a consonant without following it with a vowel sound of some sort. Practice on isolated sounds usually proves to be of very little value in oral reading which is natural. Sentences or groups of sentences make words and sound elements of these words change with changing sentences. Linguists also assign to oral reading a more prominent role, at least beyond the beginning stages. Reading is used as a tool for teaching intonation patterns and their role in determining meaning.

6. In spelling, linguists recommend the same emphasis on consistent patterns and would probably discard spell-

ing lists consisting of words selected for their interest level or frequency of use by children. If some compromise can be developed, teachers could possibly do more toward helping children learn principles they could apply to unknown words as well as learning words they need to use at present. Teachers can expect changes in spelling programs, just as they can expect changes in reading programs. Most major publishers will not want a title page printed without including the name of a linguist as an author or as a consultant to the author.

7. Children will learn to think of the dictionary as a device for recording what *is* in our language, rather than a set of standards or rules for what should be. It is with reference to the role and function of the dictionary that linguists have fought some of their most serious battles with those who hold a more traditional view of language. If the reader isn't familiar with the furor caused by publication of Webster's Third International Dictionary, he should be![9] Dictionary work will be more interesting for children if several dictionaries are used, and their systems of diacritical marking compared. This is not likely to happen if one dictionary is accepted as the arbiter of all that is good, true, and beautiful in our language.

8. Finally, teachers should find that language study is fascinating, not dull or boring. The more one knows about his language, the more one wants to know. Not only should the elementary teacher feel this enthusiasm and respond to it by wide reading, additional course work, attendance at conferences, etc., but he should share this enthusiasm with children. If it is a

genuine interest, he cannot help sharing it. Children will enjoy coining words,[10] studying the derivations of words, learning something of the history of their language, and analyzing their own sentence patterns. The problem, in a self-contained classroom, will be one of balance—other curricular areas are important, too!

SUMMARY

In establishing the objectives or purposes of this book, it was noted that the elementary teacher is told that *this* reading program, or *that* spelling series is "linguistically sound." Far-reaching changes are suggested in teaching grammar. The elementary teacher expresses some concern and wonders if it is true that standards of usage are being absolutely abolished.

Linguists are slowly making their influence felt in the language arts curricula of elementary schools. The problem facing the elementary teacher is one of selectivity, of determining *which* of the many linguistic proposals are most attuned to what we know about elementary school children and how they learn; which principles are the most durable, the most significant, those with which students of the English language should be aware. This book was written in order to help the elementary teacher gain some knowledge of his language, of linguists' efforts to study language scientifically, and to assist him in applying appropriate portions of linguistic knowledge to his teaching—his methods, techniques, and the materials he selects.

---

[9] Albert Marckwardt, "Dictionaries and the English Language," *The English Journal*, 52:336–45, May, 1963.

[10] One group of sixth-grade youngsters enjoyed observing the spread of a phrase they had coined, watching it used by children in other classrooms, and eventually by faculty members as well.

A brief history of the development of the English language was included. Points of emphasis included the contributions of the Anglo-Saxons, the Danes, the Norman French; the contribution of the Latin language was discussed. Change and flexibility were identified as significant characteristics of our language, and not undesirable characteristics.

The work of a number of linguistic scientists was described very briefly. Some linguists have devoted most of their efforts to studying the sounds of language, others to studying the structure of language. There are semanticists, interested in word meanings, and linguists who make their contribution by analyzing sounds, writing grammars, developing writing systems for the majority of the 3000 to 5000 languages of the world which have not been written.

Finally, in this chapter, the possible implications of the work of linguists for the work of elementary classroom teachers was discussed. The problem of standards received some attention. Knowing that our language is arbitrary and changing should have some effect on the elementary teacher who has previously expected a level of language in the classroom which is unnatural and unlifelike.

Reading programs, at the beginning levels particularly, and spelling programs will feel the impact of linguists' work in phonology and syntax. Language in pre-primers is likely to be more natural and childlike in the future, and reading will be taught as though it were only a visual process.

The role of the dictionary, and lessons on *how* to use it, will change somewhat; its stature is not diminished when one admits that it is a recording of a language as it is, and was, at a given point in time.

SELECTED REFERENCES

CARROLL, JOHN B., *Language and Thought* (Englewood Cliffs, N.J.: Prentice-Hall, Inc., 1964).

FODOR, JERRY A., and JERROLD J. KATZ, *The Structure of Language* (Englewood Cliffs, N.J.: Prentice-Hall, Inc., 1964).

FRANCIS, W. NELSON, *The Structure of American English* (New York: The Ronald Press Company, 1958).

FRIES, CHARLES C., *Linguistics and Reading* (New York: Holt, Rinehart and Winston, Inc., 1962, 1963).

GIRSDANSKY, MICHAEL, *The Adventure of Language* (Englewood Cliffs, N.J.: Prentice-Hall, Inc., 1963).

GLEASON, H. A., JR., "What is English?" *Linguistics, Composing and Verbal Learning* Papers from the 1962 Conference on College Composition and Communication (Champaign, Ill.: The National Council of Teachers of English). No date.

HALL, ROBERT A., JR., *Linguistics and Your Language* (Garden City, N.Y.: Anchor Books, Doubleday & Company, Inc., 1960).

HILL, ARCHIBALD, "Linguistics Since Bloomfield" (pp. 14–24), in *Readings in Applied English Linguistics*, Harold B. Allen, ed. (New York: Appleton-Century-Crofts, 1958).

IANNI, LAWRENCE, "An Answer to Doubts about the Usefulness of the New Grammar," *The English Journal*, 53: 597–602, November 1964.

JESPERSEN, OTTO, *Growth and Structure of the English Language* (Garden City, N.Y.: Doubleday Anchor Books, Doubleday & Company, Inc., 1938).

LOBAN, WALTER, *Programs in Oral English* (Champaign, Ill.: The National Council of Teachers of English, 1966).

MOULTON, WILLIAM G., *"Linguistics and Language Teaching in the United States 1940–1960"* (Washington, D.C.: U.S. Government Printing Office, 1962).

ROBERTS, PAUL, *English Sentences* (New York: Harcourt Brace & World, Inc., 1962).

ROBERTS, PAUL, "Linguistics and the Teaching of Composition," *The English Journal* 52:331–35, May 1963.

STRANG, BARBARA M. H., *Modern English Structure* (London: Edward Arnold Publishers, 1962).

STRICKLAND, RUTH, *The Contribution of Structural Linguistics to the Teaching of Reading, Writing and Grammar in the Elementary School* (Bloomington, Ind.: Bureau of Educational Studies and Testing, Indiana University, 1963).

WATERMAN, JOHN T., *Perspectives in Linguistics* (Chicago: University of Chicago Press, 1963).

WHATMOUGH, JOSHUA, *Language, A Modern Synthesis* (New York: Mentor Books, New American Library, 1956).

WOLFE, DON M., "Grammar and Linguistics: *A Contrast in Realities,*" The *English Journal,* 51:73–78, 100, February 1964.

Materials for children

The following list represents only a few of the materials related to language, its history and its structure, which are written for children and designed to stimulate their interest in language and their enthusiasm for learning more about it.

FOLSOM, FRANKLIN, *The Language Book* (New York: Grosset & Dunlap, Inc., 1963).

MARTIN, BILL, JR., *Sounds of Language Readers* (New York: Holt, Rinehart and Winston, Inc., 1966). *Sounds of Home* (pre-primer) *Sounds of Numbers* (primer) *Sounds Around the Clock* (Grade One) *Sounds of Laughter* (Grade Two) *Sounds of the Storyteller* (Grade Three).

O'NEIL, MARY, *Words, Words, Words* (Garden City, N.Y.: Doubleday & Company, Inc., 1966).

PROVENSON, ALICE and MARTIN PROVENSON, *Karen's Opposites* (New York: Golden Press, 1963).

SPARKE, WILLIAM, *The Story of the English Language* (New York: Abelard-Schuman Ltd., 1965).

VAN GELDER, ROSALIND, *Monkeys Have Tails* (New York: David McKay Co., Inc., 1966).

The Reading Process:
A Psycholinguistic View

E. Brooks Smith, Kenneth S. Goodman, and
Robert Meredith

Reading is the active process of reconstructing meaning from language represented by graphic symbols (letters), just as listening is the active process of reconstructing meaning from the sound symbols (phonemes) of oral language. Reading programs today tend to be built on principles of psychology, child growth and development, physiology, and, to some extent, sociology, but not on any systematic knowledge of language. This chapter will present a total-language, psycholinguistic view of reading. The entire process of reading can be best understood when consideration is given to the devices within language that convey meaning and the ways readers interpret and react to these devices.

PHONICS APPROACH:
ITS LIMITATIONS

A reading program based on phonics teaches children to associate sounds with letters. The reasoning in this phonics approach (sometimes mistak-

enly called phonetics) [1] is that if the child learns to associate sounds with letters, he can then sound out words and thus read. In one kind of phonics, children are taught to read *dog* by saying the sound of each letter: *duh, aw, guh.* Phonics techniques are included in many current reading programs, but for several reasons phonics *as a method* of teaching reading has fallen into disfavor:

1. The letters in written English do not each regularly represent a single sound. Some sounds may be spelled a number of different ways. For example, consider this group of rhyming words: *go, know, though, hoe, sew.* Equally confusing, some letters may represent a number of different sounds as the *o* does in *do, so, won, women,* and *not.*

2. Many successful readers do not appear to go through this letter-by-letter analysis but seem to recognize whole words by sight.

3. The generalizations contained in

[1] Phonetics is the study of the sounds of language. Because all languages are sound languages, all languages are phonetic.

most old phonics programs are unscientific. Rules not only have many exceptions, but they are often based on erroneous understandings of the language. Division of English vowels into two classes, long and short, is an example of an inaccurate view that confuses the learner and does not in any way describe the English vowel system. So-called long vowels are not single vowels at all but are compound vowels. The speaker glides from one to the other. As a person says these words, he can feel this glide: *I, bone, came, tube, extreme.*

4. Dialect accents mitigate against any attempts at standard sounding (phonics) systems.

WORD RECOGNITION APPROACH: ITS LIMITATIONS

Most current reading programs today have shifted the main emphasis from letters to words. The central task of early reading teaching in these programs is to develop a vocabulary of words that the young reader recognizes at sight. Those who prepare materials for teaching children to read by this word-recognition approach [2] must answer the question, "Which words should be taught first?" Two answers have been used singly or in combination. The words children actually use can be listed in order of frequency from those most commonly used to those rarely occurring. Alternately, a count can be made of the words used in adult speech or literature to determine the frequency and, by implication, the order of importance for early learning.

By means of these lists, basal readers

[2] Referred to by phonics advocates as the "look–say" approach.

are constructed on the principle of vocabulary control. Preprimers contain only 10 to 20 of the most frequently occurring words plus a minimum number of proper nouns. Each successive volume in the series reuses these words and adds a few. The teacher's manual lists each new word so that it may be taught to the learners. Word-attack skills, including phonics and use of contextual clues, are taught in this word-centered method so that the child will be able to "attack" new words.

Many teachers highly skilled in phonics or word-recognition methods have been successful—to a point—in teaching children to read. Enthusiastic learners with dedicated teachers can probably learn to read regardless of method—and most children *do* learn to read. But what is missing from most reading instruction is an understanding of *how* the reader reconstructs meaning from written language. Linguistics and related fields have produced new knowledge about language. To apply these new insights to reading, teachers must let go of their preoccupation with letters and words and take a broad look at reading as one phase of communication.

The child learning to read who is a native speaker of English—any dialect of English—has acquired skill in getting meaning from oral language. He responds quickly and accurately to many cues in language. Only a small fraction of this power over language is put to work through phonics or word-recognition approaches to reading.

POSSIBILITIES OF A TOTAL-LANGUAGE APPROACH

Readers can be regarded as decoders trying to reconstruct a message that has been coded. Written language has symbols, like the dots and dashes of Morse code, and complex systems of signals involved in the arrangement of the symbols.

To understand how readers utilize signal systems in language to reconstruct meaning, consider this list of nonsense words:

Gloopy	klums	poved	jonfy	klorpy
borp	Blit	Ril	rom	lofs
lof	floms	lo	bofd	

We might assume that the three words with capital letters, *Gloopy, Blit,* and *Ril,* are proper nouns; otherwise, we have no sense of meaning. But now consider this primer story in which nonsense words have been substituted for all the meaning-bearing words, with everything else left intact.

GLOOPY AND BLIT

Gloopy is a borp
Blit is a lof.
Gloopy klums like Blit.
Gloopy and Blit are floms.

Ril had poved Blit to a jonfy.
But lo had not poved Gloopy.
"To jonfy is for lofs,"
Blit bofd to Gloopy.
"Rom are a borp."
Gloopy was not klorpy.
Then Blit was not klorpy.

This story presents, in extreme, the problem of the reader's meeting words he has never seen before. Yet, there seems to be some sense to it. In fact, there are many cues to the meanings of the unknown words, and if we apply our knowledge of English, we can come close to understanding the whole story.

The title presents two nonsense words joined by *and,* so the words must be of the same class (nouns or verbs, for example); that is, *town* and *country* can be joined by *and,* as can *red* and *green, run* and *play, quickly* and *quietly,* but not *town* and *green, red* and *play.*

The first sentence provides more cues. By its position in a familiar pattern, we know that *Gloopy* is a noun, probably a singular name, because it is not preceded by a noun marker like *a, the,* or *one. Gloopy* is singular because *is* goes with singular nouns. *Borp* is a noun, we can see, because it follows *a,* a noun marker, and because it occupies a particular position in the equation-like sentence. Similarly, we know that *Blit* is most likely a name and *lof* is a noun, perhaps a category contrasting with *borp.*

Three cues tell us that *klums* is a verb: (1) its position in the sentence, (2) the inflectional ending *s* marks it as a singular verb confirming that *Gloopy* is a singular noun, and (3) it patterns with *like.*

Floms is a plural noun, we know from the plural left side of the equation, the verb *are,* and the *s* ending. We learn also that *borps* and *lofs* can be *floms.* Notice that this little story is lavish in the cues it provides. Seldom are we given only one. Note also that we are not just guessing as we decode this message. We are responding to cues.

Ril is another name. We can see that *poved* is a verb from the verb marker *had,* the inflectional ending *ed* that sets the whole sentence in the past, and again its position between two nouns, which here must be actor and object. By their positions in this sentence we know that *Ril* is the actor and *Blit* the object: it was *Ril* that poved *Blit; Blit* didn't pove *Ril.*

Lo appears to be a noun, but the printed symbols do not show intonation. The addition of appropriate intonations that cannot be represented by the graphic symbols reveals *lo* to be a pronoun with *Ril* as its antecedent. We know then that whatever *Ril* did to *Blit*, *Ril* did not do to *Gloopy*.

The reason for this becomes apparent in the next paragraph. *Blit* is addressing *Gloopy* here, we know from the quotation marks that enable us to supply proper phrasing and intonation. The reason *Gloopy* was not *poved*, *Blit bofs*, is that the *jonfy* is for *lofs* and *Gloopy* is a *borp*. *Rom* can have only one meaning, since *you* is the only singular subject that can pattern with *are*.

Finally, we learn that as a result of not being *poved*, *Gloopy* was not *klorpy* and this led to *Blit* also being *unklorpy*. If only *Gloopy* had been a *lof* instead of a *borp!* Then *Gloopy* would have been *poved* to the *jonfy*, too. We can come very close to understanding the whole little story even though the important words are all nonsense. When these were presented in list form, they meant nothing to us at all.

Adult teachers can use generalizations they have acquired about letters and sounds to say the word in the list, but that is not reading, because no meaning is involved. Reading is not reading unless it involves some level of comprehension.

Readers, even beginners, engage in the same kind of process we have just gone through, although not often on so conscious a level. By the time they start school children have internalized responses to systems of language cues.

There are really four kinds of cue systems that operate in reading to cue meaning. These are (1) cue systems within words, (2) cue systems in the flow of language, (3) cue systems within the reader, and (4) cue systems external to language and the reader.

Section 1. Cue systems within words

To understand how cue systems within words function, consider the case of a first-grader encountering *monkey* for the first time in his reading. In a phonics approach, under his teacher's urging, he would try to recall sounds he had learned to associate with the letters in the word: *m-mm, ah, nnn, ka, eh, ye* (or *ee*). He would attempt to string these sound-letter associations to make a word. Hopefully, the word would be *monkey*. Is the *ey* the same as the one in *key* or is it like the one in *they?* Aside from the problems of undependable correspondence between letters and sounds in English, this approach is quite limited. It is indeed only one of several word-attack skills.

If a child has been taught with a word-recognition method to use word-attack skills, he is basically using cues within words. He can use phonic generalizations, as just mentioned. Or he can use phonics in a modified sense, concentrating on important letters like initial and final consonants, the *m* for example.

The child may notice and remember the shape of this new world. It's high in the middle and drops down at the end: monkey.

The young reader may pick small words which he knows out of the new word and words he knows that are spelled similarly and rhyme. In this case, the only word that might help is *donkey*, which rhymes with *monkey* in some American English dialects but not in others. Children may also learn to see affixes in words and may use their recurrent meanings as cues. Ultimately, the child will rely on remembering whole words.

To recapitulate, *within words* there are these cue systems:

Letter-sound relationships (phonic generalizations)
Shape, or word configuration
Known little words in new words
Affixes
Recurrent spelling patterns
Whole known words

All proficient readers have acquired the ability to use cue systems within words. But overreliance on these cues in the early stages of learning to read leads the child away from meaning and away from the extensive knowledge of the language he brings with him to school. He focuses on minute detail and he must subsequently build back toward language. Reading, with the emphasis on words, may become a continuous series of words to attack and of meaning he lost or neglected. The child and the teacher may be so concerned with word-attack skills that the child may not even be aware that there *is* any meaning or that he is supposed to look for it.

Words. At this point, it might be well to say a few words about words. Many teachers have been amused by children's asking how to spell *hafta* (as in *I hafta go now*). Adults think of words as entities, islands surrounded by pauses or white space, but words are not nearly so distinct. *Hafta,* for example, behaves very much like a two-syllable word. It even has one-word synonyms such as *must* that can be neatly substituted for it in many cases.

The concept of language as composed of words is a useful and ancient invention. Ancient scholars no doubt noticed the perceptible pause in language that marked off recurrent patterns from each other. They noticed that these marked-off patterns had relationships consistent with meaning. The invention of written language must have predated the invention of the word concept because early written language offered no spaces to separate words. Now, however, our written language is neatly subdivided.

Teachers have tended to treat words as self-evident. They have expected children to know what words are, although it took mankind a good long time to think up the idea. With all due reverence it must be stated that in the beginning was not the word but the utterance—a glob of language. Children perceive these utterances whole long before they begin to notice the constituent elements. Only after a child has learned many utterances does he begin to sort out elements. And only after he has acquired a modicum of literacy does he begin to know and use the norms for recognizing where one word leaves off and another begins.

For the truth is that words do not really exist. It is useful and convenient to think about language as made up of words, but words have no reality extracted from language. They cannot be defined, pronounced, or classified out of the stream of language. Let us take for example the word, *white.*

Can *white* be defined in isolation? Most likely it is a color. But it could be part of a chicken egg. It could be a man's name, be a substitute for *Caucasian,* be black's foe in chess, or be red's foe in politics.

Can *white* be pronounced in isolation? Most speakers would read *white* in a list with similar intonation. But what about this sentence: *In Washington, D.C., there is a white house called the White House but the White family doesn't live there. White* has three different intonations in that sentence that must be precise. Any variation in the way *white* is stressed would change the meaning of the sentence completely.

Can *white* be classified in isolation? It is an adjective: *They waved a white flag.* But it is also a noun: *Add the white of an egg.* It can be inflected like a verb (*He will whiten his shoes*) or compared as an adverb (*Cheer washes whiter*). *White* can be classified, but only as it occurs in language.

If words cannot be defined, pronounced, or classified, they cannot be recognized. Children can learn to call their names from lists, but word recognition is a much harder task than reading language.

Section 2. Cue systems in the flow of language

The second major set of cue systems is contained in language as it flows in actual speech or writing and not in the words alone.

If the young reader encounters the new word *monkey* embedded in a story he is reading, he will have all the cues that exist within the word plus many cues outside the word itself but within language. Suppose he finds the unfamiliar word in this story fragment:

Tom saw a *monkey*. A man played some music. The little *monkey* clapped his hands. Tom gave the *monkey* a penny.

The child responds as we did with *Gloopy* and *Blit* to features that are peculiar to the English language. He began learning these responses in his infancy. Scientific linguistics has described the vital features of language to which the child responds. Psycholinguistics is providing insights into how his responses are learned and generated.

Patterns of Word or Function Order. Every language has a limited number of common patterns by which the elements in an utterance may be arranged. *Tom saw a monkey* is an example of the most common sentence structure in the English language. In formal grammar we might call it subject–verb–object or noun–verb–noun. Recent studies have demonstrated that when children come to school they have mastered all the basic patterns of the language; this is true even of children with quite meager language development. Children will know by its position in the sentence that *monkey* is something that Tom saw. In some other languages, even in Old English, *Tom saw the money* could mean *the monkey saw Tom* if *Tom* had an objective case ending and *monkey* had a nominative one. In the English of today we rely much more on position than on case or inflectional endings. So there would be no doubt that *Tom* did the seeing; the positions of *monkey* and *Tom* in the pattern make this clear even to a six-year-old.

In the brief story just given *monkey* is used in three different positions in the same basic pattern: as subject (*The little monkey clapped his hands*), as object (*Tom saw a monkey*), and as inner or indirect object (*Tom gave the monkey a penny*). The reader sees the unfamiliar word from three angles with three sets of cues.

Inflection and Inflectional Agreement. Inflectional endings on words in English are not as important as they once were, but there still are such inflectional endings, and where they exist they play an important role in cueing meaning. Certain sounds usually represented in writing by *d* or *ed* are added to many verbs as a signal that the action or event took place in the past. Similarly, *s* or *es* represents in written language a group of sounds added to many nouns to indicate plurality and to many verbs to indicate singularity. There is pattern in the use of these inflectional endings; that is, they must be consistent. *The boy sees the monkey* is acceptable; *The boys see the monkey* is equally good. But *The boys sees the monkey* would not be consistent in most dialects of English.

Children are basically aware not only of these inflectional cues but also of the need for them to be consistent. If a child reads *The boys sees . . .* it just does not sound right to him.[3]

Function Words. A small number of words in English have little or no meaning but perform key functions as structure cues. In a major language study, Fries found that 154 structure words made up fully a third of the total volume of language.

Linguists have called these words *structure words* or *function words.* LeFevre[4] calls them "empty words," referring to their lack of referential meaning as compared to nouns, verbs, adjectives, or adverbs that he calls "full words." Function words are the articles, auxiliary verbs, prepositions, and conjunctions of traditional grammar. Often they have only two or three letters. Here is a verse from Lewis Carroll's Jabberwocky with only the function words shown to illustrate how function words serve as cues to structural meaning.

[3] Of course, in dialects with no *s* forms, *He see* will sound consistent to a reader.

[4] Carl LeFevre, *Linguistics and the Teaching of Reading* (New York: McGraw-Hill, 1964), p. 80.

'Twas _____ and the _____ _____
Did _____ and _____ in the _____,
All _____ were the _____
And the _____ _____.

In the sentence "Tom saw a monkey," *monkey* is literally marked as a noun by a noun marker, *a*. If the reader mistakes *monkey* for *money*, he would be likely to realize he had made an error, because *a* does not precede a noun such as *money*. This would not be a conscious, reasoned decision but, nonetheless, it would be a sure one because the reader would be relying on his knowledge of the language.

Other function words can be verb markers (*is, has,* and *will* are examples) that cue the reader that a verb follows as in *Ril **had** poved Gloopy.*

The question marker serves much more surely as a signal that the sentence that follows is a question than does the question mark (which, lamentably, comes at the end in English writing). Words that serve as question markers are such as *who, what, did,* as in *Did Ril pove Gloopy?* or *Where is the jonfy?*

Some of these same words and others (for example, *because, that,* and *if*) can be clause markers as in *Gloopy was not poved **because** Gloopy is a borp.* Function words like *in, on, of, for, by,* and *to* can serve as phrase markers. For example, *Blit was poved **to** a jonfy **by** Ril.*

Some vital function words are literally in classes by themselves, as *Gloopy was **not** poved. Not* has no meaning of its own, but it signals that the whole statement is negative.

These function words must be present in the very simplest language passages, but their lack of meaning makes them difficult for children to learn and remember in reading. When they are presented in isolation, they are even more difficult for young readers. Many teachers have been perplexed because children could remember such words as *something,* but not *the, on, or,* or *was.* Many of the function words are also irregularly spelled; that is, they are likely to contradict phonics rules that children are taught. Some examples of function words that do not obey phonics rules are *of, for, to, do, from, was, what, can* (a homophone of *kin* when used as a function word in many dialects), *the,* and *a,* to mention just a few. Again, remember that the reading beginner is not a language beginner; he has learned to interpret these function word cues automatically in oral speech.

Intonation. Intonation is a fourth system of cues in the flow of language. It is, in a sense, the tune to which the language is sung. Intonation is only partially represented in the written language, but in speech all three parts of intonation (stress, pitch, and juncture) play a vital role in signaling meaning. To a large extent, the reader must learn to supply his own intonation. He does this by setting what he reads to a familiar tune, a common intonation pattern of English.

The parts of an English utterance are *stressed* to various degrees. Shifting these stresses from one word to another can change the meaning of an utterance completely. For instance in *Tom saw a monkey,* if unusual stress is placed on *Tom,* the reader knows that *Tom,* not Jim or Bill, saw a monkey. Shift this heavy stress to *saw* and the sentence means there is no doubt he saw it. Shift the heavy stress to the noun marker *a* and the singularity is stressed, not monkeys but *a* monkey. Stress *monkey* and the sentence means he saw not a dog, cat, or kangaroo, but a *monkey.* This kind of special stress

can be signaled in writing by underlining or italics or bold face type, but the regular, important, subtle stress differences among the words of an utterance are not represented in any way in written English.

Many words are spelled the same when used as verbs or nouns, but the stress is shifted from the first syllable for the noun to the second syllable for the verb. *Contract* and *progress* are such words. Compounds such as *blackboard* are stressed differently from the way the same two words are said when used together but not compounded. *Not all black boards are blackboards.* To understand the sense of this sentence the reader must supply appropriate stress. When a teacher says to a child, "Read that the way you would say it to a friend," he is asking the child to supply natural intonations.

Juncture refers to the ways we mark off groups of sounds with pauses of variable length to produce words, phrases, or communication units. In written language the spaces between words and punctuation such as commas and periods provide graphic cues to the reader that correspond with juncture in speech. However, this correspondence is incomplete and somewhat capricious. Our division of written language into words does not accurately reflect the oral language as children know it. *Look at the monkey* has four words, but the child normally hears no separation between *look* and *at* because there is none.

Rises, falls, and steadiness in pitch are also used to cue meaning in English. Few speakers can describe how pitch works, but all use it to get meaning. By varying the pitch pattern of the single word *what,* we can make it mean, "Go ahead, I'm listening," "I didn't hear you," or "I didn't understand you," "You're kidding," "I can't believe what you just said," and many other things.

Pitch and juncture are the cues that tell a listener that an utterance is over or continuing, that he is expected to continue listening to a series of statements, respond to a question, or act on a request. Readers must learn to associate punctuation with familiar pitch and stress patterns in oral language, so that they may supply these intonational features as they read and understand.

All three aspects of intonation—stress, pitch, and juncture—work together in oral language. When words are read from lists, the intonation is quite different from when they are read in stories. To hear this difference, read this list of words: *peaches, pears, plums.* Now read this sentence: *He bought peaches, pears, and plums.* In the list, each word has the same intonation. It is the same stress and pitch pattern as the last word in the sentence. Some children are word-callers. They read as if they were reading lists of words: *Tom, saw, the* (probably pronounced *thee*), *monkey.* Punctuation cues are of little help to these readers, because every word is the first, last, and only word in a one-word sentence.

Word-callers are so busy recognizing words by using cues within words that they make little or no use of cues within the flow of language. They may call the names of the words correctly, but they cannot get the meaning from a story without using cues that are not contained in words. They can see the trees, but they are lost in the forest.

Contextual Meaning. Earlier, full and empty words were mentioned. Full words have dictionary (lexical) definitions with some substance, but every-

one knows that a series of lexical definitions cannot be put together if one is to understand a sentence without awkward, comical, and misleading results. How could one get the sense of this sentence from dictionary definitions of the individual words: *He got up, took a dip, and shoved off.*

The lexical meaning must have added to it a contextual one. This is supplied partly by nearby function words, partly by inflectional endings, partly by the position of the word in a language pattern, partly by intonations, and partly by the lexical meaning of nearby words. Actually, only larger units of language, sentences or groups of sentences, convey meaning, and this meaning is always more than the sum of its parts. As was apparent with "Gloopy and Blit," adults who are good readers often meet unfamiliar words in their reading that they can understand because of the numerous cues that surround them. Children learn to read new words in similar fashion.

Redundancy in Language Cues. Another important aspect of language is its *redundancy.* In the story "Gloopy and Blit," the generous number of cues available was noted. Communications theorists use the word *redundancy* in a special sense to describe a tendency of languages to restrict the sequences in which language symbols can occur, to provide several cues to the same bit of information, and thus to be less than 100 percent efficient in the amount of information transmitted per unit of language.

Our language, like all other natural languages, is not very economical in the way that it transmits information. To be completely efficient (that is, to transmit the maximum amount of information per unit of language), every sound or letter would have to occur with equal frequency after every other. Likewise, every word would need to follow every other word with equal frequency. But a word like *ngopr* could not exist in English because the sequence of sounds in it is not used in our language. A sequence of words such as *To ran elephant the him not* is also not a permissible sequence in English.

Some sequences seldom occur in our language. Some never occur. This inefficiency or *redundancy* has two important effects on reading. First, it provides the reader with the repetitious cues we noted earlier. In the sentence that follows there are no less than four cues to the fact that the subject is plural: *At noon, the boys eat their lunches.*

Second, redundancy provides a narrowing of elements in the language that can fill certain slots. Only certain sounds can occur after /t/ in *Tom*. Only certain words can occur after *Tom*. After *Tom saw* still fewer words are possible. After *Tom saw a* possible correct words are more restricted. Furthermore, the unknown word *monkey* must fit equally well into a number of such restricted settings.

The process by which the child immediately or eventually knows this word is *monkey* is a kind of tentative "zeroing in." Successive sets of redundant cues narrow the number of possible words in the language that can fit. As he responds to these redundant cues, the child is not guessing. He is using his knowledge of language, his past experience, and his developed concepts. If he makes a mistake, there are almost always abundant additional cues to tell him that he is wrong and to tell him what is right.

Children do not need to know all the words before they can read stories.

In a study by Goodman, first-grade children were able to read two thirds of the words that they had missed on a list when these same words occurred in a story. Second-graders read three fourths of their list errors correctly in a story context. Third-graders got more than four out of five right in the stories.[5] They were able to do this because of the cue systems that exist in the flow of language but not in words.

Within the flow of language there are these cue systems in addition to cues in words:

Patterns of word or function order
Inflection and inflectional agreement
Function words
Intonation (pitch, stress, juncture)
Contextual meaning of prior and subsequent words and whole utterances

These cues are redundantly available to the reader.

Section 3. Cues within the reader

Obviously, learning to read depends to a very great extent on the individual characteristics of the learner. What the reader brings to the language he is reading is as important as the cues in the language itself. The message does not exist in the language. Language carries the message from the writer, but it must be re-created by the reader out of raw material within himself. A good writer always has his audience in mind. The reader must have certain associations with the language symbols in common with the writer. But he must also have some experiences in common with the writer

[5] Kenneth S. Goodman, "Cues and Miscues in Reading: A Linguistic Study," *Elementary English*, **42**, No. 6 (1965), 640.

and must have reached a level of concept development that makes communication possible.

Consider the absurd example of a six-year-old English-speaking American child trying to read an ancient Chinese philosophical tract written in archaic Chinese characters. The task is patently ridiculous, but why?

First, the child does not understand Chinese. Even if he did, the dialect he would understand would be one of many modern dialects; it would be very much changed from the ancient dialect of the Chinese philosopher who wrote the tract. Communication depends on a common language. If the young reader did overcome this handicap, he would be confronted by a system of writing he does not know. He would not have learned responses to the symbols of the written language that the writer expected to evoke in his readers. But even if he did learn the symbols, he could not read the philosophical tract because he would not have had the experiences or have developed the philosophical concepts to know what the writer intended him to know. Further, his American culture would be so different from the culture of the ancient Chinese that many of the philosophical thoughts would be literally unthinkable, even for adult Americans. The six-year-old American child learning to read English is confronted with problems that differ in degree but not in kind from this absurd example.

Language Facility. Success in any communicative transaction, including reading, depends to a great degree on the language facility of the two parties in the communication, the speaker–writer and the listener–reader. Close agreement on language between these two parties is important. Even though both may speak English, there may be large or small differences between the English of one and the other.

Differences in use of a single language are generally termed *dialects*. Groups of users separated by time, space, social or economic class, interest, political barriers, or age may develop dialect differences. Further, each user of the language develops his own idiolect, different in some respects from those of all other users.

Every child starting the first grade has mastered, for all practical language purposes, the language of his subculture—his family, friends, and community. This dialect is deeply internalized in the child; it has become a part of his personality.

Dialect Differences. When a child is learning to read, he may have problems if there is a considerable difference between his dialect and that of the basal reading series. If he does not speak a standard Midwestern dialect, he may be confused, because what he is asked to read does not sound like the language as he knows it.

But most people develop the ability to understand a wide range of dialects that differ somewhat from their own. Children in New England, New York, Chicago, and the deep South all "savvy" the lingo of the television cowpoke. In reading, the fact of dialect is reflected in a tendency on the part of the reader to translate the text language into his own dialect. Not only are the phonemes those of the oral language of the reader, but grammar, usage, even vocabulary are unconsciously shifted into the more familiar dialect. *There were a lot of pumpkins* might be read by some children as *They was a lot o' punkins*. This translation is not error, pure and simple; the child is making a linguistic leap. He is reading his own dialect from the printed page. If his teacher rejects his attempt at bridging the gap between the book dialect and his own and treats it as an error, he may be bewildered. If what he reads sounds right to him, how can it be wrong? This is not the time to be concerned about changing dialects, when reading is the goal.

Beginners, including those who speak standard dialects, are confused if basal readers use language that does not occur in anybody's speech. Older children find it difficult to read classics that employ archaic dialects. Not only have meanings changed, but structural patterns, usage, and other vital elements are different. Perhaps most difficult is that children are asked to reconstruct a dialect they have never heard spoken. This is not to suggest that all classics should be abandoned, but that special problems are involved in reading them and teachers need to help students to develop special skills to deal with these problems.

Knowledge of the language and skill in its use are important in communication. Books written without skillful use of language are hard to read. Readers whose knowledge of the language is limited, such as those who have not learned to speak it, will have great difficulty learning to read it.

Physiology. Physical factors may interfere with effective communication. Writing may be illegible because of physical disability or lack of coordination of the writer. Visual factors may interfere with the reader's ability to discern language units clearly. Hearing problems may make it difficult for children to hear sounds in language and to associate these sounds with graphic symbols. General factors of physical and mental health affect all learning, including the ability to read. These factors are of course intertwined with the total well-being of the learner

—economic, social and emotional, as well as physical.

Some medical authorities have sought to identify a pattern of physiological factors that would cause the child to fail to learn to read. This has been labeled by some *constitutional dyslexia.* Children seem to have some ability to overcome physical and perceptual disabilities, however; many of the factors that researchers have sought to link to constitutional dyslexia have been found among readers as well as nonreaders.

Learned Responses to Graphic Cues. Letters, singly or in groups, do not have sounds or meanings; they just lie there on the page. But they may evoke responses in people. Thus, people may see letters in isolation and call their names, *A, B, C,* and so forth. Or they may see letters in isolated words and call the names of the word: *peaches, pears, plums.* These responses are all learned. The important thing is that they must evoke the same general responses in all who use them.

The reading beginner has not learned these responses to graphic cues, but he has learned to respond rapidly to groups of sounds as language symbols. In reading he must become at least as facile in responding to graphic symbols. He may acquire this rapid ability to interpret graphic symbols in a "natural" manner, deriving his own generalizations just as he learned to talk and understand oral language. Or he may learn systems of reading attacks, skills, or learning strategies that he applies in a synthetic manner (phonics is such a synthetic learning strategy).

In either case, he must transfer his existing knowledge of language to the task of reading. He can only do this effectively if what he reads is real language, which differs from oral language in its use of graphic symbols rather than sound symbols.

CODE AND MEANING

If language is viewed as a code, a system for communicating meaning, then reading may be seen as a process of *decoding*. The reader uses a printed code and decodes from it the meaning that the writer had encoded.

It is also possible to go from one code to another without decoding for meaning. Such a process can be called *recoding*. That's what happens when a telegraph operator takes a written message and sends it out on his key in Morse code. He recodes the alphabetic code as dots and dashes. He need have no understanding of what he is reading to successfully recode; in fact, the original may be in a secret code that he does not know.

In oral reading, beginners and others who are not very proficient may in fact be recording graphic code (print) as oral code (speech) without decoding for meaning. Or there may be a chain sequence of this sort: [6]

$$\boxed{\text{graphic code}} \xrightarrow{\text{RECODING}} \boxed{\text{oral code}} \xrightarrow{\text{DECODING}} \boxed{\text{meaning}}$$

Eventually though, in proficient reading, the process becomes parallel to listening. There is no necessary resort to recoding print as oral language. Rather, the reader goes directly from print to meaning in the same manner that he goes from speech to meaning as a listener.

[6] Kenneth S. Goodman, *The Psycholinguistic Nature of the Reading Process* (Detroit: Wayne State University Press, 1967), p. 18.

$$\boxed{\text{graphic code}} \xrightarrow{\text{DECODING}} \boxed{\text{meaning}}$$

Even in the beginner's model where the recoding and decoding processes may be discrete and more or less sequential, they cannot be separated because the reason for reading is to reconstruct meaning. If children develop skills for recoding in school using exercises and materials that are not real, meaningful language, they will not be able to use the grammatical cues and other cues within the language but will be confined to working with cues that lead only to words. Even there they have no check on whether they have selected the right word because they cannot check their choices against cues within the flow of language.

The controversy over code emphasis versus meaning emphasis programs in reading instruction stems from the erroneous assumption that language is simply a collection of words and that all that is necessary for reading is to identify (or recognize) words. But the code that is language is a system of symbols and is not merely a collection of symbols. To decode one must respond not simply to symbols with other symbols. One must respond to the system (which in linguistic codes is called grammar) as well as to the symbols in order to arrive at the meaning. Research that has been summarized by Chall [7] and others that purports to show that code-emphasis programs are superior to meaning-emphasis programs

[7] Jean Chall, *Reading: The Great Debate* (New York: McGraw-Hill, 1967).

for teaching reading is in reality a comparison of two kinds of programs for teaching children to recode. The phonics programs focus on letter-to-sound recoding. (Chall labels these code emphasis.) The sight-word programs focus on word-shape–word-name recoding. (Chall calls these meaning emphasis.) The only sense in which the latter are more involved in meaning is that words have dictionary, lexical, definitions. But in none of these programs are all of the cues within language emphasized. They are not really decoding systems.

The Experiential Background of the Learner. The reader depends heavily on his experiential background to decode what he is reading. If the events, places, people, and objects the reader encounters are unrelated to any experiences he has had, he will have great difficulty reading about them, even though the language elements may all be familiar.

Communication depends on some base of shared experience between the sending and receiving parties. This base may be the common experience of all those who share the culture or the subculture, or may be the intimate experience shared by a small in-group or even by just two. The more intimate the base of experience, of course, the less complete must the language be, so that between close friends or family members a nod or a single word may be sufficient to communicate whole thoughts.

The following passage illustrates the kind of language composed of familiar elements that can be understood only by those who share the common experiences of the group:

If you're running a big bad AA fuelie, man, it costs dough every time you're just tripping the lights to get the tires ready.

Some slicks take ten or twelve runs to be right.[8]

Teachers of adolescents sometimes despair that their pupils can handle, with ease, passages like that above but that they bog down hopelessly in *Silas Marner* or a tenth-grade world-geography text.

Of course, reading itself is experience. This experience can be built layer upon layer, so that the armchair traveler, armchair detective, armchair scientist can come to be almost as much an initiate as his real-life counterpart. But this is all vicarious experience. Language is symbolic. It can only evoke images, feelings, thoughts, visions, which have some base in the real experience of the reader.

Recently one of the authors observed a seventh-grade boy attempting to read a work sheet in a junior high school print shop. The sheet provided directions for printing personal stationery. The boy read with difficulty but paused every time he came to the word *stationery*. Each time his teacher supplied the word, but the next time the boy was stumped again. When he had finished reading the sheet, the boy could describe the technical details involved in setting three lines of type for the job, but he had no idea what the purpose of the project was. The simple truth is that the boy had had no experience with stationery. The writer of the work sheet had assumed that all the boys had seen stationery in use and would appreciate the value of personalized stationery. This type of unwarranted assumption is frequently reflected in text material for all subjects at all levels and penalizes children whose experiences are different. Teachers who know their children

[8] LeRoi Smith, "New Drag Slick!" *Hot Rod*, July 1964, pp. 46–47.

and preread text material carefully can soften this effect somewhat by providing experiences that are needed to make text material understandable.

Conceptual Background and Ability of the Learner. Just as reading is limited by the experience of the learner, so is it limited by his conceptual development. A reader cannot read written language that expresses concepts that are far beyond his developed ability to understand. Concepts may be attained through reading, but they must be broadly within the grasp of the reader. Beyond this point, a learner must have help in understanding concepts before he can read. Indeed, teachers would be unneeded if this were not true.

Overdependence on independent study of textbooks in many classrooms is often because of a confusion between language and the concepts it conveys. Concepts are not only communicated from person to person through language; language is also the symbolic medium individuals use to manipulate their experiences and ideas in order to develop concepts. But language can be manipulated by children without their understanding the concepts involved. A child may state correctly that Michigan is a peninsula and that so is Florida, without grasping the basic significance of peninsularity. He may just be repeating, appropriately, statements he has heard. Similarly, he may read from a text and even supply correct answers to questions at the end of each chapter without in any way understanding the concepts. *Question:* What is Gloopy? *Answer:* Gloopy is a borp.

Some teachers naïvely assume that if a child can translate the written symbols in a text into oral speech, he is capable of dealing with the concepts being presented. If he cannot read a particular word, the teacher considers this a vocabulary problem. But what is labeled a "reading vocabulary problem" may involve problems on four very different levels. Here are four cases to illustrate these levels of vocabulary difficulty:

1. The reader understands a word or phrase—*monkey* or *stationery,* for example—and uses it in his oral speech, but does not recognize its graphic representation.
2. The reader does not know or use the word or phrase in his oral language but can grasp the meaning, particularly in familiar natural language. His previous experience and conceptual development have made this easy addition to his vocabulary possible.
3. The reader does not know or use the word or phrase in his oral language and cannot understand the meaning because it depends on experiences and a level of concept development that he has not attained.
4. The reader can tell the name of the word or phrase, using cues within words, but he does not know, use or understand what he is reading. Because he does not understand he is not reading.

Vital contributions to the act of reading, then, are made by the systems of cues and responses to cues that are within or must develop within the reader. To recapitulate, these are

1. Language facility the internalization of a dialect
2. The physiology of the learner, as it affects perception and expression
3. Learned response, attacks, skills, and learning strategies
4. The experiential background of the reader

5. The reader's conceptual background and ability

Section 4. Cues external to language and the reader

The fourth major group of cues that operates in reading is not directly involved in the interaction of the reader with written language. This group consists of systems of supplied extraneous cues.

Pictures. Pictures, as illustrations, give substance to descriptive language. They supplement the visual images evoked in the mind of the reader by the language. Pictures also make reading material attractive and catch the interest of the potential reader. But in most basal readers these are secondary aspects of the pictures. Pictures in basal readers are designed to carry parts of the story, to provide clues to meaning that the language is too sparse to carry. In a word-centered approach the pictures fill this role until the child acquires a substantial recognition vocabulary. Ideally, he then transfers his attention from pictures to text.

Prompting. Another form of external cue is prompting by teachers or by peers. Every time a child hesitates or errs in oral reading he is corrected and supplied with the correct form. Some teachers even make a kind of game out of this that penalizes the poor reader. A child reads orally until he is caught in an error by a classmate. Then he sits down in disgrace, and the child who caught the error reads until he is similarly apprehended. Prompting prevents the child from recognizing his own errors and from using language cues available to him to correct them. Some children become so dependent on prompting that even in silent reading they must ask a classmate or the teacher every time they meet a new word.

Concrete Objects. Teachers (and sometimes parents) often put labels on concrete objects to associate the object with the word that names it. This device is only suitable for nouns or noun phrases, but it does provide external cues to the reader.

Skill Charts. Charts showing letter-sound relationships and other generalizations are often posted in classrooms to provide reminders to the reader to help him apply particular learning strategies.

All of these external cues lead the child away from using his existing knowledge of language in the reading process. Instead of learning rapid response to the cues in written language, the reader may learn to read pictures, depend on charts, or wait for someone to supply correct responses. He gets the message, but not from the language itself.

Reading is a psycholinguistic process. While reading, the reader's thought processes interact with written language. He utilizes his store of experience, developed concepts, and learned responses to reconstruct a message that the writer has encoded in language. His responses are cued by systems of signals in language, which he has already basically mastered if he speaks the language he is learning to read. Reading comprehension is message reconstruction. Comprehension depends on the reader's using all the cues available to him. *No curriculum for teaching reading can be complete that neglects any of the cue systems. No method of reading instruction can be sound or fully successful that is not based on an understanding of the psycholinguistic process of reading.*

More Important
than the Right to Read

Donald Hugh Smith
City University of New York

One of the most significant events of my life took place in Chicago during the summer of 1967. The event began officially on the Fourth of July at the East Lansing, Michigan, home of Robert L. Green, now director of Michigan State University's Center for Urban Affairs. Throughout that day and the following, six of us—educators and community developers—made final preparations for an adult literacy and job placement program funded by the Department of Health, Education, and Welfare, to be conducted on Chicago's West Side by Martin Luther King, Jr.

By the time we met with the Reverend King in Chicago the following week, the design was complete. We would teach reading, basic mathematics, and job interview skills. Dependent on their entry levels of reading and their progress, students would be placed in jobs as rapidly as possible. With eight ministers in the Lawndale and East Garfield communities providing classrooms in their churches, the eight-week program began late in July.

Yet, as this effort to rescue 400 or 500 black people on Chicago's teeming West Side was unfolding, a larger event was being superimposed which

would have a lasting impact on all Americans. Early in the morning on the Sunday after our July Fourth meeting, the Detroit Rebellion began. By nightfall fire, violence, and death wracked the city. Within a few weeks, Newark was to become a second major battlefront as black people revolted in over 100 cities throughout America.

In this setting we attempted to teach reading in one of the nation's most neglected, abused areas. My day began early, making the rounds of the eight churches. It would be difficult to describe my feelings as I drove through the city from South to West Side, passing hundreds of "Mayor Daley's finest" in their white battle helmets, tense, anxious, poised to spring. Chicago did not burn that summer, but it felt the flames of Detroit and Newark and was terrified by the remembrance of its own holocausts in recent summers.

Surprising as it may seem in that electrifying environment, school attendance at those churches was very high. Every day teen-age dropouts sat side by side with older people, poring over the materials provided by the Behavioral Research Laboratory of Cal-

Reprinted by permission of Phi Delta Kappa, Inc. and Donald H. Smith.

ifornia. Some were learning to read; others were improving their reading skills. On several occasions when we were ready to place some of the adults in jobs they asked to remain in the reading program for a few more days. One woman said, "For the first time in my life I'm learning to read and I want to keep on just a little while longer."

For a time we were euphoric—those of us who supervised the instructional program, those who taught, those who recruited in the community, and most of all those beautiful, tortured, poverty-stricken people who found a ray of hope in the program. Before long, however, the dream was crushed and the light went out. The serpent I call "politics before people" reared its ugly head and killed the program. It is alleged that high officials in Chicago's government called the White House. Didn't President Johnson know that Martin Luther King was not to have any success in Chicago? Within a month after its opening, King's adult literacy and jobs program was closed, its grant canceled; and the director of adult education in the U.S. Office of Education, who had authorized the grant, was fired. People who wanted and needed desperately to read were denied the opportunity. One could not help but remember a similar period during the era of slavery when some plantation owners punished those who tried to teach slaves to read and write. As King discovered, the right to read is political, is controversial, and—as I intend to point out—is *not* the first priority in American education.

There can be no denying that the ability to read is a skill which offers the potential for personal independence and economic security. There can be no denying that a man who cannot read must be dependent upon

the reading skills of others and will be severely limited in the kind of work he can perform. However, as critical a need as reading is, there is something more important than the right to read. *The right to be is more important than the right to read.*

The right to be is a higher order than reading. The right to be is a God-given right. Reading is a skill, a faculty of man. The right to be recognizes the inherent worth and dignity of all human beings, of whatever color, sex, philosophy, or station in life. One can be black or white (or red, brown, or yellow), male or female, conservative or radical; no matter, one is still entitled to the right to exist, to live or work wherever one's talents or interests lie.

The right to be recognizes that man is more important than property, and that while men may own property they may not own or control other men. If our nation honored the right to be, it would give the same opportunity to have a job to a poorly educated black or Puerto Rican as it gives to a poorly educated white mountaineer or Iron Curtain refugee.

Belief in the right to be would result in a government which would protect black school children from vicious chain-wielding mobs that seek to deny them their right to read. I submit that the right to be supersedes the right to read.

Something else is more important than the right to read. More important than the right to read is the right to read the truth, for the truth shall make us free.

Thomas Jefferson held the theory that if all manner of ideas were promulgated in the marketplace of human thought and discourse, then men would have the capacity to find the truth. Such a theory, of dubious validity in America's early history, is hardly applicable to a computerized age where control of public communication by the mass media is limited to a very few who have their own cultural, economic, and political interests to protect.

At no time in our history has our national ethos been more tarnished nor our national credibility more suspect than at the present. It does not matter whether the truth is being concealed or distorted by biased historians, by the mass media, or by the President of the United States. We are all victimized by the omissions, half-truths, and out and out lies which have characterized our national history and our present life experience.

It should be clear that we are past the time when we can ignore the findings of a group so impeccably credentialed as President Johnson's Riot Commission. That commission told the rest of America what black people already knew: The principal cause of racial strife in America is white racism. Though the commission failed to point it out clearly, nowhere is racism more prevalent than in the public schools and public universities.

Racism permeates textbooks and teaching materials, teacher and administrative practices, and board of education policies. Fortunately, many of our beautiful young people, and even some older ones not beyond recall, are in open revolt against this system of human debasement. They are refusing to cooperate with an educational enterprise whose purpose has been historically and remains at present the preparation of an elitist few for dominant roles, and the rest for roles of service.

I know it has not been fashionable to discuss racism during the last few years, and I know that for a time those who will attempt to deal truthfully with the issues of slavery, exploitation, oppression, and repression will be branded as some form of traitor. And for a time we must pay that price. Our children and our country are both too precious to allow ourselves to be frightened by bugged telephones or secret dossiers. History records the fall of the Roman Empire in a period when its citizens had become too intimidated to discuss and debate the critical issues of the day. Instead, their public utterances were limited to neutral, nonpolitical, noncontroversial trivia. We cannot allow ourselves to become so decadent. We have to understand that coming to grips with national troubles and resolving them is our only real hope for national survival.

We who teach reading or any other subject must perceive the importance of developing in our students a burning desire to know their own personal and national truths. To teach them lies will turn them off, as it should.

Little does it matter, nor will it matter, that we live in the most literate nation in the world if those who can read continue to read of and believe in a nation where only white is right. Little will it matter if those who develop economic competence continue to exploit others in America and elsewhere. Little will it matter if the students we teach to read continue to solve their economic and political problems by killing women and children in distant lands.

The right to read is meaningless without its antecedent, the right to be, and its essence, the right to read the truth. The implications of this triumvirate—being, reading, and reading the truth—for our schools are fairly obvious, but the implementation is incredibly difficult in an environment which has been so well described in the recent movies *Easy Rider* and *Joe,* and in the horribly real dramas of Martin Luther King, Jr., Malcolm X, Medgar Evers, and the Kennedy brothers.

As *Easy Rider* points out, America does not permit nonconformity. Those who are free will face death if their freedom is discovered by those who remain in conformist chains. *Joe* merely underlines the issue by pointing out the murderous hysteria of those who honestly believe they are protecting America's values and best interests.

Yet with full knowledge of the dangers of change we must recognize the greater destructive potential of not owning up to the issues. Apparently the schools and the nation will never enjoy racial harmony and will continue to experience violence until the schools and the nation cease to do violence upon the minds, hearts, and bodies of its black and other minority children.

Where do we begin? Since behavior is a good deal easier to change than attitudes, it would seem that the place to start is in the materials that are being used to teach reading. The word *relevance* has become a cliché. It is rejected by those who understand it to mean discarding all that has been used in the past, and it is embraced by many who believe it implies a whole new set of values and ideas that will usher in a new world. I believe the concept includes parts of both, discarding those values and practices which are dysfunctional and adopting those new ones which promise to humanize and civilize man.

Specifically applied to reading, relevancy should mean the utilization of materials and experiences which, first, realistically and truthfully depict all races and their contributions, and, second, contain content which reflects the vital concerns and the life needs of students.

How little understood is this simple and basic concept is exemplified by action recently taken by a community school board in Queens, New York. By a 5-3 vote, the board banned *Down These Mean Streets,* by Piri Thomas, from its approved reading list. As those who have read the book know, *Down These Mean Streets* is the story of a Puerto Rican boy growing up in New York. He becomes a drug addict, then a convict, and finally is rejected by his family because his skin is black. That's where it is; that's what America's racism did to that boy and does to us all. It is the classic story of America's inhumanity to its own, a story that should be read in every classroom in America, not only for its terrible truth but also because the ultimate salvation of Piri Thomas is an inspiration for all youths who have been abused for their blackness.

The evidence is in: We are failing at all levels to teach students to read. The responsibility for failure lies with those who have controlled the schools. It lies with individual teachers who have copped out with excuses of cultural deprivation. It lies with businesses and industries that have permitted the public schools to fail with impunity. It lies with governments that continue to support all manner of reading programs designed, controlled, and operated by those who have already failed. It lies within the churches that have failed to teach a true religion. It lies within a national philosophy of white supremacy.

Finally, the responsibility lies within the local communities that have allowed professionals to earn excellent salaries with no productivity. There have been exceptions where communities have sought to control the school, but even in most of those cases all of the energy was dissipated in gaining control and in local power plays. These communities have rarely gotten around to the business of improving reading and math scores. We know that poor black, Spanish-speaking, and American Indian children *can* be taught to read.

Collectively, all of us—educators, business and industrial leaders, clergy, government, and citizenry—must assume the responsibility for holding the schools accountable.

We should recognize, however, that to produce a new generation of the best readers in the world will avail us nothing if we have not also taught our children to honor and respect themselves and others like and different from themselves. We cannot survive if we continue to turn our generations of literate Americans whose only concern is personal profit. The improvement of reading must go hand in hand with the elevation of the human condition and a search for truth. Our children have the right to read, but more importantly, they have the right to be.

Piaget and Reading Instruction

Ronald J. Raven and Richard T. Salzer
State University of New York at Buffalo

The complex process of reading includes many types of skills and abilities, from the making of simple associations to the complex analyses involved in critical thinking and problem solving. Increasingly, in recent years, students of the field of reading instruction have come to the realization that, in order to grasp the fundamental nature of the reading act, investigators must gain an understanding of the individual's perceptual and cognitive skills. Piaget has described in some detail the ontologcal development of the perceptual and logical operations which the child employs in structuring his universe (Piaget, 1963). It therefore appears advisable that students of reading seek among Piaget's findings for insights and clues which may apply to their problems of theory, research, and practice.

PIAGET'S THEORY OF INTELLECTUAL DEVELOPMENT

Piaget has convinced many psychologists and educators that it is useful to divide childhood and adolescence into

"Piaget and Reading Instruction," by Ronald J. Raven and Richard T. Salzer, *Reading Teacher* (April 1971). Reprinted with permission of Ronald J. Raven and Richard T. Salzer and the International Reading Association.

major developmental epochs or periods. One stage is followed naturally by the next, and transition is marked by the presence of well-defined behaviors of the former period and the emerging characteristics of the next.

The sensori-motor period (birth to two years, approximately) Piaget identifies as one in which the infant, at a reflex level in complete self-world totality, moves to the stage where his motor activities in relation to his environment show good organization. The infant carries on countless interactions with the things about him and notions of time-space and matter evolve. Eventually he perceives relationships and formulates primitive ideas of causality. Notions that he develops through these events are based on actions and displacements, but not thought. The complex systems of behavior and changes which occur when these interact with the environment produce representations in the form of well-developed images within the child.

The preoperational period spans the years from approximately two to seven. At this stage the child does not employ logical operations in his interactions with the environment. Rather, he tends to orient his activities on the basis of appearances; he is easily misled by what he sees. The child centers on only one aspect of an object or event at a time, on a single variable when he attempts to solve a problem. The classic Piaget experiments during this stage pose the questions of what happens to the quantity of a liquid when it is poured into a container of a shape different from that which originally held it. The preoperational child, dominated by whatever aspect of the situation has seized his attention, answers in such a way as to indicate the presence of a belief that the quantity of

liquid alters when vessels of varied dimensions are used. He cannot coordinate two related ideas, nor can he be expected to focus on attributes because of their relevance rather than their degree of obviousness. When confronted with twenty wooden beads, nearly all of which are red and two or three are yellow, the preoperational child, while he knows that all are wooden, states that there are more red than wood beads. Piaget's interpretation is that the youngster, overwhelmed by what he sees, cannot keep in mind that the beads are possessed of the two attributes at the same time.

It is important to realize that the operations which a child does develop during this stage, i.e., simple sorting by one variable and ordering of a small number of objects, depend on sensori-motor components or representations already developed in the preceding period. Although language may change the mode of the child's thinking, its development does not relieve the dependency of preoperational thought on basic sets of displacements, interactions, and representations which evolve from sensori-motor experience.

The concrete-operational period (7–11 years, approximately) is one in which the child's cognitive activities are much better organized than in the preceding stage. This greater organization has been achieved through the development of what Piaget terms the logical structure of groups. Groups are composed of elements and operations performed on these elements. The elements can be separate objects placed together because of some common attribute, e.g., size, shape, or color. The operations can be those of addition, subtraction, multiplication, division, setting elements into correspondence, or measurement.

The group, that is, the operations and the elements, possesses the properties of compositions, associativity, identity, and reversibility, and the child in this stage engages in corresponding mental operations. Composition enables the child to view the parts and represent them as contained in the whole or set; he puts one and one together figuratively as well as literally. Associativity allows him to arrange and rearrange elements in various ways while remaining secure in the knowledge that the whole has not been permanently affected. The identity operation permits him to maintain a perception of the original state or condition of elements so that, when change takes place, he can perform operations which will return them to that condition. Reversibility enables him to coordinate or compare the transformations made among the elements of a group. While identity allows one to make correspondences between a representation and another set of elements, reversibility permits a comparison of two groups that change in time or change within a group over a period of time.

These four operations enable the child to make multiple classifications, to realize that an object has many properties simultaneously and that any of these can be of greater significance than others at some point. Hierarchical classification, the formation of increasingly inclusive groupings, also becomes possible. Seriation, the placing of elements in order according to one or more criteria, is another ability that the individual comes to possess during this period.

The formal-operational period (beginning at age 11 or 12, approximately) is characterized by the ability of the youngster to control formal logic. While the concrete-operational child reasons only from directly-observed data, his older counterpart begins to deal with propositions and hypotheses apart from direct experience.

Four modes of logic enable the child to operate at this level: conjunction, disjunction, negation, and implication. The frequently recurring association of two properties expressed as "this rod is steel and bends" refers to a conjunction. Conjunctions allow the individual to say, "It is this element (x) and that element (y) that exist together" or "cause something."

The disjunction combination presents alternatives. The student can say that he has short rods that bend or short rods that do not bend. There are two possibilities, bend and not bend, and only one of these can occur in the same situation. Thus, the disjunctive operation allows the student to say, "It's got to be this element (x) or this element (y)."

The negation operation states that two variables or attributes do not exist together or are not responsible for an effect. Neither mass alone nor volume alone determines whether an object floats or sinks. In negation, the student states, "Neither element x nor element (y) causes this," or "These two elements $(x$ and $y)$ do not go together."

The last of these four combinations, implication, state that every time one variable appears a particular result occurs. When the string is lengthened, the frequency of the pendulum increases. In an implication operation, "When this element (x) occurs, then this element (y) will be true or occur."

The student in the formal-logic stage can combine these operations in various ways to produce hypotheses and deductive statements. He can determine the relevancy of variables and how these affect one another to produce a specific outcome.

RELATIONSHIP OF PIAGET'S STAGES TO READING INSTRUCTION

Sensori-motor period

While it is fashionable in some quarters to consider the possibility of offering infants instruction in reading, an examination of Piaget's theory leads to the conclusion that other activities are much more important for optimal development. Manipulative experience with a wide range of types of objects and materials during this stage appears most important for the development of images and cognitive growth. There is little reason to believe that any precisely described set of experiences should be considered crucial. The child's perceptual and intellectual abilities will develop adequately given almost any collection of artifacts that he and others may manipulate.

Preoperational period

Piaget divides this period into two stages, preconceptual (age two to four) and intuitive (four to seven). In the preconceptual phase rapid growth of language takes place for most youngsters, and it seems logical to some that reading instruction should accompany this development. This evolving language is based in the motor manipulation of the previous period. The child has, at most, mental images of objects and physical operations to which verbal labels have become attached. These labels are not abstractions in the usual sense of that term, and they certainly may not validly be attached to other labels. Preoperational thought develops through sensori-motor activities—not through language. For the preconceptual-phase child, language cannot be something apart from objects and experience. The name of the thing inheres in the thing itself, the arbitrary nature of language having yet made no impression on the child. A chair must be called "chair"; "rocker" is something else entirely.

Thought processes in the two-to-four-year-old are not sufficiently stabilized to permit him to profit much from practice on conceptual skills of any kind. Every event is new. The child thinks neither deductively nor inductively but "transductively," from point to point, making little or no differentiation concerning the degree of relevance between pairs of observations. Everything is related to about the same degree, which literally means that nothing is specifically related.

Obviously, there is little encouragement here for those who advocate systematic programs of "nursery school reading." The child's thought processes, according to Piaget, simply do not appear sufficiently stable to guarantee anything but frustration for those who would attempt didactic instruction of any kind. In the specific case of reading, there is no basis in Piaget's work for believing that the child from two to four has any interest in written language, except as it may constitute something interesting in the environment that merits whatever attention the individual youngster may desire to give it. As Almy (1967) has pointed out, the important implications for reading instruction of Piaget's work at the preoperational level relate to the necessity of providing many and varied concrete experiences, the sensory and motor activities out of which concepts and complex thinking may develop.

Such opportunities will likely influence ultimate reading achievement to a greater extent than specific perceptual discrimination training now offered in many nursery schools and kindergartens.

It is, of course, during the intuitive phase (age four to seven) that most children experience initial reading instruction. The cognitive benchmark is conservation of substance, the dawning realization that substantial change may take place in a system without the alteration of fundamental characteristics. Development of the over-all understanding of conservation of substance at approximately age seven marks, for Piaget, a major change in style of thinking on the part of the child, as he moves from near-total dependence on perception to a greater reliance on thought to check what he sees. It may be that this ability represents what most reading-instruction programs require and that its appearance constitutes "readiness." Almy, et al. (1966) have provided evidence of a rather high correlation between conservation ability and beginning-reading achievement.

Of the abilities which contribute to the development of conservation, reversibility and de-centration appear to have substantial significance for initial reading instruction. Reversibility permits the child to conserve by thinking, in the case of liquid, "If the juice is poured back into the first glass, it will come up to the top again." He solves many other problems by "undoing" some operation and coming back to the starting point. This is a mental activity which the preoperational child cannot perform, and the inference might be drawn that he should not be expected to succeed in decoding-emphasis reading programs which require him to convert graphemes to phonemes and then validate his transformations. Almy (1967) comments that the child who has not achieved reversibility "may lack the stability of perception necessary for formal reading instruction."

The characteristic of "centration" in the preoperational child's thinking refers to his inability to consider more than one aspect of a situation at a time; he is so impressed with the height of a column of water that he fails to notice how narrow it is. The beginning reading programs in most wide use continually require the child to deal with words in two almost entirely unrelated ways, however—as line puzzles to be remembered and deciphered and as signifiers of meaning. Piaget's theory leads one to believe that the child under seven cannot ordinarily be expected to engage in such mental gymnastics with facility.

The preoperational, non-conserving child cannot handle altered circumstances very well; a situation somewhat transformed is an entirely new situation. He should not be expected to view a wide variety of events and then identify their common characteristic. In presenting the young reader with upper- and lowercase letters, different type faces, manuscript and cursive writing, variations in the rendering of particular alphabet letters, and all of these in many different combinations and contexts, those responsible for initial reading instruction constantly expose children to transformed situations and expect them to isolate the single common attribute which is the key to solving the problem.

Neither can the preoperational child, since he lacks all but rudimentary classification skills, successfully engage in rule-learning and application. As Downing (1969) has noted, Piaget contends that the individual must create his own rules, assimilating new experiences into his own system and periodically accommodating by revising the system when he sees that it no longer serves adequately. The preoperational child should not be expected to pursue a reading program based on rules of grapheme–phoneme relationships. He may successfully memorize the verbal formulas but will have difficulty classifying situations to which they are appropriate.

Piaget's theory supports what might be thought of as an activity curriculum, a nursery school experience which emphasizes interaction with materials and exploration of the environment; a kindergarten in which reading and books are simply part of the general environment; and a beginning-reading program growing out of the progression through motor and perceptual functioning to symbolic activity. It should also be noted that the preoperational-period child relishes practice on evolving skills. The infant will, over and over again, put the beads into the plastic bottle and empty them out again. The somewhat older child works the same picture puzzle many times in succession. Elkind and Weiss (1967) found childen in the beginning-reading period consciously practicing left-to-right progression, even in situations unrelated to reading. Evidently, there is nothing negative with respect to repetition and drill for the child of this age; he seems to enjoy it and actually imposes such activity on himself. To criticize certain methodology or materials for reading because they appear dull or repetitious to adults or to insist that practice should be deemphasized out of a concern for the child's welfare is, in both cases, to ignore the possible validity of a Piagetian interpretation.

Piaget also emphasizes that cognitive activity should be carried out in social situations where children are working together, sharing information, and learning to take into account another person's point of view. The implications for classroom practice appear self-evident.

Concrete-operational period

Piagetian theory holds that by seven years of age the child has reached a point where he has the ability to "reason," but he reasons adequately only about direct experiences, not abstractions. One difficulty at this stage is that the child can think about and discuss matters much in advance of any content which he finds it possible to read for himself. Furth (1970) has argued that acceptance of Piaget's position should lead school people to postpone formal reading instruction for most of the elementary-school years. He stresses that the traditional emphasis on reading and writing in the early grades takes so much time and energy that over-all intellectual development may be significantly interrupted. When emphasis is placed on learning to read, the child finds himself in a position of constantly dealing with content at least five years below what his intellect could handle.

But the concrete-operational child does have the ability to study various aspects of language, including reading. Because he possesses the operations of identity and reversibility the student can view a system, make transformations upon it and, then, since he retains the original perception, return it to its previous condition. He can hold a basic idea in mind and manipulate and expand it in various ways. Specifically, rearrangement of language elements—words, phrases, sentences—becomes possible. The child can determine, through a comparison of the original with subsequent changes, whether or not various modifications of word order or substitutions have altered meaning. The concrete-operational child can make seriations and multiple and hierarchical classifications of objects and concepts close to his own life experience. He knows that objects and events have many attributes and that a word may have different meanings in various contexts. He can group words by their linguistic function and place sentence elements in various relationships with one another.

It is reasonable to infer from the findings of Piaget that reading activities during the concrete-operational period, in terms of content, can vary widely, but it should not be expected that students will reason well about what they have read unless it relates rather closely to direct experience. In any reading program organized along Piagetian lines, reading activities during the concrete-operational period would provide increased emphasis on developing logical operations by including opportunities to combine sentence and word elements, associate elements in different ways, establish correspondence or identity among elements, and would encourage students to transform the order of elements and observe the differences produced.

Formal-operational period

Many collections of reading exercises published for use in secondary schools include items which provide practice in the advanced skills of critical and creative reading and problem solving. Piaget's contribution would involve sequencing of materials to provide a correspondence between the logical operations embedded in the content and the reader's likely manner of structuring knowledge of solving a problem. For the attainment by the student of maximum comprehension of all components of a reading unit, the structure of the material should follow the pattern which Piaget has found to characterize the unfolding of the logical operations by means of which the individual manipulates or processes information. The student's pattern of processing information as he attempts to deal with novel and complex situations occurs in the following sequence: (1) classification and seriation; (2) correspondence; (3) logical multiplication; (4) tautologies; (5) implications; and (6) ratio and proportional thinking.

The student first attempts to group variables and attributes in classes and to order the elements within each class by some attribute such as weight or size. After he has produced the seriation of a possibly relevant variable and the seriation of the effect, the student makes correspondences between elements of each group of seriations. For example, he may seriate the length of a pendulum string and the period of a pendulum. He noted that a long period is associated with a long string and a short period with a short string. After making this correspondence, the student who wants to know if a change in length will bring about a change in period performs a logical multiplication. In the initial stage of logical multiplication, the individual knows that he can change the length or not change it, and observe a change in the period or not. What is called for is a two-by-two table with these four elements in the margins:

	No Period Change	Period Change
Length Change	A	B
No Length Change	C	D

After multiplying the row margin element by the column margin elements, the student notes that the products of the logical multiplication in cells A and D are found in reality. He observes a temporal association between length change and period change and between no length change and no period change. In the case of the situations represented by cells B and C, he finds no temporal association between length change and period change. The process of logical multiplication allows the student at the concrete stage to determine if an association exists between a variable and an effect.

In the stage of formal operations logical multiplication is not necessary to isolate the effect of a variable. The individual comes immediately to the four possible outcomes: (1) variable change with effect change; (2) no variable change with effect change; (3) variable change with no effect change; (4) no variable change with no effect change. The observer is simultaneously aware of all possibilities, and the operation which enables him to do this is termed a tautology.

The operations thus far described enable the individual only to determine relevant and irrelevant variables. When he deals with more variables and ones which interact among themselves, additional operations are necessary: negation, in which a change is counteracted by returning the influential variable to its original condition; reciprocity, in which a different variable is manipulated to compensate for the change; the formulation of ratios which summarize the nature of reciprocal relationships between variables; and proportional thinking in which he determines the relationships between ratios. These descriptions of the sequence in appearance of logical operations can be used to structure content in a manner which enables the student to participate actively in the process of determining the effects of variables and the relationships among these variables and effects. If the sequence is followed, all content needed to understand a given problem will be included. Merely telling the youngster, as most textbook presentations do, that length makes a difference in the period of a pendulum does not suffice; too much information remains to be acquired in some other way, probably outside of class.

The statement to a student that an association exists between a variable and an outcome may lead to correct answers in recitation or on examinations but it fails to provide information for the handling of more complex and novel situations. Inhelder and Piaget (1958) describe the sequence by which content might be so structured that various logical relationships become available to the student for analysis. In following such a pattern a learner can build a total schema which he understands very well, rather than simply learn to repeat verbal formulas. The type of associative verbal chaining found in most textbooks does not lead the learner to analyze logical relationships and thus attain a good level of comprehension.

THE IMPORTANCE OF SEQUENCE

What can be learned from Piaget has more to do with the developmental unfolding of mental operations than the age-level descriptions of cognitive skills. Whether an individual is forty years old or eleven, he still follows Piaget's sequence of logical operations when he confronts novel and complex problems or situations. He will, at these times, exhibit some preoperational-stage thinking, then go through a concrete stage, and finally progress to formal operations. Some individuals will move more rapidly than others through these stages and the progression seems less apparent in some, but it is there, nonetheless. When readers deal with content that is unfamiliar to them, it may be anticipated that their understanding will go not much deeper than the making of a few verbal associations unless steps are taken by the teacher to lead them through a sequence from unorganized focussing on first one element and then another to comprehensive analysis of all revelant relationships.

REFERENCES

ALMY, MILLIE, Young children's thinking and the teaching of reading. In Frost (Ed.) *Issues and innovations in the teaching of reading.* New York: Scott, Foresman, 1967. Pp. 89–93.

ALMY, MILLIE, CHITTENDEN, E., and MILLER, PAULA, *Young children's thinking.* New York: Teachers College Press, 1966. Pp. 139–40.

DOWNING, J. How children think about reading. Distinguished Leader's Address, Annual Convention of the International Reading Association, Kansas City, May 1969.

ELKIND, D., and WEISS, J., Studies in perceptual development III: perceptual exploration. *Child Development,* 1967, 38, 553–61.

FURTH, H. G., *Piaget for teachers.* New York: Prentice-Hall, 1970. P. 4.

INHELDER, BARBEL, and PIAGET, J., *The growth of logical thinking from childhood to adolescence.* New York: Basic Books, 1953.

PIAGET, J., *The psychology of intelligence.* New York: Littlefield, Adams, 1963.

The Task of the Teacher

William Purkey

WHAT THE TEACHER BELIEVES

No printed word nor spoken plea
Can teach young minds what men should be,
Not all the books on all the shelves
But what the teachers are themselves.

Anonymous

A basic assumption of the theory of the self concept is that we behave according to our beliefs. If this assumption is true, then it follows that the teacher's beliefs about himself and his students are crucial factors in determining his effectiveness in the classroom. Available evidence indicates that the teacher's attitudes toward himself and others are as important, if not more so, than his techniques, practices, or materials. In fact, there do not seem to be any techniques which are always associated with people who are effective in the helping relationship. Rogers reported that personality changes in therapy come about not because of such factors as professional qualifications and training, or knowledge or skill, or ideological orientation, but primarily because of the attitudinal char-

acteristics of the relationship. Attitudes play an important role, and so we need to examine the teacher's beliefs about himself and his students in some detail.

What the teacher believes about himself

There seems to be general agreement that the teacher needs to have positive and realistic attitudes about himself and his abilities before he is able to reach out to like and respect others. Numerous studies have reported that there is a marked relation between the way an individual sees himself and the way he sees others. Those who accept themselves tend to be more accepting of others and perceive others as more accepting. Further, according to Omwake, those who reject themselves hold a correspondingly low opinion of others and perceive others as being self-rejecting. From these studies it seems clear that the teacher needs to see himself in essentially positive ways. The manner in which this can be accomplished needs further investigation, but Jersild and Combs have given us some clues.

Jersild has been a pioneer in emphasizing the importance of the attitudes that teachers hold about themselves. He argues that the self-understanding of teachers is a necessary factor in coping with their feelings and in becoming more effective in the classroom. The personal problems of teachers often interfere with their effectiveness in teaching, and an understanding of the influence of these and other attitudes and emotions is vital in working with students. Jersild has suggested that we need to encourage in-service group counseling situations for teachers, in which their attitudes and feelings can be safely explored with others. This, it is hoped, would result in increased undersanding of and sensitivity to oneself, and to more effective teaching in the classroom.

A similar view is reported by Combs and his associates in their research on the perceptual organization of effective helpers. They found that effective teachers, counselors, and priests could be distinguished from ineffective helpers on the basis of their attitudes about themselves and others. Such findings as these have long-range implications for the professional education of teachers. In fact, the suggestion that teacher preparation should be based on a perceptual, self concept approach has already appeared in Combs' *The Professional Education of Teachers* (1965), and an experimental program of teacher training using the perceptual approach was introduced at the University of Florida in 1969.

The way the evidence points is that each teacher needs to view himself with respect, liking, and acceptance. When teachers have essentially favorable attitudes toward themselves, they are in a much better position to build positive and realistic self concepts in their students.

What the teacher believes about students

The ways significant others evaluate the student directly affects the student's conception of his academic ability. This in turn establishes limits on his success in school. Teachers, in their capacity of significant others, need to view students in essentially positive ways and hold favorable expectations. This is particularly important at the elementary level, but is vital in all grades. Several studies bear directly on the importance of what the teacher believes about students.

Davidson and Lang found that the student's perceptions of the teacher's feelings toward him correlated positively with his self-perception. Further, the more positive the children's perceptions of their teacher's feelings, the better their academic achievement and the more desirable their classroom behavior as rated by the teacher. Clarke reported a positive relationship between a student's academic performance and his perception of the academic expectations of him by significant others.

One of the most comprehensive studies of the self concept of ability and school success was that of Brookover and his associates which we considered, in part, earlier. Brookover and his associates conducted a six-year study of the relation between the self concept of academic ability and school achievement among students in one school class while in the seventh through the twelfth grades. A major purpose of the study was to determine whether improved self concept results from the expectation and evaluations held by significant others as perceived by students. As Brookover, Erickson, and Joiner conclude: "The hypothesis that students' perceptions of the evaluations of their academic ability by others (teachers, parents, and friends) are associated with self concepts of academic ability was confirmed." The almost unavoidable conclusion is that the teacher's attitudes and opinions regarding his students have a significant influence on their success in school. In other words, when the teacher believes that his students can achieve, the students appear to be more successful; when the teacher believes that the students cannot achieve, then it influences their performance negatively. This self-fulfilling prophecy has been illuminated by the research of Rosenthal and Jacobson.

The basic hypothesis of Rosenthal and Jacobson's research was that students, more often than not, do what is expected of them. To test this hypothesis, the two researchers conducted an experiment in a public elementary school of 650 students. The elementary-school teachers were told that, on the basis of ability tests administered the previous spring, approximately one-fifth of the students could be expected to evidence significant increases in mental ability during the year. The teachers were then given the names of the high-potential students. Although in fact the names had been *chosen at random* by the experimenters, when intelligence tests and other measures were administered some months later, those identified as potential spurters tended to score significantly higher than the children who had not been so identified. Also, Rosenthal and Jacobson found that these children were later described by their teachers as happier, more curious, more interesting, and as having a better chance of future success than other children. The conclusion drawn by Rosenthal and Jacobson is that the teacher, through his facial expressions, postures, and touch, through

what, how, and when he spoke, subtly helped the child to learn. This may have been accomplished, according to the researchers, by modifying the child's self concept, his expectations of his own behavior, and his motivations, as well as his cognitive style. They summarized their study by stating that the evidence suggests strongly that "children who are expected by their teachers to gain intellectually in fact do show greater intellectual gains after one year than do children of whom such gains are not expected." The full educational implications of the self-fulfilling prophecy remain to be explored, but it seems certain that the ways the teacher views the student have a significant influence on the student and his performance.

The attitude the teacher conveys

It is difficult to overestimate the need for the teacher to be sensitive to the attitudes he expresses toward students. Even though teachers may have the best intentions, they sometimes project distorted images of themselves. What a person believes can be hidden by negative habits picked up long ago. Therefore teachers need to ask themselves:

Am I projecting an image that tells the student that I am here to build, rather than to destroy, him as a person? (Spaulding, 1963, reported that there is a significant relationship between a student's positive self concept as reported, and the degree to which teachers are calm, accepting, supportive, and facilitative, and a negative relationship between a student's self concept and teachers who are threatening, grim, and sarcastic.)

Do I let the student know that I am aware of and interested in him as a unique person? (Moustakas maintains that every child wants to be known as a unique person, and that by holding the student in esteem, the teacher is establishing an environmental climate that facilitates growth.)

Do I convey my expectations and confidence that the student can accomplish work, can learn, and is competent? (Rosenthal and Jacobson have shown that the teacher's expectations have a significant influence on the student's performance.)

Do I provide well-defined standards of values, demands for competence, and guidance toward solutions to problems? (Coopersmith has provided evidence that self-reliance is fostered by an environment which is well-structured and reasonably demanding, rather than unlimitedly permissive.)

When working with parents, do I enhance the academic expectations and evaluations which they hold of their children's ability? (Brookover, et al. has illustrated that this method yields significant results in enhancing self concept and improving academic achievement.)

By my behavior, do I serve as a model of authenticity for the student? (Both Jourard and Rogers suggest that a most important factor in the helping relationship is the helper serving as a model of genuineness, without "front.")

Do I take every opportunity to establish a high degree of private or semiprivate communication with my students? (Spaulding found a high relationship between the pupil's self concept and the teacher's behavior when it involved personal and private talks with students.)

The above questions are samples of how the teacher may check himself to see if he is conveying his beliefs in an authentic and meaningful fashion. As Gill reported, teachers' attitudes toward students are vitally important in shaping the self concepts of their students. Gill summarized his study by saying that "teachers should consider self concept as a vital and important aspect of learning and development which the school, through its educational process, should seek to promote and foster in every child."

. . .

3

Reading-Language Achievement: Socioethnic Variation

Until recently, language arts instruction in American elementary schools has been based on the accepted dialect spoken by the majority population, the European-American cultural group. The dialects of this group, referred to as standard English dialects, have reached accepted status as a result of the favored social and political position of the people who speak such dialects.

Children of Afro-American, Mexican-American, Puerto Rican American, Indian-American, and other American minority culture groups, speaking a dialect that varies from standard English or speaking another language, were expected to perform in standard English upon entering elementary school. Such unrealistic expectations of teachers have contributed to the failure of such children to acquire the fundamental skills of reading and writing.

Because of the number of children involved, William Labov considers the problems of Afro-American children in large cities as most pressing; next, bilingual Mexican-American and Puerto Rican American children, and third, white children from Appalachian backgrounds and other underprivileged minority groups. These minority groups have experienced a high degree of neglect and require special understanding and instructional provision in the classroom.

Clearly, because such children failed to acquire the fundamental reading and expressive skills in the established reading and language curriculum, educators were forced to turn to the linguist for a redefinition of language in general and for guidance in understanding and using other forms of English. Reconsideration of language instruction for bilingual children has been long overdue.

What does the linguist say to the teacher about language variation? Roger Shuy [1] discusses the relevance of language variation for the child to learn reading and writing. He defines language variety as existing "when a member of one group uses a linguistic feature which is not shared by another group or which is not shared with the same general frequency." Variation may be geographical because of historical change or social differences. He reminds us that "variety,

---

[1] Roger W. Shuy, "Language Variation and Literacy," in *Reading Goals for the Disadvantaged,* ed. J. Allen Figurel (Newark, Delaware: International Reading Association, 1969), pp. 11–22.

118

per se, is neither bad nor illogical. In fact, it is often highly valued." Shuy urges the teacher to stop fearing language variation and start putting it to work.

In putting language variation to work, the teacher must again listen to Shuy when he states: "We now talk about black English as one of the legitimate varieties of English and we are concerned with the speakers of this variety as they come into contact with other varieties of oral language, as well as with written language." The teacher must know and understand that the language of black children is well ordered, highly structured and highly developed, which in many respects is different from standard English.

What complex set of linguistic circumstances does the black child face? Kenneth Goodman shares Shuy's concern regarding the other varieties of oral and written language. Goodman expands on this problem of the black child. The black child, with his well-developed language, his mother tongue representing the cultural values of his family and community, encounters the various kinds of language of his classmates, the informal and formal versions of standard English of his teacher, and the formal written language in reading texts. As a result of this varied language impact, Goodman maintains, the child may experience such an enormous rejection that "it endangers the means which he depends on for communication and self-expression."

How important is the teacher's attitude toward the black child's dialect? Compounding this already complex set of linguistic circumstances for the black child, at the beginning of his school career, is the attitude of the teacher toward the black child's dialect. Kenneth Johnson [2] has observed numerous faulty assumptions about dialectal variation. These assumptions have resulted in the teacher's negative attitude toward the black child's language. The main reason for these incorrect assumptions, according to Johnson, is the teacher's lack of knowledge regarding the quality of the black dialect, a well-ordered system of sound, grammar, and vocabulary. In addition to this misconception, the teacher may also believe that the black child's oral language is characterized by "sloppy speech, lazy lips, lazy tongue"—assumptions that inevitably affect the pupil–teacher relationship, damage the child's self-esteem, and lead to the adoption of teaching strategies that fail to help the child to learn to read and to acquire standard English.

What must the teacher know to help the black child learn to read? In addition to the immediate and unquestioned acceptance of the black child's dialect, the teacher must know the specific points of conflict between the black dialect and standard English. William Labov's article on sources of reading problems for black children will help teachers understand the key features of the black dialect. Labov sees the educational problem as one of reciprocal ignorance, teacher and student being ignorant of each other's language systems and lacking the know-how to translate from one language system to another. Labov deals with the structural conflicts of the dialects which interfere with reading because of a mismatch of these linguistic structures. Most helpful to the teacher are Labov's specific strategies for teaching reading that can be put into immediate practice. In summarizing these strategies, Labov maintains that the key is for the teacher to know the system of homonyms in the black phonological (sound)

2 Kenneth R. Johnson, "Teacher's Attitude Toward the Nonstandard Negro Dialect—Let's Change It," *Elementary English* 48 (February 1971): 176–84.

system and to know the grammatical differences that separate the teacher's speech from that of the child. With a knowledge of these variables, the teacher can then make the basic distinction between a genuine difference in pronunciation and a mistake in reading and can guard against calling such pronunciation a mistake.

How should black children be taught to read? Goodman lists three basic means schools have in teaching the black child to read. The first is to teach the child to read and write with materials in his own dialect. Shuy supports this approach, but Goodman finds this method impractical primarily because it would be unacceptable to some segments of the black community. In addition some linguists see many technical difficulties with this approach. The second is to teach the child to speak in the standard dialect before teaching him to read in the standard dialect. Goodman finds the second choice impractical because it would reject the black child's attained facility of language and delay teaching reading too long. The third is to let the black child read standard English materials in his dialect or the way he speaks. Goodman sees this as the only practical approach. Labov also favors this method.

When should standard English be taught? Shuy recommends placing language arts priorities for the variant speaker in a different order than currently practiced. He feels that the first priority is to teach the child to read and write and then permit a gradual acquisition of standard oral language over a period of several years, similar to the gradual acquisition of standard spelling. Johnson, too, believes that standard English should be taught at a later time than at the beginning of a child's school career and that it must be taught as an alternative dialect only when black children have a recognized need for it for vocational, social, and academic reasons.

How do the problems of bilingual children differ from those of the black speaker? How should the non-English speaking or the bilingual child be taught to read? The problem of Mexican-American, Puerto Rican American, and Indian-American children differs from that of Afro-American children in that many of the former may not hear English spoken until they enter school. Such children, whose native tongue may be Spanish or any of the various Indian languages, have all too often been given reading instruction in English immediately upon entering school, with disastrous results.

Richard Venezky[3] has helped clarify the language problems of non-English-speaking children. He has reviewed several native literacy programs currently in progress and offers a bibliography on the various specific dialects. According to Venezky two approaches have been considered for the non-English-speaking child. The first is to teach such children English first and delay reading instruction in the English language. The second is to teach such children in their native tongue. Native literacy programs logically assume that the child should be taught reading in his native tongue—the language system he has internalized by the time he enters school—thus giving the child a feeling of acceptance of his language and his cultural heritage and simultaneously or gradually teaching the national language orally until reading in the national language can also be acquired.

While he considers such native literacy programs basically appealing from

[3] Richard L. Venezky, "Nonstandard Language and Reading," *Elementary English* 47 (March 1970): 334–45.

many standpoints, especially the obvious cultural advantages, Venezky has noted the extra expense and technical difficulties in developing new materials for such programs. Without significant results that prove the native literacy approach superior to the standard language approach, Venezky tends to favor the standard language approach in which intensive oral language instruction in English is presented early in a child's life, before English reading instruction is introduced with well-established reading methods, tests, and remediation materials.

Perhaps it is not so much a question of whether major native literacy studies show superior results, or are expensive, or are technically complicated to prepare, but what the community wants and whether such children really are linguistically disadvantaged. Jack D. Forbes presents an entirely different point of view. He helps us understand the significance of the Mexican-American people, their love for their language, the advantages of being bilingual. He states that "It is true that often the knowledge of both Spanish and English is imperfect, but nonetheless the most precious of linguistic skills, the ability to switch back and forth from one language to another and the 'feel' for being comfortable in two or more languages is present as either a fully or partially developed resource. . . . What is fundamental is that Mexican-American pupils possess an entrée into two viable languages, both of which (American Spanish and American English) can be utilized as vehicles for sound linguistic development." The same may be said of many Puerto Rican American and Indian-American children.

Forbes suggests that teachers and administrators take into consideration the bilingual child's linguistic talents and create a truly bilingual–bicultural school—a position strongly supported by the Mexican-American, Puerto Rican American and Indian-American communities. Instruction in such schools, using the Forbes model for Mexican-American children would be as follows: Schools consisting of a majority of Spanish-speaking children should most likely start in Spanish, teaching English as a second language. In mixed schools both languages will need to be taught as if they were new idioms. Forbes lists published materials for classroom use on Mexican-American culture, but he does not mention Spanish beginning-reading materials available in the United States or from Mexico to be used in conjunction with teacher-made materials.

What must the teacher know to help Mexican-American children learn to read? Leonard Olguin's guide on how to unlock some of the reading problems is valuable for teachers of Mexican-American children. His teaching strategies help the teacher to understand which sounds of Spanish interfere with and impede the acquisition of English. Lack of space did not permit inclusion of Olguin's demonstration lessons but the definition of the problem, the comparison and discussion of the Spanish and the English sound systems and positional problems plus the diagnostic tests are presented.

In summary, the articles in this chapter should help the teacher understand the highly complex language problems facing minority children and the varying points of view for solving these problems. However, because understanding and accepting a problem is not enough to be an effective teacher, the chapter also includes articles that provide the teacher with information of immediate classroom application for teaching minority children to read.

Dialect Barriers
to Reading Comprehension

Kenneth S. Goodman

The task of learning to read is not an easy one. But it's a lot easier to learn to read one's mother tongue than to learn to read a foreign language, one which the learner does not speak. Actually each of us speaks a particular dialect of a language. Each dialect is distinguished from all other dialects by certain features as: some of its sounds, some of its grammar, some of its vocabulary. The dialect which the child learns in the intimacy of his own home is his mother tongue. All physically normal children learn to speak a dialect. Whatever happens to his language during his life, however fluent and multilingual he may become, this native dialect is his most deeply and permanently rooted means of communication.

Since it is true that learning to read a foreign language is a more difficult task than learning to read a native language, it must follow that it is harder for a child to learn to read a dialect which is not his own than to learn to read his own dialect.

This leads to an important hypothesis: *The more divergence there is between the dialect of the learner and the dialect of learning, the more dif-ficult will be the task of learning to read.*

This is a general hypothesis. It applies to all learners. If the language of the reading materials or the language of the teacher differs to any degree from the native speech of the learners some reading difficulty will result. To some extent also there is divergence between the immature speech of the young learner and adult language norms in the speech community. Children have mastered most but not all of the sounds and syntax of adult speech. A further divergence reflects the fact that older members of any language community are less influenced by language change than are the youth. Thus the teacher may cling to language which is obsolescent in form or meaning. Books particularly lag behind language change since they freeze language at the date of composition. Though this paper is mainly concerned with gross dialect differences it must be remembered, then, that the reading problems discussed apply to some extent to all learners because minor dialect differences are features of even homogeneous speech communities.

The divergent speaker

For purposes of discussion we'll call the child who speaks a dialect different from that which the school, text, or teacher treats as standard, *the divergent speaker*. Divergence, of course, is relative and there is by no means agreement on what standard American English is. Divergent is a good term however, because it is neutral as a value term and it is important, perhaps critical, in considering the problems of the divergent speaker to avoid labeling his language as bad, sloppy, or substandard. We need to keep clear that, though some dialects may carry more social prestige than others, they are not necessarily more effective in communication. Gleason has said, "It is a safe generalization to say that all languages are approximately equally adequate for the needs of the culture of which they are a part." Dialects represent subcultures. Therefore it can similarly be said that all dialects are equally adequate for the needs of the subculture of which they are a part.

Every child brings to school, when he comes, five or six years of language and of experience. His language is closely intertwined with the culture of his community; it embodies the cultural values and structures the way in which he may perceive his world and communicate his reactions to others.

His language is so well learned and so deeply embossed on his subconscious that little conscious effort is involved for him in its use. It is as much a part of him as his skin. Ironically, well-meaning adults, including teachers who would never intentionally reject a child or any important characteristic of a child, such as the clothes he wears or the color of his skin, will immediately and emphatically reject his language. This hurts him far more than other kinds of rejection because it endangers the means which he depends on for communication and self-expression.

Things that other people say sound right or funny to a child depending on whether they fit within the language norms of his dialect. He has become exceedingly proficient in detecting slight, subtle differences in speech sounds which are significant in his dialect and he's learned to ignore other differences in speech sounds that are not significant. He uses rhythm and pitch patterns of his language with great subtlety. He enjoys puns on language which employ very slight variations in relative pitch and stress. By the time divergent speakers are in the middle grades they have learned to get pleasure from the fact that an in-group pun based on their common divergent dialect is unfunny to an outsider like their teacher who doesn't share the dialect.

All children develop vocabulary which falls generally within the vocabulary pool of their speech community. Through repeated experience common for their culture they have begun to develop complex concepts and express them in their mother tongue.

In every respect the process of language development of the divergent speaker is exactly the same as that of the standard speaker. His language when he enters school is just as systematic, just as grammatical within the norms of his dialect, just as much a part of him as any other child's is. Most important it is a vital link with those important to him and to the world of men.

There are some differences between the problems of the divergent speaker in an isolated rural community where a single dialect is the common speech and has been for several generations and the problems of the divergent speaker in the center of one of our great cities. This latter child may live in a virtual ghetto, but his friends and neighbors represent a variety of language backgrounds. Transplanted regional dialects become social class dialects. As the city-dweller grows older he comes into increasing contact with the general culture and its language. In the home community the idiolects, the personal languages of individuals, will cluster closely around a dialect prototype. But the dialects of urban divergent speakers are much more varied and shade off from distinct divergent dialects to standard speech. Variables such as family origin, recency of migration, degree of isolation from influences outside the subculture, attitudes toward self, personal and parental goals are some of the factors which may determine idiolect.

Divergent languages or dialects

Language diversity among divergent speakers complicates the task of understanding the literacy problems which they have. The basic problems will be the same but the specific form and degree will vary among individuals.

Teachers need to give careful consideration to the separate characteristics of several kinds of language divergence. They need to first differentiate immature language from dialect-based divergence. Language which is immature is always in transition toward adult norms. Teachers need not worry too much about immaturity in language since desired change is virtually inevitable. On the other hand whatever the teacher does to speed this change is in the direction the child is moving. He can confirm the teacher's advice in the speech of his parents. But if the

teacher "corrects" the dialect-based divergent language, this is at cross purposes with the direction of growth of the child. All his past and present language experience contradicts what the teacher tells him. School becomes a place where people talk funny and teachers tell you things about your language that aren't true.

Another point that needs to be clarified is the difference between standard regional speech and some imaginary national standard which is correct everywhere and always. No dialect of American English ever has achieved this status; instead we have a series of standard regional dialects, the speech of the cultured people in each area.

It's obvious that a teacher in Atlanta, Georgia, is foolish to try to get her children to speak like cultured people in Detroit or Chicago, just as it's foolish for any teacher to impose universal standard pronunciations which are not even present in the teacher's own speech. I'm referring to such hypocrisies as insisting that *u* before *e* must always says its own name and therefore *Tuesday* is /Tyuzdey/. Cultured speech, socially preferred, is not the same in Boston, New York, Philadelphia, Miami, Baltimore, Atlanta, or Chicago. The problem, if any, comes when the Bostonian moves to Chicago, the New Yorker to Los Angeles, the Atlantan to Detroit. Americans are ethnocentric in regard to most cultural traits but they are doubly so with regard to language. Anybody who doesn't speak the way I do is wrong. A *green* onion is not a *scallion*. I live in Detróit not Détroit. I can carry my books to work but not my friends. *Fear* ends with an *r* and *Cuba* does not. Such ethnocentrisms are unfortunate among the general public. They may be tragic among educators. Too often we send children off to speech correction classes not because their speech needs correction but because it isn't like ours. Pity the poor child who finds himself transplanted to a new and strange environment and then must handle the additional complication of learning to talk all over again. And, of course, if the child is a migrant from the rural South to the urban North, his speech marks him not only as different but socially inferior. He is told not just that he is wrong but sloppy, careless, vulgar, crude. His best defense is to be silent.

In his classroom the divergent speaker finds several kinds of language being used. First is the language or bundle of idiolects within dialects which he and his classmates bring with them as individuals. Represented in their language or dialect is the language or dialect of their parents and their speech community. Next there is the language of the teacher which will exist in at least two forms. There will be the teacher's informal, unguarded idiolect and his version of correct standard speech; the way he says things off guard; the way he strives to speak as a cultured person. Another version of the standard language will be the literary form or forms the child encounters in books. To this we must add the artificial language of the basal reader. Artificial language is not used by anyone in any communicative situation. Some primarese is artificial to the point of being non-language, not even a divergent one.

The consensus of language and the uniformity of print

Two things are in the divergent child's favor. First, all speakers have a range of comprehension which extends beyond the limits of their own dialect. All of us can understand speech which differs from our own, particularly if we are in frequent contact with such speech. As they grow older, urban children are in increasing contact with a number of dialects other than their own. Secondly, the English orthography has one great virtue in its uniformity across dialects. No matter how words are pronounced printers across the country usually spell them the same. Though we get some mavericks like *guilty* and *judgment* we spell *pumpkin* the same whether we say *pəŋkin* or *pəmpkən* and *something* the same whether we say *səmpthin* or *səmpm*. This standardization of print for a multi-dialectical speech suggests that part of the problem of learning to read for divergent speakers could be eliminated if teachers let children read in their own dialects and if teachers got rid of the misconception that spelling determines pronunciation. One child asked his teacher how to spell /ræt/. "R-a-t" she said. "No, ma'am" he responded. "I don't mean rat mouse, I mean right now."

Points of divergence among dialects

Now if we examine the areas in which dialects differ we can perhaps shed some light on the barriers divergent readers face. Let us start with sound.

SOUND DIVERGENCE

Intonation

Dialects differ in intonation. Perhaps what makes an unfamiliar dialect most difficult to understand is its unexpected pitch, stress, and rhythm. Teachers often complain when they first begin to work with divergent speakers that they can't understand a word. But after a short time they seem to tune in on the right frequency. They catch on to the melody of the dialect. Since intonation is essential in understanding oral language, it is logical to assume that it must be supplied mentally by readers as they read in order for comprehension to take place. How much comprehension is interfered with if the teacher insists on intonation patterns in oral reading which are unnatural to the divergent reader can only be conjectured at this time. But there is no doubt that this is a source of difficulty to some extent.

Phonemes

Phonemes are the significant units of speech sounds which are the symbols of oral language. All American dialects share more or less a common pool of phonemes. But not all dialects use all these phonemes in all the same ways. They pattern differently in different dialects. Since phonemes are really bundles of related sounds rather than single sounds, it is likely that the range of sounds that compose a particular phoneme will vary among dialects. Vowel phonemes are particularly likely to vary. Even within dialects there are some variations. Good examples are words ending in -og, such as /dog/, /fog/, /frog/, /log/; or are they /dɔg/, /fɔg/, /frɔg/, /lɔg/? In my own idiolect I find I say /frɔg/, /fɔg/, /dɔg/, /lɔg/, but I also say /cag/, /bag/, /smag/.

Obviously phonics programs which attempt to teach a relationship between letters and sounds cannot be universally applicable to all dialects. The basic premise of phonics instructions is that by teaching a child to associate the sounds which he hears in oral language with the letters in written language he will be able to sound out words. But a divergent speaker can't hear the sounds of standard speech in his nonstandard dialect because he does not have them or because they occur in different places in his dialect than other dialects. The instruction may be not only inappropriate but confusing. When he reads the lesson he may then be forced to sound out words which are not words in his dialect. To illustrate: take a child who normally says /də/ rather than /tə/ and /nəfin/ rather than /nəθin/. Teaching him that the digraph <th> represents the first sound in *the* and the medial consonant in *nothing* makes him pronounce the words not in his dialect and throws a barrier across his progress in associating sound and print.

New reading materials and sound divergence among dialects

Recent attempts at producing beginning reading materials which have regular one-to-one correspondence between letters and phonemes will not solve this problem and may actually compound it since there will be a tendency for teachers to assume that the matched correspondence of sound and letter is to be uniform throughout the reading materials. For example, they might assume *frog* and *log* to have the same vowel sound and so teach the sounds to be the same when a student might well use /a/ as in *father* is one and /ɔ/ as in *caught* in the other. The matched phonemic–graphemic books assume that there is a uniform spoken set of sounds that can by ingenuity and counting of data be inscribed with a uniform written alphabet. This is not true, when the spoken language is viewed as a national-international phenomenon or when it is viewed as a local phenomenon in a heterogeneous cultural country as one of our urban centers.

Transcription of the sound language in ITA faces the same problems. It has a wider alphabet and can therefore transcribe the more literary and sensible English than the limited lexicon of the American linguistic readers. The British ITA materials, however, cannot be read literally except with the "received pronunciation" of the BBC. When as an American I read about "levers" in an ITA book I must say /liyverz/. The principle that spelling is the same across dialects is sacrificed and ITA spelling requires pronunciation narrowed to one special class dialect. Teachers using these materials need to make some adjustments for the dialects used by themselves and their students. There may be, no doubt is, a spoken language in common but it is not so uniform as is the common spelling system.

Another place where sound divergence among dialects affects the handling of reading materials is the traditional sets of homophones. Homophones, words that sound alike, will vary from dialect to dialect. *Been* and *bin* are homophones in my speech. In another dialect *been* would sound the same as *bean* and in still another *Ben* and *been* would be sounded alike. Bidialectal students may bring up new sets of homophones. One teacher asked her class to use *so* in a sentence. "I don't mean sew a dress," she said. "I mean the other so." I got a *so* on my leg," responded one of her pupils.

GRAMMAR DIVERGENCE

The suffix

Inflectional changes in words involve using suffixes or internal changes in words to change case or tense. In certain dialects of American English speakers say *He see me* rather than *He sees me*. They are not leaving off an *s*. There isn't any in their dialect. Similarly, plurals may not use an *s* form. *I got three brother,* is common in Appalachian speech. One teacher reported to me that her pupils could differentiate between *crayon* and *crayons* as written words and respond to the difference by selecting plural and singular illustrations, but they read the words the same, one crayon, two /kraeyen/. The problem is not an inability to see or say the *s*. It doesn't seem to belong in the pronunciation of *crayons*. The inflectional ending *s* to indicate plural is not in the grammar of this dialect.

Most Americans will add /əz/ to form plurals of words ending in /s/ /z/ /š/ /ž/ /č/ as in *busses, mazes, washes, colleges, churches,* but in the Blue Ridge Mountains this ending also goes with words ending in /sp/, /st/, /sk/ as in /waspəz/ /pohstəz/ /tæskəz/ (H. A. Gleason, *An Introduction to Descriptive Linguistics,* New York: Holt, Rinehart and Winston, p. 62). This kind of difference will be reflected in the child's reading. The differences are systematic within the child's dialect. In terms of the school and teacher they may be divergent, or as we say, incorrect, but in terms of the reader and his speech community they are convergent, that is, correct.

Not only suffixes vary, but also verb forms and verb auxiliaries. When a child says, "I here teacher," as the teacher calls the role he is not being incomplete. No linking verb is needed in this type of utterance in his dialect. There is a difference in the syntax of his dialect and other American English dialects. Fortunately such differences are minor in American English. One area of difference seems to be the use of verb forms and verb makers. *We was going, They done it, We come home* all are examples of this phenomenon.

Vocabulary divergence

An area of dialect divergence that people are most aware of is vocabulary. Most people are aware that *gym shoes* in Detroit are *sneakers* in New York, that in Chicago you may *throw* but in Little Rock you *chunk,* that a Minnesota *lake* would be a *pond* in New Hampshire. Perhaps there is less awareness of words which have similar but not identical meanings in different dialects. All words have a range of meaning rather than a single meaning. This range may shift from place to place. The meaning of *carry* may be basically the same in two dialects but some uses will be correct in one dialect but not in the other.

Vocabulary differences among dialects may cause reading difficulty and must be compensated for by the teacher who uses texts printed for a national market.

I've dealt primarily here with the barriers to learning how to read that result when the readers have divergent languages. There are of course other important problems which grow out of the differences in experience, values, and general subculture of the divergent learners. Readers can't comprehend materials which are based on experience and concepts outside their background and beyond their present development.

The reading program for
divergent speakers

Let's address ourselves to a final question. What is currently happening as the divergent speaker learns to read?

I've found that divergent speakers have a surprising tendency to read in book dialect. In their oral reading they tend to use phonemes that are not the ones they use in oral language. Their reading often sounds even more wooden and unnatural than most beginners. There is some tendency to read their own dialect as they gain proficiency, but in general it appears that teachers are more successful in teaching preferred pronunciations than reading. What is lacking is the vital link between written and oral language that will make it possible for children to bring their power over the oral language to bear on comprehending written language.

There seem to be three basic alternatives that schools may take in literacy programs for divergent speakers. First is to write materials for them that are based on their own dialect, or rewrite standard materials in their dialect. A second alternative is to teach the children to speak the standard dialect before teaching them to read in the standard dialect. The third alternative is to let the children read the standard materials in their own dialect, that is to accept the language of the learners and make it their medium of learning. The first alternative seems to be impractical on several counts. Primarily the opposition of the parents and the leaders in the speech community must be reckoned with. They would reject the use of special materials which are based on a nonprestigious dialect. They usually share the view of the general culture that their speech is not the speech of cultivation and literature. They want their children to move into the general culture though they are not sure how this can be brought about.

The second alternative is impractical on pedagogical grounds in that the time required to teach children who are not academically oriented to another dialect of the language, which they feel no need to learn, would postpone the teaching of reading too long. Many would never be ready to learn to read if readiness depended on losing their speech divergence in the classroom. The problem is not simply one of teaching children a new dialect. Children, the divergent among them, certainly have facility in language learning. The problem involves the extinction of their existing dialect, one which receives continuous reinforcement in basic communications outside of the classroom. Labov's research in New York indicates that divergent speakers do not seem to make a conscious effort to use language forms which they recognize as socially preferred until adolescence. Younger children may hear differences but lack the insight to realize which forms are socially preferred. Of course, teenagers may deliberately avoid preferred forms, too, as they reject adult ways and adult values.

In essence the child who is made to accept another dialect for learning must accept the view that his own language is inferior. In a very real sense, since this is the language of his parents, his family, his community, he must reject his own culture and himself, as he is, in order to become something else. This is perhaps too much to ask of any child. Even those who succeed may carry permanent scars. The school may force many to make the choice between self respect and school acceptance. And all this must be accomplished on the faith of the learner that by changing his language he will do himself some good. As one teenager remarked to me, "Ya man, alls I gotta do is walk right and talk right and they gonna make me president of the United States."

The only practical alternative I feel is the third one. It depends on acceptance by the school and particularly by the teacher of the language which the learner brings to school. Here are some key aspects of this approach:

1. Literacy is built on the base of the child's existing language.

2. This base must be a solid one. Children must be helped to develop a pride in their language and confidence in their ability to use their language to communicate their ideas and express themselves.

3. In reading instruction the focus must be on learning to read. No attempt to change the child's language must be permitted to enter into this process or interfere with it.

4. No special materials need to be constructed but children must be permitted, actually encouraged, to read the way they speak. Experience stories must basically be in their language.

5. Any skill instruction must be based on a careful analysis of their language.

6. Reading materials and reading instruction should draw as much as possible on experiences and settings appropriate to the children. While special dialect based materials are impractical, we may nonetheless need to abandon our notion of universally usable reading texts and use a variety of materials selected for suitability for the particular group of learners.

7. The teacher will speak in her own natural manner and present by example the general language community, but the teacher must learn to understand and accept the children's language. He must study it carefully and become aware of the key elements of divergence that are likely to cause difficulty. Langston

Hughes has suggested an apt motto for the teacher of divergent speakers: "My motto as I live and learn, is dig and be dug in return."

My own conviction is that even after literacy has been achieved future language change cannot come about through the extinction of the native dialect and the substitution of another. I believe that language growth must be a growth outward from the native dialect, an expansion which eventually will encompass the socially preferred forms but retain its roots. The child can expand his language as he expands his outlook, not rejecting his own subculture but coming to see it in its broader setting. Eventually he can achieve the flexibility of language which makes it possible for him to communicate easily in many diverse settings and on many levels.

I'd like to close with a plea. You don't have to accept what I've said. I don't ask that you believe or that you agree with my point of view. My plea is that you listen to the language of the divergent. Listen carefully and objectively. Push your preconceptions and your own ethnocentrisms aside and listen. I think that you'll find beauty and form a solid base for understanding and communication. And as you dig you'll find that you are indeed dug in return.

Some Sources of Reading Problems
for Negro Speakers
of Nonstandard English

William Labov

It seems natural to look at any educational problem in terms of the particular type of ignorance which is to be overcome. In this discussion, we will be concerned with two opposing and complementary types:

1. Ignorance of standard English rules on the part of speakers of nonstandard English

2. Ignorance of nonstandard English rules on the part of teachers and text writers

In other words, the fundamental situation that we face is one of reciprocal ignorance, where teacher and student are ignorant of each other's system, and therefore of the rules needed to translate from one system to another.

The consequences of this situation may be outlined in the following way. When the teacher attempts to overcome the first kind of ignorance by precept and example in the classroom, she discovers that the student shows a strong and inexplicable resistance to learning the few simple rules that he needs to know. He is told over and over again, from the early grades to the twelfth, that -ed is required for the past participle ending, but he continues to write:

I have live here twelve years.

and he continues to mix up past and present tense forms in his reading. In our present series of interviews with Harlem youngsters from ten to sixteen years old, we ask them to correct to classroom English such sentences as the following: [1]

He pick me.
He don't know nobody.
He never play no more, man.
The man from U.N.C.L.E. hate the guys from Thrush.

Words such as *man* and *guys* are frequently corrected, and *ain't* receives a certain amount of attention. But the double negative is seldom noticed, and the absence of the grammatical signals -s and -ed is rarely detected by children in the fifth, sixth, or seventh grades. There can be little doubt that their ignorance of these few funda-

mental points of English inflection is connected with the fact that most of them have difficulty in reading sentences at the second grade level.

There are many reasons for the persistence of this ignorance. Here I will be concerned with the role played by the second type of ignorance: the fact that the child's teacher has no systematic knowledge of the nonstandard forms which oppose and contradict standard English. Some teachers are reluctant to believe that there are systematic principles in nonstandard English which differ from those of standard English. They look upon every deviation from schoolroom English as inherently evil, and they attribute these mistakes to laziness, sloppiness, or the child's natural disposition to be wrong. For these teachers, there is no substantial difference in the teaching of reading and the teaching of geography. The child is simply ignorant of geography; he does not have a well-formed system of nonstandard geography to be analyzed and corrected. From this point of view, teaching English is a question of imposing rules upon chaotic and shapeless speech, filling a vacuum by supplying rules where no rules existed before.

Other teachers are sincerely interested in understanding the language of the children, but their knowledge is fragmentary and ineffective. They feel that the great difficulties in teaching Negro and Puerto Rican children to read are due in part to the systematic contradictions between the rules of language used by the child and the rules used by the teacher. The contribution which I hope to make here is to supply a systematic basis for the study of nonstandard English of Negro and Puerto Rican children, and some factual information, so that educators and text writers can design their teach-

[1] The research described here is a part of Cooperative Research Project No. 3091, U.S. Office of Education: "A Preliminary Study of the Structure of English Used by Negro and Puerto Rican Speakers in New York City." For much of the field work and analysis, I am indebted to Paul Cohen, Clarence Robins, John Lewis, Jr., and Joshua Waletzky of the project staff. The Final Report on Cooperative Research Project 3091 is available through ERIC, ED 010 688.

ing efforts with these other systems in mind.

PRIORITY OF PROBLEMS

Within the school curriculum, there seems to be an order of priority of educational problems that we face in large urban centers. Many skills have to be acquired before we can say that a person has learned standard English.[2] The following list is a scale of priority that I would suggest as helpful in concentrating our attention on the most important problems:

a. Ability to understand spoken English (of the teacher).
b. Ability to read and comprehend.
c. Ability to communicate (to the teacher) in spoken English.
d. Ability to communicate in writing.
e. Ability to write in standard English grammar.
f. Ability to spell correctly.
g. Ability to use standard English grammar in speaking.
h. Ability to speak with a prestige pattern of pronunciation (and avoid stigmatized forms).

I would revise this list if it appeared that the teacher could not understand literally the speech or writing of the child; weaknesses in *c* or *d* could conceivably interfere with the solution to *b*. But considering all possibilities, this list would be my best estimate, as a relative outsider to the field of elementary education; it is of course subject to correction by educators.

In dealing with children from English-speaking homes, we usually

[2] See "Stages in the Acquisition of Standard English," in Roger Shuy (ed.), *Social Dialects and Language Learning* (Champaign, Illinois: National Council of Teachers of English, 1965), pp. 77–103.

assume *a*. In the extreme cases where the child cannot understand the literal meaning of the teacher, we have to revise our approach to teach this ability first. For the most part, however, we take the first academic task of the child to be *b*, developing the ability to read and comprehend. Certainly reading is first and most urgent in terms of its effect on the rest of learning, and it is most seriously compromised in the schools of the ghetto areas in large Northern cities. The problem of reading is so striking today that it offers a serious intellectual challenge as well as a pressing social problem. One must understand why so many children are not learning to read, or give up any claim to understand the educational process as a whole.

STRUCTURAL VS. FUNCTIONAL CONFLICTS

We have dealt so far with a series of abilities. Obviously the desire to learn is in some way prior to the act of learning. Our own current research for the Office of Education is concerned with two aspects of the problem:[3]

a. Structural conflicts of standard and nonstandard English: interference with learning ability stemming from a mismatch of linguistic structures.
b. Functional conflicts of standard and nonstandard English: interference with the desire to learn standard English stemming from a mismatch in the functions which

[3] The continuing research discussed here is part of Cooperative Research Project No. 3288, U.S. Office of Education, "A Study of the Non-Standard English of Negro and Puerto Rican Speakers in New York City." The Final Report on Cooperative Research Project 3288 is available from U.S. Regional Survey, 204 N. 35th St., Philadelphia 19104.

standard and nonstandard English perform in a given culture.

In the discussion that follows, we will be concerned only with the first type of conflict.

We should also consider whose speech, and whose learning problems, must be analyzed. Here again there is an order of priority, based on the numbers of people involved, the extent of neglect, and the degree of structural differences involved. In these terms, the educational problems of the Negro children in large cities must be considered most pressing; secondly, those of Puerto Rican and Mexican children from Spanish-speaking homes; and third, the problems of white youth from Appalachian backgrounds and other underprivileged areas.

Is there a Negro speech pattern? This question has provoked a great deal of discussion in the last few years, much more than it deserves. At many meetings on educational problems of ghetto areas, time which could have been spent in constructive discussion has been devoted to arguing the question as to whether Negro dialect exists. The debates have not been conducted with any large body of factual information in view, but rather in terms of what the speakers wish to be so, or what they fear might follow in the political arena.

For those who have not participated in such debates, it may be difficult to imagine how great are the pressures against the recognition, description, or even mention of Negro speech patterns.[4] For various reasons, many teachers, principals, and civil rights leaders wish to deny that the existence of patterns of Negro speech is a linguistic and social reality in the United States today. The most careful statement of the situation as it actually exists might read as follows: *Many features of pronunciation, grammar, and lexicon are closely associated with Negro speakers—so closely as to identify the great majority of Negro people in the Northern cities by their speech alone.*

The match between this speech pattern and membership in the Negro ethnic group is of course far from complete. Many Negro speakers have none—or almost none—of these features. Many Northern whites, living in close proximity to Negroes, have these features in their own speech. But this overlap does not prevent the features from being identified with Negro speech by most listeners: we are dealing with a stereotype which provides correct identification in the great majority of cases, and therefore with a firm base in social reality. Such stereotypes are the social basis of language perception; this is merely one of many cases where listeners generalize from the variable data to categorical perception in absolute terms. Someone who uses a stigmatized form 20 to 30 percent of the time may be heard as using this form all of the time.[5] It may be socially useful to correct these stereotypes in a certain number of individual cases, so that people learn to limit their generalizations to the precise degree that their experience warrants: but the overall tendency is based upon very regular principles of human behavior, and people will continue to

---

[4] These observations are based upon experience with many teachers of English, Negro and white, at summer reading institutes, conferences on social dialects, principals' conferences, and other meetings where the speech of Negro people in urban ghettos has been discussed.

[5] Many examples of this stereotyping process are discussed in William Labov, *The Social Stratification of English in New York City* (Washington, D.C.: Center for Applied Linguistics, 1966).

identify as Negro speech the pattern which they hear from the great majority of the Negro people that they meet.

In the South, the overlap is much greater. There is good reason to think that the positive features of the Negro speech pattern all have their origin in dialects spoken by both Negroes and whites in some parts of the South. Historically speaking, the Negro speech pattern that we are dealing with in Northern cities is a regional speech pattern. We might stop speaking of Negro speech, and begin using the term "Southern regional speech," if that would make the political and social situation more manageable. But if we do so, we must not deceive ourselves and come to believe that this is an accurate description of the current situation. The following points cannot be overlooked in any such discussion:

1. For most Northern whites, the only familiar example of Southern speech is that of the Negro people they hear, and these Southern features function as markers of Negro ethnic membership, not Southern origin.

2. Many characteristic features of Southern speech have been generalized along strictly ethnic lines in Northern cities. For example, the absence of a distinction between /i/ and /e/ before nasals [*pin* equal to *pen*] has become a marker of the Negro group in New York City, so that most young Negro children of Northern and Southern background alike show this feature while no white children are affected.

3. In this merger of Northern and Southern patterns in the Northern Negro communities, a great many Southern features are being eliminated. Thus in New York and other Northern cities, we find the young Negro people do not distinguish *four* and *for*, *which*

and *witch;* while monophthongization of *high* and *wide* is common, the extreme fronting of the initial vowel to the position of *cat* or near it, is less and less frequent; the back upglide of *ball* and *hawk*, so characteristic of many Southern areas, is rarely heard; grammatical features such as the perfective auxiliary *done* in *he done told me*, or the double modal of *might could*, are becoming increasingly rare. As a result, a speaker fresh from the South is plainly marked in the Northern Negro communities, and his speech is ridiculed. Negro speech is thus not to be identified with Southern regional speech. Moreover, there are a small but significant number of features of Negro speech which are not shared by whites in the South, such as the deletion of the reduced and contracted *'s* representing forms of *is* to yield such sentences as *Ile crazy*.

4. The white Southern speech which is heard in many Northern cities— Chicago, Detroit, Cleveland—is the Southern Mountain pattern of Appalachia, and this pattern does not have many of the phonological and grammatical features of Negro speech to be discussed below in this paper.

5. Many of the individual features of Negro speech can be found in Northern white speech, as we will see, and even more so in the speech of educated white Southerners. But the frequency of these features, such as consonant cluster simplification, ·and their distribution in relation to grammatical boundaries, is radically different in Negro speech, and we are forced in many cases to infer the existence of different underlying grammatical forms and rules.

We can sum up this discussion of the Southern regional pattern by saying that we are witnessing the transformation of a regional speech pattern into a class and ethnic pattern in the Northern cities. This is not a new phenomenon; it has occurred many times in the history of English. According to H. Kökeritz and H. C. Wyld, such a process was taking place in Shakespeare's London, where regional dialects from the east and southeast opposed more conservative dialects within the city as middle class and lower class speech against aristocratic speech.[6] We see the same process operating today in the suburbs of New York City; where the Connecticut and New Jersey patterns meet the New York City pattern, in the overlapping areas, the New York City pattern becomes associated with lower socioeconomic groups.[7]

The existence of a Negro speech pattern must not be confused of course with the myth of a biologically, racially, exclusively Negro speech. The idea that dialect differences are due to some form of laziness or carelessness must be rejected with equal firmness. Anyone who continues to endorse such myths can be refuted easily by such subjective reaction tests as the Family Background test which we are using in our current research in Harlem. Sizable extracts from the speech of fourteen individuals are played in sequence for listeners who are asked

to identify the family backgrounds of each.[8] So far, we find no one who can even come close to a correct identification of Negro and white speakers. This result does not contradict the statement that there exists a socially based Negro speech pattern: it supports everything that I have said above on this point. The voices heard on the test are the exceptional cases: Negroes raised without any Negro friends in solidly white areas; whites raised in areas dominated by Negro cultural values; white Southerners in Gullah-speaking territory; Negroes from small Northern communities untouched by recent migrations; college educated Negroes who reject the Northern ghetto and the South alike. The speech of these individuals does not identify them as Negro or white because they do not use the speech patterns which are characteristically Negro or white for Northern listeners. The identifications made by these listeners, often in violation of actual ethnic membership categories, show that they respond to Negro speech patterns as a social reality.

RELEVANT PATTERNS OF NEGRO SPEECH

One approach to the study of nonstandard Negro speech is to attempt a complete description of this form of language without direct reference to standard English. This approach can be quite revealing, and can save us from many pitfalls in the easy identification of forms that are only apparently similar. But as an overall plan,

[6] H. Kökeritz, *Shakespeare's Pronunciation* (New Haven: Yale University Press, 1953); and H. C. Wyld, *A History of Modern Colloquial English* (Oxford: Basil Blackwell, 1920).

[7] Such a phenomenon can be observed in suburban Bergen County, along the boundary of the New York City dialect area. In Closter, N.J., for example, the socioeconomic differentiation of speakers by *r*-pronunciation seems to be much more extreme than in the city itself: middle-class children may pronounce final and preconsonantal /r/ consistently, while working-class children will be completely *r*-less, and this difference is maintained over a wide range of stylistic contexts.

[8] The forms of the Family Background test give the listener a limited choice of ethnic backgrounds: Irish, Afro-American, Spanish, Jewish, German, and Other White. Within each category, one can specify "S" Southern, "N" Northern, or "W" Western.

it is not realistic. We are far from achieving a complete description of standard English, to begin with; the differences between nonstandard Negro speech and standard English are slight compared to their similarities; and finally, some of these differences are far more relevant to reading problems than others. Let us therefore consider some of the most relevant patterns of Negro speech from the point of view of reading problems.

Some Negro-white differences are plainly marked and easy for any observer to note. In the following examples, the Negro forms are patterns which frequently occur in our recordings of individual and group sessions with boys from 10 to 17 years old—ranging from careful speech in face-to-face interaction with adults to the most excited and spontaneous activity within the primary (closed network) group: [9]

NEGRO	WHITE
It don't all be her fault.	It isn't always her fault.
Hit him upside the head.	Hit him in the head.
The rock say "Shhh!"	The rock went "Shhh!"
I'm a shoot you.	I'm g'na shoot you.
I wanna be a police.	I wanna be a policeman.
Ah 'on' know.	I d'know.
2 4 3 [a o no]	2 3 1 [aɪdnoʊ]

Now consider the following examples, in which Negro-white differences are less plainly marked and very difficult for most people to hear:

[9] These data are derived from series of interviews with individuals and groups in South Central Harlem and exploratory interviews in other Northern cities: Boston, Philadelphia, Cleveland, Detroit, and Chicago.

NEGRO	WHITE
He [pæsɨm] yesterday.	He [pæsd̩ɨm] yesterday.
Give him [ðeᴛ] book.	Give him [ðɛ⊥] book.
This [jɔːʏ] place?	This [jɔːᵊ] place?
[ðæs] Nick boy.	[ðæᵗs] Nick's boy.
He say, [kæːᵊl] is.	He says, [kærəl] is.
My name is [bu].	My name is [buʔ].

This second series represents a set of slight phonetic differences, sometimes prominent, but more often unnoticed by the casual listener. These differences are much more significant than the first set in terms of learning and reading standard English. In truth, the differences are so significant that they will be the focus of attention in the balance of this paper. The slight phonetic signals observed here indicate systematic differences that can lead to reading problems and problems of being understood.

Corresponding to the phonetic transcriptions on the left, we can and do infer such grammatical constructions and lexical forms as:

> He pass him yesterday.
> Give him they book.
> This you-all place?
> That's Nick boy.
> He say, Ca'ol is.
> My name is Boo.

Each of these sentences is representative of a large class of phonological and grammatical differences which mark nonstandard Negro speech as against standard English. The most important are those in which large scale phonological differences coincide with important grammatical differences. The result of this coincidence is the existence of a large number of homonyms in the speech of Negro children which are different from the set of homonyms in the speech system used by the teacher. If the teacher knows about this different set of homonyms, no serious problems in the teaching of reading need occur; but if the teacher does not know, there are bound to be difficulties.

The simplest way to organize this information seems to be under the headings of the important rules of the sound system which are affected. By using lists of homonyms as examples, it will be possible to avoid a great deal of phonetic notation, and to stay with the essential linguistic facts. In many cases, the actual phonetic form is irrelevant: it is the presence or absence of a distinction which is relevant. Thus, for example, it makes no difference whether a child says [pɪn] or [pɪᵊn] or [peːᵊn] or [pɛn] for the word *pen*; what counts is whether or not this word is distinct from *pin*. The linguistic fact of interest is the existence of contrast, not the particular phonetic forms that are heard from one moment to another. A child might seem to distinguish [pɪn] and [pɛn] in Northern style in one pair of sentences, but if the basic phonemic contrast is not present, the same child might reverse the forms in the next sentence, and say [pɪn] for *ink pen* and [pɛn] for *safety pin*. A linguistic orientation will not supply teachers with a battery of phonetic symbols, but rather encourage them to observe what words can or cannot be distinguished by the children they are teaching.

SOME PHONOLOGICAL VARIABLES AND THEIR GRAMMATICAL CONSEQUENCES

1. *r-lessness.* There are three major dialect areas in the Eastern United States where the *r* of spelling is not pronounced as a consonant before other consonants or at the ends of words:

Eastern New England, New York City, and the South (Upper and Lower). Thus speakers from Boston, New York, Richmond, Charleston, or Atlanta will show only a lengthened vowel in *car, guard, for,* etc., and usually an obscure centering glide [schwa] in place of *r* in *fear, feared, care, cared, moor, moored, bore, bored,* etc. This is what we mean by *r*-less pronunciation. Most of these areas have been strongly influenced in recent years by the *r*-pronouncing pattern which is predominant in broadcasting, so that educated speakers, especially young people, will show a mixed pattern in their careful speech.[10] When the original *r*-less pattern is preserved, we can obtain such homonyms as the following: [11]

guard	= god	par	= pa
nor	= gnaw	fort	= fought
sore	= saw	court	= caught

and we find that *yeah* can rhyme with *fair, idea* with *fear.*

[10] In New York City, the correlation of /r/ and stylistic context follows a very regular pattern, as discussed in *The Social Stratification of English in New York City,* and other references cited above. Negro speakers are especially sensitive to the prestige status of /r/. The systematic shift indicates the importance of controlling the stylistic factor, as well as socioeconomic factors, in gathering data on speech patterns.

[11] In many cases, pairs such as *guard–god, nor–gnaw,* are differentiated by vowel quality. For most Negro speakers in Northern cities, they are identical. Pairs such as *sore–saw* or *court–caught,* which oppose M.E. closed *o* before *r* to long open *o,* are differentiated more often by vowel quality, especially among older people. In any case, the lists of homonyms given here and elsewhere are given as examples of possible homonyms illustrative of large classes of words that are frequently identical.

It should be noted that words with midcentral vowels before *r* do not follow the *r*-less patterns discussed here; *r* appears much more frequently in such words as *work, shirt, bird,* even when it is not used after other vowels.

Negro speakers show an even higher degree of *r*-lessness than New Yorkers or Bostonians. The *r* of spelling becomes a schwa or disappears before vowels as well as before consonants or pauses. Thus in the speech of most white New Yorkers, *r* is pronounced when a vowel follows in *four o'clock;* even though the *r* is found at the end of a word, if the next word begins with a vowel, it is pronounced as a consonantal [r]. For most Negro speakers, *r* is still not pronounced in this position, and so never heard at the end of the word *four.* The white speaker is helped in his reading or spelling by the existence of the alternation: [fɔːfiːt, fɔrəklak], but the Negro speaker has no such clue to the underlying (spelling) form of the word *four.* Furthermore, the same Negro speaker will often not pronounce intervocalic *r* in the middle of a word, as indicated in the dialect spelling *inte'ested, Ca'ol.* He has no clue, in his own speech, to the correct spelling of such words, and may have another set of homonyms besides those listed above:

Carol　 = Cal
Paris　 = pass
terrace = test

2. *l-lessness.* The consonant *l* is a liquid very similar to *r* in its phonetic nature. The chief difference is that with *l* the center of the tongue is up, and the sides are down, while with *r* the sides are up but the center does not touch the roof of the mouth. The pattern of *l*-dropping is very similar to that of *r*, except that it has never affected entire dialect areas in the same sweeping style.[12] When *l* disappears,

it is often replaced by a back unrounded glide, sometimes symbolized [ɤ], instead of the center glide that replaces *r;* in many cases, *l* disappears entirely, especially after the back rounded vowels. The loss of *l* is much more marked among the Negro speakers we have interviewed than among whites in Northern cities, and we therefore have much greater tendencies towards such homonyms as:

toll　 = toe　　 all　 = awe
help = hep　　 Saul = saw
tool = too　　 fault = fought

3. *Simplification of consonant clusters.* One of the most complex variables appearing in Negro speech is the general tendency towards the simplification of consonant clusters at the ends of words. A great many clusters are involved, primarily those which end in /t/ or /d/, /s/ or /z/.[13] We are actually dealing with two distinct tendencies: (*1*) a general tendency to reduce clusters of consonants at the ends of words to single consonants, and (2) a more general process of reducing the amount of information provided after stressed vowels, so that individual final consonants are affected as well. The first process is the most regular and requires the most intensive study in order to understand the conditioning factors involved.

The chief /t,d/ clusters that are affected are (roughly in order of fre-

---

[12] One English dialect which shows systematic *l*-lessness is Cockney, as described in E. Sivertsen, *Cockney Phonology* (Oslo, 1960).

[13] When the /t/ or /d/ represents a grammatical inflection, these consonants are usually automatic alternants of the same abstract form //ed//. Phonetic rules delete the vowel (except after stems ending in /t/ or /d/, and we then have /t/ following voiceless consonants such as /p, s, š, k/ and /d/ in all other cases. In the same way /s/ and /z/ are coupled as voiceless and voiced alternants of the same //s// inflection. But in clusters that are a part of the root, we do not have such automatic alternation.

quency) /-st, -ft, -nt, -nd, -ld, -zd, -md/. Here they are given in phonemic notation; in conventional spelling we have words such as *past, passed, lift, laughed, bent, bend, fined, hold, poled, old, called, raised, aimed.* In all these cases, if the cluster is simplified, it is the last element that is dropped. Thus we have homonyms such as:

past = pass	mend = men
meant = riff	wind = wine
rift = men	hold = hole

If we combine the effect of *-ld* simplification, loss of *-l,* and monophthongization of /ay/ and /aw/, we obtain

[šiwa:ɣ]   She wow! = She wild!

and this equivalence has in fact been found in our data. It is important to bear in mind that the combined effect of several rules will add to the total number of homonyms, and even more, to the unexpected character of the final result:

told = told = toe

The first impression that we draw, from casual listening, is that Negro speakers show much more consonant cluster simplification than white speakers. But this conclusion is far from obvious when we examine the data carefully. Table 1 shows the total simplification of consonant clusters for two speakers: BF is a Negro working class man, 45 years old, raised in New York City; AO is a white working class man, of Austrian-German background, 56 years old, also raised in New York City but with little contact with Negroes.

The overall percentage of simplification for BF is 67 percent, not very much more than AO, 57 percent. Furthermore, the individual clusters show remarkably similar patterns; for the larger cells, the percentages are almost

Table 1. Overall Simplification of /t,d/ Consonant Clusters for One Negro and One White New York City Speaker

	BF (Negro)		AO (White)	
	Number		Number	
	Simpli-fied	Total Clusters	Simpli-fied	Total Clusters
/-st/	29	37	18	23
/-ft/	7	9	0	2
/-nt/	8	16	14	29
/-nd/	8	14	8	14
/-ld/	8	15	2	4
/-zd/	5	8	3	4
/-md/	2	3	0	1
other	4	4	1	4
Total	71	106	46	81

identical. It is true that the social distribution of this feature is wider for Negroes than for whites, but the sharpest differences are not in this particular phonetic process. As we shall see below, it is in the nature of the grammatical conditioning that restricts the deletion of the final consonant.

The other set of clusters which are simplified are those ending in /-s/ or /-z/, words like *axe* /æks/, *six* /siks/, *box* /baks/, *parts* /parts/, *aims* /eymz/, *rolls* /rowlz/, *leads* /liydz/, *besides* /bisaydz/, *John's* /dzanz/, that's / dæts/, *it's* / its/, *its* /its/. The situation here is more complex than with the /t,d/ clusters, since in some cases the first element of the cluster is lost, and in other cases the second element.[14] Furthermore, the comparison

[14] The loss of the first element—that is, assimilation to the following /s/—is most common in forms where the /s/ represents the verb *is* or the pronoun *us* as in *it's, that's* and *let's.* In none of these cases is there a problem of homonymy, even in the case of *let's* where there is no likelihood of confusion with *less.* This type of simplification will therefore not be considered in any further detail. It should be noted that "sim-

of the same two speakers as shown above shows a radical difference (see Table 2).

Table 2. Overall Simplification of /s,z/ Consonant Clusters for One Negro and One White New York City Speaker

BF (Negro)			AO (White)		
1st Cons. Dropped	2nd Cons. Dropped	Total Clus- ters	1st Cons. Dropped	2nd Cons. Dropped	Total Clus- ters
31	18	98	6	4	69

This overall view of the situation is only a preliminary to a much more detailed study, but it does serve to show that the simplification of the /s,z/ clusters is much more characteristic of Negro speakers than of white speakers. The comparison of these two speakers is typical of the several hundred Negro and white subjects that we have studied so far in our current research.

In one sense, there are a great many homonyms produced by this form of consonant cluster simplification, as we shall see when we consider grammatical consequences. But many of these can also be considered to be grammatical differences rather than changes in the shapes of words. the /t,d/ simplification gives us a great many irreducible homonyms, where a child has no clue to the standard spelling differences from his own pattern. Though this is less common in the case of /s,z/ clusters, we have

six = sick	Max = Mack
box = bock	mix = Mick

---

plification" in regard to the loss of final /s/ is merely a device for presenting the data: as we will see, there are several cases where we are forced to conclude that the /s/ is not there to begin with.

as possible homonyms in the speech of many Negro children.

4. *Weakening of final consonants.* It was noted above that the simplification of final consonant clusters was part of a more general tendency to produce less information after stressed vowels, so that final consonants, unstressed final vowels, and weak syllables show fewer distinctions and more reduced phonetic forms than initial consonants and stressed vowels. This is a perfectly natural process in terms of the amount of information required for effective communication, since the number of possible words which must be distinguished declines sharply after we select the first consonant and vowel. German and Russian, for example, do not distinguish voiced and voiceless consonants at the ends of words. However, when this tendency is carried to extremes (and a nonstandard dialect differs radically from the standard language in this respect), it may produce serious problems in learning to read and spell.

This weakening of final consonants is by no means as regular as the other phonological variables described above. Some individuals appear to have generalized the process to the point where most of their syllables are of the CV type, and those we have interviewed in this category seem to have the most serious reading problems of all. In general, final /t/ and /d/ are the most affected by the process. Final /d/ may be devoiced to a [t]-like form, or disappear entirely. Final /t/ is often realized as glottal stop, as in many English dialects, but more often disappears entirely. Less often, final /g/ and /k/ follow the same route as /d/ and /t/: /g/ is devoiced or disappears, and /k/ is replaced by glottal stop or disappears. Final /m/ and /n/ usually remain in the form of various degrees of nasalization of the preceding vowel. Rarely, sibilants /s/ and /z/ are weakened after vowels to the point where no consonant is heard at all. As a result of these processes, one may have such homonyms as:

Boot = Boo [15]   seat = seed = see
road = row   poor = poke = pope [16]
feed = feet   bit = bid = big

It is evident that the loss of final /l/ and /r/, discussed above, is another aspect of this general weakening of final consonants, though of a much more regular nature than the cases considered in this section.

5. *Other phonological variables.* In addition to the types of homonymy singled out in the preceding discussion, there are a great many others which may be mentioned. They are of less importance for reading problems in general, since they have little impact upon inflectional rules, but they do affect the shapes of words in the speech of Negro children. There is no distinction between /i/ and /e/ before nasals in the great majority of cases. In the parallel case before /r/, and sometimes /l/, we frequently find no distinction between the vowels /ih/

[15] This homonym was troublesome to us for some time. One member of the Thunderbirds is known as "Boo." We did not notice the occasional glottal stop which ended this word as a functional unit for some time; eventually we began to suspect that the underlying form was "Boot." This was finally confirmed when he appeared in sneakers labeled BOOT.

[16] The word *poor* is frequently pronounced with a mid-vowel [po] even by those who do not have a complete merger of such pairs as *sure–shore, moor–more*. One of our Gullah-influenced South Carolina informants on Saint Helena Island is named Samuel Pope or Polk, but we cannot determine which from his pronunciation.

and /eh/. The corresponding pair of back vowels before /r/ are seldom distinguished: that is, /uh/ and /oh/ fall together. The diphthongs /ay/ and /aw/ are often monophthongized, so that they are not distinguished from /ah/. The diphthong /oy/ is often a monophthong, especially before /l/, and cannot be distinguished from /ɔh/.

Among other consonant variables, we find the final fricative /θ/ is frequently merged with /f/, and similarly final /ð/ with /v/. Less frequently, /θ/ and /ð/ become /f/ and /v/ in intervocalic position. Initial consonant clusters which involve /r/ show considerable variation: /str/ is often heard as /skr/; /šr/ as [sw, sr, sø]. In a more complex series of shifts, /r/ is frequently lost as the final element of an initial cluster.

As a result of these various phonological processes, we find that the following series of homonyms are characteristic of the speech of many Negro children:

pin   = pen   beer = bear
tin   = ten   cheer = chair
since = cents   steer = stair
                 peel = pail

poor = pour
sure = shore
moor = more

find = found = fond   boil = ball
time   = Tom   oil = all
       pound = pond

Ruth = roof   stream = scream
death = deaf   strap = scrap

CHANGES IN THE SHAPES OF WORDS

The series of potential homonyms given in the preceding sections indicate that Negro children may have difficulty in recognizing many words in their standard spellings. They may look up words under the wrong spellings in dictionaries, and be unable to distinguish words which are plainly different for the teacher. If the teacher is aware of these sources of confusion, she may be able to anticipate a great many of the children's difficulties. But if neither the teacher nor the children are aware of the great differences in their sets of homonyms, it is obvious that confusion will occur in every reading assignment.

However, the existence of homonyms on the level of a phonetic output does not prove that the speakers have the same sets of mergers on the more abstract level which corresponds to the spelling system. For instance, many New Yorkers merge *sore* and *saw* in casual speech, but in reading style, they have no difficulty in pronouncing the /r/ where it belongs. Since the /r/ in *sore* reappears before a following vowel, it is evident that an abstract //r// [17] occurs in their lexical system: //sɔr//. Thus the standard spelling system finds support in the learned patterns of careful speech, and in the

alternations which exist within any given style of speech.

The phonetic processes discussed above are often considered to be "low level" rules—that is, they do not affect the underlying or abstract representations of words. One piece of evidence for this view is that the deletable final /r, l, s, z, t, d/ tend to be retained when a vowel follows at the beginning of the next word. This effect of a following vowel would seem to be a phonetic factor, restricting the operation of a phonetic rule; in any case, it is plain that the final consonant must "be there" in some abstract sense, if it appears in this prevocalic position. If this were not the case, we would find a variety of odd final consonants appearing, with no fixed relation to the standard form.[18]

For all of the major variables that we have considered, there is a definite and pronounced effect of a following

---

[17] The // // notation encloses morphophonemic forms—that is, forms of words which are the most abstract representation underlying the variants that occur in particular environments as determined by some regular process. English spelling is, on the whole, morphophonemic rather than phonemic: the stem *academ-*, for example, is spelled the same way even though it is pronounced very differently in *academy, academic, academe* and *academician.*

[The situation in regard to r is not quite this regular in white working-class speech. "Intrusive r" does appear *at* the end of *saw* in *I saw a parade,* and consonantal [r] is sometimes not pronounced in *sore arm.* But the general pattern indicated above prevails and provides enough support for the spelling forms.]

[18] This is precisely what does happen when final consonants are lost in words that have no spelling forms, no correlates in careful speech, and no regular morphophonemic alternation. Terms used in preadolescent culture will occur with a profusion of such variants (which may be continued in the adolescent years). For example, in Chicago the term for the base used in team versions of Hide-and-Seek is the *goose.* This is derived from the more general term *gu:l* with the loss of final /l/—a dialect form of *goal.* (Cf. the alternation *Gould* and *Gold* in proper names.) A similar phenomenon occurs in New York City, where the same item is known as the *dent*—related to older *den.* It is worth noting that both of these cases are characteristic of language change among the Negro speakers we are discussing, and illustrate the unchecked consequences of the homonymy we are considering. A more extreme case may be cited: in one group of teenage Negro boys, the position known elsewhere as *War Lord* (the member who arranges the details for gang fights) has shifted to a term with the underlying form //war dorf//, or possibly //waldorf// or //ward f//.

vowel in realizing the standard form. Fig. 1 shows the effect of a following vowel on final /-st/ in the speech of four Negro and three white subjects. In every case, we find that the percent of simplification of the cluster falls when a vowel follows.

The same argument, however, can be used to argue that the Negro speakers have underlying forms considerably different from those of white speakers. The white speakers showed almost as much overall simplification of the clusters before a following consonant, but none at all before a following vowel: in other words, their abstract forms were effectively equivalent to the spelling forms. The Negro speakers showed only a limited reduction in the degree of simplification when a vowel followed.

We can explore this situation more carefully when we consider grammatical conditioning. But we can point to one situation which suggests the existence of nonstandard underlying forms. In the most casual and spontaneous speech of the young Negro people whose language we have been examining, the plural //-s// inflection is seldom deleted. It follows the same

phonetic rules as in standard English: (1) after sibilants /s, z, š, ž/, the regular plural is [əz]; (2) after other voiceless consonants, [s]; and (3) elsewhere, [z]. The regular form of the plural after a word like *test, desk,* is [s], as in [desks]. If the rules were so ordered that we began with the abstract form //desk//, added the //-s//, and then deleted the /k/ in the consonant cluster simplification process, we would find the final phonetic form [dɛs:]. We do in fact sometimes find this form, in a context which implies the plural. But more often, we find [dɛsəz, gosəz, tosəz] as the plurals of *desk, ghost* and *toast.*

A form such as [dɛsəz] is consistent with an order of the rules which begins with //des//, or reduces //desk// immediately to /des/. Then the plural //-s// is added, and the phonetic rules give us [dɛsəz]. It should be emphasized that those speakers who use this form do so consistently, frequently, and in the most careful speech; it is not a slip of the tongue. On the contrary, clusters such as *-sps, -sts, -sks* are almost impossible for many Negro children to articulate. Even with direct modeling, they find it extremely diffi-

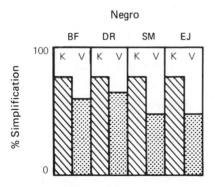
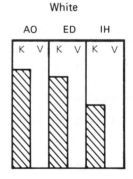

Figure 1. Effect of a Following Vowel on /-st/ Final Clusters for Four Negro and Three White Speakers

cult to repeat the standard forms of *wasps, lists, desks,* etc.[19] It is quite common for children to produce under pressure such forms as [lɪstsəsəsəs], a recursive process, as a result of their efforts to produce the *-sts* cluster.

Forms such as singular [dɛs], plural [dɛsəz] give no support for an underlying spelling form ˙*desk.* It is true that they are not inconsistent with a spelling *desk,* for an automatic rule simplifies *-sks* in 100 percent of the cases, changing -sk+s to -s+s. But there is no way for the Negro child to differentiate *mess, messes* from *des', desses,* on the basis of his own native speech forms. Therefore he can only memorize from school lessons which words have final consonants after *-s.* In the case of verbs such as *test,* and their derived nouns, there is no problem, for the form *testing* preserves the final *-t;* but most words in this class have no derived forms or inflectional forms in which a vowel follows the stem. When the next word begins with a vowel, the effect is often not strong enough to bring out the underlying final consonant in the speech of adults, and the listener does not hear the full form as regularly as he does in *testing.* There are, of course, dialects which resolve this problem in other ways by changing the rules for epenthetic vowels, yielding *deskes, testes* and *waspes,* but this is more characteristic of white Appalachian speech than Southern Negro speech.

GRAMMATICAL CORRELATES OF
THE PHONOLOGICAL VARIABLES

As we examine the various final consonants affected by the phonologi-

cal processes, we find that these are the same consonants which represent the principal English inflections. The shifts in the sound system therefore often coincide with grammatical differences between nonstandard and standard English, and it is usually difficult to decide whether we are dealing with a grammatical or a phonological rule. In any case, we can add a great number of homonyms to the lists given above when we consider the consequences of deleting final /r/, /l/, /s/, /z/, /t/, and /d/.

1. *The possessive.* In many cases, the absence of the possessive //-s// can be interpreted as a reduction of consonant clusters, although this is not the most likely interpretation. The //-s// is absent just as frequently after vowels as after consonants for many speakers. Nevertheless, we can say that the overall simplification pattern is favored by the absence of the //-s// inflection. In the case of //-r//, we find more direct phonological influence: two possessive pronouns which end in /r/ have become identical to the personal pronoun:

[ðeɪ] book   not   [ðɛ:ə] book

In rapid speech, one can not distinguish *you* from *your* from *you-all.* This seems to be a shift in grammatical forms, but the relation to the phonological variables is plain when we consider that *my, his, her,* and *our* remain as possessive pronouns. No one says *I book, he book, she book* or *we book,* for there is no phonological process which would bring the possessives into near-identity with the personal pronouns.[20]

[19] For an account of these repetition tests, see Cooperative Research Report 3288.

[20] In the Creole-based English of Trinidad, however, we do find regularly the forms *he book, she book,* etc. The grammatical differences between Trinidadian English and standard English are therefore

2. *The future.* The loss of final /l/ has a serious effect on the realization of future forms:

you'll = you   he'll = he
they'll = they   she'll = she

In many cases, therefore, the colloquial future is identical with the colloquial present. The form *will* is still used in its emphatic or full form, and the *going to* is frequent, so there is no question about the grammatical category of the future.[21] One form of the future with very slight phonetic substance is preserved, the first person *I'm a shoot you*: there is no general process for the deletion of this *m*.

3. *The copula.* The verb forms of *be* are frequently not realized in sentences such as *you tired* or *he in the way*. If we examine the paradigm, we find that it is seriously affected by phonological processes:

I'm $\neq$ I   we're   = we
you're $\simeq$ you   you're $\simeq$ you
he's   ? he   they're = they

The loss of final /z/ after vowels is not so frequent as to explain the frequency of the absence of -*s* in *he's*, and it is reasonable to conclude that grammatical rules have been generalized

___

much greater than those between nonstandard American Negro English and standard English. In the same way, we find the past tense irregular forms preserved in the dialects we are studying, but only the unmarked stem *he give, he tell* in Trinidad. See D. Solomon, "The System of Predication in the Speech of Trinidad," Columbia University Master's Essay, 1966.

[21] Given this situation, it is evident that more colloquial reading texts with contracted forms *he'll* and *you'll* will not be easy for Negro children to read. The traditional uncontracted *he will* and *you will* may seem slightly artificial to some, but will not involve the problems of homonymy discussed here.

throughout the paradigm—still not affecting *I'm* in the same way as the others, as we would expect, since phonological rules are not operating to reduce /m/.

4. *The past.* Again, there is no doubt that phonological processes are active in reducing the frequency of occurrence of the /t,d/ inflection.

pass = past = passed   pick = picked
miss = mist = missed   loan = loaned
fine = find = fined   raise = raised

At the same time, there is no question about the existence of a past tense category. The irregular past tense forms, which are very frequent in ordinary conversation, are plainly marked as past no matter what final simplification takes place.

I told him [atoɨm]
he kept mine [hikɛpmaɪn]

The problem which confronts us concerns the form of the regular suffix //-ed//. Is there such an abstract form in the structure of the nonstandard English spoken by Negro children? The answer will make a considerable difference both to teaching strategy and our understanding of the reading problems which children face. To approach this problem, we have used a variety of methods which it may be helpful to examine in detail.

THE PROBLEM OF THE -ED SUFFIX

The first approach to this problem is through a study of the quantitative distribution of the forms as spoken by Negro and white subjects in a variety of stylistic contexts. We contrast the simplification of consonant clusters in two situations: where the /t/ or /d/

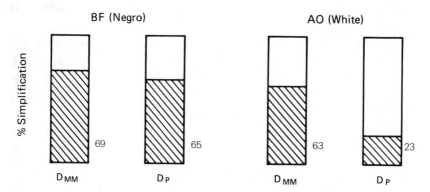

Figure 2. Effect of Grammatical Status on /t,d/ of Final Clusters for One Negro and One White Speaker

represents a part of the root form itself [D_{MM}] and where the /t/ or /d/ represents the grammatical suffix of the past tense [D_P]. Fig. 2 shows the results for the speakers BF and AO who were first considered in Tables 1 and 2.

The Negro speaker BF shows almost the same degree of consonant cluster simplification when the /t,d/ represents a past tense as when it is a part of the original root. On the other hand, the white speaker AO simplifies very few past tense clusters. We can interpret these results in two ways: (a) BF has a generalized simplification rule without grammatical conditioning, while AO's simplification rule is strongly restricted by grammatical boundaries, or (b) BF's underlying grammar is different. If we were to rewrite his grammar to show -ed morphemes only where phonetic forms actually appear, his consonant cluster rule would look much the same as AO's. Without attempting to decide this issue now, let us examine a Negro speaker in several styles, and see if the -ed is affected by the shift.

Fig. 3 shows the percent of /t,d/ clusters simplified by DR, a Negro

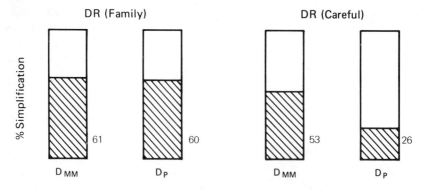

D_{MM} : / t, d/ final in monomorphemic (root) clusters
D_P : / t, d/ final as past tense -ed morpheme

Figure 3. Effect of Stylistic Level and Grammatical Status on /t,d/ of Final Clusters for One Negro Speaker

woman raised in North Carolina. On the left, we see the simplification of both D_{MM} and D_P in intimate family style, discussing a recent trip to North Carolina with a close relative. The pattern is similar to that of BF, with no differentiation of D_{MM} and D_P. But on the right we find a sharp differentiation of the two kinds of clusters: this is the careful style used by DR in a face-to-face interview with a white stranger. Fig. 3 shows that the grammatical constraint which DR uses in careful speech is quite similar to the pattern used by the white speaker AO.

Stylistic context is obviously important in obtaining good information on the underlying grammatical system of Negro speakers. We may therefore profit from considering data where this factor is controlled. Fig. 4 shows the overall consonant cluster simplification patterns for two groups of Negro boys: the Thunderbirds, 10 to 12 years old, and the Cobras, 14 to 16. These are two peer groups which form closed net-

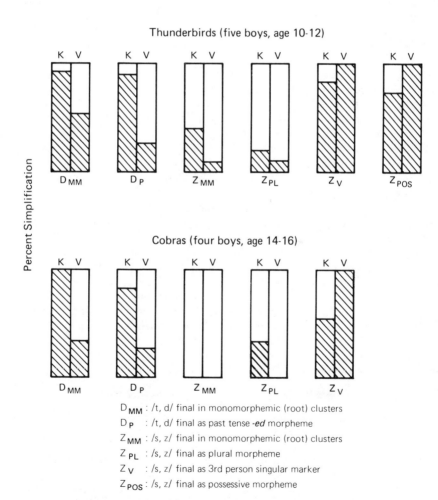

Figure 4. Simplification of /t,d/ and /s,z/ Final Clusters for Two Groups of Negro Boys from South Central Harlem

works. Most of the boys are poor readers, and they represent the groups which respond least to middle-class educational norms. In the interviews which provided this data, the groups were recorded in circumstances where they used the most excited and spontaneous speech, interacting with each other, and with only moderate influence from outsiders. Each boy was recorded on a separate track, from a microphone placed only a few inches away from his mouth. (Recordings made with a single group microphone are of little value for this type of group interaction since only a small part of the data is recovered.)

The Thunderbirds show a very high percentage of simplification of clusters before consonants: 61 out of 63 for nongrammatical clusters, and 21 out of 23 for grammatical clusters. But before following vowels, only 7 out of 14 nongrammatical clusters were simplified, and even fewer—3 out of 13—for grammatical clusters.

We can conclude from these figures that there is a solid basis for the recognition of an -ed suffix: grammatical status does make a difference when the unfavorable phonological environment is set aside. Secondly, we can see that there is a good basis for approximating the lexical forms of standard English: 50 percent of the root clusters conformed to the standard forms in a favorable environment. From another point of view, however, one might say that in half the cases, the boys gave no evidence that they would recognize such spellings as *test* or *hand* as corresponding to their [tɛs] and [hæn].

The Cobras, some four years older, are very similar in their /t,d/ pattern. The phonological conditioning has become even more regular—that is, the effect of the following vowel is more extreme. All of the root clusters are simplified before consonants, but only a small percentage before vowels. The effect of grammatical status is no stronger, however. We may conclude that the process of growing up has brought better knowledge of the underlying lexical forms of standard English, but the status of the -ed morpheme is still about the same.

Perception testing. A second approach to the problem of the -ed suffix is through perception testing. It is possible that the speakers are not able to hear the difference between [pɪk] and [pɪkt], [mɛs] and [mɛst]. If the phonological reduction rule was regular enough, this might be the case. We explore this possibility by a perception test of the following form. The subject listens to a series of three words: [mɛs, mɛst, mɛs], and is asked to say which one is different. The test is repeated six times, with various random combinations of the two possibilities. Then a second series is given with /-st/ before a vowel: [mɛsʌp, mɛstʌp, mɛsʌp], etc. A person who can hear the distinctions will give a correct response in six out of six, or five out of six trials.

The Thunderbirds had no difficulty with the perception test. Three of the boys had perfect scores, and only one showed definite confusion—in fact, the one boy who came closest to standard English norms on the other tests described below. It is true that many Negro youngsters have great difficulty in perceiving phonemic contrasts which are not made in their own dialect; but in this particular case, perception of the /-t ~ -st/ distinction has less relevance to the grammatical status of -ed than any of the other means of investigation.

Classroom correction tests. A third means of approaching the grammatical status of -ed is through the classroom correction tests mentioned earlier in the discussion. The subjects are asked to change certain sentences to correct schoolroom English, starting with easy examples like *I met three mens.* Several sentences are relevant to the *-ed* problem:

He pick me.

I've pass my test.

Last week I kick Donald in the mouth, so the teacher throwed me out the class.

As a whole, results on the classroom correction tests show that the Thunderbirds and the Cobras have little ability to detect the absence of *-ed* as a grammatical element to be corrected. They focus upon *ain't,* or *man* in *He never play no more, man,* but not upon the *-ed.* Among the Thunderbirds, only one of the five boys had this ability to supply *-ed,* and the Cobras showed no greater perception of the status of this element.[22]

The -ed reading test. The most effective way of determining the grammatical significance of *-ed* for the groups we have been working with is through a series of sentences in the reading texts used in our interviews. The relevant sentences are as follows:

a. Last month I read five books.

b. Tom read all the time.

c. Now I read and write better than Alfred does.

[22] In the classroom correction test, the same problem arises which affects any test given in the schoolroom: how hard is the subject trying to give the right answer? It is likely that the boys' general orientation toward the schoolroom would tend to reduce the amount of effort they put into this particular test; but we can base our conclusions on the type of grammatical feature which is noticed and corrected, rather than the total number corrected.

d. When I passed by, I read the posters.

e. When I liked a story, I read every word.

f. I looked for trouble when I read the news.

These sentences depend upon the unique homograph *read* to indicate whether the reader is interpreting the *-ed* suffix as a past tense signal. The first three sentences show whether the reader can use the time indicators *last month, now,* and the absence of *-s* to distinguish correctly between [ri:d] and [rɛd]. In sentences (d), (e), and (f) the reader first encounters the *-ed* suffix, which he may or may not pronounce. If he interprets this visual signal as a sign of the past tense, he will pronounce *read* as [rɛd]; if not, he is apt to say [ri:d]. The distance between the *-ed* suffix and the word *read* is kept as short as possible in sentence (d), so that here at least there is no problem of understanding *-ed* and then forgetting it.

The overall results of this test show that *-ed* is interpreted correctly less than half the time by the Thunderbirds—less often than the *-ed* suffix is pronounced. The Cobras show no material improvement in this respect. For each group, only one boy was able to approximate the standard English performance in this test.

We can conclude that the original inferences drawn from Fig. 4, based on linguistic performance in spontaneous speech, are supported by various other approaches to the *-ed* problem. The degree of uncertainty registered in the D_P column for consonant clusters, even before vowels, indicates that the *-ed* cannot function as an effective marker of the past tense for many children. Though the Cobras are four years older than the Thunderbirds, they show little change in their use of *-ed*. It is also true that some children —a minority in this case—can recognize *-ed* as a past tense marker, and use it effectively in reading, even though they usually do not pronounce it.

GRAMMATICAL STATUS OF THE //-S// SUFFIXES

The same quantitative method which was effective in interpreting the status of *-ed* can be used to analyze the various *-s* suffixes used by Negro children. Fig. 4 provides information on consonant cluster simplification as it affects four different categories of *-s*: [23]

Z_{MM} monomorphemic *-s* in root clusters: *axe, box*

Z_{PL} the plural *-s*

Z_V the 3rd person singular marker of the verb

Z_{POS} the possessive *-'s*

For each category, we can compare the extent of simplification before consonants and before vowels.

In the case of root clusters, the Thunderbirds show only a moderate tendency to drop the final element before consonants, and a very small tendency before vowels. In other words, the standard forms are intact. For the Cobras, this *-s* is always present.

The plural is rarely lost, and shows the usual effect of the following vowel.

[23] Two other types of //-s// can be isolated: the adverbial /s/ of *besides, sometimes,* etc., and the various contracted forms mentioned above: *that's, it's* and *let's*. The first is not frequent enough to provide good data for the small groups discussed here, and the second type shows a loss of the first element of the cluster with no grammatical effect.

We can conclude that the plural inflection is the same for the Thunderbirds, the Cobras, and standard English.

In the case of the third person singular marker and the possessive, an extraordinary reversal is found. For the Thunderbirds, the situation can be summarized as follows:

Z_V	-K	-V
simplified	17	12
not simplified	4	0

Not only is the extent of simplification higher in Z_V than for Z_{PL}, but the direction of influence of a following vowel is reversed. No clusters at all appeared in the most favorable environment for the phonological rule. We can infer that this is no longer effectively described as consonant cluster simplification, but rather as a grammatical fact. The third person singular marker //-s// does not exist in the particular grammar being used here. The same argument holds for the possessive //-s// marker, though as noted above, we cannot extend this argument to infer a loss of the possessive in general.

A striking fact about this situation is that the older group has gained in several respects as far as approximation to standard English forms is concerned, but their development has not affected the grammatical status of the third person singular marker.

CONSEQUENCES FOR THE TEACHING OF READING

Let us consider the problem of teaching a youngster to read who has the general phonological and grammatical characteristics just described. The most immediate way of analyzing his difficulties is through the interpretation of his oral reading. As we have seen, there are many phonological rules which affect his pronunciation, but not necessarily his understanding of the grammatical signals or his grasp of the underlying lexical forms. The two questions are distinct: the relations between grammar and pronunciation are complex, and require careful interpretation.

If a student is given a certain sentence to read, say *He passed by both of them,* he may say [hi pæs ba¹ bof ə dɛm]. The teacher may wish to correct this bad reading, perhaps by saying, "No, it isn't [hi pæs ba¹ bof ə dɛm], it's [hi pæst ba¹ boθ əv dɛm]." One difficulty is that these two utterances may sound the same to many children—both the reader and those listening—and they may be utterly confused by the correction. Others may be able to hear the difference, but have no idea of the significance of the extra [t] and the interdental forms of *th-*. The most embarrassing fact is that the boy who first read the sentence may have performed his reading task correctly, and understood the *-ed* suffix just as it was intended. In that case, the teacher's correction is completely beside the point.

We have two distinct cases to consider. In one case, the deviation in reading may be only a difference in pronunciation on the part of a child who has a different set of homonyms from the teacher. Here, correction might be quite unnecessary. In the second case, we may be dealing with a boy who has no concept of *-ed* as a past tense marker, who considers the *-ed* a meaningless set of silent letters.

Obviously the correct teaching strategy would involve distinguishing these two cases, and treating them quite differently.

How such a strategy might be put into practice is a problem that educators may be able to solve by using information provided by linguists. As a linguist, I can suggest several basic principles derived from our work which may be helpful in further curriculum research and application.

1. In the analysis and correction of oral reading, teachers must begin to make the basic distinction between differences in pronunciation and mistakes in reading. Information on the dialect patterns of Negro children should be helpful toward this end.

2. In the early stages of teaching reading and spelling, it may be necessary to spend much more time on the grammatical function of certain inflections, which may have no function in the dialect of some of the children. In the same way, it may be necessary to treat the final elements of certain clusters with the special attention given to silent letters such as *b* in *lamb.*

3. A certain amount of attention given to perception training in the first few years of school may be extremely helpful in teaching children to hear and make standard English distinctions. But perception training need not be complete in order to teach children to read. On the contrary, most of the differences between standard and nonstandard English described here can be taken as differences in the sets of homonyms which must be accepted in reading patterns. On the face of it, there is no reason why a person cannot learn to read standard English texts quite well in a nonstandard pronunciation. Eventually, the school may wish to teach the child an alternative system

of pronunciation. But the key to the situation in the early grades is for the teacher to know the system of homonyms of nonstandard English, and to know the grammatical differences that separate her own speech from that of the child. The teacher must be prepared to accept the system of homonyms for the moment, if this will advance the basic process of learning to read, but not the grammatical differences. Thus the task of teaching the child to read *-ed* is clearly that of getting him to recognize the graphic symbols as a marker of the past tense, quite distinct from the task of getting him to say [pæst] for *passed*.

If the teacher has no understanding of the child's grammar and set of homonyms, she may be arguing with him at cross purposes. Over and over again, the teacher may insist that *cold* and *coal* are different, without realizing that the child perceives this as only a difference in meaning, not in sound.

She will not be able to understand why he makes so many odd mistakes in reading, and he will experience only a vague confusion, somehow connected with the ends of words. Eventually, he may stop trying to analyze the shapes of letters that follow the vowel, and guess wildly at each word after he deciphers the first few letters. Or he may lose confidence in the alphabetic principle as a whole, and try to recognize each word as a whole. This loss of confidence seems to occur frequently in the third and fourth grades, and it is characteristic of many children who are effectively nonreaders.

The sources of reading problems discussed in this paper are only a few of the causes of poor reading in the ghetto schools. But they are quite specific and easily isolated. The information provided here may have immediate application in the overall program of improving the teaching of reading to children in these urban areas.

Mexican-Americans:
A Handbook for Educators

Jack D. Forbes

ASSETS WHICH THE MEXICAN-AMERICAN BRINGS TO THE SCHOOL

For far too long many teachers have looked upon culturally different children as being "culturally deprived." Such pedagogues have conceived of their duty as being one of filling this "cultural vacuum" with Anglo-American traits. Unfortunately, this negative (and narrow) attitude has led to the ignoring of the rich legacy which many non-Anglo pupils either bring to school or acquire outside of school through the educational processes of the folk community.

Mexican-American youth often bring to the school a varied background of experiences and skills which can be utilized as mediums for both the development of the Mexican-American pupil's potential and for the enrichment of the school experiences of non-Mexican scholastics.

The ability to speak more than one language has, in most societies, been regarded as an essential characteristic of the fully educated man. The Euro-pean educated classes have for centuries spoken French, English, German, and sometimes other languages in addition to their native idiom. American Indian groups commonly grew up speaking three or more divergent idioms, in addition to possessing some familiarity with other languages. People in the United States are today coming once again to the realization that, as in the days of Thomas Jefferson and Benjamin Franklin, a knowledge of several languages is indeed essential.

The Mexican-American child usually has a headstart over the Anglo-American because of his familiarity with two languages (and a few Mexican-Americans speak or understand an Indian language as well). It is true that often the knowledge of both Spanish and English is imperfect, but nonetheless the most precious of linguistic skills, the ability to switch back and forth from one language to another and the "feel" for being comfortable in two or more languages, is present as either a fully or partially developed resource. It is also true that most Mexican-Americans speak a dialect of

Reprinted by permission of Far West Laboratory for Educational Research and Development.

American Spanish while teachers are often acquainted with European Spanish or a standardized international Spanish. American Spanish is, nonetheless, as "correct" and legitimate as any modern idiom and has the asset of being far more "American" than standard American English, incorporating as it does thousands of words of native American origin. What is fundamental is that Mexican-American pupils possess an entrée into two viable languages, both of which (American Spanish and American English) can be utilized as vehicles for sound linguistic development.

Those educators who recognize the value of linguistic training can certainly enrich the total program of their classroom or school by making full use of the Mexican-American child's language advantage. A truly bilingual learning experience can be produced which will not only allow the Mexican child to develop both of his languages but which will make it easier for monolingual English-speaking children to *master* a second tongue.

Mexican-American children also bring to the school a variety of bicultural experiences which can enrich almost every facet of the school's program. Their knowledge of folk arts, cooking, music, literature, and dances can be utilized as vehicles for cross-cultural education and for acquainting children who are new to the region with the rich heritage of the Southwest. Additionally, Mexican-Americans, in sharing their skills with fellow pupils (being teachers, as it were), can help develop in themselves that degree of pride and self-confidence which is so necessary for successful learning generally.

Those Mexican-American pupils who come from folk-level or low-income homes will also possess valuable experiences denied to many affluent children, such as a direct knowledge of domestic arts (taking care of baby brother, et cetera) and practical work (harvesting crops, repairing tractors, et cetera). Such children often have had to assume *important* responsibilities at an early age and their relatively more mature outlook should prove of immense value to affluent children who have never had contact with life at its more fundamental level.

Needless to state, the adult Mexican-American community possesses valuable resources for school enrichment. It is not uncommon for a *colonía* (neighborhood) to possess some persons skilled in arts and crafts, folk music, folk dancing, pinata-making, costume-making, Mexican cooking, or in various commercial activities associated with Mexican arts or food. These persons can often be brought into the school as resource people and part-time instructors, thus expanding in a vast way the "bank of skills" possessed by any school district. Additionally, of course, close contacts between the school and the community can be developed or enhanced by this procedure.

In a similar manner professional-level persons of Mexican origin can be called upon to discuss Mexican history, literature, et cetera, and can suggest books, magazines, films, phonograph records, and newspapers which can be used in the school.

In summary, the quality and richness of any school's program can be greatly enhanced if the school possesses Mexican-American students and if the educators in charge are concerned enough to guarantee that all of their pupils are exposed to a multi-cultural experience which truly reflects the meaning and diversity of the Southwestern legacy.

SUGGESTIONS FOR TEACHERS
AND ADMINISTRATORS

In so far as is feasible a school serving substantial numbers of Mexican-American pupils should serve as a bridge between these students and the adult world which they will subsequently enter. This adult world will sometimes be Anglo in character, but more often it will be of mixed Anglo-Mexican culture. In any case, the school, if it is to be a bridge, must serve as a transitional experience and not as a sudden leap into a totally foreign set of values and practices.

1. The school environment should have some element of Mexican character, subject, of course, to the desires of the local Mexican-American community. Such character can be created by means of murals depicting aspects of the Mexican-American heritage, Hispano-Mexican architecture, the erection of statues depicting outstanding leaders of Mexican ancestry (such as governors of California), displays of Mexican arts and crafts, bulletin boards depicting Mexican persons and accomplishments, and by the adoption of a name for the school which is relevant to our Hispano-Mexican past. The expense involved in the above will not necessarily be great, as adults in the local Mexican-American community might well become involved in projects which would have the effect of making the school "their" school.

2. Teachers and administrators in such a school should be familiar with the Spanish language and should be encouraged to utilize this linguistic asset. At the very least, every such school must possess several professional employees capable of conversing with Spanish-speaking parents, since it is generally accepted that a successful school program demands adequate parent–school interaction and communication.

3. Communications intended for parents, such as announcements, bulletins, and report cards, should be prepared in both English and Spanish. Similarly, Parent Teacher Association groups should be encouraged to follow a bilingual pattern. Where many parents cannot understand Spanish, consideration should be given to organizing an English-speaking subsection for those parents who are not bilingual; or, more preferably, using the P.T.A. as a vehicle for teaching Spanish and English to all parents.

4. Every effort should be made to encourage full development in both Spanish and English. Until truly bilingual schools become a reality, this may mean essentially that both Spanish and English are taught in the elementary grades. On the other hand, imaginative administrators and teachers may wish to further encourage a bilingual atmosphere by the use of signs and displays throughout the school featuring both languages.

5. In schools composed primarily of Spanish-speaking pupils, and where permitted by law, instruction should probably commence in Spanish, with English being taught as a second, or foreign, language. In a mixed school both languages will need to be taught as if they were new idioms.

6. Supplementary materials utilized in the classroom, as well as library resources, should include Spanish-language and/or Mexican oriented items (magazines, newspapers, books, phonograph records, films, et cetera), in order

to provide bilingual and bicultural experiences for all pupils.

7. Curricula in the school should possess a Mexican dimension wherever appropriate. In social science courses where the development of the Western United States is being discussed, attention should be given to the Hispano-Mexican pioneers of the Southwest, to Mexican governors and explorers, and to economic and political developments taking place under Mexican auspices. Courses in state history in the Southwest should devote considerable time to the total Mexican heritage, including that of modern-day Mexican-Americans.

8. Courses in literature should include readings in Mexican literature (in translation, if necessary) and works by and about Mexican-Americans.

9. Curricula in music and "music appreciation" should give attention to all classes of Mexican music, including folk-Indian, Hispano-Mexican, and neo-classical forms. In many schools, instruction in mariachi music, Aztec music and dance, or Mexican brass band might well replace or supplement the standard band and orchestra classes.

10. Art and craft courses should acquaint all pupils with Mexican art forms and should provide instruction in Mexican ceramics, mosaic work, weaving, et cetera, wherever feasible or appropriate.

11. Mexican cooking, folk-dancing, and costume-making should be available as a part of the school's programs in home economics and fine arts wherever sufficient interest exists.

12. Mexican-American adults and youth should be involved in the life of the school as resource people, supplementary teachers, teacher's aides, and special occasion speakers. One of the primary objectives of educators should be the linking of the school with the local adult community.

13. Our Mexican cultural heritage, whenever brought into the school, should be treated as an integral and valuable part of our common southwestern legacy, and not as a bit of "exotica" to be used solely for the benefit of Mexican-American pupils.

14. In a school composed of students from diverse cultural backgrounds every effort should be made to bring a little of each culture into the school. A part of this effort might involve incorporating each major ethnic celebration into the school routine (focusing on Chinese-Americans at Chinese New Year, Mexican-Americans during Cinco de Mayo, et cetera).

15. Counselors (and to a lesser degree, the entire staff) should receive special training in Mexican-American culture and history and should have a background in anthropology and/or sociology.

16. School personnel who believe that it is important to examine pupils periodically in order to provide data on "ability" for future counseling or "tracking" should wish to obtain accurate information by the use of tests which are relatively unbiased. It is difficult to ascertain the potential of Spanish-speaking or dialect-speaking youth by means of standard English-language tests, nor can that of low-income students be predicted on the basis of tests oriented toward middle-class paraphernalia or concepts. On the other hand, biased tests will substantially predict the formal achievement level of culturally different pupils attending biased schools. Therefore, a change in tests will accomplish little unless accompanied by changes in the school, which serve

to realize and enhance the potential revealed by the new test.

The above suggestions are basically designed to change the atmosphere of the school so as to provide greater motivation for all concerned, as well as to impart useful knowledge. In addition, many curricular and methodological innovations are available which are expected to improve learning for *all* students and these new programs should certainly be made available to Mexican-American youngsters. It is to be suspected, however, that a school which is basically indifferent or hostile toward the Mexican heritage will not succeed in stimulating greater learning merely by the use of methodological innovations unaccompanied by a change in the general orientation of the school.

Shuck Loves Chirley

Leonard Olguin

As teachers, we must agree that much of the formal education a child receives must be acquired through reading. We must agree that writing is an abstract form of talking, and that reading is an abstract form of hearing and understanding what is "heard" through the eyes. We must agree that *a child cannot read what he cannot hear.*

The child with a Spanish language background has a specific set of language skills which serve him in Spanish-speaking environs, but which often turn into language problems in English-speaking surroundings.

The auditory discrimination and speaking habits—mouth muscles, tone, word order, breath control—of Spanish impede his acquisition of the English language. The interesting idea is that the limitations or impediments are identifiable, predictable, testable, and therefore vulnerable to skillful teaching.

QUICK REFERENCE SECTIONS

The following two sections are like two small dictionaries, each containing a different type of information. The first section presents a condensed "comparison and discussion" of English and Spanish alphabet sounds. The second section contains a discussion of letters that present problems to the Spanish–language-oriented because of their position within a word or utterance.

Reprinted by permission of Leonard Olguin.

Part 1.   Comparison of Spanish and English Alphabet Sounds and Discussion of Problems Encountered by the Spanish–Language-Oriented Learner

English	Spanish	Discussion
A		
There are eight basic ways to pronounce "a" in Webster's Dictionary not counting when it is silent as in "each."	There is one way to pronounce an "a." It is best produced by making the "a" sound in "ha, ha, ha" with a broad, flat smile.	The Spanish ear and mouth has the most difficulty with the schwa "a" of the variety of ways to pronounce "a" in English. The short "a" also gives much trouble.
B		
The sound of "b" in English is characteristically the same.	In Spanish, there are two sounds to "b" and two identical sounds to "v." Sometimes the sound is a clear "b" as in "boy"; other times the sound is a buzzing sound produced by both lips. (bilabial voiced fricative).	The buzzing sound of these two letters made in Spanish does not exist in English. It is quite like an English "v." The Spanish-oriented ear has no difficulty in learning the English "v" sound, but has many English problems in choosing between uttering a "v" or a "b." The untrained teacher will hear an English "v" when the Spanish mouth utters the bilabial voiced fricative sound for the Spanish "v" and "b." ("b" and "v" problems are clarified in Part 2—Positional Problems.)
C		
The "c" in English functions mainly in three sounds. It has "s" characteristics before "i," "y" or "e"; "k" characteristics before "a," "o," "u" and consonants; and in part of the digraph "ch."	The Spanish "c" functions very similarly to the English "c."	People who learn Castillian Spanish are apt to have a "th" sound, as the "th" in *thanks*, for "c's" that appear before "i" and "e." This sound variance should be regarded as a regional dialect and is generally not taught, though understood and recognized, in Western Hemispheric Spanish.
CH		
The letters "c" and "h" when written together are called a digraph in English because they together represent one sound.	In Spanish "ch" is regarded as one *letter* which stands for one sound; that of the "ch" in *champion*. It has a separate entry in the Spanish dictionary.	Spanish has a low breath level "ch" in it which offers no problem—until the high breath level English "sh" is encountered. Upon first hearing the "sh" the hearer fits the new

sound into the "ch" auditory record he has. He later produces an "sh" but at a very low breath level.

The English oriented ear upon hearing both the "ch" and "sh" produced with such a low breath level cannot clearly perceive these peculiar pronunciations since he has no receptors for such sounds.

Let's suppose a Spanish-speaking child uttered the word "choose." It would not come out with a clear "ch" sound, therefore the English hearer would hear "shoes." Inversely, if the Spanish speaker uttered "shoes," the English hearer would hear "choose."

D

Generally three sounds are attached to this symbol; the "d" as in "dog," the "t" sound of "d" as in "walked"; also the "j" sound of "d" when it appears in "soldier" and "edge."

In Spanish there are three sounds for a "d." One is like the "th" sound in "the"; another is close to the English "d" sound with the difference being that in Spanish the top of the tongue is placed closer to the front of the mouth—touching the back of the upper teeth; the third is produced by shutting off air and sound from the mouth by sticking out the tongue slightly and biting entire rim of tongue simultaneously, but gingerly.

The Spanish oriented speaker has no problem with the enunciation of "d"—his problem is in avoiding interference of the "th" sounding "d" and the quiet tongue and teeth "d." The occurrences of interference are predictable and are discussed in Part 2.

E

There are six ways to pronounce an "e" in English.

There is basically one way to pronounce an "e" in Spanish. It is like the "e" in "end." The mouth must be smiling broadly to produce the Spanish sounding "e."

No *significant* problems are encountered in learning the sounds of "e" (except for the schwa "e").

F

The sound for "f" is represented mainly as the "f" in "fish," but also occurs as a "v" sounding "f" as in "of."

There is only one sound for "f" in Spanish, and that is the sound of the "f" in "fish."

No problems.

English	Spanish	Discussion
G		
There is the "j" sounding "g" before "i," "e" or "y" and the hard sounding "g" as in "ground" in English.	In Spanish "g" has a hard sound similar to the one in English, but instead of a "j" sound before "i," "e" or "y," a Spanish "g" takes on a raspy "h" characteristic.	It is easy for the young Spanish mouth to learn the English "g."
H		
There are three ways to respond to "h" in English: 1. The silent "h" in *honest* 2. The aspirant "h" in *how* 3. The aspirant "h" in *what*	In Spanish the "h" is always silent.	There are no problems with the silent "h." The aspirant "h," in Spanish, is rasped at the throat. Therefore, practice in producing the unrasped "h" of English is necessary. The sound of "wh" must be practiced extensively because it does not exist in Spanish.
I		
There are four sounds in English for the sound of "i."	There is one sound in Spanish for the symbol "i." It is like the "i" in *police*. A smile position of the mouth is necessary to make the Spanish sounding "i."	It is very difficult for the Spanish oriented ear to learn to say the short English "I" as in *ill*. The Spanish speaker will generally say "ell," or "eel" for ill. The schwa "i" is also a problem.
J		
In English "j" generally represents one sound, although other symbols such as "g" as in *gentle* and "dg" as in "edge" produce the "j" sound.	In Spanish the "j" symbol always represents one sound; that is the rasped "h" sound.	Children of preschool and primary grade age have no special difficulty in learning the English "j." Attention must be given to adequate voicing.
K		
Sounds for "k" in English are represented by "k," "c," "ck," "ch" and "qu."	"k" sounds are represented by "c" and "qu." The symbol "k" is not used in Spanish unless it occurs in a borrowed word.	No enunciatory problem.
Basically, one sound in English.	One sound in Spanish.	The "l" sound in Spanish is crisper and sharper than the sound of the English "l." The Spanish oriented hearer has difficulty perceiving the lazy "l" of English.
LL		
Basically, one sound in English.	Although this symbol has all the appearances of a double	In Spain this symbol is sounded somewhat like the "ll" in

"l," it is not regarded as such in Spanish. It is a separate symbol which represents a distinct strong "y" sound, almost to the point of an English "j." | mi*ll*ion, and like the "ly" in ha*l*yard. In Argentina and in other countries of Iberoamerica, the "ll" has definite "j" characteristics. It is often heard as a "j" by English language ears.

M

| One sound in English. | One sound in Spanish. | No enunciatory problems. |

N

| One sound in English. | Generally sounds like English "n"; changes to "m" under conditions to be explained in Part 2. | No enunciatory problems. |

O

| There are ten entries for the pronunciation of "o" in Webster's Dictionary. | There is one way to pronounce "o" in Spanish. | Enunciatory problems not difficult to overcome (except for the schwa "o"). |

P

| One sound in English. | One sound in Spanish. | The Spanish "p" is not as heavily aspirated as the English one. Because of this, it often sounds like a "b" to English oriented ears. The Spanish oriented ear must be trained to hear and repeat the aspirated "p." |

Q

| "q" has "k" sound. | Has "k" sound. | No enunciatory problems. |

R

| "r" has one sound in English, except for regional dialect influences, where it appears to be dropped. | The Spanish "r" is unlike the English "r." It is produced by tapping the tongue lightly on the alveolar ridge, very close to the top row of teeth. An equivalent sound in English is found in the two "t's" of bu*tt*er, or Be*tt*y. | No serious enunciatory problems. Spanish speakers must learn the semi-vowel "r" of English. |

RR

| | The "rr" is a single symbol in Spanish which has no counterpart in English. | Spanish speakers must learn to "untrill" the Spanish "rr." |

S

| "s" has an "s" sound and a "z" sound. | Has an "s" and "z" sound. | No enunciatory problems. |

English	Spanish	Discussion
T		
"t" has three sounds; one as the "t" in *two*, one as part of the digraph "th" in *the* and *thin* and the "ch" sound in *venture*.	Has one sound, as the "t" in *to*.	The "t" in Spanish is barely aspirated. To the English ear it often sounds like a "d." The Spanish speaker must learn to raise the explosion level of the "t."
U		
"u" has seven sounds.	In Spanish "u" has one sound. It is like the "u" in *rude*.	Schwa "u" is a problem.
V		
"v" has one sound in English.	Same as "b."	See explanation under *B*.
W		
"w" has one main sound as in "were." It is also part of the digraph "wh" as in *why*.	"w" is not used in Spanish except in borrowed words, e.g., Washington.	A "w" spoken by a Spanish speaker will sometimes take on the sound of a hard "g" i.e., "Guashington."
X		
Has one main sound in English as in *extra*, plus the "g" sound as in *examine*.	Has same main sound as in English plus raspy "h" sound in some Spanish words.	No enunciatory problems.
Y		
Has "y" sound as in *young*, and long "e" sound as in *funny* and long "i" sound as in *shy*.	Has "y" sound as in *young*.	Children who speak Spanish, predominantly, will give the "y" a "i" sound.
Z		
Has one sound as in *hazy*.	Has "z" and "s" characteristics.	In Spain, the "z" has "th" characteristics as the "th" in *thanks*.

Part 2. Positional Problems. A quick reference of some letters that cause pronunciation problems in Spanish because of their position in words or sentences.

Letter	Problem	Discussion of Possible Training Procedure
A	(Degree of individual problems vary.) The schwa ("uh" sound) of "a" is difficult for the Spanish ear.	Exercises with schwa "a's" need to be designed to combat problems in discrimination as in: fun–fawn, shut–shot, color–collar.
B	Because words rarely end with a "b" in Spanish, it is neither heard nor reproduced by the Spanish speaker. In Spanish, when a "b" or a "v" appears between vowels, it is sounded as a bilabial voiced fricative (both lips buzz). This is carried over into English and causes pronunciation problems.	Games, poems, stories, and exercises selected with many words ending with "b" and having "b" and "v" between vowels are needed. Teacher must exaggerate pronunciation of "b" and "v" sound in both positions.
C (K&QU)	"c's" are unaspirated in Spanish. This carries over into English and causes pronunciation problems.	The untrained ear (teacher) will not notice that final "c" sounds are being omitted. Because the teacher expects the productions of the final sound, it is often heard. Many materials carefully selected (or devised) must be used to help children develop the auditory perception of "c's" (and other "k" sounds) and their proper production.
D	In Spanish: (1) initial "d's" or "d's" following a consonant are pronounced very much like the English "d" in dog, except that the tongue touches further forward on the alveolar ridge; (2) intervocalic "d's" are pronounced as the "th" in the; (3) final "d's" are (silently) produced by protruding the tongue and closing off sound by biting the tongue gingerly. The problems of "d" have a very strong carry-over into English and cause many problems in pronunciation and understanding.	Many materials selected or devised are needed to work on alleviation of this problem. A thorough understanding of the nature of the problem is necessary in order to work against it successfully. The teacher must be tuned in acutely to the production of the "d" sound.
E	When schwa sound is made for "e," the Spanish ear has trouble.	Teacher must be aware that unstressed "e's" are generally schwa sounding.
F	Final "f" must be taught.	Low breath level must be increased in production of "f."
G	The inter-vocalic (between vowels) "g" in Spanish has raspy "h" characteristics. This carries over into English causing pronunciation problems. Since Spanish	Many exercises must be designed to practice "g" in all positions; initial, medial, final, intervocalic and blends. Thorough knowledge of types of errors

Letter	Problem	Discussion of Possible Training Procedure
	words rarely end in "g," the Spanish speaker doesn't hear or reproduce final "g's" properly. The tendency is to start the "g" but fail to aspirate or voice it at the end of its production.	that can be anticipated is vital.
H	Before vowels "i," "e," and "y," takes on characteristics of Spanish "g."	Develop method to teach child to produce the breathy English "h." Not a serious problem.
I	None	None
J	The "j" sound must be installed.	In cases where a child comes from a Spanish-speaking country, he may have no "j" sound in his "sound system." Special exercises would need to be developed in order to introduce this sound meaningfully. Learners without this sound will substitute it with a Spanish "ll" which is like a strong "y."
K	Same as "c."	Same as "c."
L	In English many final "l's" are not clearly said. The Spanish ear would neither hear nor repeat this lax "l." If an English mouth would poorly produce the "l's" in the following sentence, "I'll call Paul doll," the Spanish ear would hear, "Ow cow Pow dow."	The child must learn to hear and repeat tall "l" of English. Exercises with many final "l's" are needed.
M	Since there are no words that end in "m" in Spanish, the Spanish speaker will neither hear nor reproduce the final "m." He will generally substitute this letter with an "n" or an "ng."	Exercises, games, etc., need to be selected or devised to train children in this particular problem.
N	Whenever an "n" appears before a bilabial sound (b, m, p, v) in Spanish, the "n" is pronounced like an "m." This carries over into English causing mispronunciation.	Exercises need to be designed to teach the Spanish speaker to pronounce an "n" as an "n" before bilabial sounds in English.
O	"o" is a problem when its sound is schwa.	Schwa "o's" occur most often in unstressed syllable.
P	In general "p's" are barely aspirated. Final "p's" rarely occur in Spanish and when they do they are totally unaspirated. It is difficult for the Spanish ear to distinguish the difference between final "p's" and final "b's."	Much practice is needed to learn the final aspirated "p" for the Spanish-language-oriented child.

Q	Same as "c."	Same as "c."
R	Only severe cases have a problem with the English "r."	People coming from Mexico or other Spanish-speaking countries would need to learn to untrill their "r's." Methods to help them make the new sound would need to be devised.
S	The sound of a Spanish "s" is governed by the succeeding letter. If the letter is a vowel or a voiceless consonant, the "s" has a hissing quality. On the other hand, if the next letter is a voiced consonant, the "s" has "z" characteristics. In Spanish, no words begin with an "s" followed by a consonant. These characteristics of "s" cause many pronunciation problems.	Many exercises built on the ideas of the preceding information must be designed to aid the Spanish-speaking person in learning the sounds of "s" in English.
T	In general Spanish, "t's" are only slightly aspirated. Final "t's" rarely occur in Spanish and when they do, they are totally unaspirated.	Exercises for aspirating "t's," as well as exercises having words with final "t's" must be designed to teach the English "t" sound to the Spanish-speaking student.
TH	There is no voiceless "th" sound in Western Hemispheric Spanish.	Many exercises must be devised to properly install this sound into the hearing skills of the Mexican-American child.
U	Same as "a."	Same as "a."
V	Same as "b."	Same as "b."
W	None	None
X	None	None
Y	None	None
Z	In order to produce a "z" sound in Spanish, the letter after a "z" (or an "s") must be a voiced consonant, e.g., The maze must be difficult. If it is followed by a vowel or a voiceless consonant, the Spanish ear hears it as a hissed "s."	Exercises need to be designed to teach "z" sounds as they occur in English.

THE DIAGNOSTIC TEST

First of all, this diagnostic test and its results, will be of no value if the purpose of administering it is not clearly understood.

This instrument is designed to discover which of the children tested have which problems in producing particular English sounds.

The use of the results should be utilized to help in grouping children with common difficulties so that teaching efforts can be concentrated.

In order to measure changes, the test should be given again after a reasonable period of teaching.

For Part 1, a test record has been included using a professionally trained voice. In this manner, it is assured that all the children will be tested in the same way.

The following suggestions are offered to help in setting up the testing situation:

1. Obtain the use of a good tape recorder to tape the responses given by the child.
2. Secure a clear-sounding record player on which to play the test record.
3. Make a set of earphones available to yourself as well as a pair for the child being tested.
4. Administer the test in an area that is reasonably quiet.

Tell the child he is going to hear some sentences which you would like him to repeat. Mention to him that each sentence will be given twice and that he is to repeat after the second time the sentence is given.

The instructions will be reinforced by the voice on the record.

Part 1.   Diagnostic Test for Sound Problems

Check
Below

No Problem
Inconsistent
Problem

Name _____

Grade _____ Age _____

Language spoken at

home _____

Tested by _____

Staff position _____

Date tested _____

Testing for the Sound of	Probable Problem	Test Sentence
1 schwa [ə] (uh)	ah or eh instead of [ə]	This is a girl.
2 short a	ah or eh instead of a	The pig is fat.
3 intervocalic b (between vowels)	sounds like v	Babies are cute.
4 final b	unvoiced-unaspirated (not fully produced)	Water is in the tub.
5 intial c	unaspirated (not enough air)	Cars go fast.
6 intervocalic and final c (or k)	unvoiced-unaspirated	I look at a book.
7 intervocalic d	will sound like the "th" in the or the "tt" in butter.	This is a lady.
8 final d	omitted or made as a t	The world is big.

Testing for the Sound of	Probable Problem	Test Sentence
9 ch	sounds like sh	I sit in a chair.
10 sh	sounds like ch	My shoes are new.
11 hard intervocalic g	becomes glottal fricative (buzzed in the throat)	We went days ago.
12 final g	unvoiced-unaspirated	I see a bug.
13 h	becomes glottal fricative	I see a house.
14 short i	becomes long or short e	The dog is in the house.
15 j	sounds like ch or y	I like to jump.
16 l	omitted or distorted in final positions	It is a big ball.
17 final m	unvoiced in final position	His name is Tom.
18 ng	says n instead of ng, also low aspiration level	He sang a song.
19 long o (ou)	glide-off sound omitted	We go to the show.
20 initial and inter-vocalic p	unaspirated	Puppies are cute.
21 final p	unsounded	It's time for a nap.
22 r *	distorted weak	Run like a rabbit.
23 voiced intervocalic s ("z" sounding s)	sounds like a "hissed" s	The rose is pink.
24 initial s blends	e is placed before s	Snails stroll at night.
25 all t's	unaspirated or distorted (often sound like d)	The water is hot.
26 voiceless th	becomes s or t or f	We thank you.
27 voiced th	becomes d	This is fun.
28 schwa u (uh) [ə]	becomes ah or oh	My feet are under the table.
29 intervocalic v	sounds like soft b	I count to eleven.
30 final v	unvoiced	I count to five.
31 initial w	takes g characteristics	We play with toys.
32 y	takes on j characteristics	The yellow bird sings.
33 z	sound like voiceless s's (unless followed by voiced consonant.)	The bees will buzz in the trees.

* Asterisked items do not apply to children grades K–2.

PART 2. TEST FOR FLUENCY

1. Select a picture appropriate to grade level.
2. Tell the child you would like him to tell you all about the picture.
3. Show and listen for about a minute.
4. Rate degrees of ability:

	Poor					Good				
	1	2	3	4	5	6	7	8	9	10
Fluency										

5. Other speaking problems noted.

PART 3

Comments _____

_____

_____

_____

4

Instructional Programs: An Overview

Reading programs in American schools today must inevitably reflect two major national aspirations: that every child be assured the "right to read" and that every child be given the opportunity to recognize his worth as well as to develop sensitivity to others in our pluralistic society.

In the first article Leland Jacobs explains the role of the school in fostering humanism in teaching reading. He states: "The right to read implies, as a slogan or rallying point, the rightness of the reading environment, the rightness of the teaching, the rightness of the evaluations made of his progress for keeping the child feeling, 'I can learn to read, and I'd like to learn to read better'."

To this end, the reading teacher is obligated to create in her classroom the reading environment Jacobs describes so that the child can only opt to exercise his right to read. The reading teacher must also help select and provide for each child proper teaching methods, because, as Jacobs reminds us, "the ways in which he is taught to read are a major factor in his self-image as a reader and in his perceptions of others as fellow learners." Since no one approach to reading meets the needs of all children, the teacher must be knowledgeable in all the major approaches. This chapter surveys the major approaches to reading from which the teacher can select the method that best suits the learning preference of each child.

How can the language-experience approach be used efficiently and effectively? One of the major reading approaches in the United States is the language-experience approach. Its unique features make it particularly appropriate for the beginning stages of reading. The language-experience approach permits the child to view reading as a communication process. It helps the beginning reader to understand that it is natural to communicate through print just as it was natural for him to communicate through speaking before he entered school. In the language-experience approach, the child learns to read through the whole-word method, which uses the vocabulary and speech patterns of the child.

Wilma Miller provides the background and description of the language-experience approach. In addition to listing the major advantages of the language-experience method, she points out its limitations when it is the only or main reading approach in a primary grade classroom.

What accounts for the popularity of the basal reader approach? The basal reader has been the backbone of reading instruction in the United States for many years. At present it is the most commonly used approach in this country. This approach is particularly popular because it is the most systematic tool available to the reading teacher. However, critics of the basal reader maintain that the child is restricted to the content of the reader, and consequently learning occurs at a pace that may not be consistent with his needs and interests.

As with any approach the effectiveness of the basal reader as a tool for reading instruction is determined by the expertise of the teacher. A good teacher understands that the basal reading approach does not preclude the use of supplementary and enrichment materials.

Albert Harris reviews basal readers that have appeared in the past decade and reports a number of innovations. He finds increased emphasis on decoding in beginning reading, a shift from literal comprehension toward critical and creative reading, and a statement of objectives in behavioral terms. Changes in vocabulary control, varied methods for teaching word-identification skills, increased attention to critical-interpretive reading, and study skills are some of the dimensions of these newer readers. Harris lists three new trends regarding content. The components pertaining to skill practice are broader than the traditional workbook. Many enrichment materials and visual and audio supplements are available for use with many basal series. Additionally there are changes in format.

What new alphabet approaches have been used in the attempt to increase the effectiveness of reading instruction? It is often suggested by some educators that the teaching and learning of reading English is considerably more difficult than many other languages. This, it is proposed, is due to the "irregularities" in the relationship between the sounds and symbols of the language. The traditional orthography, our twenty-six-letter alphabet, represents some forty-odd sounds. A number of alphabet approaches have been devised to provide the beginning reader with an alphabet in which one symbol represents one sound.

Edward Fry observes that alphabet reform has an extended history. He discusses a range of approaches including the Initial Teaching Alphabet (i.t.a.), Words in Color, Diacritical Marking Systems (DMS), and Uniphon. A central question posed in the discussion is whether instructional gains anticipated in the use of a new orthography may be attributed to the orthography or to the novel instructional approach.

What is individualized reading? How can the individualized reading approach be used efficiently and effectively? Individualized reading instruction began long before reading texts were published, whenever a child taught himself to read or was helped by his mother or other adult. Individualized reading in the classroom grew in popularity as a reaction to the rigid uses or misuses of basal readers that ignored individual differences in children. The individualized reading approach permits the child to perform according to his growth pattern. The child learns to read when he feels the need for such learning. He is permitted to select the materials that appeal to him, and he reads and progresses at his own pace.

Individualized reading instruction ranges from the personalized one-to-one relationship, with conference periods and teacher-pupil contracts, to small group study. It is often combined with other reading appoaches such as language experience or with basal readers.

In evaluating this reading approach, Harry Sartain recognizes the strong need for and value of individualized instruction and lists misuses of the basal program. However, he also points out the dangers observed in some individualized programs. Sartain strongly favors a reading program that combines the strengths of basal readers with the strengths of the individualized approach.

In summary, the reading teacher should select an approach or a combination of approaches that matches the child's learning preference and at the same time guarantees his "right to read."

Humanism in Teaching Reading

Leland B. Jacobs
Teachers College, Columbia University

The essence of being human is to be in charge of one's life—to assume responsibility for oneself, to be willing to renew and remake oneself on the basis of evidence that renewal and remaking are essential to one's well-being as an individual and as a man among men.

The essence of being humane is the sensitivity and thoughtfulness afforded by one to another, not in a spirit of sentimentality or tolerance but rather in a spirit of honest sentiment and a willingness to work for sense of community. To be humane is to recognize that one must contribute to the making of our world. And one contributes to that making of our world first by realizing that it is an unfinished world in need of the best efforts of the individual to re-

conceive and reconstruct it. One also contributes to the making of this world by releasing the potential of those with whom he has close contacts so that they can make their best contributions to the necessary reconstructions.

To have a major part in the development of the humanness and humaneness of the child is a major task of the school. When we, as a people, place all our children in the pluralistic school environment, we have already initiated the task of undertaking the education of the child in his humanness and humaneness. But if such an initiation is all that we do, the possibility is as great that negative learnings may result as that positive ones will be forthcoming.

Conscious, deliberate attention to the development of the child as a worthy person and as a person sensitive to the well-being of others is surely the obligation of the school when school attendance is compulsory. The child, who must give a goodly portion of his childhood to the school, has the right to expect that the school, in return, will help him cope with what he thinks and feels about being himself and with what he thinks and feels about others.

Such deliberate attention to humanism in the school experience does not call for some new subject to be added to the curriculum. It means, rather, that as the school takes its responsibility for children's knowing, simultaneously the children are experiencing the dignity of being respected as unique persons and of being respectful of the dignity of their peers.

Let us use learning to read as an example. Practically every child knows that at school he is expected to learn to read. Once he is at school, he quickly discovers that much of his success there is dependent upon his ability to cope with reading. But as soon as he is faced with the task of learning to read, he is simultaneously learning something about himself and about others, both as learners in general and as readers in particular. Thus the methods school personnel use to develop the child into a reading child are an integral part of learning to read. To put it another way, a child learns to read by reading. But he also learns to stumble in reading by stumbling in reading. Or he learns to fail in reading by failing in reading. And the ways in which he is taught to read are a major factor in his self-image as a reader and in his perceptions of others as fellow learners. Surely the child has the right to read if the school is doing its job. But even more importantly, he has the right to be a reading person—a person in whom reading is making a positive contribution to his total development as a thinker and a doer. To the extent that the obligation to learn to read robs the child of his feeling of worth, or makes him feel like an automaton, or decreases his sense of playfulness, wonder, curiosity, and constructiveness, his basic right to read has been negated rather than fostered. His desire to learn to read better, or to become a reader, may seep away. Is he learning to avoid reading whenever the compulsion is not present?

This need not, of course, be the case. Nor does the child need to be seduced into learning to read by competitive extrinsic motivations. Nor does he need to be locked into one set way of learning to read or of responding to what he has read.

The right to read implies, as a slogan or rallying point, the rightness of the reading environment, the rightness of the teaching, the rightness of the evaluations made of his progress for keeping the child feeling, "I can learn to read, and I'd like to learn to read better."

Reading is, of course, much more than pronunciation of letter sounds, although being able to recognize letter sounds may make possible, in certain instances, the unlocking of words in print. Reading is much more than decoding the little black marks on the page, although such decoding is necessary.

Reading is bringing meaning *to* and taking meaning *from* the printed page. Decoding skills (by "look and say" or general configuration; or by phonics, or by structural analysis of the root, prefix, or suffix; or by context clues) make it possible to read the lines of print, to get to what the writer is attempting to make clear. They are, to this extent, very important. And the child can get great satisfaction from being able to break the print code. But this remains only word calling unless he brings *his* meanings to bear on the meanings the writer has deposited in print. And the moment the reader brings his meanings to bear on the printed page, he is into more than decoding words. He is into sentence and paragraph and "total selection" reading. He is remembering what he has read and using this as a springboard to what he will be reading next, and then next. He is reading not only on the lines, but between the lines and beyond the lines.

Parenthetically, the child reads faster or slower depending upon not only his ability to break the print barrier but also his competence to comprehend the meanings put down by the writer within the context of his experienced meanings. In other words, skills of word recognition and abilities of comprehension and rate of reading are functions of the reading act which are so taught that the child recognizes them not as the ends of reading but rather as the instrumentalities that make real reading possible.

In order for comprehension and rate of reading to develop well in the child's mind at school, those responsible for his schooling must take into account the complexity of the reading tasks encountered by the child in learning to read. They must view reading as interrelated with speaking, listening, and writing and as embedded in man's visualizing and communicating processes. Unitary though reading may seem to be for schooling purposes, in the life of the individual it is so intermingled with the other language functions that to unhinge it from its

foundations of language and the communication process is to detract from its larger significance and to be, in the long run, miseducative.

In order that the child's right to read may be protected, those who would really teach reading create an environment, compose the teaching, and utilize assessments so that the child, in the act of reading, retains his authority in the making of his life experiences and in the management of his school learnings.

In the creation of a school setting for reading, it must be remembered that the child who finds himself in a lush reading environment is more likely to become immersed in reading. In such an environment, he is read to by his teacher, who so enjoys reading himself that he shares with children stories and poems and informative writings that whet the appetite of the child for what good writers have made available to be read. Too, since writing and reading go hand in hand, the child is encouraged to be a writer—a writer of experience charts, anecdotes and "first person" accounts, stories, poems, and informative materials. The good reading environment has many kinds of reading materials close at hand—fiction, poetry, pictures and picture books, encyclopedias, dictionaries, pamphlets, newspapers, charts, and interesting self-testing practice materials. It includes space for solitary, sustained, silent reading and writing and space for shared reading and writing in group situations. It has ready access to the school library and media center. It includes the materials for using one's reading as a springboard to one's own creative endeavors in construction, dramatization, and composition in painting, sculpture, music, dance, and puppetry, as well as in story and poem.

Different Types of Reading Methods

	METHOD	EMPHASIS ON	MAY HELP WITH	DRAWBACKS
DECODING	ALPHABETIC	*Names* of letters ar-ue-en = run see-ae-tee = cat	Letter recognition, development of left to right sequence. Durrall has suggested all the consonants' letter names, except h, q, w, and y, contain their phoneme or sound plus an extraneous vowel: e.g., b-ee, s-ee for b, c, d, g, p, t, v, z; or eh-l, eh-m for f, l, m, n, s, x.	Alphabetic sequence (a, b, c, d) may be confusing: e.g., b and d near each other in order, sound and shape similar. Child may lose interest in material read if concentrating solely on letter recognition. Some children make idiosyncratic associations with letters which are no help with sound: e.g., t is like a hammer.
	PHONIC	*Sounds* of letters ruh-uh-neh (r-u-n = run) or ruh-un (r-u-n = run) or ruh-neh (ru-n = run)	Useful for deciphering unfamiliar (from sight) word. Child can try cut a word to see if it fits. Does not have to wait to be told. Phonics can be taught *systematically*: e.g., synthesis, word building, word families; *incidentally*: analytic, beginning sounds of familiar words.	Blending or synthesizing sounds can be difficult for some children. Need for fine auditory discrimination. Boys' auditory ability appears to develop later than girls'. "Irregularity" of English may lead to restriction of vocabulary in readers, artificial style. Child can pronounce unfamiliar word, may not be in oral vocabulary.
READING FOR MEANING	WHOLE-WORD OR LOOK-AND-SAY	(symbols/pictures) run rabbit rug (not mat!)	Use of meaningful words: e.g., ice cream. Often pictorial representation an additional clue. Word/picture association. Look-and-say used for non-pictorial words, also service words: e.g., are, the, you taught as sight words.	Individual letters may be ignored, particularly word endings, medial vowels. Leads to guessing. No means of deciphering unfamiliar words. Child waits to be "told." Dependency on teacher. Difficult to differentiate between words similar in length, configuration: e.g., cat, cot must keep meaning in the foreground.
	WHOLE-SENTENCE	The girls run round the tree. (N.B. Not dance or skip)	Emphasis on whole sentence and phrases. Children's interests can be used. Meaningful. Fosters appreciation of importance of intonation, phrasing, and pitch when reading aloud.	Individual letters and words may be left out. Guessing. Written language structure may not be familiar, substitutions may be based on dialect differences: e.g., reads we was instead of we were; does not help build up letter/sound associations.
MULTIPLE CLUES	LINGUISTIC	The man will *run* in the race. The man will r . . . (letter clue) The man will *rabbit* (syntactically unacceptable) The man will *reach* (semantically unacceptable) The man will *roll* (not probable)	Language as communication. Oral language provides child with clues. Type of word which will make a good "fit." Word parts, endings, etc. Signal information, e.g., *ed* added to a word signals past tense. Written language presents letter strings which become familiar, build in sound expectations.	Reading materials sometimes based on word using common letter strings, can be artificial. Stressing letter patterns of similar form can be confusing: e.g., name, same, bane. Playing down the use of pictures (said to give extraneous cues) may make dull books. May underrate differences in speech patterns.

©Elizabeth Goodacre

Such an environment finds its rightness for reading in that it is continuously an invitation to read. It encourages self-selection of reading materials. It implies that reading is not a "period in the school day," but an integral part of all school life. It fosters curiosities. It demonstrates the many ways reading can be put to use in one's life. And, in a sense, it literally defies the child not to exercise his right to read.

So far as teaching is concerned, its rightness for the child to learn to read is paramount. That rightness implies individualization of teaching practices. The teacher so manages the classroom that the child knows he is getting individual attention in his efforts to read, and to read better. He gives attention to skills and abilities because he, as well as the teacher, knows these are the next reading tasks to work on. He knows this because his strengths and weaknesses have been demonstrated in his present reading. He is led to work with practice materials that zero in on the particular demonstrated lack that is impeding his fullest possible achievement. He is provided opportunities to work directly on these skills and abilities, as well as opportunities to read for enjoyment, reaction, and entertainment with those mechanics of reading he already possesses. He is not caught up in a mass approach to reading, in a one right way to mastery of skills, or in one kind of material to use in learning to read. In other words, the child's "life space," his "inner subjectivity," his authority of his own life, is respected, which releases him to respond to the teaching as an engagement in learning. His time and energy are conserved in applying himself to reading because he does not waste his time at school doing tasks he can already do, or going through reading rituals in prescriptive procedures that he does not in actuality use, or worrying about how he is being classified in relation to other children. He is not a "red bird," a "blue bird," or a "yellow bird" in reading. He is a reader, exercising his human right to be a child for whom the educational enterprise has about it that rightness which lets him comprehend the tasks next to be undertaken in learning to read well, participate actively in the development of plans for getting those tasks done, and enjoy the freedom to use his expertise and resources in getting the job done.

The rightness of the assessment procedures used to tell how well the child is progressing in reading, of course, directly affects his accomplishments. If he observes that practice materials or other written, informal appraisal devices are used merely to pigeonhole him into some generalized category of reading, he is not greatly helped to read better. If, likewise, more formalized testing procedures do, in fact, nothing more than grade him, he is likely to feel trapped between the testing and the real world, whether or not he succeeds on the test.

On the other hand, assessment devices, formal and informal, can be used diagnostically to help teacher and child know what he seems to be doing well, what might be best to work on next, how to work on the problem undertaken, and what materials are needed to get this job done.

In order for assessment procedures to be constructive for the well-being of the child, a broad base of instrumentalities appropriate to the various components of reading will need to be used: teacher observations; reading inventories; pupil- and teacher-made reading records; informal testing and self-testing materials; and formal, standardized tests. The spirit in which assessment is used and the ends to which it is put make the difference as to the rightness of evaluation for the child's changes of behavior in reading.

In conclusion, it would seem that the old saw about "what reading is doing in Johnny" rather than "what Johnny's doing in reading" contains considerable professional wisdom. Since reading is a distinctive, human enterprise embedded in the larger contexts of communication and language, its importance emanates from its usefulness to the person doing it. Since reading does not really exist outside a person in the process of doing it, the whole person is involved in it as a fully functioning human being. Since the school takes the major responsibility for teaching reading, the ways in which the child is taught to read have direct bearings on both his productivity as a reader and his aspirations about being a reader.

If what reading is doing in Johnny puts him further in charge of his life and increases his authority over it, it enhances his humanness. If reading in Johnny confirms and extends his ways of knowing about his world and those who live therein, he can at least potentially increase his humaneness. Then the right to read is matched by the rightness of the handling of that right. That is what schools must do.

A Critical Appraisal of the Language-Experience Approach to Reading

Wilma H. Miller

The language-experience approach is considered by reading specialists to be one of the main approaches to teaching beginning reading in the United States today. This approach has proven itself very useful in many instances, but it also has some limitations which must be carefully considered when it is used as the major reading approach in a primary-grade classroom.

BACKGROUND OF THE LANGUAGE-EXPERIENCE APPROACH

For a number of years, the experiences of first-grade children have formed the basis of some reading materials in beginning first-grade reading instructions. Every first-grade teacher is familiar with the experience chart,

Reprinted by permission of the Wisconsin State Reading Association and the author.

a group-composed manuscript. However, the language-experience approach has been refined and publicized in recent years by Dr. R. Van Allen, formerly Director of Curriculum Coordination of San Diego County, California, but now of The University of Arizona. Dr. Allen apparently first noticed this approach being used with bilingual Mexican-American children in a border area of Texas. Since these children did not have the background of experiences to bring to the interpretation of the basal readers, their teachers were using dictated or child-written experience stories as the major basis of their reading materials. The teachers of these bilingual children also discovered that they were able to read their own language patterns much more effectively than they could read the language patterns found in the basal readers.

When Dr. Allen moved to San Diego County, he brought the idea of a refined language-experience approach with him. The approach was subjected to considerable experimentation in many first grades in San Diego County. One major research study conducted there indicated that the language-experience approach, the basal reader approach, and the individualized approach were all excellent methods for teaching beginning reading. However, the results further indicated that the language-experience approach and the individualized approach also developed a keen interest in learning to read on the part of the first-grade children (1).

DESCRIPTION OF THE LANGUAGE-EXPERIENCE APPROACH

The language-experience approach can be crystallized by the following statement which Dr. Allen uses in his materials:

What I can think about, I can talk about.
What I can say, I can write.
What I can write, I can read.
I can read what I write, and what other people can write for me to read (2).

In kindergarten or in beginning first-grade, the children dictate many individual or group stories to their teacher who acts as a scribe. These stories capitalize on the in school or out of school experiences of the children and are recorded by the teacher using the language patterns of the children. The group-dictated experience charts are transcribed by the teacher on large chart paper. In using the group-composed experience charts, the teacher will read the chart to the class several times while emphasizing left-to-right progression. She will also have the children read various words or sentences from the chart. The individually dictated experience stories are often typed by the teacher using a primary typewriter and given back to the child who dictated them.

Various art media are used to illustrate the individually dictated experience stories which are the unique feature of the language-experience approach. The children occasionally use a drawing or painting to motivate the telling of an experience story, but more often the dictated story is illustrated by the child who dictated it. The illustrated experience stories are later bound into a booklet for which the child has designed a gaily decorated cover. Each child then "reads" his booklet of experience stories at school and at home.

By using both group-composed experience charts and individually dictated experience stories, the children in kindergarten or beginning first grade are able to conceptualize reading as "talk written down" and are able to learn a number of sight words in an informal manner.

As the children progress through first grade, they continue to use experience charts and stories as the major method of learning to read. They continue to dictate charts and stories to their teacher, but as they learn more and more words they can begin to write their own experience stories. Of course, in this beginning writing stage they still need considerable help from the teacher with the spelling of words, but the children are encouraged to spell the words in the experience stories as they think the words should be spelled. During the first grade, the children using the language-experience approach will read the experience stories that they themselves have composed as well as those of their classmates. The children will also read many stories from basal readers, but this reading is done on an individual basis for no ability grouping is found in the language-experience approach except for flexible short-term grouping. The children also will read many trade books in first grade.

There is no control of vocabulary in the language-experience approach for the child learns sight words found in his own experience stories or in the group-composed experience charts. Dr. Allen believes that the common service words will be learned by all children eventually since they are found in the dictated stories at some time during the early primary grades. Reading skills are taught in an incidental individual way in this approach, with phonics being taught on a "say it" to "see it" basis, the opposite of that found in the typical phonics program which empha-

sizes the "see it" to "say it" approach.

By the time the children have reached second grade, Dr. Allen assumes that they will be writing many experience stories with little help from the teacher. The children will be continuing to read their own experience booklets and the experience booklets of their classmates. They will continue to read stories from basal readers at their own reading level, whether it is the first grade, second grade, third grade, or perhaps the fourth grade levels. The second-grade children will also read trade books on their own reading level. The children will continue to learn the necessary reading skills on a basically individual basis.

The language-experience approach deemphasizes the use of experience booklets for reading material as the children approach the intermediate grades. It becomes mandatory at this level that the experience stories become supplementary instead of the basic reading materials.

ADVANTAGES OF THE LANGUAGE-EXPERIENCE APPROACH

The language-experience approach has many unique features which make it very valuable. Perhaps one special advantage of this approach is that it enables children to conceptualize "reading is talk written down" during the early stages of reading instruction. This is a concept that many more mature readers do not seem to easily attain.

Another major advantage of this approach is that it insures that children have the background of experiences to bring to their reading since the experience charts and stories utilize their own experiences. This is a very important asset to the slow learning child or to the culturally deprived child.

The children can read their own language patterns very effectively, and the use of these more mature language patterns will not lead to the language regression that is sometimes the case when the basal readers are used in first grade. It has been found that older disabled readers, even those in junior high school, can easily read their own language patterns when given an opportunity to do so by a teacher who is using the language-experience approach as a remedial method with them. The approach also has a beneficial motivating effect to the disabled reader.

The language-experience approach can also be called an integrated language arts approach since it very effectively stresses the interrelationships among the four language arts of listening, speaking, reading, and writing. It particularly stresses the relationship between oral language and reading since the dictated experience charts and stories form the integral part of the approach at the early stages. It also stresses the relationship between reading and writing effectively since the child-written experience stories play an important part in the approach at its later stage.

The children's creativity is greatly enhanced when they are using this approach. The illustrations for the experience stories and the covers for the experience booklets give the children an opportunity to effectively explore various art media. The children who have used this approach usually are very adept at writing their own creative stories and often exceed children who were taught by other reading methods in creative writing ability.

Finally, the language-experience approach seems to develop a true interest in reading in the children who have used it.

LIMITATIONS OF THE LANGUAGE-EXPERIENCE APPROACH

The major limitation of the language-experience approach is its lack of sequential skill development. Research has shown that word attack skills, perhaps especially phonetic skills, are much more effectively taught in a systematic sequential manner. Dr. Allen's belief that children will learn word attack skills when they feel a need to do so seems to be a rather naive concept.

Undoubtedly most elementary teachers are not sufficiently aware of the many facets of the complex reading process to be able to teach reading without some guidance. The language-experience approach seems to be much too unstructured to be used as the main approach for teaching reading by only but the most experienced and confident teachers of reading.

In this approach, the children do not have the control of vocabulary and systematic repetition of new words that is found in the basal readers. Using the language-experience approach the children learn vocabulary words from experience charts and stories, and the teacher can never be completely certain that they have learned the words that they will need to know how to recognize when reading basal readers and trade books.

In the language-experience approach there is no ability grouping, except for flexible short-term groups. While this may be an advantage in that it does not stigmatize the slow learning child, it certainly becomes a limitation when one considers how wasteful it is of teacher time and energy. Especially at the beginning stages when the teacher must act as a scribe for the individually dictated stories, it is almost a monumental teacher task to give each child the individual help that he needs. This is an especially important limitation when the class size is over twenty.

To function most effectively the language-experience approach assumes that primary-grade classrooms are very well equipped, and that the teachers are able to provide many enriching experiences for the children. The approach is based on the concept that the children will have much to say and to write about. Therefore, they must have an enriching and motivating classroom environment, must have the opportunity to go on many educationally valuable school trips, and must have available material with which to make their experience booklets. The classrooms must have available many basal readers and trade books also.

The language-experience approach cannot function effectively as the major method for teaching reading much beyond the primary grades since the children must begin to read in the content fields and cannot be limited to reading about their own experiences at this point.

SUMMARY

It is to be hoped that every elementary teacher has a working knowledge of the language-experience approach since it can serve many valuable purposes in the classroom. It seems particularly valuable in introducing beginning reading in first grade and as a supplementary approach in all the primary grades. It is also very valuable to use with disabled readers as one means of introducing or carrying on a program of corrective reading.

REFERENCES

1. ALLEN, R. VAN, "Three Approaches to Teaching Reading," *Challenge and Experiment in Reading.* International Reading Association Conference Proceedings, Volume 7, 1962, 153–56.

2. DEPARTMENT OF EDUCATION, SAN DIEGO COUNTY. *An Inventory of Reading Attitude.* Monograph Number 4 of the Reading Study Project. San Diego: Superintendent of Schools, 1961.

New Dimensions in Basal Readers

Albert J. Harris

City University of New York

As I began to think about this topic, the first question that occurred to me was: what does "new" mean? A dictionary disclosed several possible meanings: of recent origin; not yet used; unfamiliar; begun afresh, as in a cyclical repetition; changed for the better; different from what was before; and, recent and fashionable. Two of these seemed to fit together and be appropriate for the task. So for this paper "new" means that something is recent and different from what was before. New does not necessarily mean better, nor fashionable, nor not yet used. And the focus of this paper is on the present and recent past, not on forecasting the future.

The term "dimension" in the title is interpreted to mean an aspect or attribute or characteristic.

The third term, "basal readers," is taken to mean an interrelated set of materials for teaching fundamental reading skills. At a minimum, such a set requires a sequence of reading materials for the learners, graded in difficulty, and guides or manuals that provide directions on how to teach with these materials. Many different kinds of supplements and accessories to this basic minimum are available.

OBJECTIVES

The objectives which have guided the development of most basal reader series have not changed much since the *Report of the National Committee on Reading* published in 1925, and elaborated in *Reading in the Elementary School* published in 1949. Both of these influential yearbooks called for a balanced and comprehensive set of objectives, in which silent and oral reading, mechanics and comprehension, study skills and recreational reading, group and individual needs, were to be given balanced attention.

There have been three recent trends in regard ot reading objectives. The first is the insistence of some writers that, in the early stages of reading instruction, decoding should be stressed and comprehension should be soft-pedaled. This point of view is not new, but has received recent support from

Albert J. Harris, "New Dimensions in Basal Readers," *The Reading Teacher* (January 1972). Reprinted with permission of Albert J. Harris and the International Reading Association.

some linguists and from Chall's *Learning to Read: The Great Debate* (1967).

A second trend in objectives is increased attention to critical reading and to the development of creative thinking through reading.

A third trend is toward the reformulation of objectives into behavioral terms. A behaviorally stated objective specifies the particular behavior that a pupil has to display in order to show mastery of it. The emphasis is on what the pupil does, not on his mental processes, nor on what the teacher does to elicit this behavior.

An older statement of an objective as: "to arrange ideas in proper sequence" can be restated behaviorally as follows: "Given a reading selection and a list of statements relating to its content, the student will place these statements in order of their occurrence in the selection." (*Reading*, 4–6, p. 23) The behavioral statement specifies a way of testing for mastery of the objective. Space does not permit me to discuss in detail the merits and limitations of behaviorally stated objectives, but an opposition to their use is beginning to be heard, as in the recent paper by MacDonald and Wolfson (*1970*).

then the trend has been toward richer vocabularies.

In recent basal reader series, vocabulary is controlled in one of two ways. In readers with a phonic, linguistic, or phonic/linguistic approach, the tendency is to teach words that have in common a particular phoneme-grapheme correspondence in a group, and to restrict vocabulary to words which fit into the patterns that have been covered. Exceptions to the patterns are usually taught later. The resulting sentences at beginning level seem very artificial and contrived.

In eclectic basal readers words are introduced gradually in a sequence governed by the story to be told, and usually phonic and structural generalizations are introduced in a sequence that is based on the word stock already available. The limitations of children's knowledge of word meanings requires some continuation of vocabulary control after word identification skills have been covered, but this tends to be observed more strictly in eclectic readers than in phonic or linguistic readers. Basal readers using a revised orthography, such as i.t.a., are usually phonic or linguistic in their approach to vocabulary control.

VOCABULARY CONTROL

From the 1920s into the 1950s, publishers vied with each other in reducing the number of words introduced in a basal reading series. The bottom was reached when one series taught fewer than 1200 different words in its readers for the primary grades. Olson's study showed that in the early 1960s new words totalled fifty-four to eighty-three at preprimer level in widely used series; 113 to 173 at primer level; and 285 to 340 at first reader level. Since

HOW SKILLS ARE TAUGHT

There is quite wide variation in methods of teaching word identification skills. Among recently published basal reader series two use a modified linguistic approach, one employs a rich vocabulary but relies heavily on learning the words in context, and two introduce and apply phoneme-grapheme generalizations as new words are introduced. Eclectic basal readers have begun to use linguists and psycholinguists as consultants and to pay attention to their recommendations about the ways in which skills should be taught. Most linguistic and phonic series emphasize spelling patterns, which used to be called word families, but there is wide variation in the teaching of phonic generalizations. A small minority uses a synthetic phonics approach in which sounding and blending are emphasized.

In regard to comprehension skills, there has been a recent tendency to place less emphasis on literal comprehension and more on interpretation, inference, critical reading, and creative reading. Somewhat greater emphasis tends to be given to study skills. Rate and flexibility are still given little attention in most basal reader programs.

CONTENT

There are three main trends in regard to content. The first has been a change with regard to characters and their environments. The animals and folk and fairy tales remain, but there has been a recent rather general effort to replace the middle class white stereotype with ethnic and environmental pluralism. One finds more emphasis on urban settings, on members of minority groups, and on problems related to limited income.

A second trend has been the disappearance of the one-family cast of first grade characters from some recent series. Other series start with one family, but drop it earlier than formerly. In some series, anthropomorphic animal characters replace human characters in stories for beginners.

A third recent trend has been an increase in the amount of nonfiction, particularly for intermediate grades. This makes it possible to teach basic study skills with more appropriate con-

tent. The practice of placing fiction and nonfiction in separate books has been tried, but does not seem to be becoming a trend.

PROVISIONS FOR SKILLS PRACTICE

The traditional medium for skills practice has been a workbook to accompany each reader in a basal series. These correlated workbooks have not changed much in recent years. One series reduces the amount of teacher assistance needed by providing self-help cues at the top of each page. Self-help is also provided in some series by providing small picture dictionaries and glossaries in the readers, as low as preprimer level. Many publishers provide exercises in the form of pads of stencils that can be used on duplicating machines. Filmstrips and transparencies can be used to project skills exercises for group use. A beginning has been made in supplying recordings which give directions for exercises and then provide answers for self-correction.

Although two quite similar series of programed booklets that combine the functions of reader and workbook appeared early in the 1960s, a trend toward greater use of programed material does not seem to have been established. The computer techniques needed to teach beginning reading by computer-assisted instruction were worked out several years ago. Computer-assisted reading instruction remains at the level of experimental exploration, and is likely to remain so until two conditions can be satisfied: (1) the cost brought down to a competitive level; and (2) the software or teaching content developed to a satisfactory level in quantity and quality. There seems more promise at present in the use of computers to give and score tests as an aid in individualizing instruction, providing diagnostic information to the teacher, as in what is called "individually prescribed instruction."

ENRICHMENT

The teachers' guides for basal readers customarily provide suggestions to teachers about stories, books, poetry and music that are related to the reader content and may be used for enrichment. The new trend is to provide these materials in convenient packages as optional supplements to the program. These supplements may include such items as paperback books for use as independent supplementary reading, recordings of the supplementary books to allow children to listen to the story while looking at the print, a book containing stories for the teacher to read to the children, and boxes of games and puzzles that reinforce skills taught in the program.

VISUAL, AUDIO, AND KINESTHETIC ACCESSORIES

As has been mentioned earlier, filmstrips and transparencies have been used as optional supplements in the skills development program. Certain types of recorded materials have also been mentioned, including recorded storybooks, and recorded directions and scoring for practice exercises. Cassette tapes seem to be gaining over phonograph records. The main drawback to the expanded use of recorded accessories has been the rather high unit cost of the recordings.

Combinations of visual display units

with recordings have been developed outside of basal reading programs but have not been utilized to any extent as basal reader accessories. One form of audiovisual material is a combination of filmstrip and recording. This has been available for many trade books for some time. Another form of audiovisual presentation is provided by the Bell & Howell *Language Master* and similar machines. These use large cards with a strip of recording tape on each. When the child places the card in the machine he can hear the word spoken as he looks at its printed form. This technique, already well established in remedial work, does not seem to have been used yet as a basal reader accessory.

Three-dimensional materials, the shapes of which can be felt as well as seen, were used as an accessory reading readiness device in one series about a decade ago. After being ignored by other publishers for many years, this idea seems to be reappearing. A recent form of kinesthetic reinforcement uses stencils which guide the tracing and coloring of alphabet letters. Tracing and writing are also more often used in recent first grade workbooks than formerly.

FORMAT

The basic format pattern set by the McGuffey Readers over a century ago has lasted to the present. This pattern provided a graded series of books, hardcovered and illustrated, one for each grade of the elementary school. Of course, the series gradually became more elaborate. The first grade program evolved into one or more readiness books, preprimers, a primer, and a first reader. Two hard-covered books became customary for the second and third grades. Often the series stopped at sixth grade.

During the past decade a number of departures from this traditional format have been tried, and at this point it is not easy to discern a definite trend.

The powerful influence of the paperback has finally caught up with basal readers, with one very recent series offering schools a choice between a conventional hard-covered reader, and the same content bound in units with paper covers. It is too early to discern whether or not this will become a trend.

Print size has remained fairly constant for many years. There is an increasing use of sans serif type which resembles manuscript writing, in the first grade and sometimes higher. This has a certain logic to it, as it reduces the number of different letter forms the beginning reader has to learn. In the intermediate grades, the use of two-column pages has become common.

Illustrations have continued to be used lavishly, especially in primary grade readers. Basal reader art shows great variety. Realistic pictures, photographs, diagrams, maps, and charts may accompany factual selections, while the art accompanying fiction ranges from realistic through a simplified cartoon style to the distorted and abstract. Art tends to run to the edge of the page and indefinite boundaries are common. Vivid colors characterize the book covers and illustrations.

The influence of the nongraded school has recently been noted in the ways in which basal readers are labeled. Traditionally each reader has been marked with the grade, or part of a grade, at which it was normally expected to be used. The recent trend is to number the books in sequence by levels, encouraging teachers and pupils to get away from the idea that a particular book should necessarily be read in a particular year of schooling.

SUMMARY

While a number of innovations in basal readers have appeared in the past decade, relatively few of them have become widely adopted. In regard to objectives, there has been an increased emphasis on decoding in beginning reading, a shift from emphasis on literal comprehension toward critical and creative reading, and a very recent interest in behaviorally stated objectives. In vocabulary control recent series employ richer vocabularies, although most retain some restriction on new words through the sixth grade. There is quite wide variation in the procedures used in teaching word identification skills, while critical and interpretive reading and study skills receive increased attention.

Content shows a trend toward a multiethnic, multicultural scope. The one-family cast of characters in material for beginners is retained in some recent series but dropped in others. More nonfiction is used, especially in the intermediate grades. Skills practice is provided in several additions to, or alternatives for, the traditional workbook. Pads of stencils for use on duplicating machines, transparencies and filmstrips, and recorded directions and scoring are among the recent additions. Programed combination text-workbooks exist but most basal readers do not provide programed skills practice. Computer-assisted instruction has as yet not influenced basal reader methodology.

The recent trend in enrichment is to provide in convenient packages the kinds of enrichment materials formerly just mentioned in the teachers' guides. Visual and audio supplements exist, but combined audiovisual accessories are not available for most basal series. Kinesthetic procedures such as feeling, tracing, and writing are given increased emphasis at readiness and beginning levels. In format, new trends include use of paperback units, type which resembles manuscript writing at early levels, and two-column pages at upper levels. Illustrations have become more varied in style, and readers tend to be numbered consecutively by levels rather than identified with specific grades.

REFERENCES

CHALL, JEANNE, *Learning to Read: The Great Debate.* New York: McGraw-Hill, Inc., 1967.

MacDONALD, JAMES B., and BERNICE J. WOLFSON, "A Case against Behavioral Objectives." *Elementary School Journal,* 71 (December 1970), 119–28.

OLSON, ARTHUR V., "An Analysis of the Vocabulary of Seven Primary Reading Series." *Elementary English,* 42 (March 1965), 261–64.

Reading in the Elementary School, 48th Yearbook of the National Society for the Study of Education, Part II. Chicago: University of Chicago Press, 1949.

Reading, 4–6. Los Angeles: Instructional Objectives Exchange, P.O. Box 24095, California 90024.

Report of the National Committee on Reading, 24th Yearbook of the National Society for the Study of Education, Part 1. Bloomington, Illinois: Public School Publishing Co., 1925.

New Alphabet Approaches

Edward Fry

Perhaps the most provable thing about new alphabet approaches is that they are not new at all. One need only scratch the surface of a libary, and a cornucopia of revised alphabets, spelling reforms, and diacritical marking plans for beginning reading pours forth.

The history of the development of written language is exceedingly voluminous. There is no time in recorded history when it was not under attack and change. Probably the invention of movable type and the printing press has done more to slow down the change in written language in the last few

Edward Fry, "New Alphabet Approaches," in *First Grade Reading Programs,* ed. James F. Kerfoot (1965). Reprinted with permission of Edward Fry and the International Reading Association.

centuries than any other single factor. In these last few centuries we have attained a high degree of rigidity in written language. We now find ourselves in the somewhat strange position of having dictionaries largely agree on what letters should be used to spell each word in our language; it has not always been thus.

We could start a discussion of the need and desirability of new alphabets with a look at Cuneiform and Linear B, but let us jump ahead thirty centuries to the annual report of the National Education Association in 1910.

Your committee is able to make a report of progress that is very encouraging to those interested in the simplification of the spelling of English, as the year has been notable in the things that have been done and in the cooperation that has been secured. . . . The ridicule and the contumely heaped upon the movement five years ago has almost entirely disappeared, and the opposition to a reasonable consideration of its demands and claims is gone.

Alas the bright hopes of the educators of 1910 have been dashed on the hard rocks of history. The whole problem of alphabet reform or spelling reform is largely a political one. Any scholar could singlehandedly improve English spelling or the alphabet. However, the problem is that people with power—presidents, senators, giant corporations who publish books, even adults who vote—do not want a change because they already know the established system. On the other hand, the people who really need the change, the first-graders and the adult illiterates, have virtually no power at all. Apparently the education profession has very little power in this grave matter either.

THE READER'S PROBLEM

Lest one feel that we have gotten off the track by discussing simplified spelling in a new alphabet approaches article, let us put the whole area in "perspective." The basic problem of the first grade teacher is to train the child to decode a set of symbols which constitutes what we call written language. This set of symbols is rather closely based on spoken language. The average first grade child already possesses a good knowledge of spoken language. His vocabulary is something in excess of 5,000 words and his knowledge of the rules and structure of the English language is amazingly good. An interesting proof of the first-grader's facility with structure is to compare him with a newly arrived foreign university student who, even though well-educated, uses tortuous and often erroneous sentence structures and intonations.

Since it is the problem of the first grade student to learn to decode the written symbols, quite obviously the manner in which the language is incoded will have a profound effect. If the symbols follow strange and highly irregular principles it stands to reason that the child will have greater difficulty learning to decode them. Hence, anything that will improve the coding system, even temporarily, for beginning readers has been a concern of educators and many other intelligent people for at least centuries and probably for as long as there has been inaccurate coding systems. Thus, new alphabets, spelling reforms, and devices which temporarily add regularity, such as diacritical marks, are all part of our problem. Spelling is simply the obverse of the same problem—that of incoding, or having to write the symbol, as opposed to decoding, or having to read the symbol.

THE ALPHABET PROBLEM

A good bit of the problem of in-coding English developed during the 15th century in what scholars call "the great vowel shift." In this period between Chaucer and Shakespeare spoken English went through a notice-able change while written English failed to keep abreast. It was towards the end of this period that the spelling of English become somewhat crystal-lized due to dictionary makers like Samuel Johnson and technical inno-vators like Gutenberg.

The situation was further com-pounded by the inadequacy of the sound symbols or alphabet that the English chose to use. The alphabet which we use is really designed for writing Latin, not English. Hence, we note that modern Latin or Spanish and Italian have far fewer problems in spelling than does English. There are something like 44 different phonemes or distinctive sound units used in speaking English; however, our al-phabet has only 26 letters and at least three of these are no good at all as they overlap or duplicate the work of other letters (*C* sounds like an *S* or a *K*, *X* sounds like *KS*, and *Q* is used only with *U* and sounds like *KW*).

We get around this problem of an inadequate number of letters several ways. In consonants the situation is not too bad as we tend to use digraphs, or a special combination of two letters, to make a different phoneme. For ex-ample *CH* does not make a blend of *C* and *H*, but almost always makes the sound heard at the beginning of *chair*. But in the vowel sounds the situation is much more unpleasant, in that one letter makes many sounds. For ex-ample note the *A* in *at, all, above, ate*.

A BACKWARD GLANCE

It will perhaps help to put the modern systems in better perspective if we have a quick trip through some historical antecedents.

In 1551 John Hart wrote an essay entitled "The Opening of the Un-reasonable Writing of our English Toung." He later followed this up by suggesting a new orthography, and by 1517 he had zeroed in on the first grade problem with "A Methode of Comfortable Beginning for All Un-learned, Whereby They May Bee Taught To Read English, In A Very Short Time, With Pleasure." In the next century Charles Butler (1634) developed a phonetic alphabet for over-coming "uncertain writing and diffi-culty in learning." Because he found that the Latin Alphabet was "trouble-some to the novice reader and writer."

America's own Benjamin Franklin, that intelligent dabbler in many things, developed in 1786 his own reformed alphabet. While technically not very good, he did see the need for con-sistency and the addition of six new letters. Franklin's alphabet apparently never received any acceptance but he did manage to carry on a small cor-respondence using it.

Leaping ahead another century, we find that Benn Pitman was producing phonetic readers for the American school market using a greatly modified alphabet. Another 19th century in-novation was Fonotypy, a phonetically regular alphabet developed by Isaac Pitman and A. J. Ellis in 1884.

We have already noted the interest in spelling reforms around the turn of the century. From that time until this very day there are a number of simplified spelling organizations which actively correspond with each other in simplified spelling and regularly in-

HISTORICAL "NEW" ALPHABETS
AND
DIACRITICALLY MARKED READERS

ĭt   stănd   Ann'ș

ĭș   lămp   măt

    ĭ

a mat   the stand

The Eaſieſt and Speedieſt-way, both for the true ſpelling and reading of Engliſh, as alſó for the True-writing thereof : that ever was publickly known tô this day.

See the lamp! It is on a mat.
The mat is on the stand.

HODGES 1644

MC GUFFEY 1881

Diir Madam :—ħi abdſiekſiyn.iu meek to rektifyiiŋ aur alfabet, "ħat it uil bi atended uiħ inkanviniensiz and diſikyltiz," iz e natural uyŋ ; far it aluaz akyrz huen eni refarmeſiyn is propozed ; hueħyr in rilidſiyn,

Hwen Jərj Woſ-iŋ-ton woz a-bʏt siks yerz ɷld, hiz ſq-der gav him a haç-et, ov hwiç he woz ver-i fond, and woz kon-stant-li

BENJAMIN FRANKLIN 1768

BENN PITMAN 1855

WUNS UPON A TΛM LITƆL RCD
HCN LIVD IN A BARN WIΔ HƻR
FΛV ϵIKS. A PIG, A KΛT ΛND

ISAAC PITMAN & A.V. ELLIS   FONOTYPY 1844

But the atţic <u>windȯẉ</u> was pānǿless.   In eāmǿ the w<u>est</u> wind.   Down to the fīrǿ wĕnt the <u>litfl</u>ǿ girls. They did not want any <u>sick</u>ness.

EDWARD WARD 1894

duce some local congressman to put a bill before the United States Congress ordering that spelling in all government documents be simplified, or proposing to write into law some other scheme which will insure the modification of the American English written language.

England too has had its full share of alphabet and spelling reformers. No less a celebrity than George Bernard Shaw was so seriously interested in spelling reform that he left a major proportion of his estate to a trust which now is working on the simplification of the alphabet.

In the late 1950's Sir James Pitman, the head of the publishing firm and a member of Parliament, introduced a bill for greatly modifying the English

CURRENTLY USED NEW ALPHABET AND DIACRITICALLY MARKED FIRST GRADE MATERIALS

Sample of Primer Printed in ITA

"dœn't run awæ," ben sed tω hiſ cat.

"dœn't fiet," miek sed tω hiſ cat.

"wæt heer," sed ben and miek.

"wee will bee at scœl."

Sample of Primer Printed with DMS

"Lòøk, Bill," sảíd Lindả.

"Hērɇ cômɇs̱ Riɇky.

Hē is̱ âll reɇdy fôr schöøl.

Lòøk up and sēɇ funny Riɇky."

Sample of Primer Printed in Unifon

⊥EN M✦CT3R H✦PQ TRⱯD. HI

P✦KT UP BⱯƁI HⱮB3RT. HELD

H✦M ✦N H✦Z Ɓ✦G ORMZ AND CAⱮ

U LULUBⱯ.

Sample from first drill book for use with Words in Color

t

a̲t	ta	ut	tu
i̲t	ti	et	te
ot	to		

alphabet. This bill was defeated before it became law but, more or less as a direct consequence, Sir James did receive the blessing of the Minister of Education to experiment with An Augmented Roman Alphabet in the British Schools.

Some British parents, being not too well versed in the history of their language, prefer not to have their children learning from a "Roman Alphabet." Hence, the name of this new alphabet was changed to Initial Teaching Alphabet, or as it is popularly called the ITA. The name also reflects the current usage of this alphabet, namely that it is to be used for beginning instruction in literacy and later a transition is made to the traditional alphabet which ITA people like to call TO for

Traditional Orthography. Though it would be impolitic to say so publicly, there is probably at least a secret thought in the minds of some supporters that ITA could become *the* English alphabet to be used by everybody at all times. Needless to say, one clever way of gaining acceptance for this would be to raise a generation of children who had equal facility in TO and ITA. Some future decades from now there might be considerably less resistance to changing spelling or an alphabet if the Prime Minister, the cabinet members, the senators, the heads of corporations and a sizeable portion of the population all had equal reading and writing facility in ITA.

An interesting thing about ITA is the wide acceptance of it before adequate research results are reported. Most of the research results (see bibliography) are reported by investigators who are closely identified with the ITA movement and in many instances have authored or published materials in the ITA medium. These research results are almost uniformly glowing. Typical reports show that teachers using the ITA materials have results that are definitely superior to other teachers using the old basal reader or traditional system. While we cannot deny that high reading achievement is a good thing no matter how it is obtained, it is something else again to prove that the superior results were due to this particular alphabet rather than the fact that a new method was used.

United States educators have recently had a multitude of claims from super-phonics enthusiasts. There is little doubt that some teacher who has been graying along through her basal reading series and suddenly gets inspired by the new super-duper phonics system is going to get better results. In fact, she would probably get as good results if the situation were reversed and all the humdrum ordinary teachers were using phonics systems and she suddenly discovered a super-duper new hot-shot word reading method. In fact, it must be a little discouraging for the educational researcher to learn that in 1851 the Massachusetts Teachers Association appointed a committee to consider the subject of "Phonetics" and that this committee reported in 1852 that teachers should study the merits of the phonetic system by themselves by actual trial in their schools. When one sees such a basic problem in existence for well over a century and yet so completely unresolved, the problem of whether or not a new alphabet will really prove superior can hardly be expected to be solved in the next few years.

The Initial Teaching Alphabet is a 43 character alphabet. It uses 24 Roman or Latin characters that are used in traditional English (X and Q are missing) plus 19 augmented or additional letters. Most of the new letters are formed by a fusion of two lower case Roman letters. Five of these new letters, the long vowels, are made by placing a lower case *E* immediately adjacent to the preceding vowel. Diphthongs, other vowel sounds, and consonant digraphs are frequently similarly formed by placing two letters in close juxtaposition. Writing in the ITA is also constrained by a special set of spelling rules. Hence, some words using no new letters look different because of the spelling rules only. Both the new letters and the spelling rules add a further constraint in that so far as possible traditional word form is preserved so that in a later stage of training the students may transfer to the traditional orthography with a minimum of difficulty.

In an early paper Pitman estimated that 39.25 per cent of the words were radically changed when written in ITA, 10.50 per cent were moderately changed, 23.75 per cent had minor modifications, and 26.50 per cent were unchanged. The goal of ITA is to have a consistent phoneme-grapheme relationship so that one letter will always make the same sound, and vice versa. This goal is not always achieved, partially because of the concessions to word form, but it is a tremendous improvement over the traditional orthography.

Despite the lack of conclusive research results, the spread of the use of the Initial Teaching Alphabet has been extremely rapid. The first regular use of the ITA in the public school was in Britain in September of 1960. The experimental population consisted of approximately 600 four- and five-year-olds. The British begin reading instruction a year earlier than the Americans. In the school year 1964–65 Pitman Publishing Company, the main publishers of Initial Teaching Alphabet materials, estimates that there were approximately 60,000 British children using ITA. ITA use in the United States began in 1962 in the Bethlehem, Pennsylvania school system with a Ford Foundation grant to Dr. Albert Mazurkiewicz at Lehigh University. During the school year 1964–65 the author estimates that approximately 10,000 United States children were learning to read using the ITA. Most of these children were taking part in either continuing research in the Bethlehem schools or in research projects sponsored by the U. S. Office of Education. However, there are also many school systems "trying it out" without special foundation or government research grants. Despite these seemingly large numbers this is still far less than one per cent of the U. S. first grade population.

WORDS IN COLOR

Another British import aimed at taking advantage of some phonetic regularity principles is the Words In Color system by Caleb Gattegno. This system which has been commercially available for the past five years is used by fewer schools than is the ITA. Proponents of the Gattegno system also make some interesting statements such as, "Words In Color makes the English language phonetic through the use of color, enabling the learner to master the mechanics of reading in eight weeks or less." Forty-seven different sounds of English are taught by using different colors for each sound. Since it is difficult for children, or even adults, to distinguish 47 different colors some of Gattegno's symbols are split in half so that they are really two-colored rather than a unique color. This system does not have the color printed in children's workbook material, but rather there are 21 drill charts containing 270 letters or letter groups that make a phoneme and some phonetically regular words. The teacher drills the student to make the sounds in isolation, then blended together. For example, the first page of the first book simply contains a number of *A*'s of various sizes. The second page consists of a number of *U*'s. The third page consists of groups of *A*'s and *U*'s together which the student would blend as a word. After the five vowels are introduced (short sounds), consonants are introduced and the student can now begin to blend vowels and consonants to form short meaningful and meaningless words. The teacher is also instructed to get a large selection of colored chalk so that she can write letters and words on the board for drill.

Spache points out that this idea for the use of color to identify the common sounds was introduced by Nellie Dale in 1899.

The memorization of the 47 different sounds with their corresponding colors, as well as the 270 letter combinations which commonly are used in writing these sounds, appears at least on the surface to be the height of a mechanical memorization approach to beginning reading. Demonstrations put on by the publisher, Encyclopaedia Britannica, managed to be interesting and lively but, as yet, research proof is lacking for the superiority of this method over any other.

DIACRITICAL MARKS

Diacritical marking plans to aid beginning readers are not exactly new. One of the oldest currently-used languages, Hebrew, has a system of marks used to indicate vowel sounds for beginning readers. After a certain degree of reading maturity is established, the marks vanish and the reader and writer use only consonants.

In 1644 an English schoolmaster Richard Hodges developed a set of diacritical marks to be used with beginning readers which the publisher put forth as, "The easiest and speediest way both for the true spelling and reading of English as also the true writing thereof that was ever publicly known to this day."

In the 1890's E. G. Ward authored a set of diacritically marked beginning reading texts published by the Silver Burdett Company for the American schools. In addition to diacritical marks that made the letters-sound relationship much more regular, Ward also underlined groups of letters that were "Phonograms."

A large number of readers in the 19th century, including the famous McGuffey series, used diacritical marks for the introduction of new words.

In 1964 Edward Fry published an article in *Elementary English* describing the Diacritical Marking System (DMS) to be used for beginning reading instruction. Later that year an experiment was begun, using the DMS marks on the Allyn & Bacon readers, in seven first grades. This Diacritical Marking System has over 99 per cent phoneme-grapheme regularity and aims to achieve essentially the same goals as the Initial Teaching Alphabet without distortion in word form or change in spelling.

The DMS is somewhat simpler than diacritical marking systems found in most dictionaries, since the intention is to aid beginning readers rather than give extreme accuracy. Regular consonants and short vowels are not marked since these are the most common usages of the letters. Long vowels have a bar over them. Regular two-letter combinations which make unique sounds such as the consonant digraphs and diphthongs, have a bar under both letters. Silent letters have a slash mark through them. These marks plus a few others, such as those used for the broad *A* and other sounds of *U*, constitute the bulk of the marks used. Nearly every word the child sees in the first grade reading books is marked and likewise all work that the teacher duplicates or puts on the board has the DMS marks. In writing children have the option of using the marks or not.

UNIPHON

Another new phonetically-regular alphabet currently being used with some experiments in the Chicago area is Uniphon, developed by John Malone. This 40 letter alphabet, which the author calls "a single sound alphabet," uses block letters which have an additional interesting characteristic of being specially designed so that they can be read by computers for automatic translating purposes.

SIMPLIFIED USE OF LATIN ALPHABET

Though not really new alphabets, there are several systems of beginning reading instruction which achieve a high degree of initial phoneme-grapheme regularity by simply carefully selecting the words used in initial instruction. For example, under one type of "linguistic approach" that is put forth by Bloomfield and Barnhart, the child uses only regular consonants and short vowels. The introduction of new words is further graded so that only one short vowel is introduced per lesson. This method of controlled introduction of regular letters, while purported to be "new" in some circles, actually has as very close historical antecedent in the McGuffey Readers of the 1850's which used a similar introduction of sounds and words in its primers. While a number of other readers of the 1800's used a similar approach, one unique variation was used in the books written with words of *one* syllable published by McLoughlin Brothers in 1901. Whole books were written using only one syllable words.

METHODOLOGY

New alphabet approaches to beginning reading have some strong inferences for methodology but in and of themselves are only partially a method. For example, the most widely used set of ITA readers in the United States, written by Albert Mazurkiewicz and Harold Tanzer, have a relatively strong emphasis on the "language arts approach." These materials, which consist chiefly of a set of paperbound books with interesting stories not greatly different from a basal series, tend to have a relatively stronger *phonic* emphasis, but much of the uniqueness of method is due to the emphasis on children's writing activities in the teachers manual. While the authors would claim that it is the regularity of the ITA alphabet which facilitates children's ability to write, nonetheless the emphasis on the language arts approach is not unique to the type of alphabet used.

The DMS methods used in the current experimentation are largely overlays on the basal series. The actual pages from a basal series have been reproduced after marks have been added. The same basal series teachers manual is available, in fact required, for the teacher's use. The chief methodological feature of the DMS instructional program is the use of a number of phonic charts which accompany the basal series manual. Each time a new story is introduced in a preprimer or primer a small chart is introduced which explains one letter and its corresponding sound. The chart contains a key word (for example the word *cat* with a picture of a cat) plus several other common words which use the letter being discussed. Regular consonants and short vowels are thus introduced at the rate of one per reading lesson, and gradually digraphs, second sounds of consonants, and other vowel sounds are introduced with DMS marks. After a chart has been introduced, it is left hanging in the rooms so that the children may refer to the chart when coming across a new word. For example, if a child comes across a new word beginning with the letter *L* and he cannot remember the sound made by the letter, he needs only to look up on the board and find the *L* chart with its key picture; he may do the same with each of the letters in the word.

CONCLUSION

At the present time active experimentation is going on in the United States using the Initial Teaching Alphabet (ITA), the Diacritical Marking System (DMS), Uniphon, Words In Color, and the gradual introduction of phonetically regular letters—sometimes referred to as the linguistic approach. Of the new alphabets the only one which has published research reports is the Initial Teaching Alphabet. These published research reports, both from the United States and England, show that the ITA is definitely superior to the "old method." Whether or not this superiority is due to the special characteristics of ITA or the fact that it is a "new method" has yet to be established.

Three of these methods, ITA, DMS, and the linguistic approach, are being included in the large U. S. Office of Education Coordinated First Grade Reading Research Projects, a study now under way. The other two methods, Uniphon and Words In Color are being given field experimentation by their authors or publishers. Hence, all of these methods are being given classroom experimentation using method A classroom *vs.* method B classroom type of research design. While this type of research design may yield some interesting information, it is also quite possible for it to yield conflict information such as we have seen coming from the phonics studies over the last hundred years. It is possible that for additional valuable information the reading researcher is going to have to team up with the experimental psychologist or learning researcher who designs much smaller and much more carefully controlled studies. For example, is ITA superior to the basal reader method because it is new and because it uses a language experience approach or because it uses a phonetically regular alphabet? Current investigations will probably not satisfactorily answer this question.

A further important question might be, "If ITA or DMS or any of the other systems is superior to the traditional method, is the ITA or the DMS the best method of achieving these goals?" While each of the methods that we have discussed has gone through some developmental gesticulation, each of them is essentially the work of one man. Hence, if one of the new alphabets turns out to be definitely superior to the traditional alphabet the next question should be, "Is this the best possible alphabet to do this type of job?" American educators should seek the answer to this question before any large scale adoption of a beginning reading method utilizing a new alphabet is seriously contemplated. It is perhaps a necessary step in the evolution of new ideas that there be reasonably widespread interest in the current new alphabets and classroom experimentations of the type now under way. However, for the education profession to demonstrate itself to have achieved a reasonable degree of maturity, much more money should now be spent for research and development of new alphabets rather than wide scale adoption of them.

REFERENCES

1. DOWNING, J. A., *The ITA Reading Experiment*. London: Evan Brothers, Ltd., 1964.

2. DOWNING, J. A., *Experiments With An Augmented Alphabet for Beginning Readers in British Schools*. Pamphlet published on a talk to the 27th Educational Conference sponsored by the Educational Records Bureau, New York, November 1962.

3. DOWNING, J. A., "The Value of ITA," *NEA Journal*. Ivan Rose, Part 1; Warren Cutts, Part 2.

4. DOWNING, J. A., *The Augmented Roman Alphabet. A New Two-Stage Method to Help Children to Learn to Read*. Thirteen page pamphlet printed at Pitman Press, Bath, England, undated, circa 1962.

5. DOWNING, J. A., *Too Bee Or Not To Be, The Augmented Roman Alphabet*. London: Cassell and Company, Ltd., 1962.

6. DOWNING, J. A., *The I.T.A. (Initial Teaching Alphabet) Reading Experiment. The Reading Teacher*, November 1964.

7. FRANKLIN, BENJAMIN, "A Scheme For A New Alphabet And Reformed Mode Of Spelling With Remarks And Examples Concerning The Same and An Inquiry Into Its Uses In A Correspondence Between Miss Stephenson and Dr. Franklin Written In The Characters Of The Alphabet," 1768, reprinted in *Complete Works of Benjamin Franklin*, John Bigelow, Editor, G. P. Putnam's Sons, New York, 1887.

8. FRIES, CHARLES C., *Linguistics and Reading*. New York: Holt, Rinehart & Winston, Inc., 1962.

9. FRY, EDWARD, "A Diacritical Marking System To Aid Beginning Reading Instruction," *Elementary English*, May 1964.

10. GATTEGNO, CALEB, "Words in Color" (mimeographed). Chicago: Learning Materials Inc., circa 1963.

11. HARRISON, MAURICE, *The Story of the Initial Teaching Alphabet*. London: Pitman Publishing Co., 1965.

12. HODGES, RICHARD, *The English Primrose*. London: Richard Cotes, 1644.

13. KELLER, LINDA, *Herbert The Hippo* (children's book in Uniphon). Chicago: Peppermint Press, Inc., 1962.

14. MAZURKIEWICZ, ALBERT J., "The Lehigh-Bethlehem ITA Study" (First Year), ITA Report, mimeographed, undated, circa 1964.

15. MAZURKIEWICZ, ALBERT J., "Teaching Reading in America Using the Initial Teaching Alphabet," *Elementary English*, November 1964.

16. NATIONAL EDUCATION ASSOCIATION, *Journal of Procedures & Addresses*. Winona, Minnesota: 1910.

17. PITMAN, BENN., *First Phonetic Reader*. Cincinnati: American Phonetic Publishing Association, 1855.

18. PITMAN, SIR JAMES, *The Ehrhardt Augmented (40 sound-42 character) lower-case Roman Alphabet*. The reasons and intentions underlying its design together with a specimen. Twenty-three page printed pamphlet. London: Pitman House, 1959.

19. PITMAN, SIR JAMES, "Learning to Read," *Journal of the Royal Society of Arts*, February 1961.

20. PITMAN, SIR JAMES, "Learning to Read. A Suggested Experiment," *The Times Educational Supplement,* May 29, 1959.

21. PITMAN, SIR JAMES, "Spelling With The Augmented Roman Alphabet." Ten-page mimeographed pamphlet circulated by Mr. Downing at teacher training meetings.

22. PITMAN, SIR JAMES, "The Future of the Teaching of Reading," *Keeping Abreast of the Revolution in Education,* edited by Arthur E. Trax-

ler. Report of the 28th Educational Conference, American Council on Education, 1964.

23. SPACHE, GEORGE D., "Interesting Books for the Reading Teacher," *The Reading Teacher,* April 1964.

24. WARD, EDWARD R., *The Rational Method of Reading,* First Reader. Silver, Burdett & Co., Boston, 1894.

25. No author, *McGuffey's Eclectic Primer,* Revised Edition, copyright 1909, Henry H. Vail, American Book Company, New York.

Individual Reading—An Evaluation

Harry W. Sartain

We all have doubts about the perfection of reading methods, but there is not the slightest doubt about the need for differentiating reading instruction to fit a wide range of pupil abilities.

NEED FOR DIFFERENTIATED TEACHING

We know that when children enter the first grade they range in chronological age from about 5½ years old to about 6½ years old. There is usually is a spread of 12 months from the youngest to the oldest. However, the Stanford-Binet intelligence test norms show us that the spread in mental age is four times as great as the spread in chronological age. In any first grade class in a normal population there are children who are mentally only four years old along with others who are mentally five, six, seven, and eight. Because the most able children grow in mental ability at a faster rate than the average children, while the slower ones grow at a slower rate, this spread in inherited mental ability increases as the children move through school. By the time they reach the sixth grade the mental age range is something like seven or eight years instead of the four years that we had in first grade. This

Reprinted by permission of the University of Pittsburgh Press.

means that some sixth grade children have the mental ages of average third-graders while others have the mental ages of fourth, fifth, sixth, seventh, eighth, ninth, and tenth grade children.

Some school systems feel that they can reduce the range in academic aptitude appreciably by assigning so-called homogeneous groups to a classroom. However, these schools fail to take into account the fact that when you group children on the basis of any one average test score, you overlook the great range in ability in many specific traits that are combined in the average score.

Closer observation of testing will show that within the so-called homogeneous group there are individuals who are as weak on word analysis as any in the fastest group. In each "homogeneous" class there are individuals who are as weak in adopting speed to purpose and materials as the lowest in the slowest group and others who are as strong in this trait as the best in the fastest group. The more individual traits we look at, the more we see that there is no such thing as a truly homogeneous group. One of the more recent studies that illustrates this fact was published by Balow in the *Elementary School Journal* in October 1962 (*1*).

Time and time again studies have shown that when we attempt to adjust instruction to the capabilities of individuals, progress is significantly greater than when we teach all of the children in a class the same thing at the same rate. One of the frequently quoted studies on this topic was reported by Jones in 1948 in the *Journal of Educational Psychology* (*2*). Innumerable other studies support this finding. It is evident that reading instruction must be adopted to fit varied pupil needs and capabilities.

MISUSES OF BASAL PROGRAMS

Individualized reading has received increasing attention as a reaction to the misuse of basic programs. These misuses have resulted in poorly differentiated teaching and in the development of unfavorable attitudes toward reading (*3*). Some of these malpractices in using basic programs are:

1. *Assigning all children in the class to read the same stories at the same rate.* When we are aware of the extent of individual differences we know how ridiculous this is. Unfortunately this practice is most common at the upper grade levels where the range of individual abilities is greatest.

2. *Limiting the reading program to one series of textbooks.* This occurs in sipte of the fact that the teacher's manual of every good basal series tells us that the children learn development skills through the basic materials but that they must practice these skills in many, many other books.

3. *Requiring whole groups to follow in their books while individuals read aloud.* Oral reading should be related to listening, not to following visually in books. The practice of having children follow in books makes them bored with reading and develops unfavorable attitudes.

4. *Failing to utilize the skills program of the teacher's manual in a flexible manner to meet differing needs of pupils.* Every child does not need the same number of skills lessons.

5. *Employing practices which cause children to feel a stigma resulting from placement in inflexible reading groups.*

All of these procedures have been condemned by most reading authorities, but they are continued in situations where the teacher is uninformed or is not willing to put forth the amount of energy necessary to get to know the needs of individual children and undertake programs of instruction that provide for these needs.

VALUES IN INDIVIDUALIZED READING

Proponents of completely individualized reading have made extensive claims about the values of this approach to instruction. Among these purported values are the following:

1. Children read more books.
2. Each child's interests are given consideration.
3. The teacher learns each child's needs and provides skills programs exactly fitted to meet those needs.
4. The plan works equally well with large or small classes.
5. The plans works equally well with the slow or able student.
6. Children and parents like this arrangement.

Dozens of experimental findings are quoted in support of these claims. Unfortunately, only a few of the experiments with individualized reading have been scientifically designed, and these are seldom quoted by the people who are enthusiastic about individualized reading.

DANGERS IN INDIVIDUALIZED READING

Some teachers who have experimented with individualized reading, and have been reluctant to adopt it as the sole method, have listed certain dangers that they observe in this approach (4).

1. There is no opportunity to teach new vocabulary and concepts that are needed before reading. Those people who say that there is no need for vocabulary control in reading instruction must never have worked with children who are average and slow learners. Also they must never have studied a foreign language, for they would find how quickly one becomes swamped if he cannot keep up with the new vocabulary load.

2. In the few minutes per week that one has to work with each individual pupil, it is practically impossible to provide a really systematic and complete program of skills. When one looks at the lists of skills that are taught in some individualized programs, one is shocked by how limited and inadequate they are. In many cases an individual teacher seems to emphasize word analysis skills to the near exclusion of comprehension and work study skills (5, 6).

3. It is exceedingly difficult to identify the individual difficulties that children have during the infrequent short conferences.

4. There is some doubt about the permanence of skills that are taught so briefly and are not systematically reviewed.

5. There is less opportunity for group interaction to develop critical thinking and literary appreciation than there is when instruction is provided in groups.

6. The slow learning pupils and others who do not work well independently become restless and waste a great deal of time. It seems that those youngsters who especially need a great deal of instruction suffer from lack of the teacher's frequent attention.

7. The method is inefficient because of the time required to teach skills to individuals instead of teaching several groups of children who are progressing at similar rates. It is the same as having thirty reading groups, when it might be possible to provide basic instruction in four to six groups with additional corrective teaching in flexible groups on various days.

8. The conscientious teacher becomes very frustrated in attempting to provide individual conferences for all of the pupils who need them each day, while the careless teacher is left without adequate direction (7).

RESEARCH FINDINGS

More than three-fourths of the experimentation and research done with individualized reading is so poorly designed that it is of no help in making decisions about values and weaknesses of individualized programs (8). Some of the common errors in these studies are the following:

1. *Providing no comparison group as a control.* The fact that a person achieves some degree of success with one method does not prove that he would *not* do equally well with another method if he used the same materials, the same group of children, and the same amount of teaching effort.

2. *Failure to make the control situation exactly equivalent to the experimental situation when controls are used.* If the children in the control group do not have ready access to the same number of books, for example, as the children in the experimental group, it is not going to be possible for them to read as extensively or progress as rapidly. Other discrepancies are such things as providing more time for in-

struction with the individualized program than with the control program or providing additional assistance from student teachers with one program and not the other.

3. *The use of interested volunteers to teach one program while run-of-the-faculty-lounge teachers work with the other program.* All studies in education show that some teachers get better results than others. In a study where half-interested, average teachers employ one method and the other method is demonstrated by eager, enthusiastic teachers who are interested in individual children, there will be no doubt about the outcomes. The fact that one group demonstrates superior performance will be due largely to differences in teacher capability and performance rather than to differences in method.

4. *Comparing the experimental program with the weakest variety of standard practice rather than with the best model in standard use.* An example is the failure to provide any differentiation in the instruction of the control group. This is a way of stacking the deck in experimentation. When every child in the control group is given the same book, the experimenter can be certain in advance that the group will perform more poorly than a group where children are given books at their own differing levels of reading ability. When the experimenter claims that he compared an individualized approach with the "traditional" approach, the reader assumes that the traditional approach included both the use of basic materials and some effort to differentiate instruction through grouping within the classroom as competent teachers do. The results, when there is no attempt to differentiate teaching through grouping in the classroom, merely show a difference between differentiation

and lack of differentiation in instruction, rather than between individualized reading and a correct use of a basal program. (As an example see Reference 9.) When we claim that we are comparing basal instruction with individualized instruction it is professionally dishonest to provide an extremely poor-quality program for the control group instead of providing the quality of basal instruction that is recommended by the people who prepare the basal materials.

OBJECTIVE RESEARCH FINDINGS

A couple of years ago the more objective experiments with individualized reading were analyzed for their implications (10). Reports of studies since have not changed the conclusions that were offered then. In evaluating individualized reading one can be reasonably sure that the following statements are true:

1. The individualized reading approach can be somewhat successful under certain conditions.
2. The successful teaching of individualized reading requires especially competent teachers.
3. The less capable pupils are likely to be less successful in individualized reading programs than in programs that are more directed. (Of course, this will not be true if the comparison program makes no provision whatever for mental differences and attempts to require the same work of the slow child as the average.
4. Children read more books under the plan of self-selection with individualized instruction than they do in basal programs.
5. The personal conference between the pupil and the teacher is of special value.

6. Individualized reading does not allow adequate time for the setting of thought-provoking purposes for reading and for the introduction of new vocabulary.
7. The lack of a planned sequential skills program makes teachers uneasy about a wholly individualized organization.
8. Teachers using the wholly individualized approach are constantly pressed for time to provide conferences that pupils need.

In view of these findings, it seems wise to hesitate before we jettison every worthwhile feature of basic reading (11). At the same time, we need to recognize that basal reading programs are going to be entirely inadequate to meet the needs of individual pupils in our classes unless many adaptations are made.

A sensible approach is to combine strengths of excellent basic programs with strengths of individualized reading (12). This means that in our classrooms we should have many, many books at many, many levels in addition to the basic readers. Our children should be grouped for some standard basic instruction, but they should be stimulated to read innumerable other books independently in every spare moment. They should share their independent reading experiences individually with the teacher and with other children in personal conferences. Although the basal reading grouping might remain fairly constant during the year, there should be times every week when the children who have special interests or difficulties are brought together in temporary groups to receive the attention necessary for their continued stimulation. In this way the teacher will provide for the divergent needs of individual children without having to face the impossible task of tutoring each child separately.

REFERENCES

1. BALOW, IRVING H., "Does Homogeneous Grouping Give Homogeneous Groups?" *Elementary School Journal*, Vol. 63 (1962), pp. 28–32.
2. JONES, DAISY M., "An Experiment in Adaptation to Individual Differences," *Journal of Educational Psychology*, Vol. 39 (1948), pp. 257–72.
3. SARTAIN, HARRY W., "The Place of Individualized Reading in a Well-Planned Program," Ginn and Company Contibutions in Reading No. 28.
4. SARTAIN, HARRY W., "The Roseville Experiment with Individualized Reading," *Reading Teacher*, Vol. 13 (1960), pp. 277–81.
5. HUNT, LYMAN C., JR., "Individualized Reading: Teaching Skills," *Education*, Vol. 81 (1961), pp. 541–46.
6. MIEL, ALICE (Editor), *Individualiz-ing Reading Practices* (N.Y.: Bureau of Publication, Teachers College, Columbia University, 1958), Chapters 2, 3, and 4.
7. SARTAIN, HARRY W., *op. cit.*
8. SARTAIN, HARRY W., "Research on Individualized Reading," *Education*, Vol. 81 (1961), pp. 512–20.
9. WALKER, FREDERIC R., "Evaluation of Three Methods of Teaching Reading," *Journal of Educational Research*, Vol. 54 (1961), pp. 356–58.
10. SARTAIN, HARRY W., *op. cit.*
11. LOFTHOUSE, YVONNE M., "Individualized Reading," *Reading Teacher*, Vol. 16 (1962), pp. 35–37.
12. SARTAIN, HARRY W., *op. cit.*
13. ARONOW, MIRIAM S., "A Study to the Effect of Individualized Reading on Children's Reading Test Scores," *Reading Teacher*, Vol. 15 (1961), pp. 86–91.
14. GROFF, PATRICK, "Comparison of Individualized and Ability-Grouping Approaches to Reading Achievement," *Elementary English*, Vol. 40 (1963), pp. 258–76.

5

Enhancing Oral and Written Language Growth

This chapter examines how children develop oral and written language skills, how these skills are related, and how they are enhanced and nurtured in the elementary school.

What are the significant phases of children's language development? A review of research relating to the acquisition and development of language is pertinent. The phenomenon of rapid acquisition of language development in children has attracted the attention of child psychologists and linguists for the past four decades. Dora Smith provides a thorough overview of the research into the significant phases of a child's language development, from the cooing and babbling infant stage through language comprehension, ability to distinguish phonemes, vocabulary development and syntactical growth, to the development of abstract meanings and the use of figurative language. Understanding the acquisition and development of such major aspects of language in children will help the teacher to guide the child's progress with meaningful, realistic instruction.

What is the relationship between oral and written language development? Robert Ruddell stresses the importance of oral language and the interrelationship between oral and written language development. Ruddell states: "Understanding the contribution of oral language to the development of other basic communication skills is vital to the classroom teacher. Such an understanding should enable the teacher to better utilize the transfer potential present in the interrelatedness of all communication skills." Ruddell focuses on research dealing with these interrelationships and concludes: "The expressive skills of speaking and writing appear to parallel closely each other in developmental growth. With older children, however, some variance is noted in the types of subordination and the degree of organization utilized in oral and written composition."[1] The child's ability to express himself through written communication appears directly related to his maturity in the speaking and listening phases of language development. Ruddell's suggestions should prove helpful in teaching communication skill.

What are some oral language errors common to all children? Is direct instruc-

[1] Robert B. Ruddell, "Oral Language and the Development of Other Language Skills," *Elementary English* 43 (May 1966): 489–98.

tion necessary to help children speak with clarity and expression? Walter Loban, in his classic ten-year longitudinal study comparing the language of children from different social backgrounds found that the major problems in oral English relate to clarity of expression rather than habit or usage. In subjects speaking standard English Loban identified five categories of difficulties: inconsistency in the use of tense, careless omission of words (excluding omission of auxiliaries), lack of syntactic clarity, confusing use of pronouns, and trouble with agreement of subject and verb when using *there is, there are, there was,* and *there were.* He recommended that children with these difficulties be given language instruction which increases their coherence and effectiveness in speaking rather than drill or help in usage. Loban found a more complicated pattern of difficulties for children speaking a social class dialect. Their difficulties indicate that both usage and coherence are involved in their oral language problems. These children expend much of their energy in dealing with the standard use of the verb "to be": omission as a linking verb, omission as an auxiliary with other verbs, agreement with subject and unusual uses of the verb. Loban recommended that these children be given oral drill in usage rather than workbook drills. (See chapter 3 for additional discussion on the language of children speaking a dialect that varies from standard English.) To give all children help on coherence Loban favored more group, panel, or informal discussions so that children have an opportunity to express their thoughts and feelings.[2]

Jayne DeLawter and Maurice Eash characterize present oral language instruction as the "improvement by accident" approach. They propose that the language arts curriculum include formal, systematic oral language instruction just as in reading and writing. In such a highly structured oral language program the teacher would first identify the basic problems in oral language. DeLawter and Eash list seven basic problems in oral communication: failure to focus, poor organization of ideas, failure to clarify questions, lack of supporting ideas, inadequate descriptions, lack of subordination, and stereotyped vocabulary. At all levels of the elementary school, instruction to correct these problems would involve small-group instruction with the use of experience charts and devices such as the tape recorder which lets children hear themselves.

What methods and measures for diagnosing and measuring abilities in oral expression are available to the teacher? Assessing oral language activity, both teaching and learning, is a complex problem. However, O. W. Kopp provides the teacher with useful methods and measures for diagnosing and measuring abilities in oral expression. Kopp discusses standardized tests, both formal and informal measures and their appropriate uses. He believes that children, even in the primary grades, should be encouraged to help formulate standards for listening and speaking and should evaluate their performances on self-evaluation checklists, simple rating scales, and tape recordings.

The articles discussed thus far present review research relating to the acquisition and development of oral language. This research reveals that normal children master the sound system and the basic grammar of their language before they enter school at age five or six. Other articles in the chapter identify problems in oral language and offer suggestions or methods for correcting these problems

[2] Walter D. Loban, *Problems in Oral English,* Research Report No. 5 (Urbana, Ill.: National Council of Teachers of English, 1966).

and for furthering the development of this important language skill in the classroom.

When does written expression begin in the elementary school? Long before the child has acquired competence in reading, handwriting, and spelling, the teacher can help him to understand that he can express his ideas or thoughts through written language. Whenever the kindergarten or first grade teacher records or transcribes a caption for a painting, a verbal description of an object, or a narration of a field trip or other personal experience, she helps the child understand the importance of writing.[3] As she initiates creative writing, the teacher must extend the child's background and knowledge and encourage him to express and dictate his ideas to her. As the child feels the need to express himself in writing, the teacher should encourage him to do so with whatever limited technical skills he has acquired. The teacher should also recognize early attempts at creative and functional writing and should praise the child on his efforts without evaluating the technical skills involved in handwriting, spelling, sentence structure, or punctuation. On the contrary, the teacher may initially encourage the child to spell phonetically, working toward his independence. As the child acquires research skills, the teacher should encourage him to use picture dictionaries, charts, individual word lists, books and other sources. Such writing experiences should be pleasurable for the child.

What thought and language growth patterns in children's writing have been observed at different grade levels? Lester Golub analyzes samples of children's writing to illustrate growth patterns in language and thought problems encountered by children at different grade levels. The teacher will find the comparisons of language patterns between the grade levels most interesting. Golub suggests that the teacher deemphasize spelling and grammar problems and attend to the child's ability in using language effectively—in ordering information, conveying relationships, sequencing thoughts, shifting styles, and using metaphors. Golub also suggests that the teacher "receive" these writing abilities without criticizing the child's language, and that she provide numerous experiences as stimuli for more writing.

E. Paul Torrance, who is well known for his studies on creativity, suggests ten ways a parent might foster growth of gifted children in writing and speech. His interesting ideas, although intended for parents, can certainly be used by the classroom teacher with *all* children.

The main emphasis in these articles has been on developing written expression through creativity. However, the child must also develop the technical skill of handwriting to gain independence in written expression. Although it is easier to assess the child's written expression than his oral language skills, the teacher often has difficulty deciding whether to place emphasis on content or form, or if she is evaluating both, determining what degree of emphasis to place on each one.

What methods and measures are available to evaluate written expression? The teacher may adapt the many oral language measures Kopp discusses to evaluate skills and content in written expression.

The discussion on enhancing oral and written language growth has shown

[3] Writing is here defined as composition involving some degree of spontaneity and exercise of the imagination.

that oral language is the base for other language development: written language growth follows meaningful and effective oral language instruction, and written expression is developed early and simultaneously with oral language throughout the elementary language arts curriculum.

Developmental Language Patterns
of Children

Dora V. Smith

We in the schools face one of life's greatest challenges—to help boys and girls to lay hold on life through the development of language power, remembering that it is from the materials of experience that the child must evolve meaning and concepts by attaching them to verbal symbols.

Beginning with the birth cry, the infant gains control over volume, pitch and sound through babbling and cooing; he uses both vowels and consonants as he emits noises for their own sake. The coming of teeth paves the way for articulation as the child embarks upon a process of imitation of adult speech. Toward the end of his first year, he forms his first word, and by the age of two, he has made what one psychologist calls the greatest discovery of his life—namely, that things have names. To these he adds actions and qualities. "Dog," he says, pointing to emphasize his point, "two dogs." Perhaps a bird flies overhead. It is big and black. "What is dat?" he demands.

"A crow," his mother patiently replies—but back comes the inevitable question—"Why?" Obviously the child has begun an intensive use of language to explore his relations with people and things.

Ultimately he finds out that not all words name objects. A friend offers to bring him a present from California. What it is to be is a *secret*. He associates the word with the cricket which appeared on the hearth the night before. What the present later turns out to be is a box of mud-pie tins in the shape of animals. He picks out his storybook friends—Timothy Turtle and Old Mr. Bullfrog—and then demands emphatically, "But where's the secrick" (25)? It will take several presents from California to establish the generalization. During the second year, also, most children develop what one linguist has called "telegraphic" English—"Baby sleep." "Push car." "No, I doot!" meaning "No, I do it."

Recently, Brown and Bellugi at

Harvard studied the sentence structure used by a gifted boy and girl from highly intellectual families (5). They recorded and transcribed everything said by each child and by his or her mother in two hour interviews over a period of thirty-eight weeks. At first, a simple repetitive dialogue ensued in which the mother's sentences were structurally about a year in advance of the child's.

"I see truck," says the child.
"Did you see the truck?" asks the mother.
"There go one," says the child.
"Yes, there goes one," replies the mother (5).

The child's sentence, even with the mother's example, is a reduction of hers. He seems unable to reproduce the whole statement. "Fraser will be unhappy," says the mother. "Fraser unhappy," repeats the child. The mother's speech is always an imitation with expansion of the child's words. Later the youngster's effort to reproduce a negative results in, "No, I see a truck," to which the mother replies, "No, you didn't see a truck" (5).

At one point, when the recorders were unable to tell whether Adam understood the semantic difference between putting a noun in subject or object position, they set him two tasks: "Show us the duck pushing the boat," and "Show us the boat pushing the duck" (5). He did both without any difficulty. Later the child appeared to understand and to construct sentences he had never heard before, modelling them apparently from a latent pattern evolved from previous experience. It is clear from this example that the child's early linguistic environment is crucial.

At this stage, also, experiments in the Bank Street Nursery School re-corded the children's efforts to express cause, purpose, result, and condition in such sentences as "What for Lois crying?" or one of them takes off her coat, saying, "Janet's too warm a coat" (22).

A significant improvement in recent studies of the language of children lies in their emphasis upon positive elements of growth rather than upon so-called "errors" in English usage. The trend is due partly to the methods of study used in structural linguistics or transformational or generative grammar. Paula Menyuk at the Massachusetts Institute of Technology reports an analysis of the speech of nursery school and first grade children according to the techniques of Chomsky's transformational grammar (21). The study involved forty-eight children from a private nursery school and the same number from a first grade room. All of them came from upper class families and had IQ's of 120 or above. Selection made possible the discovery of the heights children can reach in imitation of adult speech.

Two hours of speech from a single day were recorded for all the children in addition to the language they used in response to projected pictures, individual responses in a personal interview between the experimenter and each child, and conversations within the group during role playing in a family setting. All responses were analyzed by Chomsky's techniques of transformational grammar into (1) simple, active, declarative sentences, and (2) the transformations derived from each. The recorder separated what she called "children's grammar" from adult constructions; for example:

He'll might get in jail.
I see a dog what's white.
Him's stomach hurt.

He growed.
He liketed it (21).

The nursery school children used all the basic structures employed by adults. The most common difficulties were in substituting *ed* for irregular forms of the past tense. The mean number of sentences said by the nursery school children was 82.9, and by the first grade 95.7.

Evidences of growing maturity in the first grade were complete mastery of the passive voice and partial use of *if* and *so* clauses, use of the auxiliary, *have,* of a series like S*he does the shopping and cooking and baking,* and of a participial complement such as *I like singing.* There was no difference in performance between boys and girls. Mean sentences length and total number of sentences increased with age. However, greater length was sometimes achieved by joining a series of remarks together by "and," for example, "I have a big, big teddy bear and I have a little doggie and he's named Blacky-Whitey and there's this big dog and he's named Peppermint" (21).

Dr. Menyuk summarizes her findings with this significant comment:

Most of the structures are used at an early age and used consistently. If we look at the nature of the structures which are used by all the children (for example, negation, contraction, auxiliary *be* and the like) it would seem that the theory of Piaget and others, which states that language is an expression of children's needs and is far from a purely imitative function even at a very early age, is a valid one. A need for social instrumentation and a method of categorizing the environment would motivate the usage of these structures (21).

Dr. Mildred Templin points out in her study of children three to eight that all grammatical constructions used by adults appear at least in rudimentary form in the speech of eight-year-olds, and their articulation is practically mature (27). Children from lower socio-economic levels were retarded one year. Boys matured in expression a year later than girls, a situation which has appeared less frequently in recent studies.

Ability to discriminate among sounds improves somewhat after eight while vocabulary increases to adulthood and probably throughout life in a scientifically oriented world. For most children, future growth in language, Dr. Templin notes, will be in the perfection of forms already used rather than in the introduction of new types of linguistic expression.

Comparison of her results of 1957 with those of Dr. Davis collected in 1932 is encouraging to teachers today (7). Six-year-olds today use sentences longer than those of nine-and-one-half-year-olds twenty-five years ago. Use of compound-complex and elaborated sentences increased substantially from year to year, children in 1957 using twice as many as children in 1932 (27). Deviations from standard English decreased over the years from 52 per cent at age three to 26 per cent at age six and to 23.9 per cent at age eight. There was, however, a startling increase in the use of slang and colloquialisms of fifty per cent among children from three to six and a similar increase from ages six to eight (27). Dr. Templin attributed the significant improvement over a period of twenty-five years to the increased linguistic stimulation from motion picture, radio, and television and to the greater permissiveness in the relationships of children and adults. Presumably the slang came from the same sources (27).

Dr. Walter Loban of the University

of California has in progress a fascinating study of the language of the same children from their entrance into kindergarten through their graduation from high school. Results are available for the first six years (19).

The pupils were asked in an interview to tell what they saw in a carefully selected group of pictures and what they thought about them. The responses were recorded and the language analyzed by a scheme set up by a board of linguists.

One of the major problems in any such analysis is the presence in the speech of children and young people of certain "tangles" of language. They are hesitations, false starts, and meaningless repetitions which interrupt the sentence patterns. These "tangles" were removed and studied separately from the remaining sentences. During kindergarten and the first three grades, the total group and the high subgroup showed a steady decrease in the number of mazes (35 per cent) and the number of words per maze (50 per cent) (19). The low group, on the other hand, increased both the number of mazes and the average number of words per maze during the same four year period. Throughout the study, the low group, writes Dr. Loban, "says less, has more difficulty saying it, and has less vocabulary with which to say it" (19).

The high group was distinguished from the kindergarten up by the ability to express tentative thinking as revealed by such words as *perhaps, maybe,* and *I'm not exactly sure.* The gifted sensed alternatives; the weak made flat, dogmatic statements (19). Although the pictures invited generalizations and figurative language, little of either was used by any of the children (19).

"Language," Dr. Loban points out, "is more than uttering whatever perceptions or thoughts rise by chance to the surface of expression. The content requires organization" (19). Use of the dependent clause helps to subordinate ideas, but use of dependent clauses is not in itself a sufficient index of subordination. Grammatical complexity is revealed also by use of modifiers or verbals or the clause within a clause. This latter fact is one of the chief contributions of Dr. Loban's study. Meta Bear (1), Lou LaBrant (18), Ellen Frogner (9) and others long ago found progressive use of subordinate clauses to be one measure of growing maturity in children's writing. Dr. Loban points out, however, that compression of ideas into more succinct form may represent a higher level of thinking than use of the clause. For example, one child may write, "Mary was in such a hurry that she fell over the chair," while another uses the more compact form: "In her hurry, Mary fell over the chair." One may say, "When he had finished his breakfast, Tom set off for school," while another compresses the clause into a participial phrase: "Having finished his breakfast, Tom set off for school" (19). One significant measure of growing maturity in language is ability to find more and more succinct means of expressing relationships between ideas.

Similar studies were made of the children's ability to use and to vary the basic structural patterns of English, and the dexterity each showed in varying elements such as movables within the patterns. Use of nouns amplified by modifiers, compound nouns, clauses, and infinitives was characteristic of the high as contrasted with the low groups.

Dr. Ruth Strickland used the same analytical scheme for her study of the oral language of children from sixteen public schools in Bloomington, Indiana (26). Her purpose was to contrast the intricacy of children's patterns of speech with the simplicity of sentence structure in reading textbooks commonly used in Grades 1 through 6. The latter proved to be extremely simple in contrast to forms used by the children in their own speech. Whether they should be or not seems to be a question still in the realm of dispute.

At the University Schools of Florida State University in Tallahassee Dr. Kellogg Hunt compared the maturity in sentence building of nine boys and nine girls in each of three grades, IV, VIII, and XII (13). Their IQ's ranged between 90 and 110. After trying sentence length, clause length, and frequency of subordinate clauses, he found the best index of maturity was the so-called single clause T unit, that is, a unit which is in itself a sentence. These he isolated by ignoring punctuation (of which the fourth graders had too little) and coordinating conjunctions between main clauses (of which the fourth graders had too many), and then cutting up the material into short grammatical sentences with a capital at one end, and a period or question mark at the other, with no fragment left over (13). As in Dr. Loban's study Dr. Hunt found it necessary to eliminate "mazes," which he called "garbles."

Doubtless, if one did this to the compositions of fourth graders, his respect for their achievement in language would greatly increase. Perhaps, too, if he showed the results to the children, it would increase their own respect for themselves. These "ands" Dr. Hunt thinks children use chiefly as a stopping place during which they can decide what they want to say next. Results showed that successively older boys and girls used more and more subordinate clauses and many more non-clause modifiers than the younger pupils did (13).

Dr. Hunt found fourth grade pupils employing noun clauses chiefly to indicate what people said and did, whereas older students tended to talk of what they thought or asked or believed—an interesting element in growth toward maturity (13). In all these sentences, the majority of noun clauses are direct objects. Use of noun clauses in any other position is a mark of maturity. Fourth graders used it fifteen times in such positions; twelfth graders, sixty-three times. This factor may also be related to reading difficulty.

Although practically all structures appear somewhere in the writing of fourth grade children, younger pupils tend to write as sentences what older children reduce to phrases and single words; for example, "The fireplace gave the most light in the room, but away from it they had to use the candle," as contrasted with "Aside from the fireplace, the candle was the chief source of light." This is what Hunt calls "greater density of grammatical structures" by means of which the older student "can incorporate a larger body of thought into a single intricately related organization" (13). In the work of the older students non-clauses such as infinitive or participial phrases, appositives, and the like are found in larger proportions than clauses.

Study of the growth of pre-school and elementary school children in language brings dramatically to the fore factors which are pertinent to improvement at any level of instruction. They include: (1) a social setting which stimulates constant practice in the use of language; (2) an environment rich in the things, the experiences, and the ideas for which words stand; and (3) adult example and assistance in the clearly motivated maturing of language skills. If there were time, it would be valuable to examine in the light of these criteria the setting in which language is supposed to grow in our own class-rooms.

A most telling study of this problem was carried on by Dr. Luria in Russia (20) with twins, who, finding their own phonetic grunts and gesticula-tions sufficient for their life together, hardly spoke at all with others up to the age of two, and at four barely differentiated sounds in reply to ques-tions. Sounds, separate words, direct actions, and lively gesticulations were enough for their purposes. Present ob-jects they could name, but absent ones confused them. When they entered the same kindergarten, they had no under-standing of narrative speech and re-fused to listen to storytelling, which they could not follow.

Finally, they were placed in separate kindergartens where association with others was imperative. "The new ob-jective situation," says the author, "gave rise to a need for verbal speech and became the most significant factor in its development" (20). Communica-tion through speech also led to signifi-cant improvement in the organization of their mental processes. Imaginative play, Dr. Luria believed, was a funda-mental element in lifting the children to greater heights both in thought and in language. The new situation in which speech was interlocked with ac-tion in company with other children developed first narrative and then plan-ning speech. Findings from studies such as these may have some bearing upon the question of whether reading should be taught in the kindergarten.

The influence of the home on the children's language is fundamentally important. A child of four, one in-vestigator found, is probably silent some nineteen minutes of his waking day (4). Such oral practice works won-ders, with the aid of an intelligent mother. Milner, studying the relation-ship between reading readiness and patterns of parent–child relationships, found that children who engage in two-way conversation at mealtime with parents who encourage them to talk can be distinguished from others in a reading readiness program (23). Helen Dawe, experimenting with orphanage children, who have little contact with adults, gave one group of institution-alized children of nursery-school age approximately fifty hours of (1) look-ing at and discussing pictures, (2) listening to poems and stories, (3) going on short excursions, and (4) training in understanding words and concepts (8). These children made significantly greater gains than a con-trol group in the same institution.

Enriching the child's environment, encouraging conversation about it and pushing through to adequate expres-sion of the experience in words are major elements in the growth of lan-guage. Dr. Watts, in England, also found storytelling and reading aloud to children useful for the development of language in pre-school years (28). Forty nursery rhymes, he maintains, in-troduce four hundred new words.

Together with intelligence, socio-economic status seems to be the most influential factor in the child's develop-ment of language. This problem is one of particular moment at a time when the education of the underprivileged is in the forefront of attention. Con-tact with others and an enriched en-vironment where association with the things words stand for is made possible may be the most important elements in the education of these children and young people.

Even in the kindergarten Mahmaud Khater found that upper class children talked more about themselves and their possessions while lower class youngsters talked of the outside world of people, of the immediate present, or what they would do in the future (*17*). Upper class youngsters listened to each other and commented freely and spontaneously; whereas lower class children remained silent until they were drawn out. Upper class children could discuss procedures, sticking to the subject, and contributing to the problem; whereas lower socio-economic groups tended to drop the problem and engage in narratives of personal experience. Such children often rely on gestures or on "you know what I mean" instead of coming to grips with the expression of an idea.

Bernstein in England has been much interested in this problem because differences due to socio-economic status are often progressively reinforced through the years (*3*). In the lower levels of society, he believes, the command "Shut up!" not only conditions the child's relations with his parents, but cuts off any intellectual approach to the problem; whereas in an upper class home in England, the mother's "I'd rather you'd make less noise, my dear" is less damaging to the ego of the individual and leaves room for decision on his part (*3*). Different kinds of mental functions result from such treatment.

Berg (*2*) and Havighurst (*11*) discuss this problem at length in the 1964 proceedings of the University of Chicago Reading Conference, indicating the effect of stultifying experience on language and reading at a time when one child in three in the public schools of our country's fourteen largest cities is culturally deprived.

All the evidence points to the need of psychological understanding on the part of those who presume to plan for improving the language of the underprivileged.

Martin Joos of the University of Wisconsin has penned a tirade against the grammar of correctness and the effect of it in causing school drop-outs. "Teachers must simply abandon the theory that usages differ in quality as between good and bad, correct and incorrect, and instead build their methods and reconstruct their emotional reactions on the plain facts that are already known in part to their pupils . . . that usages can be learned without condemning those which they replace, that the learner has an indefensible right to speak as he likes without school penalties, while the teacher has no rights in this respect, but only to demonstrate what usages are profitable in the adult world" (*16*).

The United States Office of Education recently called a conference on improving English skills on culturally different youth. The first seventy pages of its report set forth the need of understanding the nature, the values, and the attitudes of the culturally different, whose social backgrounds are frequently more of a detriment than their intelligence (*15*). Allison Davis of Chicago has a particularly telling article in the bulletin, emphasizing the differences in thinking to be expected of pupils from different walks of life and the danger of attempting to fit all young people into a particular academic mold (*15*).

In 1963 Frank G. Jennings wrote in the *Saturday Review of Literature* a fascinating account of Dillard University's pre-freshman program for those Negro students who wish to offset a dearth of language, little access to books and inadequate opportunity to think about and discuss current affairs with six weeks of intensive work before entering college in the fall (*14*). Requirements of the program are that the students read two hours a day from books in the library and talk over with a teacher what they have read, and that each evening they join with the group in listening to selected television broadcasts on contemporary affairs, discussing together later under the direction of a teacher what they have heard. In addition, each student may take another course of his own choosing. The program is interesting because it uses the techniques which research and common sense suggest are important for the development of language power and thinking.

Another problem in current language teaching stems from the fact that the linguist has been particularly concerned with the development of accepted forms of *structure* in the use of language, but tends to ignore the *power of words* in the expression of meaning. Does it make any difference whether a child says, "I wish you could see my nice little dog with legs four inches long," or whether he writes, "I wish you could see my beady-eyed black Scottie with the sad bewhiskered look"? The structure of these two sentences is identical, but what a world of difference there is between them as communication! Again, whereas a mature speaker says, "His ultimate destination was uncertain," an immature one remarks, "He did not know which place he would have to go to in the end" (28). The mature sentence is one of the simplest which could be found. The difference lies in the individual's command of words and of thinking.

As teachers we are deeply concerned with the development of vocabulary— not alone with how many words children know but with how well they understand those with which they are familiar, and what skills they need to increase the number, the breadth and the depth of concepts with which they have a sketchy acquaintance. Children become much interested in words from the days of Mother Goose and " 'Twas the Night before Christmas." They are captured by much more than the story of the annual visit of Santa because of the dramatic power of the words with which his housetop ride is described. From the mere names of things little children move into the realm of words which have a hypnotizing appeal to the senses. Modern poetry for boys and girls is full of such words, and children should enjoy it and the colorful picture books with stories rhythmically told, which open to them a fascinating world of language to offset the often dull vocabulary of their early readers. Both are necessary to the well-rounded development of their use of language.

In their readers, too, primary children learn to separate the roots and endings of words, to find two words in *afternoon* and *sometimes,* and ultimately to discover prefixes that alter meaning, so that large numbers of words can be made from a single root.

The intermediate grades are crucial ones for vocabulary building because words which once had a single meaning bob up in new and strange situations. An eight-year-old boy was told by his father that a building they were passing housed a Finnish bath. Incredulously, the child replied, "Is it because it's the last one he'll ever have?" Children make a game out of words with double meanings: "What is black and white and red (read) all over?" appears in every generation. And what child has not repeated the rhyme about the peach which, on falling to the ground, became a squash? Teachers should encourage such fun and participate in it.

But the real business of grades IV through XII is to lead children to a mastery in context of the significant vocabularies of the various fields of study with which they are concerned —science, geography, history, mathematics, composition and literature. One obvious tool is the dictionary, in the use of which they should be schooled in every year from the primary grades up. Children's encyclopedias are also helpful and the many books for elementary and junior high school pupils such as *The Tree of Language* by Helene and Charlton Laird (World, 1957), *The First Book of Words* by Samuel and Beryl Epstein (Watts, 1954), and *Words from the Myths, Words from Science,* and *Words on the Map* by Isaac Asimov (Houghton, 1961; 1959; and 1962).

Important vocabulary development comes from clarification of concepts in relation to the daily mastery of each subject of study. Ernest Horn has inveighed against memorization of empty words and the complacent possession of flagrant misconceptions and vague ideas which come from lack of attention to specific meanings in the social studies (12). He found one child who interpreted the sentence, "The French Revolution corresponded in a rough way with the American Revolution" (12), to mean that they wrote insulting letters to one another.

The late David Russell gave us one of the most useful studies we have of the development of vocabulary from the fourth grade through the twelfth. He called it an analysis of the *dimensions* of children's vocabulary, that is, a study of the breadth of meaning a word may have in a wide-range sampling of meanings from science, social studies, mathematics, and sports and recreation; analysis of *depth* of meaning, that is, going beyond superficial recognition of a synonym to some measure of how much a child understands about the word; *precision* of meaning, such as ability to make fine discriminations in use of the word in different situations; and finally the ability to use it in one's own, meaning vocabulary in speaking, writing, and reading. This he calls the "availability" of the word (24).

In testing for proficiency in vocabulary in Grades IV through XII he found that both boys and girls improved their scores in different subject matter areas rather consistently from grade to grade though they often slowed down somewhat in the senior high school. To test vocabulary adequately in high school requires special tests in each subject-matter. Boys in general were somewhat above girls, especially in the areas of science, sports, hobbies, and recreation. Girls' vocabularies became specialized earlier than boys'. Depth of vocabulary proved difficult to test. In breadth of knowledge of words pupils showed more growth in grades IV through VI than they did in the junior and senior high school.

Development of concepts—that is, abstract meanings—is one of the major goals of education. No one has defined this task more concretely than Dr. John Carroll (6). "For development of a concept," he says, "the individual must have a series of experiences that are in one or more respects similar. From this constellation of similarities the concept evolves. After that a mixture of positive and negative instances insures the adequate learning of the concept. For example, take the meaning of *tourist* as contrasted with that of *immigrant.* One child describes a tourist as a 'well-dressed person who drives a station wagon with an out-of-state license.' " He has seen American tourists but no foreign immigrants. To another a tourist may be well dressed and an immigrant poorly dressed. Both could be, of course, from a foreign country, and both could be American or Mexican, but the child has seen only foreign immigrants and American tourists. Ultimately, in order to develop a correct concept the reader must sense the fact that the distinction is not one of nationality or dress but of purpose, the immigrant's seeking to change his residence and the tourist in search of pleasure with no thought of altering his address. The example shows clearly what a complex task it is to help children develop accurate and specific concepts.

Finally, what is the significance of the fact that no study except Dr. Loban's mentions figurative language (19) and he found that no child used it? Figurative language is all about us. We cannot read modern advertising without it. Little children use it constantly like the child who watched the burning ashes fly up from the fireplace and come down again from the chimney. "They go up red birds," she said, "and they come down black birds." A gifted child of six once startled the writer by not understanding the expression: "Let's not cross that bridge till we come to it." "What bridge?" he asked with a puzzled look (25). Miss Gill of California has written two illuminating articles on the difficulties of teaching current American fiction to high school seniors who do not know how to respond to figurative language (10). I am not arguing for classifying and naming figures of speech, but merely for teaching how to "figure out," as the child says, "what they say." Has the reading of literature as literature with an imaginative quality to its language been neglected in our elementary and junior high schools? If so, it seems to me there is no time like the present for repairing the damage.

Study of the linguistic development of children from infancy though high school is one of the most rewarding experiences any adult can pursue. Besides that, it will guide him more expertly to help the child progress in ways that will enrich experience for him as long as he lives.

REFERENCES

1. BEAR, META, "Children's Growth in the Use of Written Language," *Elementary English Review,* XVI (December 1939), pp. 312–19.

2. BERG, PAUL CONRAD, "The Culturally Disadvantaged Student and Reading Instruction," *Meeting Individual Differences in Reading* (Proceedings of the Annual Conference on Reading, Vol. XXVI, Supplementary Educational Monograph, No. 94). Chicago: University of Chicago, December 1964.

3. BERNSTEIN, BASIL, "Social Class and Linguistic Development: A Theory of Social Learning," *Education, Economy, and Society,* Halsey, A. H., et al. (eds.). The Free Press of Glencoe, Inc., 1961, pp. 218–315; pp. 293–94.

4. BRANDENBURG, "The Language of a Three-Year-Old Child," *Pedagogical Seminary,* XXII (March 1915), pp. 89–120.

5. BROWN, ROGER, and BELLUGI, URSULA, "Three Processes in the Child's Acquisition of Syntax," *The Harvard Educational Review,* XXIV (Spring 1964), pp. 133–51; p. 135; p. 143; p. 134.

6. CARROLL, JOHN B., "Words, Meanings and Concepts," *Harvard Educational Review,* XXXIV, No. 2 (Spring 1964), pp. 178–202; p. 194.

7. DAVIS, EDITH A., *The Development of Linguistic Skill in Twins, Singletons, Singletons with Siblings, and Only Children from Age Five to Ten Years* (University of Minnesota, Institute of Child Welfare Monograph, No. 14). Minneapolis, Minnesota: University of Minnesota Press, 1937.

8. DAWE, HELEN C., "A Study of the Effect of an Educational Program upon Language Development and Related Mental Functions in Young Children," *Journal of Experimental Education,* XI (December 1942), pp. 200–209.

9. FROGNER, ELLEN, "Problems of Sentence Structure in Pupils' Themes," *English Journal,* XXII (November 1933), pp. 742–49.

10. GILL, NAOMI, "Depth Reading," *English Journal,* XLII (September 1953), pp. 311–15; "Depth Reading II: The Figures," *English Journal,* XLIII (September 1954), pp. 297–303, 323.

11. HAVIGHURST, ROBERT, "Characteristics and Needs of Students That Affect Learning," *Meeting Individual Differences in Reading* (Proceedings of the Annual Conference on Reading, Vol. XXVI, Supplementary Educational Monograph, No. 94). Chicago: University of Chicago, December 1964.

12. HORN, ERNEST, *Methods of Instruction in the Social Studies.* New York: Charles Scribner's Sons, 1937, p. 172.

13. HUNT, KELLOGG W., *Differences in Grammatical Structures Written at Three Grade Levels.* Tallahassee, Florida: Florida State University (Cooperative Research Project 1,998), 1964, pp. 11–12; p. 110; pp. 57–59; p. 139.

14. JENNINGS, FRANK, "For Such a Tide Is Moving . . ." *The Saturday Review* (May 16, 1964).

15. JEWETT, ARNO, et al. *Improving Skills of Culturally Different Youth in Large Cities.* Washington, D.C.: U.S. Department of Health, Education, and Welfare, Office of Education Bulletin 1964, No. 5, pp. 10–21.

16. JOOS, MARTIN, "Language and the School Child," *Language and Learning, The Harvard Educational Review,* XXXIV, No. 2 (Spring 1964), p. 209.

17. KHATOR, MAHMAUD, "The Influence of Social Class on the Language of Kindergarten Children": Unpublished Ph.D. dissertation, University of Chicago, 1951.

18. LABRANT, LOU L., *A Study of Certain Language Developments in Grades IV to XII, Inclusive, Genetic Psychology Monographs,* XIV (November 1933), pp. 387–491.

19. LOBAN, WALTER D., "The Language of Elementary School Children," *A Study of the Use and Control of Language Effectiveness in Communication and the Relations Among Speaking, Reading, Writing, and Listening.* Champaign, Illinois: National Council of Teachers of English (Research Report, No. I, 1963), pp. 8–32–33; p. 43; pp. 53–54; p. 58; p. 55.

20. LURIA, A. R., and YUDAVICH, F., *Speech and the Development of Mental Processes in the Child.* London: Staples Press, 1959, p. 122.

21. MENYUK, PAULA, "Syntactic Structures in the Language of Children," *Child Development* (Society for Research in Child Development, XXXIV), 1963, pp. 407–22; pp. 411–12; p. 418.

22. MERRY, FRIEDA K. and RALPH V.,

The First Two Decades of Life. New York: Harper, 1950, p. 17.

23. MILNER, ESTHER, "A Study of the Relationship Between Reading Readiness in Grade One School Children and Pattern of Parent-Child Interaction," *Child Development*, XXII (June 1951), pp. 95–112.

24. RUSSELL, DAVID, *The Dimensions of Children's Meaning Vocabularies in Grades IV Through XII*. Berkeley, California: University of California Publications in Education, Vol. XI, No. 5, pp. 315–414.

25. SMITH, DORA V., "Growth in Language Power As Related to Child Development," *Dora V. Smith: Selected Essays*. New York: The Macmillan Company, 1964, pp. 15–83.

26. STRICKLAND, RUTH, *The Language of Elementary School Children: Its Relationship to the Language of Reading Textbooks and the Quality of Reading of Selected Children*. Bloomington, Indiana: Bulletin of the School of Education, Indiana University, Vol. XXXVIII, No. 4, July 1962.

27. TEMPLIN, MILDRED C., *Certain Language Skills in Children; Their Development and Interrelationships*. Minneapolis, Minnesota: The University of Minnesota Press, 1957, pp. 83–93; pp. 99–100; p. 151.

28. WATTS, A. F., *The Language and Mental Development of Children*. London: George C. Harrap and Company, Ltd., 1964, p. 40; p. 31.

Focus on Oral Communication

Jayne Anne DeLawter and Maurice J. Eash

In the literature and in practice the improvement of oral language has received little attention in the full scope of the language arts program. Reading, seen by many as the key to academic success, is emphasized heavily in each grade of school. Spelling also has a period set aside specifically for its study, and handwriting usually is given particular attention through a period of formal instruction. Creative writing, though not a major part of the curriculum, nevertheless, is often found in extensive units throughout the ele-

"Focus on Oral Communication," by Jayne Anne DeLawter and Maurice J. Eash (*Elementary English*, December 1966). Copyright © 1966 by the National Council of Teachers of English. Reprinted by permission of the publisher and Jayne Anne DeLawter and Maurice J. Eash.

mentary years. Comparatively then, it can be seen that development of oral communication skills has been seriously neglected in relationship to the time spent in these other areas. The tragedy of this neglect is further compounded when one considers the time spent by individuals in the areas of language arts, reading, spelling, writing, and oral communication, with the latter accounting for more of the communication process than the sum total time in other areas.

With this apparent lack of emphasis in formal oral language instruction, it is inescapable that many children's ability to handle oral communication is poorly developed. Although outwardly few children have little problem communicating with other people, an analysis of language reveals repetitions, disorganized explanations, and lack of focus in ideas; all of which are a handicap to communicator and listener alike.

The approach to oral language instruction suggested in this article is an outcome of a broader study in the area of linguistic analysis of patterns of speech.[1] In this study a sample of children's language was gathered and analyzed for the structure of the language and expressions of authoritarianism. Working with these data the authors discovered common errors in oral language which would serve as a basis for oral language instruction in the classroom. The techniques used in the study can be employed in the classroom as a teacher seeks to analyze her students' speech for specific errors or problems in oral language.

In obtaining a language sample, the authors planned a situation where children were encouraged to speak freely. A method which promotes fluency in speech is the use of unfinished stories as a stimulus for oral response. Stories such as the "Anderson Incomplete Stories."[2] present a conflict situation between adults and children which the respondent must resolve in some way. An example of one of these stories is titled "The Missing Money" story. In it, a teacher finds that fifty cents has disappeared from her desk. She doesn't know what happened to it. In the interview the child is asked, "What happened to the money?" "What does the teacher do?" "How does the teacher feel?"

This type of story is desirable for several reasons. First of all, it gives the child a definite focus for his reply. It also encourages an uninterrupted flow of speech which is more easily analyzed than scattered statements in response to general questioning. Aside from the linguistic content of the responses to these stories, much can be learned about the child's cultural background and value system from a content analysis of the responses. The authors have found these stories to be of high interest to all children and to encourage lucid expression.

In order to preserve the speech samples of the children, tape-recorded interviews are essential. Previous research finds that note-taking obtains only a selective 10 per cent to 20 per cent of free flowing responses. In contrast, a taped interview captures the full response, retains the emotional tone and spontaneity of the child, and provides a listening sample which can be reviewed when desired. Certain

[1] Jayne Anne DeLawter, *A Study of Language Patterns and Expressions of Authoritarianism in Workingclass Children,* unpublished honors thesis. Ball State Teachers University, May 1964.

[2] Harold H. Anderson and Gladys L. Anderson, "Anderson Incomplete Stories," mimeograph, Michigan State University, 1959.

precautions were observed in the interviews in order to obtain reliable samples. Interviews were done individually in a school setting familiar to the students. Initial curiosity about the tape recorder was satisfied by a brief discussion, a previous experience with the machine. In this case since the interviewer was someone other than the classroom teacher, rapport with the students was built by conversation, observation, and participation in classroom procedure prior to the interview.

After the data had been collected in the interviews, the responses were typed on protocols, using a format that captured as accurately as possible the student's responses. A sample from a protocol is reproduced below.

Interviewer: What does the teacher do?

Respondent: She . . . she would just . . . she would ask 'em . . . they was doin' their arithmetic, she could just ask 'em to stop for a minute and she could say that . . . the money was gone off her desk. And if somebody had it, they could give it back to her. And nobody say nothing . . . maybe who got it would have a smile on their face or she can tell.

I. How does the teacher feel?

R. Sad . . . and mad. Because no one tell her who got it.

I. What will she do then?

R. Go around the room—look in the desks and then if nobody had it, she can say—look in their shoes. And if she still don't find it, I don't know.

I. Can you think of an ending for this story?

R. Ending of it? She feel real—very sad. She wished—she wished that she would know who'd—who were—who it was.

Linguistic studies involving elaborate analysis can be done of the prepared protocol.[3]

However, this linguistic approach does not indicate how a child can organize and handle ideas; it primarily outlines the dominant patterns in his speech.

To improve the child's language in terms of handling ideas, the teacher needs to look for basic errors in oral communication. Some of the errors which are critical to more mature speaking are:

1. Failure to focus

The ability to focus on the major point may relate to the type of stimulus given. However, the failure to focus seems to be related to immaturity of speech habits or inadequate experience in extended conversations. Failure to focus carries over into adult conversations which, when recorded, reflect tangency and indirection.[4] The ability to focus can be tested by using specific or general questions. For example, a direct question, such as "Why did the

[3] Ruth G. Strickland, "The Language of Elementary School Children: Its Relationship to the Language of Reading Textbooks and the Quality of Reading of Selected Children," *Bulletin of the School of Education,* Indiana University, 38 (July 1962).

[4] Anselm Strauss and Leonard Schatzman, "Cross-Class Interviewing: An Analysis of Interaction and Communitive Styles," *Human Organization Research,* edited by R. N. Adams and J. J. Preiss. Homewood, Illinois: Dorsey Press, 1960, pp. 205–13.

children run?" elicits a different type of response than a general directive, such as "Name three reasons why the children ran."

2. Poor organization of ideas

This error relates quite closely to the failure to focus. Many children begin speaking before they think through any organization of a response or before they examine the intent of the question or questioner. This leads to unnecessary repetition and rambling in the response. This is seen in the following interview sample:

I. Tell me more about the teacher.
R. O.K. And then the teacher . . . and then he takin' up lunch money and this boy was poor and anyway he had to get his book rent paid. He had an uncle and he was a movie star and. . . .

3. Failure to clarify questions

Again this error comes from instantaneous response with no thought about what the questioner had asked. Misunderstandings often arise from hasty replies which have little relationship to the question at hand. The protocols reflect lack of questioning before responding, or any interaction which would draw the questioner out —literally no active effort to determine the intent of the questioner. Frequently the response does not seem to fit the inquiry, and the responder seems insensitive to the questioner.

I. How would that person feel?
R. She couldda said that they shouldn'ta been playing in the yard.

4. Lack of supporting ideas

This mistake is another characteristic of immature speakers. Common to this mistake is using a general blanket statement as sufficient to prove a point or to express their position. Opinion and fact are confused in presentation. Mastery of this phase of oral communication is crucial to critical thinking and can be taught quite early in the elementary grades. Getting students to question the support for a position is essential to critical thinking on any social problem. An error of this type can be seen in the following protocol illustrating the mistaken belief that relationship means friendship, where the story implied rather poor relationships between father and son.

I. How do you know John and his father are good friends?
R. Cause that's his son.
R. Cause it's his father.

5. Inadequate descriptions

The ability to visualize and describe a scene, person, or attribute takes a high degree of awareness and mental acuity. A contributor to clear and precise detail-giving is considerable past experience in reading and analysis of reading for description. However, oral language ability will not necessarily develop from reading, if attention is not directed to the function of description. Many immature speakers tend to personalize the description if they lack words to express the ideas they hold.

In a discussion of a story involving bicycles, the substitution of personalizing the response for adequate description is seen:

I. What is a skinny wheel?
R. It's a big bike—hand brake on it.

Some of 'em have hand brakes, some have foot brakes. I like hand brakes; you don't have to put your feet back.

6. Lack of subordination

The use of subordination to divide run-on units into more precise sentences is one mark of a mature speaker. Subordination is a problem with many children as they run many sentences and ideas together. This is seen in the following example:

And then they went through it again and their mother was mad. And then they go out and play football and they wouldn't go around the house no more cause the window might get broke again and they had to stay in. And then they don't want no more whippings cause it hurts.

As the response shows, this child failed to differentiate between the level of ideas. In an attempt to maintain fluency the child has used a series of conjunctions to combine unrelated ideas.

7. Stereotyped vocabulary

The vocabulary of a child seems to be quite heavily related to his environment. An abundance of first-hand experiences is a major factor in the use of a variety of words. Children rarely use words which have no personal relevance to their own lives. Therefore, if actual experiences are not adequate, and if books or other vicarious experiences are not provided, a child's vocabulary remains that of his immediate environment, and words do not carry precise connotation. The lack of definitiveness of descriptions and stereotyp-

ing in description of human behavior is evident in the following description of a teacher's actions.

She look in her desk and look in her pocketbook again and look in the kids' desk and pockets and look in her pocket and coat pockets until she finds it.

No claim is made that these categories are mutually exclusive, and the teacher should not become bogged down in attempting to maintain a tidy classification scheme. A gross lumping of errors, however, does give a starting point for working with children on oral communication.

APPROACHES TO LANGUAGE IMPROVEMENT

After the basic errors in the children's expression have been identified and studied, the teacher is then faced with the most crucial question in the improvement of the oral language of her students—how will she use the information found in the language analysis to best approach the problem of her students? Some suggestions for beginning work are given here.

1. Small group instruction is essential for oral language development. It is advantageous to both the teacher and the student. The teacher can focus specific problems in one group and concentrate on individual communication errors. Also, more important in a small group, each child can get experience in speaking and listening. He can practice new patterns with the teacher's guidance until the patterns become almost automatic. Furthermore, the student's level of sensitivity to language can be developed without the undue embarrassment often found in speaking

and being corrected in the larger class.

2. The use of devices to help the children see and/or hear their own speech patterns can be exciting and profitable. Tape recorders offer one method in this approach. The teacher and students can listen to their own conversations and analyze oral language errors. Also, with some training, students can analyze their conversations and class discussions along the lines of the analysis in this paper.

3. Another method incorporating the children's own language is the extensive use of experience charts, even in the intermediate grades, providing teachers use the children's language. This approach involves the children as they compose stories, poems, or conversational dialogues. The content of such compositions is of immediate relevance to their lives and maintains a high degree of interest. It also allows the children to analyze their own speech patterns as a part of their language arts work.

If improvement of oral communication is to be effective, the teacher must have a program that provides for an analysis of basic errors. After discovery of the basic errors, a systematic program of instruction must be provided which sensitizes children and provides opportunity to learn better systems of expression. Improvement in oral communication is not fortuitous, although present instructional patterns have leaned heavily upon the improvement by accident approach. The framework described in this article which evolved from a research study provides a systematic approach and places the teaching of oral language upon a more secure base. There is further reason to believe that improvement in performance in oral language will carry over into the other language arts areas of reading, writing and listening.

The Evaluation
of Oral Language Activity:
Teaching and Learning

O. W. Kopp

"When I go to school, I'm going to learn to read and write." This comment reflects the aspirations of most four-year-olds about to enter the magic land of school. Their concern is centered upon the two language arts known to them. After all, they already know how to speak and listen.

Also, unfortunately, too many teachers fail to recognize the need to teach

"The Evaluation of Oral Language Activity: Teaching and Learning" by O. W. Kopp, in *Research in Oral Language*. Copyright © 1967 by the National Council of Teachers of English. Reprinted by permission of the publisher and O. W. Kopp.

speaking and listening. The term "language arts" refers to a quarternary discipline, but too often in actual practice the language arts are reduced to a binary discipline.

It is understandable and logical that much concerted effort is directed toward the teaching of reading and writing. At the same time, it is incomprehensible and illogical to assume that no further improvement is needed in the skills of speaking and listening.

Just how important is oral communication? Man in all his wisdom has discovered only two ways to settle differences—by using words or by using weapons. Democratic, peaceful resolution of problems involves discussion; listening is necessarily half of this dualism. Our world is one in which oral communication is a vitally necessary tool for understanding and learning; it frequently dominates as the primary mode of communication.

In the hope that more teachers may wish to do a better job in the teaching of speaking and listening, pertinent research has been reviewed with the aim of giving direction to the teaching of oral communication. Attention must also be given to the knowledge available from research which will assist teachers in diagnosing and measuring abilities in the oral language skills and give direction to their improvement.

LISTENING

Very little disagreement about the feasibility of teaching listening exists. Duker's extensive bibliography on listening is prefaced by a statement that listening can be improved by proper teaching.[1] Shane and Mulry, after ex-amining many references on listening, also conclude that listening can be taught and evaluated.[2] Hatfield comments that advances in teaching English include the realization that ". . . listening is an art as complex as reading and is improvable through instruction and guided practice."[3] The National Council of Teachers of English has stated that listening should be taught because it is the most used of the language arts, it is often poorly done, and evidence suggests that listening habits may be improved through training.[4]

Berry urges teachers to chart their inquiry regarding listening into four major areas.[5]

She suggests:

1. A frank analysis of your own listening experience.
2. A thoughtful study of the listening situation in your classroom.
3. A development in children of concern for their own listening competence.
4. A development of the problem in relation to communication, with listening playing its essential role—not as a value in itself but as a means to the more important meeting of minds.

[2] Harold G. Shane and June Grant Mulry, *Improving Language Arts Instruction Through Research*. Washington, D.C.: Association for Supervision and Curriculum Development, 1963, pp. 102–10.

[3] Wilbur Hatfield, "Advances in the Teaching of English," *NEA Journal*, 45 (February, 1956), 90–92.

[4] National Council of Teachers of English, *Language Arts for Today's Children*. New York: Appleton-Century-Crofts, Inc., 1954, pp. 71–105.

[5] Althea Berry, "Experiences in Listening," *Elementary English*, 28 (March, 1951), 130–32.

[1] Sam Duker, *Listening Bibliography*. New York and London: The Scarecrow Press, Inc., 1964.

Other writers agree with Berry that the first step in teaching listening is for the teacher to examine his own listening habits. Nichols has devised a self-rating scale to be used in making an analysis of one's poor listening habits.[6]

Brown has stated, "The most basic and most important element for auding competence is possessing and imparting a reliable concept of what it is that the student is being asked to improve."[7] A student must first recognize his deficiencies and then set up a plan for doing something about them.

Experiences should be provided to encourage children's use of the scientific method of inquiry into listening as well as into other subject areas. The following questions are examples of the kinds of topics which could be used as springboards for pupil discussions and pupil investigations:

1. How does listening differ from hearing?
2. What are some good listening habits?
3. What are some poor listening habits?
4. How do good listeners help a speaker?
5. How does a speaker's personality affect a listener?
6. Why does the same word often mean different things to different people?
7. How can a listener guard against accepting falsehoods for the truth?
8. How do the experiences you have had in your lives affect your listening?

9. How can wide reading improve listening habits?
10. How can you learn to tell which ideas are most important and which ones are least important?

Evaluation, of necessity, must be based upon a standard. For listening this standard is the "good listener"—one who has a wide range of interests, respect for other people and their viewpoints, and the ability to delay his own reactions. The poor listener often precludes further listening by reacting instantaneously, vigorously, and without critical thought.

Stromer suggests the following as examples of poor listening habits: tuning out one's mind; thinking we already know what is going to be said; looking for mannerisms of the speaker instead of listening; doing other things while supposedly listening; and hearing words instead of ideas.[8]

To evaluate accurately a child's listening performances, the teacher needs to recognize the importance of several factors.

1. He must take into consideration factors accounting for individual differences:
   a. Intelligence and aptitude.
   b. Reading comprehension ability and vocabulary development.
   c. Cultural background.
   d. Interests.
   e. Personality traits.
2. He must consider factors relating to attention as preparation for auditory perception:
   a. Physiological sensitivity and fatigue.
   b. Psychological sensitivity and concentration.
   c. Readiness to respond.

[6] Ralph G. Nichols, "How Well Do You Listen?" *Education,* 75 (January, 1955), 302.

[7] Don P. Brown, "And Having Ears They Hear Not," *NEA Journal,* 39 (November, 1950), 587.

[8] Walter F. Stromer, "Learn How to Listen," *This Week Magazine,* 16 (February 21, 1960), 13–15.

d. Interference of distracting elements.

e. Training of the sense organs.

3. He must consider other personal factors determining what one perceives:

a. Individual needs.

b. Perceiving what one wishes to perceive.

c. Personal bias and prejudices.

An analysis of listening problems should include diagnosis of possible hearing difficulties and a consideration of total adjustment, including personality, an element which has been found to be closely related to listening ability.[9] An analysis of listening problems should also include an assessment of the vocabulary development of the child. The teacher needs an awareness of the vocabulary development of the child and an awareness of the quality and quantity of the child's listening and speaking both in and out of school.[10, 11]

In the evaluation of listening, both formal and informal tests may be used. One is not a substitute for the other. Standardized tests or teacher-made tests can be used to evaluate such skills as listening for directions, listening for word meaning, listening to draw conclusions, listening for immediate recall of details, listening to identify the main point, and listening to identify sequence.

Standardized tests have the advantage of providing for comparison with a norm; interpretation by percentile ranks and scores; known reliability, validity, and difficulty; predetermined relationships to other test instruments; and ease of administration and scoring.[12] Brown believes that appropriate test instruments must be developed for all levels if we are to reach a needed understanding of listening.[13]

Standardized listening tests for the lower elementary grades have been almost nonexistent. The *Sequential Tests for Educational Progress* (STEP) include a listening test, but this test is not appropriate below grade four. However, Wright devised and standardized a listening test for grades two through four, which has been used by others and found reliable for grades two and three but is considered too easy for most children in grade four.[14]

Informal evaluative techniques can be designed to fit specific classroom situations. Brown reported the use of informal evaluation in three of the most common listening situations—casual listening, purposeful listening, and notetaking while listening. Students were able to assess their listening efficiency as the result of tests given in each situation. Purposeful listening resulted in better comprehension than casual listening. Notetaking seemed to lower comprehension at the time, but retesting showed that notetaking delayed forgetting.[15]

Even in the early primary grades children can formulate standards for

[9] Walter F. Stromer, "Listening and Personality," *Education*, 75 (January, 1955), 322–26.

[10] Don P. Brown, "Teaching Aural English," *English Journal*, 39 (March, 1950), 128–36.

[11] Margaret B. Parke, "Children's Ways of Talking and Listening," *Childhood Education*, 29 (January, 1953), 223–30.

[12] Don P. Brown, "Evaluating Student Performance in Listening," *Education*, 75 (January, 1955), 316–21.

[13] *Ibid.*

[14] Evan Leonard Wright, "The Construction of a Test of Listening Comprehension for the Second, Third and Fourth Grades," unpublished doctoral dissertation, Washington University, 1957. *Dissertation Abstracts*, 17 (October, 1957), 2226–27.

[15] Brown, *loc. cit.*

CHECKING UP ON MY LISTENING

	Yes	No
1. Did I remember to get ready for listening?		
a. Was I seated comfortably where I could see and hear?		
b. Were my eyes focused on the speaker?		
2. Was my mind ready to concentrate on what the speaker had to say?		
a. Was I able to push other thoughts out of my mind for the time being?		
b. Was I ready to think about the topic and call to mind the things I already knew about it?		
c. Was I ready to learn more about the topic?		
3. Was I ready for "take-off"?		
a. Did I discover in the first few minutes where the speaker was taking me?		
b. Did I discover his central idea so that I could follow it through the speech?		
4. Was I able to pick out the ideas which supported the main idea?		
a. Did I take advantage of the speaker's clues (such as first, next, *etc.*) to help organize the ideas in my mind?		
b. Did I use my extra "think" time to summarize and take notes—either mentally or on paper?		
5. After the speaker finished and the facts were all in, did I evaluate what had been said?		
a. Did this new knowledge seem to fit with the knowledge I already had?		
b. Did I weigh each idea to see if I agreed with the speaker?		

If you marked questions *NO,* decide why you could not honestly answer them *YES.*

listening and judge whether or not their performances meet their own standards. Self-evaluation checklists such as the above can help children become aware of the many factors involved in listening.

Wilt emphasized the importance of pupil participation when she stated: "Children learn best those things they live and do; they learn from each other. They cannot learn how to speak by listening entirely to the teacher speak, nor can they learn to listen to their peers when they seldom have the opportunity to listen to their peers." [16]

[16] Miriam E. Wilt, "Let's Teach Listening," *Creative Ways of Teaching the Language Arts.* Champaign, Illinois: National Council of Teachers of English, 1957.

Listening to recordings of various regional speech patterns can focus the pupil's attention on similarities and differences. Listening to tape recordings of their own voices can lead students to the realization that each individual has his own personal idiolect. Simple diagrams which show rising and falling pitch help children become aware of the intonation patterns of our language.

Each year of school should find each child progressing toward increasingly sophisticated levels of speaking and listening maturity. Each child should become more and more aware of the characteristics of good listening and his own strengths and weaknesses relative to these standards. He should realize that good listeners must have an interest in people, hear people out, respect the other person's rights to express an opinion, have an interest in the points of view of others, and be interested in broadening his own viewpoints.

Upper elementary children are capable of evaluating their own listening powers by using the following criteria:

Do I

Hold the thread of a discussion in mind?

Listen to content even though it does not affect me directly?

Watch for transitional phrases?

Try to discount bias in a speaker?

Disagree with a speaker courteously?

Reserve judgment in listening to different viewpoints in discussion?

Indicate by my remarks that I have turned over in my mind the ideas of others? [17]

Kegler has suggested that pupils keep logs of their listening activities. Analysis of these logs will prove helpful in the evaluation of listening experiences.[18]

Charting the flow of discussion may help students to recognize the importance of "equalizing" their roles as speakers and listeners. Such an activity helps develop an understanding of the communication process, emphasizes the principles of effective communication, and provides practice in the use of communication skills. Through interaction, students are given a chance to sharpen their skills as well as to exchange ideas and viewpoints.

Frazier pointed out that listening can also be taught and evaluated by means of pupil conversations and group discussions in which the teacher and pupils analyze the role of the listener and how it is being fulfilled.[19] Pupils can also determine how the group leader's role differs from that of the participants.

The alert elementary school teacher will find countless ready-made opportunities to evaluate listening as children plan units of work, give reports, give directions and make announcements, tell or read stories, and speak in verse choirs.

The evaluation of listening should also include an analysis of the school environment by such questions as the following:

1. Is the classroom climate favorable for good listening?

2. Does each child feel secure and feel that his contribution is important?

3. Is there a real purpose for listening?

4. Is the seating arrangement adequate?

5. Is frequent pupil participation encouraged?

6. Is the length of presentation appropriate for the attention span of the pupils?

7. Are children encouraged to set standards for self-evaluation?

8. Do children have the opportunity to use what they hear?

Dale has stressed the importance of making the classroom a place in which listening or not listening matters to the student. He states that to teach listening effectively it is necessary for teachers to:

1. Regard communication as sharing;

2. Earn the right to speak by listening;

[17] Wilt, op. cit., p. 88.

[18] Stanley Benjamin Kegler, "Techniques in Teaching Listening for Main Ideas," English Journal, 45 (January, 1956), 30–32.

[19] Alexander Frazier, "The Teaching of Listening: A Memo to Teachers," Elementary English, 35 (February, 1958), 111–12.

3. Create mood or disposition for others to speak;
4. Move from the simple to the complex;
5. Teach evaluation of the logic of a speech; and
6. Teach critical listening.[20]

The statement, "That to which the child is asked to listen in school should be worthy of time and thought," also emphasizes this view.[21] The school's task is to teach the child to listen objectively, appreciatively, and critically. Specific lessons for the primary purpose of teaching listening are stilted and artificial, according to Wilt. She recommends using many regular classroom activities for teaching listening skills.[22]

As a means of developing more effective listening by pupils, Dawson and Zollinger suggest that the teacher take advantage of opportunities for listening; that the classroom atmosphere be relaxed, comfortable, quiet, and thus conducive to listening; that pupils be prepared for what they are about to hear; that they be led to expect meaning whenever they listen; that opportunities be arranged for the reproduction of the materials listened to; that the children set up standards for effective listening; and that they be guided in the evaluation of what they hear.[23]

Gardner believes that "in order to listen alertly and intelligently one needs to cultivate patience, discipline, and a deeply rooted interest in others."[24] These same qualities are necessary if one hopes to teach others to listen. Even though the best way to teach listening may not yet have been established by research, everything possible should be done to improve students' listening skills.

Teaching the skills of listening involves awareness of the importance of listening; knowledge of the abilities, skills, understandings, attitudes, and appreciations acquired through the spoken word; assessment of the present listening abilities and habits of pupils; and provision for direct, systematic instruction in listening.[25]

SPEAKING

A recognition of the importance of oral communication and a realization that speaking is a part of this dualism foster a desire to improve speaking through teaching. The child enters school able to speak; but there are obvious deficiencies in his speaking skills. The need to teach speech or speaking has been accepted for many years; however, emphasis upon it and recognition of its importance have varied from time to time. Also, the swing of the educational pendulum has focused attention on different phases of speech teaching—correction of physiological deficiencies, improving mechanics of speaking, encouraging public speaking, etc.

Wagner, in a survey of speech programs, notes the increasingly broad in-

[20] Edgar Dale, *Audio-Visual Methods in Education*. New York: Dryden Press, 1954.

[21] Miriam E. Wilt, "Listening Skills Can Be Improved," *Instructor,* 72 (January, 1963), 6.

[22] Miriam E. Wilt, "The Teaching of Listening and Why," *Educational Screen,* 31 (April, 1952), 144–46.

[23] Mildred A. Dawson and Marian Zollinger, *Guiding Language Learning.* Yonkers, New York: World Book Company, 1957, pp. 160–92.

[24] John W. Gardner, "The Art of Listening," *Saturday Review,* 39 (June 2, 1956), 46.

[25] Harold A. Anderson, "Teaching the Art of Listening," *School Review,* 57 (February, 1949), 63–65.

terpretation of speech and lists the criteria which he finds are being used to evaluate the adequacy of speech programs:

1. Provision for all pupils
2. Provision for the handicapped
3. Interpretation of speech as social behavior
4. Realism in scope and sequence
5. Development of ethical standards for speech.[26]

Because the same kinds of speaking —conversation, discussion, reporting, etc.—are used at all age levels, difficulties are inherent in defining the scope and sequence of a speech program. Beauchamp feels that the main areas for emphasis should be mechanics, individual performance, and performance as part of a group.[27]

Teachers need a well planned guide to use in comparing the levels of progress of the individual pupils within their classrooms. Dawson and Zollinger recommend that these standards be formulated by a committee of teachers and give an example of a sequential listing of goals worked out by teachers of the Portland, Oregon, public schools.[28]

The level of development of speaking skills varies from individual to individual. However, Strickland states:

The standards which evolve from experience and advance progressively from level to level follow this general sequence.

[26] Guy Wagner, "What Schools Are Doing—Improving the Speech Program," Education, 8 (February, 1963), 380–82.

[27] George A. Beauchamp, The Curriculum of the Elementary School. Boston: Allyn and Bacon, Inc., 1964, pp. 95–99.

[28] Dawson and Zollinger, op. cit., pp. 138–59, 249–307.

1. Emphasis on freeing the individual and encouraging him to participate
2. Emphasis on increasing recognition of responsibility to others and the development of group consciousness
3. Emphasis on interplay of ideas and meeting of minds
4. Emphasis on responsibility for the value and the truth of one's remarks
5. Emphasis on the improvement of personal techniques such as voice and mannerisms
6. Emphasis on training for leadership in the carrying on of group processes.[29]

Evaluation of speech is a special problem, for "the transitory and usually unrecorded nature of oral communication makes systematic evaluation of it difficult."[30] A dearth of standardized tests of oral communication skills and abilities exists; therefore, it has been suggested that "in listening and speaking little dependence can be placed on standardized tests" and that "teacher–pupil-made tests, simple rating scales, tape recordings, children's own records, and observations of teachers can provide for emphasis on the improvement by each individual child in the course of each school year."[31]

The importance of the use of simple

[29] Ruth G. Strickland, The Language Arts in the Elementary School, Second Edition. Boston: D. C. Heath and Co., 1957, p. 185.

[30] National Council of Teachers of English, The English Language Arts. New York: Appleton-Century-Crofts, Inc., 1952, p. 431.

[31] Helen K. Mackintosh (Editorial Chairman), Children and Oral Language. Washington, D.C.: Association for Childhood Education International, Association for Supervision and Curriculum Development (NEA); Newark, Delaware: International Reading Association; Champaign, Illinois: National Council of Teachers of English, 1964.

rating devices—comparison of voice recordings over time or comparison of voice recordings to a scale such as Netzer's—is discussed in *The English Language Arts,* but little has been done as a follow-up to these suggestions.[32] The view generally held is that regardless of the evaluative technique used, "Methods of appraisal should be devised by teachers actually working with children, and in some of the procedures the pupil should participate in rating himself or others."[33]

Teacher–child relationship, motivation, and classroom atmosphere are important factors to be considered.[34, 35] Bolz suggests the following questions as a guide for teacher self-evaluation:

Do I recognize the need for children to practice oral expression?
Do I consistently provide opportunities for children to communicate orally?
Am I willing to work with children where I find them—willing to work patiently and understandingly with a shy child?
How can I improve my own skills in oral expression? Do I set a good example in my speech—enunciating clearly, speaking comfortably and easily, organizing my thoughts logically?
Do I listen to children? Do I give them my complete attention? Do I respond fully to their questions and comments?[36]

Hopkins believes that ". . . attainment of 'self-confidence' has been overplayed as an object of the speech course. . . . Of greater importance is his (the pupil's) knowledge of language, his skill in its use, his ability to contribute something of worth, his sense of values as expressed in the oral communication situation."[37]

Criteria for evaluation of pupil progress might be similar to Pronovost's listing of attitudes and abilities to develop in a speaking situation:

1. A desire to contribute worthwhile ideas effectively.
2. The ability to use words which express ideas clearly and accurately.
3. The ability to select and organize ideas effectively.
4. The ability to use voice and articulation so that speech will be heard and understood easily.
5. The ability to use appropriate posture, bodily actions, and visual aids.
6. The ability to adapt speech behavior and speech organization to group situations such as conversations and discussions.
7. The ability to communicate thought and mood in oral reading, choral speaking, and dramatic activities.[38]

One committee suggests that progress is being made toward the goals of speech teaching when the child shows a ". . . growing awareness of the responsibilities of both the listener and the speaker; an appreciation of the effects of oral language on oneself and others; a growing sensitivity to the influence of different purposes for communication on oral language activity; alertness to various clues and cues that

[32] National Council of Teachers of English, *op. cit.,* pp. 431–33.

[33] Mackintosh, *op. cit.,* p. 29.

[34] National Council of Teachers of English, *op. cit.,* p. 433.

[35] Carrie Rasmussen, *Speech Methods in the Elementary School,* Revised. New York: The Ronald Press Company, 1962.

[36] George C. Bolz, "Promoting Oral Expression," *National Elementary Principal,* 42 (April, 1963), 41–43.

[37] Thomas A. Hopkins, "The Spoken Word," *Education,* 84 (November, 1963), 166–69.

[38] Wilbert Pronovost, *The Teaching of Speaking and Listening in the Elementary School.* New York: Longmans, Green and Co., 1959, pp. 3–4.

are an integral part of oral communication; and growing effectiveness in discussions as shown by an increasing awareness of the importance of courtesy and relevance as well as the responsibility of knowing when to speak and when to listen." [39]

Tidyman and Butterfield have warned that one cannot stress all skills and abilities at one time, but should stress the specific language goal most needed by the individual or the group.[40] When making an evaluation, it is important to remember that specific comments about strong or weak points contribute more to growth than weak generalities.[41]

The mechanics of evaluation frequently present a problem to the teacher. The suggestion has been made that designated symbols be used as a "shorthand" notation for evaluation of individual pupils during a speaking situation; for example:

l   contributions notably relevant, pertinent

+   contributions notably for effectiveness of vocabulary, analogy imagery (as well as relevance)

g   good generalizations (induction)

e   concrete examples of illustrations of concept being discussed; application of a principle (deduction)

o   irrelevant attention-getting, foolish, ineffective oral language.[42]

Keeping a record of evaluations made of each pupil on an individual card provides opportunity for individual diagnosis and for showing evidence of progress over a period of time.

[39] Mackintosh, op. cit., p. 12.

[40] Willard F. Tidyman and Marguerite Butterfield, Teaching the Language Arts. New York: McGraw-Hill Book Company, Inc., 1959, pp. 38–63, 235–53.

[41] Mackintosh, op. cit., p. 31.

[42] Ibid.

A comparison of the teacher's evaluation of speaking performance to the pupil's evaluation can lead to a better understanding of strengths and weaknesses. Checklists such as the following might be used.

STUDENT'S SPEECH CHECKLIST

I. How do I sound?
  a. Is my voice pleasant to hear?
  b. Can others understand the words I say?
  c. Is my voice neither too loud nor too soft?

II. Is my speech interesting to others?
  a. Do I use a variety of expressions and words?
  b. Do I explain things so others understand my ideas?
  c. Do I use language correct for each speaking situation?
  d. Do I remember to take my turn to speak—talking neither too much nor too little?

I can improve my voice and speech by _____

TEACHER'S SPEECH CHECKLIST

I. Student's voice.
  a. Is the voice pleasant?
    If not, how would you describe it? _____
  b. Are articulation and enunciation satisfactory?
    If not, what needs to be improved? _____
  c. Is volume appropriate for each occasion?
    If not, is it too loud or too soft? _____

II. Student's speech.
  a. Does speech show a variety of expressions and vocabulary?
    If not, what needs improving? _____
  b. Does speech give evidence of care-thinking?
    If not, what seems to be the reason? _____
  c. Is usage acceptable?
    If not, what faults are most common? _____

d. Is there evidence that personality problems hamper speech quality?
If yes, what seems to be the problem? _____

Examples of the use of dual evaluation checklists for individual speaking situations can be found in *Children and Oral Language*.[43]

Self-evaluation based on pupil-set standards has often been recommended.[44, 45, 46] Such pupil-set standards might be similar to the following:

Do others listen when you tell a personal experience?

Can people follow the directions you give?

Can you take part in discussion without becoming angry or making others angry?

Are you tolerant and respectful of others' viewpoints?

Can you ask for information so that it is willingly given?

Are you accurate and thorough in reporting what you hear or read, so that you give true understanding to others?

Do you like to listen when others talk? [47]

Not only can children set up overall standards for improving speaking skills, but they can be led to formulate standards for each type of speaking occasion—conversation, discussion, reporting, etc. Examples of such pupil-set standards can be found in Dawson and Zollinger [48] and Strickland.[49]

Evaluation of the progress of pupils should be done with basic goals kept in mind. "As in other areas of the curriculum, a wide range of individual differences is apparent. The purpose is not to eliminate these differences—not to make every child an orator—but to help each pupil to say those things which are important to him." [50]

"When I went to elementary school I learned to read, write, *speak,* and *listen.*" It is to be hoped that this will be the comment of the adolescent of the future. With concerted teaching effort, including effort based upon adequate evaluation, it certainly should be.

[43] *Ibid.,* pp. 29–30.

[44] Robert M. Bloom, "A Program for Oral English," *Elementary English,* 41 (February, 1964), 158–64.

[45] Mildred A. Dawson, *Teaching Language in the Grades.* Yonkers, New York: World Book Company, 1951, pp. 177–78.

[46] Dawson and Zollinger, *loc. cit.*

[47] Dawson, *op. cit.,* p. 154, citing Idelle Boyce and Ethel Mabie Falk, "Judging by Results," *Childhood Education,* 14 (January, 1938), 200.

[48] Dawson and Zollinger, *loc. cit.*

[49] Strickland, *loc. cit.*

[50] Bolz, *op. cit.,* p. 43.

Stimulating and Receiving Children's Writing: Implications for an Elementary Writing Curriculum

Lester S. Golub

University of Illinois, Chicago Circle

Above everything else I would like to see our schools staffed by men and women who have poetry in their souls.*

Why not poets in the classroom as well as firemen, astronauts, physicists, candy makers, and lion trainers? But, the poet is different. He makes his living by writing, by stirring the reader's imagination by using his own imagination, by manipulating language. He is expendable in our pragmatic society, but without him there would be no song, no discovery of the inner voice of man that is in all of us. And that is what writing is all about, discovering our inner voice and expressing it in such a way, with language, that it stimulates some sort of sensitive, creative response in the listener or the reader. This explanation of writing must be kept in mind as we teach children to write, since it is the stimulating of this inner voice and the response it creates in others which be-

* Sybil Marshal, *Adventure in Creative Education.*

comes our teaching goal. In a way this goal will be too simple for those who teach from traditional language arts textbooks, where grammar, mechanics, and usage predominate. For the sake of this discussion, let us discard these texts and look squarely at the problem of stimulating and "receiving" children's writing which is their thinking in their most intimate voice.

In discarding the mechanical and grammatical dictates of language arts text we are left face to face with the child of nine through twelve who has learned to read some simple and not so simple prose, who has learned to manipulate the pencil at an excruciatingly slow rate and who has thoughts on his mind which he *wants* to express. Not only do the children in grades three through six with whom we have worked *want* to express their ideas in writing, they also *like* to express their thoughts in writing. Once the writing is done, they want to express themselves aloud with members of the class. Why, then, do children grow to detest writing in the upper grades? Can it be that their linguistic imagination and their inner voice which permit our students to know themselves have been extinguished?

Writing as a growth process. Although most children, by the time they begin school, know how to structure the English language using the rules of an introductory text in transformational grammar, rules pertaining to declaratives and interrogatives, affirmatives and negatives, active and passive voice, simple sentences, conjoined sentences, and embedded sentences, they have no explicit grammatical or rhetorical knowledge. This preschool linguistic genius still communicates like a child.

Giving a very simple stimulus of asking a child to describe a picture so that another child can identify it will offer the following difficulties for the child: (1) He will have difficulty relying exclusively on language. He wants to use his whole body for expression. (2) He will show egocentrism by using terms and experiences not shared by the listeners. (3) He will fail to use contrasts so that the listener can associate similarities and differences, assuming that the listener knows much more about the subject than he actually does.

This simple discourse situation presented to a preschool child illustrates to the teacher of children's writing just how deeply embedded are the writing difficulties which we attempt to alleviate in the process in teaching writing. In asking a nine year old child to tell a story he has heard, the teacher must be aware of the child's ability to order information so that the reader has consecutive information at each point of the narration, the teacher must be aware of the child's ability to embed sentences to convey likely figure–ground relationships in his linguistic and psychological subordination, the teacher must be aware of the child's logical conjoining of words and sentences by the use of coordination, the teacher must be aware of the child's production of a sequence of thoughts that describe a line of thought, the teacher must be aware of the child's ability to shift styles depending upon his intended reader, and the teacher must be aware of the child's ability to use metaphor to capture similarities and differences in a situation. None of these writing abilities are dependent upon grammatical knowledge, none are well developed in early childhood or in early and late adolescence. There are no definitive limits to any of these skills, and even professional writers struggle to maintain or reach these mentalistic behaviors. The struggle which professional writers encounter in surmounting these problems are at the rhetorical level rather than the grammatical level. A case in point is illustrated in Jack London's semiautobiographical novel, *Martin Eden.*

In spite of all that we know about the structure of English, there is very little which we can do to make a child write or talk like an adult, a first grader like a fourth grader, a seventh grader like a twelfth grader, and a twelfth grader like a professional contributor to *Atlantic* or *Harper's.* Yet children who are learning to read can and must simultaneously be learning to write. It does not take the child long to realize that the style of a note to Grandmother explaining that he will take off from school the day before Thanksgiving in order to have a longer visit with her is different from a note containing the same information but directed to the school principal. Even a supermarket list can be ordered in a logical order so that merchandise can be picked off the shelves in the most expedient way. In the classroom, stimuli for eliciting children's writing should in some way permit the child and the teacher to become aware of the rhetorical problems in writing. The quasi-linguistic problems such as spelling, capitalization, and punctuation, so apparent when an adult looks at children's writing, must be deemphasized by the teacher. Rather, the teacher should attend to the child's linguistic and rhetorical development which is as inevitable as the child's physical development.

The following samples of children's writing will illustrate growth patterns in linguistic and rhetorical thought problems encountered by children at different grade levels. At each level,

the stimulus for eliciting the written response was different and can be inferred from the response.

These children are retelling an experience from their reading. How might the teacher "receive" these two samples. Children 1A and 1B have done well. Linguistic errors are negligible. In reading child 1A's sample, the teacher senses an omission in the logical development in the sequence of events. This problem was not unique to child 1A. However, child 1A is able to place a time sequence in his passage with the word *then*. Child 1B allows the reader to make this logical connection by placing his sentences in

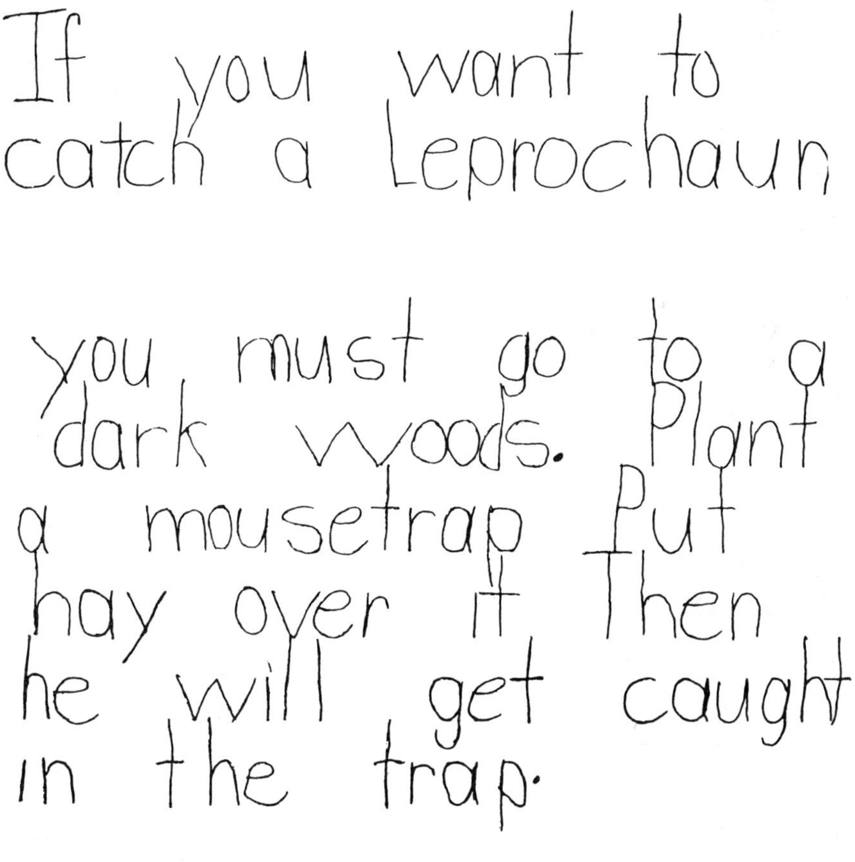

If you want to catch a Leprochaun

you must go to a dark woods. Plant a mousetrap put hay over it Then he will get caught in the trap.

Figure 1A

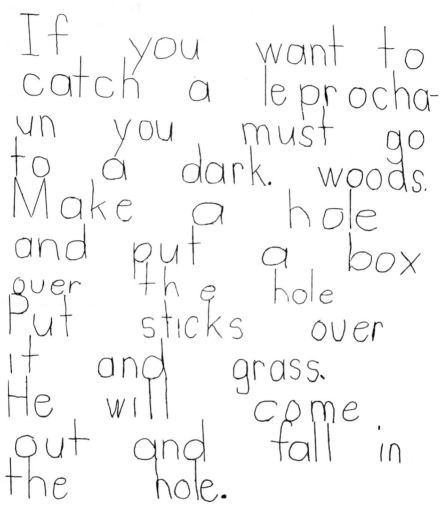

If you want to catch a leprochaun you must go to a dark. woods. Make a hole and put a box over the hole Put sticks over it and grass. He will come out and fall in the hole.

Figure 1B

a logical order. Needless to say, both children have good kernel sentence sense. The teacher need not state all of these facts to the children, but he now has a beginning for further language exercises with the children. The teacher is beginning to "receive" the children's writing. The special meaning of "receive" as used here implies that the teacher listens to or reads the child's message, he accepts the message in the mode in which it is delivered without criticizing the language of the message, and then responds to the message in such a way that his response suggests a stimulus to which the child can once again respond in either the oral or written language mode. With this communications process, the dialogue between the child, his peers, and the adults in his environment remains open and continuing.

The first impression in comparing grade one with grade two is that grade two has more information packed into each writing sample. However, syn-

Peter Rabbit

Once upon a time there lived a rabbit, his name was Peter. He lived with his mother and father under the big tree. He has wiskers as big as my little finger, then his mother died and his father had to. He has blue eyes. He has long pointed ears and he is Pink.

The End

Rusty

Mr and Mrs. Rabbit had 5 babys

Mrs. Rabbit is a Rabbit

She had 5 babys Mr Rabbit like the

little babys, I my Dord at Mrs. Rabbit

I think they are Pretty. Mr. and Mrs

Rabbit sould be Dord too. one baby

has blue eyes. two has pink eyes.

two has black eyes. the x are very Pretty

I Love Mr and Mrs Rabbit and the

5 babys they like my very best friend

She is Patty I have a lots of friend

But Patty is my very best friend. The End

I like being eight and
nine because you get to do
stuff exciting. And you join
clubs you want to be in.
And in brownies you fly
up to girl scouts. You are
trusted more when you
are eight and nine years
old. You get to do things
that big people do.

Figure 3A

tactically they are not very different. The information is apparent in the vocabulary, the coordination, and the metaphor. Student 2A is having difficulty in ordering events and in placing referents and their modifiers. Student 2B demonstrates the problem of egocentrism. The babies and the rabbit family exhibit human emotions such as love and pride and finally the student forgets the rabbits completely and is preoccupied with her friends, especially Patty. The child is no longer able to identify with the animals. As children start to write about themselves, "receiving" their writing becomes more difficult for the teacher.

The difference between thought and language in grades two and three is astounding. By grade three the child is writing cursive, he is using coordination and subordination to express relationships. His egocentrism appears appropriate to the writing stimuli offered the child. Here the teacher's knowledge of literary analysis will help him see that a value system is being displayed by both student 3A and 3B. Other people's value systems are not always easy to accept. Student 3A expresses a value in being trusted, permitted to show responsibility and to grow up so that she can do the exciting things big people do. Will the teacher's value system and the child's clash at this point if the teacher cannot understand the child's world view? How will the teacher receive these values? Student 3B expresses another set of values. First, he is impressed by the importance of decisions in his life ambition, to be a winning quarterback. He also shows appreciation for other boys who are good football players. There is a complete lack of the competitive spirit in the paper. The competitive spirit is a highly praised American value. How will a teacher receive

What are you going to do. Later throw the baum or go for it. To be a wining 2uarterback your going to think about those things. I was once a quarterback but I threw quick, and got yardeg. My team was pleased wiht me. But when Dean F. came in boy did

he do a good job. But when yougrow up go out for football. and D an S boy did make a run back.

Figure 3B

these values? Grade three appears to be the place to start teaching writing as encoding.

In these two fourth grade samples, the reader can grasp the writer's sense of audience and his ability to express his own voice. Time sequences become better defined as the children learn to control grammatical past and present tense. A real effort is made to control and order the sequence of events. These papers will not be difficult for the teacher to receive. The problems in receiving these papers is to receive

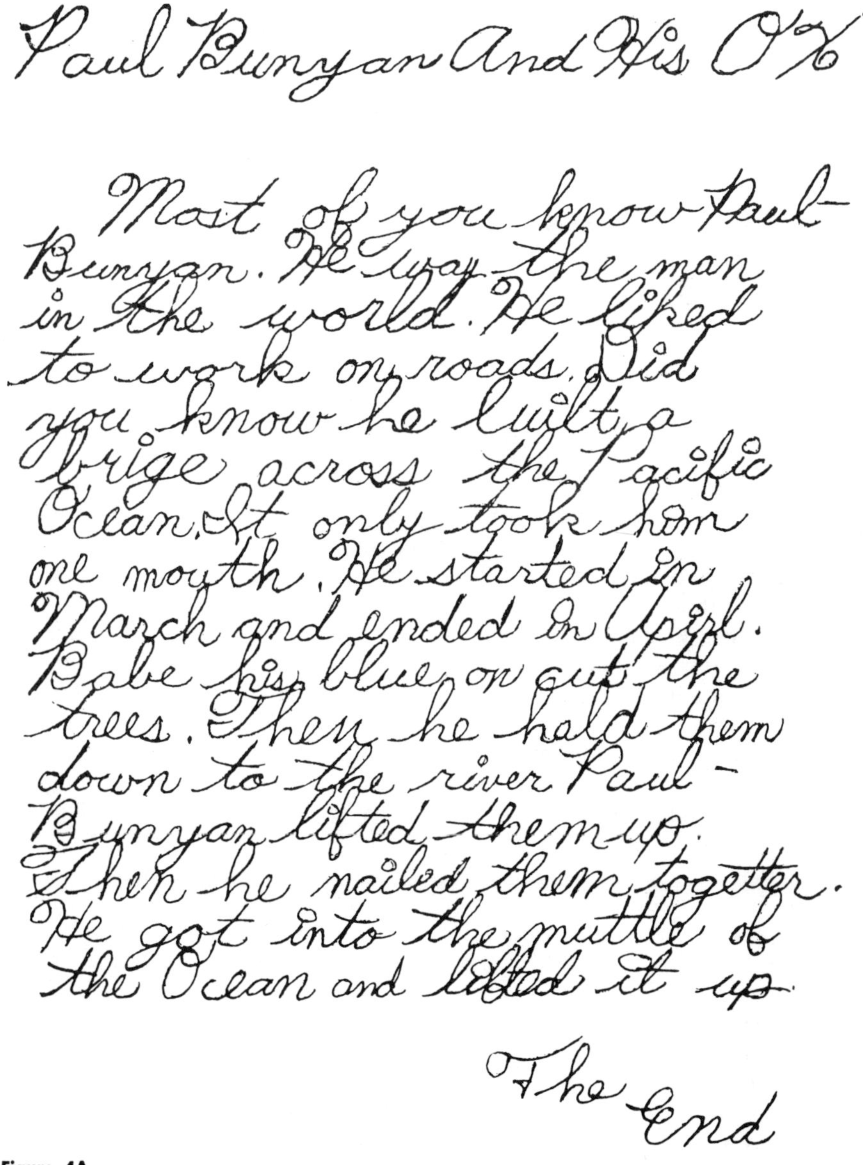

Paul Bunyan And His Ox

Most of you know Paul Bunyan. He was the man in the world. He liked to work on roads. Did you know he built a brige across the Pacific Ocean. It only took him one mouth. He started in March and ended in April. Babe his blue ox cut the trees. Then he hald them down to the river Paul Bunyan lifted them up. Then he nailed them togetter. He got into the muttle of the Ocean and lifted it up.

The End

Figure 4A

In The Woods

One day when I was walking in the woods I saw a great big thing. I didn't know what it was. So I started to walk toward it. I saw that it was Paul Bunyan's pipe. I knew it was his because it was so big. Then I walked a little bit more in the woods and do you know what I saw then? It was Paul Bunyan's axe. So I walk ahead a little bit. And then I saw Paul Bunyan in person.

The End

Figure 4B

them in such a way as to create a new stimulus which will elicit a more personal response to the next writing activity.

Something important happens between the fourth and the fifth grade in the development of the child's thought and language process. There is a complexity of events in the child's expression which is also obvious in his complex sentence structure. However, the complex of ideas seems to lack a psychological depth of field which can be obtained through a skillful use of coordination and subordination. Student 5A is involved in a cause and effect type of relationship which is somewhat successful. Student 5B might have wanted to indicate some causal relationships, but these sequences are not successfully conveyed since there are big gaps in the student's perceptions of a world of experience probably known only through vicarious experience. The teacher has to receive the

values expressed by student 5B with different psychological and sociological judgments from those used for receiving similar values expressed by a mature writer.

The thought and language growth between the fifth and sixth grades is not so striking as that between the fourth and fifth grades. If one criteria of the word "creative" is imaginative or different, this sign of creativity is present in these two writing samples. Perhaps a better sign of creativity in children is the ability to order their thoughts. This is also evident in these two writing samples. Creativity should not be confused with the bizarre and teachers should not resort to all kinds of gimmickry as stimuli for eliciting bizarre responses from their student writers. For the purposes of stimulating responses and receiving written responses from children, the most effective criteria of creativity should be the child's expression of his sincere

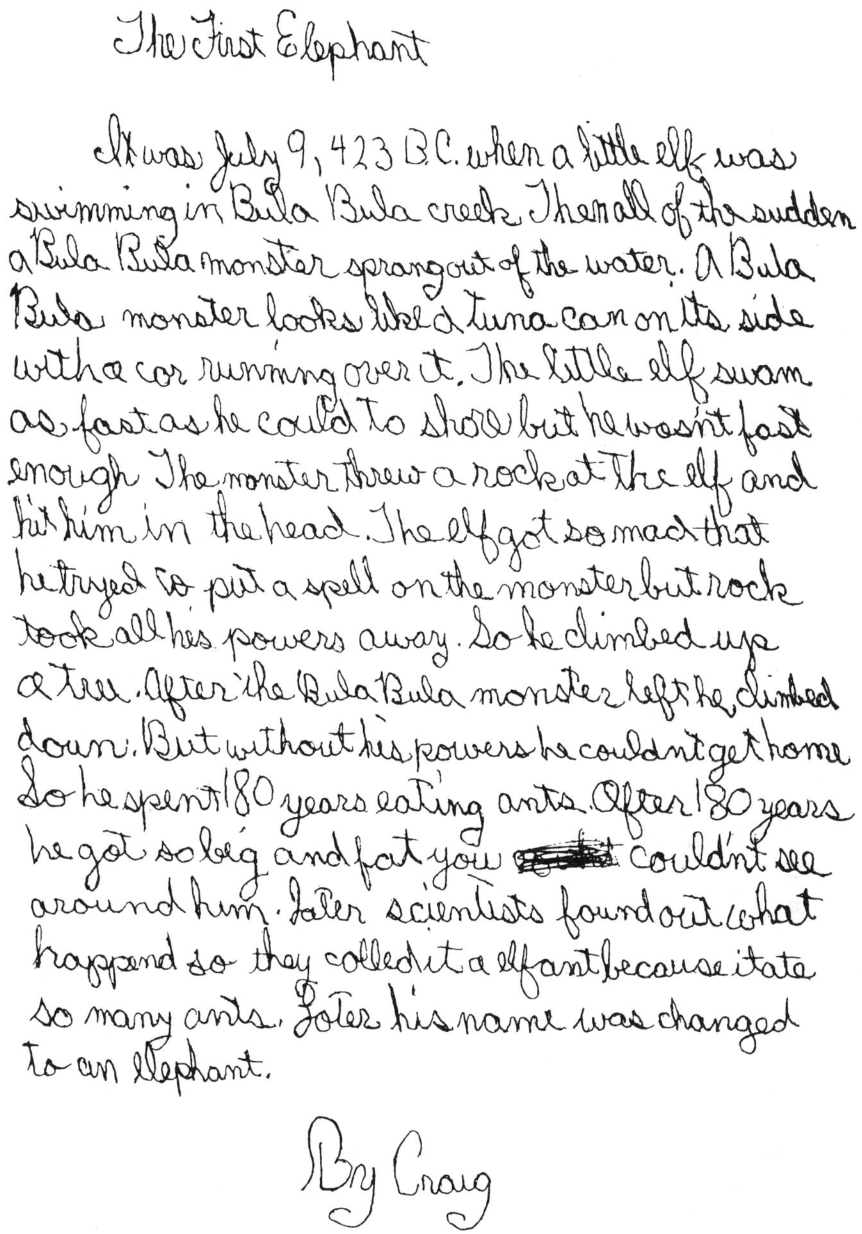

The First Elephant

It was July 9, 423 B.C. when a little elf was swimming in Bula Bula creek. Then all of the sudden a Bula Bula monster sprang out of the water. A Bula Bula monster looks like a tuna can on its side with a car running over it. The little elf swam as fast as he could to shore but he wasn't fast enough. The monster threw a rock at the elf and hit him in the head. The elf got so mad that he tried to put a spell on the monster but rock took all his powers away. So he climbed up a tree. After the Bula Bula monster left he climbed down. But without his powers he couldn't get home. So he spent 180 years eating ants. After 180 years he got so big and fat you ~~couldn't~~ couldn't see around him. Later scientists found out what happend so they called it a elfant because it ate so many ants. Later his name was changed to an elephant.

By Craig

Figure 5A

individuality, his ability to order his perceptions and his language, his ability to obtain a psychological depth of field to obtain meaningful relationships, and to test hypotheses and to reach generalizations which lead to further hypothesis testing.

In sample 6A, there is a degree of the rebel and the social critic coming through. The student is testing social

Flower Power!

One dull day I sat down in our racky rocker and started to read the News Paper. One page 4 it said join the cools at the Super Sonic Sack. So at 4 minutes after 1 minute I went to the sack and I was able to join. One Tuesday I went to the Super Sonic Sack and we yust sat around and told jokes and riddles and this cool kid said "Experience is a teacher, But here's what makes me burn, He's always teaching me things I do not care to learn. On Wild Wednesday we went camping to visit Flower Powered Boys!

Figure 5B

values, especially the superficial ones. In sample 6B, there are signs of fear and anxiety, emotions which seem different from the secure emotions of love, friendship, pride, respect, and cooperation which were apparent in the lower grades. These less welcome but important emotions are difficult for teachers to receive and deal with in class.

This discussion of the development of elementary children's thought and language has deliberately not been a statistical one. Computer programs are available for obtaining word and structure counts to measure children's language growth. These language re-sponses must be correlated against thought responses before we can completely "receive" and understand children's writing.

Children's Writing in the Elementary Curriculum. In our research on children's writing [1] we have discovered that stimulating children to write at the third through sixth grade is not a difficult problem. Certainly any kind of experience which stimulates a child's imagination will serve as a stimulus for oral or written discourse, be it a

[1] L. S. Golub and W. C. Frederick, "An Analysis of Children's Writing Under Different Stimulus Conditions," *Research in the Teaching of English* (Fall 1970), 168–81.

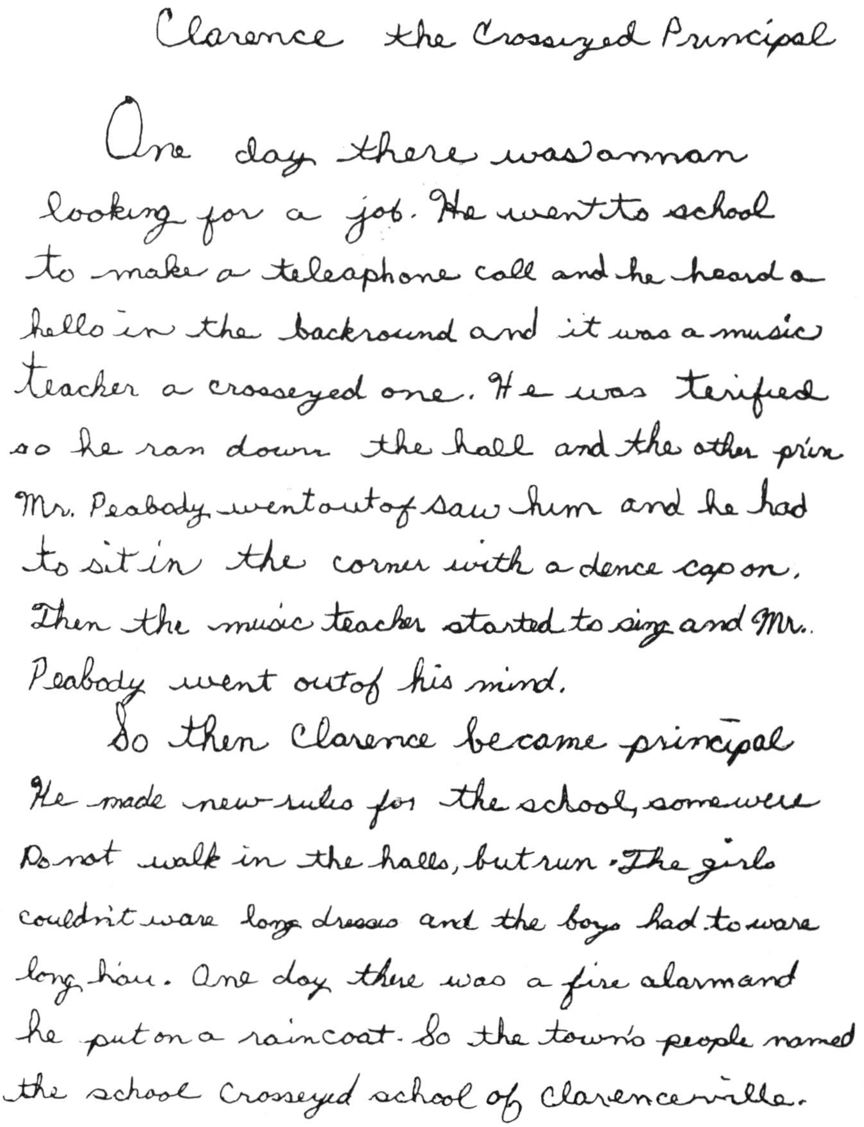

Clarence   the Crosseyed Principal

One day there was a man looking for a job. He went to school to make a teleaphone call and he heard a hello in the backround and it was a music teacher a crosseyed one. He was terified so he ran down the hall and the other prin Mr. Peabody went out of saw him and he had to sit in the corner with a dence cap on. Then the music teacher started to sing and Mr. Peabody went out of his mind.

So then Clarence became principal He made new rules for the school, some were Do not walk in the halls, but run. The girls couldn't ware long dreases and the boys had to ware long hair. One day there was a fire alarm and he put on a raincoat. So the town's people named the school Crosseyed school of Clarenceville.

Figure 6A

picture, a film, an experience from life, a retold narrative, a dialogue, a moment of creative dramatics, or simply the presence of another receptive person. In the research described here, we used picture stimuli and accompanying directions. The research was also concerned with some pedagogical questions about the pictures such as:

Does it matter if the pictures are black and white or color? Does it matter if the directions are general or specific? Does it matter if the pictures are abstract or concrete?

A set of large color photographs and paintings were duplicated in black and white as well as color. A set of general and a set of specific directions were

The Secret Cave

One night when Kevin was sleeping he heard the strangest sound. It souned like it was coming from the Secret Cave. So Kevin got up and dressed and went to the Secret Cave. When he got to the cave there was a bat in the doorway He was screaming. We scared him away. Then we went in and looked around. Down in the water hole was a young boy He was dead. Someone had trough him in the hole. And held him there for a while. But who? Keven thought Kevin went home and told his dad. And he asked Kevin if he had touched it. I said no. In the morning we called the police.

Figure 6B

prepared to accompany each picture. The pictures were then rated on an abstract-concrete scale.

Results of our study show that the black and white-concrete pictures were more successful than black and white-abstract, color-concrete, or color-abstract. The children who received a black and white-concrete picture wrote more and tended to see the narrative-descriptive possibilities in the picture. These students produced more sub-ordinate adverbial clauses, used more adverbs other than time, place, and manner modifiers, and more medial adverbs. They tended to use fewer nouns per T-unit (a T-unit is a main clause with all of its related modifying phrases and clauses), fewer words per clause, fewer words in fragments and fewer coordinated nouns. They also tended to tell a story rather than simply describe what they saw on the page. Apparently the black and white-concrete picture provided enough stimulus to energize and to direct the students' creative and linguistic imaginations. The difficulty of using a picture, a film, a play, or a literary work which is a completed composition in itself as a writing stimulus is that it does not energize the student's creative imagination even though it does produce a complete and satisfying aesthetic experience.

The type of directions, general or specific, used to accompany the stimulus makes no difference at all. The stimulus generally will capture the child's attention, and he will do what he will and can with it, no matter what the directions tell him to do.

By contrasting black and white pictures to color pictures, the black and white pictures produced fewer adjectives but these pictures produced more adverbs, more clauses but shorter ones, more types of kernel sentences, more single-base transformations, more modals, and more clauses per T-unit, thus producing longer T-units.

As one would expect, the girls wrote more than the boys, but when an adjustment was made for amount, there were fewer if any differences in structural variables. If our goals in teaching writing are clarity, economy, and directness of expression, the boys have it over the girls.

Receiving the child's written response to the stimulus is a more difficult matter and not so amenable to experimental research. However, certain conclusions from examining the development of children's writing as illustrated by the samples in this paper imply certain guidelines in receiving children's written expression.

The teacher who receives children's writing must be both a literary analyst and a psychologist. Like the literary analyst and the psychologist, the teacher must know: (1) the history of the life and times of the author, (2) what the author is actually saying on the page, (3) the psychological development of the author and the psychological clues to an interpretation of what the author is saying, and (4) the social and cultural background of the author.

The teacher cannot receive a child's writing by verbalizing to the child a historical, psychological, or sociological analysis of the child's content. Nor can the teacher receive a child's writing by criticizing and attacking the child's language. Not even a friendly, penning in red, "You have made nine spelling errors!" at the end of a child's journal entry is appropriate. The teacher must respond first to the child's writing by accepting it. The writing can be read aloud, put on an audio-tape, acted out, pinned on a wall, or stenciled and published in a school or classroom publication. In order to keep the children from going dry, the teacher must continually enrich the child's experience in the non-verbal world through art work, museum exhibits, and creative dramatics. These activities might actually result in less time for writing but in most instances they are worth the time. For example, a young child who had just read a poem about a cat and had participated in an oral vocabulary building association drill preferred to draw all of the soft, warm objects he could call to mind including his mother. Museums are nearer to our door than might be expected, especially historical, natural, and industrial museums which suit our purposes even better than art museums. Dioramas in these museums can easily be interpreted by a child's linguistic imagination.

The teacher must continually enrich the child's experience in the verbal world by reading poetry and stories, and discussing current interests and events. In providing this type of verbal and nonverbal enrichment, the teacher and the children must make a deliberate and difficult attempt to stay away from the ready made word and symbol world of advertisements so that "Let Johnny put you in the driver's seat." doesn't suddenly and seriously appear in a child's tall tale. The child's symbols must be his own so that his teacher and his peers can understand the child's true thoughts.

Frequently the symbols in the form of figurative and unique language will not be the immediate result of a stimulus. The child's inner voice may be put in after the public voice is expressed and the child can see that he has something personal to say. This should be the primary purpose of rewriting, not necessarily the cleaning up of spelling and punctuation errors.

The writing stimulus given the child must also be related to the teacher's purposes. If, for example, the teacher is attempting to evoke and analyze symbolism in the children's writing, stimuli such as apple, fire, flag, snake, lighthouse, birds can be used in a number of forms in order to observe if and how these potential symbols might manifest themselves in the children's thought. Metaphor and similes might be evoked by offering the child contrasting stimuli so that similarities and differences can be observed and figures of speech unconsciously produced.

If the teacher's purpose is to help the child understand what sincerity of expression is and to help the child discover his own inner voice, the writing stimuli might be simply forcing the child to write a parody or to imitate an easy piece such as "Casey at the Bat." A child's ability to handle realism can be examined by taking the child's treatment of a subject and contrasting it with the treatment given it by another writer. For example, a child's treatment of a topic such as "An Old Man I Knew" can be con-

trasted with a passage from *The Old Man and the Sea* or "The Man with a Hoe."

Children should also be provided with emotional human problems as their stimuli. If teachers shy away from such stimuli as a family argument, poverty, drunkenness, close personal relationships, hatred, and death, with what adults will the child ever discuss these human problems? Certainly not his parents. Discussing these human emotions with children is difficult for most teachers and can best be attempted in indirect ways such as dramatics, story telling, dialogue, and plot synopsis. Frequently, creative dramatics can get at these emotions without words before they are verbalized, but here the teacher must be a skillful director.

In the intellectual history of education, instruction in writing has been reserved for the economic and intellectual elite, whereas instruction in reading has been a central goal in the education of the masses. As a result, the ability to write has become a caste and class marker. In discussing the lower working class pupils, Bernstein[2] states:

Such children will experience difficulty in learning to read, in extending their vocabulary, and in learning to use a wide range of formal possibilities for the organization of verbal meaning; their reading and writing will be slow and will tend to be associated with a concrete, activity-dominated, content; their power of verbal comprehension will be limited; grammar and syntax will pass them by; the propositions they use will suffer from a large measure of dislocation; their verbal planning function will be restricted; their thinking will tend to be rigid—the number of new relationships available to them will be very limited.

[2] Basil Bernstein, "Social Structure, Language, and Learning," *Educational Research,* 3 (June 1961), 163–76.

Bernstein concludes that these features of lower, working-class pupil language "is a culturally induced backwardness transmitted and sustained through the effects of linguistic processing."

This linguistic, caste-class marker promises to remain in the United States as long as elementary education is directed toward reading with little or no classroom time or financial assistance given to writing. Writing instruction cannot await the last two years of high school; then it is too late to learn how to express one's thoughts in the written code. Writing instruction, the process of encoding, must begin with reading instruction, the process of decoding. Our definition of literacy must be reshaped to include reading and writing and only then will we be on the road to reducing the shocking number of illiterates (more than three million) in the United States. A child's concept attainment ability can grow only in proportion to the growth of his oral and written language ability.

RESOURCES

BROWN, ROLLO W., *How the French Boy Learns to Write* (Champaign, Illinois: National Council of Teachers of English, 1965).

COFER, CHARLES N. and BARBARA S. MUSGRAVE, ed., *Verbal Behavior and Learning* (New York: McGraw-Hill, 1963).

CONLIN, DAVID A. and GEORGE R. HERMAN, *Resources for Modern Grammar and Composition* (New York: American Book Co., 1965).

CREBER, J. W. PATRICK, *Sense and Sensitivity* (London: University of London Press, 1965).

DUNNING, STEPHEN, ed., *English for the Junior High Years* (Champaign, Illinois: National Council of Teachers of English, 1969).

HOLBROOK, DAVID, *Children's Writing* (Cambridge: Cambridge University Press, 1967).

MARSHALL, SYBIL, *Adventure in Creative Education* (New York: Pergamon Press, 1968).

MENYUK, PAULA, *Sentences Children Use,* Research Monograph No. 52 (Cambridge, Massachusetts: Massachusetts Institute of Technology, 1969).

MOFFETT, JAMES, *Teaching the Universe of Discourse* (Boston: Houghton Mifflin, 1968).

MURRAY, DONALD M., *A Writer Teaches Writing: A Practical Method of Teaching Composition* (New York: Houghton Mifflin, 1968).

PASSOW, A. HARRY, MIRIAM GOLDBERG, and ABRAHAM J. TENNENBAUM, eds., *Education of the Disadvantaged* (New York: Holt, Rinehart and Winston, 1967).

SPOLIN, VIOLA, *Improvisation for the Theater* (Evanston, Illinois: Northwestern University Press, 1963).

SWEET, HENRY, *The Practical Study of Languages* (London: Oxford University Press, 1964).

WHITEHEAD, FRANK, *The Disappearing Dais* (London: Chatto & Windus, 1966).

VYGOTSKY, LEV S., *Thought and Language* (Cambridge, Massachusetts: Massachusetts Institute of Technology, 1962).

Ten Ways of Helping
Young Children Gifted
in Creative Writing and Speech

E. Paul Torrance

Children show their giftedness in many ways—some in one way and some in another. Many children show their giftedness first through creative writing and speech. If your child shows his giftedness in this way, you may be fortunate in many ways. First, even very young children gifted in this respect provide themselves and others with much pleasure. Second, the exercise of this talent provides an excellent means for developing the creative thinking abilities and a variety of skills in creative problem solving.

Most of our studies have been concerned with ways in which schools and colleges can foster creative growth of various kinds. I believe, however, that through these studies we can suggest some rather positive ways by which parents can help children who are gifted in creative writing and speech. In this article, I shall discuss ten of them.

1. PROVIDE MATERIALS WHICH DEVELOP IMAGINATION

Parents can do much to provide materials which help *develop* the imaginative powers of children. Some parents will argue that there is no need

for this, that their problem is to keep their children from being too imaginative. It is tremendously important, however, that parents keep alive imagination and fantasy until the child's intellectual development is such that he can engage in a sound type of creative thinking. I would like to place the emphasis upon the word *development*. Parents can use the child's natural inclination to engage in imaginative activity to bring about some of this development, and to bring it about in such a way that it will lead to this sound type of creative thinking which I have been talking about.

Perhaps I can best communicate what I have in mind by talking about some specific materials through books. One of my favorites is a series of books by an Italian artist and story-teller, Bruno Munari. They are now published in the United States by the World Publishing Company. An interesting one entitled, *Who's There? Open the Door!* is good for developing both the imagination and the evaluation of judgment abilities. The cover of the book is in the form of a big door with the eye of an animal peeking out. You can have the child guess all of the things he can think of that would be so big that it would take a room for them to stand up in. The child might guess an elephant, a camel, a giraffe, a pony and the like. You open the door and it's actually "Lucy the giraffe with a large crate come all of the way from Lisbon." It might also have been some of the other things guessed. You might accept such large ones as elephant, camel, and others. You might point out, however, that a pony would not take this much space. Next, the question becomes "What's in the crate?" Again, he might guess pony, bear, hippopotamus, pig, cow, and the like. It is actually "Peggy the zebra with a trunk come all the way from Paris." Again, other things similar in size to the zebra can be accepted and those larger and smaller can be eliminated. The game continues. We have "Leo the lion with a valise come all the way from London." Next we have "Romeo the cat with a package wrapped in tissue paper, come all the way from Rome." In the package we have "Bertha, the blackbird, with a basket come all the way from Berlin." In the basket we have "Dick, the cricket, with a small parcel come all the way from Dublin." In the parcel we have "a little ant with a grain of wheat for the winter."

With such materials you are doing more than developing the imagination, you are developing the ability to think in terms of possibles, to make judgments about size, and to gain a more accurate picture of the world in which they live. Incidentally, they might on later occasions be stimulated in their curiosity to ask about the places from which these animals and insects have been shipped: Lisbon, Paris, London, Rome, Berlin, and Dublin.

Another of the Munari books that I like is *The Elephant's Wish*. The story begins: "The elephant is bored with being a big heavy animal. He wishes he could be something else. What do you think he would like to be?" This starts the guessing game. The child is asked to look into the mind of the elephant, to imaginatively put himself in the place of the elephant and think what he would want to do if he were to be tired of being an elephant. Then he is given a look into the elephant's mind by the artist and author. "He wishes he could be a little bird who flies and sings." The bird, however has his problems. "The little bird is bored with flying and singing. He is wishing too. What does he wish?" After some guessing on the part of the child, he can be given a look into the bird's mind. The bird "wishes he could be a fish and swim under water." But the fish is bored too. "He is bored with swimming under water. What does he wish?" He wishes he could go on land. How tempting it must be to him to want to go on land! "He wishes he could be a lizard sitting on a stone in the sun." The story continues. The lizard wants to be a cow, a fat, lazy ox. The ox wants to be an elephant. Thus, we return to the place where we started. Everything wants to be something else. Our problem is to accept creatively our limitations and use our abilities and resources. If we do, we will not be bored. Life will always be exciting.

There are many others. One series is E. P. Dutton's *Imagination Books*. One is *Let's Imagine Thinking Up Things* by Janet Wolff and Bernard Owett. It is a kind of duplication of one of our tests of creative thinking. For example, the child is told, "Here is a circle. Let's imagine all the things a circle can be." The child can produce some either by drawing or in words. Some examples are given in the book. I might add that the examples given are some of the most obvious and unoriginal ones: a face, the sun, the top of an ice cream cone, a ball, money, a clock, a hoop, and the like.

Other examples are Alastair Reid's *Just Suppose,* Lenore Klein's *What Would You Do, If . . .* and the monthly magazine, *Highlights for Children,* which you may have in your doctor's or dentist's office. *The Poetry-Drawing Book* by Cole and Colmore provides another innovation in children's books. It provides poems for children to illustrate and color by themselves. These materials have not been subjected to very much scientific testing, but on the basis of what we know I would assume that they provide rather sound approaches.

2. PROVIDE MATERIALS WHICH ENRICH IMAGERY

To go very far in really developing imagination or creative thinking, a child needs a rich store of imagery. This, I might add, is important not just in developing a background for writing and speaking creatively but in scientific discovery and invention, art, and the like. There are many ways of doing this. One way is through the use of the well-known classical fairy tales, folk stories, myths, and fables. I still think that the Mother Goose stories; the folk stories and fables of Italy, Germany, France, India, and other countries; the Greek and Roman myths; and the like have a very important role in developing this kind of imagery. Of course, it is also hard to beat the fact book of nature—the models of creation we have in animal and plant life. It is from this source that so many of our modern inventions come (Gordon, 1961).

3. PERMIT TIME FOR THINKING AND DAYDREAMING

Many parents keep their children so busy that they don't have time to think, much less speak and write creatively. Certainly many families would find life much more exciting and would enjoy much better mental health, if they reduced the number of activities in their schedule and gave more time for creative development. We become very disturbed, however, if children want to be alone or if they are not *visibly* busy. It is almost illegal to be busy thinking. This condition must be changed, if you are to foster creative speaking and writing in children.

I always find it very rewarding to hear stories like the following one by a graduate student. His children had always made good grades and had found school work easy before coming to the Twin Cities. Early in the school year, he found his eight-year-old son crying over his homework. He had been assigned to make up a story about a picture and couldn't think of one. He had never been asked to make up a story before. He was an outstanding reader, but making up a story was something new to him. The father was disturbed by his son's new school difficulty and decided to do something about it. The family instituted a story-telling session during the evening meal. The four-year-old led the way with some of the most delightful stories, but the mother and father also joined in. The father attests that this greatly improved mental health condition in the family had helped his son hurdle what appeared to be a difficult handicap.

We do many things which discourage children from speaking creatively —or at all, for that matter. Typical is the story of a mother who was shocked that her five-year-old daughter asked to be permitted to eat alone in her room when Mrs. Green came to lunch (Miller, 1961). The child explained that she didn't like to talk with Mrs. Green.

When asked to explain, the child said, "Oh you know. She talks to me in a baby voice—and keeps asking me hings and never gives me time to answer."

Then the mother recalled that every remark Mrs. Green made to the child was some little question she obviously did not expect answered. "Where did you get that pretty dress? What have you been doing today? What makes Julie grow so fast?"

As a result, the child clammed up tight. Then, Mrs. Green made matters worse by adding, "My, Julie is a shy one, isn't she? Are you bashful, honey? She doesn't talk much, does she?"

Many highly creative children appear to be either shy or show-offs. Shy children will talk freely with adults, if they are given time to answer questions—to take time to think and to find words to express their ideas. The show-offs will find that their acting up is unnecessary, if they are accepted as persons in conversations with adults.

4. ENCOURAGE CHILDREN TO RECORD THEIR IDEAS

Children's stories, poems, songs are valuable—they are charming and delightful and can give others great pleasure and insight. Children need encouragement, however to write down their ideas. They do not do so naturally. It is best done if some purpose is given to the writing. We found that children could be encouraged to do a great deal of writing on their own,

through the use of a magazine in which we reproduced their stories, poems, inventions, opinions, drawings, and the like. Parents cannot easily provide such an outlet. They can, however, provide many good excuses for such productions—original greetings for birthdays, important family occasions, holidays, letters to friends and relatives, and so on. To encourage children to write poems or other creative productions whenever they have something to express, give them an attractive binder, folio, or the like in which to collect their writings. Forced writing will not help. The child needs to be warmed up to his creations whatever their nature might be. He needs only to feel free to do so when he has something to express. Such writings should be done to be read, heard, or used and not to be corrected or graded. They should be enjoyed.

5. GIVE CHILDREN'S WRITINGS SOME CONCRETE EMBODIMENT

In our work with children, I have learned that they are stimulated to greater heights in their creative thinking, if their ideas find embodiment in some concrete form. There is excitement in seeing one's ideas take form. Young children in kindergarten and first grade take great pride in the murals which they paint—and I have seen some wonderful ones done by them— the inventions which they contrive, the songs and poems they compose, and the stories they write. When children find that others value and do not disparage their productions, they take courage and are eager to keep building onto their ideas, improving them, creating new words, letting one thing lead to another.

Preschool children have to tell their stories through drawings or by telling their stories and having someone else record them. In either case, their productions can be translated into some concrete form which will be appreciated. Their drawings can be placed in frames and given places of honor in the home. You can use attractive frames in which the pictures can be changed easily from time to time. These can give family and friends a great deal of enjoyment. Their drawings can also be used as designs in mother's ceramic work, sewing, and the like. I have a very treasured dinner plate which was designed by a four-year-old child. She drew a picture which she called "Snow Bubbles." Her aunt used it as the design for a set of dinner dishes for her family's Christmas gift. I liked it so much that she made a plate for me. The "Snow Bubble" title is a charming one and the dinner set is beautiful.

Children are natural story tellers and poets, and can compose charmingly and excitingly, if encouraged to do so. Seldom are these appreciated and given adequate treatment in publications. I would like to call to your attention two notable exceptions. One of these is an exciting little book by Susan Nichols Pulsifer entitled *Minute Magic* (1960). In this book, Mrs. Pulsifer presents a variety of poems by preschool children and describes her experiences in getting children to compose poems and songs. Mrs. Pulsifer joins me in contending that the drop in creative behavior which occurs at about age five is not a natural developmental change. Instead, she contends that it is due to the influence of other children, group activities, the imposition of correct techniques and facts,

rules and regulations. She believes, as I do, that with wisdom the home and school can do much to reduce this discontinuity in development and lessen this serious loss of creativity.

Another example is the work of Kathleen Wrenn and her son Robert (1949). When her son was two years of age, Mrs. Wrenn discovered that he was responding much more readily to suggestions that were sung to him than he did when the same requests were spoken. Soon, she discovered that he was responding by singing and rapidly developed a sense of rhythm and a singing scale. When Bobby was about four years old, the idea of making a book of songs began taking shape. These were simple songs about everyday happenings—songs about the fireman, the milkman, the zoo, balloons, traffic signals, and the church bell.

With new experiences, Bobby would think of ideas for songs and work them out. On one occasion, his mother asked him to put some leaves over the tulips planted in the yard so they would not freeze. He came back with the following idea for a song:

Here comes the flower out of the ground.
Spreading happiness all around,
Daffodils, hyacinths, tulips gay,
Oh, how I wish you were here to stay!

His mother suggested that "hyacinth" was a very difficult word for little children to sing and why not say "daisies" instead. His reply was, "I'm a little child aren't I and it's my word." (Yes, children dislike for others to tamper with their compositions and their reasons may be well-founded.)

One night Bobby lay for a long time listening to the sound of the rain on the roof. Then he called his mother to come quickly with a pencil and write down what he had been singing. This is what he was singing:

Pitter patter, pitter patter,
Hear the raindrops falling down.
Pitter patter, pitter patter,
Falling falling all around.
Dripping, dripping, dripping, dripping,
I can hear them overhead.
Dripping, dripping, dripping, dripping,
On the roof above my bed.

I would like to submit that the use of devices such as the ones used by Mrs. Pulsifer and Mrs. Wrenn might do much to reduce the discontinuity in creative development between the home and the school. It does not mean fixating development at a preschool level of maturity. It could mean increasing maturity.

6. ACCEPT THE CHILD'S NATURAL TENDENCY TO TAKE A DIFFERENT LOOK

For some time I had been familiar with deliberate methods for increasing creativity by looking at something in a different way. *Synectics* (Gordon, 1961), for example, stresses the principle of making the unfamiliar, familiar or the familiar, unfamiliar. One idea was sparked when one member of the team tried to imagine himself as a drop of paint, struggling to get some kind of hold on a wall which had been painted and had not been scraped or cleaned. I noted, as I began to study the thinking of kindergartners, that children use the technique of synectics and of brainstorming spontaneously and naturally all of the time. This lesson was dramatized for me through a song composed by little Catherine Babcock, "Did You Ever

Read a Clock Upside Down?" (with sound effects):

Did you ever read a clock upside down?
Upside down!
Did you ever read a clock upside down?
It is very hard to do but I think you should
Learn how to read a clock upside down.

Children think quite naturally in terms of analogy. They do not have to be *taught* the methods of synectics and bionics. Two interesting examples are given in a current advertisement of a new NBC program called "Exploring." A small boy is trying to tell us his foot has fallen asleep. He exclaimed "Gee my toes feel just like ginger ale!" Most people know exactly what he means. A little girl, discovering the woozy ribbons of color in a grease puddle, mournfully describes them as a "dead rainbow." Most people know exactly what she means, but do you know that many parents will "correct" such accurate and imaginative descriptions. If you take your cue from the amazing record of invention by the students of bionics and synectics you would do all you can to keep alive this habit of thinking by analogy. Fortunes are being made in this way!

7. PRIZE RATHER THAN PUNISH TRUE INDIVIDUALITY

Very early in our studies of creative thinking it became clear that children really prize their individuality. Just before Christmas I visited a class and admired their Santa Clauses. I commented quite informally that each one was so interesting, that no two were alike. Later in the year, they had prepared another exhibit of which they were very proud. Just as they had completed this, one little fellow said, "Dr.

Torrance would like these. No two are alike!"

Not all kindergartners and first graders received this kind of encouragement for their individuality. One mother wrote me of her son's kindergarten troubles which arose over his desire to paint his dittoed horse striped like a "z-horse" instead of brown like all of the other children's. Another mother thinks that her son's learning problems began in the kindergarten over such a difficulty. Before he started to school, he was frequently mistaken for a third or fourth grader because of his penetrating questions and conclusions, his excitement in learning. In kindergarten, however, he began bringing home failing papers. To his teacher's dittoed drawing he would add cowboy boots and hats, or even change the teacher's drawings. Now, this boy's school performance is so apathetic that he is suspected of mental retardation.

Although such things, and worse, still occur in our schools, I believe and hope that they are becoming a rarity. If your child has a teacher who is a devotee of the dittoed drawing, as parents you may have to encourage original work, as Tommy's mother did. Tommy's story can be told through four drawings. Just before Easter, 1962, Tommy and his classmates were instructed to paint "nice" rabbits for their mothers. Tommy's coloring was not the smoothest possible, so the teacher was displeased and gave him another dittoed rabbit. Again, Tommy displeased the teacher who gave him another rabbit. By now, however, it was time to flit to another activity, so in desperation she told Tommy to take the rabbit home and paint it "nice" for his mother. When Tommy reached home he was almost in tears. How could he paint a rabbit "nice" for his mother! Quite wisely his mother gave

him a blank sheet of paper and told him to draw whatever kind of rabbit he wanted. He drew a delightfully different rabbit which his mother loved.

8. BE CAUTIOUS ABOUT EDITING CHILDREN'S WRITINGS

Adults sometimes think they can improve the writings of children by editing them—"correcting them," they say. Sometimes we think we are improving them when we really do not. In fact, we may spoil some of their beauty and honesty, and this disillusions children. We learned a very painful lesson on this score in one of our studies which involved the production of a weekly magazine of children's writings.

I had instructed the editor to be careful to maintain the integrity of the children's ideas but to correct spelling, punctuation, grammar, and the like—errors which might prove embarrassing to the children when it appeared in the magazine. This was not enough caution, however, and the fifth-graders let us know about it in no uncertain terms. One of them wrote as follows:

Dear Editors:

I don't think that you should change our poems, stories, etc. I know you are trying to make them better, but sometimes the way people write things—no matter whether it makes sense or not—is the way people want them.

In poems this is especially true. Sometimes certain punctuation marks express an awful lot.

Please try and understand the way we feel about it.

It was the following paragraph in another letter which really sobered me:

Dr. Torrance, you told us that our ideas are important. The way our stories and poems have been changed around makes us wonder.

This doesn't mean that children aren't willing to proofread and polish their creative productions for publication. They are. Nevertheless, the experience has taught me how easy it is for adults unknowingly to communicate to children that their ideas are *not* really important.

9. ENCOURAGE CHILDREN TO PLAY WITH WORDS

Children and adults enjoy word games, and there are a number of good ones on the market in a number of forms. Almost all of them involve the creation of new relationships. Since the ability to see or to create new relationships is at the very core of every creative act, this can be an important skill to develop in children. These make interesting family entertainment and provide one way in which parents can help. One delightful book about word play is Alastair Reid's *Ounce Dice Trice* (1958).

10. LOVE THEM AND LET THEM KNOW IT

Children will never reveal their intimate imaginings unless they feel that they are loved and respected. As I observed teachers and pupils during my first year of study, I was almost immediately impressed by the obvious importance of the feeling of affection between teacher and pupils and the development of what I have chosen to call the creative relationship. I like to

call it the creative relationship because it operates so much like the creative thinking process. I think it works the same way with parents and children. The adult has to be willing to let one thing lead to another in this relationship, to embark with the child on an untraveled pathway, not knowing where the relationship will lead. It is something that parent or a teacher can desire fervently and for which they can work hard. Then suddenly, it seems to "just happen," but the teacher or parent has to be willing to let it happen, just as the inventor or scientific discoverer does when the solution to his problem "just happens."

For some time I had observed that a certain teacher seemed to have such a relationship with almost all of her pupils, especially Brian. One day she showed me this picture that Brian had drawn of her one day when he became angry with her. He did not show the picture to her until several days later. When she asked him what were all of the scattered lines in the background, Brian explained, "That's your brains. I was so mad with you that day I thought your brains had fallen out." I felt that this was a good test of relationship. The teacher was not threatened by it. She knows that Brian loves her and Brian knows that she loves him.

REFERENCES

Babcock, Catherine Marly, *Did You Ever Read a Clock Upside Down?* Danbury, Conn.: Reeves Soundcraft Corp., 1962.

Cole, W. and Julia Colmore (Ed.), *The Poetry-Drawing Book.* New York: Simon & Schuster, 1960.

GORDON, W. J. J., *Synectics*. New York: Harper and Brothers, 1961.

KLEIN, LEONORE, *What Would You Do If* . . . New York: William R. Scott, 1961.

MILLER, JOYCE, How to Talk to Children. *Home Life,* November 1961, *15 (11),* 13.

MUNARI, B., *Who's There? Open the Door!* Cleveland: World Publishing Company, 1957.

PULSIFER, SUSAN NICHOLS, *Minute Magic*. Boston: Chapman and Grimes, 1960.

REID, A., *Ounce, Dice, Trice*. Boston: Little, Brown, 1958.

REID, A., *Supposing*. Boston: Little, Brown, 1960.

WOLF, JANET and B. OWETT, *Let's Imagine Thinking Up Things*. New York: E. P. Dutton, 1961.

WRENN, B. and KATHLEEN WRENN, *Fun For Everybody: Songs for Children*. Cincinnati, Ohio: Willis Music Company, 1949.

6

Decoding Instruction

Writing is a code for speech. If children are to read, they must be able to break the code. To succeed academically, they must be able to decode the printed symbols in a wide range of reading materials. To help children learn to decode more efficiently, teachers must understand the factors that facilitate this process: phonology, word structure, syntax, and intonation.

There are varying opinions on how the decoding process should be developed. Chapter 4 discussed a variety of approaches to reading instruction, many of which differ particularly in their strategies for teaching the child to decode. The selections in this section discuss one or more of the strategies used for decoding.

What does research indicate about teaching decoding skills? Nila Banton Smith sums up some of the more recent research in this area. While her research analysis compares programs that emphasize decoding with those that emphasize meaning, she concludes that the teacher, the school, and the child are more important to success than either code or meaning emphasis. As a result of having reviewed research on auditory and visual discrimination, Smith reports that both types of discrimination have a high relationship to reading success as does the use of context clues. She offers strategies for teaching discrimination, the use of context clues, and decoding skills in general. She also reports on research that relates phonic generalizations and knowledge of word structure to reading success. Contributions made by linguistics to reading instruction, including the use of spelling patterns and structural linguistics, are identified. Smith concludes her analysis by discussing newer dictionaries and technological devices available for teaching reading skills.

In many instances when children are taught to decode using a phonic approach, they are required to learn many phonic generalizations. After reviewing much of the research on the subject, Lou Burmeister concludes that many of these generalizations have only limited usefulness.[1] She determines which of these generalizations have greatest utility and suggests that these be central to phonics instruction.

[1] Lou E. Burmeister, "Content of a Phonics Program Based on Particularly Useful Generalizations," *Reading Methods and Teacher Improvement*, ed. Nila Banton Smith (Newark, Del.: International Reading Association, 1970), pp. 27–33.

How does the viewpoint of the linguist concerning phonics instruction differ from that of many educators? As a linguist, Ronald Wardhaugh maintains that so many of the phonic generalizations are not useful "because they are inaccurate, unordered, or circular. . . ." Wardhaugh explains that the difference in the linguist's viewpoint of how children learn to read is indicated by their asking three pertinent questions: What abilities do the children already have? What is the nature of the reading task? and What can the linguist do about it? Like Charles Fries,[2] Wardhaugh emphasizes the confusion concerning *phonics* and *phonetics.* Closely related to this confusion, he feels, are the procedures teachers use in phonics instruction. In his conclusion he stresses certain points; for example, a child can speak and has a vast knowledge of the language he is learning to read. Such points, Wardhaugh contends, must provide a basis for phonics instruction.

Central to decoding instruction is an understanding of the relationship between letters and sounds. Although the sounds represented by consonant graphemes are relatively stable with relatively minor variation, each vowel grapheme represents several different sounds. *How then can vowel sounds be stabilized for beginning readers?* Richard Wylie and Donald Durrell report on an investigation of phonogram recognition among first grade children. They sought answers to six questions relating to phonograms and reported the results. The questions concerned how easily the child learned phonograms in comparison to separate vowel sounds, what influence the type of vowel in the phonogram had on the ease with which the child learned it, whether a single consonant or a consonant blend made learning the phonogram easier, and what effect the frequency of occurrence of the phonogram had on ease of learning.

Are other aspects of word structure useful in word attack? Roger Shuy discusses two such aspects, affixes and syllables. Like Wylie and Durrell, Shuy feels that emphasis on the phonogram or "graphemic base" is an important approach to teaching decoding skills. Shuy's treatment of syllabication varies in several respects from the traditional approach. He feels that the child must already be an accomplished reader to use the traditional rules for syllabication. In addition Shuy suggests other reading strategies based on linguistic knowledge: the use of word order, punctuation and capitalization, and sentence structure. He has broadened the topic of structure beyond the word to the structure of language. He feels that this structure should more nearly resemble the structure children use in their spoken language.

How can the teacher make use of the child's natural knowledge of the structure of his language? One way is through the use of context clues based on this knowledge. Most experienced readers use a context-based strategy to determine the meaning of unfamiliar words. Robert Emans explores the ways readers use context clues in word recognition. He finds four such uses: (1) to help the child remember forgotten words, (2) to check the accuracy of words identified by other means, (3) to anticipate what a word might be, and (4) to identify the meaning of homographs. Emans then explores how context clues work and offers a classification of the wide variety of these clues. Hoping to encourage more

---

[2] Charles C. Fries, *Linguistics and Reading* (New York: Holt, Rinehart and Winston), 1963.

varied approaches to the use of context in word recognition, he offers several suggestions for teaching children to use context clues to improve their reading.

There is some indication that excessive use of context to aid in word attack leads to guessing. It is usually recommended that teaching the use of context clues be a part of a well-rounded program for the development of decoding skills. Obviously the amount and kind of decoding skill instruction provided will vary with the child; however, most children will profit from special attention in this area.

Strategies for Improving the Teaching of Decoding Skills

Nila Banton Smith
University of Southern California

The decoding skill had its inception when primitive man stood on a hillside and made gestures to his tribe which they "read" as a warning that the enemy was approaching, or when he stood on the other side of a river and made gestures indicating that game was plentiful in that vicinity. Next followed the decoding of picture-writing on sand, bark, or stone as the exigency of the occasion demanded. Finally, the alphabet was invented; then came centuries of decoding words with the use of the alphabet method.

Insofar as American schools are concerned, during the three-and-a-half centuries of our existence a great variety of decoding methods have been used at different times: the conventional alphabet method of course, but also methods using several modified alphabets; the word method; diacritical marking systems; and several phonic methods—the analytic method, the synthetic method, and the "family" method of blending initial consonants with phonograms. These methods have come and gone in cycles through the years of our past but at this moment every one of them can be found somewhere in the classrooms of the United States. Several other approaches have been added recently: modified alphabets have appeared again, of which i.t.a. is an outstanding example; the linguistic approach; the language experience approach; programed instruction; words in color; and technological

Nila Banton Smith, "Strategies for Improving the Teaching of Decoding Skills," in *Reading Methods and Teaching Improvement* (1971). Reprinted with permission of Nila Banton Smith and the International Reading Association.

approaches. Diversity in decoding approaches has never been so great in the schools of our country. Never has so much research been conducted in this area as that which has issued forth in recent years. The decoding skills are the focus of unprecedented attention at the present time and this attention is well deserved for nothing is more fundamental to the reading process than ability to "crack the code."

I will briefly sum up some of the recent research in this area with the hope that from it some strategies for improvement may emerge directly or through inference.

THE CODE EMPHASIS VERSUS MEANING EMPHASIS QUESTION

There have been varying points of view expressed of late in regard to the code emphasis versus the meaning emphasis in primary reading. Therefore, it seems advisable to touch upon this topic in discussing decoding skills.

In 1967, Chall (7) reported the results of an extensive analysis of research studies, interviews, and classroom visitations in her book *Learning to Read: the Great Debate*. This book included a discussion of the USOE First Grade Reading Studies as reported by Bond and Dykstra in *The Reading Teacher,* May 1966. (This was the first and only one of the USOE First Grade Reading Studies that had been reported at the time Chall's book was published.)

As a result of her research Chall reached several conclusions, one of which is quoted in part:

. . . a code emphasis—one that combines control of words on spelling regularity . . . produces better results with unselected groups of beginners than a meaning emphasis, the kind incorporated in most of the conventional basal-reading series used in schools in the late 1950s and early 1960s.

I will now briefly discuss the results of the USOE First Grade Reading Studies, themselves, as they proceed through not only the first grade but also through the second and third grades.

During the first year of this series of studies, data were compiled from 27 individual projects in which different methods and materials were used including basal, basal plus phonics, i.t.a., linguistic, language experience, and phonic-linguistic (4).

Bond and Dykstra concluded at the end of this first year of experimentation that code emphasis programs tend to produce better overall achievement for beginners than do meaning emphasis programs.

Following the first year of experimentation, 13 of the 27 projects were continued for another year to assess the relative effectiveness of these programs after two years of instruction (12). The results of the second grade study indicated that early and relatively intensive teaching of sound-symbol correspondences appeared to be highly related to reading achievement at the end of second grade, also. This was true of programs labeled i.t.a., linguistic, and phonic-linguistic.

However, when the third grade was reached researchers found a different situation. Six of the investigators (15, 22, 23, 32, 33, 37), of the original 27 projects followed their pupils through the third grade. These projects included basal readers, i.t.a., linguistic readers, diacritically marked readers, supplemental phonics, and phonic-linguistic readers. In five of the six methods being compared, the reading test results at the end of third grade showed no consistent and statistically significant superiority for any one of the methods. In one project (23), the phonic-linguistic method, there were the highest mean adjusted reading scores. However, this method also had the highest nonpromotion rates in first and second grades so removal of the poorest readers from the group because of promotion policies in the school might have affected the scores in this one case.

To sum up: according to the projection of the USOE Cooperative Studies into the third grade, the code emphasis in beginning reading does not show superiority over other methods. There was no consistent advantage for any of the methods studied when pupils were followed through to the end of the third grade.

We find similar conclusions resulting from studies conducted in other countries.

Morris (27) made a study in Great Britain in which she found a slight difference in favor of the phonics-first method in infant school, i.e. in the first three grades. For the next three grades she found achievement was somewhat greater for those whose introduction to reading had been the whole word method.

She concluded, "The teacher's competence, the children's intelligence, the classroom facilities were factors found to be more important influences on later reading success than the method used in the initial phases of reading instruction."

Müller (28) conducted a study to compare three different methods that had been taught in first and second grades: synthetic (i.e., letter phonics), word method, and sentence-story method, using a sample of 587 second grade pupils in Wiesbaden and Frankfurt, Germany. He found that the synthetic method was superior to the sentence method at the end of the second year. However, at the end of the fourth year there were no significant differences among the three groups.

The samplings of research presented above support the contention that in the long run factors relating to the teacher, the children, and the school are more important to reading success than reliance on any one particular method.

In regard to decoding skills, specifically, it seems appropriate to mention that several of the original conclusions of the investigators (5) who directed the USOE studies may well serve as useful strategies in improving decoding skills in general. I will quote three of these conclusions and add comments of my own.

1. "Word study skills must be emphasized and taught systematically regardless of what approach to initial reading instruction is utilized."

As a result of their studies the investigators were quite positive in advocating the strategy of *emphasizing* decoding skills and teaching them *systematically* rather than incidentally.

2. "Combinations of programs, such as a basal program with supplemental phonic materials, often are superior to single approaches."

Games, devices, auditory and visual materials, and supplemental programs designed for use in improving the decoding skills are available in great variety. We rarely find scientific evidence in regard to the effectiveness of these aids and we realize that we should not depend upon such materials solely to do the teaching job. On the other hand these aids offer reinforcement, motivation, and opportunity for individual progression—all desirable qualities which should be recognized and utilized.

One additional conclusion from the USOE studies was the following:

3. "A writing component is likely to be an effective addition in a beginning program."

Several of the methods that produced superior decoding results in first grade children included a considerable amount of writing. Perhaps receiving the perception of the symbol or word through the kinesthetic sense offered an additional avenue which strengthened recognition. Writing symbols for phonic elements and writing sight words should be helpful. No doubt a useful strategy in many cases would be to have children do more writing of sound-symbol correspondences and of difficult sight words.

STRATEGIES IN REGARD TO AUDITORY AND VISUAL DISCRIMINATION

Auditory and visual discriminations are major factors in the perceptual processes. Studies indicate that these factors have special significance during the readiness and first grade periods.

Several investigators have found a high relationship between ability to recognize the letters of the alphabet and readiness for reading. Nicholson (29), Olson (31), and Gavel (16) for example, found that recognizing the letters was the best predictor of beginning reading success.

Durrell (11) concluded that auditory and visual discriminations of word elements appear to be more closely related to the acquisition of the primary grade reading vocabulary than is mental age.

Sister Nila (30) stated that the four chief factors related to reading readiness were auditory discrimination, visual discrimination, range of information, and mental age—in that order.

Hackney (18) and Benz and Rosemier (3) made studies of fourth grade children which involved word recognition skills. Several of the elements tested entailed the use of visual and auditory discrimination. Investigators in both cases divided their subjects into three groups—high, middle, and low. Hackney divided subjects on the basis of reading ability; Benz and Rosemier, on the basis of comprehension. In both cases the high group was significantly superior in the word recognition skills to the average and low groups. There was still opportunity for growth in average and low ability groups.

These and many similar studies support the following strategies in regard to the importance of auditory and visual discrimination:

1. The fairly new procedure of giving auditory and visual discrimination practice on letters of the alphabet to preschool children.

2. Giving auditory and visual discrimination practice on phonic elements early and throughout the first grade.

3. Placing continued emphasis upon auditory and visual discrimination of word recognition skills *throughout* the grades with students who still need help in using these skills.

USE OF CONTEXT CLUES AND ANALYSIS OF WORD STRUCTURE

All through the years phonics was considered to be the one technique which children should be taught to use in finding out the pronunciation of unrecognized words. However, in the late forties and early fifties two new techniques appeared and were widely accepted—those of using context clues and structural analysis.

With the almost exclusive emphasis on sound–symbol relationships in some of the recent approaches perhaps we might ask, "Are there some teachers who are losing sight of, or at least greatly deemphasizing, the context and structural analysis techniques? Should they?"

The use of context clues

Does the use of context clues have value in word recognition? Many primary teachers have been teaching the technique of finding unrecognized words through the use of context clues beginning early in first grade by asking children when they meet an unrecognized word, "What would it have to be to make sense in this sentence?"

While the use of context clues probably serves its greatest function in middle and upper grades, and while most of the research on this technique has been conducted at higher levels, primary teachers who have emphasized this procedure have found that through skillful comments and questions their pupils have developed a high sensitivity to the use of context clues in finding out the pronunciation and meaning of unfamiliar words. This should provide a good foundation for more extensive use of this technique in later grades.

Now to discuss some studies that indicate the usefulness of the context technique. Goodman (17) tested second grade children on reading lists of isolated words. Then he had them read text in which these same words appeared. The study indicated that primary children can read many words in context which they cannot read from lists.

Hafner (19) tried teaching context clues to fifth graders for a month. This instruction caused them to make gains in comprehension.

McKee (26) found that the average child in fourth grade can use context clues to identify the meaning of an unrecognized word about once in three times.

Dunn (10) analyzed word identification skills used by fourth grade pupils to identify unfamiliar words. He found that context clues accounted for 30.5 percent of unfamiliar words identified.

Several people have attempted to devise classification schemes of different types of clues which can be found in context as aids in recognizing unknown words. Two of the most recently reported schemes will be mentioned.

Dulin (9) has grouped context clues which would probably be useful in the middle and secondary grades under two heads: "Format or Typographical Aids" and "Syntactical and Structural Aids." Under the latter he names contrast, synonyms and opposites, direct description, cause-effect relationships, tone or mood, and combinations of these.

Ames (1) made an analysis of 334 contextual situations in which college graduate students had been judged to have successfully determined the meanings of unknown words. A fourteen category classification scheme of contextual aids was developed from the readers' introspective reports of what portions of context had been used to determine word meanings. The investigator then made an analysis of the unsuccessful attempts to use context in applying the fourteen category classifications scheme developed from the successful use of 222 situations which elicited incorrect responses. He found that 93 percent of the incorrect responses could be categorized by the same scheme developed from the correct responses. [See *Journal of Reading*, 14 (October 1970), 5–8.]

Ames does not recommend the aids he has listed as priorities for teaching because his research is too limited. Besides, he believes that teachers should de-emphasize the use of classification schemes in teaching students to use contextual aids. The various schemes are too unscientific at present, and there is a danger of children just learning labels or names of aids rather than making use of them. He suggests using examples informally to help children become "context-wise."

Some suggested strategies for teaching context clues follow:

1. By all means teach the use of context clues. Research indicates that it is a valuable technique in finding out the meaning and pronunciation of unrecognized words.

2. Most authorities recommend teaching the use of context clues through discussion whenever an opportunity is favorable rather than devoting special periods to context instruction.

3. It is advisable for the teacher to familiarize herself with several of the classification schemes of contextual aids and then present examples from these schemes to the children upon opportune occasions so that they may become aware of the great variety of aids that are available to them.

The use of structural analysis

Should we continue to teach structural analysis? Research in regard to the use of this technique is scant so we will have to resort to discussion for the most part in considering this topic.

Several years ago studies were made in regard to the frequencies of pre-fixes (35) and of suffixes (36) in Thorndike lists. A study was made with college students by Hunt (21) in 1951 in which he found a positive relationship between ability in structural analysis and scores in vocabulary and in reading comprehension.

Examination of research reveals but one recent study, reported by Hanson (20) in 1966. Hanson attempted to find when the teaching of the use of the variant word endings could most profitably be given. She concluded ". . . that the teaching of generalizations concerning the use of variant word endings is possible and effective in the second half of first grade."

With this brief presentation of research, we'll proceed with a discussion of other considerations.

First, let us consider the increased frequency of the changed structure of words. In our frantic search for words to express new meanings in this rapidly changing world, and in our haste to say everything in the quickest possible way, we are adding prefixes and suffixes to thousands of words which heretofore have not been so modified. Furthermore we are compounding and hyphenating words at a tremendous rate as short cuts to various ways of saying things. If you will pause to count the number of words whose structure has been modified in current literature, you will find that from one-third to one-half have been changed from the stem form.

This increase in changed structure of word forms is apparent in textbooks, also. Beginning in third grade, structurally-changed words become long and often look difficult to children. On one page in the beginning of a third grade geography book, the reader may find *railroad, rainfall, mountainous, descendants, irrigation, reservation, canneries, agricultural, specializes, tropical, population, continent*—quite an array of variant word structures for just one page.

At the secondary level, multisyllabic words are highly prevalent and students benefit by studying foreign derivations as well as reviewing the skills of syllabication.

In primary texts there are problems. For example, in one first reader the vocabulary list in the back of the book shows *soup* and *thin* as the only new words on a certain page, but when the children read the page they find *helping, boxes, hardly,* and *scared* all met for the first time in the changed forms. Even though the children have been taught the endings, *ing, es,* and *ly,* they haven't attached them to these particular words before and many of them may need help in doing so. Particularly they may need help with the word *scare* which they are supposed to know because they had the compound word *scarecrow* in the primer.

STRATEGIES IN REGARD TO ANALYSIS OF WORD STRUCTURE

1. It would appear to be good strategy for us not only to teach analysis of word structure at the present time but to stress it because of the increased usage of changed word forms in everyday reading and in textbooks, and because readers do not list structurally changed words as new words, after the element of change has once been introduced and is attached to a known word which has not previously appeared in the text in its changed form.

2. Insofar as the recent study presented at the beginning of this section is an indication, it appears that we can begin to teach analysis of word struc-

ture effectually as early as second half of first grade.

STRATEGIES IN REGARD TO PHONIC GENERALIZATIONS

During the past few years phonic generalizations has been the subject of much research and discussion. I refer to those rules which we have taught for years such as "When two vowels are together in a one-syllable word the first one usually has the long sound and the second one is usually silent."

In 1963 Clymer (8) reported a study in which he selected forty-five generalizations and developed a word test from four widely used sets of readers in primary grades. He then set two criteria for judging the utility of the generalizations as applied to this primary vocabulary. Only eighteen of the forty-five generalizations met the criteria of usefulness in Clymer's study. Following this study, there appeared to be a hesitancy on the part of many to teach phonic generalizations at all, even though this was not the import of the Clymer research. The important contributions which the study made were those of causing us to question the value of generalizations which have been in the literature on reading for years, and to stimulate research to determine strategies for the selection and application of the most useful phonic generalizations.

Since Clymer's study, many additional studies have been made, and we now have a summary list of "Especially Useful Generalizations." This list was prepared by Lou E. Burmeister as a result of summarizing and comparing findings of seven recent studies designed to investigate the value of many commonly found phonic, structural analysis, and accent generalizations, plus extensive linguistic studies. (The list appears in the article which Dr. Burmeister wrote for this volume. See also reference 6).

Both Winkley (38) and Emans (14) found that a higher utility of generalizations might be realized if the original statements of many of the rules used in the former studies were modified. For example, "When a vowel is in the middle of a one-syllable word, the vowel is short." This generalization was found to have a much higher utility when modified to read "When a vowel is in the middle of a one-syllable word, the vowel is short except that it may be modified in words in which the vowel is followed by *r*."

To sum up strategies for the content of phonic generalizations: keep on teaching them, but teach only those that are especially useful, and feel free to revise the wording in some of the old ones to make them more inclusive and more useful.

As for methodology, the method most widely used appears to be the inductive method in which children are introduced to a rule through generalization from several examples rather than through memorization of the rule as an isolated item in itself to be applied later.

SOME VIEWPOINTS OF SOME LINGUISTS

Linguistics is the scientific study of language. Linguists are concerned with the broader aspects of language in its several dimensions. Many linguists believe that reading teachers can make the best use of linguistics only by becoming more familiar with this subject as a whole—by taking courses in linguistics, reading and studying about linguistics, and applying their more ex-

tensive knowledge of language throughout their curriculum activities, including reading. Others have some rather specific ideas about things that might be done in teaching reading that would apply theories drawn from linguistic science. Still others have expressed ideas which they have interpreted from linguistic theory concretely into reading materials. All linguists feel that the science of linguistics has contributions to make to reading, but because of the wide variation of opinion in regard to the nature of this contribution it seems advisable to limit this section to "*Some* Viewpoints of *Some* Linguists."

The regular spelling approach

Most linguists who have prepared basal readers have made use of the regular spelling principle. They believe that it is of advantage to use word patterns of regular spelling as the content of beginning reading. These word patterns, such as *cat, hat,* and *sat,* introduce consonants as systematically as vowels. As many as twenty patterns are used in some cases, and some irregular spellings which tend to pattern are also included, such as *right, sight,* and *might.* A valid word pattern is considered to be one which functions not only for identifying one-syllable words such as *sat,* but also for identifying embedded patterns in the stressed syllables of multisyllable words, such as *satisfaction.* In learning to decode, authors of linguistic readers believe that perception should proceed from the spoken word to the written word. When the pupil applies his word recognition skill he feeds back from the written word to the spoken word.

Of the many patterns used, Sabaroff (34) writes of five basic vowel patterns that she has discerned in linguistic materials and which she considers to be of great advantage to children in decoding words. She enumerates these five basic patterns as (1) the single vowel followed by a single consonant, *cat;* (2) the open vowel pattern, *go;* (3) the vowel with final *e* pattern, *ride;* (4) the double vowel pattern, *seed* and *rain;* and (5) the vowel with *r* pattern, *for* and *harm.* Then there are other special vowel–consonant combinations, *all, old, igh,* and multisyllable words. She feels that each "new pattern opens up a whole new array of words that draw on all previously learned information." The linguistic method, however, centers on the *pattern* as a whole, not on the vowel alone.

Structural linguistic approach

Structural linguistics is concerned with how language functions when used by persons who learned it as their native tongue. Speech is the primary concern of these linguists in the teaching of reading. They point out that single words rarely bear meanings, that strings of words work together to produce larger wholes in speech. Instead of beginning with words in reading, the structural linguist would begin with oral reading of the larger language patterns or sentences with emphasis on "melodies of speech." They feel that these melodies of speech are cues both to word recognition and meaning. Lloyd (25) says, "The ability to relate the melody of speech to the written page is the key to good reading." The "melodies" of speech fall under the general heading of *intonation* which in turn involves *stress, pitch,* and *juncture.* Some who have produced reading materials have made use of these elements.

Stress is the degree of loudness or softness with which syllables are uttered. According to linguists there are four levels of stress. In reading, stress may have a lot to do with questions as "*What* was she doing? What was *she* doing? What *was* she doing? What was she *doing?*"

Pitch refers to the rate of vibration of air while speaking. If air vibrates rapidly we have a high pitch; if slowly, a low. Linguists recognize four levels of pitch. Varying pitch can change a declarative sentence into a question as "He is going." "He is going?" It may change a declarative sentence into an exclamatory sentence expressing excitement. "Tom was coming to visit us." "Tom was coming to visit us!"

Juncture is the breaking off or interrupting of speech according to the structure of the sentence—the breaks or pauses in the succession of sounds. For example, "That lady is a queer bird" may have a different meaning if we pause after "That." "That, lady, is a queer bird." The linguists recognize four levels of juncture according to the length of pauses. Punctuation usually signals these pauses.

The chief skill contribution of intonation is in the area of meanings, but it also contributes to word recognition through the use of context clues to words that are necessary in completing meanings in sentence patterns.

On this topic of *intonation,* another use which an English professor has found for it in the field of remedial reading might be mentioned. Jean G. Pival has written an interesting article on "Stress, Pitch and Juncture: Tools in the Diagnosis and Treatment of Reading Ills." It appeared in *Elementary English,* 45 (April 1968), 458–63. The reader might be interested in learning how this teacher gains insights into the difficulties for her remedial readers and how she helps to remedy difficulties through observation and study of intonation patterns.

STRATEGIES FOR WORKING WITH THE NEW DICTIONARIES

There is a galaxy of new dictionaries being published, including many new picture dictionaries for use in kindergarten and primary grades, as well as simplified dictionaries for the middle grades. These are great boons from the standpoint of establishing dictionary habits, but they are adding confusion to the already perplexing situation in word attack skills, largely because they are using new marking and pronunciation symbols and because they vary so much, one from another. They vary in diacritical markings, location of accent marks, as well as respellings and usage.

One thing that the several new dictionaries do have in common is what, at first sight, seems to be an overabundant use of the schwa sound—that very short vowel sound which occurs in unaccented syllables and is alike for all vowels, such as *a* in about, *e* in problem, *i* in engine, *o* in gallop, and *u* in circus. The new dictionaries mark this sound with a symbol looking something like an upsidedown *e*. Glancing through recent dictionaries, we may find from 10 to 20 or more of these schwa sound markings on a single page. Perhaps this reflects a modern speech tendency to slur the short vowels in unaccented syllables until all of them sound even shorter than a short *u*: for example, the two *e*'s in "Los Angeles," the first *i* in "Louisville."

What strategies may we use in meeting these new dictionary situations?

1. For one thing we had better give a lot more attention to teaching the schwa sound than we have in the past.

2. Let's provide classrooms with small sets of dictionaries from different publishers. Instead of having thirty dictionaries that are just alike for a class of thirty children, we should provide five sets of six each of dictionaries from different publishers. Let the children compare pronunciation keys, placement of accent marks, and respellings so that they will be able to use any dictionary at hand in their future school and life work.

TECHNOLOGICALLY ASSISTED INSTRUCTION

They tell us that technology is going to give us a great boost in improving instruction in all fields in the future, including reading. I will briefly describe some of the technological devices now in use in teaching reading, including decoding.

The talking typewriter is used in teaching reading in several places. The typewriter, itself, looks like an ordinary typewriter with a large keyboard. Above the typewriter there is a screen for visual presentation and also a microphone. There is a recorder inside the machine which is computer-controlled. Both audio and visual responses are made through the use of slides and tapes.

The talking-typewriter is under experimentation in several public schools where it is being used in teaching nursery school children and older remedial students. For directed teaching the machine is programed with coordinated visual and audio instructions. For example, when the letter *A* appears on display and is sounded by the speaker, the child can depress the *A* key only. None of the other keys will work for him. If the speaker asks the child to spell *cat* he can depress only the correct letters in the correct order. None of the other letters on the keyboard will respond to his touch.

Results reported from Chicago, Philadelphia, and New York where the typewriter is being used with nursery school children indicate that the children learn to recognize the letters and their sounds. In some cases children can type out short stories dictated to them.

I shall mention the *electronic* teaching machine next as falling within the automated category and being used in teaching reading. (The tachistoscopes, rate controllers, accelerators, and other devices which we have commonly been calling "machines" will not be discussed in this section.) Most of the present electronic teaching machines look something like television screens in open-face boxes, with accompanying equipment consisting of an audiovisual system conveyed by the screen and speaker. Some have earphones, and a typewriter. Materials used in the machines vary. Some companies prepare their own materials, some use commercial materials, some use a combination of their own materials and commercial materials. Therefore, the decoding skills are taught in different ways and with different emphases in the programs of different companies.

The Dorsett Machine is one of these teaching machines. It was used in a highly innovative situation, beginning in October 1969. According to an arrangement between the Dorsett Educational Systems and Texarkana Schools, the company agreed for a fee of $80 to raise the grade level of 200 ninth and tenth grade potential dropouts one grade level in 80 hours. The company agreed to be paid on a sliding scale—more if the student's level was raised in

60 hours or less, less if it took 105 hours or more for the student to succeed, nothing if the student made no progress.

This was the first experiment in which a producer of equipment or publisher took over the teaching of remedial reading in a public school on a contractual basis paid by the school or an educational funding agency. Many other school systems have followed and are now engaging in accountability experiments.

The computer is now being used to teach reading to first graders at East Palo Alto, California. This is how the computer device works: there are sixteen terminals from the one computer which serve each of sixteen children. Each child works at the end of his particular terminal. While all children work simultaneously, each one may be working on individual material and progressing at his own rate.

The child has an opportunity to make three different kinds of responses: he may make a response on the picture screen with a light-projection pen or on the typewriter, or he may make an oral response according to the instructions given to him by the audio system of the computer or directions on the screen.

Insofar as decoding in word recognition is concerned, the computer will prove to be valuable in providing practice in recognizing whole words, phoneme–grapheme relationships, word-structure elements, syllabication, diacritical marks, respellings, and the application of useful generalizations. However, I think the greatest contribution of the computer to decoding may lie in the diagnostic area. By keeping an exact record of each child's achievements teachers will know on what particular elements or phases of decoding each child is weak, and if the computer's programed instruction cannot take care of these weaknesses, teachers will have to correct them.

The most exciting innovation of the near future will probably be cassettes which will permit the recording and playback of televised material through conventional television sets from small, easy to use disks inserted in portable electronic devices attached to the antenna ends of television sets. Everything necessary will come in one package. These cassettes will have many innovating classroom uses in science, speech, drama, music, and reading.

Insofar as the decoding skills are concerned, two possibilities might be mentioned. For remedial homework they should be very useful. For example: the teacher may be televised teaching lessons which can be used by children independently and which are based on various aspects of decoding which usually cause difficulty. When children experience one or more difficulties, they can be given the disks for the various lessons, one by one, to be plugged into their home TV sets and used for reinforcement, providing the home video cassette set is of the same design as the one at school.

In practice teaching it would be very helpful if student teachers could view and analyze video cassettes of their own teaching of different decoding skills; and it would be of great assistance both in teacher training and inservice courses if personnel in both groups might view and discuss the teaching of several master teachers, as they teach lessons on different aspects of the decoding program. The video cassettes would be easy to transport and sufficiently economical to facilitate a sizable number of such viewings.

We do not know what the wonderful future of technology may hold for us. Whatever it holds, all of us will welcome assistance in helping children to master the foundation on which all other parts of the reading structure depend for support—that foundation skill area of decoding written and printed symbols.

REFERENCES

1. AMES, WILBUR S., "The use of Classification Schemes in Teaching the Use of Contextual Aids," *Journal of Reading*, 14 (October 1970), 5–8.

2. BAILEY, MILDRED HART, The "Utility of Phonic Generalizations in Grades One through Six," *Reading Teacher*, 20 (February 1967), 413–418.

3. BENZ, DONALD A., and ROBERT A. ROSEMIER, "Word Analysis and Comprehension," *Reading Teacher*, 21 (March 1968), 558–563.

4. BOND, GUY L., and ROBERT DYKSTRA, "The Role of the Coordinating Center in the Cooperative Research Program," *Reading Teacher*, 19 (May 1966), 565–568.

5. BOND, GUY L., and ROBERT DYKSTRA, "The Cooperative Research Program in First Grade Reading Instruction," *Reading Research Quarterly*, 2 (Summer 1967), 26–142.

6. BURMEISTER, LOU E., "Usefulness of Phonic Generalizations," *Reading Teacher*, 21 (January 1968), 349–356.

7. CHALL, JEANNE, *Learning to Read: The Great Debate*. New York: McGraw-Hill, 1967, 178–179.

8. CLYMER, THEODORE, "The Utility of Phonic Generalizations in Primary

Grades," *Reading Teacher*, 16 (January 1963), 252–258.

9. DULIN, KENNETH L., "Using Clues in Word Recognition and Comprehension," *Reading Teacher*, 23 (February 1970), 440–445.

10. DUNN, JAMES, "A Study of the Techniques of Word Identification," doctoral dissertation, Brigham Young University, 1970.

11. DURRELL, DONALD D., "First Grade Reading Success Study: A Summary," *Journal of Education*, 140 (February 1958), 2–6.

12. DYKSTRA, ROBERT, Summary of the Second Grade Phase of the Cooperative Research Program in Primary Reading Instruction," *Reading Research Quarterly*, 4 (Fall 1968), 49–70.

13. EMANS, ROBERT, "When Two Vowels Go Walking and Other Such Things," *Reading Teacher*, 21 (December 1967), 262–269.

14. EMANS, ROBERT, "The Usefulness of Phonic Generalizations above the Primary Grades," *Reading Teacher*, 20 (February 1967), 419–425.

15. FRY, EDWARD, "Comparison of Beginning Reading with i.t.a., DMS and t.o. after Three Years," *Reading Teacher*, 22 (January 1969), 357–362.

16. GAVEL, SYLVIA R., "June Reading Achievements of First Grade Children," *Journal of Education*, 140 (February 1958), 37–43.

17. GOODMAN, KENNETH S., "A Linguistic Study of Cues and Miscues in Reading," speech given at an AERA Convention, February 1964.

18. HACKNEY, BEN H., JR., "Reading Achievement and Word Recognition Skills," *Reading Teacher*, 21 (March 1968), 515–518.

19. HAFNER, LAWRENCE E., "One Month Experiment in Teaching Context Aids to Fifth Grade," *Journal of Educational Research*, 59 (July–August 1965), 472–474.

20. HANSON, IRENE W., "First Grade Children Work with Variant Word Endings," *Reading Teacher*, 19 (April 1966), 505–507.

21. HUNT, JACOB T., "The Relationship of Structural Ability in Word Analysis and Ability to Use Context Clues to Vocabulary and Reading," doctoral dissertation, University of California, at Berkeley, 1951.

22. HARRIS, ALBERT J., and COLEMAN MORRISON, "The Craft Project: A Final Report," *Reading Teacher*, 22 (January 1969), 335–340.

23. HAYES, ROBERT B., and RICHARD C. WUEST, "A Three Year Look at i.t.a, Lippincott, Phonics and Word Power, and Scott, Foresman," *Reading Teacher*, 22 (January 1969), 363–370.

24. HILLERICH, ROBERT L., "Vowel Generalization and First Grade Reading Achievement," *Elementary School Journal*, 67 (February 1967), 246–250.

25. LLOYD, DONALD J., *Reading American English Sound Patterns*, Monograph No. 104. New York: Harper and Row, 1962.

26. MCKEE, PAUL, *The Teacher of Reading*. Boston: Houghton Mifflin, 1948, 427–472.

27. MORRIS, JOYCE M., "Teaching Children to Read—III: The Relative Effectiveness of Different Methods of Teaching Reading, B. The Place and Value of Whole-Word Methods," *Educational Research*, 1 (1959), 61–75, IV, A.

28. MÜLLER, RUDOLF, "Fehleranalytische Diagnose bei Legasthenikern," in K. Ingenkamp (Ed.), *Lese- und*

Rechtschreibschwäche bei Schulkin-dern. Weinheim and Berlin: 1966, 98–104, II, C.5.

29. NICHOLSON, ALICE, "Background Abilities Related to Reading Success in First Grade," *Journal of Education,* 140 (February 1958), 7–24.

30. NILA, SISTER MARY, O.S.F., "Foundations of a Successful Reading Program," *Education,* 73 (May 1953), 543–555.

31. OLSON, ARTHUR V., "Growth in Word Perception Abilities as It Relates to Success in Beginning Reading," *Journal of Education,* 140 (February 1958), 25–36.

32. RUDDELL, ROBERT, "A Longitudinal Study of Four Programs of Reading Instruction Varying in Emphasis on Regularity of Grapheme-Phoneme Correspondences and Language Structure on Reading Achievement in Grades Two and Three," final report, Project Nos. 3099 and 78085. University of California at Berkeley, 1968.

33. SCHNEYER, J. WESLEY, "Reading Achievement of First Grade Children Taught by a Linguistic Approach and a Basal Reader Approach—Extended into Third Grade," *Reading Teacher,* 22 (January 1969), 315–319.

34. SABAROFF, ROSE E., "Improving Achievement in Beginning Reading: A Linguistic Approach," *Reading Teacher,* 23 (March 1970), 523–527.

35. STAUFFER, RUSSELL G., "A Study of Prefixes in the Thorndike List to Establish a List of Prefixes That Should Be Taught in the Elementary School," *Journal of Educational Research,* 35 (February 1942), 453–458.

36. THORNDIKE, EDWARD L., *The Teaching of English Suffixes.* New York: Bureau of Publications, Teachers College, Columbia University, 1941.

37. VILSECK, ELAINE C., and DONALD L. CLELAND, "Two Approaches to Reading Instruction," final report, Project No. 3195. University of Pittsburgh, 1968.

38. WINKLEY, CAROL K., "Which Accent Generalizations Are Worth Teaching?" *Reading Teacher,* 20 (December 1966), 219–224 .

Linguistics and Phonics

Ronald Wardhaugh
University of Michigan

Recent years have witnessed a renewal of interest in phonics, as evidenced by the publication of such books as Diack's *The Teaching of Reading, in Spite of the Alphabet* (6), Matthew's *Teaching to Read: Historically Considered* (10), and Chall's *Learning to Read: The Great Debate* (4). The old "phonics" versus "look-and-say" controversy appears to be almost dead; for, to believe the critics, research findings seem to indicate that some instruction in phonics in the beginning stages of reading produces better results than no instruction in phonics. To a student of language, of course, this claim about the usefulness of phonics would appear to make sense in spite of what research says. It seems quite obvious that in order to learn to read, a child must somehow become aware of the connection between the sounds of human voices and marks made by human beings on paper to represent these sounds. In recent years, too, certain people engaged in studying the reading process and devising methods for teaching reading seemingly have discovered linguistics. I use the

phrase "seem to have discovered linguistics" quite deliberately because I am not sure that they really have discovered linguistics. I note a lot of mouthing of linguistic terms at conferences; a readiness to use these terms in literature advertising various kinds of courses, texts, and reading series; and some willingness on the part of teachers and teacher-trainees to take a course or two in linguistics. Phonics is *in* and linguistics is *in*. To me, they are two very strange bedfellows, and it is my purpose in this paper to comment on the relationship and to offer certain observations.

Let me begin by turning my attention to what people in reading who have investigated some of the language content of phonics have had to say about that content. For example, Clymer (5), Emans (7), Bailey (1), and Burmeister (3) have been concerned with examining a body of lore called phonic generalizations. For many teachers, it would appear that a large part of phonics consists of a set of statements, or phonic generalizations, about language. Children must learn

Ronald Wardhaugh, "Linguistics and Phonics," in *Language and the Communication Process* (1971). Reprinted with permission of Ronald Wardhaugh and the International Reading Association.

these generalizations so that they can use them to work out what sounds are represented by the marks seen in books. If the children can apply the generalizations to the marks, the children should be able to read. The work on phonic generalizations by these investigators is of interest to us in various ways. First of all, it is of interest because the generalizations have been examined for their usefulness and found to be quite deficient. Many of the generalizations are useless because they are inaccurate, unordered, or circular: that is, they are based on a misunderstanding of linguistic facts, or they are presented randomly to children, or they cannot readily be applied. And, finally, of course, as Stauffer (*11*) has pointed out, investigations have shown that teachers themselves do not know the generalizations; and, presumably, since teachers can read, one must ask if children really need to know the generalizations in order to learn to read anyway.

As a linguist, I could explain why much of the research on phonic generalizations achieved the inevitable results it did achieve and, also, why some of the research should not have been done at all; but this is not the place to pursue those issues. What *is* important for me to note is that reading experts themselves, not linguists, produced the evidence which suggests that much of the content of phonics instruction is valueless. Let us turn, then, away from the reading experts' evaluations of phonics in order to look at the total issue of phonics instruction from the viewpoint of a linguist.

When a linguist approaches the problem of understanding just what five- or six-year-olds must accomplish in learning to read, he asks himself, what abilities do children bring to the task? what is the nature of the task

itself? and what special contribution can he make to helping both children and teachers in the task? First of all, what abilities do children bring to the task of learning to read? It so happens that there is one very obvious ability that is generally overlooked: every child speaks the language. In fact, unless a child is very unusual—and by "unusual" I mean pathologically afflicted—he has usually been using an extremely sophisticated linguistic system for about three years when he faces the task of learning to read. This linguistic system is so complicated that no adequate grammars exist to describe it, and no one knows exactly how it works. It seems presumptuous then to a linguist that anyone would attempt to teach something that no one knows very much about. And yet it seems that teachers regularly treat six-year-olds as though they were linguistically naive and attempt to teach them the language.

The second point to remember is that in learning to read, children must learn a new system—a writing system— and the relationship of that system to one that they know already—the linguistic system. Every child must learn to relate the marks in books in front of him to the meaningful arrangements of sounds that he hears around him. Of course, he might not care to learn this relationship if such learning does not seem to have any payoff for him; but, in every case, whether willing or unwilling, the task is the same. It can be conceived as either one in which the child starts from the spoken language he knows and finds out how it is written—essentially the approach advocated by such linguists as Bloomfield (2) and Fries (9)—or one in which he figures out how certain written symbols may be pronounced—the typical phonics approach and the approach advocated from time to time by various students of language, such as Wijk (14) and Venezky (12). There are good arguments to support either approach, and the choice of approach depends on one's preferences rather than on conclusive evidence from any discipline known to the writer, linguistics included. However, even though linguistics provides no grounds for making a choice, it does provide certain understandings which seem to be absolutely necessary in implementing that choice once it has been made. So the third and major point of this paper will be concerned with the nature of these understandings.

A very basic understanding that teachers must have, if they employ any kind of phonics approach, is a knowledge of the differences between *phonics,* a way of teaching reading; *phonetics,* the study of speech production; and *phonemics,* the study of how sounds function to convey meaning differences. In *Linguistics and Reading,* Fries (9) made much of the importance of teachers' achieving an understanding of the distinctions among these terms, and it would be well to revisit Fries frequently on this point so as to clarify the distinction. It would be well to do so because confusion in this area is endemic in reading, as any linguist can observe, usually after less than five minutes' reading in the literature. I have already remarked that teachers have trouble enough with parts of phonics, but this trouble is compounded by the misinformation that abounds about phonetics. It would not be an overstatement to say that many books on phonics betray the fact that their writers know almost nothing about phonetics, or have never thoroughly understood what they have been told, or have some kind of hearing difficulty. In working with teachers,

I often find it extremely difficult to get them to hear how people really speak. Yet the same people quite often teach phonics and advise others on such matters as speech correction, remedial instruction, and so on.

Phonetic misinformation abounds, as do unproductive ways of looking at problems. For example, the whole mythology of long and short vowel sounds, as usually taught, can work only if some meanings other than the usual meanings of "long" and "short" are given to those terms. Likewise, the use of terms like "blending" and "digraph" seems to a linguist to be less than useful, for the best way of dealing with the beginnings of words as *bread* and *bled* is surely not to set up sets of special blends but to show the relationship of these words to such words as *bed, red,* and *led* and to deal with the *bread, bled* problems as consonant sequences, not as mysterious blends. And the term digraph seems to derive from a mixture of orthographic and phonetic information, a hopeless mixture to which I shall return shortly.

Even worse does the phonetics become when the teacher meets the dual phenomena of dialect and maturation. There is little attempt to acknowledge the fact that every child controls a remarkably systematic phonology. Instead, almost every child is found wanting; for it is the rare child, indeed, who does not get his speech "corrected" in one form or another. He is exhorted not to slur words, not to be sloppy in his enunciation, not to articulate sounds in one way but in another; not to mispronounce certain words which are said to be "habitually mispronounced," and so on. If he is really unlucky, he gets special attention in pronouncing final *r*'s in *here* and *far,* even though he is from New England; or in differentiating *which* from *witch,* even though both words sound alike to him; or *pin* from *pen*, even though the teacher has her problems with these words herself, being careful to specify whether she wants a *writin'* one or a *stickin'* one—except, of course, when she's also working on final *ng*'s, in which case she says *writing* and *sticking*. All this is so unnecessary, for there is absolutely no need for teachers to behave in such a manner. A child who comes to school in kindergarten or first grade has a phonological system which is quite adequate for him. He does not need improvement of that system, even if we knew how to improve it; and writing itself is systematic. The task in phonics instruction is one of systematically relating the two systems for the child, not one of trying to change the first system—a doubtful goal—or of making it like the second system—an impossible goal. Let me add that this second goal is impossible because the task is one of teaching children to read and not one of teaching books to talk.

A final basic objection is to any notion that a child has to be taught his sounds or taught the language. Time and time again we hear that little Johnny doesn't "know his sounds" and little Johnny is enjoined to work harder to master them. It never occurs to the teacher to ask herself how little Johnny understands what she is saying to him or what, in other words, little Johnny must know in order to understand that he is being told to do something. What the teacher means is quite different from what she says. She wants little Johnny to be able to dissect words into patterns that she herself only dimly comprehends and that often as not violate good linguistic sense for a purpose which she believes is good but of which she has a totally inadequate understanding. It is rather surprising that so many Johnnys *do* learn

to read even when they are taught by phonics methods, for most phonics instruction is a good testament to the resilience of children: they learn, as it were—Flesch (8) notwithstanding—in spite of it rather than because of it.

The procedures used by teachers in phonics instruction often deserve as much criticism as do the levels of phonetic awareness of teachers. Perhaps the biggest problem with the procedures in general is that they betray so much confusion about the relationship of sound and symbol. Letters are said to have sounds; children are supposed to speak like talking books, and normative judgments abound. Even when more enlightened writers devise exercises for teaching certain aspects of phonics intelligently, the classroom teacher can step in the way and destroy the good work. One fourth grade boy was asked in which word, *suit* or *wool,* did he hear the same vowel as in *boot*. His answer *suit* was crossed out by the teacher who wrote, in bright red ink for all the world to see, the word *wool*. Who should be teaching and who should be taught in such a case? But it is easy to see what the problem is: a confusion in the teacher's mind between writing and speech.

Again, a linguist must protest the almost vicious circularity of some of the instruction. By this I mean that the children must already have the skills they are being taught if they are to understand what the teacher is trying to teach them. For example, one writer on phonics gives a rather complicated rule for syllabication which says that "when there is one consonant between two vowel sounds, the consonant usually goes with the next syllable, if the preceding vowel is long, and with the preceding syllable, if the vowel is 'short' or has a sound other than 'long.'" The words *robot* and *robin* are used as examples. It should be obvious that the rule cannot be used unless one already knows the values of the vowels in question; and, if one knows the values, there is no need to use the rule to pronounce the words.

I have deliberately taken a rather harsh view of phonics instruction for two reasons. One is very simply that such a view is required by what goes on in phonics. But the second reason is a mere personal one. Linguists have to some extent been associated with a method which looks like phonics instruction: elsewhere (13) I have called this method a neo-phonics approach. Both Bloomfield and Fries were extremely critical of phonics as it was practiced, but both wanted to stress the sound–symbol relationship which is at the heart of phonics. However, both approached the relationship from sound-to-symbol whereas phonics instruction has proceeded in the direction of symbol-to-sound. I would argue that an equally valid approach for a linguist to take would have been a symbol-to-sound one, as Wijk and Venezky have done. So all that Bloomfield and Fries did, in effect, was to look at the old problem from the opposite direction; hence, my use of the term neo-phonics. I think that the greatest contribution of Bloomfield and Fries was not so much the idea that the direction might well be changed—for I am not convinced it need be—but their bringing to the problem of the sound-symbol relationship a good knowledge of linguistics and phonetics. I am sorry to say that this latter knowledge has been almost completely ignored.

Let me conclude then by emphasizing certain points which must provide the basis for any kind of phonics or neo-phonics instruction and which must be recognized in any kind of meaningful research activity.

The first point is that a child learning to read can speak the language and has a vast knowledge of that language. He may speak a different dialect from the teacher, but that dialect is systematic. He may also be going through some maturational developments in his articulatory abilities, but we can do almost nothing about these and probably should not try to either.

A child's language is a fully integrated, well-functioning system. The written language that he must eventually read is also systematic. Teachers must try to understand *both* these systems, for the task is one of helping the child to relate them. Phonics should provide a systematic way of relating the two systems.

In order to provide this relationship, phonics instruction should not involve speech correction because most of this effort is wrongly motivated; should not demand dialect change, because such change is almost certainly quite unnecessary; and should not perpetuate linguistic and phonetic misinformation.

Finally, the whole notion of deductive teaching needs to be reassessed in the light of a better understanding of the child's task and abilities, and those parts in such teaching which obviously contradict one another or are viciously circular must be abandoned immediately.

If "phonics" instruction, as Chall suggests, has indeed proved to be better than "look-and-say" instruction, when the two have been put into competition, this is a remarkable fact; but I suppose a fact. How much better a "scientific" phonics would be than the pseudoscientific one that we have at present I can only speculate. In this paper I have suggested that some basic insights from linguistics can be of use to teachers who use phonics and to researchers who wish to investigate the usefulness of phonics as a way of teaching reading. Let me conclude on a lighter but not really less serious note by saying that I marvel very often how wonderful children are to do what they do and to achieve what they do in spite of teachers, parents, look-and-say, phonics, linguistics, and all the rest of the mad world we surely live in!

REFERENCES

1. BAILEY, MILDRED H., "The Utility of Phonic Generalizations in Grades One Through Six," *Reading Teacher,* 20 (1967), 413–18.
2. BLOOMFIELD, LEONARD, and CLARENCE L. BARNHART, *Let's Read.* Detroit: Wayne State University Press, 1961.
3. BURMEISTER, LOU E., "Usefulness of Phonic Generalizations," *Reading Teacher,* 21 (1968), 349–56, 360.
4. CHALL, JEANNE, *Learning to Read: The Great Debate.* New York: McGraw-Hill, 1967.
5. CLYMER, THEODORE, "The Utility of Phonic Generalizations in the Primary Grades," *Reading Teacher,* 16 (1963), 252–58.
6. DIACK, HUNTER, *The Teaching of Reading, in Spite of the Alphabet.* New York: Philosophical Library, 1965.
7. EMANS, ROBERT, "The Usefulness of Phonic Generalizations Above the Primary Grades," *Reading Teacher,* 20 (1967), 419–25.
8. FLESCH, RUDOLPH, *Why Johnny Can't Read—and What You Can Do About It.* New York: Harper & Row, 1955.
9. FRIES, CHARLES C., *Linguistics and Reading.* New York: Holt, Rinehart and Winston, 1963.
10. MATTHEWS, MITFORD H., *Teaching to Read: Historically Considered.* Chicago: University of Chicago Press, 1966.
11. STAUFFER, RUSSELL G., *Directing Reading Maturity as a Cognitive Process.* New York: Harper & Row, 1969.
12. VENEZKY, RICHARD L., "English Orthography: Its Graphical Structure and Its Relation to Sound," *Reading Research Quarterly,* 2 (1967), 75–105.
13. WARDHAUGH, RONALD, "Linguistic Insights into the Reading Process," *Language Learning,* 18 (1968), 235–52.
14. WIJK, AXEL, *Rules of Pronunciation for the English Language.* London: Oxford University Press, 1966.

Teaching Vowels Through Phonograms

Richard E. Wylie
Temple University

Donald D. Durrell
Boston University

Vowels have long been labeled the unreliables and the undependables. In written English each vowel stands for several different sounds and most vowel combinations represent additional sounds. As a result, the teaching of vowels is difficult because of the varied spelling of vowel sounds.

Many proposals for vowel learning are found in reading practice. Textbook authors and teachers of reading have depended on vowel rules to help with the numerous variations of vowel sounds. The limited value of such rules for primary words was shown by Clymer (1963). Bailey (1967) found similar lack of dependability for vowel rules in intermediate grade words. Hanna and others (1966) programmed a computer with 111 vowel rules and ninety-two consonant rules, with the result that the computer spelled only half of 17,000 words from the Thorndike–Lorge list correctly. The rules approach to vowels seems unpromising.

Other attempts to deal with the complexities of vowels include: (a) respelling of words for initial teaching, as in the Initial Teaching Alphabet in which major vowel phonemes are always represented by the same letters; (b) representing different vowel sounds by different colors in print; and (c) controlling the introduction of vowels, beginning with short vowels which are considered more regular. These are just a few of the many attempts to adjust or control vowels to make them more stable and hopefully more easy to master.

Millions of children have learned to read and spell despite the unreliability of rules and without the aids of respelling, colored letters, or the control of vowels in introductory material. How have they found their way through vowel complexities? What are their approaches to stabilizing vowel sounds through materials which use standard spellings and standard print?

STABILITY OF VOWELS
IN PHONOGRAMS

Ending phonograms appear to stabilize the vowel sounds for the begining reader. In Durrell's list of 286 rhyming phonograms which appear in primary grade words, 272 or 95% have stable sounds of vowels (1963). These 272 phonograms with stable vowel sounds are contained in 1,437 words of the Murphy (1957) list of words appearing in the speaking vocabulary of primary grade children. Among the phonograms in which vowel sounds were dependable, the following appeared in ten or more primary grade words: -ack, -ail, -ain, -ake, -ale, -ame, -an, -ank, -ap, -ash, -at, -ate, -aw, -ay, -eat, -ell, -est, -ice, -ick, -ide, -ight, -ill, -in, -ine, -ing, -ink, -ip, -it, -ock, -oke, -op, -ore, -ot, -uck, -ug, -ump, -unk. Nearly 500 primary grade words are derived from these thirty-seven high-frequency phonograms.

Of the fourteen phonograms in which vowel sounds varied, only ten produced more than one varying primary grade word. These were the following: -ead (bead, head), -ear (dear, wear), -ive (five, give), -one (done, bone), -ost (lost, post), -ove (clove, love), -ow (blow, how), -own (town, grown), -ull (dull, pull), and -ush (brush, push). Only 109 primary grade words are derived from these phonograms in which the vowel sound varies. Clearly, the beginning reader can find much security in vowel sounds through rhyming phonograms, without depending upon temporary or doubtful aids to simplify the task.

Phonograms which combine the vowel with the initial consonant offer no such stability. The *a* is stable in the phonogram -*ang* (sang, bang, hang, rang), but it has many sounds in *ca*- (cat, car, came, call). The *e* is stable

in -*ell* (bell, tell, well, fell), but not in *be*- (bet, because, beach). The ability of children to recognize rhyming words may account in part for the ease of learning rhyming phonograms.

The fact that many rhyming phonograms are spelled differently (-aid, -ade; -ain, -ane; -air, -are) appears to be little bother to children in reading. Santeusanio (1962) found that direct teaching of such homophones led to little confusion in reading. The different spellings are easily recognized in reading; spelling, however, asks the child to choose between such homophones, which is a more difficult task.

STUDIES IN PHONOGRAM
LEARNING

A study of phonogram recognition among first grade children in May was undertaken to find answers to the following questions:

1. Is it easier to identify separate vowel sounds or whole phonograms?

2. Are short vowel phonograms more readily learned than long vowel phonograms?

3. Are long vowel phonograms spelled with "silent *e*" easier to learn than those formed with vowel digraphs?

4. Are phonograms containing vowels other than long or short more readily learned?

5. Are short vowel phonograms with a single consonant more readily learned than those with consonant blends?

6. Does ease of phonogram learning depend upon the number of words based on the phonogram?

A population of nearly 900 first grade children taking part in the study of Murphy (1965) was available to the author. Among these thirty classrooms it was possible to select for this study those which showed normal intelligence and reading progress. All children followed the Scott-Foresman basal reading program, but in half of the classrooms Speech-to-Print Phonics (1964) replaced the Scott-Foresman word service. In the studies which follow, children were drawn equally from both treatment groups.

1. Is it easier to identify separate vowel sounds or whole phonograms?

It is possible that the phonogram as a unit of recognition is easier to learn than the separate vowel within the phonogram. To study this question, a thirty-two item test of phonogram identification was constructed and used with 230 children in May. Each item consisted of five phonograms in which only the vowel varied; the consonants were the same for all five phonograms. The first two items are illustrative:

ack	ick	ock	eck	uck
ed	id	ud	od	ad

All phonograms were based on short vowels. The ability to identify whole phonograms was tested by asking the children to "circle the one that says *ock*." The ability to identify separate vowel sounds within the phonogram was tested by using the same test form on the following day. This time the children were asked to "Circle the one that has an *o* in it,"—the short sound of *o* was pronounced. All short vowels were tested in each test form.

The mean score for identifying whole phonograms was 14.14; the mean score for identifying separate vowel sounds was 10.80. The difference of 3.34 was significant at the .01 level. Apparently the whole phonogram is easier to identify than the separate vowel it contains. If the child can recognize the phonogram more accurately than the separate vowel, one may question the desirability of teaching vowels separately.

2. Are short vowel phonograms more readily learned than long vowel phonograms?

To answer this and the remaining questions, a test of the ability to identify 152 phonograms was given to the entire population in May. The test consisted of four-choice items, with distractors designed to force accurate response to both vowels and consonants. For example, when the child was asked to "Find *irt* and circle it," the test item was the following:

art   ort   int   irt

While it is recognized that the difficulty of the item may be determined by the distractors, there were many samples of each type of them. To avoid fatigue, this test was given in several sittings.

For each of the questions, a random sample of one hundred tests were analyzed and the *per cent* of correct responses for each item was determined.

Short vowels are often taught before long vowels on the assumption that the short vowel sound is more regular. If this is true, it would seem that short vowel phonograms would be easier to master than long vowel phonograms. In the phonogram test of 152 items, there were fifty-eight short vowel phonograms and forty-one long vowel phonograms. The long vowel phonograms were identified slightly better than short vowel phonograms: the per cent of correct answers was 68.25 for long vowel phonograms, as compared to 67.19 for short vowel phonograms. Since the difference of 1.16

was not significant, it is apparent that short vowel phonograms and long vowel phonograms are equally easy to learn. This study finds no support for teaching short vowels first.

3. Are long vowel phonograms spelled with "silent *e*" easier to learn than those formed with vowel digraphs?

It might be thought that the "silent *e*" phonograms represented a more regular spelling of long vowels and that such phonograms would be more readily mastered. Of the 152 test items, there were eighteen "silent *e*" phonograms (-ace, -ate, -ade, -ite, -ine, etc.) and fourteen phonograms with vowel digraphs representing long vowel sounds (-ear, -aid, -ail, -oat, -ean, etc.)

The "silent *e*" phonograms were no easier to identify than the vowel digraph phonograms. The per cent of correct answers for "silent *e*" phonograms was 68.44; for vowel digraph phonograms, 67.00.

4. Are phonograms containing vowels other than long or short more readily learned?

There were thirty-one phonograms which contained vowels other than long or short (-all, -arm, -ool, -urn, -alk, -aw, etc.). These were less well mastered than phonograms which contained vowels that were clearly long or short. The per cent of identification for varied vowel sounds was 63.11, as compared to 68.25 for long vowel phonograms and 67.19 for short vowel phonograms. The difference was significant at the .01 level. Although this might lead to the conclusion to teach phonograms with vowel variations later than long or short vowel phonograms, there were many phonograms with varied vowel sounds quickly identifiable.

5. Are short-vowel phonograms with a single consonant (-at, -ig, -ot) more

readily learned than those containing consonant blends?

Among the 152 phonograms tested, there were twenty-four short vowel phonograms ending in a single consonant; thirty-four ended in consonant blends. The phonograms with single consonant endings were more easily identified; they showed 71.13 per cent of passes as compared to 64.41 for phonograms ending in consonant blends. This difference was significant at the .01 level.

6. Does the ease of phonogram learning depend upon the number of words based on the phonograms?

While the above studies of ease of identification of phonograms produced general findings, in each comparison there were many exceptions to the generalization. Some long vowel phonograms were much more readily learned than short vowel phonograms, some vowel digraph phonograms ranked higher than "silent *e*" phonograms; some consonant blend phonograms were more easily identified than those with single consonant endings. Perhaps the ease in learning rests in part upon the number of primary grade words stemming from each phonogram, providing more practice in the year's reading.

The phonograms were divided into "high frequency" and "low frequency" depending upon the number of primary grade words in which they appeared. Phonograms which yielded more than ten primary grade words were classified as "high frequency," those which yielded between five and ten words were listed under "low frequency." There were thirty-seven "high frequency" phonograms and 115 "low frequency" phonograms among the 152 included in the test.

The per cent of identification of

high frequency phonograms was 70.69 as compared to 65.70 for phonograms of low frequency. The difference of 4.99 was significant at the .01 level. High frequency phonograms were more readily identified than low frequency phonograms, but again, there were many individual exceptions to this rule.

SUMMARY

In learning to read, the child may find stability in vowel sounds through ending phonograms. Nearly 1,500 primary grade words stem from phonograms which have stable vowel sounds. Whole phonograms are more easily identified by first-grade children than the separate vowels contained in the phonograms, suggesting that the recognition unit is the phonogram rather than the separate vowel. Long vowel phonograms and short vowel phonograms are equally easy to learn; no support is found for teaching short vowel phonograms first. Long vowel phonograms "regularly" formed with "silent e" are no easier to learn than long vowel phonograms formed with

vowel digraphs. Short vowel phonograms ending in a single consonant are more readily mastered than those ending in consonant blends. Phonograms which yield ten or more primary grade words are more readily learned than those which yield between five and ten words. Individual phonograms show many exceptions to the above generalizations; apparently the ease of learning phonograms depends upon a combination of the above factors as well as others.

REFERENCES

BAILEY, MILDRED H., The utility of phonic generalizations in grades one through six. Reading Teacher 1967, 20, 413–18.

CLYMER, THEODORE, The utility of phonic generalizations in the primary grades. Reading Teacher 1963, 16, 252–58.

DURRELL, DONALD D., Phonograms in primary grade words. (mimeo) Boston University, 1963.

HANNA, PAUL R. and others, Phoneme-grapheme correspondence as cues to spelling improvement.

Some Relationships of Linguistics to the Reading Process

Roger W. Shuy

Is there more information available from the field of linguistics for reading instruction than that involving sound–symbol correspondences? If so, how can we use this information to improve our reading programs? In the selection which follows Roger Shuy presents a number of linguistic insights which are of basic importance to decoding instruction. As a part of his discussion of the relationship of linguistics to reading, the author includes the contribution of language structure to both the decoding and comprehension processes. He also provides new ideas related to syllabication and the decoding process.—J. Ahern

. . .

THE STRUCTURE OF LANGUAGE

At the early levels the child depends greatly on his knowledge of sound–letter relationships. But as he learns, he must rely less and less on decoding and more and more on something else. This "something else" might be called underlying linguistic structure. By this I mean the ability which even beginning readers have that enables them to avoid misreading via any manner other than by the phonological and gram-

matical rules of their native language. They do not read *spot* as *psto* (and impossible phonological realization in English), although they quite possibly could realize it as *stop, spat, spet,* or any other sequences of sounds permissible in English. In addition, the child is relying heavily on his knowledge of the grammar of his language to guide him in the reading process. He will do well to utilize his knowledge of the meaning units of language from the smaller affixes and inflections to the principle involved in embedding a relative clause in the nominal part of the sentence ("Charles, who lives in Washington, visited New York.") In his reading, a child will rely on his cumulative knowledge of how spoken language works to anticipate the message of the written page. Therefore, it is probably wise to offer the child reading matter with sentence constructions as much like his own language as possible, in order to take advantage of the reinforcement which predictability can produce. For example, recent research in the oral language of primary school children indicates few sentences beginning with prepositional phrases. A preposition at the beginning of the sentence might be read by a young reader as though it were part of the previous sentence:

Larry goes to school. At his desk he has some books.

might be misread

Larry goes to school at his desk. He has some books.

In addition, complex sentences, the passive voice, and heavy use of nominal constructions should be avoided in beginning reading materials. Sentence patterns unlikely to appear in the child's oral language should be delayed until the reader is far enough along in his learning to be able to tolerate them. To those who object to the possible monotony such restrictions might yield we might say that monotony is a less decisive factor for children who have not yet become familiar with the printed page than it is for adults.

GRAMMATICAL CLARITY AIDS IN COMPREHENSION

Readers still in the development stage should not have to face ambiguity, cultural or structural. Such sentences as "Flying planes can be dangerous" are ambiguous and should be avoided at this stage.

For further clarity, beginning reading materials should also include as much linguistic redundancy as possible. This means that unexpected constructions like metaphors and similes should be put off for awhile. Familiar words and concepts should be used in different sentence settings, so that the child becomes aware that familiar words may be used in various ways and with various meanings.

The function of intonation in sentence meaning should be revealed to the child, too. Children can experiment by reading a sentence in different ways with the stress on different words, to obtain slightly different meanings.

LEARNING WORD STRUCTURE

Words, too, have a discoverable structure, and a child should be shown how recognizable word-parts are put together in English. He needs to be aware of affixes (a term covering both prefixes and suffixes), inflections (such as plurals with *s* and tense changes with *ed* and *ing*), contractions, and compounds.

He should be led to discover the learning value of a word-part such as the graphemic base, which may be defined as a word-part consisting of a vowel and a consonant which has high utility in decoding, particularly in initial consonant substitution—for example, *at,* which is a graphemic base useful in building words like *bat* and *flat,* as well as in decoding long words like *atmosphere.*

Another aspect of word structure that the child needs to know is syllabication. Once thought to be simply a matter of pronunciation, syllabication has been shown in recent research to involve a complex network involving compounding, affixation, and phonology. If approached in the right way, syllabication can be more than just a curiosity of language; it can help in the decoding of new words. The teacher can help the child view syllabication as an aid rather than as an end in itself. For this purpose, I have devised a set of rules for syllabication which are taught as an integral part of this reading series. They are appended to this article.

Past experience in teaching syllabication has been built on dictionary word-division which is often inconsistent and which is more concerned with where to divide a word when writing it at the end of a line than with the decoding of new words. But for a child to succeed in using syllabication to analyze a new word, he needs to know compounding, affixation, inflection, and the difference between glided and unglided vowels.

First reaction to such a proposal might suggest that teaching syllabication is really the function of the language arts, since a child who wants to find the proper syllable divisions needs to know the subject matter of what we have been labelling "language arts" (as opposed to reading). But this simplification of the task overlooks a very important aspect of the reading process—namely, that it proceeds along the lines of units larger than the sound–letter relationship. A child who has learned syllabication as an interweaving of sound, word-parts, and word classes has a distinct advantage over one who hasn't.

AIDS TO COMPREHENSION

As the child becomes less dependent upon sound–symbol relationships, he becomes more able to utilize knowledge of complex language concepts such as the role of word-order in comprehension. He uses cues such as punctuation and capitalization to assist in getting meaning, and he utilizes his knowledge of the structure of sentences in the reading process.

In summary, then, an effective reading instruction program will recognize that children begin with a well-developed language system. We are not teaching them their language. We are only teaching them to read it. Such a program will attempt to begin where the child is and to see the learning situation from the child's point of view. It will take advantage of the child's as yet undimmed ability to hear language—for example, to distinguish glided vowels from unglided ones. Furthermore, an effective program will utilize the regularity found in the English language while, at the same time, recognizing the child's ability to handle diversity with ease.

However effective a program may be, the instructor is still crucial to its success. The teacher must realize that the reading process is a complicated matter requiring of the child many skills such as visual and auditory discrimination, decoding of sound-letter correspondences, and taking advantage of his underlying knowledge of the structure of his language. Linguistics is one of several academic fields which may help reading programs become more efficient.

RULES FOR SYLLABICATION

Reading 360 introduces syllabication for decoding on the basis of the following linguistically-ordered rules. To decode long or unfamiliar words, pupils are to start with Rule 1. If it does not apply, they are to go on to Rule 2. If necessary, they will try Rule 3 and possibly Rule 4.

1. First see if a word is a compound word, one made up of two or more words you know or can easily decode (*playmate* = *play* + *mate*). If it is, read its parts. Try saying it with the stress on the first part:

PLAYmate. It must make sense in the sentence you are reading.

2. Then look for prefixes, such as *de,* and suffixes, such as *ly,* and other word-endings you know, such as *ed.* Look for any larger word-parts you know, such as *ible.* If there are any, divide the word by removing that part and decoding the rest (the "root" word) as usual. Try putting the stress on the "root." Remember that some word-endings like *ed* don't always stand for a separate syllable (as in *stopped*).

3. Look in the middle of the word for a consonant cluster, such as the *sk* in *basket,* or a consonant digraph, such as the *sh* in *bushel* or the *ll* in *bellow.* (A syllable which includes a doubled consonant letter is usually a stressed syllable.)

   a. If you find a cluster of 2 consonant letters, such as the *sk* in *basket,* divide the word into parts between the two letters of the cluster (*bas/ket*).

      If the cluster is made up of three consonant letters, such as the *mbl* in *grumble,* divide after the second of the three consonant letters (*grumb/le*).

   b. If you find a consonant digraph, such as the *sh* in *bushel,* or the *ll* in *bellow,* divide after the digraph.

      The spelling pattern of the first syllable will probably be CVC or some variation of this pattern (*bas* = CVC; *grumb* = CCVCC), so try decoding this syllable with an unglided vowel sound. Try putting the stress on the first syllable; vowel letters in the syllables other than the stressed syllable will often stand for the unglided vowel sound /ə/.

4. If there is no cluster of consonant letters in the middle of the word (*lizard*), try the following steps. Divide the word after the consonant that follows the first vowel letter (*liz/ard*), and decode the VC- or CVC-pattern syllable as a word in this pattern is decoded—by giving the vowel an unglided sound. Give stress to this syllable. Vowel letters in the other syllables will usually stand for the unglided vowel sound /ə/. If this strategy does not result in a word you know, try dividing after the first vowel letter (the *i* in *tiger*), or after the first vowel digraph (the *ai* in *raisin*), and decode the first syllable as a CV-pattern word is decoded—by giving the vowel a glided sound. Give stress to this syllable. Vowel letters in the other syllables will usually stand for the unglided vowel sound /ə/.

BIBLIOGRAPHY

TRAGER, GEORGE L., and HENRY LEE SMITH, *An Outline of English Structure.* New York: A.C.L.S., 1957.

VENEZKY, RICHARD F., "English orthography: its graphical structure and its relation to sound," *Reading Research Quarterly,* Vol. II (Spring 1967), pp. 75–105.

Use of Context Clues

Robert Emans

Ohio State University

Mary had a little lamb,
Its fleece was white as _____..

Few four-year-old children would be unable to complete the sentence with *snow*. Likewise, Becky and her mother wanted to go shopping. They climbed into the _____ to go to the store." Few children, even before entering school, would have difficulty with supplying any one of several words which would make sense: *car, automobile, bus, streetcar.* Children use context in their oral language, easily and naturally. Children, and adults too, use context clues to aid them in their reading.

It is easy to find testimonials to the importance of context clues in reading. Open almost any textbook on the subject and there are such statements as

It would be difficult to overestimate the value of the context in children's word perception in reading (7:16).

Contextual clues provide one of the most important aids to word identification and interpretation (6:84).

Context clues are perhaps the most important single aid to word perception (11:25).

The person who has not developed skill in the use of verbal context has not become a mature reader (22:23).

It is important to know, however, that many children who are thought to be in difficulty in reading because of limited skill in analytical techniques or because they have insufficient knowledge of phonetic, structural, or visual elements are usually in difficulty because they are not using context clues well (4:321).

Obviously, statements praising the worth of context clues are easily found. Much has been written about how the use of context helps the reader develop the meaning of words. As important as it may be this topic is not the concern of this paper. Rather, the purpose is to attack the more elusive problem and explore what aid the use of context clues gives the reader in respect to word recognition.

There are at least four uses of context clues in word recognition. These can be summarized as follows:

1. Context clues can help children remember words they have identified

"Use of Context Clues," by Robert Emans, in *Reading and Realism,* Proceedings of the Thirteenth Annual Convention, 13 (1) (1969), 76–82, ed. J. Allen Figurel. Reprinted with permission of Robert Emans and the International Reading Association.

earlier, but forgotten. Most teachers can cite examples of a child's having difficulty with a partially known word and then recognizing the word in a new setting after being told that the word is a familiar one and that it makes sense. For example, if a child reads "Bill was a cow" for "Bill saw a cow," asking him if what he reads makes sense will often enable him to correct himself.

2. Context clues may be combined with other word-analysis clues (phonic and structural analysis) to check on the accuracy of words tentatively identified by the use of other clues. Bond and Wagner state that context clues serve as "checks on the accuracy of all the other techniques that are used" (5:172).

3. Context clues help in the rapid recognition of words for all readers by helping one anticipate what a word might be. The ability to draw an accurate inference to what a word is can serve as a time-saver. It is a faster technique than other word recognition aids such as phonics. It enables the reader to use only those phonic and other analytical techniques which are necessary to distinguish one word from another. For example, instead of having to sound out a word, the efficient reader uses only enough phonic clues to recognize the word quickly when combined with the meaning clues.

4. Context clues are required for the correct identification of some words. Gray states, "The pronunciation of many words (permit, for example) depends upon their meaning in a given context" (11:148). Other words which require the use of context clues are lead in a pencil or lead the way, wind a ball of string or the wind blew, tear a piece of paper or a tear flowed down her cheek, and piggy bank or a bank to fish from.

HOW DO CONTEXT CLUES WORK IN WORD RECOGNITION?

Following the importance of context clues and some of the uses of context clues in word recognition, one should ask how context clues work? By answering this question, one can gain a better idea as to how to teach the use of context clues.

To understand how context clues work it must be recalled that the child brings to reading a background of experience and oral language. Likewise, the child must bring to the reading situation a habit of demanding meaning from his reading. A child must combine his experience, his oral language, and the meaning he gets from his reading if he is to use successfully context clues in recognizing words. When he meets a word which he cannot recognize, he uses his experiences, oral language, and the meaning of the words, phrases, sentences, and paragraphs surrounding the word to anticipate what the word might be. Bond and Wagner state, "Instead of having to recognize the word from the total of words in the English language, the use of context clues limits the choice of words to the few that would fit the meaning of the passage being read" (5:172). By also using the other word recognition skills the child has at his disposal, he tentatively identifies the word and checks to see if the word makes sense. For example, if a child reads the sentence, 'Jenny picked up her _____ to draw," he can, from his experience, limit the words to such possibilities as pen, crayon, pencil, or chalk. He would not have to select the word from the 800,000 or so possible words in the English language. By combining this information with various phonic clues, the child could recognize the exact word more quickly than by using only phonics.

With respect to the point that context clues may be used in conjunction with other word recognition techniques, Bond and Tinker state, "Meaning clues alone are not enough for good reading at any level. They must be accompanied by the use of a flexible set of word recognition skills. It is the interaction of all the word-study skills that forms the foundation on which a competent reader builds his reading structure" (4:322). DeBoer and Dallmann state, "Context clues are most effective when they are employed along with other methods of word attack" (8:111). In actual reading, the use of context clues is probably so closely tied in with other word recognition techniques that neither can be separated. Context clues alone are seldom adequate because they provide only one aid to word recognition. They may suggest one of several possible words but seldom point to the specific word. For example, in the sentence. "The mouse nibbled a piece of _____," any number of possible words could fit the meaning. However, by combining the sense of the sentence with the phonic clue that the word begins with a *ch* sound, the reader can readily supply the word *cheese*. Children should probably be discouraged from using context clues alone. By combining them with other word recognition techniques a child would be discouraged from wild guessing. Therefore, in relation to the discussion that follows, it should be remembered that whenever context clues are taught, they should probably be combined with other word recognition aids.

Some people might regard the use of context clues as untutored or guessing; and in a sense it is. However, it is probably more accurately described as inferential reasoning which must be developed, guided, and used in many areas of life. Nila Banton Smith states, "Surely this process of examining meanings, reasoning, and deducing an unrecognized word is not just a matter of chance guessing" (20:186). Kolson and Kolinger state, "Guessing is the mainstay of the contextual clue skill and should be encouraged, but wild guessing is a symptom of a disability in contextual clue use" (14:65). The sophisticated use of context clues, therefore, should probably be developed along with reasoning and the use of other word recognition skills.

THE CLASSIFICATION OF CONTEXT CLUES

Various attempts have been made to classify the wide variety of context clues. Although these classification schemes may be closely related to those for developing word meanings, they also have relevance for the use of context clues in word recognition. Artley (3) identified ten types of contextual aids the reader might find in printed matter: typographical (e.g., quotation marks, parentheses), structural (e.g., appositives, nonrestrictive clauses), substitute words (synonyms, antonyms), word elements (roots, suffixes, prefixes), figures of speech (similes, metaphors), pictorial representation (e.g., pictures, diagrams, charts), inference, direct explanation, background of experience of the reader, and subjective clues (e.g., tone, mood, intent). Likewise, McCullough (15) identified two general classes of clues, idea and presentation. Idea clues included pictorial illustration, verbal, experience, comparison and contrast, synonym, summary, mood, definition, and familiar expression. The presentation clues included the position of words, the sequence of a sentence or paragraph, and the general organization of a selection. From a study of 500,000 running words Deighton (9) identified four *key words* classes (definition, examples, modifiers, and restatement) and *inferential clues* for which the reader has no direct clue except his ability to draw inferences. In his dissertation, for which he won the IRA research award, Ames (1) found fourteen clues from his case studies of mature readers using a variety of contextual situations:

1. Clues derived from language experience or familiar expressions
2. Clues utilizing modifying phrases or clauses
3. Clues utilizing definition or description
4. Clues provided through words connected or in series
5. Comparison or contrast clues
6. Synonyms clues
7. Clues provided by the tone, setting, and mood of a selection
8. Referral clues
9. Association clues
10. Clues derived from the main idea and supporting details pattern of paragraph organization
11. Clues provided through the question-and-answer pattern of paragraph organization
12. Preposition clues
13. Clues utilizing nonrestrictive clauses or appositive phrases
14. Clues derived from cause and effect pattern of paragraph and sentence organization

Concerning the Artley and McCullough classifications, Russell states, "These are often too technical for systematic use in the elementary school. . . . " (19:300–301). Likewise, Ames states in respect to his own study that that "It must be stressed that much more research is necessary and one would be ill-advised to try to develop elaborate instructional procedures based on the present classification scheme" (2:81). An appropriate task regarding the implementation of context clues in word recognition would appear to be the development of a simplified scheme for classifying the numerous kinds of context clues identified. The next few paragraphs will suggest such a possible scheme.

Most context clues for use in word recognition seem to fall into one of three main categories: meaning bearing clues, language bearing clues, and organization clues. The meaning bearing clues use the sense of the sentence or sentences surrounding the unrecognized word. The category includes such clues for recognizing unknown words as familiar expressions and idioms, definitions, descriptions, examples, synonyms, antonyms included in the text, as well as comparisons and contrasts, and the tone, mood, and setting of what is being read.

The language bearing clues use knowledge of syntax, the structure of sentences, as aids in word recognition. Hildreth states, "The use of context clues has its roots in linguistics" (13: 156). There are a number of examples of language bearing clues. One such aid is the noting of phrases which may serve as a clue in recognition of modified unknown words. Another such aid is the recognition of unknown words through referral signal words, such as *these* and *same,* which refer to what has been stated previously. The associating of known words of one part of speech with closely related unknown words of another part of speech (such as nouns and verbs or adjectives and nouns) may serve as another clue.

For example, birds fly and fish swim; grass is green, and old ladies usually have gray hair. Finally the recognition of the relationship of nonrestrictive clauses, appositive phrases, or prepositional phrases to other parts of a sentence may serve as another language clue.

Another group of clues involve how sentences or paragraphs are organized. Within this group are such aids as the realization that an unknown word is part of a series of words and an appreciation of the relatedness of main idea to details, of questions to answers, and of cause to effect within sentences or paragraphs.

Therefore, it would appear that many context clues fall within one of these three classifications: meaning bearing, language bearing, and organization. The scheme is not all inclusive. For example, the scheme does not include contextual aids from pictures or the typography. However, it seems to simplify the complex classification schemes previously suggested.

Possibly to date, sufficient emphasis has not been placed on the role that context clues play in word recognition because the classification schemes have appeared to be too complex. The preceding simplified, yet comprehensive, scheme for the classification of context clues is proposed in the hope that it will foster further investigation in this area. Because of the simplification, teachers may feel encouraged to teach the use of context clues as knowledge of the structure and implications for teaching context clues is more attainable.

TEACHING CONTEXT CLUES

Although the teaching of context clues seems complex, there is evidence that teachers should attempt to do so. McCullough (15) concluded that adults fail to use context clues because they were never taught how to use them. In a study by McKee, children were found to use context clues effectively in only about one third of the opportunities presented (17:73), while Porter (21:316) found that third grade children could give an appropriate meaning of a word left out of context in about 80 percent of the cases. Since children may not develop the skill of using context clues without specific training, they should be given help in its development. Hester states, "Systematic guidance is necessary to help him learn this important technique for recognizing words" (12:138).

The goal of instruction for the use of context clues in word recognition is probably to develop such skill that context clues are used easily and automatically. If a child makes as many errors in contextual reading as he does in reading a list of words, he is probably failing to make extensive use of context clues. The problem becomes one of developing instructional procedures.

There is little evidence that children will use context clues more effectively if they have knowledge of sentence patterns. McKee states, such knowledge "contributes little if anything to the pupils' comprehension of the sentences" (18:185). However, children will probably benefit from knowing that (1) a word makes sense within a sentence; (2) readers can use sentence meaning to help recognize an unrecognized word; and (3) more than one word may fit the meaning of a sentence and, therefore, structure and phonic clues are often necessary.

In preparing to teach the use of context clues, materials should be carefully scrutinized to determine if the content gives adequate clues to words which children have not yet learned to recognize in their reading but possess in their speaking-listening vocabularies. Only a few such words should be presented at any one time, as too many unknown words make using the context difficult and might encourage wild guessing. The exact ratio of unknown words to known words probably depends on the children's intelligence, maturity, and background, although Bond and Tinker suggest that about one word in every forty running words should be unknown (4:321). Nevertheless, the materials used should be easy enough for children to recognize the unknown word without too much difficulty.

The materials should reflect the language patterns of the child whenever possible, be at a concept level appropriate to the children, and have the unknown words evenly distributed throughout the text.

After the materials have been selected, provisions need to be made, as in any reading activity, to assure that children have the background to read the materials through prior direct and vicarious experiences, including discussions, explanations, demonstrations, and field trips. The children need then to be given direct guidance in reading using context clues. Such guidance may include talking about the idea so that knowing the meaning of a sentence or paragraph will help in recognizing unknown words; encouraging children to read the entire sentence before deciding on an unknown word, showing how context clues can be combined with other word recognition techniques, such as phonics; reading the exercises orally to the children and having the children supply the unknown word; covering a few lines in a story and having the children anticipate what will come; asking which part of a sentence or paragraph gives a clue to an unknown word; and showing that some words must be recognized in context, such as, *wound* the clock and *wound* a deer.

Pictures may be used in the lower grades to develop an orientation toward the use of context clues. Hildreth states, "The use of picture clues is similar to the use of context clues for deriving the meaning of new or forgotten words" (13:156). In the lower grades much of the content is carried by pictures in the readers. However, Weintraub found that children do not make as much of illustrations as they might (23). Therefore, children may be taught to look at pictures to get clues for unknown words since pictures are a part of the total context and since they may be helpful in demonstrating to children the concept of using context clues. Picture-word cards, picture dictionaries, and introducing new words in advance of reading with the aid of pictures can be helpful in getting children to use pictures as aids in word recognition.

As soon as children have developed enough sight words to read sentences, pictures become less and sentences become more important for developing the use of context clues. Sentences, paragraphs, riddles, and stories with parts of words omitted may be given to children. Emans (10) found the following hierarchy of exercises, easiest to most difficult, to be significant at the .001 level of confidence for children from grades three to ten:

1. No clues given other than context
2. Beginning letter given
3. Length of word given
4. Beginning and ending letters given
5. Four word choice given
6. Consonants given

Teachers can probably think of variations to the exercises. For example, in the multiple-choice type of exercise, words with the same sounds or words with similar configurations may be used.

In summary, this paper shows the importance of helping children develop skills in the use of context clues in word recognition and makes suggestions as to how to teach these skills.

REFERENCES

1. AMES, W. S., "A Study of the Process by which Readers Determine Word Meaning Through the Use of Verbal Context," unpublished doctoral dissertation, University of Missouri, 1965.

2. AMES, W. S., "The Development of a Classification Scheme of Contextual Aids," *Reading Research Quarterly,* 2 (1966), 57–82.

3. ARTLEY, A. S., "Teaching Word-Meaning through Context," *Elementary English Review,* 20 (1943), 68–74.

4. BOND, G. L., and M. A. TINKER, *Reading Difficulties: Their Diagnosis and Correction.* New York: Appleton-Century-Crofts, 1967.

5. BOND, G. L., and EVA B. WAGNER, *Teaching the Child to Read* (3rd ed.). New York: Macmillan, 1960.

6. CARTER, H. L. J., and DOROTHY J. McGINNIS, *Teaching Individuals to Read.* Boston: D. C. Heath, 1962.

7. CORDTS, ANNA D., *Phonics for the Reading Teacher.* New York: Holt, Rinehart and Winston, 1965.

8. DE BOER, JOHN J., and MARTHA DALLMANN, *The Teaching of Reading.* New York: Holt, Rinehart and Winston, 1964.

9. DEIGHTON, L., *Vocabulary Development in the Classroom.* New York: Teachers College, Bureau of Publications, 1959.

10. EMANS, R., and GLADYS MARY FISHER, "Teaching the Use of Context Clues," *Elementary English,* 44 (1967), 243–246.

11. GRAY, W. S., *On Their Own in Reading.* Glenview, Illinois: Scott, Foresman, 1960.

12. HESTER, KATHLEEN B., *Teaching Every Child to Read.* New York: Harper and Row, 1964.

13. HILDRETH, GERTRUDE, *Teaching Reading: A Guide to Basic Principles and Modern Practices.* New York: Holt, Rinehart and Winston, 1958.

14. KOLSON, C. J., and G. KOLUGER, *Clinical Aspects of Remedial Reading.* Springfield, Illinois: Charles C Thomas, 1963.

15. McCULLOUGH, CONSTANCE M., "Learning to Use Context Clues," *Elementary English Review,* 20 (1943), 140–43.

16. McCULLOUGH, CONSTANCE M., "The Recognition of Context Clues in Reading," *Elementary English Review,* 22 (1945), 1–5.

17. McKEE, P., *The Teaching of Reading.* Boston: Houghton Mifflin, 1948.

18. McKEE, P., *Reading: A Program of Instruction for the Elementary School.* Boston: Houghton Mifflin, 1966.

19. RUSSELL, D. H., *Children Learn to Read* (2nd ed.). Boston: Ginn, 1961.

20. SMITH, NILA BANTON, *Reading Instruction for Today's Children.* Englewood Cliffs, New Jersey: Prentice-Hall, 1963.

21. SPACHE, G. D., *Reading in the Ele-*

mentary School. Boston: Allyn and Bacon, 1964.

22. TINKER, M. A., *Bases for Effective Reading*. Minneapolis: University of Minnesota Press, 1965.

23. WEINTRAUB, S., "The Effect of Pictures on the Comprehension of a Second-Grade Basal Reader," unpublished doctoral dissertation, University of Illinois, 1960.

7

Comprehension and Thinking Strategies

No one denies that one ultimate aim of reading instruction is to produce readers who comprehend what they read. There is, however, some debate whether decoding or comprehension should receive primary emphasis during beginning reading instruction or whether each should receive equal emphasis.

Closely related to reading comprehension is listening comprehension. Research indicates that listening may also be improved by the same kinds of instructional procedures used to improve reading comprehension; in fact, training in listening has been shown to have a beneficial effect on reading comprehension.

Robert Ruddell defines comprehension as ". . . the process of thinking in response to symbolic representation which ranges along a meaning continuum from factual to interpretive to applicative. . . ."[1] In his investigation of a literacy teaching model, Ruddell discusses basic components of comprehension ranging from vocabulary development to relational meaning.

Examining the definition and the components of comprehension, the reader will become acutely aware of the complexity of the comprehension process. In all probability most individuals use a variety of comprehension and thinking strategies in the reading and listening process.

Does the child's development of thinking strategies follow a pattern? Jean Piaget has provided a framework for the development of thought, a process which he divides into five stages: the period of sensorimotor intelligence (birth to two years), the period of preconceptual thought (two to four years), the period of intuitive thought (four to seven years), the period of concrete operations (seven to eleven years), and the period of formal operations (eleven to fifteen years).[2] In the first selection, Piaget discusses the dynamics of thought. He feels that to explain the development of thought one must rely on three principal factors—maturation, physical experience, and social interaction—to

[1] Robert B. Ruddell, *A Research Investigation of a Literacy Teaching Model: Project DELTA.* U.S. Department of Health, Education and Welfare, Office of Education, EPDA Project No. 005262 (Berkeley: University of California, 1972).

[2] Jean Piaget, *The Psychology of Intelligence* (London: Routledge and Kegan Paul, 1950).

which, Piaget believes, a fourth and intervening factor, equilibrium, *must* be added. According to Piaget the child seeks to establish an equilibrium, or balance, between what he understands and what he experiences in his environment. This balance may evolve from any of the three principal factors identified. If he has learned that a ball can be soft and round, the child must adjust his schema to reestablish equilibrium when he learns that a ball may also be *hard* and round.

As she directs the child's learning in the classroom, the teacher must remind herself of the factors that influence the child's development. In addition, the teacher can help the child to establish the needed equilibrium between what he already knows and the new ideas and experiences with which he is confronted.

What implications do Piaget's theories and research have for the reading teacher? Millie Almy discusses some of the implications these theories have for beginning reading. Among these implications, she believes, are the role of play in learning, the problems of visual and auditory discrimination and left–right orientation, and other aspects of learning to read which may be tied to the stages of cognitive development proposed by Piaget.

Russell Stauffer views reading as a learning process influenced by a large number of variables, both independent of the reading act and dependent on its efficiency. *What are these reading related variables and how do they influence reading instruction and learning?* Stauffer discusses the variables and then describes the reading–thinking process as it relates to them. He contends that reading efficiency can be attained if teachers and students are acquainted with the reading–thinking process. Stauffer also differentiates between *meaning reception learning* and *discovery learning* and discusses the difference in the ways in which the two modes of learning proceed.

David Russell calls attention to the caution that has characterized the study of thinking in the United States. Only recently have American psychologists given substantial attention to the study of the intellect. *But what constitutes thinking behavior?* Russell divides thinking behavior into six categories: perceptual thinking, associative thinking, concept formation, problem solving, critical thinking, and creative thinking. He then proceeds to discuss the various studies that have been undertaken in each of these categories.

After reviewing the research, Russell concludes that even in the higher level categories, skills can and should be taught. He is concerned that perhaps too much attention is being given to the perceptual aspects of word identification and to children's responses to literal meaning. Today some educators with a behavioristic orientation are suggesting that too much attention is being given to critical and creative thinking (and not enough to the decoding skills and factual material). Unfortunately however, standardized reading test data, which serve to support such viewpoints, measure only the lower levels of thinking and often reflect a distorted picture of children's reading performance.

Not all comprehension takes place as a result of reading. Far more of a child's time in the classroom is spent listening to information. *What is the relationship between listening and reading?* Paul Hollingsworth reviews this relationship and discusses the effect of training in listening on reading performance. A positive relationship indicates the necessity of providing better instruction in listening.

If a child's ability to listen with comprehension is positively related to his ability to read with comprehension, how can comprehension in both areas be improved simultaneously? Ralph Nichols discusses the problem of inefficient listening, which he feels is the result of poor listening habits. Nichols outlines three skills in concentration which the good listener must practice. He also provides suggestions for teaching listening in the primary grades and for reinforcing good listening behavior.

Helping children to comprehend what they read and what they hear is a continuous process. The teacher cannot say, "Today I'll teach comprehension," and then forget it for the rest of the week. She must become aware of the many facets of comprehension and of the strategies children use to understand verbal material. This knowledge can be used to improve the comprehension abilities of students at all levels of educational experience.

The Genetic Approach to the Psychology of Thought

Jean Piaget

From a developmental point of view, the essential in the act of thinking is not contemplation—that is to say, that which the Greeks called "theorema"—but the action of the dynamics.

Taking into consideration all that is known, one can distinguish two principal aspects:

1. The formal viewpoint which deals with the configuration of the state of things to know—for instance, most perceptions, mental images, imageries.
2. The *dynamic* aspect, which deals with transformations—for instance, to disconnect a motor in order to understand its functioning, to dis-

associate and vary the components of a physical phenomenon, to understand its causalities, to isolate the elements of a geometrical figure in order to investigate its properties, etc.

The study of the development of thought shows that the dynamic aspect is at the same time more difficult to attain and more important, because only transformations make us understand the state of things. For instance: when a child of 4 to 6 years transfers a liquid from a large and low glass into a narrow and higher glass, he believes in general that the quantity of the liquid has increased, because he is

Jean Piaget, "The Genetic Approach to the Psychology of Thought," *Journal of Educational Psychology*, 52, 1961, 271–76. Copyright (1961) by the American Psychological Association and reproduced by permission.

limited to comparing the initial state (low level) to the final state (high level) without concerning himself with the transformation. Toward 7 or 8 years of age, on the other hand, a child discovers the preservation of the liquid, because he will think in terms of transformation. He will say that nothing has been taken away and nothing added, and, if the level of the liquid rises, this is due to a loss of width, etc.

The formal aspect of thought makes way, therefore, more and more in the course of the development to its dynamic aspect, until such time when only transformation gives an understanding of things. To think means, above all, to understand; and to understand means to arrive at the transformations, which furnish the reason for the state of things. All development of thought is resumed in the following manner: a construction of operations which stem from actions and a gradual subordination of formal aspects into dynamic aspects.

The operation, properly speaking, which constitutes the terminal point of this evolution is, therefore, to be conceived as an internalized action reversible (example: addition and subtraction, etc.) bound to other operations, which form with it a structured whole and which is characterized by well defined laws of totality (example: the groups, the lattice, etc.). Dynamic totalities are clearly different from the "gestalt" because those are characterized by their nonadditive composition, consequently irreversible.

So defined, the dynamics intervene in the construction of all thought processes; in the structure of forms and classifications, of relations and serialization of correspondences, of numbers, of space and time, of the causality, etc. One could think at first glance that space and geometry add to the formal aspect of thought. In this way one conceived of the geometric science in the past, considering it impure mathematics, but applicable to perception and intuition. Modern geometry, since *Le Programme d'Erlangen* by F. Klein, has tended, like all other precise disciplines, to subordinate the formal to the dynamic. The geometries are, indeed, understood today as relying all on groups of transformation, so that one can go from one to the other by characterizing one less general "subgroup" as part of a more inclusive group. Thus geometry too rests on a system of dynamics.

Any action of thought consists of combining thought operations and integrating the objects to be understood into systems of dynamic transformation. The psychological criteria of this is the appearance of the notion of conservation or "invariants of groups." Before speech, at the purely sensory-motor stage of a child from 0 to 18 months, it is possible to observe actions which show evidence of such tendencies. For instance: From 4–5 to 18 months, the baby constructs his first invariant, which is the schema of the permanent object (to recover an object which escaped from the field of perception). He succeeds in this by coordinating the positions and the displacements according to a structure, which can be compared to what the geometricians call "group displacements."

When, with the beginning of the symbolic function (language, symbolic play, imagerie, etc.), the representation through thought becomes possible, it is at first a question of reconstructing in thought what the action is already able to realize. The actions actually do not become transformed immediately into operations, and one has to wait until about 7 to 8 years for the child to reach a functioning level. During this preoperative period the child, therefore, only arrives at incomplete structures characterized by a lack in the notion of combinations and, consequently, by a lack of logic (in transivity, etc.).

In the realm of causality one can especially observe these diverse forms of precausality, which we have previously described in detail. It is true that a certain number of authors—Anglo-Saxon above all—have severely criticized these conclusions, while others have recognized the same facts as we have (animism, etc.). Yet, in an important recent book (which will appear soon) two Canadian authors, M. Laurendeau and A. Pinard, have taken the whole problem up once again by means of thorough statistics. In the main points they have come to a remarkable verification of our views, explaining, moreover, the methodological reasons for the divergencies among the preceding authors.

At about 7 to 8 years the child arrives at his first complete dynamic structures (classes, relations, and numbers), which, however, still remain concrete—in other words, only at the time of a handling of objects (material manipulation or, when possible, directly imagined). It is not before the age of 11 to 12 years or more that operations can be applied to pure hypotheses. At this latter level, a logic of propositions helps complete the concrete structures. This enlarges the structures considerably until their disposition.

The fundamental genetic problem of the psychology of thought is hence to explain the formation of these dynamic structures.

Practically, one would have to rely on three principal factors in order to explain the facts of development: maturation, physical experience, and social interaction. But in this particular case none of these three suffice to furnish us with the desired explanations—not even the three together.

Maturation. First of all, none of these dynamic structures are innate, but they form very gradually. (For example: The transitivity of equalities is acquired at approximately 6½ to 7 years, and the ability of linear measure comes about only at 9 years, as does the full understanding of weights, etc.) But progressive construction does not seem to depend on maturation, because the achievements hardly correspond to a particular age. Only the order of succession is constant. However, one witnesses innumerable accelerations or retardations for reasons of education (cultural) or acquired experience. Certainly one cannot deny the inevitable role which maturation plays, but is determined above all by existing possibility (or limitation). They still remain to be actualized, which brings about other factors. In addition, in the domain of thought, the factors of innateness seem above all limitative. We do not have, for example, an intuition of space in the fourth dimension; nevertheless we can deduce it.

Physical experience. Experiencing of objects plays, naturally, a very important role in the establishment of dynamic structures, because the operations originate from actions and the actions bear upon the object. This role manifests itself right from the beginning of sensory-motor explorations, preceding language, and it affirms itself continually in the course of manipulations and activities which are appropriate to the antecedent stages. Necessary as the role of experience may be, it does not sufficiently describe the construction of the dynamic structures—and this for the following three reasons.

First, there exist ideas which cannot

possibly be derived from the child's experience—for instance, when one changes the shape of a small ball of clay. The child will declare, at 7 to 8 years, that the quantity of the matter is conserved. It does so before discovering the conservation of weight (9 to 10 years) and that of volume (10 to 11 years). What is the quantity of a matter independently of its weight and its volume? This is an abstract notion corresponding to the "substance" of the pre-Socratic physicists. This notion is neither possible to be perceived nor measurable. It is, therefore, the product of a dynamic deduction and not part of an experience. (The problem would not be solved either by presenting the quantity in the form of a bar of chocolate to be eaten.)

Secondly, the various investigations into the learning of logical structure, which we were able to make at our International Center of Genetic Epistemology, lead to a very unanmious result: [1] one does not "learn" a logical structure as one learns to discover any physical law. For instance, it is easy to bring about the learning of the conservation of weight because of its physical character, but it is difficult to obtain the one of the transitivity of the relationship of the weight:

$$A = C \text{ if } A = B \text{ and } B = C$$

or the one of the relationship of inclusion, etc. The reason for this is that in order to arrive at the learning of a logical structure, one has to build on another more elementary logical (or prelogical) structure. And such structures consequently never stem from experience alone, but suppose always a coordinating activity of the subject.

Thirdly, there exist two types of experiences:

[1] See Etudes d'epistomologie genetique, Vols. 7 and 10.

1. The physical experiences show the objects as they are, and the knowledge of them leads to the abstraction directly from the object (example: to discover that a more voluminous matter is more or less heavy than a less voluminous matter).

2. The logicomathematical experience supposes to interrelate by action individual facts into the world of objects, but this refers to the result of these actions rather than to the objects themselves. These interrelations are arrived at by process of abstractions from the actions and their coordinates. For instance, to discover that 10 stones in a line always add up to 10, whether they are counted from left to right or from right to left. Because then the order and the total sum have been presented. The new knowledge consists simply in the discovery that the action of adding a sum is independent of the action of putting them in order. Thus the logicomathematical experience does not stem from the same type of learning as that of the physical experience, but rather from an equilibration of the scheme of actions, as we will see.

Social interaction. The educative and social transmission (linguistic, etc.) plays, naturally, an evident role in the formation of dynamic structures, but this factor does not suffice either to entirely explain its development, and this for two reasons:

First, a certain number of structures do not lend themselves to teaching and are prior to all teaching. One can cite, as an example, most concepts of conservation, of which, in general, the pedagogs agree that they are not problematic to the child.

The second, more fundamental, reason is that in order to understand the adult and his language, the child needs means of assimilation which are formed through structures preliminary to the social transmission itself—for instance, an ancient experience has shown us that French-speaking children understand very early the expression *"quelques unes de mes fleurs"* [some of my flowers] in contrast to *"toutes mes fleurs"* [all my flowers], and this occurs when they have not yet constructed the relation of inclusion:

Some *A* are part of all *B;*
therefore *A* < *B*

In conclusion, it is not exaggerated to maintain that the basic factors invoked before in order to explain mental development do not suffice to explain the formation of the dynamic structures. Though all three of them certainly play a necessary role, they do not constitute in themselves sufficient reason and one has to add to them a fourth factor, which we shall try to describe now.

This fourth factor seems to us to consist of a general progression of equilibration. This factor intervenes, as is to be expected, in the interaction of the preceding factors. Indeed, if the development depends, on one hand, on internal factors (maturation), and on the other hand on external factors (physical or social), it is self-evident that these internal and external factors equilibrate each other. The question is then to know if we are dealing here only with momentary compromises (unstable equilibrium) or if, on the contrary, this equilibrium becomes more and more stable. This shows that all exchange (mental as well as biological) between the organisms and the milieu (physical and social) as composed of two poles: (a) of the *assimilation* of the given external to the previous internal structures, and (b) of the *accommodation* of these structures to the given ones. The equilibrium

between the assimilation and the accommodation is proportionately more stable than the assimilative structures which are better differentiated and coordinated.

It is this equilibrium between the assimilation and accommodation that seems to explain to us the functioning of the reversible operations. This occurs, for instance, in the realm of notions of conservation where the invariants of groups do not account for the maturation and the physical experience, nor for the sociolingual transmission. In fact, dynamic reversibility is a compensatory system of which the idea of conservation constitutes precisely the result. The equilibrium (between the assimilation and the accommodation) is to be defined as a compensation of exterior disturbances through activities of the subject orientated in the contrary direction of these disturbances. This leads directly to the reversibility.

Notice that we do not conceive of the idea of equilibrium in the same manner as the "gestalt theory" does, which makes great use of this idea too, but in the sense of an automatical physical equilibrium. We believe, on the contrary, that the mental equilibrium and even the biological one presumes an activity of the subject, or of the organism. It consists in a sort of matching, orientated towards compensation—with even some overcompensation—resulting from strategies of precaution. One knows, for instance, that the homeostasis does not always lead to an exact balance. But it often leads to overcompensation, in response to exterior disturbances. Such is the case in nearly all occurrences except precisely in the case of occurrences of a superior order, which are the operations of reversible intelligence, the reversible logic of which is characterized by a complete and exact compensation (inverted operation).

The idea of equilibrium is so close to the one of reversibility that G. Brunner, in a friendly critcism of one of our latest books appearing in the *British Journal of Psychology*, proposes to renounce the idea of equilibrium because the notion of the reversibility seems sufficient to him. We hesitate to accept this suggestion for the following three reasons:

First, reversibility is a logical idea, while the equilibrium is a causal idea which permits the explanation of reforms by a means of a probabilistic schema. For instance, in order to explain the formation of the idea of conservation, one can distinguish a certain number of successive stages, of which each is characterized by the "strategy" of a progress of compensation. Now it is possible to show [2] that the first of these strategies (only bearing upon one dimension, to the neglect of others) is the most probable at the point of departure, and further, that the second of these strategies (with the emphasis on a second dimension) *becomes* the most likely—as a function of the result of the first. And, finally, that the third of these strategies (oscillation between the observed modifications upon the different dimensions and the discovery of their solidarity) *becomes* the most likely in the functioning of the results of the preceding, etc. From such a point of view the process of equilibration is, therefore, characterized by a sequential control with increasing probabilities. It furnishes a beginning for causal explanations of the reversibility and does not duplicate the former idea.

Secondly, the tendency of equilibri-

[2] *Logique et equilibre* (Vol. 2 of *Etudes d'epistomologie genetique*).

um is much broader for the operation than the reversibility as such, which leads us to explain the reversibility through the equilibrium and not the reverse. In effect, it is at this level of the obvious regulations and sensory-motor feedbacks that the process of equilibration starts. This in its higher form becomes intelligence. Logical reversibility is therefore conceivable as an end result and not as a beginning and the entire reversibility follows the laws of a semireversibility of various levels.

Thirdly, the tendency to equilibrate does not only explain this final reversibility, but also certain new synthesis between originally distinct operations. One can cite in this regard an example of great importance: the serial of whole numbers. Russell and Whitehead have tried to explain the basic set of numbers through the idea of equivalent classes, without recourse to the serial order. This means that two classes are believed to be equivalent, if one can put their respective elements into a reciprocal arrangement. Only when this relationship relies on the quality of the objects (an *A* put into relation with an *A*, a *B* with a *B*, etc.) one does not get the quantity. If this relationship is made exclusive of the qualities (an Individual *A* or *B* put into relationship with an Individual *B* or *A*) then there exists only one way to distinguish the elements from each other. In order not to forget one, or not to count the same twice, one must deal with them in succession and introduce the serial factor as well as the structure of classes. We may then say, psychologically speaking, that the sequence of whole numbers is synthesis between two groupings qualitatively distinct, the fitting of the classes and serialization, and that this synthesis takes place as soon as one excludes the qualities of the elements in question. But how does this synthesis occur? Precisely by a gradual process of equilibration.

On the one hand the child who develops his ideas from numbers is in possession of structures enabling him to fit them into classes (classifications). But if he wants to be exclusive of qualities in order to answer to the question "how many," he becomes unable to distinguish the elements. The disequilibrium which appears, therefore, obliges the child to resort to the idea of order and take recourse to arranging these elements into a lineal row. On the other hand, if the child arranges the elements as 1, 1, 1, etc., how would he know, for instance, how to distinguish the second from the third? This new disequilibrium brings him back to the idea of classification: The "second" is the element which has but one predecessor, and the "third" is one that has two of them. In short,

every new problem provokes a disequilibrium (recognizable through types of dominant errors) the solution of which consists in a re-equilibration, which brings about a new original synthesis of two systems, up to the point of independence.

During the discussion of my theories, Brunner has said that I have called disequilibrium what others describe as motivation. This is perfectly true, but the advantage of this language is to clarify that a cognitive or dynamic structure is never independent of motivational factors. The motivation in return is always solidary to structural (therefore cognitive) determined level. The language of the equilibrium presents that activity, that permits us to reunite into one and the same totality those two aspects of behavior which always have a functional solidarity because there exists no structure (cognition) without an energizer (motivation) and vice versa.

Young Children's Thinking
and the Teaching of Reading

Millie C. Almy
University of California, Berkeley

When does an American child begin to learn to read? When he watches his mother prepare his food from a can or carton covered with reading material? When he first pays attention to television? When he responds to his mother's "don't touch?" When he says his first word? When he encounters his first book?

Perhaps we cannot pinpoint such beginnings, but increasing knowledge of the way in which language develops and the processes involved in auditory and visual perception suggests that such incidents as these are important steps in learning to read.

When I studied beginning reading in 1948, an important issue concerned the function of the kindergarten program. Was it to focus on preparing children for formal reading instruction and, if so how? The issue as I saw it then was not between "all reading and no reading, but rather between two conceptions of reading in child development. One viewed it as a series of stages or levels, at each stage of which certain experiences were appropriate. The other viewed it as a more

continuous process of reorganization, in which the reaching out for new experience was, at least in part, dependent on what had gone before." [1]

Recent interpretations of the work of Piaget, current studies of infant learning, and new appraisals of earlier studies of maturation and training lend considerable support to the latter point of view. They also open up, as Hunt points out in his provocative volume *Intelligence and Experience* the possibility that it might be feasible to discover ways to govern the encounters that children have with their environments, especially during the early years of their development, in order to achieve a substantially faster rate of intellectual development. Moreover, inasmuch as the optimum rate of intellectual development would mean also self-directing interest and curiosity and genuine pleasure in intellectual activity, promoting intellectual development properly need imply nothing like

[1] M. C. Almy, *Children's Experiences Prior to First Grade and Success in Beginning Reading* (New York: Teachers College Bureau of Publications, 1949).

Reprinted by permission of United States Department of Health, Education, and Welfare, Office of Education.

the grim urgency which has been associated with "pushing" children.[2]

Viewing the process of learning to read as one that both reflects and contributes to progress in intellectual development, I should like to examine some of the implications for beginning reading instruction that may be drawn from Piaget's theories and research related to them.

Piaget was concerned primarily with various aspects of children's thought in relation to the evolution of the mental operations involved in the adults' abstract logical thought. He traced this evolution from the earliest reflex behavior of the infant, describing how he thought such initially diverse functions as looking, grasping, and sucking gradually become organized into increasingly complex patterns, or "schemata." These schemata, originally occurring as actions, were eventually internalized and became mental pictures or ideas, to which words were attached, according to Piaget.

Once the ability to comprehend and to use words has developed, these ideas, it appears, are similarly organized into increasingly complex patterns and associations. For example (the illustration is mine), in infancy the child, in looking at, reaching for, and grasping a large ball, adjusts his prehension to its size and contour differently than for a small cube. Given enough of such sensorimotor experiences and the added stimulation of hearing these experiences described by others, he can ultimately apply the words *cube, ball, large, small, big, little, round,* and *square* appropriately.

We say that he is developing concepts. But such concepts remain for a long time highly personal and indi-

[2] J. McVicker Hunt, *Intelligence and Experience* (New York: The Ronald Press Co., 1961).

vidualistic. They are, as some authors have termed it, "embedded" in objects. The child tends to make direct comparisons between objects, or his recollections of them, in his testing of whether a particular concept applies in a new situation. To illustrate, a 3½-year-old remarked while polishing apples, "These is round like marbles is round." When confronted with some candy "jawbreakers," he actually substituted them for marbles in a game.

At this low level, many concepts are still not freed from the examples in which they appear. However, this child's awareness of and verbalization of the property of roundness suggests that she had the rudimentary framework of associations or "schemata" necessary to handle incoming information relating to a variety of instances. Presumably, the impact of many such encounters finally transforms the notion so that it becomes a more adequate and somewhat more abstract concept of roundness.

The difficulties the child under the age of 6 has in dealing with properties or attributes apart from objects are epitomized in Piaget's experiments dealing with "conservation."

Here he asks at what point in development and through what kinds of environmental encounters a child comes to grasp the idea that a given amount or quantity is not changed by transformations in appearance. For example, does the child, confronted by an array of cubes that are spaced close together and then spread far apart, focus on the number of cubes, or is he distracted by the area they occupy? In the first instance he will "conserve," indicating that the quantity remains the same. In the second, he will maintain that these are "more" when they are spread out. (Those of you who have taught kindergartners have probably encountered children who wish to break up their snacktime crackers so they will have more to eat.)

Again, given two vessels of liquid that he has agreed contain the same amounts, does the child "conserve" the amount when that in one vessel is poured into another of different shape? Or does he pay attention to the height and width of the vessel successively (rather than dealing with the relationship between the two dimensions), so that he maintains that there is more in one than in the other?

These are but two of a variety of demonstrations that Piaget uses to test whether or not a child has achieved conservation, or in terms of the mental processes involved—"reversibility."

Piaget's collaborator, Barbel Inhelder, describes two forms of reversibility: "(a) negation, . . . in which a perceived change in form is canceled by its corresponding negative thought operation; and (b) reciprocity, as expressed in the child's discovery that 'being a foreigner' is a reciprocal relationship, or that left–right, before–behind spatial relationships are relative." [3]

Transition to operational thinking begins, according to Piaget, at around the age of 6. Changes in the concrete–abstract dimension of thinking represented in this transition are more or less paralleled by changes in the subjective–objective dimension of thinking. The older child is ordinarily less preoccupied with personal and emotional concerns, or perhaps better able to extricate himself from them and to consider the viewpoints of other people. His thinking is less often autistic and less often dominated by fantasy and imagination.

[3] William Kessen and Clementina Kuhlman. "Thought in the Young Child," *Child Development Monograph,* 1962, vol. 83, no. 2.

The research in which I am currently engaged has been concerned with the period of transition from a preoperational and subjectively oriented thought to a more operational and objective kind.

YOUNG CHILDREN'S THINKING: "CONSERVATION" IN RELATION TO OTHER VARIABLES

We interviewed 330 children from kindergarten and from the first and second grades of two New York City schools, one middle and one lower class. Demonstrations and questions used to establish the presence or absence of conservation concerned a number of cubes following transformation in their appearance. In each instance the interviewer, prior to posing the crucial questions, used a series of training procedures to establish the child's ability to describe what he saw.

The interview also included demonstrations and related questions about the floating and sinking of a variety of objects. We gave the Stencil Design Test and the Ammons Picture Vocabulary Test. From school records we obtained measures of reading readiness and achievement, understanding of mathematical concepts, and Pintner–Cunningham IQ scores.

The general trends described by Piaget are substantiated by the results. In the middle-class school 10 percent of the kindergartners, 30 percent of the first graders, and 46 percent of the second graders gave substantial evidence of the ability to conserve. In the lower class school, where bilingualism was a complicating factor, the trend toward increasing ability with age appeared to be less clear and much slower. The percentages were 4, 7, and 22.

The measures of reading ability

were those used in the New York City schools, the New York Tests of Reading Readiness and Reading Growth. Since we did not administer the test ourselves and have had access to only a portion of the test booklets, we can only regard our results as suggestive of relationships that might be examined through further research. At the first-grade level in the middle-class school, the children who "conserved" did significantly better in the reading readiness tests than those who did not "conserve." The differences were not statistically significant at the second-grade level.

We are now trying to determine the role of verbal intelligence and other factors in the ability to conserve. Our present feeling is that whatever is tested by the Stencil Design Test is contributing more to conservation ability than is sheer verbal ability.

IMPLICATIONS FOR BEGINNING READING INSTRUCTION

Many of the implications for beginning reading instruction that emerge from Piaget-inspired research have to do with concept formation. To neglect providing many and varied concrete experiences in the period of preoperational thought may later hinder the adequate development of abstract thinking and may possibly interfere with the development of reading comprehension.

Piaget's theory further implies the necessity that the child discover his own errors in thinking in such fashion that he, himself, attempts to correct them. The adult cannot think for the child nor can he impose adult answers on him. Rather, he paces the child's understanding with increasingly varied and complex problems so that the child

becomes aware of his own error, rearranges his information, and moves gradually to a new synthesis.

This emphasis on active experimentation clarifies the role of play in the intellectual life of the young child. From it, some support might be found for the postponement of reading instruction.

More apropos is a consideration of the ways young children deal with printed words and letters. Given a reading environment, a child may begin as early as the nursery school years to search for meaning in printed symbols. When he confronts a word similar in configuration to one he has already learned, he tends to assume it is the same until he has learned to search the surrounding text or picture for confirming or negating information.

As to specific training for the visual and auditory perception aspects of learning to read, it may be that many of the discriminative abilities that go into the reading process are developed, or fail to develop, long before the child is brought to kindergarten, even prior to nursery school. What goes into the typical reading readiness program at the first grade, or in the kindergarten, may represent for some children too little and too late; and for others, too much and too soon. For example, exercises to facilitate the perception of gross differences may come long after a child has learned to make such distinctions accurately. On the other hand, exercises in noticing subtle differentiations in detail, such as those involved in distinguishing a *p* from a *g*, or in maintaining a left–right orientation, may come before a child has had the variety of experiences requisite for the development of such skills. A child who has not achieved "reversibility" in his thought processes and who does not understand reciprocal relationships may lack the stability of perception necessary for formal reading instruction.[4]

A recent study by David Elkind, replicating earlier Piaget experiments, indicated that a majority of children under the age of 7 lacked a differentiated concept of left–right.[5]

We can speculate on the most effective way to insure steady progress

[4] David P. Ausubel, "Stages of Intellectual Development and Their Implications for Early Childhood Education," paper presented at the First Institute on the Concept of Development and Early Childhood Education, New York City, September 1962.

[5] David Elkind, "Children's Conceptions of Right and Left," *Journal of Genetic Psychology*, 1961, Vol. 99, pp. 269–78.

toward learning to read in the years before formal instruction. An environment that provides the child with many opportunities for varied sensory and motor experiences is essential. So too is the presence of people who talk *with* (not merely to or at) the child, people who read and write and who share these activities with children.

Current research in young children's thinking indicates that it is desirable for those responsible for the child's instruction to be skilled in appraising his discriminative and thinking abilities. Thus, the experiences provided him can be more effectively designed to further both his intellectual development and his progress toward learning to read.

Reading as a Cognitive Process

Russell G. Stauffer

University of Delaware, Newark

Comprehension is the function of a large number of variables. When the value of a variable changes, the value of comprehension changes also. Mathematically it can be said that $c = (f)x$; or that c (comprehension) is a function of x (a variable). When the function of x changes, the efficiency of c may also. Even though the exact relationships among variables cannot be stated precisely, it is possible to identify the principal variables that influence the teaching-learning process in purposeful learning.

Undoubtedly certain independent variables in a reading instruction situation influence learning: the teacher—her actions and interactions with the children; the student—his abilities and motivation; the instructional materials—their nature and difficulty; and the group and its cohesiveness. The dependent variable—reading efficiency—is also dependent upon processes essential to purposeful learning. The processes include setting a goal, gathering and processing information, accepting or rejecting information through critical thinking, reaching or not reaching a goal, and experiencing feelings of success or failure. It is with reading–thinking processes that this presentation is primarily concerned.

THE INDEPENDENT VARIABLES

The history of research in teaching and learning shows that the single most significant independent variable in a purposeful instructional situation is the teacher. The findings reported by the twenty-seven USOE studies of first-grade reading instruction reconfirm this (*10*). Encouraging and guiding pupil discovery (6:247) is not only the trend in recent years but is also the salvation of the learner caught up in the midst of a series of knowledge explosions (3). Rote learning and lock-step practices are giving way before teaching and learning which encourage the student to raise questions and find answers and *use* the answers in different situations. Adler says (*1*:43) "The art of reading, in short, includes all the same skills that are involved in the art of discovery: keenness of observation, readily available memory, range of imagination, and, of course, a reason trained in analysis and reflection . . . To whatever extent it is true that reading is learning, it is also true that reading is thinking."

The role of the teacher takes on new dimensions when the art of discovery is taught. A delicate balance is required between giving too much direction to students and giving too much freedom and responsibility. The immediate teaching situation determines largely how much help a teacher should give as well as when and why to give help. "Where students are assisted in discovery, usually three features are incorporated into motivation: bringing to the students a problem that is real and meaningful, (2) encouraging and guiding students in gathering information, and (3) providing a responsive environment in which students get accurate feedback promptly so they can ascertain the adequacy of their responses" (*4*:247).

Efficiency of learning is influenced by several factors in the cognitive domain; particularly intellectual ability both general and specific, and previous experience. In the affective domain such variables as interests, attitudes, values, and so on are determiners of readiness for learning and efficiency of learning.

While it is true that the knowledge and experience that students bring with them materially influences their learning, it is considered equally true that motivation or set or intention to learn strongly influence meaningful learning. The highest form of motivation in inquiry learning seems to be intrinsic to the process itself (*14*). The excitement inherent in gathering and processing information is tremendously satisfying. Focusing on the cognitive aspects of learning, by involving the learner intellectually—his questions, his hypotheses, his processing of information, his evaluation—mobilizes pupil effort and concentration of attention. As a result the information processed is more clearly differentiated, more functional in new situations, and more resistant to forgetting.

The material to be read must be potentially meaningful to the student. In other words, the material may not be too discrepant. It must be discriminable from what is already known, because students process data in terms of their established conceptual systems. As long as the information encountered consists of reasonably familiar events and situations, the process of assimilation occurs without too much difficulty (9). When faced with conceptual categories that can be readily assimilated, conceptual reorganization needs to occur. This process of reshaping and reorganizing conceptual structures is known as accommodation. The learner experiments and may attempt to break down data into component parts and analyze it in terms of variables he already knows. Material that can be organized so as to be assimilated is retained for a longer period of time. This is especially so if the conceptual models have stability and clarity.

When the experience and knowledge of the reader are not sufficiently broad or relevant so that ready assimilation can be accomplished, a promising technique is to help the reader gain a better grasp of the material by presenting to him advance-organizer type passages (2). Advance organizers are short expository passages that provide a general overview of the material, its organizational elements, and show how concepts already learned are similar to or different from the new concepts being presented.

Group cohesiveness can be guided to achieve useful goals. The nature of the task at hand and the group temperament or interaction can foster desired interactions among the pupils. Children performing at about the same level and capable of maintaining group prestige tend to develop group cohesiveness. To accomplish this, teachers may divide a whole class so that each member experiences success and secures prestige for a job well done.

Each of the independent variables described significantly influence reading instruction and learning. Efficient reading skills to be accomplished, must be taught. This means that if efficient pupil learning is to be accomplished expert teaching is required. Needed are teachers who are not only well-educated but also thoroughly acquainted with the reading–thinking process.

THE DEPENDENT VARIABLE

Comprehension as the dependent variable takes on a different significance when viewed from a teaching–learning point of view. Now comprehension efficiency becomes the major objective of reading instruction. Some of the criteria used to determine efficiency of comprehension are accuracy, thoroughness, speed, and style. The abilities that need to be developed are to be versatile and to think critically.

The versatile reader is one who has the ability to adapt his rate of reading to his purpose for reading and to the nature and difficulty of the material. The thinking reader attains his goal through productive thinking and sound judgments.

Comprehension efficiency is inferred from performance during and immediately after reading instruction, at a later time, and in different situations. Instructional effectiveness is a composite of many characteristics and varies from one directed reading activity to another. Much depends upon teacher behavior, pupils' cognitive abilities, and intellectual characteristics;

and the materials used. Much depends also on how a reader performs in the library, at home, in the curriculum areas of the school program, and so on.

Efficient reading blends process, content, and product in such a way that the purposes for reading are accomplished in the most economical time and way. This happens only when the reader knows why he is reading what he is reading, and tries to do it well.

THE NATURE OF THE
READING–THINKING PROCESS

A moment's reflection calls to mind many illustrations to support the fact that language and reading embody concepts used to communicate about objects, events, and principles. It is readily apparent, too, that much of the knowledge one gains throughout life and many of the conclusions one reaches are based upon concepts of a second-hand variety. Historical concepts are particularly illustrative. No one can go back in time and meet or see Caesar or experience living at the time of Caesar. The concepts any scholar has of that period in time are based on perceptual experiences that have had to be transformed and used abstractly. The same may be said when projecting plans into the future. The net result is that the cognitive structures a student forms perceptually by seeing, manipulating, and experimenting need to be established with the greatest of care, since it is on these structures or schemas that concepts learned by reading and study are based. If the inclusiveness and generality of these experienced happenings, events, and actual state of affairs are not thoroughly and thoughtfully

established, the subsequent concepts based on these mental structures will be all the more arbitrary and faulty. In other words, if the things we see and manipulate in our everyday affairs are examined only casually, they will provide schema of limited usefulness.

Dewey (4) considers reflective thinking an essential learning aim because it emancipates the student from merely impulsive and merely routine activities. Reflective thinking requires a turning over of ideas in the mind and giving them serious and consecutive thought so as to find something new or to see what is already known in a different light. In turn, he does not give the name *thinking* to the automatic, unregulated, and autistic ideas that course through the mind.

In school it is assumed that students read and study textbooks and similar expository materials in a reflective way and without rotely memorizing the content. By so doing they acquire new concepts and extend and refine old concepts. Of course, they may also read just to be entertained and may do so in such a way that a minimum of intellectual effort is required. Even so, books written primarily for entertainment can be examined as they are in literature appreciation courses.

When *meaningful reception learning* is compared with *discovery learning*, noteworthy distinctions can be identified (7:Chaps. 7 and 8). The virtues of discovery learning seem readily apparent, but the utility value of the method takes on a different perspective when it is realized that a student does not have to discover all concepts independently and that he does not have time to do so. In discovery learning a student attains concepts by observing their common attributes through active searching and productive thinking, by using them in new situations, and by evaluating their usefulness. In meaningful reception learning ". . . the entire content of what is to be learned is presented to the learner in final form" (4:85). He is asked to internalize it so that it will be available and reproducible at some other time. The process of meaningful reception learning, like that of discovery learning, requires the student to have a meaningful purpose and to use material that is potentially meaningful.

Undoubtedly, the reading-thinking process as a way to operate takes on major significance as the prime independent variable in the learning activity of a student. It does so because it focuses on the cognitive aspects of learning and is an indispensable condition of *meaningful learning* as well as a principal way of attaining concepts *by discovery learning.*

Setting a goal influences retention of meaningful material more than intention to remember after a goal has been reached. Retention is better, too, when practice is done with intent to learn, rather than incidentally. When learning is done with intent it is called purposeful learning.

Discovery type reading, motivated by pupil purposes, can be taught in a *group* situation where all the material is presented at one time to be internalized, as well as in *individualized* reading instruction where the reader is on his own and materials are made available, and he has to select what he needs to meet his purposes.

In the former procedure all the pupils are presented at the same time the same selection or the same textbook to be read. Now the teacher must direct the activity in such a way that the major responsibility for purposes for reading rests with the student (12). This is necessary because the learner has to know how to bridge the gap between what he already knows and what he is about to learn.

The use of advance organizers is one way of doing this. Subconcepts are provided which increase the familiarity and meaningfulness of the new material (2). Purposeful mental activity is developed by focusing on the cognitive aspects of the material to be learned and relying on a motivation that is developed retroactively from successful learning.

A survey of the material can be made so that a set can be obtained. Such a survey is made with the intent to raise questions and speculate about answers. A question well asked is half the answer and this, along with the speculation, helps the student marshall his knowledge and experience and compare it with what the context leads him to anticipate (11). Or one may ask students to note similarities and differences between the material to be studied and what they already know (15).

Questions can be raised for the learner. Then the students must be instructed to speculate about the answers (13). This speculation causes them to mobilize their knowledge, compare and contrast it with the nature of the question, and in turn help them make the question more or less their own. Such a procedure focuses on the motivational aspect of the students' intellectual commitment and concentration of attention.

Purposeful intellectual involvement of a student asked to reorganize his conceptual systems by reading is an indispensable condition of the reading process. The learner must be given an opportunity to try out his conceptual models by using them to make predictions, design objectives, or to set goals. Lorge (8:173) defines the teacher's task in a practical way and supports the need for learner involvement.

The teacher's task in the development of thinking is important and significant. The steps must, by suggesting, hinting, or questioning, lead the learner through the phases of understanding the problem, suggesting hypotheses or reasons for the existence of the problem, and formulating hypotheses for the solution of the problem. Here the teacher can help the learner by asking him to formulate questions. Good questioning is good hypothesis formulation.

This procedure implies a disposition to incorporate new ideas into the existent level of the student's cognitive structure by starting at and with the learner's level of ignorance.

In an individualized situation, inquiry reading is dictated by pupil interest, and material is selected by the pupil. The pupil decides on what conceptual changes he wishes to accomplish and how discrepant they are. He gathers and selects data, and processes the information in whatever sequence is meaningful to him. He programs and paces his own learning. Of course, teaching is involved. The teacher keeps a constant check on the purposes for reading—their nature and complexity. Skillful questioning by the teacher may help clarify the learner's purposes or bring them into better focus. Furthermore, to avoid having the pupil proceed randomly and inefficiently, the teacher arranges the learning situation so that productive inquiry-type individualized reading can be accomplished.

The gathering and processing of information varies from one arranged reading instruction situation to an-

other. In a meaningful reception type situation in which the material or textbook to be learned is given to the students to read, all of the information has been programmed for him. Now the great importance of cognitive structure is readily apparent because the data have been gathered and assembled for the reader. How he processes the information depends largely on the degree to which the reader focuses upon a problem. If a situation or problem has been intellectualized by the reader and stated, or restated, in such a way as to be clear to him, then the reading and thinking may be productive.

On the other hand, when the mode of learning is inquiry and the gathering of data takes as its limits all sources available, efficient learning proceeds differently. Now the learner must know when to select material, how to select it, and how to determine its reliability. In order for instruction to be effective, the teacher must be thoroughly acquainted with a learner's existing conceptual structures so that the gathering and processing may start at the level of the learner and not be too discrepant. In addition, the teacher must keep a check on the conceptual modifications that are occurring and must do so at every step along the way. In some situations the solutions may be readily found and processed; in others the search may require continuous effort for a week or a month or longer.

When the production aspect of reading or learning has been accomplished and a solution has been tentatively accepted, it must be tested out or evaluated. This is done through *critical thinking;* and the teaching of critical thinking is thought to be a most important teaching job.

Ennis (5:84) viewed critical thinking as the correct assessing of statements. He declared twelve aspects of critical thinking that would help a student perform at the various stages in the process of assessment:

1. Grasping the meaning of a statement
2. Judging whether there is ambiguity in a line of reasoning
3. Judging whether certain statements contradict each other
4. Judging whether a conclusion follows necessarily
5. Judging whether a statement is specific enough
6. Judging whether a statement is actually the application of a certain principle
7. Judging whether an observation statement is reliable
8. Judging whether an inductive conclusion is warranted
9. Judging whether the problem has been identified
10. Judging whether something is an assumption
11. Judging whether a definition is adequate
12. Judging whether a statement made by an alleged authority is acceptable.

It is to be noted that the judging of value statements is not included in this list. Neither does the list allow for those aspects of thinking that would be grouped under creative or divergent thinking.

In addition, Ennis proposed a three-dimensional model of critical thinking: a logical dimension, a criterial dimension, and a pragmatic dimension. A person competent in the logical dimension knows what follows from a statement or group of statements because he has examined their meaning. He is particularly alert to such logical quali-

fiers as "all," "some," "if . . . then," and so on. A person competent in the criterial dimension is capable of using a set of rules or criteria for judging the adequacy or reliability of statements about the world of things, men, and events. These criteria must be applied with discretion.

The pragmatic dimension covers the impression of the background purpose on the judgment. It also includes the decision as to whether the statement is good enough for the purpose. This dimension recognizes the necessity for the balancing of factors preceding the judgment, because it is the purpose that helps the reader judge how important it is to be right and when there is enough evidence. Since complete criteria can most likely never be established, an element of judgment is needed over and above the ability of applying criteria and knowing logical meaning.

Confirming or rejecting, testing, verifying, require application of: logical dimensions by the recognition of instances and the application of principles; criterial dimensions through the knowledge of criteria or judgmental yardsticks; and pragmatic dimension in deciding that there is or is not enough evidence and how strict one must be about the evidence, to satisfy the purposes of the inquiry. Teachers can arrange learning situations to facilitate this kind of critical reading and thinking. Even in the lowest grades children can be given the challenge of dealing with fiction by recognizing problems and organizing information so as to suggest solutions or hypotheses.

Cognitive processes can be directed toward finding a logical conclusion or an already accepted conclusion, as in convergent thinking or critical thinking. Or, the cognitive processes can be directed toward finding the new or the novel conclusion, as in divergent thinking.

The experiencing of feelings of success or failure comes to be regarded by students as an intrinsic aspect of the reading–thinking process and the making of judgments. In finding the path from what is known to what is unknown and is to be discovered, the learner obtains satisfaction from verifying his thinking or solving a problem. It is an active process of seeking and searching, collecting and organizing, generalizing and solving. The activity is exciting and pleasurable in its own right. Overcoming obstacles within a student's range of assimilation and accommodation has as its concomitant the feelings of genuine learning of the sage.

The cognitive abilities that have been emphasized do not develop unrelated to the personality of the students. Children must be taught to test their own attitudes, habits, and interests to try to find out why they act as they do, or why they treat certain people as they do. Teachers must examine their attitudes toward children to determine which are associated with firm, stimulating, warm, and productive learning situations.

CONCLUSION

Reading, thinking, problem solving, and creating always occur in a context. Reading is about something. Purposeful reading is directed toward a solution or goal, as is problem solving. Creativity is involved in expressing something in a new form or another form.

The cognitive processes involved are those of assimilation and accommodation. The first of these two processes consists of taking in and incorporating what is perceived in terms of what is known and understood at the time. The second paves the way for conceptual reorganization. It may require the reshaping and reorganizing of conceptual structures until they fit and/or account for the new circumstances.

Inquiry is native to the mind. Children are by nature curious and inquiring, and they will be so in school if they are so directed and if they are permitted to inquire. It is possible to direct the reading–thinking process in such a way that children *will* be encouraged to think when reading—to speculate, to search, to evaluate, and to use.

The dependent variable—reading efficiency—can be accomplished if teachers and students are thoroughly acquainted with the reading-thinking process. The process can be taught in a small group situation where it can be honed and sharpened as the various members bring a variety of purposes to bear upon the outcome. However, the object is to prepare scholars who can work alone, who can initiate searches, locate and process data, and arrive at solutions.

REFERENCES

1. ADLER, MORTIMER J., *How to Read a Book.* New York: Simon and Schuster, 1940.

2. AUSUBEL, D. P., *The Psychology of Meaningful Verbal Learning.* New York: Grune and Stratton, 1962.

3. BRUNER, J. S., "The Act of Discovery," *Harvard Educational Review,* 31 (1961), 21–32.

4. DEWEY, JOHN, *How We Think.* Boston: D. C. Heath and Co., 1933.

5. ENNIS, ROBERT H., "A Concept of

Critical Thinking," *Harvard Educational Review,* 32 (Winter 1962), 81–111.

6. HEATH, R. W. (Editor), *New Curricula.* New York: Harper and Row, 1964.

7. KLAUSMEIER, HERBERT J. and WILLIAM GOODWIN, *Learning and Human Abilities.* New York: Harper and Row, 1966.

8. LORGE, IRVING, "The Teacher's Task in the Development of Thinking," *The Reading Teacher,* 13 (February 1960), 170–75.

9. PIAGET, J., *The Origins of Intelligence in Children.* New York: International Universities Press, Inc., 1952.

10. *Reading Teacher, The,* R. G. STAUFFER, Editor. May 1966 and October 1966.

11. ROBINSON, FRANK, *Effective Study.* New York: Harper and Brothers, 1941.

12. STAUFFER, R. G., "Reading as Reflective Thinking" (Proceedings of Schoolmen's Week Conference, University of Pennsylvania, Philadelphia, Pa.), 1961.

13. STAUFFER, R. G., ALVIN T. BURROWS and DILYS M. JONES, *Skillbook for Skyways to Tomorrow.* New York: Holt, Rinehart and Winston, Inc., 1962.

14. SUCHMAN, J. R., "The Child and the Inquiry Process," *Intellectual Development: Another Look.* Papers and Reports from the ASCD Eighth Curriculum Research Institute. (Washington, D.C.: ASCD, NEA, 1964), pp. 59–77.

15. WITHROCK, M. C., "Effects of Certain Sets upon Complex Verbal Learning," *Journal of Educational Psychology,* 54 (1963), 85–88.

Research on the Processes of Thinking with Some Applications to Reading

David H. Russell

Research on the so-called "higher mental processes" has been a dubious, even precarious enterprise in this country for much of this century. Scholars in most disciplines, and even psychologists themselves, have had doubts about attempts to study cognitive functioning. In the *Scientific American,* Barron (4) reports sending letters to writers asking them to contribute to

David H. Russell,"Research on the Processes of Thinking with Some Applications to Reading," in *Language and the Higher Thought Processes* (1965). Copyright © 1965 by the National Council of Teachers of English. Reprinted by permission of the publisher.

studies of creative thinking. He comments as follows on the replies:

In trenchant and not particularly orderly prose, about a fifth of those who responded to our original letter pointed out the intrinsically evil character of psychological research. The objections to such research are mainly on these counts: it is vivisection; it is an expression of the effort of organized society to encroach upon the individual and rob him of his freedom; it is presumptuous because it seeks to describe and to understand what is intrinsically a mystery.

The suspicion of studies of thinking has extended beyond artists, writers, college professors, and atomic scientists to psychologists themselves. Despite the brilliant exceptions of James, Thorndike, and the transplanted Lewin, American psychologists in general have been wary of studies of mental life. We have careful laboratory investigations of conditioning eye-blink and elegant procedures for recording the maze-running ability of rats, but we have often shied away from the study of the complex intellectual life of children and adults. This has probably not been true of European psychology to nearly the same degree. The Gestaltists, and Burt, Bartlett, and Piaget have been concerned with cognitive processes. Here in America, as Edna Heidbreder put it, we have not always been asking the important questions about human behavior—or at least not until quite recent times. Within the last ten years, however, there has been a discernible shift of emphasis in psychological research toward some of the many phases of intellectual functioning.

It is now about ten years since I attempted to put together, in some sort of organized fashion, the scattered work of the last sixty years on higher mental processes. In the book *Children's Thinking* (45) I agreed with Johnson (30) that, in surveying research on children's thinking, it is possible to distinguish between the materials of thinking, which are multitudinous, and the processes of thinking, which are very few. I suggested that it is feasible to describe, and to some extent to discover, unique characteristics of each of six types of thinking. These categories I am using in this article because I believe they all can be applied directly to the learning of language abilities and especially to learning to read, the area from which my examples will be drawn. Here then is the hypothesis—that most thinking behavior can be categorized into one or more of the six categories: perceptual thinking, associative thinking, concept formation, problem solving, critical thinking, and creative thinking. It is not the purpose of this article to be taxonomic—to define and distinguish these types—although this can be done. Instead, I should like to indicate a few outstanding researches or research results in the various categories, with an occasional hint of how these may be applied to the process of reading. There are, of course, many other labels that could be used—thinking has been described as relational, fluent, logical, structural, scientific, evaluative, inferential, deductive, and artistic. Spearman (51) wrote of eduction of relations and correlates. Guilford (22) uses terms like convergent and divergent thinking. Bruner (7) distinguishes between intuitive and analytic thinking. The possibilities are many but this paper uses six labels which are particularly relevant to the work of the teacher.

1. *Perceptual Thinking.* Perceptual thinking is learned; it goes beyond relatively unlearned sensation to an

awareness of objects and events which are interpreted. It may be relatively simple as in pitch discrimination or complex as in a recognition of emotional meanings. It may be objective as in naming a primary color or subjective as in interpreting pictures or in the "Johnson image" during an election. Perceptual research flourished early in this century, moving from introspection to nicely controlled laboratory responses. Applications to letter, word, and phrase recognition are obviously related to reading and therefore researches and theories of perception probably need more attention in educational psychology.

Some of the theories of perception are physiologically based as in Hebb's (24) cell-assembly theory and some are functionally based as in Helson's (26) adaptation level or Brunswik's (10) perceptual constancy. The last ten years has seen emphasis on the influence of set, attitude, and other personality factors in perception as in the work of Ames (2), Bruner and Postman (9), and Blake and Ramsey (5). The well-known Ames' studies illustrated the influence of habit in visual perception of space relationships. The Bruner–Postman three-step cycle of expectancy, input of information, and checking of hypothesis would seem to offer many leads to reading research. For example, they say the stronger the set or hypothesis, or category, the less information needed to confirm it, the more needed to change it. The Blake and Ramsey book explores some of the relationships between perception and personality.

More recent summaries of research on perception are represented by Wohlwill's (60) review of the development of perception abilities in childhood and by the Gibson and Olum (18) chapter on experimental methods of studying perception in children. They find that the research on the question of part *versus* whole discrimination is inconclusive with results depending upon the materials used in the experiments. Langman (33) listed sixteen visual perception skills and five auditory perception skills needed in reading and added seventeen generalizations used in letter–sound analysis. Gibson (19) studied the role of grapheme–phoneme correspondences in perception of words and concluded that pseudo-words constructed according to rules of invariant spelling-to-sound correlation are perceived more accurately in tachistoscopic presentation than their matched words with variable spelling–sound prediction. Gibson also reports several other studies in the volume by Levin et al. (34), which contains accounts of twenty-two separate studies, most of them dealing with some form of perception. In the collection Levin has two other studies of variable grapheme–phoneme correspondences and, in addition to the study mentioned, Gibson deals with the perception of letters.

The analysis of some of the more complex perceptions of children as they read paragraphs or stories is currently not an active area. Earlier studies by McKillop (39), Groff (21), and others illustrated that perception of the meaning of paragraphs may be affected by attitudes toward the subject matter read. Reed (44) has traced some of the relationships between personality scores and reading choices in the sixth grade. Studies are needed, for example, of children's perceptions of different types of fictional characters or of different kinds of poems.

2. *Associative Thinking.* Associative thinking is a broad term which includes such theories or constructs as conditioning, S–R bonds, primacy,

and reinforcement. With the exception of the study of reinforcement, research on this topic has declined from the interest of the 1920s but there seems little doubt that the label describes much thinking of a rather routine sort in which simple relationships are established. It may be the most accurate description of children's learning names of letters or a sight vocabulary.

Both McCreary (38) and Otto (43) have studied associative learning in relation to reading ability. A number of other studies within this framework have been reported in the new publication *The Journal of Verbal Learning and Verbal Behavior.*

In his book, *Learning Theory and Personality Dynamics,* Mowrer (41) extended the concept of association in a two-factor exposition to include both contiguity theory and drive-reduction theory. Current interest in the area is also evident in Skinner's reinforcement theory and its application to teaching machines. In the Soviet Union, Luria (36) is continuing the Pavlov tradition with studies of children's thinking based on theories of conditioning and association.

3. *Concept Formation.* Research in this area goes back at least to the 1890s and G. Stanley Hall. It has always been pursued with some diligence and has recently flourished with even more prominence as certain scientists, mathematicians, and scholars in structural linguistics have become interested in the concepts children can learn. One problem nagging today's primary teacher is whether young children understand more than they did a generation ago as a result of television, travel, and other phases of modern life. Another problem in curriculum planning is that of selection of the most important concepts in a discipline. A

third one concerns the current tendency to introduce concepts earlier; children can learn them sooner than we once thought but is the earlier gain worth the extra effort?

Research on concept formation has been summarized in general articles by Russell (46) and by Carroll (12) and in specific subject-matter fields by research workers with interests in particular areas. The research on concepts can be divided into three categories: (1) concept discovery, (2) gradual concept attainment and enrichment, and (3) children's knowledge of concepts at various age levels. Carroll believes the first phenomenon is the result of inductive thinking, the second of deductive thinking. The first is usually used in laboratory experiments; the second and third are closely related to the usual teaching and learning procedures in school.

The laboratory studies of concept discovery began with the work of Hull (27) in 1920 on learning nonsense names for pseudo-Chinese characters. This type of study was continued in the 1940s by Heidbreder (25) and expanded in the book, *A Study of Thinking* by Bruner, Goodnow, and Austin (8). Bruner hypothesizes that the subjects use different "selection strategies" and "reception strategies" in sorting out a sequence of events or group of examples so they can categorize them. He uses such terms as simultaneous-scanning, conservative-focusing, and focus-gambling to describe ways the category may be established. In many of his more recent books Piaget has been concerned with concept discovery in simple science experiments. Although the relationship between concept discovery and the reading process is not clear, Kress (32) has shown that there are differences between good and poor readers, who have been matched on general intelligence, in the ability to discover concepts in some of the well-known, clinical type, non-verbal sorting tests. The retarded readers preferred concrete to functional or abstract methods and scored lower on versatility and flexibility in concept formation.

The second main area of concept acquisition seems to have much significance for reading instruction. Undoubtedly many children beyond the ages of seven or eight learn many concepts, at least partially, by reading about them. The series of studies by Welch and Long (58) suggest that children can use a two-step hierarchy between two and four years and that most kindergartners can grasp a three-step hierarchy (people–man–soldier). In the spiral curriculum or through reading, children may add "layers of meaning" to their concepts. The most important work in the area of concept learning is that of Piaget who is also concerned with the third division of concepts typically known at various developmental levels. His numerous experiments have been summarized and evaluated in part by Flavell (16) and by Hunt (28).

There are scores, perhaps hundreds, of respectable investigations of concepts known, or not known, at various stages. For example, Russell (48) has summarized some doctoral studies at the University of California on the development of social concepts, conservation concepts, the self concept, the concepts of liberty and justice (as contained in the Pledge of Allegiance), concepts of God, and concepts understood by middle class and culturally deprived children. Among other things, in The Measurement of Meaning, Osgood (42) suggests the importance of connotative meanings and personality factors in any analysis of a store of concepts.

Such investigations raise theoretical questions of interest. For example, if certain concepts, as in mathematics or science, are not typically grasped at some age level, should the teacher, forsaking all others, make strenuous efforts to have the children understand these concepts if they have been labelled important by the mathematicians or scientists? Since some concepts seem to be harder than others, but also more fundamental than others, in what sequence should concepts be studied? A third question is whether children, adolescents, and adults think alike or differently in concept formation. There is considerable agreement in the literature that thinking is similar at all levels. In The Process of Education, for example, Bruner (7) writes of a central conviction "that intellectual activity anywhere is the same whether at the frontier of knowledge or in a third-grade classroom" (p. 14). On the other hand, Piaget believes that the preschool child relies on what he calls "intuitive thought" based largely on perceptual experience, that the child of elementary school ages shifts into a stage of "concrete operations" or ways of getting information which begin with the objective world but are internalized and symbolized. It is not until eleven or twelve years, Piaget believes, that the child becomes capable of "formal operations," of understanding "reversibility," or grasping possibility as effectively as reality. It is therefore not until this stage, Piaget believes, that the child can fully grasp the abstractions of mathematics or physics or other disciplines. These problems are examples of some of the questions about concept formation which must be studied in relation to the whole curriculum, including reading.

4. *Problem Solving.* The psycho-

logical view of problem solving is one of a complex operation involving several specific types of thinking. Problems may exist in any field, including those on the printed page, where there may be a question for the child of deciphering strange words, of grasping an author's argument, or of judging a fictional character. Modern psychology still accepts Dewey's (13) classic five steps in problem solving but regards them as a general, somewhat idealized picture rather than an exact description of some of the frustrations and circumlocutions of the individual who cannot find an immediate solution. For example, today we use many labels to describe the solver's behavior. These include (1) relational thinking (Maier's combining the essentials of two isolated experiences), (2) logical reasoning (Guilford tests for this factor), (3) rigidity (Werner and Kaplan and Bloom and Broder find this a useful concept, but some research indicates it is a specific rather than a general trait), and (4) anxiety (Fattu reports a negative relationship between anxiety and number of problems solved). A number of studies such as that of Mc-Nemar (40) have found that good problem solvers excel poor problem solvers in ability to overcome an induced set and to do deductive thinking. Harootunian (23) found that reading ability, intelligence, judgment, and problem recognition were important predictors of problem solving ability; closure, word fluency, and ideational fluency made little independent contribution to variance in problem solving ability.

As indicated elsewhere, the research suggests that problem solving behavior varies with (1) the nature of the problem, (2) the methods of attack used, (3) the characteristics of the solver, and (4) the group or social factors in the situation. Problem solving has been studied most thoroughly in science situations (14, 29) and with mathematical materials (Wertheimer, 59), but each of these four areas may apply in the reading situation. For example, the first (the nature of the problem), might include the numbers of unknown words in the selection, the second (methods of teaching), the pupil's ability to outline, the third, the attitudes of the reader to the content, and the fourth (influence of the group), may be of interest in terms of current views about individualized and group reading. What we know about the dynamics of groups (6, 31) has not been tested in groups organized for reading instruction. But a number of writers including Stauffer (52) have shown that problem solving in the areas of word recognition and simple comprehension may be encouraged as early as the first grade.

5. *Critical Thinking.* From the psychological point of view, critical thinking is the most dubious of the six labels by which I am attempting to summarize research in thinking. Usually it is part of some other process, as in evaluating the kinds of evidence collected in problem solving or judging the original result in creative thinking. The nearest the psychologist comes to allowing the term is in his use of the word *judgment.* Educational writings, on the other hand, are full of the two words, and the term "critical thinking" is especially the darling of the social studies people. One trouble in educational writing has been that critical thinking has had so many meanings. It has been made synonymous with the ability to abstract and organize information, to draw inferences, to search for relevant materials, to evaluate data, to compare sources, to employ a from-Missouri attitude, to distinguish fact

from opinion, to detect propaganda, and to apply the rules of logical reasoning (49). Perhaps the time has arrived when we should be critical of our use of the phrase "critical thinking."

As a research area, the field of critical thinking accordingly suffers from this lack of precision. The exploratory study of Glaser (20) is still about the best at the high school level. A number of studies of propaganda analysis are closely related to reading. The bulletin published by the National Conference on Research in English and entitled *Critical Reading* (50) is correctly subtitled as an introduction. Some of the confusion in terms is shown in the book from England by Abercrombie (1) entitled *The Anatomy of Judgment* and subtitled "An Investigation into the Processes of Perception and Reasoning." This may be one more bit of evidence that psychologists confuse terms, or the whole picture may be interpreted to mean that critical thinking is not a separate process so much as part of other cognitive functioning. Like some psychologists in this country, Abercrombie reasons that in receiving information from a given stimulus pattern we select from the total amount of information available and from our own store of information. Thus the perceptual process involves selection and judgment with the subject sometimes deliberate, sometimes unaware of what he is doing. Abercrombie used a tape recorded, group discussion method with university students and found that some of the factors influencing judgment became apparent and the judgments improved. The group discussion method may be one way of getting at assumptions or preconceptions and thus of improving critical thinking.

Recent attempts to clarify the concept of critical thinking have been made by Ennis (15) who divides the activity into some twelve overlapping categories along logical, critical, and pragmatic dimensions, and by Saadeh (49) who related his analysis to some of the rules of logic. Saadeh taught critical skills to sixth graders with considerable success as did Lundsteen (35) in another investigation of the possibility of teaching critical listening abilities.

6. *Creative Thinking.* In these days of emphasis upon intellectual attainment, curricular rigor and the "pursuit of excellence," creative thinking, and creativity are fashionable topics. In addition to individual researches, well-supported team studies are being made in a half-dozen centers throughout the country. Guilford includes creativity in his studies using factor-analysis at the University of Southern California. At Chicago, Getzels and Jackson (17) have differentiated between adolescents scoring high on intelligence tests and adolescents rated as creative, but have not studied cases where the two groups overlap. In Berkeley, MacKinnon and his associates (37) have a series of studies of personality factors related to creativity in various professions, and in Minnesota, Torrance (56, 57) is heading work on a group of studies more closely related than most to creative behavior in classroom settings. Such studies assume that creative thinking is not the province of a gifted few but exists on some sort of continuum for much of the population. In addition to certain skills, production of originality in some of these studies seems to involve three general factors which may be labelled perceptual, integrative, and emotional. MacKinnon finds different amounts of these in artistic creativity, scientific creativity, and what he terms "overlapping" creativity. Artistic creativity

involves externalization of an internal state; emotion and personality may be heavily involved. In scientific creativity the scientist functions as a mediator between an external problem and its solution and is, presumably, less involved emotionally. Creativity in the "overlapping" category includes performers, interpreters, and high-grade individuals in such pursuits as architecture and engineering.

In some of their research memoranda, Torrance and his students report trouble in establishing the reliability of his tests of creativity in elementary school children but have certain findings about the personalities of children rated as creative. As some of us might suspect, the so-called creative child is not well accepted by his peers or his teachers in the first four grades; he is often rated as limelighty and bossy. By the sixth grade a better status has usually been achieved.

On the positive side, the upsurge of interest in creativity may be documented by the publication, within five years, of at least six substantial volumes collected by various editors and reporting research in various aspects of creativity. Alphabetically by editor or author, these include Anderson's *Creativity and Its Cultivation* (3), MacKinnon's *The Creative Person* (37), Stein and Heinze's *Creativity and the Individual* (53), Taylor's *Creativity: Progress and Potential* (54), Taylor and Barron's *Scientific Creativity: Its Recognition and Development* (55), and Torrance's *Creativity: Second Conference on Gifted Children* (56). Combined with scores of research articles, the books represent increasing interest in, instead of final conclusions from the empirical study of creativity.

In the above research, two important problems are unsolved: the unique characteristics of creativity in childhood and youth, and some valid and reliable measures of creativity itself. As one reviewer put it, "creativity is a construct in search of a generally acceptable objective referent." Most of the tests of creativity have been developed by Guilford and his associates or adapted from his work. These lend themselves to factor analysis, which may be regarded as one step on the way to complete understanding, but some of them do not seem to correlate highly either with retest scores, with teachers' or supervisors' judgments of creativity, or with rating of students' creative products by independent judges.

The books and articles are samples of work in progress which suggest four domains of research in creativity: (1) the nature of the creative process, (2) the characteristics of the creative person, (3) the qualities of creative products, and (4) the social-cultural milieu, including classrooms, which block or foster creative responses. The whole area of creative thinking thus bristles with problems. Is there such a thing as teaching creativeness? Does creativity in play, rhythms, and language occur before creative thinking about social or scientific problems and are they different things? What can teachers do to achieve some sort of balance between conformity and spontaneity in the classroom? How can we get more "discovery" into a reading lesson? What are the places of production *versus* appreciation in reading and in other curricular areas?

The act of reading has usually been regarded as a receptive process rather than a creative one. There seems to be some justification, however, for the use of the term "creative reading" to signify behavior which goes beyond word identification or understanding of literal meaning to the reader's interpretation of the printed materials (47). Such reading may be productive of new ideas, critical of old ones, or appreciative of the art of literature. Research studies suggest that certain mechanics of reading must be well in hand before the child or adolescent achieves these higher levels of reading and that they, like the skills, can be developed by the right kinds of instruction.

CONCLUSION

The above examples suggest that language abilities should be defined not merely as perceptual skills nor as the ability to grasp a communication, nor as competence in solving verbal problems. Probably all types of thinking are involved in the learning and use of language and these I have subsumed under six labels. Other general descriptive terms could be used and more precise designations of specific verbal behavior are undoubtedly needed. Furthermore, this account neglects such topics as emotional factors in thinking, the role of memory, and attempts to derive a comprehensive theory or model of thinking as in the work of Burt (11) or Guilford (22). It is probably not too important in the study of the reading process, from which the examples are drawn, to distinguish between the types of thinking, here called perceptualizing and conceptualizing. Behavior which involves the apprehension of events or objects such as printed symbols may be profitably conceived as a categorizing, whether perceptual or conceptual. As Bruner has put it, "There are examples in which it is almost impossible to differentiate perceptual and conceptual categorizing, notably in language learning" (8). In addition to its use in the

discovery of concepts, reading seems to be one of the best ways we have of deepening and enriching concepts.

Similarly, there is overlap of critical thinking with the processes of problem solving and creative thinking. A child or a scientist must be critical of his proposed solutions to a problem. An adolescent or an adult must sometimes be critical about his creative production, whether an original story or an interpretation of A. E. Housman. Despite this blending of critical thinking into problem solving and creative thinking, it is my bias that some aspects of critical thinking can be taught directly as such. (See the article by Stauffer in this series.) Similarly, I believe the other five types of thinking can, to some extent, be isolated and taught in relation to the school curriculum, including reading.

In reading instruction of the past, most of a reading teacher's time and energy have gone into perceptual aspects of word identification and conceptual responses to literal meaning. These are necessary bases for more sophisticated approaches to reading, but perhaps the time has come when we can use our psychological knowledge of the processes of problem solving and critical and creative thinking to help teachers develop a more demanding set of goals for reading instruction.

BIBLIOGRAPHY

1. ABERCROMBIE, M. L. JOHNSON, *The Anatomy of Judgment*. London, England: Hutchinson, 1960.
2. AMES, ADELBERT, "Visual Perception and the Rotating Trapezoidal Window," *Psychological Monographs* 65: No. 324, 1951.
3. ANDERSON, HAROLD H. (ed.), *Crea-*

tivity and Its Cultivation. New York: Harper, 1959.

4. BARRON, FRANK, "The Psychology of Imagination," Scientific American 199:151–166, September, 1958.

5. BLAKE, ROBERT R. and G. V. RAMSEY (eds.), Perception: An Approach to Personality. New York: Ronald, 1951.

6. BLAKE, ROY, "Small Group Research and Cooperative Teaching Problems," National Elementary Principal 43: 31–36, February, 1964.

7. BRUNER, JEROME S. and LEO POSTMAN, "Symbolic Value as an Organizing Factor in Perception," Journal of Social Psychology 27:203–208, May, 1948.

8. BRUNER, JEROME S., JACQUELINE GOODNOW, and G. A. AUSTIN, A Study of Thinking. New York: Wiley, 1956.

9. BRUNER, JEROME S., The Process of Education. Cambridge: Harvard University Press, 1960.

10. BRUNSWIK, EGON, Perception and the Representative Design of Psychological Experiments. Berkeley: University of California Press, 1956.

11. BURT, CYRIL, "The Differentiation of Intellectual Ability," British Journal of Educational Psychology, 24:76–90, June, 1954.

12. CARROLL, JOHN B., "Words, Meanings and Concepts," Harvard Educational Review, 34:178–202, Spring, 1964.

13. DEWEY, JOHN, How We Think. Boston: Heath, 1910.

14. DUNCKER, KARL, "On Problem Solving," trans. by Lynne S. Leer, Psychological Monographs, 58, No. 27, 1945.

15. ENNIS, ROBERT H., "A Concept of Critical Thinking," Harvard Educational Review, 32:81–111, Winter, 1962.

16. FLAVELL, JOHN H., The Developmental Psychology of Jean Piaget. Princeton, N. J.: Van Nostrand, 1963.

17. GETZELS, JACOB W., and PHILIP W. JACKSON, Creativity and Intelligence. New York: Wiley, 1962.

18. GIBSON, ELEANOR N. and V. OLUM, "Experimental Methods of Study in Perception in Children," P. H. Mussen (ed.), Handbook of Research Methods in Child Psychology. New York: Wiley, 1960.

19. GIBSON, ELEANOR, et al., "The Role of Grapheme-Phoneme Correspondences in the Perception of Words," American Journal of Psychology, 75: 554–570, December, 1962.

20. GLASER, EDWARD M., An Experiment in the Development of Critical Thinking. Contributions to Education No. 843. New York: Teachers College, Columbia University, 1941.

21. GROFF, PATRICK J., Children's Attitudes Toward Reading and Their Critical Reading Abilities in Four Content-Type Materials, doctor's dissertation. University of California, Berkeley, 1955.

22. GUILFORD, JOY P., "Three Faces of Intellect," American Psychologist, 14:469–479, August, 1959.

23. HAROOTUNIAN, B. and M. B. TATE, "The Relationship of Certain Selected Variables to Problem Solving Ability," Journal of Educational Psychology, 51:326–333, December, 1960.

24. HEBB, DONALD O., The Organization of Behavior: A Neuropsychological Theory. New York: Wiley, 1949.

25. HEIDBREDER, EDNA, "The Attainment of Concepts: IV, The Process,"

Journal of Psychology, 24:93–138, July, 1947.

26. HELSON, HARRY (ed.) and others, *Theoretical Foundations of Psychology*. New York: Van Nostrand, 1951.

27. HULL, CLARK A., "Quantitative Aspects of the Evolution of Concepts," *Psychological Monographs*, 28, No. 123, 1–86, 1920.

28. HUNT, JOSEPH McV., *Intelligence and Experience*. New York: Ronald, 1961.

29. INHELDER, BARBEL and JEAN PIAGET, *The Growth of Logical Thinking from Childhood to Adolescence*. New York: Basic Books, 1958.

30. JOHNSON, DONALD M., "A Modern Account of Problem Solving," *Psychological Bulletin*, 41:201–229, April, 1944.

31. KELLEY, H. H. and J. W. THEBAUT, "Experimental Studies of Group Problem Solving and Process," *Handbook of Social Psychology*, Vol. II (Gardner Lindzey, ed.). Cambridge, Mass: Addison-Wesley, 1954.

32. KRESS, ROY, "An Investigation of the Relationship Between Concept Formation and Achievement in Reading." Abstract of Dissertation; private communication from author, 1960.

33. LANGMAN, MURIEL P., "The Reading Process: A Descriptive Interdisciplinary Approach," *Genetic Psychology Monographs*, 62:3–40, August, 1960.

34. LEVIN, HARRY, ELEANOR GIBSON, and others, *A Basic Research Program in Reading*. Cooperative Research Project No. 639. Ithaca, New York: Cornell University, 1963. (Mimeog.)

35. LUNDSTEEN, SARA W., *Teaching Abilities in Critical Listening in the Fifth and Sixth Grades*, doctoral dissertation, University of California, Berkeley, 1963.

36. LURIA, ALEKSANDR R., *Speech and the Development of Mental Processes in the Child*. London, England: Staples Press, 1950.

37. MacKINNON, DONALD W. (ed.), *The Creative Person*. Proceedings of Conference of IPAR and University Extension. Berkeley: University of California Extension Division, 1961.

38. McCREARY, ANNE P., "A Study of Association, Reinforcement and Transfer in Beginning Reading," *Journal of Experimental Education*, 31:285–290, Spring, 1963.

39. McKILLOP, ANN S., *The Relationship Between the Reader's Attitude and Certain Types of Reading Responses*. New York: Bureau of Publications, Teachers College, Columbia University, 1952.

40. McNEMAR, OLGA W., "An Attempt to Differentiate Between Individuals with High and Low Reasoning Ability," *American Journal of Psychology*, 68:20–36, March, 1955.

41. MOWRER, O. HOBART, *Learning Theory and Personality Dynamics*. New York: Ronald, 1950.

42. OSGOOD, CHARLES E., G. J. SUCI, and P. H. TANNENBAUM, *The Measurement of Meaning*. Urbana: University of Illinois Press, 1958.

43. OTTO, WAYNE, "The Acquisition and Retention of Paired Associates of Good, Average and Poor Readers," *Journal of Educational Psychology*, 52:241–248, October, 1961.

44. REED, CHARLES H., *Relationships of Personality and Reading Choices of Sixth-Grade Children*, doctoral dissertation, University of California, Berkeley, 1962.

45. RUSSELL, DAVID H., *Children's Thinking*. Boston: Ginn, 1956.

46. ———, "Concepts," *Encyclopedia of Educational Research,* 3rd edition (C. W. HARRIS, ed.). New York: Macmillan, 1960.

47. ———, *Children Learn to Read* (2nd ed.). Boston: Ginn, 1961.

48. ———, "Six Studies of Children's Understanding of Concepts," *Elementary School Journal,* 63:255–260, February, 1963.

49. SAADEH, IBRAHIM Q., *An Evaluation of the Effectiveness of Teaching for Critical Thinking in the Sixth Grade,* doctoral dissertation, University of California, Berkeley, 1962.

50. SOCHOR, E. ELONA (ed.), *Critical Thinking: An Introduction.* Bulletin of the National Conference on Research in English, Champaign, Illinois: National Council of Teachers of English, 1959.

51. SPEARMAN, CHARLES E., *The Abilities of Man.* New York: Macmillan, 1927.

52. STAUFFER, RUSSELL G., "Children Can Read and Think Critically," *Education,* 80:522–525, May, 1960.

53. STEIN, M. I., and S. J. REINZE (eds.), *Creativity and the Individual.* Glencoe, Ill.: The Free Press, 1960.

54. TAYLOR, CALVIN W., *Creativity: Progress and Potential.* New York: McGraw-Hill, 1964.

55. ———, and FRANK BARRON (eds.). *Scientific Creativity: Its Recognition and Development.* New York: Wiley, 1963.

56. TORRANCE, E. PAUL (ed.), *Creativity: Proceedings of the Second Minnesota Conference on Gifted Children.* Minneapolis: University of Minnesota Extension Division, 1959.

57. ——— (ed.), *Talent and Education: Present Status and Future Directions.* Minneapolis: University of Minnesota Press, 1960.

58. WELCH, LIVINGSTON, and L. LONG, "The Higher Structural Phases of Concept Formation in Children," *Journal of Psychology,* 9:59–95, January, 1940.

59. WERTHEIMER, MAX, *Productive Thinking.* New York: Harper, 1945.

60. WOHLWILL, JOACHIM, "Developmental Studies of Perception," *Psychological Bulletin,* 57:249–288, July, 1960.

Can Training in Listening Improve Reading?

Paul M. Hollingsworth
Arizona State University

This question has been asked many times by teachers, administrators, and researchers. Will training in listening improve the pupil's reading abilities? Edna Lue Furness (6) in her study stated: "The modern academic term 'communication' acknowledges a basic relationship between reading and listening." Does this basic relationship between listening and reading mean, however, that improvement in the one skill will make an improvement in the other skill? To answer these questions, various studies in this area have been made.

INTERRELATIONSHIP BETWEEN LISTENING AND READING

Dow (5) reported approximately eighteen factors of reading comprehension that seem sufficiently similar to listening comprehension to consider these two receptive skills closely related. Just because they may be similar, however, does not indicate that they are identical. Wiksell (16) wrote that in reading one is able to adapt his own rate to the difficulty or nature of the reading material; however, listening demands a great deal more, inasmuch as the listener must follow the speaker no matter what the rate of speaking may be. Thus, in listening there is little time for reflection, which is so important in reading.

Hampleman (7) reported in his study of fourth and sixth grade pupils that skill in both listening and reading requires that active thinking be applied to symbols and that listening should be distinguished from mere hearing and reading from mere seeing.

Reading and listening do have things that they share in common, and they are interrelated. Austin (1) reported that listening and learning to organize spoken language play an important role in understanding what is read. In her work with the primary grades she indicated that the listening program is an important aid to reading comprehension.

Cleland and Toussaint (4) determined the degree of relationship be-

Paul M. Hollingsworth, "Can Training in Listening Improve Reading?" *The Reading Teacher* (November 1965). Reprinted with permission of Paul M. Hollingsworth and the International Reading Association.

tween selected tests of listening and reading. They found that the measure showing the closest relationship with reading was Sequential Tests of Educational Progress Listening Test.

Vineyard and Bailey (15) did a study similar to that of Cleland and Toussaint, but this study was done with 114 second-semester freshmen students of Southwestern State College. Vineyard and Bailey found that reading ability, listening skill, and intelligence are highly related to one another.

LISTENING AND ITS EFFECTS ON READING

Betts (2) reported a study in 1940 done at the fifth grade level. He found a greater incidence of hearing impairment among the low achievers than among the high achievers. He felt that these findings may indicate a possible causal relationship, or that they reveal merely another difficulty for which the nonachiever must compensate. Hildreth (8) indicated that reading comprehension depends on comprehension of spoken language and that listening to correct English helps to improve recognition of the same expressions in print. Spache (13) suggested that measures of auding ability mark potential ceilings for reading ability.

Marsden (12) conducted a study to determine the effect of practice in listening (1) to decide upon the main idea of a selection, (2) to get the details on a given topic presented by a selection, and (3) to draw a conclusion from material presented. He tested ability of 254 fifth and sixth grade pupils to read for these pur-

poses. The lessons consisted of several short stories which were read by the teacher. Marsden concluded that the skills of reading a selection to note its main idea, to draw conclusions, and to note details were improved when opportunity to practice listening for these three purposes was given.

Lewis (10) conducted a study with intermediate grade pupils to determine the effect of training in listening (1) to get the general significance of a passage, (2) to note details presented on a topic by a passage, and (3) to predict the outcomes from a passage. Three hundred fifty-seven intermediate pupils in twelve classrooms were used. The program of training in listening consisted of thirty lessons of approximately fifteen minutes each. One lesson was given each day for six weeks. The teachers read the selections to the pupils. Each lesson included a listening exercise for each of the three purposes stated above. Lewis concluded that training in listening for the three purposes seemed to have a significant effect upon the ability of intermediate grade pupils to read for those same purposes.

Stromer (14) conducted a study to examine some of the relationships between reading, listening, and intelligence. He utilized three groups of students. These groups were: a listening group, a reading and listening group, and a reading group. The data collected seemed to indicate that the reading-listening method of training tends to increase the reading rate of the subjects.

Another research project, similar to those of Marsden and Lewis, was done by Kelty (9) in 1953 to determine the effect that training in listening for certain purposes had upon the ability of 188 fourth grade pupils to read for those same purposes. The purposes referred to were: (1) deciding upon the main idea of a selection, (2) deciding upon the supporting details given in a selection, and (3) drawing a conclusion. The experimental group of ninety-four pupils was given thirty fifteen-minute lessons over a period of thirty days in listening. The control group received no instruction in listening. Kelty concluded that practice in listening for certain purposes favorably affects the ability of fourth grade pupils to read for those same purposes.

Brown (3) pointed out that auditing ability supports reading ability during the first years in school, in which children learn to recognize the visual representation of words whose sound and sense already are familiar to a large extent.

Lubershane (11) conducted a study to determine if training in listening can improve reading ability. He had thirty-five pupils in the experimental group and thirty-seven in the control group, both groups from the fifth grade. The control group were given no listening exercises. The Metropolitan Reading Test for reading achievement was given before and after training. The experimental group was given auditory training exercises designed to improve written responses to oral commands. He concluded with a statement that auditory training may prove of value in reading programs, although no definite statistical proof of the value of these exercises in improving reading ability was found. The generally greater growth in reading ability in the experimental group suggested strongly that the auditory exercises had a positive effect on reading growth.

CONCLUSION

Can training in listening improve reading? Many of these research reports show that through the improvement of listening abilities reading can be improved. Listening does have a positive effect on reading achievement.

REFERENCES

1. Austin, Martha Lou, "In Kindergarten Through Grades 3," *Methods and Materials for Teaching Comprehension*, pp. 57–73. Conference on Reading. Chicago: University of Chicago Press, 1960.

2. Betts, Emmett A., "Reading Problems at the Intermediate-Grade Level," *Elementary School Journal*, 40 (June 1940), 737–46.

3. Brown, Don, "Auding as the Primary Language Ability." Unpublished doctor's dissertation, Stanford University, 1954.

4. Cleland, Donald L., and Isabella H. Toussaint, "The Interrelationships of Reading, Listening, Arithmetic Computation and Intelligence," *Reading Teacher*, 15 (Jan. 1962), 228–31.

5. Dow, Clyde W., "Integrating the Teaching of Reading and Listening Comprehension," *Journal of Communication*, 8 (Autumn 1958), 118–26.

6. Furness, E. L., "Improving Reading Through Listening," *Elementary English*, 34 (May 1957), 307.

7. Hampleman, R. S., "Comparison of Listening and Reading Comprehension Ability of 4th and 6th Grade Pupils," *Elementary English*, 35 (Jan. 1958), 49–53.

8. HILDRETH, GERTRUDE, "Interrelationship Among the Language Arts," *Elementary School Journal,* 48 (June 1948), 538–49.

9. KELTY, ANNETTE P., "An Experimental Study to Determine the Effect of 'Listening for Certain Purposes' Upon Achievement in Reading for those Purposes." Unpublished doctor's field study, Colorado State College of Education, 1953.

10. LEWIS, MAURICE S., "The Effect of Training in Listening for Certain Purposes upon Reading for Those Same Purposes." Unpublished doctor's field study, Colorado State College of Education, 1951.

11. LUBERSHANE, MELVIN, "Can Training in Listening Improve Reading Ability?" *Chicago School Journal,* 43 (Mar. 1962), 277–81.

12. MARSDEN, WARE, " A Study for the Value of Training in Listening to Achievement in Reading." Unpublished doctor's field study. Colorado State College of Education, 1951.

13. SPACHE, GEORGE D., "Construction and Validation of a Work-Type Auditory Comprehension Reading Test," *Educational and Psychological Measurement,* 10 (Summer 1950), 249–53.

14. STROMER, WALTER FRANCIS, "An Investigation into Some of the Relations Between Reading, Listening, and Intelligence." Unpublished doctor's dissertation, University of Denver, 1952.

15. VINEYARD, EDWIN, and ROBERT BAILEY, "Interrelationships of Reading Ability, Listening Skill, Intelligence and Scholastic Achievement," *Journal of Developmental Reading,* 3 (Spring 1960), 174–78.

16. WIKSELL, WESLEY, "The Problem of Listening," *Quarterly Journal of Speech,* 32 (Dec. 1946), 506.

What Can Be Done About Listening?

Ralph G. Nichols

Of the four language arts—reading, writing, speaking, and listening—listening is quantitatively the most important by far. Forty-five percent of the time we spend in verbal communication is spent listening. Yet up to about ten years ago, very little was known about listening. Only a few research studies had been made, and almost no schools were teaching listening. Since then, however, dramatic developments have been taking place.

One landmark was the publication in 1952 of *The English Language Arts,* a report based on a five-year study by the Commission on the English Curriculum of the National Council of Teachers of English. This report stated clearly that good listening habits must be taught, not left to chance; that, just as there is a need for continuous instruction in reading throughout the school years, so there is a need for carefully graded training in listening.

Today listening as a basic medium of learning is getting increasing attention in elementary and high schools, and most of the notable universities in America are teaching courses in lis-

tening. Scores of industries have instituted their own listening-training programs.

What lies behind this tremendous surge of interest in effective listening? It seems to me that it springs from an attempt to find answers to two questions, both of great importance to teachers: Is inefficient listening a problem, in and out of school? Can anything be done about it?

IS INEFFICIENT LISTENING A PROBLEM?

If we turn to the schoolroom for evidence as to whether inefficient listening is a real problem, the answer is a resounding "Yes."

Much of the research on this question has been done at the universities. For example, a number of experiments have tested students' ability to answer questions about material presented to them in a ten-minute lecture. Almost without exception the students answered only about half the questions correctly. Retests from two weeks to two months later showed about 25 percent of the answers correct.

This kind of evidence from the universities is shocking enough. But let us turn for a moment to industry. Is inefficient listening a problem there? Again the answer is an unequivocal "Yes." There are studies which indicate that because of poor communication often neither management nor workers understand very much of each other's hopes and aspirations.

I think it is accurate and conservative to say that without training in listening most of us operate at precisely a 25 percent level of efficiency when we listen to a ten-minute talk. And we know from research that the longer the talk the less the comprehension of it.

WHAT CAN BE DONE ABOUT INEFFICIENT LISTENING?

Is there anything we can do about inefficient listening? The answer is fortunately "Yes." If we want to become good listeners, if we want our pupils to become good listeners, we can get results.

Currently every fall on the St. Paul Campus of the University of Minnesota we give training in listening to the 25 percent of the incoming freshmen who are the poorest listeners. We have never trained a group that did not gain at least 25 percent in listening efficiency.

Primarily the business of becoming a good listener consists of getting rid of bad listening habits and replacing them with their counterpart skills.

TEN BAD LISTENING HABITS

Several years ago I identified what seemed to me to be the ten worst listening habits in America today. Though my discussion of them here is in relation to the ways they may affect us in a formal listening situation, the effects of these habits can be just as devastating in less formal listening situations at home, at school, in business or social groups.

Teachers will perhaps get the most from this discussion if they think back to recent lectures they have listened to at educational meetings or public forums.

1. Calling the subject dull. The bad listener often finds a subject too dry and dusty to command his attention and he uses this as an excuse to wander off on a mental tangent. The good listener may have heard a dozen talks on the same subject before, but he quickly decides to see if the speaker to be heard has anything to say that can be of use to him. The key to good listening is that little three-letter word *use.* The good listener is a sifter, a screener, a winnower of the wheat from the chaff. He's always hunting for something practical or worthwhile to store in the back of his mind to put to work in the months and years ahead. G. K. Chesterton said many years ago that in all this world there is no such thing as an uninteresting subject, only uninterested people.

2. Criticizing the speaker. It's the indoor sport of most bad listeners to find fault with the way a speaker looks, acts, and talks. The good listener may make a few of the same criticisms, but he quickly begins to pay attention to what is said, not how it is said. After a few minutes the good listener becomes oblivious to the speaker's mannerisms or his faults in delivery. He knows that message is ten times as important as the clothing in which it comes garbed.

3. Getting overstimulated. Listening

efficiency drops to zero when the listener reacts so strongly to one part of a presentation that he misses what follows. At the University of Minnesota we think this bad habit so critical that, in the classes where we teach listening, we put at the top of every blackboard the words: *Withhold evaluation until comprehension is complete —hear the man out.* It is important that we understand the speaker's point of view fully before we accept or reject it.

4. *Listening only for facts.* I used to think it was important to listen for facts. But I've found that almost without exception it is the poor listeners who say they listen for facts. They do get a few facts, but they garble a shocking number and completely lose most of them. Good listeners listen for the main ideas in a speech or lecture and use them as connecting threads to give sense and system to the whole. In the end they have more facts appended to those connecting threads than the catalogers who listen only for facts. It isn't necessary to worry too much about facts as such, for facts have meaning only when principles supply the context.

5. *Trying to outline everything.* There's nothing wrong with making an outline of a speech—provided the speaker is following an outline method of presentation. But probably not more than a half or perhaps a third of all the speeches given are built around a carefully prepared outline. A good listener is flexible. In his note taking he adapts to the organizational pattern of the speaker—he may make an outline, he may write a summary, he may list facts and principles—but whatever he does he is not rigid about it.

6. *Faking attention.* The pose of chin propped on hand with gaze fixed on speaker does not guarantee good listening. Having adopted this pose, having paid the speaker the overt courtesy of appearing to listen to him, the bad listener feels conscience free to take off on any of a thousand tangents. Good listening is not relaxed and passive at all. It's dynamic; it's constructive; it's characterized by a slightly increased heart rate, quicker circulation of the blood, and a small rise in body temperature. It's energy-consuming; it's plain hard work. The best definition I know of the word *attention* is "a collection of tensions inside the listener," tensions that can be resolved only by getting the facts or ideas that the speaker is trying to convey.

7. *Tolerating distraction.* The poor listener is easily distracted and may even create disturbances that interfere with his own listening efficiency and that of others. He squirms, talks with his neighbors, or noisily shuffles papers. He makes little or no effort to conceal his boredom. The good listener tries to adjust to whatever distractions there are and soon finds that he can ignore them. Certainly he does not distract others.

8. *Choosing only what's easy.* Often we find that poor listeners have shunned listening to serious presentations on radio or television. There is plenty of easy listening available, and this has been their choice. The habit of avoiding even moderately difficult expository presentations in one's leisure-time listening can handicap anyone who needs to use listening as a learning tool.

9. *Letting emotion-laden words get in the way.* It is a fact that some words carry such an emotional load that they cause some listeners to tune a speaker right out. I have pinned down a few: *mother-in-law, landlord, landlady, automation, clerk, big business, communist*—these are all fighting words to some people. I sometimes think that

one of the most important studies that could be made would be the identification of the one hundred greatest trouble-making words in the English language. If we knew what these words were, we could bring them out into the open, discuss them, and get them behind us. It's so foolish to let a mere symbol for something stand between us and learning.

10. *Wasting the differential between speech and thought speed.* Americans speak at an average rate of 125 words per minute in ordinary conversation. A speaker before an audience slows down to about 100 words per minute. How fast do listeners listen? Or, to put the question in a better form, how many words a minute do people normally *think* as they listen? If all their thoughts were measurable in words per minute, the answer would seem to be that an audience of any size will average 400 to 500 words per minute as they listen. Here is a problem. The differential between the speaker at 100 words per minute and the easy thought speed of the listener at 400 or 500 words a minute is a snare and a pitfall. It lures the listener into a false sense of security and breeds mental tangents.

However, with training in listening, the difference between thought speed and speech speed can be made a source of tremendous power to the listener. He can hear everything the speaker says and note what he omits saying; he can listen between the lines and do some evaluating as he goes along. To do this, to exploit this power, the good listener must automatically practice three skills in concentration:

1. *Anticipating the next point.* A good listener tries to anticipate the points a speaker will make in developing a subject. If he guesses right, the speaker's words reinforce his guess. If

he guesses wrong, he'll have to do some thinking to discover why he and the speaker failed to agreee. In either case, his chance of understanding and remembering what was said is nearly double what it would have been if he had simply listened passively.

2. *Identifying supporting material.* A good listener tries to identify a speaker's supporting material. After all, a person can't go on making points without giving his listeners some of the evidence on which he bases his conclusions, and the bricks and mortar that he has used to build up his argument should be examined for soundness.

3. *Recapitulating.* With the tremendous thought speed that everyone has, it is easy to summarize in about five seconds the highlights covered by a speaker in about five minutes. When the speaker stops to take a swallow of water or walks over to the blackboard to write something or even takes a deep breath, the experienced listener makes a mental summary. Half a dozen summaries of the highlights of a fifty-minute talk will easily double the listener's understanding and his ability to retain the important points in the talk.

LEARNING TO LISTEN IN THE PRIMARY GRADES [1]

This informal review of the bad listening habits that too often block the listening efficiency of adults leads us right to a question tremendously important to us as teachers. How can we keep children from developing the bad listening habits that plague too many

[1] Adapted from an article by Dr. Nichols in the Guidebook section of The Teacher's Edition of *Learn to Listen, Speak, and Write,* Book 1/1.

of us? And conversely, how do we go about teaching the counterpart listening skills?

When we think about primary children, these questions are all the more important, because to them getting information from listening is a necessary substitute to getting information from reading. Until they learn to read well, children must receive the bulk of their instruction, guidance, knowledge, and entertainment by ear. Ability to follow directions, to respond to signals—indeed, every school activity—is largely controlled by listening efficiency, and the thinking children do must be done in the language they have heard.

Certainly, then, we need to give early attention to teaching children how to listen. Fortunately, during the past years, we have made considerable progress in identifying the skills that underlie efficient listening and in working out techniques and materials that develop specific listening abilities—for example, listening to directions, organizing ideas while listening.

Interpreting oral reports

In addition to giving children formal listening exercises, we can also use their day-by-day experiences for the direct teaching of listening. Children spend hundreds of hours in primary classrooms just listening, and every one of these hours can help them improve in ability to listen if we will but bring the act of listening into conscious focus for them. Children need to be challenged to think as they listen and to organize and interpret what they hear.

In general our goal in teaching listening should be to develop the same levels of comprehension and interpretation in listening that we work for in reading. To this end, good use can

be made of the accounts children give of things that happen on the playground or at home.

For example, suppose Nancy tells about going home to find that her mother had baked a cake. She wasn't allowed to eat any, because it was for her grandmother's birthday, but her mother let her decorate the cake, and after supper they took it to her grandmother's for a surprise.

To help children interpret Nancy's report, the teacher asks the same kinds of questions she would ask if she were helping the children interpret a story in their readers.

What did Nancy talk about? (Interpreting the main idea.)

What did she say first, next, and last? (Understanding sequence.)

How did Nancy feel when her mother wouldn't let her have a piece of cake? (Understanding emotional reactions.)

Recognizing good performance

In teaching listening as in teaching anything else, it pays to recognize a good performance. Children should be praised whenever they demonstrate that they have listened carefully and perceptively. If Jim's answers to questions about Nancy's story of the surprise party for her grandmother show that he caught the fun and the excitement of the event, this should be commented on. If Susan is asked to deliver a message to a teacher and does so successfully, this should be noted.

Demonstrating good listening

In developing good listening habits in children it is also important for a teacher to demonstrate these habits herself. If she is attentive to the words of her pupils, if she thoughtfully considers statements made by them, her influence for the good is tremendous. She should frequently ask pertinent questions and heed the answers given. And she should be highly sensitive to the great and truthful generalization that most teachers talk too much (about half of all classtime).

Eliminating bad practices

In addition to praising good performances and setting a good example herself, the primary teacher will undoubtedly have to work to overcome four bad practices that often interfere with children's learning to listen effectively. Two of these are things that children exhibit, two are things to which teachers are prone.

Inattention (or faked attention). Just as adults sometimes daydream when they seem to be paying attention, so do children. There are several ways a teacher can help them overcome this bad habit. She can alert the class ahead of time to specific things for which to listen. She can read or tell part of a story and ask each youngster to provide his own ending for it. She can use round-robin listening drills: One child says a word, a second child repeats it and adds another, the third repeats both and adds a word, and so on until some child misses a word, when the whole process starts again.

The important thing in meeting the problem of inattention is to keep listening an active process by specifying how the things learned are to be used. When a listener intends to put to use the things he hears, his listening efficiency at once increases.

Overstimulated response. Another bad habit that children, like adults, may exhibit is the overstimulated re-

sponse. When Mary waves her hand throughout Frank's discussion or Dick breaks into a sentence to correct a "have did," the moment has arrived for some direct listening instruction.

Pupils need to learn to make their comments after, not before, a speaker finishes. A teacher must make it clear that an effective response to a speaker depends on an understanding of all that he has said—an understanding not likely to exist when the listener has been preoccupied with his own thoughts or with his reaction to but a part of what was said. One condition of good listening is listening to the "WHOLE THING."

There are one or two bad habits of which teachers themselves may be guilty.

Needless repetition. In an earnest attempt to make sure that everyone understands, a teacher may repeat things several times. This kind of repetition breeds bad listening habits by creating boredom or a false sense of security. If repetition is necessary, a good listener in the class should be asked to do the repeating.

Demanding pupil attention. The second bad practice a teacher may be guilty of is demanding pupil attention. At the end of a hard day she may find herself sternly saying, "Pay attention, please." This is certainly understandable, but it is also regrettable. To be able to listen should consistently be regarded as a pleasant privilege.

To help children develop a positive attitude toward listening, several techniques may be used. Children might make an illustrated chart or booklet of what they think are good listening manners and practices. On an occasion when youngsters have listened especially well, their teacher might reward their good performance by reading another chapter in a story they enjoy.

Dividends for teachers and pupils

There is no denying that giving thought to listening practices throughout the school day will require an investment of time, effort, and ingenuity by the primary teacher. But the use of techniques like those described will help children develop responsive attitudes toward listening. And pupils can get practice in some of the specific skills that enter into efficient listening. The investment is sure to pay dividends in terms of teaching effectiveness for the teacher and learning efficiency for the children.

All of us, children and adults alike, will profit from utilizing to the fullest extent every means of learning at our disposal. And we need to develop competence in all four of the language arts if we are to achieve true efficiency in communication. The 45 per cent of communication time that we spend in one kind of listening or another should be time well spent. Twenty-five per cent listening efficiency is not enough for any of us. We can do better than that; children can, too. Let's take steps to make sure that they do.

8

The Reading Program
Gains Purpose
Through Literature

This chapter gives attention to the importance of literature in a meaningful reading-language program. The decoding act is not an end in itself; it is a means of attaching thought to symbols. Decoding and comprehending words, phrases, and sentences are valuable skills because of the information and vicarious experiences awaiting those who unlock the printed word. The world of literature supplies content giving this skill meaning.

If reading is a tool, how should this tool be used for the elementary school child? The unfamiliar language patterns and controlled vocabulary of some beginning basal readers provide children a rather narrow picture of what is awaiting them in the world of print. A wide range of literature can be made available to children as listeners and beginning readers, the range expanding as they become independent readers.

In offering literature to children, educators should be clear about the benefits. The values of literature are often taken for granted or in some other way overlooked, but such values must be articulated in setting up goals for a reading program. In approaching this section, ask yourself *What are my goals in using literature with children?* Then compare your statements to those of Leland Jacobs who discusses why he believes children's literature serves to:

1. entertain
2. refresh the spirit
3. explore life and living
4. act as a guidance resource
5. stimulate creative activities
6. model beautiful language.

What daily evidence can children be given for why they should read? Not only must the teacher be clear about her literature goals, but she must be able to translate those goals into meaningful terms for children. One way the teacher can help children formulate their own reasons and motivations for reading is through the practice of offering literature. Since a literary experience occurs as

342

a result of interaction between a reader (or listener) and literature, such an experience cannot be forced or even assigned. Louise Rosenblatt refers to the reading experience as a "happening," resulting from "a live circuit between the reader and the text." Her description of the teacher's task varies considerably from the idea that the teacher is responsible for planning and administering each part of the experience so that it is virtually the same for all participants. She relates how she picked up a poetry text and was drawn into reading the old Scottish ballad "Edward, Edward," in which the son is doing penance for killing his father.

I found myself re-living the step-by-step revelations of the crime and its aftermath. As I finished the poem, it was as though I had been participating in a Greek tragedy in capsule. Associations with Oedipus and Orestes were a measure of my emotional involvement. And then, I turned the page:

1. What is the name of this kind of poem?
2. What was the effect of the refrain? [1]

After being totally involved in a drama, these two questions shock the reader into an observer position and ask for analysis of this work as a piece of literature. How does this reaction affect the student's involvement in the content of the poem? When students come to expect this type of concluding question, how might it affect their reading? Although it may be important that such information be learned, it can be done at another time, outside the emotional involvement of a particular work. Once teachers conceptualize literature as an adventure with unlimited chances, dependent on the vision of the participant, rather than as a body with dissected parts, there are numerous means of carrying on a "Why read?" campaign with students.

The articles in this chapter concentrate on the issues the teacher must face in teaching literature: selection of literature for children, and the uses of literature in the reading program. The underlying theme is how to motivate children to be readers, not just to learn about reading. The reader can compare his/her list of priorities with those identified in the ensuing articles.

One priority, says Charlotte Huck, is to be a teacher who reads. Just as it helps children to see reading as an enjoyable pastime in their homes, it is also beneficial for them to see teachers reading and sharing their vast knowledge of children's literature with students. Huck also says that the teacher should make available a wide range of books to satisfy many interests and reading levels. Equally important is the reading environment. A physical setting conducive to comfortable reading and daily provision for reading time demonstrate to children that the teacher supports this activity. Finally, according to Huck, the teacher should allow children to follow their own reading interests, even if they appear one-tracked at times. She maintains that forcing children to read all types of literature around a library wheel or other charting device may discourage many children from finding out what reading could have held for them.

Leland Jacobs, on the other hand, believes that teachers should expose chil-

[1] Louise M. Rosenblatt, "A Way of Happening," *Educational Record*, 49 (Summer 1968), 339.

dren to a good balance in literature so they might know the range available to them. A child does not know whether he will enjoy folktales unless he has read (or heard) folktales. However, Jacobs' phrase, "Give children literature" exemplifies the antithesis of forcing children to read various literature types. The clue to ensure the welcome reception of giving is to choose literature *for* children, not adult literature *about* children, a practice of past years.

Two aspects of the issue literature for children, not about children, will be dealt with here. One is the matter of allowing children to select their materials, and the other is the problem of finding literature that appeals to each child's basic needs and interests. The first has been explored by Helen Darrow,[2] who wanted to see if there was value in having children choose their own reading content.

Darrow examines traditional three-group reading instructional plans as well as individualized reading[3] situations with the child selecting literature. She discovered distinct contrasts in the way the children functioned during the reading period and the way they articulated what they were doing. In the individualized plans, reading was treated as one of the language arts, and activities involved all communication modes; whereas in the traditional plans, the skills were isolated, with children reading as a group, writing as a group, listening, and so on, but rarely integrating these skills naturally.

A second distinction related to programming found children in an individualized program involved in planning and making independent choices regarding their activities. Darrow relates that when they were questioned about tomorrow's plan, the children knew what it would be because it would build on what they had chosen to be involved with that day. In traditional grouping, with assigned reading content in texts, children reported that tomorrow would be the same as every other day, or that they did not know what they would be doing because the teacher planned it. Darrow's data would eliminate the need to ask those self-directed children, "Why read?" They have their personal reasons for reading and they are doing it!

Literature *for* children rather than *about* them can be acquired another way. Of course, the teacher will find examples of literature for children daily, simply by reading to them and learning directly what they like and why. This takes a long time, however, and can be hit and miss. One particular form of literature—folklore—can be used as a natural bridge for children to go from their oral and written language to published literature. Anthropologist Alan Dundes discusses how the teacher can use rhymes, jingles, folktales, and songs familiar to children to build a base toward the introduction of other forms of literature for children, such as poetry and fiction. Folk literature can provide content for the reading program. The teacher can use jump rope rhymes or jingles for matching configurations, creating word families by rhyming, examining structural elements,

---

[2] Helen Fisher Darrow, "Reality, Morality and Individualized Reading," *Claremont Reading Conference Yearbook, 1968,* ed. Malcolm P. Douglass, pp. 278–85.

[3] Individualized reading, as used in this context, refers to a program in which students choose their reading material, then plan and carry out activities that communicate the content and the reader's interpretation and/or response to it. The implication here is that the students assumed this responsibility gradually, as they were guided in making intelligent choices, and that they continued to need guidance in varying degrees.

and so on. By reciting these jingles, children are manipulating words and phrases they have spoken many times, so the patterns are familiar. Because of this familiarity, children's folklore also helps to enhance self-esteem and confidence. The teacher who has such regard for the child's words, which she not only listens to but records (in writing or on tape) and reads back, will greatly enhance the child's feeling about his self-worth and the worth of his family group.

Dundes supports this use of folklore by stating the importance of this literature to its cultural group. He points out the absurdity of the phrase "culturally deprived." All groups have their own culture, which may simply be different from the dominant culture.

This discussion leads to the question of whether culturally different or minority group children need different literary experiences from other children. Patricia Cianciolo [4] has reviewed studies that show a universality in interests and preferences of children. These findings suggest crystallized principles that would be well applied to all children:

1. Make available a large amount of literature depicting the child's culture, but do not limit him to such literature;
2. Make picturebooks available to nonreaders and as yet dependent readers.

The potential of literature as a primary transmitter of culture is raised. Cianciolo sees it as an opportunity for minority cultures to become aware and informed of the dominant culture so that they gain confidence and feelings of security in their total surroundings. Dundes expands this idea: he believes that all groups should have the opportunity to gain an appreciation of commonalities and to be aware of the differences; he opposes the practice of labeling "right" and "wrong." In this way, knowledge, awareness, and sensitivity can flow both directions to bring mutual understanding and appreciation.

If a literature program is to be accountable to anyone, it must first be accountable to the students. It will then carry the potential for fulfilling the educators' criteria, as well. As Huck says, "The measure of the total reading-language program, which has now been described as including literature as a major component, is no longer *can* the children read, but *do* they read?"

[4] Patricia Jean Cianciolo, "A Recommended Reading Diet for Children and Youth of Different Cultures," *Elementary English*, 48 (November 1971):779–87.

Give Children Literature

Leland Jacobs

From the beginnings of the movement for free public education in this country, literature has held a place as a curriculum experience for boys and girls. It is true that, in the beginning, it was a rather sad and sorry kind of literature. One of the first bits of verse which colonial children were expected to learn reminded them dolefully that "In Adam's fall, we sinned all."

It's probably characteristic of so much of the literature that was given to those poor little Puritans that, as Dorothy Baruch has said, "One would think from the kinds of reading experiences which were given to the young in those days that the adults of the community were in momentary fear of an infant revolt, and so they dangled them over hell-fire and brimstone to keep them in line."

As our country first looked to the Old World for its traditions and culture, so, similarly, we looked to the Old World for our first children's literature. Later, we developed a literature for adults that represented our declaration of intellectual freedom from other parts of the world. In the absence of a truly children's literature, we gave to children some of the masterpieces of this adult literature.

ADULT LITERATURE NOT APPROPRIATE FOR CHILDREN

It is tragic that to this day, in some schools in the United States, the children's literary heritage is confined pretty much to the old classical adult material. In some third grades one still finds children reading:

Between the dark and the daylight,
When the night is beginning to lower,
Comes a pause in the day's occupations
That is known as the Children's Hour.

As one looks at that poem inside out, he discovers that it is the reminiscences of an old man looking back upon the joys of having children in his household. If, in your school systems, you have any such individuals in the third grade, I recommend that you look at your promotional practices rather critically!

Or, along in the fourth grade—because, I presume, the title is "Little Boy Blue"—one still finds nine-year-olds trying to get into the experiences expressed by "The little toy dog is covered with dust, but sturdy and staunch

Reprinted by permission of Illinois State University.

he stands." Now if you analyze those lines sympathetically, you discover that this is the emotion of an adult who has lost a child. It is *about* a child—but not *for* a child.

As we moved on toward the twentieth century, there began to develop a movement for literature that was distinctively *for* children. It was prompted by men and women who believed firmly that the boys and girls of America deserve as significant a literature for *them* as do the adult readers in our culture. Our present age has seen the full flowering of this movement. The literature is here. This is truly the Golden Age of children's literature.

If we follow in the tradition of literature as an experience for boys and girls in the elementary schools, then, our job is so to provide it that, increasingly with their maturity, they grow in taste in reading. Without literature as a vital experience for children, I have the suspicion we have spent so much time on other aspects of reading, that we are in part to blame for the low level of adult reading habits in American life today.

There are six good reasons why children need literature in their lives.

1. Literature is entertainment. The first reason why children need literature is that literature is entertainment. I have no fear of entertainment as a noble end to education. The shortening of the working hours—for everybody but members of our profession, it seems—gives more time for leisure. Certainly, along with radio, picture magazines, movies, and television, some time ought to be reserved for reading. Unless children at school learn to love to read and enjoy reading for its own sake as entertainment, we are missing one of our wonderful citizenship opportunities. I would never apologize to anybody coming into my classroom

and finding me enjoying literature with children. Literature as entertainment is a perfectly valid reason for it as a curriculum experience.

2. Literature refreshes the spirit. Literature sometimes helps to take us away from the urgencies of life that have become too urgent. Through the experience of reading fine prose and fine poetry, for the moment one learns to escape from the immediate cares and comes back to them recreated and refreshed. Unless children have many opportunities for this experience at school, they may never learn this wonderful value of literature in the refreshment of spirit.

Nor is that all of literature's contribution to the spirit. In all of our lives there are some books which—long after we have forgotten their titles, the incidents and the names of the characters—if one comes in contact with them again, they recall what I term a "residue of meaning," an overtone of spiritual values. Because such books have such vital meanings to us, the spiritual quality of their entertainment comes to the fore. We cannot expect that of every story or of every poem, but it is only as children have experiences with literature that this great potential is at least a possibility.

3. Literature helps explore life and living. Children need literature in order to explore life and living. There is no other medium—television, radio, or any of the rest—that quite compares with that wonderful experience of getting into the life situations of another person in the ways that one can do it with literature. A fine author is so cautious, in the sense of being careful with life—the realities of life—that somehow or other he reaches out to the young reader, and together, they go exploring into the life and the living, the customs, the mores, the habits of thinking of another character. Sometimes, first-hand experiences are best, but there are certain kinds of experiences that can come only vicariously through this kind of experience with literature. So, children need literature as an exploration of life.

4. *Literature is a guidance resource.* Literature can serve as a guidance resource for letting a person get insights into himself so that he can possibly change behavior. Not all literature can do it, nor can it always be done prescriptively. But everyone of us has in his life probably at least one book that helped to give him insight about himself at a time when he needed it.

5. *Literature stimulates creative activities.* Children need literature as a springboard to creative activities in other areas. Creative reading of literature, coupled with a rich program in the other arts, gets one art to feed another art. Reading stimulates drawing and rhythmic interpretation in dramatics. The richer the children's experiences in reading and dramatics, the richer they all become in the creative aspects of living.

6. *Literature is beautiful language.* Children need literature in order to enrich their own language. Literature is beautiful language, and who among us would not want children to get the beauty of their mother tongue at its best?

BUT WHAT LITERATURE?

But what kind of literature will provide the kind of values children need? I have three great parallels, which, if followed consistently, will provide the kind of literature program the children of today need.

Parallel 1: The new and the old. Today's literature program needs a balance of new literature and old literature, for one's literary heritage has its source in the combination of the two. A child needs a great deal of the modern literature—the things that have been written for children in his own generation—because it is written in the idiom and in the style, mood, and tempo that he understands because he's living it. The great modern writers for children know what the inside of a child's mind is like, and they write with a tempo, style, and spirit that is twentieth-century modern.

The child needs a wealth of this material, but if his heritage is to be rich, he needs to know that before his time there came to us great stories, too —stories like "The Elephant's Child," who went down by the "great gray-green, greasy Limpopo River, all set about with fever-trees, to find out what the Crocodile has for dinner." Kipling is gone, but "The Elephant's Child" is with us yet. The child needs the old, old tales of Grimm, Asbjornsen, Joseph Jacobs, and all the rest of the wonderful crew of folklorists who collected the old stories of the world. Children love this old literature. They particularly love it if they can share it with an adult who had it, too, as a child. This is the kind of literature that May Lamberton Becker said is like the measles going through an orphanage. Generation after generation, the continuity of the literary experience going from the old to the young, and from the young to the younger is a great experience and a great combination of new and old reading experience.

Parallel 2: Realistic and fanciful literature. My second parallel is the balance between realistic and fanciful literature. Now, the child loves the kinds of stories that acquaint him with his own world, whether he is close to it in time and space, or far from it.

He loves animal stories. He wants stories that take him out to the various parts of the United States, where people live like him as an American and yet different from him because they belong to an area that is different. This balance of realistic literature, which we call regional literature, he needs and wants tremendously.

But he also wants at this age to go out in time and space belond our own country to the Orient, to Europe, up into the hills of Switzerland with Heidi, over into Japan with the little farmer boy who was saved from the tidal wave.

He wants to go back into time—to the time of Abraham Lincoln, when a little girl wrote and recommended that Lincoln would look much better on a platform if he had whiskers. So he raised whiskers, and she saw that he had them and met him in those days, as Hertha Pauli has written.

But along with these kinds of experiences in time and space with realistic literature, he also wants the kind of literature which takes him out of this world into the world of the impossible, the improbable, and the fanciful. So there is "Mary Poppins"; there are the "Three Wishes"; there are the fairy tales that transcend time and space. I think these are terribly urgent. Look what the child can do with such literature. He can get out of the plausible and the possible and look back on the real to get a greater perspective on both.

Parallel 3: Prose and poetry. I am sad that in so many schools today there is so little time for poetry. There are some good reasons for this. For, in the past, you know some of the things we did. "Mass memorization," for example—forty times around the room, "I wandered lonely as a cloud that floats on high o'er vales and hills," until you hope you never see a daffodil again. Or, "verse vivisection," where you tear it to pieces to see how it ticks. Or, "poetic preachment," where you give children poetry to improve their spirits, their souls, and their characters.

That isn't our idea of poetry for children. Today, we give them their wonderful heritage of poetry where they can read it and see it beautifully on a page, or hear it joyously.

THE PLACE OF LITERATURE IN THE CURRICULUM

Children need literature, then, for entertainment, for refreshment of spirit, for the exploration of life and living, for guidance, for creative activities, and for the enrichment of language. We deprive them of these values at our peril.

There are some people who like to say that the social studies are the backbone of the curriculum. That's all right with me. Then there are some who think that mathematics give muscle to the curriculum. That's all right with me, too. Because, deep down inside, I am quite sure that literature is mighty close to the *heart* of the curriculum; and, as Edna St. Vincent Millay has said so well:

The world stands out on either side,
No wider than the heart is wide.

Give children literature!

A Way of Happening

Louise M. Rosenblatt

New York University

What should be understood by the term *literature* when we speak of the literature program or of teaching literature? Underlying assumptions about the nature of literature will profoundly affect the organization of the literature program and the day-to-day procedures for carrying it out. Especially important are the implicit assumptions about literature prevailing in the colleges and graduate schools, since these ideas will influence the character of the literature curriculum down to the earliest levels. That shockingly few graduates of our schools and colleges are readers of literature is a frequent criticism of our educational system. Efforts are therefore being made to produce new literature curricula. Unfortunately, the theories of literature prevalent in the colleges and universities today fail to provide sound theoretical bases for literature programs that will educate a reading public capable of participating in the benefits of literature.

What, then, should be understood by *literature*? What do we teach when we teach literature? A personal experience may provide a springboard for discussion: As I was leafing through a poetry text, I came upon the old Scottish ballad, "Edward, Edward" and found myself drawn into rereading it.

In the dialogue between Edward and his mother, he reveals the fact that the blood on his sword is that of his "Father deir." He expresses his desperate, remorseful decision to do penance wandering over the seas, leaving his towers and halls to fall into ruin, his wife and children to beggary. I found myself reliving the step-by-step revelations of the crime and its aftermath. As I finished the poem, it was as though I had been participating in a Greek tragedy in capsule. Associations with Oedipus and Orestes were a measure of my emotional involvement. And then, I turned the page:

1. What is the name of this kind of poem?
2. What was the effect of the refrain?

The shock of these questions drew me away from all that I had lived through in reading the text—the structure of feelings called forth by the pattern of events, my darkening mood as I evoked the image of the destruction of the

Reprinted from *Educational Record,* Summer 1968, copyright American Council on Education, Washington, D.C. 20036.

family through the son's desperate crime and terrible penance, the horror of the final interchange between the two voices.

Is this not typical of what often happens in literature classrooms at all levels? Out of the best intentions in the world, out of misguided zeal, the student is hurried as quickly as possible into some kind of thinking and discussion or writing that removes him abruptly—and often definitively—from what he has himself lived through in relation to the text. Often, he is asked to destroy the actual effect of the poem, novel, or play through focusing his attention on a reduction of it to some clumsy paraphrase of its "literal meaning." Or he may be involved at once, as with "Edward, Edward," in classifying the work as a ballad or a lyric or an epic. Or, again as in the question about the refrain in "Edward, Edward," the effect of the work may be taken for granted and his attention focused at once on a totally analytic consideration of the function of various technical devices or underlying images. Or he may be asked to write on the theme of the work. All of these may be respectable questions about the poem, but only in their appropriate place. And their appropriate place is decidedly not as a substitute for, or an evasion of, the actual experience of the poem as a work of art.

NEGLECT OF ESSENCE

The danger is that at all levels, from kindergarten through the graduate school, in some such way the essence of literature is neglected. W. H. Auden, in his elegy on William Butler Yeats, provides powerful reminders of the essential quality of poetry (and *poetry,* for our purposes throughout this dis-

cussion, can be used interchangeably with the terms *literature, literary work of art,* and *imaginative literature*). Auden writes, "For poetry makes nothing happen: . . . it survives, a way of happening." We forget that literature is "a way of happening."

Certainly, in 1939, Auden had no notion of the newest use of the word "happening." The Random House dictionary includes this latest meaning of "a happening" as an event, and then adds that often the audience is also participating in what is going on. This seems to add another level of meaning to Auden's phrase. Yet, perhaps this meaning was already, to some extent, implicit. The poem is a happening, an event, because of the participation of the reader or the listener. The reader *makes the poem happen* by calling it forth from the text. This is why Auden, earlier in the poem could say of Yeats, "he became his admirers."

But, one may object, this is true of all readers, the reading of any kind of text, scientific, informative, as well as imaginative. In all kinds of reading, the reader is active. He must bring his own past experience to bear on the text, and thus "make something of" the symbols, the little black marks that he sees or the sounds that he hears. Because this is true, much that we say about the reading or teaching of poetry or imaginative literature has implications for the teaching of any kind of reading.

Auden's phrase reminds us, however, that poetry is a particular way of happening. Poetry, he says, *makes* nothing happen—that is, poetry is not a tool, an instrument for accomplishing some end or purpose or task beyond itself. Informational, expository, argumentative writings are instrumental in that sense. When we read such a text, our attention is focused on the outcome, on what will be left with us when the reading is over. Hence, a paraphrase or a summary of a piece of information often is quite as useful as the original. Someone else can read the newspaper or a scientific work for us and summarize it quite acceptably. But no one can read a poem for us. Accepting a summary of a poem, an analysis of someone else's reading or interpretation or experience of it, is analogous to having someone else eat your dinner for you. You can use someone else's summary of a biology text, you can benefit from the rephrasing of the technical language of a law, but a work of art, as art, must be a personal experience.

ACTIVE PARTICIPATION

This "way" of a poem or any literary work of art is what differentiates it from ordinary reading. In other kinds of reading, we are amply concerned with the information or ideas that will be left with us once the reading has ended, as, for example, when we are reading a text that gives us directions about how to do something. In reading the poem, we not only bring about the "happening" by responding to the verbal symbols that make up the text, but also our attention is focused on the qualities of the very happening that we are bringing to pass. We are directly involved, we are active participants in the "happening." We are aware of what the symbols call forth in us. They point to sensations, objects, images, ideas. These we must pattern out of the material that we bring to the work from our past knowledge of life and language. And these in addition call up in us associated states of feeling and mood.

The text is the guide and control in all this, of course. We must pay atten-

tion to the order of the words, their sound, their rhythm and recurrence. Our attention oscillates between the texture of the sound and rhythm of the words, and all that these evoke in us. We vibrate to the chiming of sound, sense, and associations. We focus on this electric charge set up between the text and us. The verbal symbols stir much more in us than is relevant to the text; we must crystallize out and organize those elements that do justice to the particular words in their particular places.

This live circuit between the reader and the text is the literary experience. Literature is, first of all, this sensing, feeling, thinking, this ordering and organizing of feeling, image, and idea in relation to a text. The quality and structure of the reader's experience in relation to the text becomes for him the poem, the story, or the play. The task of teachers of literature is to foster this particular "way of happening," this mode of perceptive and personal response to words, this self-awareness in relation to a text.

The sense of literature as "a way of happening," then, must be central to any sound literature program. An underlying and pervasive principle, important for every stage of the program, from the earliest years to the last, should be this: No practice or procedure, no pattern or sequence, should hinder the student's growth in capacity to create literary experiences for himself. Constant alertness is required to avoid methods and programs emphasizing concerns that may become substitutes for, rather than aids to, the sense of the personal meaningfulness of the literary experience.

TO ENRICH RESPONSE

This in no way denies the responsibility of the reader to the text: On the contrary, the literature program should be directed toward enabling the student to perform more and more fully and more and more adequately in response to texts. This means fostering both the capacity for literary experiences of higher and higher quality and the capacity to reflect on these experiences with increasing insight and maturity. Literary sensitivity and critical maturity, it will be seen, cannot be divorced from the individual's rhythm of growth and breadth of experience.

Ironically, at this time, when there is a laudable impulse towards a general revision of the literature curriculum, certain influences have tended to obscure these fundamental considerations. Current critical theories, on the one hand, and current educational theories, on the other, converge to reinforce an analytic, theoretical approach to literature.

One needs only to recall the various schools of critical theory that have prevailed in our universities and literary circles during the past half-century. All of these are reflected in some degree in the literature programs and the approaches to the teaching of literature in our schools and colleges at this time. There is the didactic and moralistic approach, which stems from a long and flourishing tradition, but is perhaps now most in eclipse in the universities. There is the still widespread emphasis on viewing the literary work as a document in literary history and in the author's biography. There is the approach to the literary work as a document reflective of political, social, and economic developments. There is the psychological approach, treating the work as symptomatic of the author's psychic structure or as an embodiment of archetypal patterns or myths.

In recent decades, the general approach associated with the label of the "New Criticism" has, in some quarters, become a literary orthodoxy. The "New Critics" have looked upon the literary work as a self-contained system of words, and they have emphasized technical and stylistic analysis. The "Chicago group" have diverged somewhat from this, emphasizing especially the approach in terms of Aristotle's categories, but they also are mainly concerned with analysis of literary types and the author's methods. Despite the extremely valuable contributions of these and other critical schools, and despite their differences among themselves, they share with the older approaches the tendency to divert attention from the literary event, the individual literary "happening" itself. The personal involvement of the reader, the engagement in the actual process of bringing the work into being from the text, has been taken for granted. All, no matter what their emphasis, usually consider the work as given—as an object for study and analysis.

DISREGARDING THE READER

Thus, the New Critics' concern with "the work itself" led, unfortunately, to disregard of the reader's contribution. Perhaps the model or the competing image of the impersonality and systematic objectivity of the sciences lurked somewhere in the background. At any rate, these critics did not work out a sound theoretical basis for relating their formalist or contextualist method to the other approaches, especially the psychological and the social. Even more important, they did not work out—or even see the need for —a thoroughly developed theory of the relationship between the reader and the text.

Hence, current critical doctrines could not offer an adequate theoretical framework when the educational environment generated a much-needed impetus toward rethinking of the literature curriculum. Jerome Bruner's *The Process of Education*[1] can be cited as one of the most influential of the various expressions of the need for cumulative and sequential curricula. A number of his formulations have become part of the general vocabulary of the field. Starting with the assumption that any subject could be taught effectively in some intellectually honest form to any child at any stage, Bruner developed the notion of the "spiral curriculum," in which the fundamental structure, the basic ideas or principles, of a discipline would be taught from the very earliest level and would be encountered repeatedly in more and more complex forms throughout the years. This curricular model was admittedly based on experimentation in the sciences and mathematics.

The dominant emphases in the theory of literature fostered a rather uncritical application of this model to the development of literature curricula. The laudable effort to build up sequential and cumulative literature programs has been largely vitiated by the tendency to structure the spiral around a set of broad theoretical or intellectual concepts. Too little attention was paid to the fact that, unlike disciplines such as mathematics or the sciences, literature does not present itself as a structure of generally agreed upon basic concepts. Intent on finding something analogous to, say, the concepts of *number* or *set* in mathematics, curriculum planners have fixed on theoretically-formulated concepts such as, to illustrate the range, *form,* or *irony,* or

tragedy. Based on one or another critical approach, structuring concepts have been drawn from subjects or themes or patterns treated in literature, from the genres or types into which they can be classified, or from the techniques or methods that can be analyzed.

BACK INTO ABSTRACTION

Thus planners of a literature curriculum build a spiral program in which *satire* is to be studied at various levels. Menippean satire is a unit in the third grade, for example, and increasingly complex units on satire are encountered at intervals throughout the subsequent nine years of the literature program.[2] Such planning tends to develop more and more complex theoretical formulations, classifications, and distinctions. Because these curricula have been produced by people of literary culture, one encounters at times evidence of a need to protest the importance of taste, of the intrinsic value of the work itself. But the absence of a theoretical basis for handling this seems to throw the planners back into the realm of abstract or theoretical con-

---

[1] Cambridge, Mass.: Harvard University Press, 1961; see also Bruner, *Toward a Theory of Instruction* (Cambridge, Mass.: Harvard University Press, 1966); and Bruner et al., *Studies in Cognitive Growth* (New York: Wiley & Sons, 1967).

[2] These comments are intended to characterize a general weakness in the patterns of various sequential curricula produced in recent years, especially by the Curriculum Study Centers sponsored by the Office of Education. I have seen a number of these at various stages, and have consulted the materials distributed by the Materials Center of the PMLA. No program is singled out here, since any one curriculum should be accorded a full study of its strengths and weaknesses. Individual units and sections are sometimes more adequate than the weak theoretical scaffolding of the total sequential program.

Stoddard Malarkey, "Sequence and Literature: Some Considerations," *English Journal,* March 1967 (56), pp. 394–400, is typical of the kind of theoretical weakness discussed here.

cepts as the sign of progression—i.e., a progression based on concepts or information *about* literature apart from readers.

In a lecture at New York University in March 1967, the great psychologist, Jean Piaget, referred to Bruner's contention that any subject could be taught to any child at any stage, and then remarked that, after all, the child as well as the discipline has a sequential development. Even the child's ability to grasp concepts in mathematics or physics, Piaget's work has demonstrated, follows a growth process—a series of stages of development—that may, perhaps, be accelerated (if, he added, this is desirable) but cannot be bypassed.[3] If this is true for logical reasoning, how much more important it is to consider the emotional, intellectual, and social equipment of the student in planning the sequence of the literature program! The "way" of literature should not be ignored; the literature program deals with literary texts which primarily represent—not a structure of intellectual concepts to be assimilated—but a body of potential literary experiences to be participated in.

UNHEEDED WARNINGS

Surely, much more searching consideration should have been given to

[3] Brunner, in his chapter "Readiness for Learning," in *The Process of Education* also recognizes the need for further research on the problem of tailoring material to the capacities and needs of students, but much more attention has been given to his idea that a spiral or sequential curriculum can be devised once the basic concepts or forms are established.

No attempt is being made here to deal with the extremely complex relationship between the work of Bruner and Piaget. See Bärbel Inhelder, et al., "On Cognitive Development," *American Psychologist*, February 1966 (*21*), pp. 160–64.

the question: In what sense can the study of literature be viewed as a theoretically structured discipline? Bruner's use of the terms *idea, principle,* or *basic concept,* derived from the example of mathematics and the sciences, is not applicable without qualification to literature, for which the intellectual or theoretical concept does not have the same kind of fundamental priority. Bruner's own tentativeness about his extrapolations to literature—his references, for example, to tragedy, comedy, and farce, or his comments on *Moby Dick*—should have been taken more seriously, and his few warnings about the difference between the sciences and other disciplines, such as literature, should have been heeded. Instead, often under the influence of the New Criticism or of theoretical classifications such as those found in Northrop Frye's *Anatomy of Criticism,* the tendency has been to assume that theoretical categories provided the basic pattern for a spiraling complexity of analysis and classification in the literature program.

But should this program be conceived as a body of concepts to be learned and applied in increasingly complex ways? Is satire—to return to an earlier example—to be thought of as primarily a concept to be clarified? Certainly a most challenging critical problem is the formulation of a clear definition that will do justice to all the works thus designated. But prior to such a concept, should not satire be *experienced?* Is it not basically a way of viewing represented personalities, situations, and behavior in the light of feelings about what they should be and are not? Even a very simple satiric animal story requires the relating of different planes of thought and feeling about personalities and behavior. This is a complex operation involving ideas and emotional attitudes, rather than primarily an analytic, reasoning, classifying operation. Under certain conditions, even young children are able to have such an experience, but the emphasis should be on the actual literary event or happening, on a vivid evocation of image, action, and attitude from the text. We need to discover the emotional and intellectual structure of such a literary experience. Generalizations *about* it, even about its satiric meaning for human beings in general, may be beside the point, to say nothing of theoretical notions about a label called *satire*. Satiric works, whether in the ninth grade or in college, should be read primarily as structures of experience which have present meaningfulness for the student reader. Given the capacity to organize experience in this way under the guidance of the printed page, the concept of *satire* can emerge ultimately as relevant to actual literary experiences and a useful way of designating them.[4]

INTUITIVE LEARNING

Instead of a structure or sequence of theoretical concepts to be achieved through analysis of literary works, the literature program, then, should be seen primarily as a structure of modes of linguistic and literary experience. The focus should be on what the child or youth may be equipped—sensuously, emotionally, intellectually, and linguistically—to evoke and organize from the spoken word or the printed page at each stage of his development.

In opposition to the pressures toward the analytic and theoretical approach to the literary work, I should like to suggest the principle that

[4] The nature of relative complexity in literature also requires much fuller study through systematic research in the classroom.

throughout the entire literature program, the primary emphasis should be on an intuitive acquisition of literary habits and literary insights. I am using the term *intuitive* in the manner of students of language who tell us that the child acquires a language intuitively.[5] By the time he comes to school, if he has been exposed to users of English, say, he will have acquired a command of the basic structure and the signal system or cues of that language. Theoretical analysis, diagramming, labeling of parts, as the experimental evidence indicates, have little relation to his actual original acquisition of the spoken or written language. Once he possesses the basic structure of the language, as a mode of behavior, he can understand a system of grammatical analysis that may be taught him as an explanation of what he already does. First, we are told, let the child acquire intuitively the habit of the structure of the language and its way of generating sentences. Then later (if necessary) he can learn intellectually and theoretically to analyze or describe this linguistic behavior.

MORE SENSITIVE EXPERIENCES

In the same way, in literary training, the prime essential is the intuitive

[5] Bruner and other scientists use the term *intuitive thinking* to designate "hunches" or sudden insights into the solution of a problem, which has been preceded by logical analysis of the problem and for which logical proof must subsequently be developed. This tends to stress the absence of logical analysis. In the discussion above *intuitive* implies absence of formal analysis, but includes also conscious attention to responses to verbal signs and their organization into a mode of immediately apprehended experience. Theoretical analysis may be applied to this kind of intuitive event, but should not be equated with it.

development of habits of responding to the literary text. The literary "way" of responding to a pattern of verbal signs has to be firmly assimilated. This, we have seen, is not only learning how to relate word and referent into a meaningful organization, but also learning how to look at, to savor, the structure of image, idea, feeling, attitudes, during the process of evoking it from the text. Out of the feelings and experiences with life and language which even the young reader brings to the text, he makes the new experience which is the poem or the story. For the youth as for the young child, there should be a continuing reinforcement of habits of sensitive and responsible organization of literary experiences. The sequence to be generated in a literary program is thus a sequence of more and more complete, more and more sensitive, more and more complex experiences.

After the reader has felt the sensuous, emotional, and intellectual impact of the work reverberating within him, he can be led further to pull his experience together and to reflect on it. This indeed is the beginning of the critical process. At any level of the curriculum, what he should study first of all is the relation between himself and the text. This is what he has to learn to be "critical" of.[6] And on that kind of critical relationship can be based later the more complex kinds of self-conscious critical activity. Surely, before the New Critic can make his refined analysis of metaphor or irony or structure, he has undergone a sensitive intuitive experience in relation to

[6] This is insufficiently recognized in the discussion of criticism as central to the literature program in *Freedom and Discipline in English,* Report of the Commission on English (New York: College Entrance Examination Board, 1965).

the text. This is the object of his criticism, and not some impersonal external object. The path into literary mastery will not, therefore, be primarily through analysis, the naming of parts, the labeling of types, the identifying of figures of speech, the definition of themes, the evaluation of techniques, or the formulation of aesthetic concepts. *Literary experience, intuitive assimilation and reinforcement of habits of responding to the verbal text, should at all times provide the living context for relevant or appropriate interpretation or critical analysis.*

Under the guidance of these fundamental principles, the contributions of both the literary and educational theorists can become welcome grist to our mill. Critical and theoretical concepts will need to be constantly translated into the kinds of experience and the kinds of processes involved. Thus, we may start by bouncing the child on our knee as we chant nursery rhymes with him, and as time goes on expose him to more and more complex rhythms and patterns of the language. This ability to hear the rhythmic patterns and recurrences of verse and prose is the essential accomplishment; the laborious counting out of syllables or naming of verse patterns is an analytic exercise whose value, even for the older student, seems often obscure. Again, as a story is read, the young reader must learn to link together in a meaningful way a series of episodes experienced through time. When one finds a high school youngster who calls an essay a story or vice versa, is this due to failure to have taught him the terminology, or is it not due to the fact that he has not *felt* a narrative linkage so fully that the name of that kind of experience becomes permanently linked with it? Or as the child grows older, he must fix his attention on the interplay of the qualities of setting and situation and personality. These capacities to evoke experience from the text and to interrelate these felt experiences into a structure surely are more basic than the meaning of a "novel of manners" or a "picaresque novel."

AN INDUCTIVE PROCESS

Recognition of the primacy of the intuitive assimilation of habits of literary response will provide, then, the basis for building a sound sequential literature program related both to the student's development and to the basic modes of literary activity. This also offers a rationale for inductive learning and teaching in the literature program. In one sense, every reading of a text constitutes an inductive process, since the student reader must through trial and error seek to organize the many sensations, emotions, and ideas that present themselves. Any reading involves such creation of tentative interpretations which are either rejected or strengthened by the new elements encountered in the text.

But here I am thinking rather of the inductive process as it leads ultimately to the development of critical or technical concepts. The soundest inductive learning seems to arise when the student is given the conditions which lead to his asking the question for which later he discovers the solution. I have been seeking to develop the image of a literature program in which the student is given the opportunity again and again to stay close to his literary experience, to reflect on it, and to do greater justice to the text and what he makes of it. After repeated experiences in which it has been important, for example, to pay attention to who is speaking in the poem or the

story, the term *persona* may become both meaningful and useful. After many sensitive perceptions of the rippling-out of figurative meanings, the concept of *metaphor* can be more than a rote learning of (usually a distorted) definition. Repeated individual literary experiences can lead to analytic insights and groupings under broader critical categories. Concepts such as *epic* or *irony* or *sonnet* represent three very diverse kinds of such conceptual groupings.[7]

Probably one of the most challenging requirements for this kind of teaching is that after creating the conditions for discovery, we should have the faith and the patience to permit this process to develop. The more insecure we are, the greater the tendency to thrust the answers and the theoretical terminology upon the student. The greater also the tendency to deceive ourselves by the kinds of questions that rush the student away from the experience and lead him into impersonal and abstract formulations. Space does not permit a fuller discussion of classroom techniques here. My principal purpose is to underline the emptiness of the current tendency to think that the way to do justice to literature is through analysis or categorizing of it. When this trend reveals itself even in the earliest grades, the need for this *caveat*

---

[7] The primary stress here on literary experience as against analytic talk about literature seems to have some analogies with the psychologists' emphasis on the stage of "concrete operations" as preliminary to developing mathematical concepts, or on experience with geometric configurations and intuitive methods of dealing with them as a prelude to grasping theorems and axioms. But in the literary context, the ability to handle the intuitive phase is central, and the theoretical insights are supplementary (although some present day critics might claim that literature exists to make critical analysis possible!).

is obvious. (Recent articles [8] deal with "literary analysis" of a picture book in the second grade and "literary criticism" in the third grade.) Usually, teachers of the very youngest children have seemed best aware of the individual's need to perceive and to pay attention to his perceptions—his need to feel and to pay attention to his feelings. Teachers at all levels have the responsibility of honoring such needs of all readers, if literature is to be a bulwark against the dehumanization of so much of our adult lives.

A LIFE ACTIVITY

More than ever, the contemporary world affirms our democratic dream of a society in which each real human being can come to fruition as an honored individual. The Civil Rights Act has committed us once and for all to compensating for the cultural deprivation suffered by many children. In the field of literature, this has forced a recognition of something that many of us have been saying for decades: If we wish children to learn how to participate in literature, we have to be concerned about the experience the child brings to the literary work. We must offer him works to which something in his own life, his own preoccupations, and his linguistic experience may serve as a bridge.[9] Only then can he have a literary experience. Once the child or

[8] See *Elementary English,* January 1966 (43), and January 1967 (44).

[9] The work in literature of the Hunter College Curriculum Study Center, dealing with an inner city group, illustrates this approach.

the young reader has had the literary experience, he should not be misled into thinking that the literary work exists primarily as an object for analysis and classification. He should understand it as a life activity that has value in itself and that can offer him personal satisfaction. In addition, on this basis, it should be possible for us to have the courage to present literature as a source of personal and ethical and social insights.

In a sense, practically all of our children are in one way or another culturally deprived. All, we have seen, are in need of nourishment for their powers of sensuous and aesthetic perception. (Recently, the director of a summer program in the humanities in Connecticut found that his pupils, drawn from all socio-economic segments of the community, were equally "deprived" so far as the arts were concerned.) Or practically all may be "deprived" because of a narrow environment—whether of poverty or wealth, of a totally urban, suburban, or rural life, through immersion in an ethnic or regional subculture. or, at the very least, through lack of an international culture in this at once one-and-divided world. Literature can compensate, thus, for the limitations of time and place and class and nation; can compensate, too, perhaps, in some degree, for the limitations and the sorrows of the human condition. If we think of every reading of a literary work as a "happening," as something lived through sensuously, emotionally, and intellectually, then sequential and cumulative literature programs may indeed make an important contribution to American culture.

Planning the Literature Program
for the Elementary School

Charlotte S. Huck

Elementary school teachers have all but forgotten that the most important reason for teaching boys and girls to read is to help them become *readers*. Controversies continue to be waged over methods of teaching reading, the most appropriate age for beginning instruction, and machines versus basic materials. Many primary teachers report that they spend over one half of the total school day on reading instruction alone. Teachers proudly point to the results of reading achievement tests to prove the effectiveness of their teaching. As a nation we take pride in the 98% literacy rate of our population. Recent criticism to the contrary, the majority of the evidence points to the fact that our schools are teaching children the skill of reading. And yet our schools have failed miserably in helping boys and girls develop the habit of reading. In many instances we have developed an illiterate group of literates—adults who know *how* to read but do *not* read. In one study,[1] nearly one half (48%) of the adults in the United States had not read one

book during the year. Another study[2] which contrasted American reading habits with that of adults in other countries revealed that only 17 percent of the Americans had been reading from a book the previous day whereas 55 percent of the English sample had been engaged in this activity. Despite the rising educational level and the high standard of living, a large proportion of the American public expresses little interest in reading.

Although there are many factors which are responsible for the small amount of book reading in the United States, one major factor may well be the overemphasis of the instrumental or basic reading program to the neglect of the literature program in the elementary school. In fact, some elementary school teachers would maintain that literature was something one studied in high school, not the elementary school. Others would say that reading and literature are synonymous. Still others would claim that the literature program is cared for by the "free

[1] David H. Russell, "We All Need to Read," *Saturday Review* 39:36, February 18, 1956.

[2] Lester Asheim, "A Survey of Recent Research," *Reading for Life*, edited by Jacob M. Price. Ann Arbor: University of Michigan Press, 1959, pp. 3–4.

reading" period on Friday afternoon when teachers are free to complete their attendance records while the children are free to develop appreciation and discrimination for fine literature by reading a Nancy Drew mystery! We have no literature program in the elementary school when we compare it with our carefully planned developmental programs in reading, spelling, and arithmetic. All our efforts are directed towards teaching children to read—no one seems to be concerned that they *do* read or *what* they read. The means have become the end. We have developed better and better basic readers, we have even cut some of them apart and boxed them! Yet few children ever developed a love of reading by reading a basic reader or by progressing from one colored reading card to another. It is almost as if we had put our children in link trainers for reading, and then focused our attention on producing bigger and better link trainers and methods of using them without ever giving the children a chance to use the skill they have developed by discovering the thrill of flying. Link trainers do play an important role in training pilots; basic readers play an important role in helping children to learn to read. However, the ultimate goal of both of them should be self-elimination.

Teachers and children must not prize the skill of reading as an end in itself; they must see it as a beginning of a lifetime pleasure with books. There are no values in knowing how to read; only values which are derived *from* reading. As teachers recognize the values which result from wide and varied reading, they will see the need for a planned literature program in the elementary school.

The first major value of literature is enjoyment. Personal enjoyment of reading *is* a respectable activity and should be encouraged. Adults read for pleasure and not to produce a book report. Children too should discover the joy of just reading for fun. They *may* want to share their enjoyment in many different ways, but children should not feel that they always have to *do* something with a book to celebrate its completion. Reading books should be a natural part of children's lives and not such a momentous occasion that we must shoot off firecrackers in the form of book reports, mobiles, or dioramas each time a book is completed. This practice is a remnant of the past when books were scarce and precious and reading ability was limited to a few. A wide variety of experiences in interpreting children's literature may deepen children's appreciations, but they should never become the required penalty for reading a book. Alert teachers know when children's needs have been met through reading; they do not ask for tangible verification. One fourth-grader, whose mother had just died, was introduced to Corbett's *The Lemonade Trick*. This book contains some delightful spoofing of boys' and dogs' behavior. You may remember the part where Waldo, the dog, drinks some of the magic lemonade and immediately becomes so good that he goes out in the backyard to *fill in* the holes which he had dug the day before. For two days, this fourth-grader was completely absorbed in this book. Once he was observed reading it while he walked to the coat closet. Escapism, yes, but he had found an acceptable way to contain his problem, and in the midst of sorrow, a book had been able to make him laugh.

Personal-social growth may also be influenced by *what* children read. Probably many of us experienced death and its accompanying feelings of loss and separation as we read of Beth's death in *Little Women*. American children today may realize some of the personal horrors of war as they identify with Tien Pao in De Jong's starkly written book, *The House of Sixty Fathers*. Some of our overprotected white children may experience the hurts of prejudice for the first time as they read and identify with Mary Jane, the main character in Dorothy Sterling's fine story by the same name which tells of desegregation in our public schools in the South. Or books may help children with the developmental task of growing-up and fulfilling their adult roles. They discover as they read such books as *Nkwala* by Edith Lambert Sharp that this is a universal experience, and they identify with the Salish Indian boy whose "childhood itched him like a goatskin robe." Books help children explore living, "to try on" various roles and accept or reject them as they search for their own identity.

Children may satisfy their desire for information and intellectual stimulation through wide reading. Willard Olson has identified what he calls the "seeking behavior" of boys and girls. Certainly this is revealed in children's response to the recent flood of factual books. Informational books are no longer disguised by the fictional trappings of a trip to the farm with a favorite uncle. Children are hungry for knowledge about the physical and social world in which they live. Many well-written informational books contribute to the thrill of helping children discover specific facts by presenting them clearly and in a meaningful way. These books satisfy, but they do not satiate; they supplement and extend texts in science and social studies. Such fine books as the special edition of Rachel Carson's *The Sea Around Us*

widen children's vision and open new vistas of beauty and mystery.

Only as children are exposed to much fine writing will they develop an appreciation for a well-chosen phrase, rich descriptive prose or convincing characterization. After a story has been finished, the teacher and children may take time to reread and relish particularly enjoyable words or paragraphs: The beautiful but quiet story of *Miracles on Maple Hill* by Virginia Sorensen contains many such descriptive phrases. In one lovely passage Marly ponders the multiplicity of feeling which can be associated with one sound, sight or word:

How so many things could be in a few words was something else Marly didn't know. But it was the same way the whole feel of school can be in the sound of a bell ringing. Or the way the whole feeling of spring can be in one robin on a fence post.[3]

One of the most unique books published this year is *Hailstones and Halibut Bones*[4] by Mary O'Neil. In twelve different poems the author explores the various dimensions of sight, sound, and feeling conveyed by different colors. She describes purple as "sort of a great Grandmother to pink" and suggests that "the sound of green is a water-trickle." Her richest contrasts are in her poem "What is Black." This delightful book will help children to appreciate fine writing which creates vivid word pictures and describes emotions. One first grade teacher[5] had read selections from *The Lonely Doll, A Friend Is Some-*

[3] Virginia Sorensen, *Miracles on Maple Hill*. New York: Harcourt, Brace and Company, 1956, p. 4.

[4] Mary O'Neil, *Hailstones and Halibut Bones*. Garden City, New York: Doubleday and Company, Inc., 1961, p. 11.

[5] Mrs. Jack Holloway, Lincolnwood School, Evanston, Illinois.

one Who Likes You, Bears on Hemlock Mountain, and *Love Is a Special Way of Feeling* to initiate discussions about love, friendship, sorrow, hate, and fear. Following the discussion on loneliness, a group poem was composed from the children's various contributions. It shows the sensitivity of these mature first-graders to the books they had heard and to the insights which they had concerning their own feelings.

A LONELY FELING

When I am lonely there's no one to walk
  with me.
No one loves me.
I feel sad and want to cry.
This feeling comes when:
  I move away and a friend doesn't come
  too.
  or I wake up and am alone in the dark.
It's there when:
  No one eats with me,
  No one greets me after school
  A friend calls me a hurt-name or I'm
  sick in bed.
When I am lonely I am so by myself, it
  makes the me, inside, afraid.

Books can provide the stimulus for children's writing about their own joys, fears, and problems. Constant exposure to fine writing will be reflected in children's increased skill in their own oral and written expression and in their deepened appreciation for truth and beauty.

Another major value of wide and varied reading is that it acquaints children with their literary heritage and provides a firm foundation for future literary experiences. Bruner, in his much discussed little book *The Process of Education,*[6] maintains that the basic

[6] Jerome S. Bruner, *The Process of Education.* Cambridge, Mass.: The Harvard University Press, 1960, p. 13.

principles and concepts of each discipline should be identified and taught to children. He suggests that children can grasp the idea of tragedy and basic human plights as they are represented in myth. Children may become acquainted with various forms of literature as they are read and discussed. They may begin to build appreciation for the well-written biography or for poetry, that most neglected area in children's literature today. Some of our children literally jump from Mother Goose to Tennyson, without ever hearing of the fine poetry of David McCord, Walter de La Mare, or Eleanor Farjeon. Teachers need not be afraid to introduce such literary terms as anthology, autobiography, or allegory to our modern day child whose TV vocabulary includes such words as "ammoniated" and "supersonic." Then there is a whole body of children's literature which forms a common background in our culture. Think of the many modern day expressions which have been derived from the field of children's literature:

He was as mad as a Hatter
I won't be your man Friday
He has a Midas touch
She was filled with "insatiable curiosity"
His life is a good Horatio Alger Story

The period of childhood is limited. If children miss reading or hearing a book at the appropriate age for them, it is missed forever. No adult catches up on his reading by beginning with *Peter Rabbit* or *Homer Price.* There is no one book which must be read by all children, but there are many fine books which we would hate to have children miss. These include some of the classics but also, many of our modern books which may become the classics of tomorrow. There is a body of children's literature which is worthy of a solid place in the curriculum.

Finally, the true value of the effects of the literature program for today's children will be seen in the reading habits of adults in 1985. The explosion of knowledge makes it essential that our children become readers. The natural obsolescence of materials has so increased that adults must become constant readers if they are to stay abreast of new developments. The mark of the informed man is no longer whether he can read or what he *has* read, it may be based upon what he is currently reading. Our sociologists are predicting amazing increases in the amount of leisure time for the average person (not in our profession). The acid test of the reading program in our schools will be the cause which children and adults will make of books in this increased time.

Obviously, these six values of literature will not be fulfilled by an instructional reading program or by a Friday afternoon recreational reading period. As teachers, librarians, and administrators become committed to these values—to the worth of literature in children's lives, they will plan a comprehensive literature program for every elementary school. The planning must start with teachers who read themselves, who enjoy reading and recognize its values for them. Their first task will begin with making books, many books and fine books available for boys and girls. The recent recommendations in the *Standards for School Library Programs* [7] suggest that all schools having two hundred or more

[7] American Association of School Librarians, *Standards for School Library Programs*. Chicago: American Library Association, 1960.

students need well-organized central libraries *and* a qualified librarian. In 1958-59 some two thirds of our elementary schools did not have central libraries and the ratio of qualified school librarians to pupils was one librarian to some 4,261 pupils! When may we look forward to the day that parents and educators will begin to view libraries as being as worthy of school funds as multipurpose rooms and $40,000 cafeterias! Books are the tools for learning, the very bread of knowledge. Must our children continue to be like Alice at the Mad Hatter's party, prepared to feast at the table of reading with no room and no books?

We must do more than make books available for boys and girls, we will want to create a climate which will encourage wide reading. While visiting schools during Book Week this year, I observed several classrooms that had small displays of new books on the window sills. I watched and I waited for two whole mornings and I never saw a single child have time to look at or read any one of those books. Like the mathematician counting his stars in the *Little Prince,* they were too busy with "matters of consequence" to take time to enjoy reading. A planned literature program does take time. It provides time for children to read books of their own choice every day. It allows time for children to share their experiences with literature in many ways. In the planned literature program, time is provided for the daily story hour regardless of the age of the group. For we know that most children's reading ability does not equal their appreciation level until sometime in the junior high school. During this daily story hour, the teacher will introduce the various kinds of literature which children might miss otherwise. Certain books need to be savored together in order to heighten children's appreciation. This seems to be particularly true of such fantasy as *The Gammage Cup*, *The Borrowers* and even that most American of all fantasy, *Charlotte's Web*. Teachers will not want to read books which children themselves will ordinarily read. It is fun to read a chapter of *Henry Huggins*, but children will eagerly finish this book themselves once they have been introduced to it. A variety of books should be presented in order to at least expose boys and girls to different types of books. Children in the middle grades go on reading jags—they read series books with the same avidity with which they collect bottle tops. This is characteristic of their development patterns and should not be a cause for concern. If fifth grade girls only want to read horse stories, let them. Could you fill in a balanced wheel for your reading pattern this year? A lifetime of reading will show a certain balance, but even an adult follows particular reading interests, completely absorbed in biography for a while, or perhaps plunging into theology for the first time, or avidly reading everything which has been written by a newly discovered author. Can't we extend children the same freedom of selection which we allow ourselves?

In planning a literature program, teachers will not only provide for separate times for literature experiences but they will make wide use of certain trade books to enrich and vitalize learning experiences in *all* areas of study. Children should be encouraged to verify, extend, or contradict the presentation in their textbook by contrasting it with facts found in other books. Social studies is greatly enriched by the many excellent books about children in different lands, by biography, and by fine historical fiction, those books which clothe the factual bones of history and make it come alive. Children who read Fritz's *The Cabin Faced West* or *The Courage of Sarah Noble* by Dalgleish will have a better understanding of their historical heritage than the children who are limited to a single textbook approach. History, by its very nature, is interpretative. Children need to read books with many different viewpoints in order to become critical assayers of the contemporary scene. The flood of factual books in science has been gratefully received by children and teachers. Future space pilots can find the most recent information in trade books rather than texts. For example, Beeland and Wells' book *Space Satellite, the Story of the Man-Made Moon* came out in a third edition, three years after its first printing! Very few texts can be that up-to-date. Arithmetic, art, and music may all be enriched through the use of exciting books in children's literature. The day of the single text for all is gone, as many fine books find their rightful place in the curriculum.

The planned literature program will only be as effective as the teachers who make it. This means teachers will have to know children's literature; it means they will want to keep informed of the new developments in the field. A continuing in-service study group might read and review some of the 1500 juvenile titles which come off the press yearly. Some faculty meetings might well be devoted to discussions of the place of children's literature in the curriculum and the development of lifetime reading habits of boys and girls.

Vertical planning of teachers from

kindergarten through grade six might result in a guide for a literature program either as an integral part of the total curriculum or as a separate program. Such a guide might include purposes, plans for selection of books, recommended books for reading to children and by children, suggested experiences with literature and evaluation procedures. Texts in children's literature and such journals as *Elementary English, The Horn Book*, and the *School Library Journal* should be a part of every school's professional library. Teachers and librarians might prepare recommended buying lists for Christmas and birthday gifts. Lists of books for reading at home could also be prepared, for children who become enthusiastic about books at school will want to continue their reading at home.

Finally, we may agree as to the values of a planned literature program, but unless we evaluate that program, it probably will not be included in our curriculum. Provision should be made for a staff evaluation of the total literature program, values of it, time devoted to it, and the success of the program. Children's reading habits should be evaluated as well as their reading skill. Interest in reading is not as intangible as it may sound, it can be measured; not in terms of how many books boys and girls have read, although that is a part of it, but in terms of the depth of understanding and new insights which they have gained from their reading. Reading achievement tests do not measure this, nor do citywide comparisons of grade level standings. But teachers, librarians, and parents know if children are reading. Hopefully, we would wish that all children might echo the feelings of this child in the third grade who wrote about her world of books.

MY OWN WORLD [8]

When I open up my book I go into a world
all my own
Into a world of sorrow or joy,
    but wherever it is I don't hear the things
about me.
I could be reading in a busy noisy factory,
    but my world keeps me away, My world
of books.

This then is the acid test of our literature program—not do children know how to read, but *do* they read, *what* do they read, and more important, do they *love* to read.

This enthusiasm for books doesn't just happen. It results from an effective instructional program which is well balanced by a literature program that has definite purposes and a definite place in the curriculum. It requires a teacher who is dedicated to the values of literature, and it demands that we lift our sights from our basic reading programs in the elementary school to a planned literature program for all!

BIBLIOGRAPHY OF CHILDREN'S BOOKS

ANGLUND, JOAN WALSH (author-illustrator), *A Friend Is Someone Who Likes You*. New York: Harcourt, Brace and Company, 1958.

ANGLUND, JOAN WALSH, *Love Is a Special Way of Feeling*. New York: Harcourt, Brace and Company, 1960.

BEELAND, LEE and ROBERT WELLS, *Space Satellite, the Story of the Man-Made Moon*. Illustrated by Jack Coggins. Third Edition. Englewood Cliffs, N.J.: Prentice-Hall, Inc., 1960.

[8] From Wickliffe School, Upper Arlington, Ohio. Mrs. Donna Waldeck, teacher.

CARSON, RACHEL LOUISE, *The Sea Around Us.* Special edition for young readers adapted by Anne Terry White, New York: Simon and Schuster, 1958.

CLEARY, BEVERLY, *Henry Huggins.* Illustrated by Louis Darling. New York: William Morrow and Company, 1950.

CORBETT, SCOTT, *The Lemonade Trick.* Illustrated by Paul Galdone. Boston: Atlantic-Little, Brown and Company, 1960.

DALGLIESH, ALICE, *The Bears on Hemlock Mountain.* Illustrated by Helen Sewell. New York: Charles Scribner's Sons, 1952.

DALGLIESH, ALICE, *The Courage of Sarah Noble.* Illustrated by Leonard Weisgard. New York: Charles Scribner's Sons, 1954.

DE JONG, MEINDERT, *The House of Sixty Fathers.* Illustrated by Maurice Sendak. New York: Harper and Brothers, 1956.

FRITZ, JEAN, *The Cabin Faced West.* Illustrated by Feodor Rojankovsky. New York: Coward McCann, Inc., 1958.

KENDALL, CAROL, *The Gammage Cup.* Illustrated by Erik Blevgad. New York: Harcourt, Brace and Company, 1959.

O'NEIL, MARY, *Hailstones and Halibut Bones.* Illustrated by Leonard Weisgard. Garden City, New York: Doubleday and Company, Inc., 1961.

NORTON, MARY, *The Borrowers.* Illustrated by Beth and Joe Krush, New York: Harcourt, Brace and Company, 1953.

SHARP, ELIZABETH LAMBERT, *Nkwala.* Illustrated by William Winter. New York: Harcourt, Brace and Company, 1956.

STERLING, DOROTHY, *Mary Jane.* Illustrated by Ernest Crichlow. New York: Doubleday and Company, Inc., 1959.

WHITE, ELWYN BROOKS, *Charlotte's Web.* Illustrated by Garth Williams. New York: Harper and Brothers, 1952.

WRIGHT, DARE (author-illustrator), *The Lonely Doll.* New York: Doubleday and Company, Inc., 1957.

Folklore as a Mirror
of Culture

Alan Dundes

University of California, Berkeley

The various forms of folklore: myths, folktales, legends, folksongs, proverbs, riddles, gestures, games, dances and many others can provide a vital resource for a teacher who seriously wishes to (1) *understand* his students better, and (2) *teach* those students more effectively about the world and about the human condition. For folklore is *autobiographical ethnography*— that is, it is a people's own description of themselves. This is in contrast to other descriptions of that people, descriptions made by social workers, sociologists, political scientists or anthropologists. It may be that there is distortion in a people's self image as it is expressed in that people's songs, proverbs, and the like, but one must admit that there is often as much, if not more, distortion in the supposedly objective descriptions made by professional social scientists who in fact see the culture under study through the culturally relative and culturally determined categories of their own culture. Moreover, even the distortion in a people's self image can tell the trained observer something about that people's values. Out of all the elements of culture, which ones are singled out for distortion, for special emphasis?

Folklore as a mirror of culture frequently reveals the areas of special concern. It is for this reason that analyses of collections of folklore can provide the individual who takes advantage of the opportunities afforded by the study of folklore a way of seeing another culture *from the inside out* instead of *from the outside in,* the usual position of a social scientist or teacher. Whether the 'other culture' is far from the borders of our country or whether the 'other culture's is lodged within these borders, a world shrunk by modern technological advances in transportation and communications demands that education keep pace. We need to know more about Vietnamese worldview; we need to know more about American Negro values.

One of the greatest obstacles impeding a better understanding of Vietnamese, American Negro or any other culture is what anthropologists term "ethnocentrism." This is the notion, apparently held in some form by all the peoples of the earth, that the way *we* do things is "natural" and "right" whereas the way *others* do them is "strange," perhaps "unnatural" and maybe even "wrong." The Greek historian Herodotus described ethnocentrism, without of course using the term, as follows:

If one were to offer men to choose out of all the customs in the world such as seemed to them the best, they would examine the whole number, and end by preferring their own; so convinced are they that their own usages surpass those of all others.

One of the purposes of studying folklore is to realize the hypothetical premise. Man cannot choose out of all the customs in the world until he knows what these customs are. Traditional customs are part of folklore. Obviously the point in collecting, classifying, and analyzing the customs and other forms of folklore is not necessarily to allow the investigator to choose a way of life other than his own. Rather by identifying the similarities, the actual historical cognates such as hundreds of versions of Cinderella, a tale which folklorists label as Aarne-Thompson tale type 510 in the internationally known index of Indo-European folktales first published in 1910, or by identifying the near-similarities, the probably noncognate folkloristic parallels which seem to depend upon universal or quasi-universal human experiences (such as the introduction of death into the world because of some unthinking or foolish action on the part of a culture hero or trickster figure), one has convincing data which can effectively be used to promote international understanding. If only the Turks and Greeks realized that they had the same folktales and the same lovable wise fool of a Hodja figure in many of these tales. The same

holds for the Arabs and the Jews. In this light, it is sad to think that folklore, instead of being used as a constructive force for internationalism has all too frequently been the tool of excessive nationalism.

The history of folklore studies reveals that folklorists in many different countries have often been inspired by the desire to preserve their national heritage. The Grimms, for example, at the beginning of the nineteenth century, imbued with nationalism and romanticism, and armed with the fashionable methodology of historical reconstruction, collected folktales and legends with the hope of rescuing something ur-German, that is something truly Teutonic, before it faded from the scene altogether. The Grimms were surprised and probably more than a little disappointed when they discovered that many of their "Teutonic" tales had almost exact analogues in other European countries. The Grimms incidentally, like most nineteenth century collectors, rewrote the folklore they collected. This retouching of oral tales continues today in the children's literature field where reconstructed, reconstituted stories written in accordance with *written not oral conventions* are palmed off as genuine folktales.

One can see that the basic mistrust of folk materials is part of a general ambivalence about the materials of oral tradition, the materials of the folk. On the one hand, the folk and their products were celebrated as a national treasure of the past; on the other hand, the folk were wrongly identified with the illiterate in a literate society and thus the folk as a concept was identified exclusively with the vulgar and the uneducated. (The folk to a modern folklorist is any group of people whatsoever who share at least one common linking factor, e.g., religion, occupation, ethnicity, geographical location, etc. which leads to Jewish folklore, lumberjack folklore, Negro folklore, and California folklore. As an American I know American folklore; as a professor I know campus folklore; as a member of a family, I know my own family folklore.) The equation of folklore with ignorance has continued. The word 'folklore' itself considered as an item of folk speech means fallacy, untruth, error. Think of the phrase "That's folklore." It is similar to the meaning of 'myth' in such phrases as "the myth of race." This is *not*, however, what folklore and myth mean to the professional folklorist. A myth is but one form or genre of folklore, a form which consists of a sacred narrative explaining how the world and man came to be in their present form. Folklore consists of a variety of genres most of which are found among all peoples of the earth. Nevertheless, the association of folklore with error (consider 'folk' medicine as opposed to 'scientific' medicine') has made it difficult for the study of folklore as a discipline to gain academic respectability and has generally discouraged the use and study of folklore by educators.

It is still mistakenly thought that the only people who study folklore are antiquarian types, devotees of ballads which are no longer sung and collectors of quaint customs which are no longer practiced. Folklore in this false view is equated with survivals from an age past, survivals which are doomed not to survive. Folklore is gradually dying out, we are told. Moreover, since folklore is defined as error, it is thought by some educators to be a good thing that folklore is dying out. In fact, it has been argued that one of the purposes of education is to help stamp out folklore. As man evolves, he leaves folklore behind such that the truly civilized

man is conceived to be folkloreless. From this kind of thinking, one can understand why education and folklore have been on opposite sides and also why when well meaning educators move into other cultures, e.g., in Africa or in a ghetto school, they actually believe they are doing their students a service by helping to suppress local customs, superstitions, folk speech, and other folkloristic traditions. So it is that African students are taught Shakespeare and Chaucer as great literature while their own superb oral literature is not deemed worthy of classroom treatment, assuming that the western educated teacher even knows of its existence. How many teachers of literature, of the epic in particular, are aware of the fact that the epic is a living oral form and that epics up to 13,000 lines are now being sung in Yugoslavia, among other places? How many teachers of American Negro children have ever heard of the "dozens" (or "rapping and capping" or "sounding" etc.) or of the "toast," an important Negro folklore genre in rhyme reminiscent of epic form? Yet the technique of verbal dueling known as the "dozens" and the epic toast are extremely viable forms of American Negro folklore and they encapsulate the critical points and problems in Negro family structure and in Negro–white relations. One could teach both literature and social studies from such folkloristic texts (were they not 'obscene' by *our* standards) with the advantage that these texts would be known by the students from their own lives and experience.

Why not teach children about the nature of poetry by examining their own folk poetry: nursery rhymes, jump rope rhymes, hand clap rhymes, ball bouncing rhymes, dandling rhymes, and autograph book verse among others. There is almost no method or approach found in the study of literature which could not also be applied to folk materials. One could discuss formal features such as metrics, rhyme, alliteration; one could discuss content features such as characterization, motivation, themes. By using the materials of folklore as a point of departure, the educational process may be comprehended as dealing with the real world rather than with a world apart from the world in which the students live. With folklore, the classroom becomes a laboratory or forum for a consideration of "real life" as it is experienced and perceived by those being educated. Let me briefly provide just a few examples of folklore and try to illustrate how they might be used to enliven and stimulate classroom discussions.

One technique which can immediately show children something important about the nature of oral tradition is to select one item of folklore and ask each child to tell the other members of the class his *version* of the item. It doesn't matter what the item is: when Christmas presents are opened (Christmas Eve, Christmas morning, one on Christmas Eve and the rest on Christmas day, etc.) or what one says near the end of *Hide and Seek* to summon all the other players: Olly, olly oxen free, Olly Olly Ocean free (All ye, all ye 'outs' in free?????), Home free all, etc. After a number of versions have been elicited, the students should be able to see that although there is considerable diversity, there is also considerable uniformity. If there are differences— such as how many candles are placed on the birthday cake (some have the number of candles equal to the number of years old while others have that number plus one with the extra to grow on, etc.), even those differences are

traditional. How many children believe that the number of candles left burning after the attempt to blow them out signifies the number of children one will have? How many believe the number left burning signifies the number of years to pass before one's wish (made right before the blowing attempt) comes true? Through such devices, the children can learn that there are frequently subtraditions within traditions. Then the teacher may ask the children, "Which version is correct?" "Which version is the right one?" Normally, there will be extended debate on this, individual students championing their own individual versions, perhaps pointing to the statistical evidence available within the classroom to support one version over another. Gradually, the children will come to realize that in folklore as in life, there is often no one correct or right version. One traditional version is just as traditional as another version. *A*'s way of observing Christmas or birthday rituals is no better and no worse than *B*'s. Isn't this a marvelous way of showing what ethnocentrism is: people insisting that the way they know is best and proper while the strange unfamiliar way is wrong? And isn't this a marvelous way of teaching tolerance? If children can learn that their fellows' ways are not "wrong" but "alternative, equally traditional" ways of doing things, this could be one of the most important lessons they are ever likely to learn.

Having illustrated the nature of variation in folklore, the teacher might wish to discuss why there is variation. Here the difference between oral and written (or printed) traditions is crucial. Folklore is passed on by means of person to person contact. And an item of folklore may be changed by different individuals in accordance with their own individual needs, the demands of a particular social context—the make-up of the audience—is it boys and girls, just boys, children and grown-ups, etc. or the requirements of a new age. So it is that each item of folklore is passed on through time, sometimes remaining the same, sometimes changing. This is why the task of collecting and ana-lyzing folklore can never be completed. Tomorrow's version of a folksong may or may not be the same as the one we know today which in turn may or may not be the same as the one which was known in the past. This is in marked contrast to the products of written tradition. If one reads a play of Shakespeare or a novel of James Joyce today, one can be reasonably sure that one hundred years from now, the identical text will be read by others.

There is a tendency to underestimate the differences between a visual/written record and an aural/oral record. It has only recently been suggested that the mass media, radio, television, motion pictures, etc. have, by discouraging or impinging upon time formerly spent in reading, made us an oral rather than a written culture. Actually, one should say, has made us an oral culture *again*. In evolutionary terms, pre-literate society which was orally oriented became literate, but now we have 'post-literate' man who is influenced by oral communication once more. Yet the education system has not always kept pace. The traditional emphasis has been upon "reading and writing." What about "speaking"? Oratory, valued so much by oral cultures around the world, has become almost a lost art in literate societies. Interestingly enough, in American Negro culture there is tremendous value placed upon rhetoric as one aspect of style. The "man of words" is highly esteemed and anyone who has heard

American Negro preachers use their voices surely recognizes the eloquent power of that oral style.

It is a pity that our educational philosophy continues to worship the written word. Note that "literacy" is still thought by some to be a *sine qua non* for an individual to be able to vote. The fact that intelligent peoples all over the world are capable of reaching decisions without anything more than oral communication seems to be overlooked. We tend to trust what is "down in black and white." "Put it in writing," we say; we tend to distrust oral testimony, regarding it as unreliable. We forget that much of what is written down—in newspaper, in books, circulated as oral communication first. Even the Bible was in oral tradition before it was committed to written form! With such bias in favor of written tradition, it is easy to see why there has been relatively little interest in the study of oral tradition. But by failing to recognize the differences between oral and written traditions, we do a disservice to ourselves as well as our students. Who has never heard someone give orally an address which was written out in advance? Yet relatively few written works read well aloud. Similarly, students taking written notes from an instructor's free-flowing oral classroom delivery are often dismayed by the sentence fragments, the agreement errors, etc. There are major lexical and stylistic differences between oral and written tradition. "Indeed, Moreover, One cannot escape the conclusion . . ." are acceptable written conventions, when *seen* on a printed page, but they may *sound* stilted when heard in speech. A word or phrase may *look* right, but *sound* wrong. But by the same token, a word or phrase which sounds fine, may look terrible in print.

In oral speech, one can use slang, folk similes (as cool as a cucumber) and folk metaphors (to fly off the handle). In written tradition, these are branded as "clichés" by diligent teachers of English composition. Such teachers are wont to warn their students to "avoid clichés." The folklorist would urge that children *not* be told never to use clichés but rather that they be taught the difference between oral and written traditions and *not* to confuse the conventions of each. In oral tradition, originality is neither desired nor expected. The more traditional (=unoriginal) the better. However, in our written tradition, originality is essential. But children can not avoid clichés. Do they not learn to speak before they learn to read and write? The point is simply that children should not be taught to write as they speak and they should not be taught to speak as they write. The unfortunate confusion of oral and written conventions is one reason why most printed collections of folklore are spurious. They have been edited and rewritten to conform to written rather than oral style. The expletives, meaningful pauses, the stammers, not to mention the eye expressions, the hand movements and all the other body gestural signals are totally lost in the translation from oral to written tradition. This is why it is impossible to learn what folklore is by *reading* books. If one is interested in learning about folklore, one must elicit oral tradition. A useful class exercise might be to have a child tell a joke or legend to his classmates whose task it becomes to write it down. One could then discuss at length just what was "left out" in the written version that had been in the oral version.

In order to more fully understand and utilize folklore, one must have some idea of the functions of folklore.

Folklore reflects (and thereby reinforces) the value configurations of the folk, but at the same time folklore provides a sanctioned form of escape from these very same values. In fairy tales, the hero or heroine is inevitably told not to do something; don't look in the secret chamber, don't answer the door, etc. Of course, the protagonist violates the interdiction. He may be punished for his disobedience, but usually he comes out ahead in the end. For example, the hero marries the princess. The escape mechanism is equally obvious in traditional games. On the one hand, educators urge that games be played to teach "teamwork," "cooperation," and "fair play." On the other hand, once in the game, children can compete and they can compete aggressively. One can "steal" the bacon or "capture" the flag of the opposing team. In "King of the Mountain," boys can push rivals off the raft. In adolescent games such as "Spin the Bottle" "Post Office," or "Padiddle," the rules *require* the participants to do that which they would very much like to do but which they might not otherwise do. Folklore provides socially sanctioned forms of behavior in which a person may do what can't be done in 'real life.' One is not supposed to push anyone around in real life—at least if one believes the "Golden Rule," but in games one is supposed to take a chair and leave someone else without one to sit on (in "Musical Chairs"). As a young adolescent, one cannot kiss a casual acquaintance without feelings of guilt or hearing cries of derision. Yet in kissing games, one *must* do so. The folkloristic frame not only permits, but *require* the taboo action and it also thereby relieves the individual from assuming the responsibility (and guilt) for his actions. The individual has no choice; it is a mere spin of the bottle or some other act of chance (such as seeing a car with only one headlight working) which dictates the sexual behavior. In children's games, the drama of real (adult) life is often enacted. Yet neither teacher nor student may be fully aware of just what is involved in a particular game. In much the same way, folk—and social—dances allow for heterosexual body contact in a society which true to its Puritan heritage has consistently condemned the body and its domain. The fact that boys can dance with girls, girls can dance with girls, but boys cannot dance with boys in American culture reflects our great fear of homosexuality. This is striking when one recalls that most societies even have men's dances from which women are excluded. Americans remain slaves to a tradition in which the body is seen as dirty, as something to be denied or repressed. Note that we still insist on *physical* (corporal) punishments for intellectual/mental lapses. The body is punished, not the mind, every time a child is struck or spanked!

As a specific example of how folklore functions, let me cite one riddle text. A child comes home from school and at the dinner table asks his parents: "What is black and white and red all over?" The parent, if he's alert and has a good memory, replies: "A newspaper" which in fact is one of the older traditional answers to this riddle. But there are other modern traditional answers. Some of these are: a sunburned zebra, an embarrassed zebra, a zebra with measles, a wounded nun, a bloody integration march, and for the sophistocate: *Pravda,* the *Daily Worker,* or the *New York Times* which involves an interesting play on the original 'newspaper' answer. Now what precisely is going on? What function, if any, does this riddle or the hundreds like it serve? I believe that this kind of riddle provides an effective mechanism for reversing the normal adult-child relationship in our society. In our society, it is the parent or teacher who knows all the answers and who insists upon proposing difficult if not 'impossible' questions to children. However, in the riddle context, either the parent doesn't know the answer to the elephant or little moron joking question—in which case the child can have the great pleasure of telling him what the answer is *or* the parent gives the 'wrong' answer (e.g., 'newspaper' would be considered 'wrong' by the child who has *another* answer in mind —and aren't there plenty of instances where the child answers an adult's question perfectly well but fails because his answer was not the particular answer the adult desired? This is also what happens whenever an unthinking adult asks the kind of questions which can be labelled as being "Guess what's in my mind" questions. In this instance where the parent has given the 'wrong' answer, the child has the even more exquisite pleasure of *correcting* rather than merely informing the parent.) Children also use riddles with their peers where a similar function is evident. A child goes one up if he has a riddle which stumps a friend. I should perhaps mention that riddles or joking questions are by no means confined to children's usage. Many adults use such devices in daily interpersonal rituals. Some of these riddling questions provide serious reflections of our culture. Do you remember the 'knock-knock' cycle? Well, have you heard the World War III knock-knock joke? No? Okay, "Knock-knock" (audience): "Who's there?—(long silent pause—signifying that no one would be left to answer in the event of total nuclear world war.)

LITERATURE FOR CHILDREN OR
LITERATURE OF CHILDREN

The analysis of the content of children's folklore could help anyone seriously interested in understanding children. I refer specifically to that portion of children's folklore which is performed *by children for other children*. This is distinct from that portion of children's folklore which consists of materials *imposed upon children by parents and teachers*. The analysis of the latter kind of children's folklore would probably give more of an insight into parents' and teachers' worldview than the worldview of children. I suspect that in courses dealing with children's literature, it is this latter category which receives most of the attention. In other words, the emphasis is on 'literature for children' rather than 'literature of children'! (By 'literature of children' I mean their oral literature, their folklore, their traditions, not their little *individual* written compositions or poems.) This is, in my opinion, the same kind of thinking that makes Peace Corps teachers teach Shakespeare and Chaucer to African students instead of utilizing African folktales and proverbs, that is, using some of the 'native' literature as the basis for an understanding of the nature of prose and poetry. Educational, as well as foreign, policy is invariably made in accordance with the value system of us, the teacher or the American. Such decisions may be rational from our point of view; they may even prove to be 'correct,' but in the majority of cases, these decisions are probably all to often made without sufficient knowledge of the groups we honestly want to help. We tend to think of the 'other' people be they inhabitants of villages in Asia or children in our classroom as poor little sponges who need to soak up as much of our material as they possibly can.

The phrase "culturally deprived" is a prime example of this faulty kind of thinking. From an anthropological perspective, of course, there can be no such thing as culturally deprived. Culture in anthropological usage refers to the total way of life of a people, and not to a very select group of elitist materials such as opera, the great books, etc. All human beings have culture in general; some people share one culture rather than another. Hopi culture is different from Vietnamese culture. So it is impossible in this sense for any individual to be "culturally deprived"; our minority groups have just as much culture as anybody else. The point is simply that it is another culture, a different culture. To call a minority group 'culturally deprived' is a kind of survival of nineteenth century 'white man's burden' thinking. The real question is: Do we want "them"—and 'them' could be American Negroes, South Vietnamese, children in our classroom, etc. to give up their culture and accept our culture in its place or do we not insist on a melting pot metaphor with the pot to take on the consistency of the dominant ethos? In my opinion, the 'unmelting pot' might be a more apt metaphor. If so, then perhaps we should allow or better yet, encourage 'them' to enjoy, understand, and take pride in their own culture. Obviously, the culture of our children is closer to our adult culture than the culture of a distinct ethnic minority or some foreign population to our culture in general. Nevertheless, the principle in terms of educational philosophy is the same.

What kinds of things do we see in our children's own folklore?

Teacher, teacher, I declare
I see *so and so's* underwear.

Charlie Chaplin went to France
To see the ladies' underpants . . .

I see London; I see France
I see *so and so's* underpants.

We see the child's curiosity about the body and the immediate body covering. The child finds it difficult to accept the adult's apparent rejection of the body and its natural functions. Consider the following jump rope rhyme:

Cinderella, dressed in yellow
Went downtown to see her fellow.
On the way her girdle busted.
How many people were disgusted? 1, 2, 3, etc.

Clearly, children, in this instance little girls, are fascinated by a particular undergarment, the girdle. Note that the girdle busts while Cinderella is on the way to see, or in some versions to kiss, her fellow. Do children really know what they are saying?

FOLKLORE AND SIBLING RIVALRY

Less symbolic, but equally important are the sentiments underlying these familiar jump rope verses:

Fudge, fudge, tell the judge
Mama's got a new born baby.
It ain't no girl, it ain't no boy
Just a newborn (or 'common,' or 'plain ol', or 'ordinary') baby
Wrap it up in tissue paper
Throw (send) it down the elevator.
First floor, miss
Second floor, miss, etc. (until the jumper misses)

This is really an extraordinarily revealing rhyme. First of all, why is the judge informed about the newborn baby? Is the judge the person who can take away children from parents or the person who has the power to punish parents for mistreating children? In any case, here is explicit sibling rivalry. What child does not resent the arrival upon the scene of the newborn child who threatens the previously existing relationship between the older children and the mother? Notice how the poor baby is demeaned. It is sexless. It's not a girl, not a boy, in other words, it's *nothing*. It's just—and that word 'just' tells all—an ordinary baby, nothing exceptional, nothing to make a fuss about. And what does the jumper–reciter recommend should be done with the baby? *Throw* it down the elevator. The jumper then jumps as many floors as she can without missing. Thus by being a skillful jumper, a girl can send her baby sibling far away. The more jumps without misses, the further the baby is sent away. Thus through jumping rope, a young girl is able to do something 'constructive' about getting rid of her inevitable aggression against the new sibling rival. This inter-sibling hostility, I submit, is an integral part of American children's worldview. Look at the following jump rope rhyme:

I had a baby brother
His name was Tiny Tim.
I put him in the bathtub
To teach him how to swim.
He drank up all the water;
He ate up all the soap.
He tried to eat the bathtub
But it wouldn't go down his throat.
He died last night
With a bubble in his throat.

This is an equally blatant example of an expression of sibling rivalry.

Note the tense of the verb in the first line. I *"had"* a baby brother. Here is wishful thinking, a common element in all folklore. The baby rival is gone, and before the rhyme really gets started. What of the rest of the rhyme's content? Precisely where is it that the newborn baby gets so much obvious physical attention? In American culture, it is the bath. It is during and after bathing that the baby is fondled, powdered, played with, etc. So the older child takes things into his own hands. He puts the baby into the tub pretending to teach him how to swim. What does the baby do in the tub? He tries to eat everything. Babies are in fact orally inclined as it is this body zone which provides the initial point of contact with the world, a body zone which operates by incorporating what is needed, i.e., mother's milk. From the older child's point of view, the baby is always being fed—hence it appears to have an insatiable appetite. What then is more appropriate from the older child's perspective than to have his baby brother choke to death from eating something he shouldn't be eating, from trying to eat too much, that is, symbolically speaking, from trying to take too much, more than his share of their common parent's bounty. Of course, children hate their parents too:

Step on a crack (line)
Break your mother's back (spine)

SYMBOLISM IN FOLKLORE

No doubt many people who are unsympathetic to psychology and symbolism may doubt the validity of the above interpretations of children's folklore. Such interpretations, they would argue, are *being read into* innocent folklore rather than being *read out* of the folklore. Yet the astonishing thing is that much the same symbolism is contained in the folklore *for* children as communicated by parents and teachers. It has long been wrongly assumed that folktales—e.g., Grimms' *Kinder und Hausmärchen* and *nursery* rhymes are strictly children's fare. This is not true. These materials were related by adults to other adults as well as children. If adult males have Oedipus complexes, then it is clear why it is they who relate the story of Jack and the Beanstalk. A boy lives alone with his mother, throws beans out of a window at his mother's request, climbs a tall magic beanstalk, hides from the threatening giant in the friendly giant's wife's oven, kills the giant by cutting the giant stalk with an axe which is often helpfully provided by his mother waiting at the foot of the stalk, and finally lives happily ever after with his mother! (Parents, of course, to the infant's eye view of the world appear to be giants!) For women with Electra complexes, it is normally a girl versus a wicked stepmother or witch. Whereas the donor figure in male folktales may be a female (cf. Jack's mother, the giant's wife); in female folktales, the helper may be a male (cf. the woodsman in "Little Red Riding Hood"), although to be sure sometimes kind father figures help boys and kind mother figures (e.g., fairy god-mothers) help girls. In Hansel and Gretel, the children are tempted orally and they nibble at the witch's house. (The children were not given food by their parents.) The witch, like so many cannibalistic villains in fairy tales, intends to employ the infant's first weapon (eating, sucking, biting) by devouring the children. In this tale, the heroine, Gretel, succeeds in duping the witch into being burned up in her own oven. The female-oven symbolism is consistent. In Jack and the Beanstalk, the boy hides in the giant's wife's oven to escape the giant; in Hansel and Gretel, a tale featuring a girl's point of view, the heroine eliminates the female villain by making her enter her own hot oven! And what of Cinderella who we noticed in jump rope rhymes? What is the significance of the story of a girl who marries a prince because of a perfect fit between a foot and a glass slipper? What has the ideal marriage to do with a foot fitting into a slipper? And why do we still tie old shoes on the bumpers of cars carrying newlyweds off on their honeymoon?

One clue to the symbolism of slippers and shoes comes right from Mother Goose. One of the rhymes which parents read to children is:

There was an old woman who lived in a shoe.
She had so many children she didn't know what to do.

A literal, historical interpretation would have to locate a place where women once lived in actual shoes. But how would one explain the stated connection between "living in a shoe" and "having lots of children." Fortunately, another verse to this rhyme reported in the Ozarks in the 1890s makes the symbolism even more overt:

There was another old woman who lived in a shoe
She didn't have any children; she knew what to do.

With symbolic systems, it is never a matter of one isolated instance. Within a given culture, there are whole consistent patterns of symbolism. The symbolism of a culture will be manifested in the folklore of that culture.

So we should not be surprised to find other nursery rhymes:

Cock a doodle doo
My dame has lost her shoe
Her master's lost his fiddling stick
They don't know what to do.

Remember these are part of the children's folklore which is transmitted to children by parents and teachers. I do not necessarily believe that parents are aware of the symbolic content of folklore any more than I believe that children are consciously aware of all the symbolism. Clearly, folklore could not function successfully as an outlet if there were conscious awareness of its being so used. Folklore is collective fantasy and as fantasy, it depends upon the symbolic system of a given culture. I should be remiss if I did not state my conviction that the communication of collective fantasy and symbols is a healthy thing and I would strongly oppose those educators who advocate placing Mother Goose and fairy tales on a high shelf or locked case in the library. Folklore is one way for both adults and children to deal with the crucial problems in their lives. If our folklore sometimes deals with sexuality and the interrelationships between members of a family, then this is obviously something of a problem area in our daily lives. We know that folklore in all cultures tends to cluster around the critical points in the life cycle of the individual (e.g., birth, initiation, marriage, death) and the calendrical cycle of the community (e.g., sowing, harvesting, etc.) In fact, if one collects the folklore of a people and then does a content analysis of that folklore, one is very likely to be able to delineate the principal topics of crisis and anxiety among that people. So if American folklore, both adult and children's folklore has a sexual element, then we must face the problem which is reflected in the folklore. Squelching folklore as if such a thing were really possible—it is impossible to censor oral tradition as opposed to print—would not help in solving the original problems which generated the collective fantasies in the first place.

FOLKLORE ABOUT TEACHERS

There can be no doubt that folklore reflects culture and as a final example, I will briefly mention teacher folklore. The folklore of and about teachers reflects both teachers' attitudes about themselves and students' attitudes about teachers. There is the resentment of administrators as illustrated in the numerous dean stories, e.g., "Old deans never die; they just lose their faculties." There are the parodies of teaching methods. An English teacher is explaining to her class how to write a short story: It should have religion, high society, sex, and mystery. Within a few moments, a little boy says, "O.K., I'm finished." The teacher, surprised at the speed of the boy's composition, asks him to read his short story aloud to the class. "My God," said the duchess, "I'm pregnant! Who did it?" There are also commentaries on teachers who run their classes without any regard for what their students might like or think. A professor gives an advanced seminar in algebraic functions. Only one student shows up. However, he strides to the lectern and reads his hour-long lecture. Each day, the professor does the same thing. He sets up his notes and reads his lecture. One day, while at the blackboard writing a long series of equations and formulas, the professor sees the one student's hand raised.

"Excuse me, professor, but I don't see why x cubed equals y cubed. Why wouldn't x cubed equal y cubed plus z cubed?" The professor replied, "That's a very interesting question but I don't want to take up valuable class time with it. See me at the end of the hour." In a variant of this joke, it is a professor of art history who offers a seminar in advanced Burmese vase painting. Again there is one student and again the professor reads his lecture. This time, the professor is at the faculty club talking to his colleagues. When they discover that he has only one student for the seminar, they ask him what he is doing in the class. He tells them that he reads his lecture just as he always has. "Good heavens," one colleague exclaims, "with just one student why don't you run the class as a discussion?" whereupon the professor replied, "What is there to discuss?" Of course, I don't have to say how distasteful modern students find this philosophy of education.

The folklore of teaching includes elementary school teachers too. For example, there's the story of the elementary school teacher who taught look–say reading. One day in backing her car out of a parking place on the street, she banged into the car parked behind her. She immediately got out to survey the possible damage and looking at her rear fender she said, "Oh, oh, oh, look, look, look, Damn, Damn, Damn!" Notice the threefold repetition in the punchline. There are three words each of which is repeated three times. Is this unusual? Certainly not. Three is the ritual number in American folklore. Whether it's three brothers in folktales, three wishes, a minister, a priest, and a rabbi, or the fact that there are frequently three action sequences in jokes and three repetitions of lines in folksongs: John

Brown's body lies a moulderin' in the grave, Polly put the kettle on, Lost my partner what'll I do?, etc., the pattern is the same. This pattern is *not* universal; most American Indian peoples have the ritual number *four*. Here is yet another illustration of how by analyzing the folklore we gain insight into the culture which it mirrors. Three is a ritual number not just in American folklore, but in all aspects of American culture: time—past, present, future; space—length, width, depth; and language—good, better, best, etc. This is why we have the three R's (Reading, 'Riting and 'Rithmetic), Primary, Secondary, and Higher Education, the latter with its three degrees B.A., M.A. and Ph.D., the first of which can be cum laude, magna cum laude, and summa cum laude. This is why we have such pedagogical principles as: "Preview, Teach, and Review" which retains its tripartite form in the folk translation: tell 'em what you're going to tell 'em; tell 'em and tell 'em what you told 'em.

Folklore as a subject of study can be a most rewarding one. It does serve as a mirror of culture and it is a mirror well worth looking into. The teacher who encourages his class to examine their own folklore or better yet sends them out with collecting projects, such as collecting the folklore of a group from another 'culture' can give his students as well as himself an educational experience of immeasurable value. We need to use every available means to better understand ourselves and our fellow men. Folklore is one such means, one available for the asking. We are all folk. All one needs to begin such work is people, people to ask and people to listen. Whether an individual asks about his own folklore or asks others about their folklore, if he listens, he will learn.

SUGGESTED READINGS

Those interested in general folklore theory should consult Alan Dundes, ed., *The Study of Folklore* (Englewood Cliffs: Prentice-Hall, 1965). For American folklore in particular, one may look at Jan Harold Brunvand, *The Study of American Folklore: An Introduction* (New York: W. W. Norton, 1968) and Richard M. Dorson, *American Folklore* (Chicago: University of Chicago Press, 1959). Those curious about the number three may enjoy Alan Dundes, "The Number Three in American Culture," in *Every Man His Way: Readings in Cultural Anthropology* (edited by Alan Dundes) Englewood Cliffs: Prentice-Hall, 1968), pp. 401–24.

9

Evaluation, Diagnosis, and Remediation of Reading Difficulties

Most children in public schools receive their reading instruction from the classroom teacher. For this reason these teachers should have training and experience in diagnostic and remedial techniques as well as in the other aspects of reading instruction. Because it is a time-consuming procedure, indepth diagnosis is often left to the reading specialist. However, the classroom teacher should have knowledge of the procedures involved in informal diagnosis, and she should be aware of what to do to implement the findings of the complete diagnosis.

What basic tools are available to the reading teacher or the reading specialist to evaluate a child's reading progress? Robert Ruddell focuses on one of the most commonly used instruments—the standardized reading achievement test. He analyzes the problems encountered in using this device to measure the reading progress of all students. Some of these problems are inherent in the tests themselves; others relate to the ways the results of testing programs are used. Ruddell's discussion leads the reader to conclude that standardization tests must be greatly revised; they must be used to enhance reading instruction rather than as a device to compare one school with another; and they are only one tool to be used for evaluation of reading performance.

The current emphasis on accountability has brought to the foreground another type of measurement—criterion-referenced testing. However, this procedure need not be associated only with accountability. Its primary value is for instructional evaluation and diagnosis. As M. I. Chas. Woodson declares, criterion-referenced testing is most useful in making short-range instructional decisions. These tests are usually based on instructional objectives. They do not compare children; instead they identify the degree to which a child has achieved a predetermined level of competence in a skill. Woodson compares the information yielded by criterion-referenced tests and norm-referenced tests. He also outlines the purposes of criterion-referenced testing and discusses the interpretation and use of such evaluation. However, he cautions against the limited generalizability of criterion-referenced testing.

Informal diagnosis is another useful procedure for classroom teachers. Often such diagnosis will involve no more than daily observation and interpretation of the child's reading progress as he uses the materials of the classroom.

The classroom teacher can obtain a substantial amount of instructional information from an informal reading inventory. *How does the teacher prepare an individual informal inventory?* Marjorie Johnson and Roy Kress provide some answers in their directions for preparing, administering, and recording a word-recognition test. They also discuss the preparation of a reading inventory, its administration, and the procedure for recording results. The suggestions for measuring listening skills parallel those for oral reading, where the two communication skills involve the comprehension process.

Although preparation of an inventory like that outlined by Johnson and Kress may be time-consuming initially, the inventory can be used many times and can be constructed from familiar, readily available materials.

What kinds of oral reading performance reveal reading problems? Kenneth Goodman has conducted extensive research into a type of oral reading analysis identified as "miscue analysis." He feels that these "miscues" are produced in response to the same kinds of clues that produce so-called "correct responses." Burke and Goodman discuss these "miscues" in the context of one child's reading of a story. They apply a series of questions to the child's performance, which seek to determine what kinds of "miscues" the child makes. Although a study of the reading process itself seems to have been the primary purpose, the taxonomy of questions can also be used to determine the possible reasons for a child's errors in his oral reading.

Diagnostic teaching should be an ongoing process for all children in the classroom; the teacher must not wait until a child is failing.

What approaches are available to prevent reading problems and provide remediation? Schell makes several recommendations concerning sight words, including three approaches which, he maintains, will help children remember problem words. He also recommends several sources of remedial material and of information concerning vocabulary problems. In addition he provides suggestions concerning phonic and structural analysis—when these skills should be taught, how much to teach, and how to teach them—as well as instructional guidelines which, he feels, are so relevant that every teacher should use them. Not everyone would agree with all of his suggestions, particularly the inclusion of only phonemically regular words in early reading material. Other suggestions, however, such as the importance of auditory discrimination, are almost universally accepted.

Finally, Dorothy McGinnis discusses the treatment of reading disability on both an individual and a group basis. Although many of her suggestions are general, she does provide an overview of the area. She not only emphasizes procedures to remediate reading difficulties but also stresses the importance of certain psychological variables to reading success.

We do not yet know why some children learn to read without apparent difficulty, while others with equal ability have considerable trouble mastering the process. It is certain, however, that many reading problems would not exist if reading teachers were alert to the early signs of developing difficulties, if they knew what to look for and how to adjust reading instruction to meet the needs of their youngsters.

Achievement Test Evaluation— Limitations and Values

Robert B. Ruddell

University of California, Berkeley

Evaluation of reading instruction in the public school setting should be basically concerned with the degree to which instructional objectives are being realized through pupils' reading ability. If achievement tests are used to provide one index of reading performance, then test items must be carefully examined for fit with instructional objectives. It is not uncommon to find reading achievement instruments used in public school settings with little concern for the nature of the test objectives as reflected by the test items.

In recent years accountability in reading instruction has come to be equated with achievement test scores—regardless of what the reading achievement test may measure. Such scores are considered by many legislators, public school administrators, and teachers to represent the pupil's reading competence. This viewpoint fails to realize that the test scores are at best a rough reflection of a child's reading performance and not his competence. Further this rough reflection of performance relates only to those specific

objectives identified by the test maker and may match the objectives of the instructional program only to a slight degree.

Language performance of minority group youngsters speaking a nonstandard dialect is rarely considered in assessment. Language control typically presents no great problem to the middle-class urban child entering the public school. He has already learned to effectively communicate in oral language having mastered for the most part the various structural patterns and transformations typically used by adults. There is undoubtedly a wide range of relational and lexical concept development present in a class of thirty plus youngsters. In addition, there are special problems encountered by low-income Black, Chicano, and Indian children who use nonstandard and second language forms. Variations in the sound system, the grammatical system, and the lexical system may result in confusion between standard English speakers and nonstandard and second language speakers in test situations where sentence context is not sufficient

Robert B. Ruddell, "Achievement Test Evaluation—Limitations and Values," position paper prepared for the School Psychologist Conference on Testing, University of California, Berkeley, December 1971.

to clarify the intended meaning. If we are to understanding the relationship between these various systems and reading performance, it becomes clear that dialectal variation must be accounted for; otherwise, the assessment makes false assumptions about the language performance of the nonstandard speaker.

The selection of test instruments should thus be carefully examined relative to the objectives of instruction and the nature of the pupil population. Achievement performance level may be attributed to a variety of factors including the following:

1. pupil unfamiliarity with labels and concepts used in test situations, i.e., failure to understand the task required to respond to test items,
2. unfamiliarity with labels and concepts being evaluated by the instrument,
3. difficulty in attending to and processing oral stimuli presented in standard English dialect,
4. difficulty in correctly interpreting picture test items in response to oral stimuli, and
5. little understanding of test-taking behavior, e.g., elimination of an obvious detractor item to enhance the possibility of selecting the correct response.

When interpreting test results, the classroom teacher and the reading specialist should pay careful attention to these dimensions. For example, factors 1, 3, 4, and 5 could partially explain the relatively low performance by minority children in test situations. It is important that teachers examine these behavior dimensions in relation to children's performance.

Reading achievement test items which present words and phrases in isolation should be viewed with caution. The child is deprived of familiar grammatical clues and a normal language context in performing on such test items. Evaluation instruments should also be carefully examined for possible penalties resulting from value-based "right answers"—a situation where the child's experience, his concepts, his labeling system fail to match that of the test maker.

Educators must become acutely aware of the limitations of achievement tests by carefully examining the manuals and data related to the formulation and standardization of the instrument. Many of the test limitations are clearly stipulated but receive little attention by those using a given instrument. Six cautions which should be observed in using group achievement tests follow: [1,2]

1. Because standardized reading achievement tests are designed to measure highly generalized skills, they do not measure the specific objectives for a particular student or class.
2. Because only a few of the complex skills and arts of reading can be sampled in any one measurement instrument, achievement tests cannot be used as the basis for planning a complete instructional program.
3. Because standardized reading achievement tests include tasks closely related to those used to measure intelligence, they reflect

[1] California Test Bureau/McGraw-Hill, "Improving Instructional Programs through Process Evaluation." A report prepared for the Office of Program Evaluation, California State Department of Education, 1972.

[2] Kenneth S. Goodman, "Testing in Reading: A General Critique." An unpublished position paper for the Commission on Reading, National Council of Teachers of English, 1971.

many factors other than the effectiveness of classroom instruction.

4. Because the "objective" scores students receive on a standardized reading achievement test are determined by the norm group to whom they are compared, these tests tell little about student achievement unless this norm group is completely and accurately defined. Boards of education, the community, parents, and even professional educators often misinterpret achievement test scores for this very reason.

5. Because of pressure for high achievement test scores, standardized tests are subject to corruption. Since each test in a limited time can only sample specific areas of student achievement, these areas can be noted and selected for special emphasis in an instructional program making the results an invalid measure of total student achievement.

6. Although reliability measures for group achievement tests when not corrupted by special preparation give assurance of the comparability of results if administered in the same manner and at the same time to a group equivalent to the norm group, the test score of any one individual student is subject to a significant error of measurement. Group tests can measure accurately achievement of groups, but the achievement of any one individual is not necessarily measured accurately. Yet the results of group achievement tests are frequently used in schools for the assessment and educational placement of individuals.

Achievement test evaluation in reading should account for several dimensions of the reading process in order to obtain improved understanding of the nature of reading progress. Data collected on reading comprehension, word analysis skills, and listening comprehension provide an opportunity to identify relative achievement strengths and weaknesses exhibited by a specific group of pupils. For example, an achievement pattern identified by relatively weak reading comprehension, relatively weak word analysis skills, and relatively high listening comprehension achievement provides important clues for the instructional program. In this pattern the relatively high listening comprehension score suggests well-developed oral attending and comprehension ability. The pupils, however, are unable to utilize this comprehension ability when confronted with printed material which may be due to the inability to decode the written words for comprehension purposes. This inference is supported by the relatively weak word analysis skills achievement level. This achievement pattern would suggest that the teacher should concentrate on the word analysis in the reading program in order to enable the pupils to decode words for comprehension purposes. Reading growth in word analysis skills should facilitate the reading comprehension achievement level bringing the latter achievement area closer to the relatively high listening comprehension achievement level. The use of achievement patterns based on several measures thus represents one positive use of achievement instruments for group evaluation.

The design for future reading achievement instruments must search for answers to a range of basic questions. Several such questions follow: What are the basic skills and strategies that a successful reader must possess? What role does the reader's motivation play in successful reading? How are reading skills and strategies related to language development and use? Is the reading process different at various developmental levels? Are some skills or strategies learned before others? And how does the reading process differ across languages and cultures? [3]

Until such time that these questions can be answered, reading achievement tests as we know them today should represent only one of several tools for evaluating pupils' reading performance.

Future evaluation of reading progress must focus on reading as it occurs in a natural reading-language context. Emphasis must be placed on identifica-

tion of pupil strengths as well as weaknesses. Further, we must move from simply counting errors to a careful analysis of student performance as we attempt to relate to the student's underlying competence. This can best be accomplished in small group or individual settings. The purpose of achievement assessment must shift from the use of test results as a political statistic, as has been the case in recent California history, to the use of assessment to provide insight leading to an improved instructional program for our students. Only then do we become truly accountable in the educational enterprise.

[3] *Ibid.*

Criterion-Referenced Measurement

M. I. Chas. E. Woodson
University of California, Berkeley

THE NATURE OF
CRITERION-REFERENCED TESTS

A criterion-referenced test is one designed to yield measurements that are directly interpretable in terms of specific performance standards. For example, a criterion-referenced test may yield the conclusion "Johnny can identify the topic of a paragraph 90 percent of the time." Notice it does not tell the teacher anything about how he com-

pares with other students. It is up to the teacher to decide whether such a conclusion is favorable or unfavorable. The conclusion also rather directly implies instructional efforts which might be used. A decision as to whether he should receive instruction in this area would be based on his achievement in terms of the task described.

Criterion-referenced tests may be contrasted with norm-referenced tests which are designed to provide a rela-

Reprinted by permission of the author and California State Department of Education.

tive ordering of individuals with respect to their test performance. For example, a norm-referenced test may yield the conclusion "Johnny can identify the topic of a paragraph better than 60 percent of the children his age." Note this statement does not tell the teacher he is skillful or unskillful at the task, but simply compares him with others in a norm group. A decision as to whether he should receive instruction in this area, based on a standardized test score, would be based on a comparison among children.

A standardized test may be either norm-referenced or criterion-referenced, though essentially all available today are designed as norm-referenced tests. This situation is rapidly changing. Standardized tests are "standardized" in the sense that their procedures have been carefully planned so that many persons may be tested in essentially the same way and a common interpretation given to the scores. They usually include information as to how certain groups perform in the form of norms.

Standardized tests of the norm-referenced type are not easy to develop. Frequently a great deal of work is necessary to develop a set of test items which are effective in measuring an educational objective. Many proponents of criterion-referenced measurement feel that it will be easy to construct effective items and tests. This remains to be seen.

The objectives associated with most norm-referenced standardized tests are rather global. These have important uses. They tend to be of some use in making comparisons across different instructional systems, to the extent that the tests represent common objectives. They are, however, of relatively little use in day-to-day, short-range instructional decisions. They tend to be influenced little by instruction over a short period of time. Norm-referenced standardized tests tend to be more useful over long periods of time and from the school, district-wide, or state-wide point of view.

It is not usually possible to tell a criterion-referenced test from a norm-referenced test by examining the items. The difference lies primarily in the way items are developed and selected, and the way the test is interpreted. The range of usable item types is great. Items can range from familiar pen and pencil items of the traditional types, to check lists, teacher ratings, observation scales, tasks which involve several children, and tasks which involve student and teacher interaction (e.g., looks up word in dictionary when puzzled in a conversation by a concept or word he does not know).

THE PURPOSES OF
CRITERION-REFERENCED TESTING

1. Criterion-referenced tests are intended to be directly interpretable into instructional prescriptions.

2. Criterion-referenced tests are intended to be more useful in the moment to moment decisions about instruction than norm-referenced tests.

3. Criterion-referenced tests are intended to yield information more specific to the objectives of a local program by being adaptable to local goals and methods.

4. Criterion-referenced tests aim at describing reading achievement in a large variety of dimensions. Such global concepts as "comprehension" and "vocabulary" usually do not help much with the immediate decisions regarding instruction. "Proportion of the time *mat* is transposed to *mit*" has immediate and clear implications for instruction. A

standardized norm-referenced test may measure "reading comprehension" but give little help in describing particular learner behaviors or selection of appropriate instructional decisions.

THE INTERPRETATION AND USE OF CRITERION-REFERENCED TESTING

1. There is some limitation to comparisons between nonstandardized tests. When one teacher constructs a test and concludes a students can "identify the topic of a paragraph 90 percent of the time," it is not clear if some other teacher would reach the same conclusion on the basis of a test he or she designed for a similar objective. To the extent such conclusions differ, there is some error of measurement.

Standardized tests are not without error either, but the kind of error mentioned above seems not to be independent of persons giving and using the tests. Standardized tests have the virtue of giving nearly the same result no matter who gives them and are relatively independent of the teacher's judgment. Teachers often desire information independent of their judgment as an aid or augmentation to their judgment in making decisions. To the extent a test simply reflects the teacher's judgment, it does not give new information useful to the teacher.

2. A common way to develop criterion-referenced tests is to specify objectives in such a way that they imply a rule for generating a large number of appropriate items. If our instructional objectives was "to use the letter pattern cvce to identify the appropriate vowel value," we can easily see that this objective implies a set of test items. We have only to select a number of these. (Note the selection needs to be independent of the instruction given.

We would want to test on items other than those on which instruction was given.) But if our objective is "to be able to identify the emotion expressed in a passage," the set of test items implied is much less clear.

This procedure may be implemented by a teacher making a list of instructional objectives and associating with each a selection of items or rules for generating items. The teacher's judgment is a key factor here, but consulting published lists of objectives and even standardized tests may be useful. Most teachers will want to use a broad selection of behaviors as possible indicators of the objectives of interest.

It is important that teachers distinguish between objectives as instructional tools and the measurements used to assess them. When the behaviors to be observed are specified in fine detail, behaviors easy to measure or observe tend to become the sole objectives of instruction. Teacher-prepared objectives may be a very important tool to help the teacher plan instructions even if they do not easily lead to measurement techniques.

CAUTIONS REGARDING CRITERION-REFERENCED TESTING

1. Criterion-referenced tests are limited in generalizability. Unless they are standardized and represent common objectives, they cannot be used for comparisons between classes, teachers, teaching methods, or schools.

2. The selection of the items and their scoring depends heavily upon teacher judgment.

3. Most teacher-made tests are too short for the purpose intended. This conclusion is based upon norm-referenced tests but probably will also be true of criterion-referenced tests.

4. It may be that teachers can be trained to prepare their own nonstandardized criterion-referenced tests. For example, a list of rules for generating criterion-referenced items from instructional objectives may be developed by a group of teachers or rules found to be effective distributed to teachers for their consideration. In certain content areas such as arithmetic this seems relatively easy. In basic reading skills it may be possible. In complex skills it is still uncertain how to do this.

SOME CONCLUSIONS

It seems likely that:

1. Criterion-referenced tests will not replace norm-referenced tests; both will be important tools for teachers, and they will, in general, serve different purposes.
2. Criterion-referenced tests will be most useful in making short-range instructional decisions. Norm-referenced tests will be most useful when the teacher wishes to compare a student or a class with others of a norm population.
3. Teacher-made criterion-referenced tests will be of great use to teachers in making decisions about how well they meet their own instructional objectives.

REFERENCES

GLASER, R., Instructional technology and the measurement of learning outcomes. *American Psychologist,* 1963, *18,* 519–521.

GLASER, R., & NITKO, A. J., Measurement in learning and instruction. In R. L. Thorndike (Ed.), *Educational Measurement.* Washington: American Council in Education, 1970.

POPHAM, W. J., *An Evaluation Guidebook.* Instructional objectives exchange, Box 24095, Los Angeles, Calif. 94004, 1971.

Procedures for Individual Inventory

Marjorie Seddon Johnson and Roy A. Kress

The total process of an individual informal inventory of reading ability may be divided for convenience into four major sections. These might be labeled pupil and examiner readiness, the word recognition test, the reading inventory, and the listening inventory. All four must be included if a thorough and competent job is to be accomplished.

PUPIL–TEACHER READINESS

Two major purposes are to be accomplished during this period. There is, of course, a need to enlist the cooperation of the person being examined if the inventory is to give valid and reliable results. Consequently, this period must be one during which rapport is established between pupil and teacher, and the examining technique to be used is explained. It is important that the pupil have at least some understanding of the method to be used to evaluate his accomplishments and needs in the reading area.

During this period, the examiner has an opportunity to appraise the child's oral language facility in many different ways. As they engage in informal conversation, he can pick up any actual defects in speech, appraise the degree of spontaneity in informal situations, determine the child's ability to respond to specific questions, and get some measure of the maturity level of the child's vocabulary, sentence structure, and pronunciation. Likewise, there will be some reflection of the child's ability to concentrate on oral language activities and to respond appropriately. While all of this is going on, a great deal can also be learned about the child's attitude toward himself and the reading process. All of this material is significant in the total evaluation of his strengths and weaknesses in the reading area.

With the new information gained and any previous data on the child, the examiner should be able to estimate the possible level at which to begin with the word recognition test. The materials which the child is currently using for instruction, for instance, may give some clue. The child's own evaluation of the problems that he faces in reading may be indicative of the kinds of needs which will be uncovered, and may well dictate that

Marjorie Seddon Johnson and Roy A. Kress, "Procedures for Individual Inventory," in *Informal Reading Inventories* (1965). Reprinted with permission of Marjorie S. Johnson and Roy A. Kress and the International Reading Association.

testing should begin at a very low level.

One guiding theme in the course of this period should be the attempt to make the child as serious, and yet relaxed, as possible about the job which faces him. He should understand that he is going to face tasks of increasing difficulty, so that he may go as far as his abilities will allow at this particular time. He should become aware of the fact that, if it is at all possible, the examiner will begin with materials which are quite easy for him, so that he will be able to demonstrate skills and understandings he has in the reading area.

WORD RECOGNITION TEST

To appraise the child's immediate recognition vocabulary and use of word analysis skills, words are presented in isolation. Lists of words from preprimer at least through sixth grade level should be available for this testing. In a clinical word recognition test, these lists should be samplings of common vocabulary at the various levels. For classroom use, however, the sampling is more often from the specific instructional materials. Twenty to twenty-five words appear to constitute an adequate sampling at each of the reader levels.

For actual test material, these lists of words should be typed clearly, at least double-spaced, so that they can be flashed with a manual tachistoscopic technique for immediate recognition purposes. Clear, readable type should be provided so that there is no possibility of difficulty which results from the vagueness of the visual stimulus rather than from the child's inability to handle the particular word recognition task required. From each list of words two scores will be derived, one

representing the child's immediate recognition of the words (flash presentation), and the second, his performance in working words out in an untimed situation. In each case, the percentage of words correct is the score. On the flash test, only those correct responses which are given immediately are counted in the basic score. If corrections are made spontaneously, without a re-exposure of the word, credit is given for independent correction, but the basic score does not change. Thus if a child, on a list of 20 words, pronounced 19 correctly and one wrong, his basic score would be 95%; if he made an immediate correction of the twentieth word without seeing it again, a plus one would be added to the record of the scoring. The 95% + 1 would indicate, then, that he had corrected his one error without teacher aid.

The manual technique for flashing the words to the child is a relatively simple one, but requires practice so that it can be executed smoothly. Two cards (3 x 5 index cards are suggested) comprise the materials needed. Seated next to the child, the teacher places the word list directly in front of the child. To flash a word to the child, the two cards are held together immediately above the first word form in the list. The lower card is moved down to expose the word; the upper card is then moved down to close the opening between them. This complete series of motions is carried out quickly so that the child gets only a flash presentation of the word. However, it is important that the word be exposed completely and clearly. A tendency in inexperienced examiners is to follow the lower card with the upper one, thus never really giving a clear exposure of the word. If a child responds correctly on the flash presentation, the examiner goes on to repeat the performance with the next word. If, however, an incorrect response is given, the word is re-exposed by pushing up the upper card so that the word can again be seen. No clues are given but the child has the opportunity to re-examine the word and to apply whatever word analysis skills he has at his command.

Immediately responses are recorded in a flash response column. The responses for re-exposures of the word appear in the untimed column. The untimed score is the basic sight vocabulary plus all corrections made without examiner help. It is important that responses be recorded immediately, so that there is complete accuracy in the record of the performance. Delay in writing down the child's response for even a few seconds may lead to confusion and incorrect reporting on the part of the examiner.

The word recognition test is continued, moving from level to level until the point is reached at which the child is no longer able to function adequately at any given level. Unless the situation is extremely frustrating to the child, it is advisable to continue the test until the child is able to recognize only three or four of the words in the list at the level then being administered.

The following example shows two levels of one boy's word recognition test as his responses were recorded. A check indicates a correct response; zero, no response; d.k., a statement that he did not know the word; separated letters, a naming of the letters. Single letters or phonetic symbols represent attempts to reproduce the indicated speech sound. Where an incorrect response was recorded and followed by a check, Robert made a spontaneous correction. A zero preceding a word or a check mark indicates an unusual delay before responding.

The seventy-five per cent score, plus one, at preprimer level, for example, indicates that Robert had fifteen words of the twenty correct initially, during the flash presentation, and made one spontaneous correction without seeing the word again. His eighty per cent untimed score represents credit only for sixteen words which were recognized at flash because Robert made no additional corrections during the untimed presentation. At primer level, however, he worked out three in the untimed exposure. Here, his untimed score represents forty per cent correct during the flash presentation plus an additional twelve points for those three corrected when he had unlimited time to consider the word.

THE READING INVENTORY

A wise procedure for starting the reading inventory is to begin at least one level lower than that at which the child first encountered difficulty in the word recognition test. The one situation in which this might not be suitable would be that in which the child has definitely revealed in his conversation or in his past history severe difficulties with comprehension. In this case, it would be best to begin at the very lowest level in order to present as few comprehension problems as possible on the initial selection.

Once the starting level has been determined, the procedure at each level is the same. Before any reading is done, a definite readiness for the particular selection should be established. In the course of this readiness, a purpose for reading should be brought out. The examiner must be careful not to reveal so much in the way of vocabulary used in the selection or ideas contained that he gets no opportunity to measure the child's actual reading performance.

Word Recognition Test [1]

Name _Robert_   Age _9_   Date _1/8/64_

Pre-Primer Level			Primer Level		
Stimulus	Flash	Untimed	Stimulus	Flash	Untimed
1. little	✓		1. Good	oh-oh-dog	0 "What story was it in?"
2. you	✓		2. Run	✓	
3. can	✓		3. are	can	oh- and
4. Play	✓		4. like	little	0
5. said	0	something	5. one	✓	
6. Want	0	0	6. Away	"never saw that word!"	0
7. come	✓		7. All	0	dis
8. it	✓		8. duck	0	b-b-b/0
9. comes	came	0	9. yes	y-e-s ✓	
10. Come	✓		10. get	0	0
11. for	✓		11. She	her	✓
12. see	✓		12. make	0	m-m/0
13. play	✓		13. my	✓	
14. It	✓		14. No	oh-oh-✓	
15. I	✓		15. This	0	they
16. to	✓		16. am	it/at	0
17. in	m-✓		17. red	✓	
18. Big	✓		18. run	✓	
19. not	down	0	19. Do	✓	
20. big	✓		20. he	d. remember	0
	75⁺¹	80%	21. yellow	✓	
"Only four wrong! I did good. I'm reading."			22. Will	what	✓
			23. home	✓	
			24. went	0	0
			25. they	0	came ✓
				32⁺²	52%

[1] First two levels of the Individual Word Recognition Test, Form C, based on the Daniels' Reading Vocabulary Study, Philadelphia: The Reading Clinic, Temple University, 1963.

Instead, some orientation should be given which will give the child a reason for reading, and a set in the right direction. As soon as this is accomplished, the selection designed for oral reading at sight is read aloud by the child in order for him to accomplish the established purpose. The examiner times the reading accurately (with a stopwatch) and keeps a careful record of the exact way in which the selection was read. Each hesitation or error is recorded, for example. If there is need for examiner help with pronunciation of words, this is given, but the amount is very carefully checked. As soon as the reading has been completed, the comprehension check is administered. The examiner must keep in mind that his purpose here is to evaluate the child's comprehension, and not to teach him. If a question is answered incorrectly, this does not mean that the examiner should help the child arrive at the right answer. Instead, he should go on to the next question. Responses to the comprehension questions should be recorded verbatim wherever this is possible. If such recording is not done, the immediate reaction to the adequacy of the response is oftentimes in question.

When the check on the reading of the first selection is completed, readiness for reading the second selection should be established immediately. Again, a purpose must be set for the reading. This time, the child reads the second selection at the same level silently. While this reading is being done, the examiner should observe carefully, keeping track of the time required for the reading as well as any signs of difficulty or specific reactions to the material. The comprehension check on the silent reading should be administered in the same fashion as was that for the oral reading at sight. When this has been completed, a new purpose should be established for re-reading a portion of the selection orally. Here, the performance should be recorded exactly as was done during the oral reading at sight.

This same procedure is followed at each level until a frustration point has been reached. When this occurs, the reading inventory itself is discontinued.

The following example is one child's performance on oral reading at sight at primer level. The notations indicate that he hesitated twice during the reading, apparently to give some thought to the words. Two actual errors were made. He read *cows* for *cow* and repeated to correct the error. He read *so* for *too* and apparently never noticed his error. Generally, he showed

good fluency with the rest of the selection.

On the comprehension check, he responded freely, and showed ability to handle various types of questions. He forgot one bit of necessary information for the inference about the boy's name—the father's name. However, he made it clear that if he had remembered this, he would have been able to make the inference. His other error seemed to be one of failing to realize that the boy showed no signs of expecting to help until he was told he could and then went to bring the cow to his father rather than milk her himself.

All in all, indications are that the performance certainly meets the criteria for an instructional level. This is not to say that he might not also meet these criteria at a higher level or demonstrate similar needs at a lower level.

THE LISTENING INVENTORY

The process of determining the highest level at which the child can understand materials read to him is usually begun at the next level following the one at which frustration was reached. In this process, the examiner again develops a readiness for the handling of the selection, and sees that a purpose is established just as it was for the reading of the materials by the child himself. In this case, however, the actual reading is done by the examiner. When this has been completed, listening comprehension is evaluated in a manner similar to that used for measuring the child's reading comprehension. This process is continued at successively higher levels until the child fails to maintain a level of 75 per cent accuracy in comprehension. When difficulties with understand-

Primer -
Oral at sight
56 words

AT THE BARN

Bob and his father came out of the house.

They went to the big red/barn.

They were going to get some milk.

"You can help me," said Mr. /Black.

"I will get the cow," called Bob as

he ran on into the barn.

"Don't go too fast," called Mr. Black.

"You will make her jump."

[handwritten left margin: Good rhythm / Expressive / W.R. 96%]

[handwritten right: sec. 120 WPM 28)3360 28 56]

[handwritten right: .03571 % error 56)2.00 168 32 0 280 40]

√How do you know Bob and his father had not been outside? *they came out of the house*

√Where had Bob and his father been? √

√Where were they going? *to the barn*

√What did they want to get? *milk*

√In what were they going to put the milk? (picture clue) *a bucket*

○ What was Bob's last name? *I forgot - it told his father's name, but I forgot*

√ Did Bob expect to milk the cow? How do you know? *He went right to the barn. Q to milk the cow*

√ How did Bob feel about being allowed to help? How do you know? *he was happy. I guess he liked it. Q-t ran right away & he his father told him he cried his*

√ What warning did Mr. Black give Bob? *Not to go real fast*

√ How do you know Mr. Black was afraid Bob might scare the cow? *he yelled at him to slow up or she'd jump.*

[handwritten left margin: Comp. 80% Quick, natural responses Questions weren't ready to push for thinking - what did he do when.]

Recapitulation

WR	96	Oral Comp.	80	ORR:	Time	
Oral WPM	120	Silent Comp.			Correct?	
Silent WPM		Avg. Comp.			Rhythm	

ing are at the root of the reading problem, the child may be able to do no better in the hearing comprehension test than when he is doing the reading himself. In such cases, it may be necessary to use alternate selections at lower levels to establish a hearing comprehension level.

CONCLUSION

The individual informal reading inventory is a clinical device. It is designed to reveal extensive information about a child's reading strengths and needs as well as to establish the levels at which he can function independently and with instruction. The results obtained from administration of such an inventory are as good as the examiner, no better. Specific criteria for the establishment of levels have been indicated. However, the powers of observation and the standards of judgment of the examiner are the final determinants of the adequacy of the information gained.

When a Child Reads:
A Psycholinguistic Analysis

Carolyn L. Burke and Kenneth S. Goodman

Wayne State University

Starting from the rather simple premise which states that nothing a child does when he reads orally is accidental or random, we have attempted to describe deviations between the child's actual oral reading and his expected oral reading. Some refer to this type of study as an analysis of errors; we prefer to call the phenomena we are studying "miscues" because we have come to believe strongly that they are produced in response to the same cues which produce expected responses, and that the same mental processes are involved in generating both expected and unexpected responses.

No intelligible description of a set of phenomena as complex as children's oral reading miscues is possible, however, without some kind of theoretically based framework. Unless categories of related phenomena are developed and some attempt is made to articulate these categories into a general framework, the descriptive study becomes a mere listing and some phenomena may go undetected because their significance is not realized. Over the last five years of descriptive studies, Good-

man's Taxonomy of Cues and Miscues in Reading has evolved. Since reading involves the interaction of thought and language this taxonomy organizes miscues according to linguistic and psychological characteristics. A constant process of refinement and modification has resulted from the attempts to use the taxonomy in categorizing the miscues of children reading basal text stories, moderately difficult for them which they had never seen before.

This article will deal primarily with one child's reading of one story. With it we hope to illustrate our analysis and at the same time demonstrate the order within complexity that we have found in the reading process.

Our subject, whom we shall call Daniel, was nine-years-old and in the fourth grade at the time he was taped. He is caucasian, of French-Canadian background. The home is bi-lingual. Recent tests at the time of his reading indicated an IQ of 120 and reading achievement at 5th grade—8 month level (roughly a year ahead of actual grade placement). The story he read for the study came from the latter part

"When a Child Reads: A Psycholinguistic Analysis," by Carolyn L. Burke and Kenneth S. Goodman (*Elementary English*, January 1970). Reprinted by permission of the National Council of Teachers of English.

of the sixth grade book of a basal reading series and was thus ostensibly two years above his actual grade placement and a year above his reading test grade placement.

Daniel had 179 miscues on eleven pages, or 8.7 miscues per 100 running words of text. This was high among 8 fourth grade children who read the same story, but his comprehension (based on scoring his retelling of the

Table 1. Miscues Per Hundred Words & Comprehension Rating for Eight Fourth Grade Readers

Subject	M. P. H. W.	Comprehension
Daniel	8.7	27
2	2.6	30
3	2.7	34
4	3.3	27
5	1.9	26
6	8.5	22
7	6.3	15
8	6.9	25

story) was average for the group and exactly the same as the child with the fewest miscues, 39. This is but the first bit of evidence to support the conclusion that all miscues are by no means of equal significance and that little can be learned about the reading ability of Daniel or any child merely by counting his miscues.

APPLICATION OF THE TAXONOMY

At present, in applying the taxonomy to description of an oral reading corpus, we answer 28 questions about each miscue. Since we can deal with many characteristics at the same time the need for subjective decisions is minimized. This contrasts with common

procedures in standardized achievement and diagnostic tests where, if errors are categorized at all, it is on the basis of single characteristics, usually based on assumed cause–effect relationships. When a child reads, there are complex interactions of reader and written language which cannot be understood if the process is oversimplified.

It is impossible, within the limits of an article, to touch upon all of the data which emanates from the 28 questions of the taxonomy. For this reason 18 of of the questions have been pulled out for examination here.

THE QUESTIONS

1. Did he correct his miscue?
2. Of what type was the miscue? (substitution, insertion, omission, reversal, or complex combination)
3. What language level was involved? (sub-morphic, bound morpheme, free morpheme, phrase, sentence or larger unit)
4. Did the response involve divergent dialect?
5. What was the grammatical function of the response?
6. What was the grammatical function of the expected response?
7. Was there graphic similarity between the stimuli for the response and for the expected response?
8. Was there phonemic similarity between the response and the expected response?
9. Did the miscue involve a bound morpheme or syllable?
10. Was the expected response a function word?
11. Was the response a function word?
12. Was the meaning of the response related to the meaning of the expected response?
13. Was intonation involved in the miscue?

14. Was the syntax of the response acceptable?

15. Was the meaning of the response acceptable?

16. Was the syntax changed in the response?

17. Was the meaning changed in the response?

18. Was the intonation of the response acceptable?

Most answers involved several possibilities rather than just yes or no. For example responses to question 7, graphic relationship, may be classified as (0) No; (1) Differ in a single grapheme; (2) Similar spelling; (3) Key elements in common; (4) General configuration; (5) Non-word; (6) Homographs; (7) Splitting syllables; (8) Allographs. It is not possible to discuss the precise ways in which decisions are made about the answers to each of these questions. That, and a more explicit spelling out of terms we use, must wait for publication of the taxonomy, which is still in development. Here we will focus on some of the key things we have learned about Daniel from the application of this analysis.

It may help to make the procedure more understandable if we look at one of Daniel's miscues and some of the statements we can make about it. In response to this sentence in the book:

He was *folding* the check.

Daniel said:

He was *holding* the check.

Though this seems relatively simple, there are a number of items of information which emerge from our analysis of this one miscue:

1. He did not correct it.

2. *Folding* and *holding* both are functioning as verbs.

3. A substitution was made.

4. The substitution was on a word level.

5. Actual response and expected response differed by one grapheme.

6. Actual response and expected response differed by one phoneme.

7. Syntax was acceptable and unchanged.

8. Meaning was acceptable but changed.

ONE CHILD'S MISCUES

Table 2 presents selected data indicating the percentages of Daniel's miscues. The first bar, for example, indicated that Daniel did not correct or attempt to correct 75% of his miscues. He successfully corrected 22% and made unsuccessful corrections of 3%. In itself this is interesting but its meaning is open to speculation. We have already indicated that Daniel's 8.7 miscues per 100 words did not keep him from a fair comprehension of the story. Now we must add that he did not attempt to correct ¾ of these miscues. Rather than speculate about why he did not correct more often and how he still was able to comprehend we can look for further information.

Bar graph 9 in Table 2 indicates that the syntax of 82% of Daniel's miscues was fully acceptable in the passages in which the miscues occurred, while only 4% were not syntactically acceptable with prior context. An additional 10% resulted in meaningful sentences that did not make sense in the passage. In other words we must deal with the significance of the frequency of Daniel's miscues and his infrequent corrections within the

Table 2.   Perception of Miscues

	0	10	20	30	40	50	60	70	80	90	100	N
Corrections	0 Not Corrected								1 Corrected	9		179
Response Function	1 Noun			2 Verb	3 Adj.	4A d.v. / 5	Function Word			6 Indeter		122
Expected Response	1 Noun			2 Verb	3 Adj.	4 Adv.	5	Function Word		6 Indeter		139
Type	1 Substitution					2 Insert.		3 Omission	4 5 6 Sub.w/ Ins.&Omit			177
Level	1 Sub-Morphemic	2 Bound Morphem.	3 Free Morpheme						4 Phrase	5 Sent.		179
Graphemic	0 Not Involved				1 Differ in single grapheme		2 Similar Spelling	3 Key Element	4 5 6	7		130
Dialect	0 Not Involved							1 Dialect Involved	2 9			177
Phonemic	0 Not Involved							1 Sing. Vowel	2 Single Consonant	4 5 6		130
Syntactic Acceptability	0 No	1 Only w/ Prior	3 4	In Passage								177
Semantic Acceptability	0 No	1	Only w/ Prior	3 In Sentence	4	In Passage						176
Semantic Change	0 Meaning Not Changed						1 Meaning Changed					176
Syntactic Change	0 Syntax Not Changed					1	Syntax Changed					176
Intonation Acceptability	0 No	1 Acceptable							2 Only w/ Prior			176

understanding that his responses had a strong tendency to be semantically acceptable and an even stronger tendency to be syntactically acceptable.

Additional insight is provided by examining the miscues which Daniel corrected. Tables 3 & 4 indicate the percentage of miscues in the various categories of syntactic and semantic acceptability that Daniel corrected. While he corrected almost half of the miscues that were fully or partially unacceptable in syntax, he corrected only 17% of those that were fully acceptable. Daniel corrected or attempted to correct only 15% of those that were semantically, fully acceptable. He corrected 22% of those that resulted in meaningful sentences only. But he corrected or attempted correction in 41% of his totally unacceptable miscues and

Table 3.   Contingency Table With Syntactic Acceptability and Corrections

Correction	No	Yes	Unsuc-cessful	Total
Syntactic Acceptability				
Not Acceptable	4 .571	3 .429	0 .000	7 .040
With Prior	11 .500	11 .500	0 .000	22 .125
Only after	0	0	0	0
In Sentence	1 .500	1 .500	0 .000	2 .011
In Passage	117 .807	24 .166	4 .028	145 .824
Total	133 .756	39 .222	4 .023	176

Table 4. Contingency Table With Semantic Acceptability and Corrections

Correction	No	Yes	Unsuccessful	Total
Semantic Acceptability				
Not Acceptable	10 .588	6 .353	1 .059	17 .097
With Prior	16 .500	16 .500	0 .000	32 .183
Only After	1 1.000	0 .000	0 .000	1 .006
In Sentence	14 .778	4 .222	0 .000	18 .103
In Passage	91 .851	13 .122	3 .028	107 .611
Total	132 .754	39 .223	4 .023	175

50% of his miscues that made sense only with what preceded them.

Bar graphs 12 and 13 of Table 2 show that a little less than half of Daniel's miscues resulted in changed meaning, while a little more than half resulted in changed syntax. Again this underscores our earlier statement that not all of Daniel's miscues are of equal significance. Table 5 and Table 6 provide an interesting contrast with the information on acceptability of his mis-

Table 5. Percentage of Corrections and Syntactic Change

Correction	Syntactic Change		
	No	Yes	Doubtful
No	64 .49	68 .52	0
Yes	17 .44	22 .56	0
Unsuccessful	4 1.00	0	0

Table 6. Percentage of Corrections and Semantic Change

Correction	Semantic Change		
	No	Yes	Doubtful
No	79 .60	52 .39	1 .01
Yes	10 .26	29 .74	0
Unsuccessful	3 .75	1 .25	0

cues. About 52% of those he did not correct involved changed syntax. And about the same percent of those he corrected or attempted to correct did not involve changed syntax. But in 75% of the miscues he corrected, the meaning had been changed; whereas only 40% of those he did not correct had changed meaning.

To sum up what we have learned so far: Daniel makes frequent miscues. These miscues are generally acceptable in regard to meaning and grammar. He tends not to correct them. He appears to be using syntactic acceptability and semantic acceptability as tests of his responses because he is more likely to correct those that are not acceptable. Syntactic acceptability appears to be a somewhat stronger test of the two. On the other hand those that he corrects are very likely to involve changes in meaning, which is perhaps an indication that Daniel is ultimately concerned wtih understanding the total meaning of the story and thus he tends to correct miscues which are not in keeping with his developing comprehension.

RECOGNITION OF GRAMMATICAL FUNCTION

The 2nd and 3rd bar in Table 2 indicate the grammatical function of

Table 7. Grammatical Function of Expected Response and Grammatical Function of Observed Response for Daniel

Grammatical Function of the Observed Response	Grammatical Function of the Expected Response							Percentage of Grammatical Functions in Story
	Noun	Verb	Adj.	Adv.	Funct. Word	Ind.	Total	
Noun	31	0	0	0	2	0	33	30%
	.939	.000	.000	.000	.061	.000	.303	
Verb	0	17	0	0	0	0	17	17%
	.000	1.000	.000	.000	.000	.000	.156	
Adjective	0	0	8	0	0	0	8	8%
	.000	.000	1.000	.000	.000	.000	.073	
Adverb	1	0	0	3	1	0	5	6%
	.200	.000	.000	.600	.200	.000	.046	
Function Word	5	1	0	0	32	1	39	36%
	.128	.026	.000	.000	.821	.026	.358	
Indeterminate	0	0	0	0	0	7	7	2%
	.000	.000	.000	.000	.000	1.000	.064	
Total	37	18	8	3	35	8	109	
	.339	.165	.073	.028	.321	.073		

the response and of the expected response. The similar distribution is obvious. But what is more important is the information provided by Table 7. If a reader is operating with a very strong sense of grammatical function we would expect 100% of all substitutions to be of the same function as the expected response. This in fact comes close to being true in Daniel's case. Of 109 miscues which involved word substitutions, only 11 varied in function. He achieves 100% in verbs, adjectives and indeterminates; and comes close in nouns and function words. Adverbs, though few in number, show an expected variability. Since they are usually movable within patterns, their syntactic function is less easily predicted.

We should also be interested in whether Daniel's miscues involving any grammatical function are dispropor-

Table 8. Percentage of Occurrence of Grammatical Function

Grammatical Function	Text	Daniel's Miscues
Noun	30%	30%
Verb	17%	16%
Adjective	8%	7%
Adverb	6%	3%
Function Word	36%	36%
Indeterminate	2%	6%

tionate to actual distribution of these functions in the story. Such disproportion might indicate a potential difficulty.

The percentage of occurrence for each grammatical function involved in Daniel's miscues is, in fact, very close to the percentage of occurrence in the text. In only one area, words where grammatical function cannot be determined, is the percentage involved greater than the occurrence within the text. Involved here are nonword responses.

The data would seem to indicate that Daniel has no special difficulty in handling any of the grammatical functions and runs into difficulty only when he is unable to determine grammatical function.

GRAPHIC AND PHONEMIC MISCUES

Bar 6 on Table 2 indicates that of 130 miscues in which it was relevant to consider graphic similarity between actual and expected responses almost 40% involved no graphic similarity at all. A bit less than ¼ involved differences of only a single grapheme. Another ¼ involved less similarity (similar spelling and key elements).

The information on phonemic involvement presented in bar 8 of Table 2 is not directly parallel. Here only close similarities are categorized and all others are classed as "not involved." Again it will be noted that a bit less than ¼ involve deviations by a single phoneme.

One needs to be careful in interpreting the data. On the one hand there appear to be some miscues that are based on misperceptions of graphic shapes and misapplication of phonic relationships. But on the other hand, the large volume of Daniel's responses which were expected (not miscues) and the very use of graphic and phonic information in miscues which did involve graphic and phonemic relationships indicates that he is using graphophonic information as he reads. He uses it, however, within the twin contexts of meaning and grammar. He

corrects not when he has made a misperception or misapplication of a phonic principle but when meaning or syntax is disturbed or unacceptable.

Daniel does not appear to be totally dependent on grapho-phonic information. In fact he appears to sample from it rather than using it all, and he appears to be ready to abandon phonics when it doesn't work. Some insight into how he does this is provided in his treatment of unknown, out-of-context, words in the story. *Philosophical* occurs as a word read by the main character from a dictionary. Subsequently, it reoccurs several times, always out of any meaning or grammatical context.

Daniel's first attempt at the word was *phi lo so puh cal*. Next he said *phizosophicly*. His third try was *physicol*. Not satisfied, he moved to *physical* on the fourth trial; evidently this was a familiar word to him because he stuck to that throughout the remainder of the story.

INTONATION

Another area which is invested with importance in the classroom is that of intonation. We had some hypotheses that revolved around the ideas that better readers would have better oral intonation, and that there should be some correlation between syntactic acceptability, semantic acceptability and intonational acceptability.

A look at bars 9, 10, and 11 on Table 2 shows that miscues were totally syntactically acceptable about 80% of the time, totally semantically acceptable 60% of the time, while total intonational acceptability was around 88%. In Daniel's case our theory would seem to be upheld. Daniel is, however, already a very proficient reader. When examining younger children, who are still in the initial reading phases, or children who are experiencing some reading difficulty we found that syntactic and semantic acceptability can drop low while intonation remains quite high.

It seems as if intonation is a much more stable factor. Children seem to supply some kind of acceptable English intonation even when they fail to comprehend. A developmental fact which might be important here is that intonation is probably the first aspect of speech which an infant develops and, as such, should be stable. This is not to say, though, that Daniel's oral reading sounded smooth and fluent.

Acceptable intonation is not the same as preferred intonation. It can be slightly awkward but still acceptable within English patterns. Many teachers, when they ask the child to "read with feeling" are really asking for preferred intonational patterns, in fact, for an almost dramatic reading of the material.

Oral and silent reading at Daniel's level of proficiency are not the same. There are techniques involved in oral reading which are non-existent in silent reading. Most of these techniques revolve around the fact that in oral reading an audience, other than the reader himself, is present. The desired slow down in rate of reading is not to aid the reader's comprehension, but to accommodate the audience. In silent reading the reader is not held to so slow a pace.

This fact suggests that the basic purposes of oral reading are different from those of silent reading. In oral reading there is an attempt to communicate with others while in silent reading the communication exists only between the reader and the author (through the material). If differences exist between these two modes of reading then proficiency in silent reading does not always mean proficiency in oral reading.

DIALECT

Daniel showed little outward evidence of any divergence in his dialect. (Operationally we classify as dialect miscues, any consistent deviation in phonemes, morphemes, syntax, and vocabulary from our own preferences.) But Daniel's French-Canadian background showed in a number of his miscues. Some examples are substitutions of *harms* for *arms,* *shair* for *chair, shoose* for *choose, dat's* for *that's, de* for *the, shuckled* for *chuckled, dere* for *there.* In addition *hankachief* appeared for *handkerchief, coun't* for *couldn't, din't* for *didn't, idear* for *idea,* and *bissy* for *busy.* Altogether, more than 20% of his miscues were involved.

Only one of these dialect-involved miscues was corrected. Obviously the subject was quite unaware of these miscues. Further, they caused no disruption to his comprehension since they represented his own *preferred* forms. It seems that if a teacher should make him conscious of these miscues he might become so self-conscious in oral reading that his comprehension would suffer. These same observations, of course, pertain to the Negro speakers of low divergent dialects we have studied.

OTHER DATA

Bar graph 4 indicates the type of miscue made. Substitutions proved to be the most frequent miscue type

(45%). Substitution involving omissions and insertions accounted for another 13% of the miscues.

For Daniel then, it can be predicted that over half of his miscues will involve some kind of substitution. It would seem that he is well aware of the relationship between a written symbol and a necessary oral response.

The structural level of the miscues is indicated in bar graph 5. Miscues were at the free morpheme level 57% of the time. The sub-morpheme and bound morpheme levels accounted for 27%, the phrase and sentence levels for 16%.

Daniel's miscues seem most likely to involve single words in the printed text. This does not indicate however, the syntactic level at which Daniel was operating. To gain insight into the syntactic level, some comparison would have to be made between the structural level at which the miscue occurred and the structural change which the miscue caused.

IN CONCLUSION

The developing reading theory with the accompanying taxonomy of reading miscues offers a new framework against which to examine the reading process. As the preceding analysis of Daniel's reading indicated, the analysis offers a very complete profile of an individual child's reading. Individual miscues can be examined from different levels at the same time so that the full complexity of the reading process can be considered.

Using a multi-level analysis we can obtain data about the relative importance and the relationship to cognition processes of differing miscues. For example, such an analysis of Daniel's reading indicated the following complex relationships:

1. There was little relationship between the number of miscues and comprehension.
2. Some miscues did not result in changed meaning.
3. Miscues were more apt to be corrected when meaning had been affected.
4. Miscues tended to be corrected when resulting syntax was unacceptable.
5. Over half of the miscues involved substitution, from 60% to 100% of the substitutions did not involve a change in grammatical function.
6. Dialect involved miscues did not cause meaning change.

As we apply this analysis of miscues to groups of readers at varying stages of development and with varying backgrounds we should be able to draw some conclusions about the process of reading, its development, and the effect of various kinds of instruction on this development.

SELECTED BIBLIOGRAPHY

Bormuth, John R., "Readability: A New Approach," *Reading Research Quarterly*, Vol. 1, 1965–66, p. 79.

Carterette, Edward C. and Margaret Hubbard Jones, *Contextual Constraints in the Language of the Child*. Co-op. Research Project 1877, 1965, U.S. Office of Education.

Clay, Marie M., "Emergent Reading Behavior." Unpublished Doctor's thesis, University of Auckland, New Zealand, 1966.

Goodman, Kenneth, "A Linguistic Study of Cues and Miscues in Reading," *Elementary English Journal.* October, 1965.

GOODMAN, KENNETH S., "Reading: A Psycholinguistic Guessing Game," *Journal of the Reading Specialist,* May, 1967.

GOODMAN, YETTA M., "A Psycholinguistic Description of Observed Oral Reading Phenomena in Selected Young Beginning Readers." Unpublished D.Ed. dissertation, Wayne State University, 1967.

HAYES, WILLIAM, "My Brother is a Genius," *Adventures Now and Then,* Betts Basic Reading Series, ed. Emmett Betts and Carolyn Welch (3rd edition; New York, American Book Company, 1963).

HUNT, KELLOGG, *Grammatical Structures Written at Three Grade Levels.* National Council of Teachers of English, Research Report No. 3, 1965.

KOLERS, PAUL A., "Reading is Only Incidently Visual." A paper presented at I.R.A. Preconvention, Boston, April, 1968.

LOBAN, WALTER D., *The Language of Elementary School Children.* National Council of English, Research Report No. 1, 1963.

Project Literacy Reports. Harry Levin, director. Ithaca, New York: Project Literacy, Cornell University, No. 1–8.

SPACHE, GEORGE D., *Reading in the Elementary School,* Allyn and Bacon, 1964.

STRICKLAND, RUTH G., *The Language of Elementary School Children: Its Relationship to the Language of Reading Textbooks and the Quality of Reading of Selected Children.* Bulletin of the School of Education, Vol. 38, No. 4, Indiana University: Bureau of Studies and Testing, School of Education, 1962.

WEBER, ROSE-MARIE, "Errors in First Grade Reading." Unpublished Research Report, Cornell University, 1967.

Preventing and Correcting
Word Identification Problems

Leo M. Schell

Kansas State University

In corrective and remedial situations, the two biggest problems that teachers typically face are (1) small and unreliable sight vocabulary and (2) deficient and inconsistent word attack skills. Specific suggestions for helping prevent or correct these problems are too numerous to detail comprehensively, but all teachers, classroom or remedial, should be aware of some basic ways of coping with these problems.

SIGHT WORDS

Which words to stress?

Words from three different sources must be recognized quickly and accurately if anything resembling true reading is to occur. These sources are the basal reader, content field textbooks, and service words.

Teachers should make lists of words which pupils, individually or corporately, *repeatedly* miss when reading orally from a basal reader. Specific review time should be regularly provided for concentrated practice on these words using one or more of the approaches mentioned below.

Some words in content field textbooks are so common that students should recognize them without hesitation. Examples of these words are shown below.

Mathematics—*length, numbers, many, less*

Social studies—*country, president, forest*

Science—*experiment, electricity, temperature, liquid*

These words can be handled in the same manner as basal words. However, technical or infrequently occurring words such as *acre, plateau, asteroids, oxygen,* and *minuend* should not be considered essential and worthy of review.

Some words, because they occur so frequently in all kinds of material, must be recognized instantly and without confusion if the child is to read independently beyond basal and content field textbooks. Two valuable lists

Leo M. Schell, "Preventing and Correcting Word Identification Problems," in *Reading Difficulties: Diagnosis, Correction, and Remediation,* ed. William K. Durr (1970). Reprinted with permission of Leo M. Schell and the International Reading Association.

of such service words are Dolch's 220 "Basic Sight Vocabulary" words and Fry's 600 "Instant Words." Dolch's list can be found in

DOLCH, *Psychology and Teaching of Reading*. Garrard Press, 1951, 507–08.

DOLCH, *Teaching Primary Reading*. Garrard Press, 1960, 255.

ERICKSON, *Handbook for Teachers of Disabled Readers*, Sernoll, 1966, 63.

ROSWELL and NATCHEZ, *Reading Disability*, Basic Books, 1964, 239.

ZINTZ, *Corrective Reading*, Wm. C. Brown, 1966, 42.

Fry's list can be found in

FRY, "Word List for Remedial Reading," *Elementary English,* November 1957, 456–58.

ERICKSON, op. cit., 65–68.

SCHELL and BURNS, *Remedial Reading,* Allyn and Bacon, 1968, 361–66.

Children with sight vocabulary problems need to be tested on these service words and appropriate remediation begun for any words which are unknown or on which there is hesitation.

Which approaches to use?

Three basic approaches can be used to help children remember words with which they have problems. These, in rank order for treating mild to severe problems, are (1) oral rereading, (2) supplementary practice, and (3) a visual-motor approach.

Troublesome words may be focused on after a basal selection or context field passage has been read silently by asking children to read orally sentences containing these words. (This procedure assumes the teacher knows or can guess those words which may present more than average memory problems.) Prevention, not correction, is the key attribute of this procedure; it will not help the child who habitually confuses *fill* and *full* or who never remembers *that.*

With some children, memory is so unreliable that mere reseeing is insufficient to embed the visual image deeply enough for unhesitating recall at a later time. These children must have their attention focused on a printed symbol while saying or trying to recall its oral equivalent. For these children, supplementary practice is essential and may be provided in at least three ways: worksheets, games and activities, and tachistoscopic practice.

Three levels of worksheets are possible. The lowest level would provide as many context clues as possible. For example, pupils confusing *want* and *went* could work a sheet such as the following:

WANT   WENT

1. Tom _____ to school.

2. Did Rover _____ to go?

3. Who _____ with Tom?

This worksheet forces the child to write each word while saying it and thus helps him remember minor details in the appearance of the word.

A somewhat more difficult level includes words presented in isolation with some kind of contextual clue such as an illustration or a categorical name. (See examples below.)

The most difficult level would include rows of words from which children would select and underline those said by the teacher. Obviously, these exercises can be varied in level of difficulty to match the capability of the children.

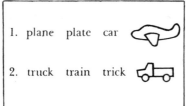

Write the words that belong together.

Animals   *Buildings*   *Actions*

walk   horse   jump   run   house

fish   school   store   bird   throw

Games and activities help take the drudgery out of what could be boring, repetitive drill. Some serious disadvantages must be considered: (1) The activities may not focus sufficiently on reading. Pupils may be so interested in *flying to Mars, picking apples,* or *adding feathers to a headdress* that they pay little attention to word learning. (2) The games may demand too little actual reading. For example, a "fishing" game may consume a disproportionate amount of time in hooking a "fish" (cardboard fish with word on it), passing the pole, etc. (3) The activities may involve too much competition among students and result in the lowest pupil's sinking even lower in self-esteem and initiative. (4) Words are usually presented in isolation, thus minimizing contextual clues and word meaning. Or, a combination of several of these drawbacks may be involved in the activities.

Judicious selection and use of these activities can overcome these disadvantages and contribute enormously to the ease and enjoyment of learning. Two sources of commercial materials and possible teacher-made games and activities are

SPACHE, *Good Reading for Poor Readers,* Garrard Press, 1968, Ch. 7.

SCHUBERT and TORGERSON, *Improving Reading Through Individualized Correction,* Wm. C. Brown, 1968, 86–94.

Children who need to study a word before finally recalling its oral equivalent can frequently profit from work with a tachistoscope of which there are three common kinds. One is homemade from oak tag, has a hand-operated shutter, and should be operated by the teacher. Directions for making two different kinds can be found in

BOND and TINKER, *Reading Difficulties,* Appleton-Century-Crofts, 1968, 313.

DURRELL, *Improvement of Basic Reading Abilities,* Harcourt, Brace and World, 1956, 177.

One advantage of commercial tachistoscopes is that they can be operated by the pupil. And, as with homemade ones, motivation is high and attention excellent. The most widely used model is the *Flash-X* manufactured by Educational Development Laboratory (EDL), Huntington, New York, which also has extensive word lists at different grade levels to fit into a hand-held device. Most filmstrip projectors can be converted into tachistoscopes by a special attachment with variable speed shutter, or a card held in front of the lens can serve the same purpose. Some suitable filmstrips (and their producers) are

THE SOCIETY FOR VISUAL EDUCATION (Chicago),
  Speed-i-o-Strip Series (10 strips)
  Graded Word Phrases (56 strips)
LEARNING THROUGH SEEING (Sunland, Calif.),
  Word Mastery (12 strips)
  Phrase Mastery (12 strips)
  Instant Words & Word Phrases (48 strips).

A last resort for children unable to remember words from memory is some kind of a visual-motor approach in which the child traces a word after scrutinizing it intensely. Bond and Tinker discuss several different tracing procedures and conclude that such methods are of primary value to the severely disabled readers and should be used in conjunction with other methods. Harris recommends adaptation of a tracing system and states that it has been highly successful in his Queens College reading clinic. Readers interested in finding out more about this procedure may examine

BOND and TINKER, *Reading Difficulties*, 471–80.

HARRIS, *How to Increase Reading Ability,* McKay, 1961, 391–93.

OTTO and MCMENEMY, *Corrective and Remedial Teaching,* Houghton Mifflin, 1966, 166–68.

ROSWELL and NATCHEZ, *Reading Disability,* 82–83.

Attention is called to the fact that the lowest level of worksheet suggested earlier uses a modified visual-motor approach, and the suggestions for coping with severe cases of word confusion on the following pages embodies elements of such an approach also. When we consider that much of spelling has parts of this procedure in it, it becomes obvious that this is a practical way of preventing many sight recognition problems and deserves widespread use in the primary grades.

Even though these three basic approaches provide additional practice for children with problems, all three should be buttressed and supplemented by a painless approach too often overlooked by teachers addicted to the idea of intensive work as the only solution to distinct problems. This painless approach is independent reading of easy and pleasurable material. A book matched to the child's appropriate reading level will, of necessity, repeat many of the words the child has trouble remembering. If selected by the child, it will hold his attention, force him to try to understand it, and demand that he read each word rather than skipping or substituting words. Primary grade teachers have repeatedly reported that independent reading plays too small a role in their total reading program. For many children, perhaps extensive use of artificial and contrived games, devices, and activities is unnecessary; a natural situation may better provide the necessary review while concomitantly exposing children to quality literature.

What special problems to expect?

Children with a small and unreliable sight vocabulary typically have two special problems: (1) they confuse words of similar configuration and (2) they have exceptional trouble remembering small words with highly abstract meanings.

Almost all children tend to identify a word by looking at the first and/or last letter(s) of a word while paying little attention to the medial letter(s). This overreliance on word configuration is the primary cause of children confusing *full, fill, fall; wander, wonder; scare, score;* and numerous other highly similar appearing words. One factor over which teachers have some control which may contribute to this problem is the typical phonics program in basal readers which introduces initial and final consonant letter sounds early in the sequence but postpones vowel letter sounds until second grade. Vowel letters are almost always the cause of confused words; consonant letters rarely are. It may be that earlier introduction of medial vowel letter sounds might help children focus attention on the internal parts of words, thus preventing later problems. But, as inoculation does not help children already afflicted with a disease, neither do preventive suggestions help pupils already suffering from word confusion; corrective measures are required.

Authorities agree that children with this problem should be presented with situations which demand that they visually scrutinize words that are minimally different, rather than merely relying on the *gestalt* of the word. A sample exercise follows:

We went for a ride in a _____.
                                 beet boat
Then we _____ home.
          came come

Two excellent sources of practical ideas for practice exercises are

Bond and Tinker, *Reading Difficulties,* 324–27 and 342–44.

Wilson, *Diagnostic and Remedial Reading,* Chas. E. Merrill, 1967, 127–29.

Not only are there more words highly similar in configuration than we generally realize, but many of these have abstract meanings which seem to compound the problem many children have of remembering them. For example, *there, their, then, these,* and *those* are repeatedly confused or not remembered as are *on, no, own, how, now,* and *won* or *where, when, were, ever, even,* and *every.* Wilson, the only major author who specifically discusses this common problem, suggests that since these words derive meaning almost totally from context, they should not be taught in isolation but in context. He recommends three ways to meet these criteria: (1) composing an experience story, (2) drill on prepared phrase cards, and (3) construction of sentences from word cards (7:129–31). The experience story seems equally appropriate as a preventive and as a corrective measure and should be seriously considered by primary grade teachers. Brown and Loper note that self-illustrated picture cards can be used by a child to build a sight vocabulary even though no publisher could get away with pictures as ambiguous as those children would produce. But, they ask, what difference does it make as long as "the child's illustrations make sense to him—and he learns the words" (2:94–95).

With severe cases of word confusion, instruction should be as simplified as possible. Teachers should focus on one word at a time and proceed by small steps from easy to more difficult learnings. The following suggested procedure should be adapted to each child's problems and capabilities.

1. Have child *trace* the word.
2. Have child *copy* the word
   a. from a model.
   b. from memory.
3. Have child *match* the word with similar words
   a. simultaneously (*while* looking at the confused word).
   b. successively (*after* looking at the confused word).
4. Have child *read* the word in context.
5. Have child *pronounce* the word in isolation
   a. untimed.
   b. flashed.

After the child has mastered two confused words individually by this procedure, two more steps can be added to assure absolute mastery.

6. Present two or more similar (confused) words in context to be read orally.
7. Present two or more similar (confused) words in isolation to be pronounced.

Children with less severe confusions may benefit from tachistoscopic work. Some filmstrips (and their producers) are

PSYCHOTECHNICS (Glenview, Ill.)
Look-A-Like Words

D-P-B Words
Word Discrimination

Teaching Technology Corp. (North Hollywood, Calif.)
Confused Words (with correlated workbooks)
Confused Word Phrases (with correlated workbooks)

Comments

Even children who have no problems learning to read require numerous presentations of words to reach memorization mastery. The procedures mentioned above are merely different ways of repeating the words children have difficulty remembering. Three things seem evident about the repetition of words and the approaches: (1) It seems reasonable that if a child has failed to learn to remember a word by one procedure, correction should not be based solely on the repeated use of that procedure. A change, possibly tentative and temporary, is in order. (2) With children requiring an unusually large number of word repetitions, variety is essential. Several of the described approaches should be used to alleviate monotony and to maintain interest in learning. (3) Even though word repetition is usually successful, mere repetition is insufficient. Children need a variety of ways other than sheer memory for attacking an unrecognized word. And the more weapons a child has to attack an "enemy," the shorter the battle, the fewer the casualties, and the surer the victory. Beginning or disabled readers need a whole arsenal of weapons, and teachers who fail to teach phonic and structural analysis, context clues, and dictionary usage are merely handing the child a pop gun while requiring him to storm an enemy stronghold.

PHONIC AND STRUCTURAL ANALYSIS

Which elements to teach when?

How to determine which phonic and structural analysis elements to teach—and when to teach them—is a real and practical problem. For most classroom teachers, an essential tool in answering these questions is the skills chart accompanying the basal reader or in the local curriculum guide. After determining the child's appropriate instructional level, the teacher can use this outline to see what skills were (or should have been) introduced previously and at what level they were taught. This chart provides a rough idea of the skills in which the child most likely is deficient and gives some general clues as to the sequence in which these skills should be taught. Further testing and observation can refine these initial judgments and help zero in on the most deficient and crucial skills. Similar guides can be found in

EDWARD FRY, "A Frequency Approach to Phonics," *Elementary English,* 41 (November 1964), 759–65.

JACK BAGFORD, *Phonics: Its Role in Teaching Reading,* Sernoll, 1967.

WILLIAM S. GRAY, *On Their Own in Reading,* Scott, Foresman, 1960.

ARTHUR W. HEILMAN, *Phonics in Proper Perspective,* Chas. E. Merrill, 1968.

Without such references, few teachers know the skills taught at earlier levels which must be retaught in a corrective or remedial situation. Thus, such resources play a fundamental role in any remediation program.

How much should be taught and how?

A fourth grader capable of grade level reading but performing at a low second grade level is so far behind, lacks so many skills, and presents so many classroom problems that the temptation is great to present all the missing skills in a short period of time to boost him to his potential level. But if such a temptation prevails, the skills will probably only be presented, not learned. McCullough warned against this temptation by noting, "Rabbits don't become kangaroos by eating carrots faster" (7).

It is easy to assume that children with reading skill deficiencies have been malnourished on a meager diet of sight words and have not had a rich, balanced diet of varied word attack skills. Such is usually not the case. Rather, they probably have been presented three balanced, but skimpy, meals daily and have only picked at these and never really cleaned up their plate and have never asked for, or been given, seconds! They require regular meals with large, balanced portions—eaten slowly and thoroughly digested. One way to assure digestion and to avoid gastric hyperacidity is to use the PPAR cycle, which simply means that one element or principle is presented, practiced, applied, and reviewed before another one is introduced. Corrective and remedial readers have myriad unrelated bits and pieces of word attack skills floating about in their memory which they are unable to use because they never really gained mastery in applying them in realistic situations. Using the PPAR cycle of skills instruction should transform the unintelligible into the usable by assuring mastery of an element or principle before introduction of another one.

In the PPAR cycle, practice should be in a situation structured to assure a maximum degree of success; ease, not difficulty, and definiteness, not ambiguity, should characterize such exercises. Just as we deliberately select reading materials guaranteed to minimize frustration, so should we choose or design practice activities to do the same. Worksheets and other practice activities should be judged by standards similar to those used in an informal reading inventory to determine the proper level of reading materials.

"Mrs. Smith, what's this word?" is a persistent litany in many classrooms and the ubiquitous response is, "Johnny, we worked just yesterday on how to sound out words like that." Phonic elements recently presented and practiced just are not (can't be?) applied. A prime cause of this difficulty may be that practice, of necessity, occurs in an artificial situation, usually on a worksheet or a similar exercise, and there is little or no carryover of this learning to actual reading situations. Teachers should repeatedly show pupils how learned skills can be used in reading. In introducing words prior to reading a selection, the teacher can select words which embody recently studied elements or principles and ask pupils how they were able to figure out the pronunciations. Or, after reading a selection, the teacher can list or have pupils find words that can be attacked using newly learned skills. Not only should this procedure encourage children to actually use their knowledge, but it should also promote their feeling of independence and confidence—major components in reading success. Thus, two birds with one stone.

An integral part of the PPAR cycle should be periodic, cumulative review of several elements. The memory of the average child is faulty, subject to partial forgetting and inconsistent performance even under the most fortuitous circumstances, so it is not surprising that problem readers respond identically. For best retention, these reviews should stress the application of elements or principles by using unknown words. Re-using words from prior practices facilitates mere recall, a lower level cognitive behavior than application of knowledge. Unknown words more truly correspond to realistic situations children will face in which they must independently figure out a new word. Psychology has unanimously affirmed that the more practice situations resemble use situations, the better the learning will function in the use situations. Ignoring so fundamental a principle only impedes mastery and attests to slovenly unprofessionalness.

Some comments on instruction

Research and experience have shown some instructional guidelines that are gaining such increased acceptance and widespread use that they should be known and practiced. Some of the more significant ones follow.

1. Two auditory aspects are so fundamental to learning both phonic and structural analysis that ignoring or slighting them virtually ensures the failure of this approach. These are auditory discrimination and auditory blending.

A child who can't differentiate auditorily between /red/ and /rid/ may pronounce pet as /pit/ because he assigns the short i sound to the letter e. Such a minor event may have major consequences if the erroneous pronunciation distorts the whole meaning of the sentence, "That is my pet." Auditory discrimination ability must be evaluated and, if deficient, be trained before intensive instruction in highly similar phonemes is undertaken. So much material for instruction is available in basal reader readiness books and other commercial materials, that there seems little need to list sample exercises or possible sources. For evaluation, even though numerous readiness tests measure auditory discrimination, there are only a few standardized tests with appropriate subtests. Some of these are

Stanford Diagnostic Reading Test, Level I. Harcourt, Brace and World, 1966.

Gates–McKillop Reading Diagnostic Tests. Bureau of Publications, Teachers College, Columbia University, 1962.

Wepman Auditory Discrimination Test. Language Research Associates, 1958.

Auditory blending is an old skill receiving renewed attention, possibly because Chall, Roswell, and Blumenthal found it a good predictor of beginning reading success (3). After dividing an unrecognized word into either its constituent phonemes or syllables, these elements must be fused to form an auditorily familiar word. Children deficient in this ability flounder miserably in learning and applying either phonics or syllabication. Both levels of the Stanford Diagnostic Reading Test measure this ability, as does the Gates-McKillop Reading Diagnostic Tests, both listed above. Two other tests valuable in assessing this skill are

Diagnostic Reading Scales, California Test Bureau, 1963.

Roswell–Chall Auditory Blending Test, Essay Press, 1963.

Suggested specific practices for helping children synthesize these separate sounds in words may be found in

ROSWELL and NATCHEZ, *Reading Disability*, 90–91.

BOND and TINKER, *Reading Difficulties*, 337–39.

BROWN and LOPER, "Word Recognition in the Elementary School," in Marjorie Johnson and Roy Kress (Eds.), *Corrective Reading in the Elementary Classroom*, Perspectives in Reading No. 6. Newark, Del.: International Reading Association, 1967, 106.

2. Undoubtedly the inconsistent phoneme-grapheme relationship in English spelling is one cause of children's inability to apply word attack skills consistently. One way to have children use these skills in a functional situation is to have them practice in materials containing only phonemically regular words, i.e., material in which words such as *come, are, once,* and *have* are intentionally omitted or their occurrence strictly controlled. Most linguistic readers can be used or adapted for this purpose. Some publishers of such readers are Harper and Row; Harcourt, Brace and World; Chas. E. Merrill; Science Research Associates; and D. C. Heath. Some materials written expressly for this use are

Phonics in Rhyme, Teaching Technology, 1967.

Phonic Readers, Wenkart, 1961.

Easy Road to Reading Improvement Series, Marand, 1966.

3. Numerous recent studies such as Clymer's (4) have shown that some of the widely taught phonic and structural analysis principles have feet of

clay. In corrective and remedial situations, confusing or infrequently used elements or principles should be stringently avoided. Even though each teacher will have to decide this on the basis of the particular children being taught, the author has reason to question whether the following learnings should be included in most remedial instruction: (1) the "soft" sound of g, (2) r-controlled vowels, (3) accenting, and (4) meanings of affixes. Teachers should be discriminative in what they teach; they should feel free to omit a principle that has little applicability or to revise one so it has greater utility.

4. Children deficient in word attack skills need more than normal repetition and practice to attain satisfactory competency—just as is necessary in learning sight words. Varied repetition is highly important for the sake of both learning and motivation. To meet the wide range of individual learning modalities and to assure adequate repetition without boredom, media of all kinds should supplement textual materials. Games, filmstrips, transparencies, records and tapes, and programed materials are all available for providing practice with word attack skills. The best bibliographies of such materials and ideas are

DECHANT, *Diagnosis and Remediation of Reading Disabilities*, Parker, 1968, ch. 7.

SCHUBERT and TORGERSON, *Improving Reading through Individualized Correction*, 97–121.

Comments

Individual word attack skills cannot function in isolation. Initial consonant letters cannot be sounded accurately without sounding the following vowel letter; there is no sense in syllabicating a word if the reader can't blend the parts together; and syllabication may produce only unintelligible gibberish without correct accentuation. Since all these skills must work together, instruction cannot focus only on one skill without incidentally incorporating several other facets. The only time skills can be isolated is in a textbook on reading instruction. Piecemeal, unrelated instruction tends to produce highly competent "sounders" who are unable to apply their knowledge functionally in true reading situations, thus negating the ultimate purpose of instruction. A limited program which lacks balance is therefore, in the long run, self-defeating.

REFERENCES

1. BOND, GUY L., and MILES A. TINKER, *Reading Difficulties: Their Diagnosis and Correction*. New York: Appleton-Century-Crofts, 1967.

2. BROWN, DON A., and DORIS J. LOPER, "Word Recognition in the Elementary School," in Marjorie Johnson and Roy Kress (Eds.), *Corrective Reading in the Elementary Classroom*, Reading Aids Series. Newark, Del.: International Reading Association, 1967.

3. CHALL, JEANNE, FLORENCE ROSWELL, and SUSAN BLUMENTHAL, "Auditory Blending Ability: A Factor in Success in Beginning Reading," *Reading Teacher*, 17 (November 1963), 113–18.

4. CLYMER, THEODORE W., "The Utility of Phonic Generalizations in the

Primary Grades," *Reading Teacher,* 16 (January 1963), 252–58.

5. DECHANT, EMERALD, *Diagnosis and Remediation of Reading Disability.* West Nyack, New York: Parker, 1968.

6. HARRIS, ALBERT J., *How to Increase Ability* (4th ed.). New York: David McKay, 1961.

7. McCULLOUGH, CONSTANCE, "Meeting Individual Needs by Grouping for Reading," Ginn Contributions to Reading No. 19, 1962, 4.

8. ROSWELL, FLORENCE, and GLADYS NATCHEZ, *Reading Disability: Diagnosis and Treatment.* New York: Basic Books, 1964.

9. SCHUBERT, DELWYN G., and THEODORE L. TORGERSON, *Improving Reading through Individualized Correction* (2nd ed.). Dubuque, Iowa: Wm. C. Brown, 1968.

10. WILSON, ROBERT M., *Diagnostic and Remedial Reading.* Columbus, Ohio: Charles E. Merrill, 1967.

11. ZINTZ, MILES V., *Corrective Reading.* Dubuque, Iowa: Wm. C. Brown, 1966.

The Teacher's Treatment of the Disabled Reader

Dorothy J. McGinnis
Western Michigan University

Treatment, whether applied by physician, therapist, or teacher is determined by diagnosis. This paper defines and discusses the nature of treatment both from an instructional and therapeutic point of view. It suggests and illustrates eight factors essential in treatment and sets forth a flexible grouping plan for meeting the reading needs of thirty, second grade children whose reading performance ranges from that of a nonreader to that of a reader at the fifth grade level. It illustrates the use of a projector in providing a visual-visual-auditory approach in the treatment of a second grade boy who is a disabled reader.

DEFINITION OF TREATMENT

Treatment, as applied to reading, is the act, method, and manner of helping an individual attain better adjustment by means of psychotherapeutic aid, counseling, and instruction. It is designed to remedy or mitigate the individual's disability in order to assist him in the realization of his goals. Treatment can be general, specific, pal-

Dorothy J. McGinnis, "The Teacher's Treatment of the Disabled Reader," in *Reading Difficulties: Diagnosis, Correction, and Remediation* (1970). Reprinted with permission of the International Reading Association.

liative, or preventive in nature. It must, however, be a direct response and sequence of a diagnostic study of the individual or of an immediate anticipation of his needs.

SOME PRINCIPLES ESSENTIAL TO TREATMENT

Treatment, as applied by the classroom teacher, involves both instruction and therapy. Some principles underlying its application are briefly summarized.

Pay attention to the individual

Each child needs to be accepted as a person and at his level of development. He needs to be understood, respected, and liked. In working with the child the teacher needs to know the child's abilities, his interests, his attitudes, his goals, and the reading skills he possesses and those he does not possess. The teacher can identify early manifestations of physical, psychological, and environmental factors affecting his progress. She can stimulate his interest in reading and help him to build up his self-concept. If necessary, she can aid him in developing more wholesome attitudes toward reading, books, the library, and the school. The teacher must do more than "go through the basal text" or follow a ritualistic approach to informal reading.

Stimulate, inform, guide

In providing treatment the teacher can utilize a goal-oriented process which will permit her pupils to develop their reading skills as they carry on projects and activities of interest and of value to them. Young and Young (1) have shown how a writing program has culminated in the production of "books" containing stories written by children in their own "unique and unrevised wording and speech patterns." Such projects are the outcome of superior teaching resulting from stimulation, information, and guidance. The whole process is goal oriented and results in "feedback" and even more stimulation which can lead to additional projects and purposeful learning.

Emphasize interpretation rather than evaluation

Remediation involves treatment which is based upon diagnosis, and diagnosis is a continuous process never complete until the disability has been eliminated. The teacher must interpret the child's performance rather than merely evaluate his achievement. Tests are only tools designed to determine facts which must be explained. The teacher must constantly ask *why* does the child respond in this manner. First one explanation and then another must be investigated. Each "hunch" should be considered, and if found relevant it can be tentatively accepted. In a further study of the problem this "hunch" may be found material or essential to an explanation of the child's disability. His reactions to instruction and therapy must be subject to continuous interpretation.

Secure adequate materials

Materials must be selected in terms of the goals they are designed to accomplish and not because of their availability. The perceptive teacher will ask, "What materials will best accomplish my objectives for the child? Which will be of the greatest interest to him? Are the materials appropriate to his reading level? Which will be most effective?" Materials are to be considered as tools designed to accomplish a specific goal essential to the growth of the child's ability to read. They require careful selection and continuous adjustment.

Select and modify instructional procedures

No one method is adequate for teaching all children to read. Some children learn by a visual–visual approach, some by a visual–auditory, some by a visual–kinesthetic, and some by a visual–tactual approach. It is the responsibility of the teacher to discover how the child learns and then to teach him in the way he learns. Furthermore, she must select and modify instructional procedures so as to meet the reading needs of each student. The emphasis in instruction must be placed upon the skills and abilities which the student does not possess but which are essential for his *immediate* success in reading. In fact, a child with a marked reading disability should be assured of some degree of laudable achievement. A flexible grouping plan described in this paper can become an effective means of achieving this goal. Instructional procedures in all instances must be meaningful to the child and should be related to *his* goals.

Guide step by step

In working with the individual and with groups of children the experienced teacher has in mind the *goals* she plans to accomplish, the *materials* she expects to use in achieving these goals, and the *procedures* she will employ. She has a plan of attack, and her treatment will involve a sequence of instructional activities which are dependent one upon the other. In teaching chapter reading, for example, she will show her students how to identify main ideas, how to convert major headings into questions, and how to read for answers to these questions, and then she will show her pupils how to make the new facts their own. Her instruction advances step by step.

Avoid frustration and emotional set

The teacher's main task is to arouse within each child the desire to improve his reading. Motivation is essential to success in learning. The instructional period must be one in which the student can make progress. Success must be assured, for every child needs satisfaction, security, and recognition. The successful teacher will accentuate the positive and eliminate the negative. In successful treatment the individual will be given an opportunity to experience success early and continuously.

Emphasize wholeness and continuity of learning to read

The successful teacher of reading will emphasize the integration of reading skills rather than merely an accumulation of skills. She will understand that reading skills, if they are to be functional, must "go together" as hydrogen and oxygen unite to form water, H_2O. This means, of course, that basic reading skills will be utilized by the student as he accomplishes his purposes and achieves his goals. Furthermore, the teacher will understand that learning to read is a continuous process. It is a way of life and an essential aspect of purposeful living in an ever-changing world.

TREATMENT OF CHILDREN AND GROUPS

Miss Rose, the teacher of thirty, second grade children, has worked with her students for nearly six weeks. After determining the individual reading needs of the students, she has decided to make use of a flexible grouping plan in order to instruct them adequately. This plan makes it possible to provide boys and girls, whose reading achievement is at different grade levels, with an opportunity to carry on reading activities suited to their different and varying needs. In flexible grouping children are brought together to achieve a purpose and remain together until their purpose has been accomplished. The groups are not permanent and in many instances may change weekly. For example, during one week Miss Rose had four groups of children. One group was composed of eight boys and girls who needed to learn how to read for detail. A second group contained twelve children who were given instruction in word attack. A third group was made up of four children who received instruction in reading for main ideas. A fourth group was composed of six children who needed instruction in how to follow printed directions. Four of these came from underprivileged homes and had little experience with written materials. They were, however, interested in making witches for Halloween, and this involved cutting, coloring, and pasting. In order to accomplish these objectives, they needed to learn how to read for the purpose of following directions.

It will be observed that the children in each of the four groups have specific objectives to accomplish. In achieving these objectives they make use of materials suitable to the purpose and to their reading levels. Furthermore, procedures vary with each group as the teacher brings her instruction to a sharp focus. This flexible grouping plan will continue for several instructional periods, and then regrouping will occur so as to achieve new objectives. This grouping plan is based upon the assumption that the instructor is cognizant of the reading needs of her children. Such a plan can easily lead to individualized instruction.

SUGGESTIONS FOR USING FLEXIBLE GROUPING

In making use of flexible grouping, the changing needs of each child and the determination of adequate reading objectives should be given primary consideration. Materials designed to accomplish these objectives should be selected in terms of the child's purpose, interest, and reading level.

Teachers experienced in the use of flexible grouping report that at least forty-five minutes are required for reading activities. The work of the smaller groups can be started first and left for a time with a chairman or group leader. It is frequently necessary to have the groups with which the teacher is not working carry on an activity which does not require guidance from the instructor. Time spent within a group is dependent upon objectives accomplished and the interest of the individuals making up the group. Generally, group activities extend from two to five instructional periods.

Teachers having an experiential background in grouping have found it advisable to make use of anecdotal records. Others have found it expedient to list the reading needs of each child on a 5″ x 8″ card. The teacher inexperienced in grouping should work with one group and gradually extend her instructional activities to two and, if advisable, to three or more. Teachers who have difficulty in keeping several groups functioning simultaneously may do so because of a lack of careful planning, inadequate control of children, or faulty work habits on the part of their students. Flexible grouping is not recommended for the inexperienced teacher.

TREATMENT OF A CLINICAL PROBLEM

Miss Rose reports that one of her students, Stephen, was referred to the Psycho-Educational Clinic at Western Michigan University, not only because of his reading disability, but because of its duration and the fact that she believed him to be a boy of average mental maturity. At the time of his referral he was nine years and eight months old. He has been enrolled in the public schools for four years and has made two years of progress. It is obvious that he dislikes reading and any activity related to books. A former teacher reports the possibility of mental retardation and suggests a hearing loss. Neither of these inferences has been substantiated. It is said that he loves animals and can "express himself through art."

The report of the clinical study of Stephen made by the reading clinic provides the following diagnosis. "Stephen is a boy of average intelligence who has achieved at a low level in the language arts, especially reading, primarily because of a mental set against reading which has resulted from for-

mal instruction before he had reached a sufficient degree of readiness. Sibling rivalry can be a contributing factor."

Before examining the results of remedial treatment, let's briefly examine the clinic's recommendations.

1. Utilize a visual–visual–auditory approach.
2. Reduce sibling rivalry.
3. Do not *require* oral reading.
4. Emphasize *why* and *how* questions.
5. Have parents provide aid only when asked.
6. Stress praise and commendation.

In applying the treatment suggested by the staff of the Psycho-Educational Clinic in the remediation of Stephen's disability, the visual–visual–auditory approach was utilized. In implementing this process, a picture of a cowboy actively engaged in the roundup of steers was projected upon the chalkboard. Because of his interest in animals, this picture immediately captured Stephen's attention and that of two other boys in his class. The children were encouraged to discuss the picture, and in this manner background and mental content were built up. Objects in the picture were labeled on the chalkboard. The children were encouraged to make visual–visual–auditory associations and when the current was turned off, they were asked to identify the word symbols. If errors were made, the picture was restored. The children were taught to use the words in sentences, and later were encouraged to dictate a story concerning the action shown in the picture. Their sentences were written by Miss Rose on the chalkboard, using as few helping words as possible. After careful planning, a title was selected for the story. Stephen and his two friends read the story as a whole, and later they read to answer questions asked by the teacher. When expedient, word study was introduced making use of structural analysis and phonics. Miss Rose emphasized phrase reading and the use in sentences of the words she had previously taught. Stephen and his associates were shown how to design and construct binders which were used to hold a reproduction of the story the children had written. Stephen, who was now an author, experienced great satisfaction in reading *his* story to his parents and to his grandparents. This visual–visual–auditory approach to reading was continued for five weeks, and during this time Stephen added over two hundred new words to his reading vocabulary and actually developed an interest in stories and books. His parents reported that he read aloud his "books" to visitors and anyone who would listen. Frequently they said he urged that his listeners ask him questions concerning the material he had read. Evidently, in Stephen's case this goal-oriented approach paid off. It enhanced the value of instruction and provided therapy as his self-concept was actually increased. A conference between Miss Rose and the parents made possible the discussion of sibling rivalry, reading instruction in the home, and the importance of reinforcement of desired responses by means of praise and commendation. It is apparent that Miss Rose has demonstrated her ability to provide treatment following a clinical study of a disabled reader. Furthermore, she has shown a high degree of creativity in meeting the reading needs of her boys and girls.

SUMMARY

This paper has shown how treatment in the form of instruction and therapy can be applied to a group situation and also in an individual case. Eight principles underlying remediation have been explained. Flexible grouping and the teaching of reading as a goal-oriented process have been illustrated.

REFERENCE

1. YOUNG, VIRGIL M., and KATHERINE A. YOUNG, "Special Education Children as the Authors of Books," *Reading Teacher*, 22 (November 1968), 122–25.

Author Index